Fourth Edition

Introduction to Forensic Anthropology

Steven N. Byers

Foreword by Stanley Rhine

Boston Columbus Indianapolis New York San Francisco Upper Saddle River
Amsterdam Cape Town Dubai London Madrid Milan Munich Paris Montréal Toronto
Delhi Mexico City São Paulo Sydney Hong Kong Seoul Singapore Taipei Tokyo

Editorial Director: Craig Campanella
Editor in Chief: Dickson Musslewhite
Publisher: Nancy Roberts
Editorial Assistant: Nart Varoqua
Senior Manufacturing and Operations Manager for Arts & Sciences: Nick Sklitsis
Operations Specialist: Renata Butera
Director of Marketing: Brandy Dawson
Senior Marketing Manager: Laura Lee Manley
Marketing Assistant: Lisa Krilick
Senior Managing Editor: Ann Marie McCarthy
Senior Project Manager: Denise Forlow
Creative Art Director: Jayne Conte
Cover Design: Bruce Kenselaar
Cover Photograph: Background Image: © Peter Ptschelinzew/Lonely Planet Images. Skull: © Julie R. Angel.
   Courtesy of the State of New Mexico, Office of the Medical Investigator
AV Project Manager: Mirella Signoretto
Full-Service Production, Interior Design, and Composition: PreMediaGlobal
Printer/Binder: Edwards Brothers
Cover Printer: Edwards Brothers
Text Font: Palatino 10/12

Credits and acknowledgments borrowed from other sources and reproduced, with permission, in this textbook appear on appropriate page within text.

Library of Congress Cataloging-in-Publication Data
Byers, Steven N.
   Introduction to forensic anthropology / Steven N. Byers ; foreword by Stanley Rhine.—4th ed.
      p. cm.
   Includes bibliographical references and index.
   ISBN 10: 0-205-79012-7
   ISBN 13: 978-0-205-79012-8

1. Forensic anthropology,   I. Title.
   GN69.8.B94 2011
   614'.17—dc22

                                                                                    2010043080

10 9 8 7 6 5 4 3 2 1

Prentice Hall
is an imprint of

Exam ISBN 10: 0-205-79015-1
Exam ISBN 13: 978-0-205-79015-9

Student ISBN 10: 0-205-79012-7
Student ISBN 13: 978-0-205-79012-8

*To Michael Charney, an anthropologist of the old school
and forensic anthropologist* par excellence

CONTENTS

PREFACE

The nascence of this book dates to 1998 when I was given the opportunity to teach an undergraduate course in anthropology dealing with forensics. Feeling comfortable teaching it only as an introduction to forensic anthropology, I discovered two things that gave me the idea to write this book. The first was the absence of a textbook in the field. Although Krogman and Iscan's *The Human Skeleton in Forensic Medicine* and Stewart's *Essentials of Forensic Anthropology* were available, I deemed both of them too complex for the lower-division class that I had been asked to teach; also, both were quickly becoming outdated. In addition, I reviewed Rathbun and Buikstra's *Human Identification* as well as Reich's *Forensic Osteology* but decided that the cases presented were both too spotty in their coverage of the topics germane to forensic anthropology and, again, too complex for an introductory class. The second thing was my rediscovery of Clyde Snow's article entitled "Forensic Anthropology" in the 1982 *Annual Review of Anthropology*. In this article, Snow codified the forensic anthropology protocol by listing all the issues surrounding the death of an individual that should be elucidated by the forensic anthropologist (if warranted by the available data). To me, the topics listed in the protocol constituted a nearly perfect outline for a course on this subject, and I began writing lectures following that protocol. As anyone who has developed a class such as this knows, preparing lectures on topics as diverse as determining demographics from the skeleton and time since death from partially or fully decomposed remains leads one to review the works of many prominent forensic anthropologists. Thus, the writings of Wilton Krogman, T. Dale Stewart, Clyde Snow, William Bass, Ellis Kerley, Douglas Ubelaker, Stan Rhine, and many others figured prominently in my classroom preparations. At the end of the semester, I looked over my lecture notes and realized that they had the makings of a textbook on forensic anthropology. Since one did not exist, I was inspired by the founders and the many fine workers in the field, to embark on this venture. So if this work reaches its goal of providing a comprehensive overview of forensic anthropology to date, it is because (to paraphrase Isaac Newton) I have stood on the shoulders of giants.

Introduction to Forensic Anthropology is meant to be a self-contained textbook for a lower-division, college-level course. Therefore, I have endeavored to keep complex terminology to a minimum. Only the most basic anatomical terms, as given in *Gray's Anatomy*, are used. Also, because forensic anthropology is an applied science, this book emphasizes the *hows* of this field, leaving the *whys* unexplored. For example, although the reason for the lumbar curve in the human vertebral column is interesting from an anatomical and evolutionary standpoint, this and other such issues are not discussed. Rather, these features are only described as they relate to the forensic anthropological process. Also, when discussing relevant aspects of the human skeleton, I focused on the central tendency of these features, while paying only a little attention to human variation. My reasoning is that students first must understand what "typical" specimens look like before approaching how individual specimens can vary from the norm. Although some would disagree with this approach, I think that it is appropriate to the intended audience of this work.

In a book of this nature, it is difficult to determine the number of references that are appropriate. Since it is a textbook, I followed the guideline that, if a subject is generally accepted, I did not provide sources. In addition, references are not given for observations from my own experience. I also took the opportunity to document many aspects of human osteology that are generally known by skeletal biologists but are not treated formally. Thus, information on differentiating prehistoric from contemporary remains, which is scattered in single sentences in the literature, is compiled and given full treatment in the text. These include the skeletal studies that I have performed over the years, as well as observations on the fine forensic osteological collection of the New Mexico Office of the Medical Investigator. However, whenever available, I have provided references to summary articles when describing methods.

Since the publication of the first edition of this textbook, forensic anthropology has become more and more focused on objective methods (e.g., logistic regression for determining sex), as opposed to the more subjective techniques of the past (e.g., anthroposcopic viewing of the classic traits of the pelvis for determining sex). This trend is due to important U.S. Supreme Court decisions (e.g., *Daubert v. Merrell Dow Chemical* [as in Chapter 1 text]) as well as federal legislation (i.e., Federal Rules of Evidence) and programs aimed at developing "best practices" for the field (e.g., Scientific Working Group for Anthropology [SWGANTH]). This natural evolution toward greater methodological rigor has influenced the contents of this book in the following manner. First, if a method was well accepted, it was included here no matter what problems might exist with its formulation (e.g., unknown nature of sample on which it was based). Despite the greater emphasis placed on objectivity, well-accepted methods will continue to be used by forensic anthropologists even as researchers provide supporting data confirming their value. Thus, it is appropriate to include them here. Second, methods employing large ($n \geq 100$) and diverse (Whites, Blacks, Asians) samples were incorporated if the demographics of the sample members were known unequivocally. This helped ensure that only rigorously tested methods are presented. Third, methods were included only if they were based on samples from the United States; inclusion of those based on worldwide samples would make this book too cumbersome. Fourth, only simple methods involving few measurements are included. As methods become more rigorous, by necessity they become more complex (e.g., Fourier analysis), sometimes too complex for a book of this nature. Thus, to keep with the purpose of presenting the basic methods of the field but keeping in mind the level of the intended audience, only those methods that involve a few basic measurements (e.g., skull length, skull width, skull height) and simple computations (e.g., addition, multiplication) are presented. For the interested reader, citations to references that provide the more complex methods are provided. Fifth, a newer method was described if it had been studied by at least two independent researchers; my thinking was that most methods need confirmation before inclusion in a book of this nature.

Despite the above, however, I did break these rules on occasion. When I felt a topic should be included, even if only one study without a large and varied sample was available, it is described here (e.g., Ann Ross's study of caliber and cranial entrance wound size). I also violated these rules when a method was based on more appropriate samples (e.g., the stature formula of Rebecca Wilson and colleagues that are based on a modern forensic sample) even when more classic studies were available (e.g., the Trotter and Gleser formulas). I even included studies that used samples outside this country when I felt the results would be applicable to all humans (e.g., Cynthia Wilczak and Kenneth Kennedy's study of marker's of occupational stress).

The following six points represent what is new for this edition:

- Greater discussion in Chapter 1 on legislation and court decisions affecting forensic anthropology
- Increased emphasis on quantification of error rates of both old and new methods
- Addition of logistic discriminant functions for sexing skulls based on visual traits in Chapter 8

- Revised stature reconstruction formulas in Chapter 10 based on data in the Database for Forensic Anthropology
- Inclusion of stature reconstruction formulas for fleshed body parts in Chapter 10
- Reorganization of Chapter 18 around positive, probable, and other methods of identification

As with any large manuscript, this book represents the result of the work of many individuals. Although I accept full responsibility for omissions and errors, I thank with all my heart the following people. First, I thank Stan Rhine, who read every word of this text with the sole purpose of ensuring that the field that he loves so well is not misrepresented. His suggestions greatly improved this text and, on more than one occasion, saved me from writing a book that was not properly focused. Second, I thank the reviewers who provided helpful comments and suggestions to the first edition: Kenneth Kennedy, Cornell University; Eugene Giles, University of Illinois; Anthony Falsetti, University of Florida; Murray Marks, University of Tennessee; and A. Midori Albert, University of North Carolina at Wilmington. My thanks also goes to the reviewers of the second edition: Midori Albert, University of North Carolina at Wilmington; George Gill, University of Wyoming; Michael Pietrusewsky, University of Hawaii; Mary K. Sandford, University of North Carolina at Greensboro; and Michael Warren, University of Florida. This book is better because of their efforts. Third, I thank the Office of Contract Archeology of the University of New Mexico's Maxwell Museum of Anthropology for the use of an office; their hospitality is greatly appreciated. Fourth, I thank the New Mexico Office of the Medical Investigator, which provided access to its collection of forensic cases that figures prominently in the photographs presented in this text. Fifth, I thank the Museum of Southwestern Biology at the University of New Mexico for allowing me to photograph their documented collection of nonhuman skeletal remains that appear in Chapter 3. Sixth, I thank the Maxwell Museum of Anthropology at the University of New Mexico for allowing me to photograph their documented collection of human skeletal remains. Seventh, I thank Dr. Murray Marks for the loan of two skulls of persons of African-American descent, whose photographs appear in Chapter 7. Eighth, I thank Julie R. Angel for her fine photography; her attention to detail ensured that all pictures appearing in this book illustrate those aspects that I wanted to show. Ninth, I thank Jay R. Alexander of I-hua Graphics for his drawings that are virtually photo quality. Last (and certainly not least) I thank my editors, Sarah Kelbaugh, Jennifer Jacobson, David Repetto, and Nancy Roberts, their editorial assistants, Lori Flickinger, Amy Holborow, Emma Christensen, and Jack Cashman; my production editors, Pat Torelli, and Joseph Malcolm, my project managers Tom Conville and Denise Forlow, and all the people at Allyn and Bacon and Prentice Hall who allow me to continue to write new editions. Without them, this work would not have been possible.

Steven N. Byers

FOREWORD

Just as forensic anthropology is clearly too critical to be left to amateurs, so is the business of writing forewords. However, I will try, as few foreword writers can claim to have known their subject for as many years as I have known Steven Byers. He arrived at the University of New Mexico in 1983, ready to launch his Ph.D. work. But I had met him some years earlier, as an undergraduate.

You might expect Byers to have been an enthusiastic follower of matters forensic. But he was not. He pursued his own quiet path, winding through thickets of forensic anthropology students busily boiling down bones, examining gunshot wounds, and gathering to talk in hushed tones about the latest case. Byers shied away from such applied matters to concentrate on the osteology of extinct peoples rather than extant ones. However, it was impossible for him to avoid forensic anthropology entirely, and he became a participant in a number of research projects that had application to prehistoric osteology as well as to forensic anthropology.

Eventually he, too, succumbed to the siren call of forensic anthropology, and found himself teaching such courses at the undergraduate level. He quickly realized that forensic anthropology cannot simply be learned from a text and put immediately into practice. Long-term commitment and guided study are essential. He also learned that this burgeoning field had no real textbook and set about to remedy that defect. Over the next couple of years, our frequent lunch-time discussions centered evermore on the details of forensic anthropology as he worked his way through the intricacies of osteological analysis in a medicolegal context. Eventually he began to hand me bits and pieces, then entire chapters of what has now become the book that you, the reader, hold in your hands.

Forensic anthropology is a serious field of endeavor; it is much more than merely applied osteology. It requires comprehension of the limits of one's knowledge. It requires keeping interpretations within the boundaries of the data. It requires recognition that to mishandle data could imperil another person's life or freedom. The forensic anthropologist must live by the realization that to venture beyond those bounds could not only harm his reputation and by extension, tarnish the field, but, more important, could put another person into unwarranted jeopardy.

The world of forensic medicine is divided into a large number of specialties, each of which adds its own particular insights and understandings to the resolution of a case. The forensic anthropologist sees only a small part of the total caseload. However, some of those cases may involve the forensic anthropologist not only in recovery and examination of remains and the writing of a detailed report, but testimony in court. That is what makes forensic anthropology "forensic." For every case carries with it the potential of courtroom testimony as an expert witness, whose duty it is to provide the jury another piece or two of the puzzle to fit into place. With that duty comes the requirement to say only what can be said, to say it succinctly, clearly, and unambiguously. The ultimate decision belongs to the jury. But it is the forensic anthropologist's obligation to provide them the data and *interpretation* that will help to illuminate the matter before them.

Not everyone who reads this book, or even those who also take additional coursework in forensic anthropology at one of those few institutions offering such training, will become a forensic anthropologist. And a good thing it is, since the work tends to be sporadic, difficult to find, and derided by colleagues who claim to be doing "real" science. But it is rewarding in other ways. In a sense, forensic anthropology is to the rest of anthropology as nuclear physics is to theoretical physics: It is committed to interdigitation with the real world.

However, to take a course (or courses) in forensic anthropology is valuable in itself. Such courses show the student how a rather esoteric subject (the study of human bones) can be applied to modern life. They show how a detailed examination of bones can reveal much about the identity of a person, how he or she lived, and, in some cases, how that person died. They illustrate, time and time again, that knowledge is not static and that, as we slowly push back the boundaries of ignorance, we engage in that most human of all activity, rational thought.

So for those of you who are reading this book who will never take another course in forensic anthropology, read it carefully. You will find it to be a sure guide into the labyrinth of forensic anthropology. For those few who prevail against all reason and logic to pursue a career in this field, this book will provide you a good introduction to what will become a critical force in shaping your life. You will also help other people (many of whose names you will never know) to come to grips with trauma in their lives. It is a specialized and noble application of human osteology. It is science in the service of humanity.

Stanley Rhine

Introduction

In 2009, a woman walking her dog in the area known as the West Mesa of Albuquerque, New Mexico, discovered human bones that eventually lead the police to the skeletal remains of 11 bodies (plus one fetus) believed to be prostitutes. In 1991, a fully clothed skeleton was found lying on an open-coil box spring mattress beneath the front porch of a house in Jefferson Parish, Louisiana. In the basement of a burned-out house in Tennessee, a charred skeleton was discovered among the debris left from a fire. In 1979, the partially skeletonized remains of a young adult male, exhibiting a crushing blow to the side of the skull and cut marks to the bones of the thorax, were recovered from a wooded area in the Midwestern United States. Despite the differences in time and geographic location, all of these cases had one thing in common: one of the most important persons involved in the investigation of these remains was a forensic anthropologist.

Forensic anthropology is the field of study that deals with the analysis of human skeletal remains resulting from unexplained deaths. Experts in this discipline, because of their understanding of skeletal biology and associated subjects, examine human bones with the goal of extracting as much information as possible about persons represented by skeletal remains and about the circumstances surrounding their deaths. Since forensic anthropology employs the principles of anthropology to analyze legal problems involving human osteological material, it is an applied science that embraces both anthropological and forensic studies.

Forensic anthropologists attempt to accomplish five main objectives in their work. First, when soft tissue has deteriorated to the point that demographic characteristics of a body cannot be determined by visual inspection, these forensic specialists attempt to determine ancestry (i.e., race or ethnic group), sex, age, and living height from the skeleton. Second, when there is evidence of traumatic injury (e.g., bullet holes, stab wounds, fractures) to human bone, forensic anthropologists attempt to identify the nature of the traumas and their causative agent(s) with the intent of gathering information pertaining to the cause and manner of death. Third, since forensic anthropologists have studied the amount of deterioration that occurs in cadavers over time, they often can render a determination of the postmortem interval, that is, the amount of time that has passed since persons have died. Fourth, because they are acquainted with the methods of archaeology, these specialists can assist in locating and recovering buried or surface remains in such a manner that all evidence relevant to a forensic investigation is collected. Finally, forensic anthropologists, using the unique features present in virtually all skeletons, can provide information useful in obtaining positive identifications of deceased persons.

As mentioned above, forensic anthropology intersects with both anthropological and forensic studies. Anthropology is the study of the biological and cultural aspects of all humans in all places in all times. One subdivision of this discipline is biological anthropology, the study of the biological evolution and development of humans. Forensic anthropology is one of the specialties within this subdiscipline. The forensic sciences are those fields of study in medicine and jurisprudence that deal with legal issues, both criminal and civil. Since forensic anthropology is the study of skeletal material that comes under the jurisdiction of law enforcement and other similar agencies, it also is one of the forensic sciences.

Forensic anthropologists usually study skeletons of deceased persons (i.e., **decedents**) that the **medicolegal community** (e.g., medical investigators, coroners) has defined as requiring investigation. Generally, these are people who have died within the last 50 years when not in the care of a physician. Fifty years is the appropriate period for investigating deaths, because this is the time in which it is probable that those personally knowledgeable of decedents and the circumstances surrounding their deaths might still be alive. (This would include the perpetrator of a crime in cases of homicide.) Thus, forensic anthropologists deal with the skeletonized remains of persons whose deaths could be the result of criminal activity within the present adult human life span.

As stated above, the traditional role of forensic anthropologists is to work with cases of human deaths when soft tissue has degenerated to the point that other medical forensic specialists (e.g., pathologists) cannot determine demographics, time since death, and cause and manner of death. Forensic anthropologists step in when decomposition is so advanced that these characteristics can be determined only from skeletal remains. However, forensic anthropologists increasingly are becoming involved as consultants even when soft tissue is present. Thus, law enforcement agencies may ask forensic anthropologists to view the bones of a "fleshed" body to determine if there is fracturing under tissues that have not decomposed. Similarly, forensic anthropologists may help to untangle the sequence and trajectories of multiple bullet wounds to "fresh" bodies. In addition, when age cannot be determined from a cadaver, forensic anthropologists harvest parts of bones to determine this demographic characteristic. Finally, because of their knowledge of bone and tooth changes during growth, they have been asked to estimate the age of living young persons accused of crimes to determine if they are old enough to stand trial as adults.

In addition to the above-described work, forensic anthropologists fulfill a number of other roles in modern society. First, these specialists are consulted in the identification of victims of mass disasters. Airplane crashes, wars, acts of nature, or any phenomenon in which a large number of people perish and their remains are dismembered or disfigured are events that may need the skills of forensic anthropologists. Thus, when the Big Thompson River in north-central Colorado unexpectedly flooded in 1976 killing 139 people, a forensic anthropologist (Michael Charney), working as a deputy coroner with other specialists, helped organize the effort that lead to the positive identification of all victims. Similarly, a forensic anthropologist (Stanley Rhine) assisted the Office of the Medical Investigator in 1980 when riots at the State Penitentiary in Santa Fe, New Mexico, left a number of inmate bodies burned beyond recognition.

Another area in which forensic anthropologists work is the study of atrocities committed during warfare. Civil unrest has resulted in the deaths of numerous victims of political violence in many countries, particularly those in Central and South America, as well as in various countries in Africa and Europe. A number of organizations, such as Physicians for Human Rights and the United Nations Commission on Human Rights, provide funding for consultants to travel to various countries to investigate these deaths. And forensic anthropologists are often in the group that performs this work. In the Americas, one major figure in these types of investigations is Clyde Collins Snow. This famous forensic anthropologist has done much to bring to light the circumstances

BOX 1.1
The Analysis of Francisco Pizarro

In 1984, William R. Maples was part of a team that analyzed the skeleton of Francisco Pizarro, the conqueror of the Inca Empire. Pizarro was assassinated in 1541 by the son of a dead rival who wished revenge for the death of his father and the loss of his lands, for both of which Pizarro was responsible. Using swords and perhaps a crossbow, the assassins assaulted Pizarro while he was eating his Sunday meal. Accounts of the assassination, told by conspirators who confessed, indicate that Pizarro was disabled by a sword cut to the throat; then, as he lay on the ground, his body was pierced by multiple sword thrusts and possibly shot by a crossbow. Over the years, the body of Pizarro was moved and reburied on several occasions, causing his remains to become lost. Several skeletons were attributed to the conqueror of Peru, resulting in a request by Peruvian historians for Maples and others to examine remains in an attempt to provide an identification.

When Maples went to Lima, he was confronted with two boxes, one of which contained the mixed remains of several adults and children; the other contained human bones and a lead box with a traumatized human skull. After viewing the material, Maples determined that the skull in the lead box belonged to a headless skeleton in the other box. This skeleton was of a 5-foot, 5-inch to 5-foot, 9-inch white male who was over 60 years old at the time of his death. All of these demographic characteristics agreed with what was known of Pizarro at the time of his death. The skeleton showed no less than 11 and as many as 14 cut marks to the vertebral column, arms, and head. Most of the cuts were concentrated on the head and neck area, which agreed with the description of the assassination provided by the conspirators. One cut indicated that a double-edged instrument (probably a sword) was thrust from the right side, cutting the right vertebral artery and nicking the first neck (cervical) vertebra. The skull also manifested a thrust wound to the left eye orbit that exited through its outside wall. Similarly, a thin-bladed instrument had been thrust up through the neck where it entered the braincase; it was twisted in place and then withdrawn and thrust in again. Given the demographics of the skeleton and the agreement of its trauma with the recorded death of Pizarro, the identification of these remains as the conqueror of Peru was considered "positive."

surrounding the deaths of victims of political violence, as well as helping to organize and educate local authorities on the methods used to investigate atrocities.

Finally, forensic anthropologists have become involved in the study of persons of historical interest but of no medicolegal significance. For example, William R. Maples brought his expertise to the study of the skeleton of Francisco Pizarro, the conqueror of the Inca Empire, who in 1541 was murdered by political rivals (see Box 1.1). He also studied the remains of the last czar of Russia and his family, who were executed by firing squad in 1918, as well as the remains of President Zachary Taylor, who some persons have suspected of dying by poisoning. Similarly, Douglas H. Ubelaker studied the skeleton of Carl Weiss, the accused assassin of Senator Huey P. Long of Louisiana in 1935. His work, showing the trajectory of the bullets fired by Long's bodyguards that killed Weiss, helped lay to rest questions about the authenticity of the official reports of the time.

This field holds a fascination for all who work in it, or for those who simply come in passing contact with it. The analysis of human skeletal remains for information on deceased persons is an area that is only slowly becoming known to law enforcement and the general public. Therefore, it is the purpose of this book to provide an overview of the methods used by forensic anthropologists to examine human skeletal remains. Specifically, the goal of the author is to describe each step in the forensic anthropological process with equal intensity and detail so that a clear understanding of the field will result. After reading this work, although they will not become experts, students will

FIGURE 1.1   Thomas Dwight, the father of American forensic anthropology. (Photo by Julie R. Angel; reprinted from: Thomas Dwight, M.D., L.L.D., John Warren, *The Anatomical Record*, Copyright © 1911. Reprinted by permission of Wiley-Liss, Inc., a Subsidiary of John Wiley & Sons, Inc.)

have an appreciation of what can and cannot be determined from human skeletal remains.

HISTORICAL BACKGROUND

For his pioneering work concerning the medicolegal aspects of the human skeleton, Thomas Dwight (1843–1911) has been credited as the "Father of Forensic Anthropology in the United States" (Stewart, 1979). Dwight (Figure 1.1) was the first to write articles and essays, as well as to give lectures, on the topic of human skeletal identification, which was the original designation of forensic anthropology. During his lifetime, he researched methods for determining age, height, and sex from the sternum (breastbone); estimating stature without using bones of the arms and legs; determining age at death from closure of joints between the bones of the skull; and estimating sex from joints of long bones. His papers are the first of their kind that apply knowledge of the human skeleton to forensic situations in the United States.

From these beginnings, American forensic anthropology began a slow evolution that, through the efforts of many persons over the years, led to a new subdiscipline within anthropology. Several histories of this subdiscipline, as practiced in the United States, are available both in the popular (Joyce and Stover, 1991; Ubelaker and Scammell, 1992; Maples and Browning, 1994) and scientific (Stewart, 1979; Snow, 1982) literature. Readers are encouraged to consult these works for further details concerning the past events of this young science. The following discussion is based on the work of T. Dale Stewart (1979) and others as noted in the text. Since the history of this subdiscipline can be divided into formative, consolidation, and modern periods (Ubelaker and Scammel, 1992), these subdivisions will be discussed separately.

Formative Period: Early 1800s to 1938

Although Thomas Dwight is considered to be the founder of American forensic anthropology, the origin of this science in the United States can be traced to the Parkman murder of 1849 (Maples and Browning, 1994), where two anatomists first demonstrated the effectiveness of methods regularly used in forensic anthropology today. In 1849, Oliver Wendell Holmes I and Jeffries Wyman were professors of anatomy at Harvard University when they were asked to investigate the death of Dr. George Parkman. This prominent physician purportedly was killed by a Harvard University chemistry professor named John W. Webster. Webster had borrowed money from Parkman but committed murder rather than repay the debt. Webster then dismembered Parkman's body, placing segments in his anatomy lab and privy (similar to a septic tank) and burning the head in a furnace. Holmes and Wyman, with the help of their anatomy colleagues, were able both to reassemble the body and to determine that it was a 5-foot 10½-inch white male who was between 50 and 60 years old when he died. All this information was consistent with what was known of Parkman. In addition, dentures found in the furnace matched the molds of Parkman's mouth made by his dentist when the plates were fabricated. Thus, through the work of these scientists, an identification of the decedent was made, which (with the help of other evidence) helped to convict Webster of Parkman's murder.

Another famous crime of the formative period was the Leutgert case of 1897. In this highly publicized murder, Adolph Leutgert was accused of killing his wife Louisa and placing her body in a vat of potash located in his sausage factory. The body dissolved leaving only a greasy jelly, four small pieces of bone, and a ring belonging to Mrs. Leutgert (Maples and Browning, 1994). The four bone fragments were so small that they could fit on a present-day quarter. The prosecution called anthropologist George A. Dorsey (1868–1931), who appears to have been aware of Dwight's work, to determine if the bones could be identified. In a notable courtroom testimony, Dorsey was able to prove that the four fragments were from a human hand, foot, and rib. Although this evidence would not withstand the rigors required by modern courts, nonetheless, his testimony coupled with other evidence helped to convict Leutgert of the murder. Unfortunately, after this successful entry into the field, Dorsey never again consulted on criminal cases, apparently because he was severely criticized by opposing anatomists (Stewart, 1979).

After these promising beginnings, there was a period during which there were few writings and no cases receiving sensational publicity dealing with medicolegal aspects of the human skeleton. Harris H. Wilder (1864–1928) published, with Bert Wentworth, a book outlining the aspects of human identification from his work on dermatoglyphics (configuration of fingerprints) and reproduction of the face from the skull (a method used by forensic anthropologists today). Also, Paul Stevenson (1890–1971) wrote two articles on human skeletal identification, one on determining age from the epiphyseal union of the long bones (see Chapter 2 for an explanation) and the other on the stature of Chinese from long bone measurements. The theory underlying both of these methods is heavily used in present-day forensic anthropology.

Although the foregoing works represent the total of publications from Dwight's time to the middle part of the 1900s, several prominent anthropologists worked quietly on forensic cases, giving little importance to their work (Ubelaker and Scammell, 1992). Ales Hrdlicka (1869–1943), at the Smithsonian Institution, and Earnest Hooton (1887–1954), professor of anthropology at Harvard University, worked on a number of cases involving human skeletal identification without publishing any of their findings or receiving public recognition for their work.

Although not stated by most historians of forensic anthropology, two physicians of the formative period played prominent, albeit unwitting, roles in the development of this discipline. T. Wingate Todd, a physician in Cleveland, Ohio, started what was to become the Hamann–Todd collection of human skeletal remains (it also contains a large number of nonhuman primate skeletons). From 1912 to 1938, he was able to acquire the bones of approximately 2600 persons (Stewart, 1979). For many of these, the demographics are known unequivocally, making this collection heavily used for developing standards for determining ancestry, sex, age, and stature from various aspects of the human skeleton. Robert J. Terry and his successor Mildred Trotter performed a similar task in St. Louis, Missouri. Between 1914 and 1965, the Terry collection of 1636 human skeletons was compiled from dissecting-room cadavers, many of known age, sex, and ancestry (Stewart, 1979). This collection, which bears his name, is now housed in the Smithsonian Institution, where it is used regularly for human skeletal research.

A final well-known murder occurring toward the end of the formative period that is often described in the forensic anthropology literature (Stewart, 1979; Ubelaker and Scammell, 1992; Maples and Browning, 1994) is the Ruxton case from Great Britain. Although, like the Parkman murder, the principal investigators were not forensic anthropologists, the methods used by the medicolegal specialists of this homicide are still in use today. The case involved the murder of two women: Isabella Van Ess, the common-law wife of physician Buck Ruxton, and Mary Rogerson, Ms. Van Ess's personal maid. The facts of the case are recorded in John Glaister and J. C. Brash's *Medico-Legal Aspects of the Ruxton Case*, published in 1937. In this volume, the authors describe how the disappearance of the women from the Ruxton home in Lancaster occurred around the same time that foul odors were described as emanating from the Ruxton residence. Also at this time, Dr. Ruxton rented a car, and stated that his wife and her maid had taken a vacation. When the dismembered, mutilated, and decomposed bodies of two persons were recovered from a gully in Scotland, the authors undertook to re-assemble the body parts and place them in positions similar to those of photographs of the women when alive. The antemortem and postmortem images were then compared, point by point, to show the similarity between the bodies and photographs of Ms. Van Ess and Ms. Rogerson. Based on this, and other evidence, Dr. Ruxton was found guilty of the murders and hanged in 1936. An interesting aside to this case, pointed out by Stewart (1979), is that Glasiter and Brash used the ratio between portions of the breast-bone (i.e., manubrium and sternal body; see Chapter 2 for information on the sternum) as positive proof that this bone from one of the mutilated bodies belonged to a woman. Their statement is in marked contrast to Thomas Dwight's finding in 1881 that this ratio is of little value in determining sex (see Stewart, 1979:94–95, for direct quote). Despite this error, Glasiter and Brash appear to have been right in their identifications, and their method of superimposing living photos on skeletonized remains is currently in use by forensic anthropologists.

Consolidation Period: 1939 to 1971

The formative period is considered to have ended with the publication of *Guide to the Identification of Human Skeletal Material* by Wilton Marion Krogman (1903–1987) in 1939 (Rhine, 1998). This landmark work, written as a pamphlet for the Federal Bureau of Investigation (FBI), summarized what was known about the human skeleton up to that time. In 1962, Krogman (Figure 1.2) expanded this work into what is considered the seminal publication in skeletal identification: *The Human Skeleton in Forensic Medicine.* This text, as well as its second edition with co-author M. Y. Iscan (Krogman and Iscan, 1986), was the first book to be devoted to the application of the study of human bone to forensics.

FIGURE 1.2 Wilton Marion Krogman. His FBI manual on skeletal identification ushered in the consolidation period of forensic anthropology. (Photo courtesy of Mark Krogman)

As discussed by T. Dale Stewart (1979), several events took place in the 1940s and 1950s that were to have a great impact on forensic anthropology. First, during World War II, the bodies of killed service men often could not be recovered from the battlefield fast enough (and thus were badly decom-posed) or were so severely disfigured that identification was difficult. To deal with this situation in the Pacific, the U.S. Army Office of the Quartermaster established the Central Identification Laboratory in Hawaii (called CILHI for short) with Charles E. Snow (1910–1967) as its first director (Stewart, 1979). When Snow returned to teaching on the mainland in 1948, Mildred Trotter (1899–1991) took over the lab, where she began working on improving ways of determining stature from the lengths of long bones, using the skeletons of killed servicemen and records of their heights. The result of her work at CILHI and as professor of anatomy at Washington University in St. Louis, Missouri, over the next quarter century is a standard set of formulas used for many decades for determining stature from skeletonized remains.

The second event of this period that increased the knowledge base of skeletal identification was the Korean War. Faced again with the problem of identifying servicemen killed in action, the U.S. Army established an iden-tification laboratory in Japan with T. Dale Stewart (1901–1997) as its direc-tor. Under his guidance, Thomas McKern undertook a definitive study for determining age from aspects of the skeletal remains of deceased soldiers. Their ensuing publication, *Skeletal Age Changes in Young American Males* (McKern and Stewart, 1957), still provides the standards for determining age at death from osteological remains.

One last person of importance during this period is T. Dale Stewart, who, while working at the Smithsonian Institution, contributed much to the development of forensic anthropology. He wrote numerous articles on the aspects of skeletal identification that applied to the forensic situation. Also, early in the modern period he wrote one of the most influential books in the field: *Essentials of Forensic Anthropology* (Stewart, 1979). Stewart also contributed to the development of the discipline by organizing a number of seminars over a 20-year period on skeletal identification that became increasingly concerned with forensics through time. Finally, with Mildred Trotter, he was largely responsible for persuading the U.S. Army to allow for research on the human remains from World War II and the Korean War under their care.

Modern Period: 1972 to the Present

The modern period is considered to have begun when the Physical Anthropology Section in the American Academy of Forensic Sciences (AAFS) met for the first time in 1972 (Rhine, 1998). The founding of this section was the result of work by Ellis R. Kerley (1924–1998) and Clyde Collins Snow (1928–present) (Figure 1.3), who in the previous year had solicited enough interest among their colleagues to meet the minimum number of members required by the AAFS. Five years later, the American Board of Forensic Anthropology (ABFA) was created with the purpose of ensuring the competence of persons who practice forensic anthropology in the United States, Canada, and their territories. As of this writing, it is composed of 70 diplomates (board certified forensic anthropologists), while the Physical Anthropology Section of the AAFS has almost 400 members.

FIGURE 1.3 Ellis Kerley *(left)* and Clyde Collins Snow *(right)*. Their efforts to form the physical anthropology section within the American Academy of Forensic Sciences signaled the beginning of the Modern Period. (E. Kerley photograph, courtesy of W. M. Bass. C. C. Snow photograph, courtesy of Dr. Snow; original taken by Daniel Hernandez, retaken by Julie R. Angel)

Two last events of note in the modern period are the founding of the Forensic Anthropology Data Bank at the University of Tennessee, Knoxville, and the founding of the Scientific Working Group for Forensic Anthropology (SWGANTH). As more and more information was accumulated on modern human skeletons, it became obvious that contemporary people were deviating from the norms established by the skeletal material of the Terry and Todd collections, as well as the World War II and Korean War dead. This prompted the Physical Anthropology section of the AAFS to form a committee that eventually created a computer database of information on modern skeletons (Moore-Jansen et al., 1994). This forensic data bank, started in 1986, is continuing today to collect information on documented forensic cases so that new standards for determining demographic and other characteristics from the human skeleton can be updated continuously. The data collected here has been used to develop a series of computer programs, called FORDISC, which can be used to calculate ancestry and sex.

SWGANTH was founded in 2008 by the FBI and Department of Defense Central Identification Lab (DOD CIL) to recommend "best practices" in the discipline. With the greater emphasis on verifying methods and their error rates in the forensic disciplines in general (see discussion of *Daubert* later), this working group is in the process of identifying and codifying existing standard and developing standards where they do not exist. The ultimate goal is to write guidelines for the methods and make them available to all practicing forensic anthropologists. Since this body is fairly new, guidelines have not yet been issued; however, these will be published on their website (www.swganth.org) in the future.

FORENSIC ANTHROPOLOGISTS AND THE MEDICOLEGAL COMMUNITY

Forensic anthropology is just one field within a group of specialties in the medicolegal community that deals with human death. The main experts in this community are medical examiners, coroners, and forensic pathologists. Medical examiners and coroners are persons who have the legal responsibility to certify the deaths of people dying within their jurisdiction when not in the care of a physician. Coroners are elected officials who may, or may not, have medical training, while medical examiners are licensed physicians who have specialized in forensic work. Assisting these specialists are forensic pathologists, who are medical doctors that perform autopsies and other procedures with the purpose of discovering any information that can help determine the cause and manner of death. All these specialists usually perform their functions on "fresh" bodies, that is, decedents who are visually recognizable and whose soft tissue can be used to determine matters relevant to their deaths.

Once human remains are badly decomposed, skeletonized, or heavily burned, other specialists must be consulted in the investigation of unknown deaths. Three specialties that are useful particularly with these types of remains are forensic anthropology, forensic archaeology, and forensic odontology. As described earlier, **forensic anthropology** deals with the identification of persons from their skeletons. Its function is to provide law enforcement officials with a demographic profile of decedents that can be checked against people listed in their missing persons' files. By limiting the number of cases to examine (e.g., only white males around 20 years of age and approximately 6 feet tall at the time of death), the likelihood of finding a match is enhanced. After such a match is discovered, forensic anthropologists sometimes perform a second function by helping to supply data for the positive identification of the deceased.

Another specialty that deals with decomposed human remains of medicolegal significance is **forensic archaeology**. Specialists in this field use archaeological methods to locate and retrieve human skeletal material while following the rules of evidence established by law enforcement agencies. Since most forensic anthropologists are knowledgeable in the methods of forensic archaeology, many anthropologists do not consider this a separate specialty (Rhine, personal communication). Finally, **forensic odontologists** are dentists who specialize in identifying persons from their dentition (i.e., teeth). Whereas forensic anthropologists use information from medical records to determine a positive identification, forensic odontologists match dental records with the dentition of decedents to accomplish this function. These specialists perform the bulk of positive identifications from skeletonized remains.

From this description, it can be seen that forensic anthropologists are part of a team of specialists concerned with matters of deaths of unknown cause. These specialists, keenly aware of the extent of their knowledge, regularly emphasize teamwork in the forensic process (Charney and Wilber, 1984; Rhine, 1998). Typically, experts from many forensic specialties work with human remains and the associated physical evidence. This not only includes the authorities mentioned previously, but also experts in **ballistics** (the study of firearms), **forensic entomology** (the study of insects on human remains), **forensic botany** (the study of plants in relation to crime scenes), and any number of other forensic specialties.

FORENSIC ANTHROPOLOGY AND JURICEPRUDENCE

In recent years, much has been published concerning legislative and judicial events that have heavily influenced the forensic disciplines, and consequently forensic anthropology. Although a detailed history would not be appropriate to a book of this nature, a simplified outline of the most important of these events is presented in chronological order:

1. *Frye v. United States* – This 1923 case, called *Frye* for short, involved a person found guilty of murder, James Frye, who appealed his conviction based on the trial judge's exclusion of the results of a "Deception Test" that was part of his defense. This test, a crude precursor of the Polygraph or Lie Detector, involved the use of a blood pressure cuff to read systolic pressure (the pressure exerted by the heart when it contracts and forces blood out of the left ventricle). It was believed by the psychologist William Moulton Marston (oddly enough, the creator of the comic book character, Wonder Woman) that systolic blood pressure would automatically increase when a person lies. When James Frye passed this test, Marston accepted his claim of innocence. The Washington DC Circuit Court was asked to determine if the trail judge erred when he excluded Marston's testimony, with its assertion of Frye's innocence. This court concluded that the trial judge had not erred and that ". . . while courts will go a long way in admitting expert testimony deduced from a well-recognized scientific principle or discovery, the thing from which the deduction is made must be sufficiently established to have gained general acceptance in the particular field in which it belongs." This ruling is credited with developing the "general acceptance" criterion for expert testimony that influences American jurisprudence to this day. The most common interpretation of *Frye* is that expert testimony can be admitted if the principles upon which it is based are generally accepted by other professionals in the field of study. Unfortunately, this ruling made it difficult for new methods that have not yet gained general acceptance to be admitted in court.

2. *Federal Rules of Evidence (FRE)* – The FRE were passed in 1975 as a means "to secure fairness in administration, elimination of unjustifiable expense and delay, and promotion of growth and development of the law of evidence to the end that the truth may be ascertained and proceedings justly determined." Although it contains numerous rules, the most important for the forensic sciences is Rule 702, which states:

If scientific, technical, or other specialized knowledge will assist the trier of
fact to understand the evidence or to determine a fact in issue, a witness

qualified as an expert by knowledge, skill, experience, training, or education, may testify thereto in the form of an opinion or otherwise, if (1) the testimony is based upon sufficient facts or data, (2) the testimony is the product of reliable principles and methods, and (3) the witness has applied the principles and methods reliably to the facts of the case.

The "trier of fact" is the jury or trail judge, and this rule was written to provide the court with general criteria on which to base a decision as to the admissibility of experts and their testimony. Notice that Rule 702 not only recognizes the importance of the experience of the expert providing testimony, but also that the expert's testimony is based on data and methods that are supported scientifically. Just as importantly, notice that it does not include the "general acceptance" criterion.

3. *Daubert v. Merrell Dow Pharmaceuticals, Inc.* – This case, called *Daubert* for short, was brought against the Merrell Dow Pharmaceuticals Company by parents of children with birth defects. In it, they allege that an anti-nausea drug taken by the mother of Jason Daubert, and manufactured by the company, caused that child's birth defects. (Another minor child, Eric Schuller, was a co-defendant.) In 1993, the Supreme Court heard the case as a means of determining the standard(s) for the admission of scientific evidence in federal court. This case helped reduce the influence of the "general acceptance" criterion (but did not eliminate it) when it agreed with the lawyers for Daubert and Schuller that the FRE had superseded *Frye*. The opinion helped interpret the FRE when it noted that, for a scientific theory or technique to be admissible, five guidelines needed to be considered by the court:

1. The theory or technique can be (and has been) tested
2. It has been subjected to peer review and publication
3. It has a known or potential error rate
4. It has standards controlling its operation
5. It has attracted widespread acceptance within a relevant scientific community

An important part of this ruling is its insistence on flexibility in these criteria; that is, they are not absolute preconditions for the acceptance of expert testimony by the court, but guidelines to be considered by the trial judge.

4. *General Electric v. Joiner* – Robert Joiner sued General Electric (GE) and other companies complaining that the chemicals used by them had caused his small cell lung cancer. Joiner worked around transformers made by GE that contained a chemical coolant contaminated by polychlorinated biphenyls (PCBs). Since these chemicals are considered hazardous to human health, experts contended that the PCBs and their derivatives caused Joiner's illness. The court did not allow their testimony because the judge felt that the experts did not show a link between exposure to PCBs and small cell lung cancer. In 1997, the Supreme Court ruled that the trial judge did not abuse his discretion as gatekeeper when he ruled that the expert testimony was inadmissible because there was ". . . too great of an analytical gap between the data and the opinion proffered." The Supreme Court further ruled "that abuse of discretion is the proper standard by which to review a district court's decision to admit or exclude scientific evidence."

5. *Kumho Tire Company, Ltd., v. Carmichael* – This case was brought by Patrick Carmichael after a tire on his minivan failed, causing an accident in 1993 where one passenger died. A tire failure analyst alleged that the tire, manufactured by the Kumho Tire Company, was defective. In 1999, the Supreme Court heard the case because lower courts disagreed on the admissibility of the analyst's testimony. Specifically, one court discarded the tire failure analyst's testimony on the grounds that it did not meet the

Daubert standards. However, a higher court ruled that the analyst's testimony was technical not scientific, and therefore not subject to the *Daubert* standards. The Supreme Court ruled that the lower court was correct when it asserted that all expert testimonies were subject to the *Daubert* standards, since the distinction between scientific and technical was not simple and clear-cut. In addition, this decision re-emphasized the role of the trial judge as gatekeeper as to the admissibility of expert testimony.

In the past, forensic anthropology testimony was allowed in court because the persons offering opinions generally had advanced (usually doctorate) degrees in anthropology, thereby meeting the requirement of Rule 702 (even before it was written). Additionally, the methods they used met the category of "general acceptance" (*Frye*) and/or the three criteria of Rule 702. Recently, the discipline has begun to (re-)analyze all methods, including those generally accepted, to help ensure that they fit the guidelines given in the FRE and *Daubert*, so that the ruling of *Joiner* is not violated. Thus, there is a greater emphasis on standardization and quantification in the field. This helps to ensure that the methods of forensic anthropology are acceptable in a court of law, whether judged to be scientific or technical (*Kumho*).

In the following chapters of this textbook, every attempt will be made to present methods that have been tested on samples of known human (and sometimes, nonhuman) remains (Guideline 1 of *Daubert*). The results of these tests (studies) will be cited from the peer-reviewed scientific journals in which they were published (Guideline 2 of *Daubert*); the primary journals that publish the results of research in forensic anthropology are the Journal of Forensic Sciences (published by the AAFS) and the American Journal of Physical Anthropology (published by the American Association of Physical Anthropologists). The presentation of these methods will include the standards used when collecting data (part of Guideline 4 of *Daubert*), including end points of measurements (e.g., stature is measured from the bottom of the foot to top of the head) and scales of measurement (e.g., ordinal-level categories, centimeters, kilograms). Methods of analysis also will be described as a number of these have become standard in the field (also part of Guideline 4 of *Daubert*). Similarly included will be error rates when known (Guideline 3 of *Daubert*); these take many forms but the most common are standard errors of measurements and/or statistical parameters, and ranges of values between the highest and lowest value of a measurement or observation (see Methods of Forensic Anthropology section in this chapter). While perusing this textbook, readers will see these aspects described for most of the methods of forensic anthropology. When missing, the readers should remind themselves that *Daubert* does not completely disclaim *Frye*, with the inclusion Guideline 5; that is, generally accepted methods are satisfactory in some cases. Notice also that, by following the *Daubert* guidelines, forensic anthropologists reduce the risk of trial judges feeling there is "too great of an analytical gap between the data and the opinion proffered," and not allow forensic anthropological findings to influence a case (*Joiner*).

THE FORENSIC ANTHROPOLOGY PROTOCOL AND THE LAYOUT OF THIS BOOK

When confronted with decomposed bodies or skeletonized remains, forensic anthropologists attempt to provide law enforcement officials with as much information as possible about the decedents and the circumstances surrounding their deaths. In a now classic article, Clyde Collins Snow (1982) codified a protocol for gathering this information. In it he listed those aspects about deceased persons that forensic anthropologists should attempt to determine when working with human remains. Snow's protocol, presented as a series of questions, is quoted here:

1. Are the remains human?
2. Do they represent a single individual or the commingled remains of several?
3. When did death occur?
4. How old was the decedent?
5. What was the decedent's sex?
6. What was the decedent's race?
7. What was the decedent's stature? body weight? physique?
8. Does the skeleton (or body) exhibit any significant anatomical anomalies, signs of old disease and injuries or other characteristics which, singly or in combination, are sufficiently unique to provide positive identification of the decedent?
9. What was the *cause of death*? (e.g., "gunshot wound," "blunt force trauma," "tuberculosis," "unknown," etc.).
10. What was the *manner of death*? (i.e., "natural," "accident," "suicide," "homicide," "unknown").[*]

Although not all these questions can be answered in all cases, forensic anthropologists are enjoined to determine as much of this information as possible from human skeletal remains.

While this list presents the major points of concern, several additions and modifications can be made. First, differentiation of recent from prehistoric humans is part of the larger problem of establishing the forensic significance of skeletal remains. Thus, in addition to Snow's "Are the remains human?" can be added, "Are the remains of medicolegal significance (i.e., no more than 50 years have passed since death)?" In this manner, those skeletons that are too old (e.g., prehistoric) can be eliminated from further forensic analysis. Second, since most forensic anthropologists are trained in archaeological techniques, the proper recovery of decomposed or skeletonized remains is an important part of the forensic process. When present during recovery, forensic anthropologists can prevent the loss of information that may be helpful in determining answers to the 10 questions posed above. Third, because the word *race* engenders too many negative connotations (especially among professional anthropologists), the term *ancestry* is coming into wider use to designate what is known to the general public as race or ethnic group. Finally, the sequence of questions 4 through 6 should be rearranged due to methodological necessities. For example, some characteristics for estimating sex from the skeleton can be affected by ancestry (e.g., males of Asian ancestry often have more "female-looking" skulls than those of European ancestry). Also, many methods for determining sex, age, and stature require knowledge of ancestry to be properly applied. Therefore, ancestry should be considered first when analyzing the demographic aspects of decedents (Pickering and Bachman, 1997). A similar situation exists with age; many methods for determining this characteristic require knowledge of the sex (and occasionally ancestry) to be properly applied.

This list, modified as discussed, provides the subject matter of the chapters in this book. After an overview of the human skeleton in Chapter 2 (required of anyone who wishes to understand forensic anthropology), the chapters follow the adjusted sequence of the protocol. Chapter 3, Establishing Forensic Significance, discusses the methods for resolving the two questions of whether the remains are human and do the remains have medicolegal significance. Chapter 4, Recovery Scene Methods, describes the methods used to locate, map, and recover human remains in the forensic context. Chapter 5, Estimating Postmortem Interval, deals with the question of when the death occurred. Chapter 6, Initial Treatment and Examination, deals with the question of whether the remains represent a single individual or the commingled remains of several, as well as issues involved in preparing skeletal remains for examination.

---

[*]Used with permission from the *Annual Review of Anthropology*, Vol. 11, © 1982, by Annual Reviews. www.AnnualReviews.org

Once these preliminary functions are performed, the demographic characteristics of the skeleton can be determined. Thus, Chapter 7, Attribution of Ancestry, deals with the question of the decedent's ancestral group. Chapter 8, Attribution of Sex, describes methods for determining the decedent's sex. Chapter 9, Estimation of Age at Death, deals with the age of the decedent when he or she died, while Chapter 10, Calculation of Stature, deals with the first part of Snow's question 7, the decedent's stature.

After the demographics have been established, other issues concerning individuals or their deaths can be considered. Chapters 11 through 14 present information relevant to questions of the *cause of death* and the *manner of death*. These chapters individually deal with the different types of skeletal trauma encountered in forensic anthropology, and describe methods for determining their timing in relation to death. Chapter 15, Antemortem Skeletal Conditions, and Chapter 16, Postmortem Changes to Bone, describe aspects of the human skeleton that might be mistaken for skeletal trauma (thereby leading to a false indication of cause of death) or that could be used to help in the process of determining an identification. Chapter 17, Additional Aspects of Individualization, deals with the later part of question 7 (i.e., body weight and physique); additionally, it deals with any feature discernible only from the bones that can help identify the individual in a general sense (e.g., the decedent's facial features). Chapter 18, Obtaining an Identification, provides information needed to answer question 8; in this chapter methods that can "provide positive identification of the decedent" will be described. This chapter is also conceptually different from those preceding it; Chapters 3 through 17 involve gleaning as much information from the skeleton as possible without knowing the identity of the decedent. However, Chapter 18 presents methods that can be used to determine if the remains match those of a specific person. These methods therefore require that antemortem (premortem) medical or dental records of an actual person be available for comparison. Finally, Chapter 19, Conclusion, deals with issues surrounding the forensic anthropological process not described in previous chapters.

METHODS OF FORENSIC ANTHROPOLOGY

Like all other sciences, the methods used by forensic anthropologists can be divided into two (somewhat overlapping) types: those used to gather data, and those used to analyze data. Data-gathering methods involve techniques used to collect information from human skeletal remains and the circumstances surrounding their discovery. These vary from simple visual examination of skeletal (and to a lesser degree, soft tissue) traits and characteristics of the recovery site to complex methods, such as determining age from microscopic examination of thin sections of teeth. By contrast, data analysis methods involve techniques used to analyze the gathered data for the purpose of answering the questions posed by the forensic anthropology protocol. Thus, after data are gathered for determining the living height of a person from a skeleton, methods of stature reconstruction are employed to estimate this trait. Within each of these two types, there is a set of methods that is used regularly by forensic anthropologists. Since these techniques figure prominently in the following chapters, it is appropriate to describe them before proceeding further.

Data-Gathering Methods

Because the forensic anthropological process involves gathering information in both the field and the laboratory, the methods used in these areas are different, with some overlap. In the field, the general method is to observe and map the area around human remains and collect any items that appear to be related to the individual(s). This will be described in Chapter 4, so it will not be discussed further here.

Laboratory methods are those used to gather data on the (mainly) skeletal remains and (to a lesser extent) associated items. Although forensic anthropologists have an almost endless number of methods for gathering data, generally these techniques can be divided into four types: anthroposcopic, osteometric, chemical, and histologic. Each of these methods use one or more of the scales of measurement codified by S. S. Stevens (1946): **nominal**, **ordinal**, **interval**, and **ratio**. Since these pervade the four data-gathering types, they will be defined first.

The nominal scale of measurement involves the classification of data into discrete (usually) non-overlapping categories. In forensic anthropology, sex and ancestral group can be considered to be "measured" on a nominal scale. That is, sex is measured as either male or female (with genetic pathological conditions such as Klinefelter's syndrome overlapping the two groups); ancestral group is White, Black, or Asian (with groups such as Hispanics having characteristics of two of these categories). Ordinal scales also involve discrete non-overlapping categories but they can be ordered, such as small, medium, or large. Thus, the size of the mastoid process of the skull (the downwardly pointing knob of bone behind the ear) can be measured on a five-point scale from small to large (see Figure 8.13). An important aspect of this scale is that the distance between categories is not fixed; thus, in Figure 8.13 the difference in mastoid size between categories 1 and 2 is not necessarily the same as between 2 and 3. Both nominal and ordinal scales are called qualitative because they divide into categories that are non-numerical; the use of numbers to represent them is a mere convenience. Thus, it is just as reasonable to use M – Male and F = Female, as 1 = Male and 2 = Female; similarly, the five-point scale for the mastoid process (as well as those for other cranial characteristics) in Figure 8.13 could be represented by smallest, small, medium, large, and largest.

Interval levels of measurement are rare, with only two usually recognized: time and temperature. These scales have units of measurement that, unlike ordinal categories, are fixed; thus, the difference between 1° and 2°C is the same as between 101° and 102°C. A distinctive characteristic of these scales is that there is no natural zero point; thus, 0°C is the freezing point of water, not the absence of all heat. Similarly, AD 0 is not the start of time; it is a mere convenience for measuring time. Another characteristic of these scales is that the ratio between values is not meaningful. Thus, an object that is 40°C is not twice as hot as an object that is 20°C; similarly, an object dated AD 2000 is not twice as old as an object from AD 1000. The ratio level scale is that which one normally associates with measurement. These scales have a zero point and are comprised of units of measurement that are fixed. Thus, an inch is a set unit of measurement, as is a millimeter. Each of these units can be combined into other set units of measurement such as the foot (12 inches) and yard (36 inches) or the centimeter (10 mm) or the meter (100 cm). Stature (height) is measured on this type of scale (i.e., a person who is 5' 11" tall). Other measurements of the skeleton which involve the use of feet and inches, or (the more common) metric measures of centimeters, millimeters, and kilograms, are also measured using ratio scales. Unlike the interval level, in these scales, the ratio between measurements is meaningful; a person who is 200 lbs is twice as heavy as a 100 lb person. Also, the zero point has the meaning of the absence of a measured trait; a population with 0% blood type "A" means the absence of this blood type. These two levels of measurement are called quantitative because they use numerical categories.

Anthroposcopy is the visual inspection of the human body, sometimes with the aid of x-rays or a hand-held lens, for the purpose of identifying traits of a qualitative (i.e., nominal or ordinal scale) nature. Because it is the most accessible (i.e., does not require special instruments), it is the most common method used by forensic anthropologists to determine various characteristics of a skeleton. For example, visual examination of the human skulls pictured in Figure 1.4 would reveal that the one on the left (a) is larger and more heavily built than the one on the right (b). This would lead to an opinion that the

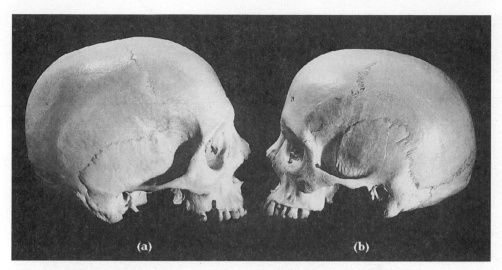

FIGURE 1.4   **(a)** Male and **(b)** female skulls showing the larger and heavier construction of the former. (Photo by Julie R. Angel; courtesy of the University of New Mexico–Albuquerque, Maxwell Museum of Anthropology, #39 and #21)

skull on the right was from a female because, on average, females are smaller and more delicate than males. Although this visual examination is somewhat subjective (e.g., "larger and more heavily built" versus "smaller and more delicate"), it is a powerful tool that, when used by experienced people, leads to proper identification of sex 80% to 90% of the time. Since the chance of a correct guess when choosing between two alternatives (i.e., male or female) of equal probability is 50%, this is a significant increase in the likelihood of being right. As will be seen in subsequent chapters, there are a number of anthroposcopically visible traits of the skeleton that, when viewed by forensic anthropologists, will lead to the determination of demographic (i.e., ancestry, sex, and age) and other characteristics of the skeleton with greater accuracy than predicted by probability theory.

Osteometry is the measurement of human bone on a quantitative scale (usually millimeters and centimeters) using calipers or an osteometric board (see Figure 1.5). **Metric methods**, as they often are called, attempt to quantify using ratio level scales many of the anthroposcopic characteristics helpful in the identification of aspects of the skeleton. Thus, forensic anthropologists will often take measurements to determine ancestry, sex, age, stature, and other characteristics of a living person from their skeletal remains. For example, simply measuring the humerus (the upper arm bone) of a person (see Figure 1.6) and multiplying its length by 5 will yield a rough estimate of the height of the individual from whom the bone was derived. Results of the analysis of metric data are often expressed in terms of probability (e.g., 80% probability that the person was male) or ranges of values (e.g., stature is between 5 feet, 3 inches, and 5 feet, 7 inches).

Chemical methods involve analyzing the chemical makeup of certain structures of the skeleton and associated matter (e.g., the ground beneath a decomposing body). These methods involve sampling matter and applying special techniques to determine their nature. **Histology** is the study of the microstructure of bone and teeth. This usually involves cutting off thin slices and staining them for viewing under a microscope to determine demographic characteristics (especially age). Both of these methods require special instrumentation that is not always available to forensic anthropologists. Thus, this book will concentrate mainly on the anthroposcopic and osteometric methods used in forensic anthropology, with only limited reference, where appropriate, to chemical and histological methods.

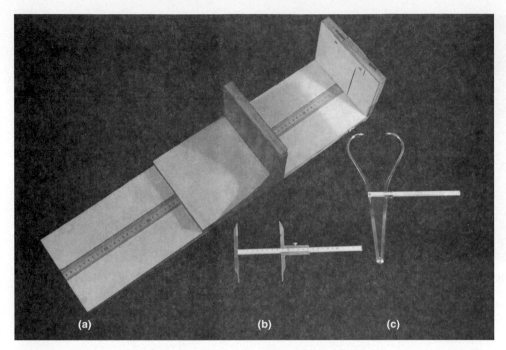

FIGURE 1.5 Instruments used by forensic anthropologists to measure bones: **(a)** osteometric board, **(b)** sliding caliper, and **(c)** spreading caliper. (Photo by Julie R. Angel)

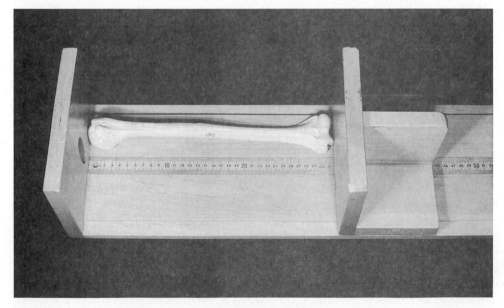

FIGURE 1.6 Measuring the upper arm bone (humerus) of a human being. By multiplying its length by 5, a rough estimate of the height of a person can be calculated. (Photo by Julie R. Angel)

Data Analysis Methods

Although each step in the forensic anthropology protocol has its own specific techniques, five methods are used most commonly to analyze data derived from the skeleton: decision tables, range charts, indexes, discriminant functions, and regression equations. The **decision table** helps researchers to judge the importance of conflicting information so that they can arrive at a single conclusion (e.g., although the skeleton has some characteristics of males, the most likely sex is female). The second method, **range chart**, involves making a visual representation of multiple ranges of estimates (e.g., age ranges) so that a central tendency can be determined. The third technique is a method for standardizing skeletal measurements for two dimensions; **indexes** are developed so that numerical expressions of the shape of a structure (e.g., nose opening) can be compared between different groups.

The last two methods are borrowed from statistics. **Discriminant function analysis**, like using indexes, is a method for calculating a numerical expression of shape; however, it can be used when more than two measurements are available. Finally, **regression** is a method by which the value of one characteristic (e.g., stature) can be determined from the values of other characteristics (e.g., lengths of long limb bones). Since these five methods are used extensively in forensic anthropology, they will be discussed separately next.

DECISION TABLES   One of the most common problems faced by forensic anthropologists is how to make a single determination from ambiguous data developed from skeletal remains. For example, when viewing indications of sex, some skeletons will manifest both male and female characteristics. The simplest method for deciding between conflicting information is the decision table. In this technique, the various decision options are listed across the top of the table, while the characteristics for determining these options are listed down the side. The user marks those columns where the characteristic indicates agreement with one of the options; and the column with the most marks represents the decision that is most likely to be correct.

As an example, suppose that a forensic anthropologist is given a skeleton and asked to determine if it is contemporary (i.e., could be of medicolegal significance) or noncontemporary. As will be seen in Chapter 3, a number of characteristics of bone can aid in this determination. These are listed down the left side of Table 1.1, while the options (i.e., contemporary and noncontemporary) are listed across the top. In each of the columns, the expression of the characteristics within each option is listed. Thus, contemporary skeletons are usually light in color (i.e., the color of fresh bone), whereas noncontemporary bones are often darkened by the soil in which they were buried. Similarly, the surface texture of contemporary bone is usually smoother than bone that is older (i.e., noncontemporary). Statements such as these can be made for all the characteristics listed in the table.

After creation of the table, it is only necessary to circle the expression of each characteristic seen in the skeleton at hand and count the number of traits supporting each option. Table 1.2 presents the results of a fictitious forensic case. As can be seen, the

TABLE 1.1   Decision Table for Determining Noncontemporary from Contemporary Remains

	Noncontemporary	Contemporary
Color	Dark	Light
Texture	Rough	Smooth
Hydration	Dry	Wet
Weight	Light	Heavy
Condition	Broken	Solid
Fragility	Fragile	Tough
Soft tissue	Absent	Present

TABLE 1.2 Decision Table for Noncontemporary versus Contemporary Example

	Noncontemporary	Contemporary
Color	Dark	(Light)
Texture	Rough	(Smooth)
Hydration	Dry	(Wet)
Weight	Light	(Heavy)
Condition	(Broken)	Solid
Fragility	Fragile	(Tough)
Soft tissue	(Absent)	Present

majority of the characteristics indicate that this skeleton is contemporary; therefore, it is likely that the specimen is medicolegally significant. Use of tables such as these can help untangle conflicting data when making a decision.

Several words of warning are necessary concerning this method. First, when constructing a decision table, it is important to ensure that all relevant characteristics are listed on the left side of the table. Incomplete information is one of the easiest ways to make an improper decision. Second, key characteristics must be remembered when using the decision table. These are traits that, when present, allow for an unequivocal decision to be made. For example, although not given in the fictitious case, if the teeth of the skeleton being analyzed were found to contain plastic crowns, all the characteristics marked in the Noncontemporary column are irrelevant. These types of crowns indicate contemporary remains even if **all** other traits denote an older age.

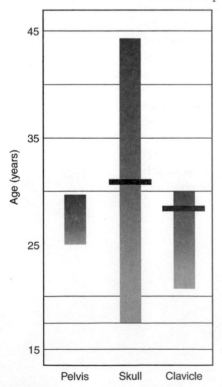

FIGURE 1.7 Range chart of skeletal age example. (Horizontal bars are averages.)

RANGE CHARTS Another common problem faced by forensic anthropologists is how to combine several sources of information to arrive at a single estimate. For example, in the coming pages, the reader will be faced with problems such as determining the age of an individual from features of the skull, as well as pelvis. When different characteristics from different structures provide data relevant to a single determination, some method must be developed for combining this information. There are many techniques for handling this situation, most of which are based on probability theory and are very complex. However, the simplest method is to chart the ranges of the features and see where the most overlap occurs. In this manner, the most likely estimate can be obtained.

An example will best illustrate this approach. Suppose that the age at death of a decomposed body is to be assessed from skeletal data. As will be seen in Chapter 9, there are various methods for determining this parameter. For the purposes of this discussion, the skeleton in question exhibits fusion of the growth center at the end of the clavicle (collar bone) where it attaches to the sternum (breastbone). Previous studies of growth have shown that this indicates an age at death of 21 to 30 years with an average around 28 years. Also, it is known that the lines that separate the various bones of the skull (called suture lines) fuse and disappear over time; in this fictitious example, the state of fusion indicates an age of 18 to 44 years, with an average around 31 years. Finally, features from the pelvis indicate an age of 25 to 29, with no average. To determine the most likely age at death from these data, the construction of a chart similar to that shown in Figure 1.7 is useful. The first step is to draw a time line that starts at the lowest value from the ranges given by the data and ends with their highest value; in our example, the low is 18 years, while the high is 44 (see vertical axis). Next, the ranges for each of the data sources (clavicle, skull, and pelvis) are drawn (vertical bars) and the averages are marked (horizontal crossbars).

This simple chart helps to illustrate the areas of overlap between the various ranges so that the most probable estimate can be made. From this example, the majority of the overlap is from 25 to 30 years, indicating an age at death in the mid- to late-twenties. As will be seen in the following chapters, this method is useful for estimating time since death, age at death, and any other parameter for which multiple sources of data are encountered. In addition, as shown in Box 1.2, this method has value in distinguishing the remains of one person from another.

BOX 1.2
The Oklahoma City Child Disappearances

Clyde Snow and James Luke (1984) present a use of the range chart for attributing skeletal remains to one of two missing children. In the summer of 1967, two children disappeared from the area of Oklahoma City. The first was a 5-year-old called "Anna" by Snow and Luke, who vanished while playing near her home in the late afternoon. The second, named "Barbara," was 6 years old when she disappeared 4 weeks later while riding her bicycle.

Despite massive searches, neither girl was located until the fall of that year, when the skeletonized remains of a child were discovered on an abandoned farm south of Oklahoma City. Along with some items of clothing, approximately one-third of a single skeleton was recovered; this included the skull, vertebrae of the neck and upper back, and at least one bone from each of the limbs.

Range chart of age changes

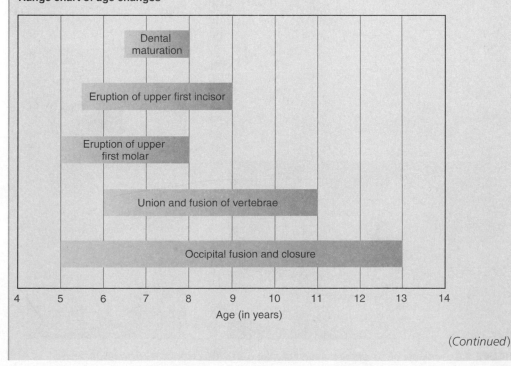

(*Continued*)

BOX 1.2 (Continued)

Because both girls were so close in age and general physique, it was not immediately obvious to Snow which was represented by the skeletonized remains. One area that he concentrated on was the determination of age. Consulting accepted methods for estimating age from the skeleton, he began charting age characteristics that he could observe on the remains. First, he determined that the four parts of the rear bone of the skull (called the occipital) that are separated at birth were fused in the specimen. Since this occurs between 5 and 13 years of age, he diagrammed this span first on a range chart (see bottom line on chart on page 19). Second, he looked at the vertebrae that also are divided into separate segments at birth. Here he noticed that the age indicated was between 6 and 11 years of age (next bar up on chart). Third, he noticed that the first upper molar was present and fully in place. Since this tooth erupts in most children between 5 and 8 years of age, he drew a line between these two ages on his chart (see third bar up on chart). Fourth, also looking at the teeth, he determined that the fully erupted upper first incisor indicated an age between 5½ and 9. Finally, using information on unerupted teeth, he determined an age between 6½ and 8 (see top line on chart). From this information, he concluded that the bones were those of Barbara's, because her age of 6 at disappearance fell closer to the midpoint of all the ranges. Since Anna's age of 5 was closer to the lower end of the ranges, it was less likely that her bones were those that were recovered.

INDEXES Indexes are simple, but powerful, statistics for quantifying anthroposcopic traits. When two measurements express visually identifiable characteristics, one can be divided into the other to obtain a single number. This number, when multiplied by 100, yields an index. Generally, the values of indexes vary among groups. Thus, calculating the index on an unknown skeleton can lead to a determination of group membership.

A good example of this method is the nasal index. This statistic is calculated by dividing the width of the nasal opening of the skull (Figure 1.8a) with the height of the nose (Figure 1.8b) and multiplying the result by 100:

$$\text{nasal index} = \frac{\text{nasal width}}{\text{nasal height}} \times 100 \tag{1}$$

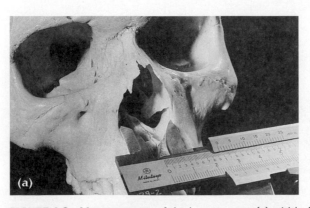

FIGURE 1.8 Measurements of the human nose: **(a)** width; **(b)** height. (Photo by Julie R. Angel)

Because persons of African descent (i.e., Blacks) generally have wide noses, the resultant index usually is 85% or higher (Olivier, 1969); this means that the nose is almost as wide as it is high. However, persons of European descent (i.e., Whites) with their narrower noses generally have indexes that are less than 70% (Olivier, 1969). From this information, a skull with a measured index of 90% would most likely be Black because this value falls within the range of this ancestral group while being above that of Whites.

DISCRIMINANT FUNCTIONS   Unlike indexes, discriminant functions use any number of measurements to distinguish two or more predetermined groups. The most famous application of this method in biological (and forensic) anthropology was by Eugene Giles and Orville Elliot (1962), who used a number of measurements of the skull to distinguish ancestral groups from each other. These authors calculated discriminant functions from measurements of samples of Whites and Blacks from the Terry Collection and of Native Americans from the archaeological site of Indian Knoll. Their functions are still used today by forensic anthropologists.

To understand how this statistical method works, consider the two measurements used in the nasal index: nasal width and nasal height. Generally, Blacks have wide noses (and therefore large nasal widths), while those of Whites are more narrow. The distribution of this measurement is graphically represented in Figure 1.9; notice that the average width value for Blacks is around 27 mm, while it is 24 mm in Whites. By looking at this graph, it is easy to see that a skull with a nasal width less than 23 mm is most likely to have come from a person of European descent. Similarly, a measurement greater than 28 mm would indicate a Black individual. However, nasal height also can be used to distinguish these two ancestral groups. By plotting these two measurements on a graph (instead of dividing one by the other), the distribution in two-dimensional space between Whites and Blacks can be seen (Figure 1.10). Notice that the members of the sample form rough ellipses (dashed lines) that are fairly separate on the chart.

When confronted with situations such as this, statisticians devised a family of techniques, called **discriminant functions**, for calculating the best way to distinguish the groups represented. One such calculation is illustrated in Figure 1.11. Here, through a series of complex mathematical calculations, a discriminant function (line I originating at zero) is calculated such that a line drawn perpendicular to it (line II drawn between the two ellipses) separates the two groups with a minimal amount of

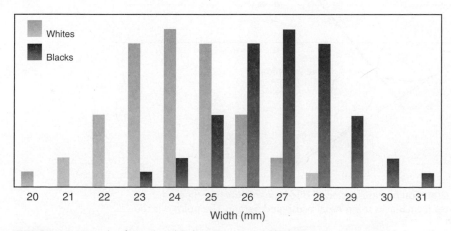

FIGURE 1.9   Graph of nasal width for Whites and Blacks.

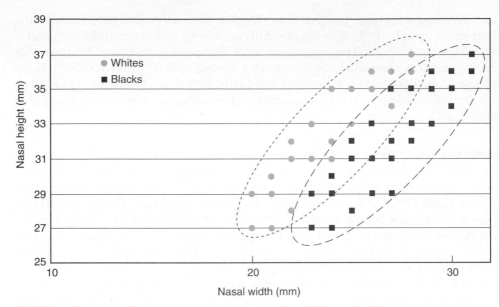

FIGURE 1.10 Graph of nasal width and nasal height for Whites and Blacks.

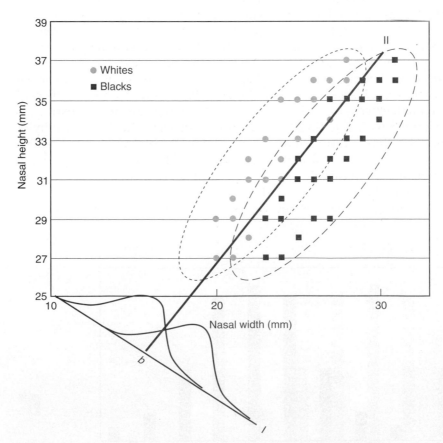

FIGURE 1.11 Graphical representation of discriminant function (line I) for separating Whites from Blacks using nasal width and height. The point *b* is the sectioning point.

misclassification. This function has one value for all members in the sample, making it analogous to the example given for nasal width. Thus, by calculating the value of the function from measurements of an unknown skull, the ancestral group can be determined within a level of probability.

Although not immediately obvious from this example, discriminant functions are more valuable than indexes, because any number of measurements can be used. For example, the graph in Figure 1.11 can be augmented with any third dimension that might aid in distinguishing Whites from Blacks. Since the faces of persons from the latter group generally have more projection than those of Whites, plotting facial jut would cause the ellipses in Figure 1.11 to form three-dimensional "clouds" of points of Blacks and Whites. In this case, the discriminant function would calculate a plane that provides maximum separation of the two clouds from each other. Although difficult to visualize, any number of other measurements (usually no more than 10) can be added and the discriminant function calculated.

The usual form of this procedure is a formula consisting of coefficients (multipliers) and sometimes constants. Formula (2), taken from Giles (1970), is a discriminant function that can be used to determine sex from the height of the chin and the height and width of the lower jaw of a White person:

$$F = 1.390(\text{chin height}) + 2.304(\text{jaw height}) + (\text{jaw width}) \qquad \textbf{(2)}$$

In this formula, there is no constant, but the numbers 1.390 and 2.304 represent the coefficients, which are multiplied by jaw measurements and all values added together. If the resultant value is greater than 287.43 (called a **sectioning point**; that is, point b, where the line separating the ellipses in Figure 1.11 contacts the discriminant function), the jaw is considered to be from a male; results under this value are considered female. For example, suppose that the chin of a lower jaw is 32 mm, while the height is 64 and the width is 118. Formula (2) becomes

$$F = 1.390(32) + 2.304(64) + 118 = 309.9 \qquad \textbf{(3)}$$

Since this value is above the sectioning point, the jaw would be considered to be male.

Discriminant functions figure prominently in forensic anthropology. From cranial measurements, these functions are used to distinguish males from females, as well as members from different ancestral groups (e.g., Whites, Blacks, Asians). Similarly, measurements of the lower jaw (as in the previous example), as well as dimensions of the limb bones and other postcranial structures, can be entered into discriminant functions to determine both of these demographic characteristics. In short, this method is used whenever there are discrete categories that can be distinguished using metric measurements.

REGRESSION EQUATIONS   One last data analysis method used by forensic anthropologists involves predicting the size of one characteristic from the size of another. The most popular method for doing this is the regression equation, an idea developed by Sir Thomas Galton in his studies of inheritance (Snedecor and Cochran, 1967). When Galton thought he saw that children shared characteristics with their parents, but to a lesser degree (e.g., children were shorter in stature than their parents), he used the term "regression toward the mean" to characterize this phenomenon. This outcome has since been disproved, but the term "regression" has endured.

To best understand how regression works, an example published by the author (Byers et al., 1989) will be used. Figure 1.12 presents a plot of the length of the inside bone of the foot (called metatarsal 1) against stature for 22 Black persons of both sexes. As can be seen, longer foot bones are associated with taller people (this is why the band of points rises from the lower-left corner to the upper-right corner of the graph).

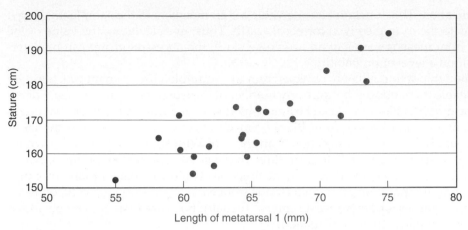

FIGURE 1.12 Graph of length of metatarsal 1 against stature.

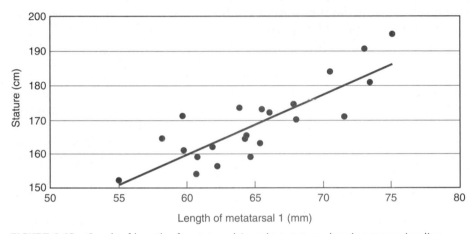

FIGURE 1.13 Graph of length of metatarsal 1 against stature showing regression line.

To better define this relationship, a line that best fits this association (see Figure 1.13) can be computed through a series of mathematical calculations not displayed here. The equation of the line that best fits the relationship between metatarsal 1 length and stature is

$$\text{Stature} = 51.85 + 1.799(\text{length of metatarsal 1}) \qquad \textbf{(4)}$$

This formula can be used to calculate the height of persons from only the first bone in their foot. For example, if a partial skeleton is found with a 60-mm metatarsal, the height of the individual in life was

$$\text{Stature} = 51.85 + 1.799(60) = 51.85 + 107.94 = 159.79 \text{ cm} \qquad \textbf{(5)}$$

This translates to approximately 5 feet, 3 inches tall.

Unfortunately, because regression equations are based on samples, they contain three sources of error. First, the value in equation (4) of 51.85 (called the **intercept**) is only one of many such values; other samples might yield intercepts of 53.12, 49.33, or similar values. For example, if the sample accidentally included only persons with long feet in relation to their heights, the intercept might be smaller than that of equation (4). Second, the value 1.799 (called the **slope** of the regression line) is also only one approximation of any number of slopes. In the example just given of long-footed people, this slope would be less than that calculated from a sample of normal-footed people. Finally, notice that none of the data points falls on the regression line displayed in Figure 1.13; however, by calculation, the predicted value always will. This seemingly contradictory situation constitutes the third source of error in these types of equations. The usual approach in forensic anthropology is to ignore the first two sources of error, while accounting for the last with the standard error of the estimate.

The **standard error** of predicted values is a quantification of the amount of scatter of points about the regression line. This statistic has been used to determine a range of statures that could be possible, given a certain calculated value, by multiplying it by 2 and adding the resultant value to, and subtracting it from, the predicted stature to arrive at a 95% confidence interval (CI). For example, the error for equation (4) is 6.25 cm; thus, its 95% CI is ±12.50 (i.e., 2 × 6.25) cm. This means that the true stature of the person in the example fell between 147.29 and 172.29 mm (4 feet, 10 inches, and 5 feet, 8 inches). This technique shows the imprecise nature of most estimates in forensic anthropology.

Unfortunately, although this method is commonly used in forensic anthropology, it is incorrect, since it does not account for the increasingly unknown nature of points away from the middle of the line (Klepinger and Giles, 1998). An estimate of the 95% CI depends on five factors: the standard error of the predicted value, the sample size from which the equation was calculated, the square of the distance of the predictor variable (in our example, the first foot bone) from its average, the variance of the variable to be predicted (in our example, the stature), and an appropriate value from the t-distribution. Although these must enter into any correct calculation of CIs, the resultant computations are too complex for a book of this nature. Therefore, readers are encouraged to consult the article by Klepinger and Giles (1998) or any introductory statistics book for a complete discussion of the correct method for calculating these values in regression equations.

Summary

1. Forensic anthropology is a subfield within anthropology that deals with the analysis of medicolegally significant human skeletal remains (i.e., skeletons of persons dead less than 50 years).
2. Although the history of forensic anthropology in the United States starts in the 1800s with Thomas Dwight and others, the discipline did not form as a field separate from the rest of anthropology until the mid-1900s.
3. Forensic anthropologists follow a protocol that defines the information that should be retrieved from the human skeleton.
4. Demographic characteristics (i.e., ancestral group, sex, age, and stature) can be estimated from human skeletal remains.
5. Forensic anthropologists often try to determine cause of death from skeletal trauma induced by any number of outside forces.
6. Special characteristics of the human skeleton can be identified by forensic anthropologists to help in obtaining a "positive" identification.
7. Determining time since death and properly recovering skeletonized remains are the province of forensic anthropologists.
8. Anthroposcopy (visual identification) is one of the main methods for gathering data relevant to forensic anthropology.
9. Other data-gathering methods include osteometry (measurement of bones) and histologic and chemical methods.
10. Forensic anthropologists use several methods to make a decision between two or more alternatives (decision table) and to combine multiple ranges of information to arrive at a single estimate of a characteristic of interest (range chart).
11. Forensic anthropologists use indexes, discriminant functions, and regression formulas to calculate parameters of interest from metric data.

Exercises

1. Suppose a body is found that is only partially skeletonized. Under these circumstances, would it be appropriate to call in a forensic anthropologist? Why?

2. Suppose that a forensic pathologist, in attendance when the body in Exercise 1 is brought in, says that he or she could not perform an autopsy. Would it be appropriate now to call in a forensic anthropologist?

3. The skeleton of Jesse James has been examined on several occasions in the past to determine the aspects surrounding his death. Since little of the soft tissue was left, a forensic anthropologist (Michael Finnegan) has done much of this analysis. Why do you suppose a forensic anthropologist, who is normally interested in bodies of medicolegal significance, would get involved in such work?

4. In an attempt to determine whether they were victims of cannibalism, the skeletons of the companions of explorer Alferd Packer, the "Colorado cannibal," were examined by a team of forensic anthropologists. Why was it more appropriate for this work to be done by these specialists as opposed to a forensic pathologist?

5. Forensic anthropologists have been involved in investigating atrocities that occurred during the Bosnian War. What steps in the forensic anthropology protocol and its additions do you think that these specialists perform?

6. On what steps in the forensic anthropology protocol did Thomas Dwight attempt to provide information? On what steps did Paul Stevenson provide information?

7. Box 1.2 describes how Clyde Snow determined that the bones of a child discovered near Oklahoma City were those of "Barbara" rather than "Anna." From the information provided, what method of data collection did he use to arrive at his conclusion? What method of data analysis?

8. Mildred Trotter developed formulae for calculating stature from the lengths of long limb bones. Which method did she probably use to determine these equations?

9. Diane France, a forensic anthropologist in Colorado, analyzed the upper arm bone (humerus) to determine if metric measurements could be used to distinguish males from females. What data analysis method did she probably use to determine if this was possible?

Basics of Human Osteology and Odontology

Although they should be acquainted with methods from various disciplines, all forensic anthropologists must be fully knowledgeable in human osteology and, to a lesser extent, odontology. Human **osteology** is the study of the bones of the skeleton, including their names, placement, articulations with other bones, visible features, and so forth. **Odontology** is the study of dentition; this entails the recognition of the deciduous (baby) and permanent teeth as well as their placement in the mouth, their major features, and the variations seen in persons of different ancestry. This knowledge must be so extensive that not only can complete skeletons and dental arcades be analyzed for information concerning decedents, but also skeletons with missing and fragmented bones as well as incomplete dentitions and damaged teeth can be recognized as human and examined for personal data.

An understanding of human osteology and odontology is important for two reasons. First, bones and teeth contain many indicators of the basic demographic characteristics of persons. As mentioned in Chapter 1, the sex of individuals can be attributed from traits visible on the skull; in addition, as will be seen in Chapter 8, the pelvis and long bones also can be used for this purpose. Similarly, the skeleton contains features that can be used to evaluate ancestry and age at death, as well as the living height of a person. The second reason for studying human osteology and odontology is to gain an understanding of what is considered "normal" in the human skeleton and teeth. By knowing these standards, deviations can be identified that are useful for developing a positive identification and for providing information concerning the life and circumstances of death of individuals.

The purpose of this chapter is to provide a brief overview of human bones and teeth. Because entire books have been written on these structures, a single chapter cannot provide more than the most basic aspects of these subjects. Therefore, only those topics in human osteology and odontology that are specifically addressed in later chapters will be discussed here. For example, there are approximately 40 identified landmarks of the skull that are used as end points for measurements (as well as other purposes). However, only the 16 points that are referenced in subsequent chapters will be described here. Although this makes the discussion relatively brief, the reader will obtain enough knowledge to understand the information presented later in the book. Those interested in greater detail on these subjects can refer to either Bass (1995), Steele and Bramblett (1988), White (1991), or the osteology section of any anatomy textbook (e.g., *Gray's Anatomy*).

OVERVIEW OF THE HUMAN SKELETON

Although a variety of anomalous conditions can add to the number, the adult human skeleton ordinarily is composed of 206 bones (Goss, 1973). These range in size from small, angular polygons (e.g., the bones of the wrist) to long, heavy limb bones with straight or gently curving shafts. Each bone in the body is given a name as well as a side designation (if paired). Thus, the bone of the upper arm is called the humerus and persons normally are born with one on the right and one on the left side. Some bones and skeletal structures are actually aggregations of a number of smaller bones; for example, the wrist is composed of eight separate bones, while the skull consists of 22. Finally, with the exception of only one (the hyoid suspended below the mouth), all bones connect to (**articulate** with) at least one (and in many cases more than one) other bone.

To aid in describing the skeleton, a useful standard is the **anatomical position**. This is the position of the body, either standing or lying, with the arms arranged straight along the side and the palms of the hands facing forward. In addition, the legs are extended straight, with the feet arranged as though they were flat on the ground (as in standing). In relation to this position, there is a nomenclature for anatomical (also called cardinal) directions and planes, which further simplify discussions of the skeleton; this terminology is presented in Table 2.1.

Although some of these terms are not necessary when studying the skeleton (e.g., front can be used instead of anterior), most ease the complexity of the description of skeletal elements. For example, the term **proximal** refers to the segment of a bone that is closest to the articulation point of the body, that is, closest to the point of attachment. Thus, the top (**superior**) end of the humerus (upper arm bone) where it articulates with the shoulder is its proximal end. Conversely, the bottom (**inferior**) end of the humerus where it connects to the bones of the lower arm is called the **distal** end. In a like manner, the inside bone of the lower arm (the ulna) is called the **medial** bone because it is closest to the middle of the body, while the outside bone (the radius) is called the **lateral** bone. Notice also that several of the directions have two terms (e.g., anterior and ventral, posterior and dorsal); although the words in each pair can be used interchangeably, generally the first term listed is the most commonly used for its particular direction (e.g., superior is more common than cranial). Mastery of this nomenclature will significantly help the reader to comprehend the information presented in this book.

TABLE 2.1   Cardinal Directions and Planes Used in Describing Osteological Structures[1]

Cardinal Directions

Superior (cranial)	Up; point or region lying above another point or region
Inferior (caudal)	Down; point or region lying below another point or region
Medial	Point or region lying closest to the midline of the body
Lateral	Point or region lying away from the midline of the body
Anterior (ventral)	Front; point or region lying closest to the front of the body
Posterior (dorsal)	Back; point or region lying closest to the back of the body
Proximal	Point closest to an articular point with body
Distal	Point farthest from an articular point with body

Anatomical Planes

Frankfort	Plane that aligns the lower border of the eye with the upper border of the ear opening; also called the Frankfort horizon
Sagittal	Plane, cutting through body from front to back, that divides it into left and right halves
Coronal	Plane, at right angles to the sagittal plane, that divides the body into front and back halves
Transverse	Plane that divides the body at the waist into upper and lower sections

[1]After Rhine (1970).

Figure 2.1 presents a line drawing of the human skeleton showing the articulations and names of the major bones. The skeleton can be divided into two areas for ease of study: cranial and postcranial. Because of its complexity, the **cranial** skeleton is often studied as a separate unit; this includes the skull, the mandible (lower jaw), and the ear ossicles. The **postcranium** (all bones below the skull) is divided for ease of study into two segments: the **axial** skeleton and **thorax** (those bones making up the vertebral column and rib cage) and the **appendicular** skeleton (composed of the bones of the arms, legs, shoulder, and pelvis). Learning the important features of each of these segments and the bones within them is essential to understanding all other chapters of this book.

Cranial Skeleton

The skull is composed of 22 outwardly visible bones (there are three ear ossicles on each side that cannot be seen easily). Except for the lower jaw, these articulate tightly at suture lines so that there is little movement between adjacent bones. Because it is the most widely studied structure in the skeleton, the discussion of the cranium is divided into four topical areas. The first concerns the bones that make up the cranial skeleton and the various prominences and other features visible on their exterior surface. The second deals with the sutures, which separate these bones, and the third topic involves the landmarks on the cranium. Fourth, the various sinuses within bones of the skull deserve consideration because of their value in developing positive identifications of individuals.

BONES   Figure 2.2a illustrates the skull from the anterior aspect, where the bones of the face and the anterior braincase are identified. Starting superiorly, the **frontal** is the forehead bone that comprises the front part of the braincase and the upper part of the eye orbits. In some skulls, especially those of males, there are thickened areas above each eye orbit called **supraorbital tori**. Articulating with

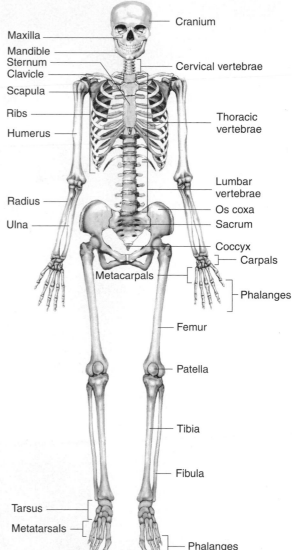

FIGURE 2.1   Drawing of the human skeleton showing the names of the main bones and their articulations.

the frontal inferiorly are the right and left **zygomatic** bones (plural: **zygomatics**), which compose the lateral walls of the eye orbits. Forming the floor of each of these orbits is the **maxilla** (plural: **maxillae**); this paired bone also comprises the upper jaw. Notice that the maxillae articulate laterally with the zygomatics and medially with a pair of bones that forms the bridge of the nose, the **nasal** bones (plural: **nasals**). Visible inside the nose are turbinal bones called **nasal conchae** that supply the structure for the soft tissues involved in the sense of smell. Similarly, far to the rear of the nose is a vertical bone, the **vomer**, which divides the posterior nasal opening roughly in half. Finally, the lower jaw (**mandible**) contacts the maxillae along the dental arcade.

Figure 2.3 illustrates the lateral view of the skull, where the main bones of the braincase are clearly visible. Starting anteriorly and forming the medial walls of the eye orbits are the paired **lacrymal** bones (plural: **lacrymals**), which exhibit a vertical ridge (**crest**), and the single **ethmoid**. Next, the side of the frontal is seen as the front of the

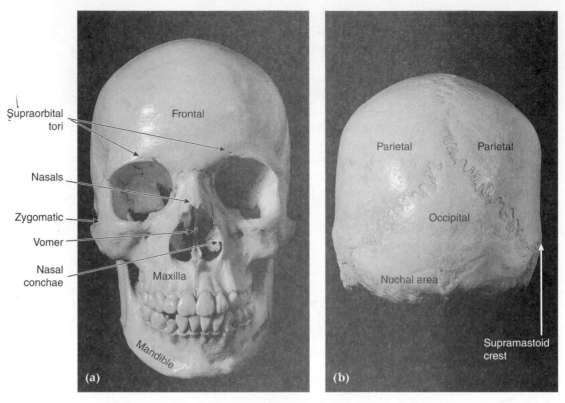

FIGURE 2.2 **(a)** Anterior and **(b)** posterior views of the human skull. (Photos by Julie R. Angel; specimen courtesy of the State of New Mexico, Office of the Medical Investigator)

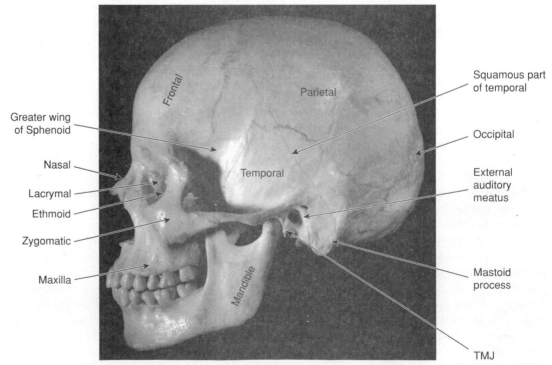

FIGURE 2.3 Lateral view of the human skull. (Photo by Julie R. Angel; specimen courtesy of the State of New Mexico, Office of the Medical Investigator/Illustration by Jay R. Alexander, I-hua Graphics)

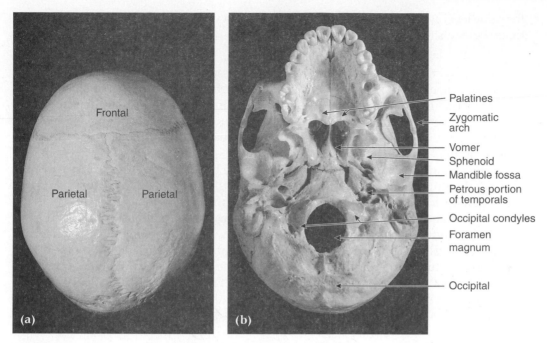

Palatines

Zygomatic
arch

Vomer

Sphenoid

Mandible fossa

Petrous portion
of temporals

Occipital condyles

Foramen
magnum

Occipital

(a)   (b)

FIGURE 2.4   **(a)** Superior and **(b)** inferior views of the human skull. (Photos by Julie R. Angel; specimen
courtesy of the State of New Mexico, Office of the Medical Investigator)

braincase, composing the forehead. Articulating with the frontal posteriorly are
the **parietal** bones (plural: **parietals**); these paired bones make up the middle of the
braincase. Posterior to the parietals is the **occipital** that forms the back part of the vault;
it also contributes significantly to the base of the braincase. As viewed from the rear
(Figure 2.2b), this bone displays a prominent wing, called a **squamous**, the lower part of
which contains the **nuchal** (neck) area. The **temporal** bone (plural: **temporals**) forms the
lower part of the sides of the braincase (Figure 2.3); the most important features of these
paired bones are the ear opening (called the **external auditory meatus**), the **mastoid
process**, the flared upper part (called the **squamous** portion), and the **styloid process**.
The temporals articulate anteriorly with an extremely complex bone called the
sphenoid; the greater wing of this bone is located between the temporal and the zygomatics. Finally, the lower jaw articulates posteriorly
with the temporals at the **temporomandibular joint** (TMJ); this is the
only moveable bone in the skull that is easily visible.

Inferior and superior views of the skull are illustrated in
Figure 2.4. The inferior view (Figure 2.4b) shows the occipital, inferior parts of the temporals, and lower part of the sphenoid.
Important features of this view include the sockets for the **condyles**
of the mandible (**mandibular fossa**), the **foramen magnum** (which
allows for passage of the spinal nerves into the brain), the occipital
condyles (for attachment to the vertebral column), and the **palatine**
bones (plural: **palatines**). These latter bones form the posterior part
of the hard palate (the anterior part is formed by the inferior maxillae). The superior view (Figure 2.4a) shows the main bones of the
cranial vault: frontal, right and left parietals, and occipital.

The last bone to consider in the cranial skeleton is the hyoid. This
is a small U-shaped bone (Figure 2.5) that is suspended in the neck, at

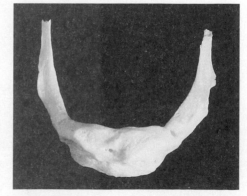

FIGURE 2.5   Superior view of the hyoid
bone. (Photo by Julie R. Angel; courtesy of the
University of New Mexico–Albuquerque, Maxwell
Museum of Anthropology, #53)

the same level as the inferior edge of the mandible. In young individuals, it is composed of three segments, which fuse later in life.

SUTURES As can be seen from the preceding discussion, the skull is formed from multiple bones that, except for the mandible, join with each other by special joints that appear as lines incised into the cranium. These lines are referred to as **sutures**. Understanding of the sutures is important, because most of these structures close with time and may become completely obliterated in old age. Thus, this feature can help determine the age at death of individuals from their skeletons.

The majority of the sutures are named for the bones that they separate. Thus, the internasal suture separates the nasal bones, and the zygomaxillary suture separates the zygomatics and maxillae. However, seven sutures are not named in this manner. The **coronal suture**, visible in Figure 2.6, separates the frontal and parietals; it ends at the point where the frontal meets the greater wing of the sphenoid. The **sagittal suture**, also visible in Figure 2.6, separates the right and left parietal bones; it starts at the coronal suture and ends where the parietals meet the occipital. The **lambdoid suture** separates the parietals and occipital bone (see Figures 2.6 and 2.7); it curves across the back of the skull, ending where the occipital and parietals meet the temporals. The final specially named suture separates the squamous portion of the temporals from the

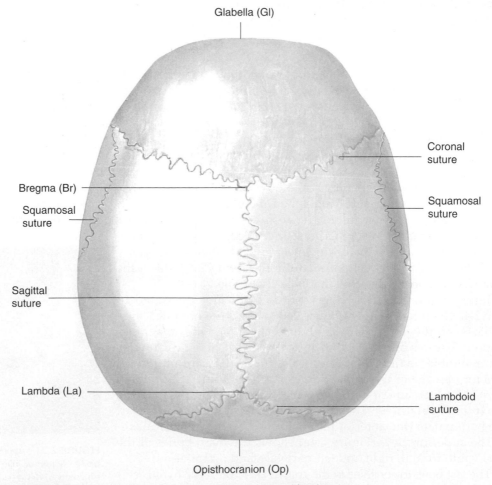

FIGURE 2.6 Superior view of skull showing sutures and landmarks.

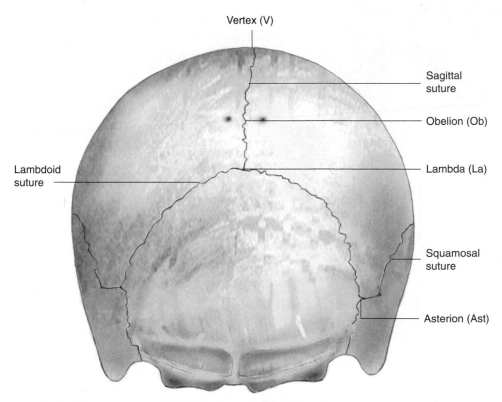

FIGURE 2.7   Posterior view of skull showing sutures and landmarks.

parietals (see Figure 2.8); this is the **squamosal suture**. The palate has three distinct sutures visible in Figure 2.9. The **incisive suture** separates that part of the maxillae that contain the incisors (called the premaxilla) from the rest of the bone. In addition, the **transverse palatine suture** separates the maxillae from the palatines while the **median palatine suture** separates the two maxillae and the two palatines.

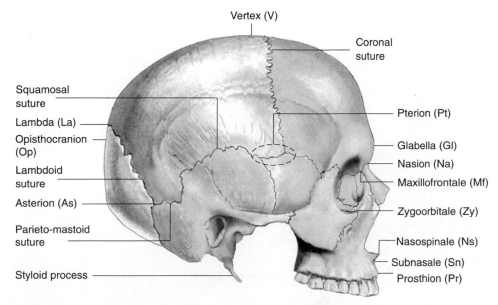

FIGURE 2.8   Lateral view of skull showing sutures and landmarks.

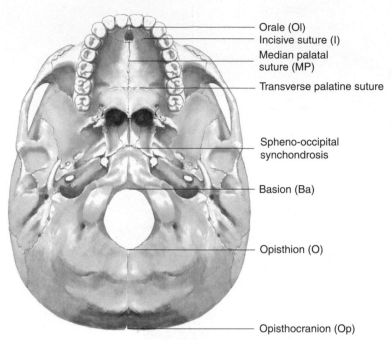

Orale (Ol)
Incisive suture (I)
Median palatal suture (MP)
Transverse palatine suture

Spheno-occipital synchondrosis

Basion (Ba)

Opisthion (O)

Opisthocranion (Op)

FIGURE 2.9 Inferior view of skull showing sutures and landmarks.

LANDMARKS Over the years, it has been convenient to designate points on the skull for use in description or in measurement. There are many of these **landmarks** depicted in Figures 2.6 through 2.10; however, only 16 are important for the purposes of this text. **Bregma** is the point where the sagittal suture ends anteriorly at the coronal suture in the sagittal plane (Figure 2.6); **basion** (Figure 2.9) is the most inferior point on the anterior border of the foramen magnum. **Nasion** is the point where the internasal suture meets the nasofrontal suture in the midsagittal plane (Figure 2.10), and **subnasal** is the point on

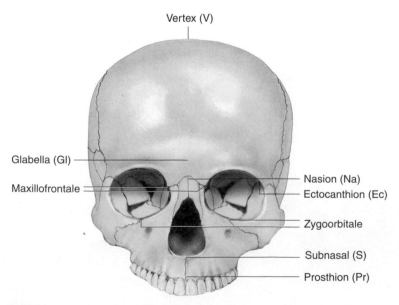

Vertex (V)

Glabella (Gl)

Maxillofrontale

Nasion (Na)
Ectocanthion (Ec)

Zygoorbitale

Subnasal (S)

Prosthion (Pr)

FIGURE 2.10 Anterior view of skull showing sutures and landmarks.

the lower margin of the nasal aperture in the midline. **Glabella** is the most anterior point on the frontal on the midline (Figure 2.8); this point is located between the supraorbital tori (when present). **Opisthocranion** is the farthest point on the back of the skull from the glabella in the sagittal plane (Figure 2.8). Near this landmark on the rear of the skull is the point where the sagittal and lambdoid suture meet; this point, called **lambda** (see Figures 2.6 and 2.7), also is in the midline. **Prosthion** is the most anterior point on the intermaxillary suture in the midsagittal plane (Figure 2.8); it differs from **orale**, in that it is located on the anterior part of the maxillae, whereas the latter is on the inferior part of those bones. **Pterion** is not an actual point; rather it is the region where the greater wing of the sphenoid meets the frontal, parietal, and temporal. **Obelion** is located in the midsagittal plane where a line drawn between the right and left parietal foramina bisects the sagittal suture. **Ectocanthion** is the point where the upper border meets the lateral border of the eye, and **asterion** is the point where the squamosal suture ends at the lambdoid suture. **Zygoorbitale** is the point at which zygomaxillary suture contacts the lower border of the eye (see Figure 2.10) and **maxillofrontale** is the point at which the fronto-maxillary suture meets the anterior lacrymal crest. Two final landmarks both occur on the mandible: **gnathion** is the lowest point on the mandible on the midline (not illustrated), and **gonion** is the point where the ascending ramus meets the horizontal ramus.

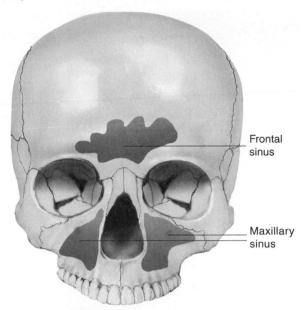

FIGURE 2.11   Location of the major sinuses of the human face.

SINUSES   The final structures relevant to the study of the human skull are the pockets of air, called **sinuses**, within sections of some of the cranial bones. The frontal, ethmoid, temporals, sphenoid, and maxillae all exhibit such pockets. The **frontal sinus** (Figure 2.11) is a complex open area that lies both above the upper border of the eye orbits and in the lower portion of the frontal in the midline (i.e., toward nasion). The **maxillary sinuses** are large, uncomplicated areas in the upper jaw (Figure 2.11) that appear to lighten these bones without sacrificing structural integrity. The sinuses of the other three bones are more complex in nature and difficult to illustrate; these structures in the ethmoid, sphenoid, and mastoid processes of the temporal bone are composed of multiple cells that are not easily seen even in x-ray. Research into sinuses, especially in the frontal, has indicated that their configuration is unique enough in individuals that they can be used to positively identify a skeleton when antemortem radiographs are available for comparison.

Axial Skeleton and Thorax

This segment of the postcranium is composed of the sternum and the bones of the vertebral column and rib cage (Figure 2.12). The **sternum** (Figure 2.13) is the breastbone that serves as an anchor for the anterior ends of the ribs. This bone is composed of a rectangular lower part, called the **body,** and an upper, roughly triangular part called the **manubrium.** It is easily felt in the living, but often not

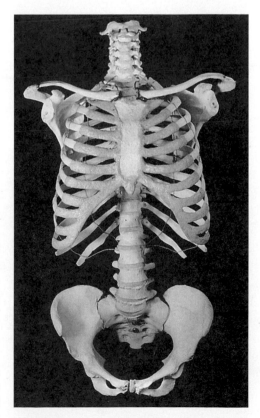

FIGURE 2.12   The axial skeleton pictured with the hyoid as well as bones of the shoulder, pelvis, and thorax. (Photo by Julie R. Angel)

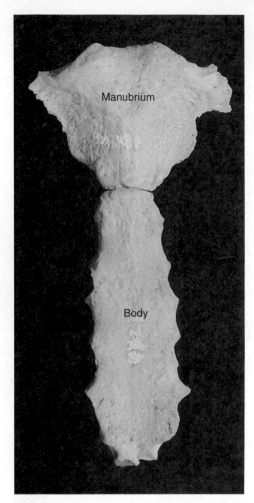

FIGURE 2.13   Anterior view of the sternum. (Photo by Julie R. Angel)

remembered as a separate bone. The other structures of the axial skeleton and thorax are described separately next.

VERTEBRAL COLUMN   Generally, each **vertebra** (plural: **vertebrae**) is composed of two segments, a **body** and a **neural arch** (Figure 2.14). The latter structure arches away from the body, forming the **vertebral foramen** that allows for passage of the nerve column down the spine. On most vertebra, this arch has three processes; the **spinous process** extends posteriorly, while transverse processes extend laterally from the right and left sides. In addition to these structures, each vertebrae has (at least) four areas of articulation (called **facets**), two on top for joining with the bone above and two on the bottom for the bone below. Finally, the vertebrae of the middle rib cage contain extra facets for articulating with the ribs, both on the body and on the transverse processes.

The three types of vertebrae are definable by their location in the spine: cervical, thoracic, and lumbar. The **cervical vertebrae** comprise the top seven bones of the spinal column, corresponding to the neck. The uppermost of this set is called the **atlas** (Figure 2.15a), a uniquely constructed vertebra that has no body and appears ringlike when viewed from above. The superior surface of this bone has facets that contact the skull at the occipital condyles, while the facets of the inferior side contact the second cervical vertebra, called the **axis** (Figure 2.15b). This latter bone also is distinct from other vertebrae in that it has a superiorly projecting knob of bone called the **dens** or **odontoid process**. The remaining cervical vertebrae are built along the general pattern of other vertebrae, in that they have bodies, neural arches, articular facets, and spinous and transverse processes. Figure 2.16a shows the anterior and lateral views of two middle cervical vertebrae, and Figure 2.16b shows these vertebrae from the inferior and superior aspects. Note the foramen through the transverse processes (**foramen transversarium**); these are unique in the vertebral column and can be used to easily separate cervical vertebrae from others in the spinal column.

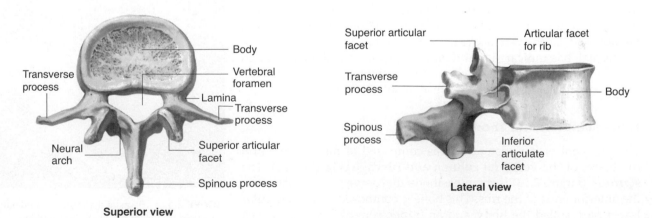

FIGURE 2.14   Superior and lateral views of a vertebra, showing its component parts.

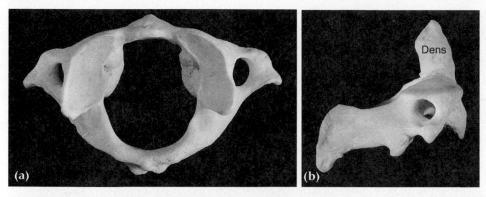

FIGURE 2.15   The first two vertebrae of the spinal column. **(a)** Superior view of the atlas and **(b)** lateral view of the axis.   (Photos by Julie R. Angel)

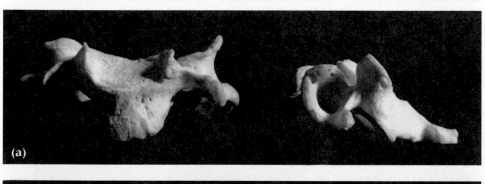

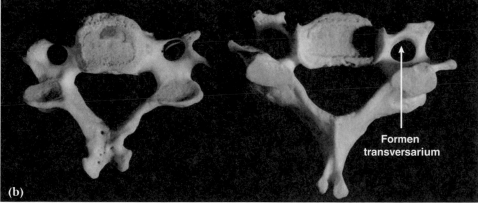

FIGURE 2.16   Four views of the cervical vertebrae: **(a)** anterior and lateral; **(b)** inferior and superior.   (Photos by Julie R. Angel)

The middle of the vertebral column is usually composed of 12 **thoracic vertebrae** that exhibit all the major structures described previously (Figure 2.17). These vertebrae have the facets on both the body and the transverse processes for articulation with the ribs. The long spinous processes of these vertebrae slant inferiorly to the point that they allow only limited posterior movement of the upper back. The **lumbar vertebrae** (Figure 2.18) are the five bottom bones of the spinal column, above the sacrum. These do not have articular facets for the ribs and have shorter and wider transverse and spinous processes as well as **mammillary processes** for the superior articular facets.

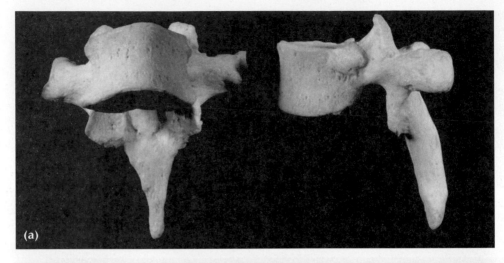

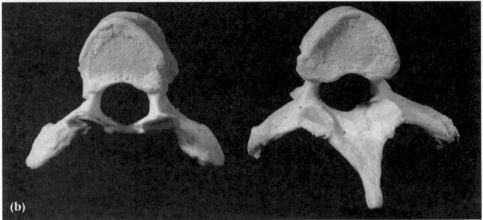

FIGURE 2.17   Four views of the thoracic vertebrae: **(a)** anterior and lateral; **(b)** superior and inferior. (Photo by Julie R. Angel)

In addition, these have very large bodies which survive well when exposed on the ground or when buried.

RIB CAGE   The rib cage is composed of 12 **ribs** (singular: **rib**) on each side (men and women have equal numbers; see Box 2.1), which connect posteriorly to the vertebral column and anteriorly to the sternum. Each rib has two basic components (Figure 2.19), the neck and body. The **neck** of the rib is the posterior part of the bone that has articular facets for both the body of the vertebrae and their transverse processes. The **body** of the rib is the rest of the bone extending from the neck to the midline anteriorly, where it articulates with the sternum by way of cartilage (called the **intercostal cartilage**). The top two and bottom two ribs generally are easily distinguished. The first rib is small and flat; it articulates medially with the seventh cervical and first thoracic vertebrae and anteromedially with the manubrium. The second rib is larger and less flat than the first, but is still easily distinguished from others by its smaller size. The eleventh and twelfth ribs, also called **floating ribs**, can be identified by their short length and somewhat pointed ends that lack the squared-off appearance of other ribs.

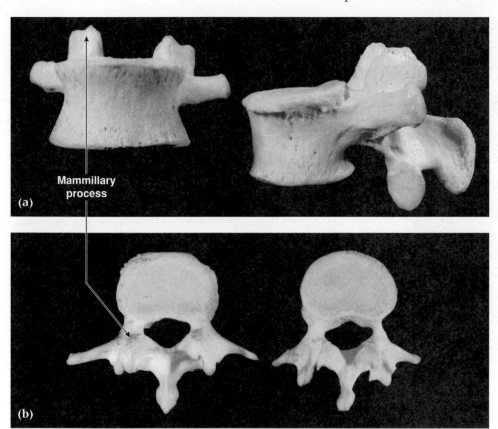

FIGURE 2.18   Four views of the lumbar vertebrae: **(a)** anterior and lateral; **(b)** superior and inferior. (Photo by Julie R. Angel)

BOX 2.1
The Number of Ribs in Men and Women

It is fairly common for people who, remembering their catechism, think that men have one fewer rib than women. The author has encountered this belief on many occasions while teaching various courses in anthropology, as well as in everyday conversation. The source of this belief is the Bible, specifically Genesis 2, verses 21 and 22:

> So the Lord God caused a deep sleep to fall upon the man, and while he slept took one of his ribs and closed up its place with flesh; and the rib which the Lord God had taken from the man he made into a woman and brought her to the man.

What is most interesting about the people who believe this is their lack of examination of the subject. For example, why is it expected that men would have one fewer rib than women? Why wouldn't women simply have only one rib, since that is all that was used to make them? Indeed, why are women composed of any bones other than that one rib? Similarly, was this rib taken from only one side? And, if it was, why don't men have uneven numbers of these bones on the left and right sides. All these speculations are of no importance, because research has shown that men and women have the same number of ribs. Although sex can be differentiated in many cases from the skeleton, one method used for this purpose is not the number of ribs (or any other bone, for that matter).

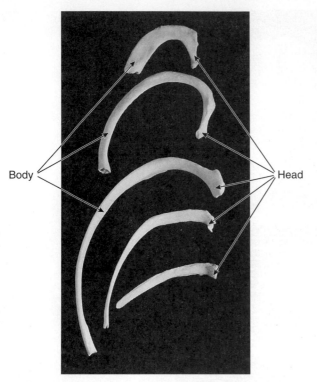

Body   Head

FIGURE 2.19 Superior view of the first, second, eighth, eleventh, and twelfth ribs. (Photo by Julie R. Angel)

Appendicular Skeleton

The appendicular skeleton is composed of the bones of the upper and lower limbs. These include not only the long bones of the arms and legs but also those of the terminal appendages (i.e., hands and feet). Since it is convenient to divide this skeleton into upper and lower halves, each of these will be described separately.

UPPER LIMBS Each shoulder girdle (right and left) is composed of two bones: the clavicle (collarbone) and the scapula. The **clavicle** (plural: **clavicles**), which is S-shaped when viewed from above or below (Figure 2.20), articulates medially with the manubrium and laterally with the scapula. The triangular shoulder blade (Figure 2.21), called the **scapula** (plural: **scapulae**), has five important features. First, the **spine** is a raised area of bone that angles superiorly on the dorsal surface from the medial to the lateral edge. It ends in the **glenoid cavity**, which is the articular surface for the head of the humerus (see Appendicular Skeleton); the configuration of this structure allows for movement in all planes, making the shoulder joint unique in the human skeleton. In addition to these features, the scapula has two processes. The **acromion** tips the spine, where it allows for articulation of the lateral end of the clavicle. The **coracoid process** projects anteriolaterally from the superior end of the glenoid cavity. A final feature of this bone is the **ventral infraspinous plane**. This is the plane formed by the body of the scapula below the spine on the anterior surface. The body of the scapula is very thin, making it prone to puncture wounds and fractures and to postmortem loss and cracking.

Additionally, the upper limbs are composed of three long bones (called the humerus, ulna, and radius) and the bones of the hands. The **humerus** (plural: **humeri**) is the upper arm bone (Figure 2.22) that articulates proximally with the scapula (specifically the glenoid cavity) and distally with the ulna. Its major features are the **head** (for articulation with the glenoid cavity), the **greater tuberosity**, the **lesser tuberosity**, the **deltoid tuberosity**, the **trochlea**, and the **olecranon fossa**. This latter structure accepts the process by the same name of the ulna and prevents the elbow from bending backward.

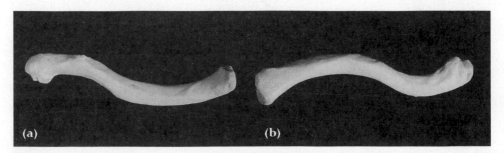

(a)   (b)

FIGURE 2.20 **(a)** Inferior and **(b)** superior views of the clavicle. (Photo by Julie R. Angel)

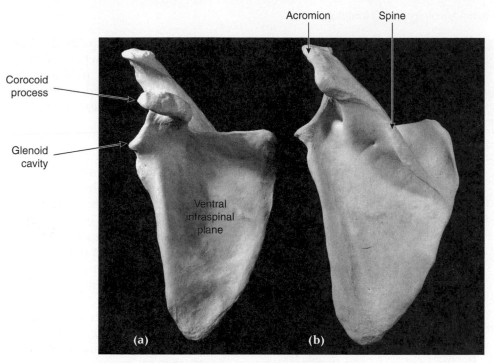

FIGURE 2.21 **(a)** Anterior and **(b)** posterior views of the scapula. (Photo by Julie R. Angel)

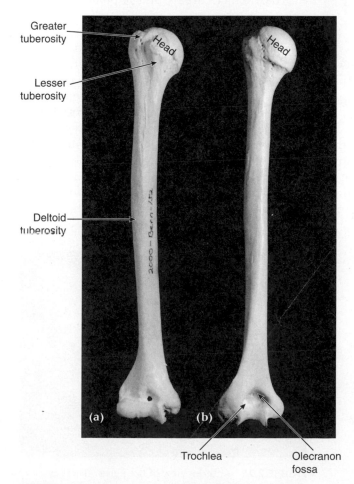

FIGURE 2.22 **(a)** Anterior and **(b)** posterior views of the humerus. (Photo by Julie R. Angel)

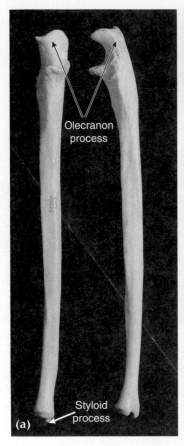

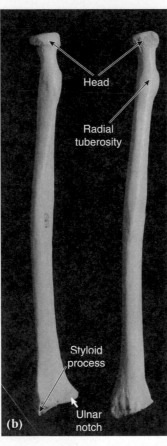

FIGURE 2.23 The bones of the lower arm: **(a)** anterior and lateral views of the ulna; **(b)** anterior and posterior views of the radius. (Photos by Julie R. Angel)

The **ulna** (plural: **ulnae**) is the medial bone of the lower arm (Figure 2.23a) when the skeleton is laid in the anatomical position. The **olecranon process** articulates with the trochlea proximally, and the **styloid process** of the **head** points toward the wrist.

The **radius** (plural: **radii**) is the outside bone of the lower arm (Figure 2.23b) when the body is laid in the anatomical position. Its **head** articulates medially with the **radial notch** of the ulna and superiorly with the lateral portion of the trochlea. Its **styloid process** also points toward the wrist; medial to this feature is the **ulnar notch**, for articulation of the head of the ulna. In addition to these features, notice the **radial tuberosity** just below the head; this is for attachment of the biceps muscle.

The bones that make up the hand (Figure 2.24) are those of the wrist (**carpals**), palm (**metacarpals**), and fingers (**phalanges**). There are a total of 27 of these bones in each hand: 8 carpals, 5 metacarpals, and 14 phalanges.

LOWER LIMBS The pelvis (Figure 2.25) is composed of four bones, a right and left os coxa, the center bone called the sacrum, and the coccyx. Each **os coxa** (plural: **ossa coxae**) in turn is composed of three bones (see Figure 2.26): the **ilium**, **ischium**, and **pubis**. Figure 2.27 illustrates the important features of this bone: the **greater sciatic notch** (formed by the posterior extension of the ilium), the **pubic symphysis** (the medial part of the pubic bone), and the hip socket (called the **acetabulum**). This latter structure forms an area for articulation with the head of the thigh bone (called the *femur*).

FIGURE 2.24 Anterior (palmar) view of the bones of the hand. (Photo by Julie R. Angel)

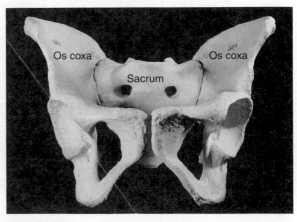

FIGURE 2.25 Anterior view of the pelvis. (Photo by Julie R. Angel)

When viewed medially, the inferioposterior part of the ilium manifests a roughened L-shaped area, called the **auricular surface**. Both the auricular surface and the pubic symphysis undergo changes through time, which makes them useful for the estimation of age at death. In addition to these structures is the **preauricular sulcus**. When present, this groove runs along the superior margin of the greater sciatic notch on the ilium. Finally, the **obturator foramen** is the open area encircled by the ischium and pubis. The sacrum (Figure 2.28), which is the bone that attaches the vertebral column to the pelvis, usually is composed of five vertebrae that are fused both between the bodies and the neural arches. Finally, the coccyx (not pictured) usually is composed of four undeveloped vertebrae that fuse into a single bone later in life (i.e., after 25 or 30 years). This bone attaches to the inferior end of the sacrum.

Below the pelvis, each lower limb is composed of three long limb bones (the femur, tibia, and fibula), the knee cap (the patella), and the bones of the foot. Figure 2.29a displays the **femur** (plural: **femora**), or thigh bone, in anterior and posterior views. Notice the balllike end (the head) for articulation with the hip socket joint (the acetabulum), the two greater and lesser **trochanters**, the **linea aspera** on the posterior side, and the large **condyles** at the distal end (with a space between them called the **intercondylar fossa**) for articulation with the tibia. In addition, notice the supracondylar lines that converge into the linea aspera about a quarter of the way up from the distal articular end; these enclose a triangular area called the popliteal surface.

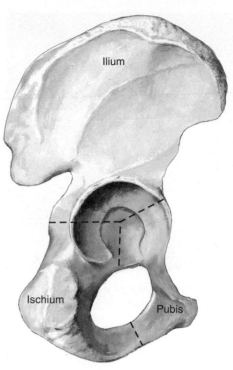

FIGURE 2.26   Lateral (external) view of the os coxa showing its three bones: ilium, ischium, and pubis. (See also Figure 3.5.)

The **tibia** (plural: **tibiae**) has several features of interest (Figures 2.29b). First, the proximal end displays a flared metaphysis (the condyles) for articulation with the distal

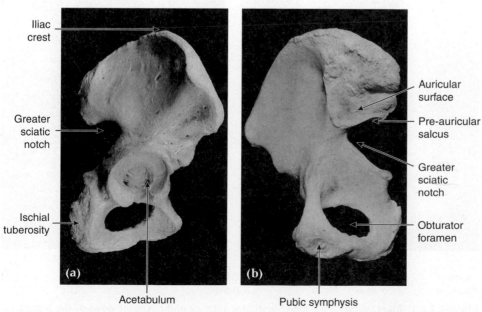

FIGURE 2.27   **(a)** Lateral and **(b)** medial views of the os coxae. (Photo by Julie R. Angel)

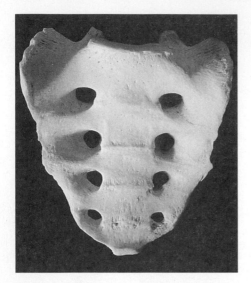

femur; located between these is a pair of prominences called the **intercondylar eminence**. Also, the anterior surface displays a **tuberosity** that starts just below the condyles and a raised area (the **anterior crest**) that extends from below this tuberosity down approximately two-thirds the length of this bone. Finally, notice the process that extends inferiorly on the distal end; this **malleolus**, located on the medial side, helps to stabilize the ankle by preventing sideways movement.

The **fibula** (plural: **fibulae**) is a thin bone that articulates with the tibia on the lateral side (Figure 2.30). It is composed of a somewhat triangular head for contacting the tibia below the lateral condyle and a **malleolus** to oppose this same structure on the tibia. Finally, lying on the anterior aspect of the knee (covering the inferior femur and superior tibia) is the **patella** (plural: **patellae**), or kneecap (Figure 2.31).

The foot (Figure 2.32) is composed of bones of the ankle (**tarsals**), foot (**metatarsals**), and toes (**phalanges**). The total number of bones in this structure is 26: 7 tarsals, 5 metatarsals, and 14 phalanges. Two of

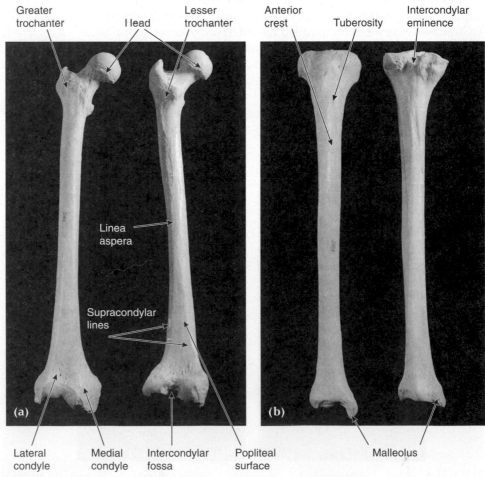

FIGURE 2.29   Main bones of the lower limbs: **(a)** anterior and posterior views of the femur; **(b)** anterior and posterior views of the tibia. (Photos by Julie R. Angel)

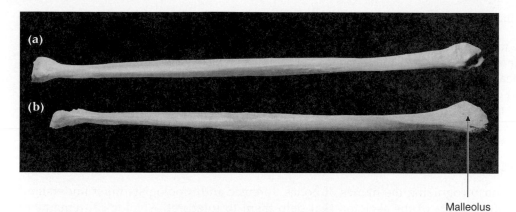

Malleolus

FIGURE 2.30 **(a)** Lateral and **(b)** medial views of the fibula. (Photo by Julie R. Angel)

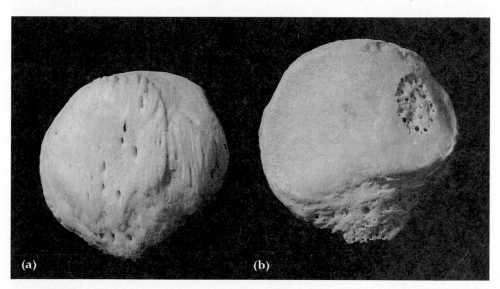

(a)   (b)

FIGURE 2.31 **(a)** Anterior and **(b)** posterior views of the patella. (The pores visible in the posterior surface represent a pathological condition.) (Photo by Julie R. Angel)

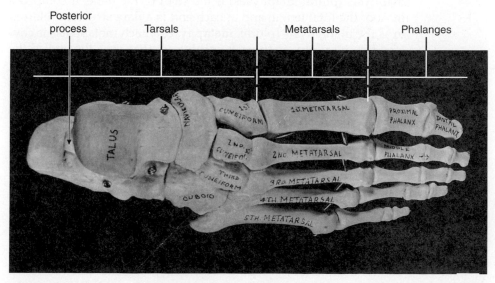

Posterior process   Tarsals   Metatarsals   Phalanges

FIGURE 2.32 Superior view of the bones of the foot. (Photo by Julie R. Angel; specimen, courtesy of the University of New Mexico–Albuquerque, Maxwell Museum of Anthropology, Osteology laboratory)

the tarsal bones are particularly important. The top bone is the **talus**, which has a superior and medial articular facet for the tibia and lateral facet for the malleolus of the fibula. A feature of this bone is the **posterior process**, which is the most posteriorly projecting part of this bone. Just inferior to the talus is the **calcaneous**; it comprises the heel of the foot and articulates superiorly with the talus and anteriorly with many of the remaining bones of the ankle.

BASIC TOPICS IN OSTEOLOGY

Beyond recognizing the names of bones, forensic anthropologists must understand various aspects of the skeleton that help them to interpret osteological remains of medicolegal significance. Two subjects are particularly important: anatomy and growth. Anatomy refers to aspects of bone beyond those described previously; thus, beyond being able to identify external structures, internal and even microscopic features must be learned. The process by which bones grow also is important to forensic anthropologists; by knowing the stages through which the skeleton passes, age and other aspects of persons can be determined from their osteological remains. Due to their importance, each of these subjects will be discussed separately next.

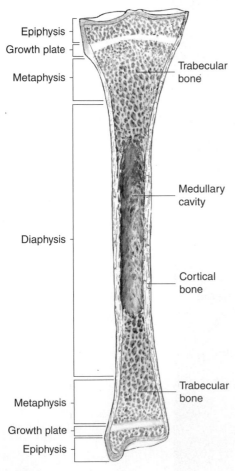

Epiphysis
Growth plate
Metaphysis
Trabecular bone
Diaphysis
Medullary cavity
Cortical bone
Trabecular bone
Metaphysis
Growth plate
Epiphysis

FIGURE 2.33 Components of a long bone: diaphysis, metaphysis, and epiphysis. (From Figure 11, Ortner and Putschar, 1981)

Anatomy of Bone

The anatomy of bone can be divided into three areas: gross external, gross internal, and microscopic. Gross external anatomy starts with the components of whole bone that are visible without magnification. These include the structures described previously for individual bones, such as articular ends, prominences (called **tubercles** and **tuberosities**), holes for blood vessels (called **foramen**), and orbits (eye, nose, ear openings). In addition, there are a number of lesser structures, such as grooves (indicating the presence of overlying blood vessels) and lines (for the attachment of muscles by tendons).

Besides these, three gross structures of long bones are recognized (Figure 2.33): diaphysis, metaphysis, and epiphysis. The **diaphysis** (plural: **diaphyses**) is the shaft of the bone. It composes most of the total length and at each end is a flare structure referred to as the **metaphysis** (plural: **metaphyses**). Each metaphysis is covered by an **epiphysis** (plural: **epiphyses**) that caps the end of the bone. This latter structure is separate from the other two during development, becoming fused after growth has ceased. (This phenomenon, called epiphyseal union, is useful for estimating the age of individuals as well as for disentangling commingled remains; see Chapters 9 and 6, respectively.) A thorough knowledge of these structures increases the ability of forensic anthropologists to identify bones that are represented only by fragments.

Gross internal anatomical structures refer to those elements visible when a bone is cut open. The smooth, exterior of all skeletal elements is referred to as the **cortex** or **compact** bone (see Figure 2.33). It is composed of a strong, well-organized tissue called **lamellar** bone that is laid down in thin layers that run parallel to the long axis of a bone. In contrast to the exterior cortex is the **cancellous** or **trabecular** bone of the interior (see Figure 2.33). This spongelike structure occurs in the metaphyses of long bones, within the ribs and all bones of the hands and feet, inside the bodies of the vertebrae, and between the inner and outer cortical surfaces of the cranial vault (where it is called the **diploe**). Its primary function is to reinforce the bones without adding excess weight. A final internal structure is the **medullary cavity** (see Figure 2.33), which is the opening that runs through the center of all long bones. In life, it is filled with fatty tissues that are the target of carnivores when they gnaw on the skeleton after death.

Viewing the final anatomical structures of bone involves engaging in a field of research called **histology**, the study of microscopic features of biological tissue. By cutting off thin sections of bone for inspection under a microscope, a number of features become visible that are useful for such activities as distinguishing human from nonhuman bone fragments (see Chapter 3) and estimating age at death (see Chapter 9). When cortical bone is magnified, linear fibers of collagen can be seen running parallel to the long axis (if present) of a bone. These layers appear under a microscope as dashed lines in an otherwise relatively featureless area (see Figure 2.34) and comprise what is called primary lamellar bone. Interspersed within these layers are **primary vascular canals** (arrows C in Figure 2.34) that carry minerals and nutrients to and from the osseous tissues. Also seen within the cortex are **osteons** (bone cells) that are seen throughout the lamellar bone of the cortex. Osteons contain an opening through their centers for the passage of a blood vessel. These cells first appear during growth where they are called **primary osteons**; however, over time they die and become fully or partially replaced by other osteons, called **secondary osteons**.

During growth, lamellar bone is deposited in circumferential layers due to the **osteogenic** (bone forming) activity of cells within a tissue that covers all bones during life. This tissue, called the **periosteum**, not only forms bone during growth but also creates new bone that bridges the gap between broken segments after fracture. As collagen fibers are laid down, separate mineral crystals are deposited within these fibers adding strength to the structure of the bone. (Because of this construction, fractures move along even planes within the mineral crystals making straight and/or angular lines rather than wavy lines with rounded corners.)

After growth ceases (i.e., after the epiphyses have fused to their respective bones), large-scale modifications to bone shape, called **modeling**, stop except in cases of fracture repair, pathological conditions, or heavy use and overuse. However, the processes that caused modeling continue, resulting in **remodeling** where some structures are removed by bone cells while other cells replace these structures. Bone is removed during remodeling in hollow areas (called resorptive bays or Howship's lacunae) that

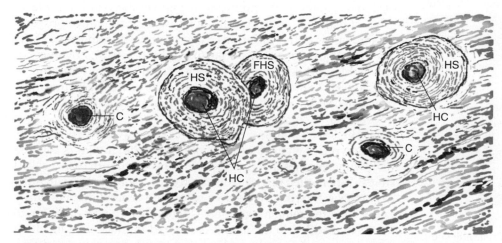

FIGURE 2.34 Histological structures of cortical bone: (C) primary vascular canals, (HS) Haversian systems, (HC) Haverisan canals, and (FHS) fragmentary Haversian system.

appear as if holes had been purposefully drilled into the primary lamellae. This removed bone is subsequently replaced by layers of secondary lamellar bone that is laid down centripetally inside these holes. When replacement ceases, the resultant structure resembles a bull's-eye, with the center spot being a blood vessel-like passage called a **Haversian canal** (arrows HC in Figure 2.34). These circular layers and canals, collectively called **Haversian systems** (HS in Figure 2.34), continue to form through life such that new ones encroach on old ones leaving fragments (fragmentary Haversian system, FHS, in Figure 2.34). Also, because these structures take up more and more space as age increases, the amount of original lamellar bone and number of primary vascular canals decrease through time.

Bone Growth

Early in life, bones form within **cartilaginous precursors** by the deposition of bone matrix (the fiber and mineral crystals described previously). Generally, this process follows a pattern where **primary centers** form (**ossify**) first. Next, **secondary centers** of ossification form, which eventually will unite with the primary centers, forming a complete bone. This information is important when recovering subadult remains to ensure that all centers are found and to enable a good estimate of age. Also, as will be seen in subsequent chapters, occasionally these centers do not fuse, resulting in the formation of accessory bones, which might be confused with traumatic injuries.

Long bones grow by **apposition** (deposition) of bony matrix onto the ends of their metaphyses. By a complex mechanism that is poorly understood, bone is applied to the ends and edges of the metaphysis, while it is removed from that part of this structure that will become the narrower diaphysis. Similarly, the diaphysis grows outward by deposition of bone on the cortex and removal of bone from the inner surface of the medullary cavity.

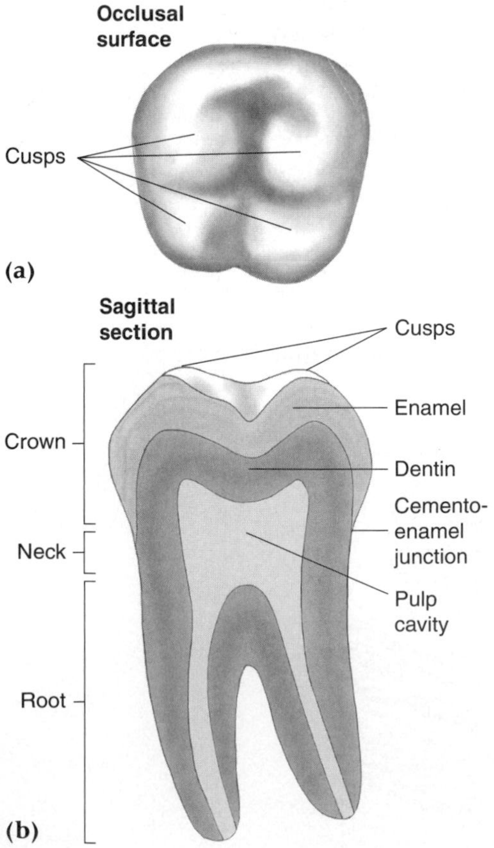

OVERVIEW OF THE HUMAN DENTITION

Although the analysis of teeth in the forensic situation is not strictly within their purview, all forensic anthropologists must have a basic knowledge of human dentition to properly perform their work. This knowledge must include an understanding of dental anatomy, the ability to recognize the types and placement of teeth, an understanding of how dentition develops, and an awareness of the variations that can occur within teeth. These are the subjects of entire books (e.g., Taylor, 1978); however, an accessible and relatively complete summary can be found in Bass (1995). The following section will cover only the most fundamental elements needed to comprehend the topics introduced in later chapters.

The basic anatomy of a tooth is illustrated in Figure 2.35. The **crown** is the part that is visible above the gum; it is covered with white **enamel** that is peaked in some teeth into points called **cusps**. Where the crown meets the rest of the tooth is termed the **neck**; this is the constricted area below the enamel that is slightly wider than the remaining tooth. The **root** is that part of the tooth that is embedded in the jaw; it is secured in place by a ligament that prevents it from becoming dislodged during **mastication** (chewing). The number of roots depends on the tooth; generally,

FIGURE 2.35 (a) Occlusal and (b) lateral line drawing of tooth showing the basic anatomical structures.

the front teeth have only one, while those toward the back of the mouth have two, three, and even four of these structures. The root and that part of the crown covered by the enamel are both made up of a bonelike material called **dentin**.

When studying teeth, five basic directions (similar to the cardinal directions used in the body) are distinguished for the tooth surfaces. The **mesial** surface refers to those parts of the teeth closest to the midline, while **distal** refers to surfaces away from the midline. Also, the inner parts of teeth are referred to as **lingual** (toward the tongue), while the outer parts are either **labial** (near the lips) or **buccal** (near the cheeks). Finally, **occlusal** refers to the chewing surface of teeth.

Another convenience when studying teeth is to divide the mouth into **quadrants**: upper left and right, and lower left and right. Within each of these quadrants, the sequence of teeth is the same (Figure 2.36); starting at the midline (mesially) are the incisors, followed (distally) by the canines, premolars, and molars. The **incisors** are the flat, chisellike

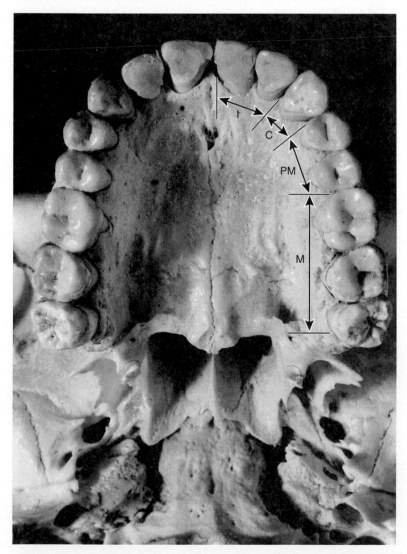

FIGURE 2.36 Human permanent dentition showing the four different tooth types. I = incisors; C = canine; PM = premolars; M = molars. (Photo by Julie R. Angel)

teeth in the front of the mouth that are easily visible when persons are smiling or talking. Their crowns are wider (mesial-distally) than they are thick (labial-lingually). Because they have only one root, they are often lost postmortem, which is unfortunate because these teeth are valuable in determining ancestry (see Chapter 18). **Canines** are the pointed teeth next to the second incisor; these single-cusped teeth, sometimes called "eye teeth" or cuspids, also have a single root; however, it is so long that it brackets either side of the nasal opening, anchoring it securely in the jaws.

The next teeth in line are the **premolars** (called bicuspids by some dentists), which usually have two cusps and one or two (usually joined) roots. The final, most distal teeth are the **molars**; these are the square to rectangular chewing teeth found at the rear of the mouth. The upper molars generally have three roots, while the lower molars have two; these are often fused in both the upper and lower third molar.

Humans have two sets of teeth during life, the deciduous dentition (also called baby or milk teeth) and permanent teeth. **Deciduous dentition** is composed of five teeth per quadrant: two incisors, one canine, and two molars. (Notice that there are no deciduous premolars.) This results in a total of $5 \times 4 = 20$ teeth. The **permanent dentition** is composed of eight per quadrant: two incisors, one canine, two premolars, and three molars. This results in a total of $8 \times 4 = 32$ teeth. Occasionally, variations in these numbers occur. Extra (**supernumerary**) teeth appear as small, peglike structures usually located in the area between the normal teeth. Similarly, some teeth never erupt (the missing wisdom tooth; see Box 2.2) or never develop (congenitally missing teeth).

Deciduous can be distinguished from permanent teeth by their size and color. Since baby teeth are smaller than their adult counterparts, it requires little experience to distinguish the two. Also, the crowns of deciduous teeth often will have a slight yellowish tint; this is caused by their thin enamel, which allows the color of the underlying dentin to show through. However, the crowns of permanent teeth generally are the white color of their enamel because this substance is so thick that the underlying dentin is fully hidden.

The sequence by which teeth form and erupt follows a relatively set pattern. Formation entails the coalescence of enamel into cusps, followed by apposition of this substance as well as dentin from the occlusal surface toward the tip of the root. When

BOX 2.2
Wisdom Teeth

The emergence of wisdom teeth is often accompanied by a discomfort that borders on (even intrudes deeply into the realm of) excruciating pain. A wisdom tooth is simply a third molar that is found in some persons but not in others. The pain is caused by the crowns of these teeth bumping against the second molars due to a lack of space in both the upper and lower jaws. Although dentists and other oral health care professionals visualize these teeth as several payments for their BMWs or Mercedes Benzes, their arrival in most persons is greeted with no small unhappiness.

Persons of European ancestry are afflicted most often by problems associated with wisdom teeth. This is because these people have the smallest faces and therefore the smallest space in their jaws for these teeth. Blacks and persons of Asian descent rarely have trouble with the third molars due to their larger and more spacious palates and jaws. They also are the most likely people to have these teeth simply because there is enough space for them. Unfortunately, this is small consolation for those afflicted with the pain of the emergence of the third molar. To make matters worse, these teeth do not necessarily impart wisdom, despite their name. This has to be earned the old-fashioned way through experience and an open and active mind; the pain of emerging teeth does not help much in that arena.

approximately one-half of the root is formed, the tooth emerges into the mouth through what is called the alveolare margin of the jaws, where it continues to grow until it reaches a genetically determined length. Thus, by knowing the schedule by which the different parts of the teeth form and the timetable for their eruption, the age of subadults can be estimated fairly accurately (see Chapter 9).

Summary

1. The adult human skeleton normally is composed of 206 bones.
2. A number of cardinal directions and planes simplify the process of examining the human body.
3. Important features of the skull include the bones, the sutures that separate these bones, landmarks (used to identify various points and regions on the skull), and the sinuses found within various bones.
4. The axial skeleton is composed of the hyoid, the vertebrae (7 cervical, 12 thoracic, and 5 lumbar), the ribs (12 on each side), the sternum, the right and left scapulae and clavicles, and the pelvis.
5. The pelvis is composed of four bones: right and left ossa coxae, the sacrum, and the coccyx; each os coxa likewise is composed of three bones that fuse in early adolescence: ilium, ischium, and pubis.
6. The upper limbs are composed of three paired long limb bones (humeri, ulnae, and radii) and the bones of the hand: wrist (carpals), palm (metacarpals), and fingers (phalanges).
7. The lower limbs are composed of three paired long limb bones (femora, tibiae, and fibulae), the kneecaps (patellae), and three bone sets at the terminus of the leg: ankle and heel (tarsals), foot (metatarsals), and toes (phalanges).
8. There are four types of teeth in the human mouth: incisors, canines, premolars, and molars.
9. Normal humans have two sets of teeth: deciduous (also called baby or milk teeth) and permanent.
10. Similar to studying bones, cardinal directions are used when examining and describing teeth.

Exercises

1. Define and describe the three components of a long bone. What component would seem most likely to fracture when impacted by an outside force (e.g., fall from a high place or blow from a club).
2. Name the bones of the cranial vault and their respective locations. Which of these would seem the most and least likely to be the target of a gunshot wound by an assailant and why?
3. Name the major bones of the facial skeleton and their locations. Given the morphology of the soft parts, which would you expect to vary among individuals from different ancestral backgrounds?
4. Name the major sutures of the cranial vault and their location. Given their appearance, would they be likely to be mistaken for fracture lines and why?
5. Name the major bones of the upper limbs and their location. Considering how persons protect themselves when falling or being attacked, which bones (if any) are most likely to be broken and why?
6. Name the major bones of the lower limb and their location. Considering how persons protect themselves when falling or being attacked, which bones (if any) are most likely to be broken and why?
7. Name the major histological structures of bone. Considering the changes that occur during life, what (if any) structures may be useful for determining the age of a person at death?
8. Name the landmarks of the facial skeleton and cranial vault. Which pairs would be most likely to be used to determine the length of the skull? Which two for the height of the face? The height of the skull?
9. Name the bones of the thorax. Of these, which are most likely to be fractured during a fall or an attack by an assailant using a blunt instrument (e.g., club) and why?

3

Establishing Forensic Significance

The first issue usually faced by forensic anthropologists involves recognizing the forensic significance of osteological material. Forensic significance refers to remains that the medicolegal community has defined as needing investigation (i.e., persons who have died within the last 50 years while not in the care of a physician). Given this, forensic anthropologists first must determine if the remains presented to them for analysis are osteological in nature, rather than made of a material that looks like bone. This normally is only a problem with highly fragmented material. Next, if the remains are bone, they must be determined to be from a human, rather than a nonhuman animal. If the bones are from a nonhuman that is unrelated to a forensic case, they can be discarded (although some workers add them to a comparative osteology collection at their university or college). However, if they are human, the last step is to determine if they are from a person who has died within the last 50 years.

This chapter addresses the issue of how to identify these three aspects of osteological remains. The first part deals with distinguishing bone from nonbone; this is necessarily short because of the rarity of the problem. The second part discusses the differences between human bones and those of nonhumans that are most likely to be encountered in the forensic context (i.e., quadrupedal mammals). The last part details those characteristics that differentiate the remains of persons who died within the last 50 years from those who died earlier; the term **contemporary** will be used for those in the former category, while **noncontemporary** will refer to remains from the latter category.

While reading these topics, it must be remembered that in a forensic analysis all osteological remains should be treated as medicolegally significant when in doubt. This assumption should be maintained until a medical examiner or coroner is convinced that the remains are not related to a criminal case. This is particularly relevant to this chapter since establishing forensic significance usually can be done in the field (e.g., Why bring cow bones back to the lab for further analysis?). Thus, by retrieving all suspected or doubtful specimens, no important data will be ignored inadvertently; and only time is lost if a more detailed examination reveals that the remains do not fit the definition of medicolegal significance.

BONE VERSUS NONBONE

Douglas Ubelaker (1998) was one of the first forensic anthropologists to point out the value of microscopic analysis in distinguishing bone from nonbone. He has noted that in cases of extreme fragmentation and few remains, there may be a question as to the nature of the material. In these cases, he recommends examining the fragments under a microscope to better see the surface features of the specimen(s) in question. Bone, when magnified, will reveal a fairly compact surface with some graininess (especially in the elderly). However, nonosteological material may have features not consistent with this expectation. In two cases reported by Ubelaker, fibrous material was visible in one specimen, and a complex-layered structure filled with cell-like openings was seen in the other. These, and other similar unexpected findings, can lead an experienced forensic anthropologist to conclude that such specimens are not composed of bone and probably are not of forensic significance.

For more difficult to distinguish materials, Ubelaker and associates (2002) describe a method by which the chemical makeup of a sample is compared with that of the Spectral Library for Identification and Classification Explorer (SLICE) at the Federal Bureau of Investigation (FBI) laboratory in Washington, D.C. The technique involves obtaining micro-slices of the specimen and submitting it to scanning electron microscopy (SEM) and energy dispersive X-ray spectroscopy (EDS) to determine its chemical makeup. This makeup is compared with approximately 1800 different entries in the SLICE database to determine which of the materials is the most similar to the unknown sample. The calcium to phosphorous ratio is useful particularly to distinguish bone from nonbone since only ivory, mineral apatite, and some types of coral have similar ratios of these substances. As with simple microscopy, this method is useful with small fragments of materials of unknown nature.

HUMAN VERSUS NONHUMAN

Distinguishing human from nonhuman bones is one of the easiest methods for eliminating forensically insignificant finds. Although human beings are distinctly different anatomically from other animals, nonhuman bones (especially in the absence of the skull) often are confused with those of humans. William Bass (1995) summarizes the results of two studies from Tennessee showing that between 25% and 30% of cases brought to the attention of forensic anthropologists were nonhuman bones. Thus, for the sake of saving time, the ability to recognize nonhumans is an important skill needed by all forensic anthropologists. Both Ubelaker (1989) and Bass (1995) present useful sections dealing with human and nonhuman bones. For readers with a greater interest in this topic, Schmid (1972) extensively illustrates nonhuman bones alongside their human counterparts, while the works of Cornwall (1956), Gilbert (1973), and Gilbert et al. (1981) present extensive information on the osteology of nonhumans.

Three aspects of bones help to make the distinction between human and nonhuman possible: histology, maturity, and architecture. **Histology** is the study of microscopic structures of living tissue. In forensic anthropology, this specialty involves the size and arrangement of Haversian systems, osteons, and other such structures that can be used to distinguish human from nonhuman bone fragments. **Maturity** helps to distinguish animals whose mature bones are approximately the same size as subadult humans; subadult human bones will have unfused or missing epiphyses (see Chapter 2), while those of nonhumans will display fused epiphyses (Bass, 1995). When bones are approximately the same size as adult humans, **architecture** (i.e., shape) can be used to make the distinction (Ubelaker, 1989). Dissimilarities in shape generally are so distinct that differentiation between human and nonhuman is one of the easiest skills for forensic anthropologists to master. Finally, there are two nonhuman animals, bears and pigs, that deserve special treatment because of the similarity between some of their anatomical parts and humans. Thus, this section is divided into four parts. The first summarizes histological structures that help distinguish human from nonhuman bone fragments. The second deals with differences between small animals whose remains might be confused with infants and children, while the third deals with the differences in architecture between adult humans and nonhumans. The last section deals with bear paws and pigs teeth which can appear similar to human hands and teeth, respectively.

Histological Differences

Histology has shown some promise for distinguishing human from nonhuman bone when osteological fragments are too small to be identified by maturity or architectural differences. The techniques used for obtaining bone samples that can be viewed microscopically are largely outside the scope of this textbook; however, a short discussion of this subject is warranted. In a fine review article, Maria Hillier and Lynne Bell (2007) summarize the multitude of studies concerning the qualitative and quantitative differences between the cortical bone from (mainly) the ribs and long bones of humans and nonhumans. They state that human bone is characterized by dense Haversian systems while large mammal bone has both Haversian bone and plexiform bone (see Figure 3.1). In immature large mammals, plexiform bone can be seen throughout the cortex from the periosteal to endosteal surfaces but, by adulthood, Haversian bone has replaced it near the endosteal surface. In humans, plexiform bone is found only in fetal remains and pathological bone (e.g., bone that appears at the site of a traumatic injury). Given this, the appearance of plexiform bone in non-fetal and non-pathological bone would seem an excellent criterion for distinguishing human osteological fragments from those of large mammals. Unfortunately, since the plexiform structures appear close to the periosteal surface in mature mammals where taphonomic forces may degrade or remove evidence of their presence, this criterion is somewhat limited.

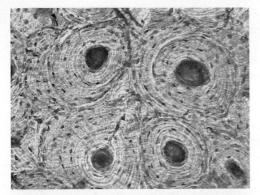
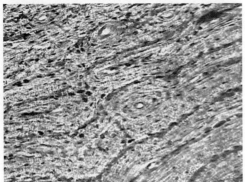

FIGURE 3.1 Histological structures of human and nonhuman bone. **(a)** Human; **(b)** nonhuman (*Bos taurus*). (Photos courtesy of Monika Martiniaková)

Hillier and Bell (2007) further state that, when Haversian bone is found, it can be distinguished from nonhumans by the diameter of the Haversian systems and their concomitant canals. In humans, the diameter of Haversian systems ranges from approximately 180 μm to 325 μm, while the size of this structure in rats, hares, raccoon dogs, badgers, cats, dogs, horses, and old world and new world monkeys lies below this range. Similarly, the size of human Haversian canals ranges from approximately 30 μm to 175 μm, while it is smaller in rats, rabbits, cats, deer, and old world and new world monkeys. Unfortunately, data not available to Hillier and Bell indicate that these variables may not be as useful as they appear, in that the ranges of (at least) some of these animals overlap with humans (see Martiniaková et al., 2006; Cattaneo et al., 2009). Thus, more research needs to be done in this area before humans can be distinguished from nonhumans based on histological structures.

Maturity Distinctions

Nonhuman bones are distinguishable from human infants and children by the level of osteological maturity. This immaturity in the bones of subadults is expressed as nonunion of the epiphyses with their diaphyses, which gives them an unfinished appearance. Through knowledge of this fact, small nonhuman bones are distinguished from infants and children. Figures 3.2 to 3.4 present the limb bones of a human infant compared with those of a mature fox and a coyote. Although the bones are all approximately the same length, notice that the lack of epiphyses on the human remains

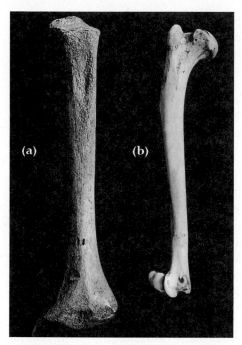

FIGURE 3.2   **(a)** Humerus of human infant compared to that of **(b)** a fox (*Vulpes macrotis*). (Photo by Julie R. Angel; fox courtesy of the University of New Mexico, Museum of Southwestern Biology)

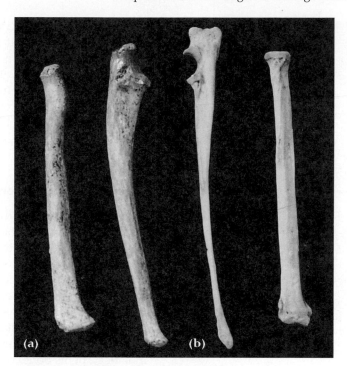

FIGURE 3.3   **(a)** Ulna and radius of human infant compared to that of **(b)** a fox (*Vulpes macrotis*).   (Photo by Julie R. Angel; fox courtesy of the University of New Mexico, Museum of Southwestern Biology)

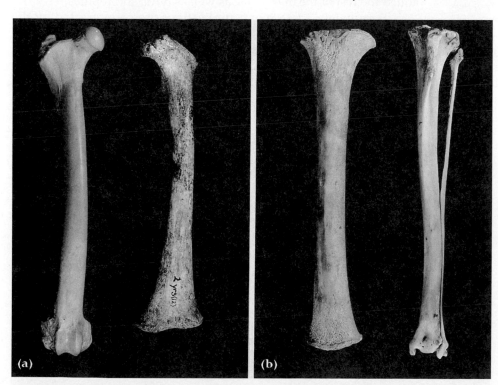

FIGURE 3.4   Limb bones of a human infant compared with those of canids. **(a)** Femur of human infant *(right)* compared to that of a coyote (*Canis latrans*); **(b)** tibia of human infant *(left)* compared to that of a fox (*Vulpes macrotis*).   (Photos by Julie R. Angel; coyote and fox courtesy of the University of New Mexico, Museum of Southwestern Biology)

FIGURE 3.5 Half of a rib cage of
(a) a human infant compared with that of
(b) a coyote (*Canis latrans*). (Photo by Julie R.
Angel; coyote courtesy of the University of New
Mexico, Museum of Southwestern Biology)

makes them easily distinguishable from the two animals. Similarly, Figure 3.5 presents half of the left side of a rib cage from an infant compared with that of a coyote; the lack of epiphyses on the human ribs (coupled with the architectural difference of greater curvature) distinguishes them from this creature. Figure 3.6 shows the differences between an os coxa of a human infant and that of a fox; the former manifests unfused ilium, ischium, and pubis, while the latter is a single unit with barely a trace of the lines that originally separated these three bones.

Architectural Differences

Architectural (shape) differences are the main method for distinguishing human from nonhuman bones of equal size. Unfortunately, the process of defining these differences is complicated by several factors. First, all mammals (including humans) have the same bones, with only a few additions and subtractions. Thus, humans, cows, sheep, deer, coyotes, elk, and pronghorns (antelope), as well as **canines** (doglike animals), **felines** (catlike animals), and bears all have two femora, tibiae, humeri, radii, and so forth. Consequently, there are only a few bones whose presence indicates definitely nonhuman (e.g., penis bone) or whose size indicates definitely human (e.g., large clavicle). Another complicating factor is the large number of different animals that may be encountered; to those just listed can be added the rest of the mammals, as well as birds and reptiles.

Fortunately, these two complications are counteracted by the fact that the majority of nonhuman bones brought to forensic anthropologists come from **quadrupedal** (four-footed) mammals, all of whom share a similar bone architecture required by their four-footed stance. This causes a number of skeletal similarities among these otherwise different creatures, thereby simplifying the task of identifying nonhumans. Also, to make matters easier, humans have distinctive skeletal

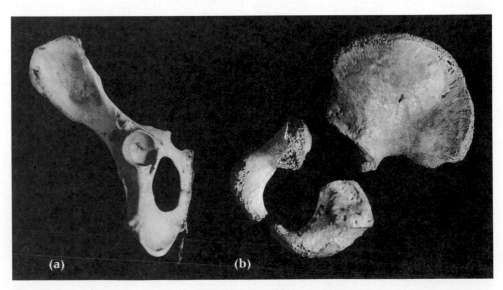

FIGURE 3.6 Pelvis of **(a)** fox (*Vulpes macrotis*) and **(b)** human infant. (Photo by Julie R. Angel; fox courtesy of the University of New Mexico, Museum of Southwestern Biology)

BOX 3.1
Will the Real Turkey Please Stand Up?

Stan Rhine (1998) describes a case in which the ability to determine human from nonhuman ended with some embarrassment to an Albuquerque physician. This man was digging in his backyard and discovered what he thought was a partial human skull. To quote:

> He proudly bore his find to the Anthropology Department at the University of New Mexico for verification and elaboration. He was directed to the late Dr. Harry Basehart . . . (who) turned the specimen over in his hands, slowly withdrew the pipestem from between his teeth, and, with a friendly smile tugging at the corners of his lips, suggested heading down to the basement.
>
> A huge rack of drawers in one dingy hallway contained the comparative skeletal collection. Sliding open a drawer labeled "Turkey Bones," he reached in and extracted one—a pelvis. Ever the gentlemen, he slowly rotated the two identical specimens before the physician, one in each hand. He gently suggested to the discoverer that instead of a human skull, he had dug up "the pelvis of some large avian species."

Concluding their consultation, Basehart asked for his visitor's business card. He was not trying to find a family physician, but to ensure that if a personal medical emergency should develop he did not make the mistake of consulting a physician who could not distinguish between a human skull and the south end of a northbound turkey.*

_____

*From S. Rhine, *Bone Voyage,* University of New Mexico Press, Albuquerque, 1998, p. 15.

configurations related to their **bipedal** (two-footed) stance that are readily distinguished from those of quadrupeds.

In this section, shape differences between humans and commonly encountered nonhumans will be illustrated and discussed. The section is divided into three parts; the first, which deals with differences in skulls, is short for reasons that will become evident. The second deals with the more complicated task of differentiating the human from nonhuman elements of the axial skeleton. The last part presents a comparison of the limbs of these animals.

CRANIAL SKELETON   As pointed out by Rhine (1998), the human skull is so distinctive that even the uninitiated are unlikely to confuse it with the cranium of nonhumans. (However, see Box 3.1 for a humorous example in which this was not the case.) This probably is due to the popularity of the skull as a symbol of death (e.g., the skull and crossbones for poisons) and other terrors that makes it a fairly commonly pictured structure. Also, the large braincase with small face and the absence of a prominent snout makes the human skull virtually unique in the animal kingdom. Even the crania of our closest relatives, such as chimpanzees, are not easily mistaken for human (even in the unlikely event that they are encountered in a forensic situation). Thus, because of its notoriety and shape, little needs to be said about the human skull and how it is distinguished from those of nonhumans.

Figure 3.7 displays anterior views and Figure 3.8 displays lateral views of the skulls of deer, wolf, and mountain lion compared to a human. The deer skull is typical of many **ungulates** (hoofed animals), while the coyote represents the canines and the mountain lion represents felines. The reader need only study these briefly to notice the larger snouts and smaller braincases of these quadrupeds when compared to the human skull. Additionally, the presence of projecting, saberlike teeth on the **felid** (feline) and **canid** (canine) distinguishes these animals from humans.

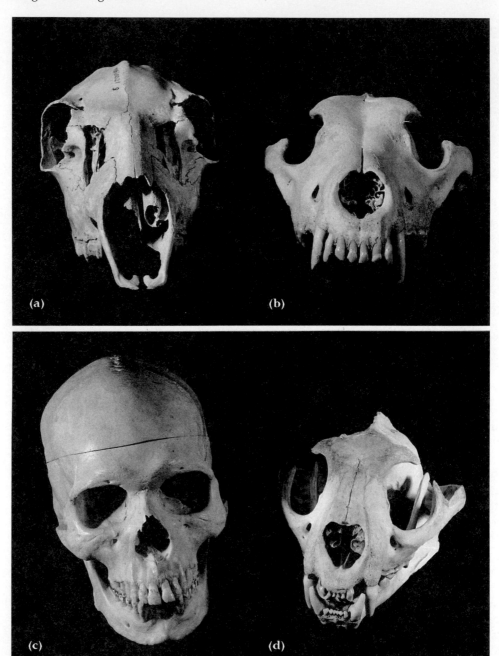

FIGURE 3.7 Front view of skulls: **(a)** deer (*Odocoileus hemionus*); **(b)** wolf (*Canis lupus*); **(c)** human (*Homo sapiens*); and **(d)** mountain lion (*Felis concolor*). (Photos by Julie R. Angel; nonhuman skulls courtesy of the University of New Mexico, Museum of Southwestern Biology)

AXIAL SKELETON AND THORAX   Unlike the skull, humans and nonhumans are not as easily discerned on the basis of the bones of the axial skeleton, despite their great differences. (This probably is due to lack of exposure in school, a problem faced by many of the sciences.) Thus, in this section, a comparison of quadruped against human will be made for each of the bones that comprise the axial skeleton, with an emphasis on those differences that easily distinguished the two. Again it is worth mentioning that forensic

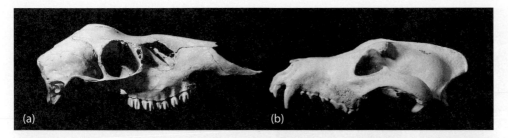

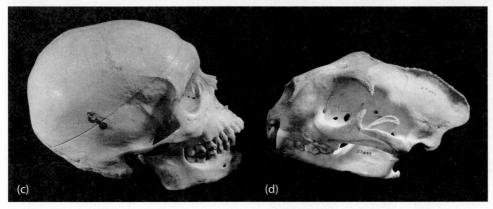

FIGURE 3.8   Side view of skulls: **(a)** deer (*Odocoileus hemionus*); **(b)** wolf (*Canis lupus*); **(c)** human (*Homo sapiens*); and **(d)** mountain lion (*Felis concolor*).   (Photos by Julie R. Angel; nonhuman skulls courtesy of the University of New Mexico, Museum of Southwestern Biology)

anthropologists should be consulted whenever bones of unknown origin are encountered in a forensic situation.

Starting with the vertebral column, Figure 3.9 illustrates this structure from the lateral aspect in both a human and a sheep. Notice that the quadruped has larger cervical vertebrae and longer spinous processes than seen in the human. Also, the sheep has two curves, one through the neck, which is concave, and the other between the head and the pelvis, which is convex. However, in humans, a third exists in the lower part (lumbar vertebrae) that is concave. Figure 3.10 illustrates the differences between the human sacrum and that of a sheep. Notice the somewhat triangular outline of this structure in humans when viewed anteriorly; this outline is less noticeable in the sheep. The differences in the number and configuration of the ribs between sheep on the left and human on the right is shown in Figure 3.11a. Despite the similarity in size, the human ribs are almost C-shaped, while those of the sheep have only about half of this curvature. Figure 3.11b illustrates the sternum of these two species in the anterior aspect; notice the wider top (the manubrium) of the human bone when compared with the more linear nature of the entire sternum in the quadruped.

APPENDICULAR SKELETON   Although most people will recognize nonhuman bones when structures such as claws, fur, or hooves are present, the bones of the quadrupedal appendicular skeleton have been confused with those of humans. These bones include the arms and legs in people, which are analogous to those of the forelimbs and hind limbs of quadrapedal animals, respectively. Humans and quadrupeds have the same bones in these structures, albeit in different configurations. Thus, this section will treat each limb bone and other structures of the appendicular skeleton (i.e., shoulder, pelvis) in turn so that the differences between the human and nonhuman will be obvious.

Figure 3.12 displays the scapulae of human and sheep, both in anterior and in posterior aspects. Although both are triangular, notice that the widest section of the bone is

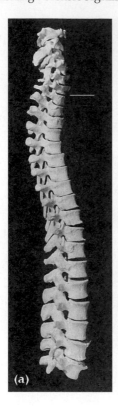
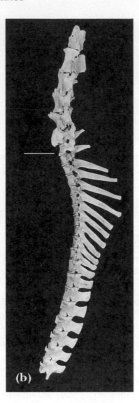

FIGURE 3.9 Vertebral column of **(a)** human and **(b)** sheep (*Ovis canadensis*). The sheep's spine is arranged vertically to better demonstrate the differences from the human in both structure and form. A line is drawn at the base of the neck of each. (Photo by Julie R. Angel; sheep courtesy of the University of New Mexico, Museum of Southwestern Biology)

farthest from the glenoid fossa in the sheep, while in humans this structure is located on one of the corners of the widest part. Figure 3.13a displays the humeri of a human and four quadrupeds: deer, sheep, cow, and elk. Notice at the proximal end that the equivalent of the greater tubercle in the quadrupeds is more developed and projects beyond

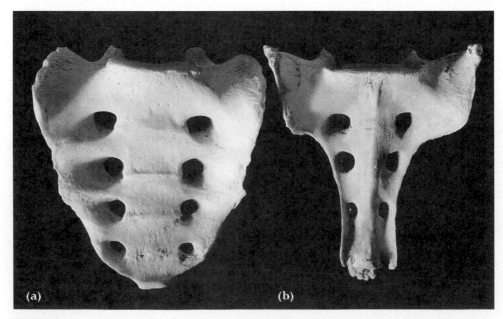

FIGURE 3.10 Sacrum of **(a)** human and **(b)** sheep (*Ovis canadensis*). (Photo by Julie R. Angel; sheep courtesy of the University of New Mexico, Museum of Southwestern Biology)

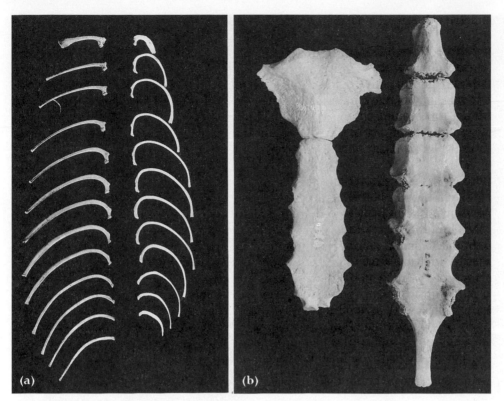

FIGURE 3.11 **(a)** Ribs of human *(right)* compared with those of a sheep (*Ovis canadensis*).
(b) Sternum of human *(left)* and sheep (*Ovis canadensis*). (Photo by Julie R. Angel; sheep courtesy of
the University of New Mexico, Museum of Southwestern Biology)

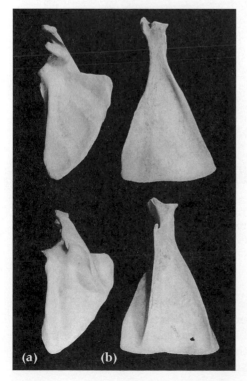

FIGURE 3.12 Scapula of **(a)** human and **(b)** sheep
(*Ovis canadensis*) from anterior and posterior aspects.
(Photo by Julie R. Angel; sheep courtesy of the University of
New Mexico, Museum of Southwestern Biology)

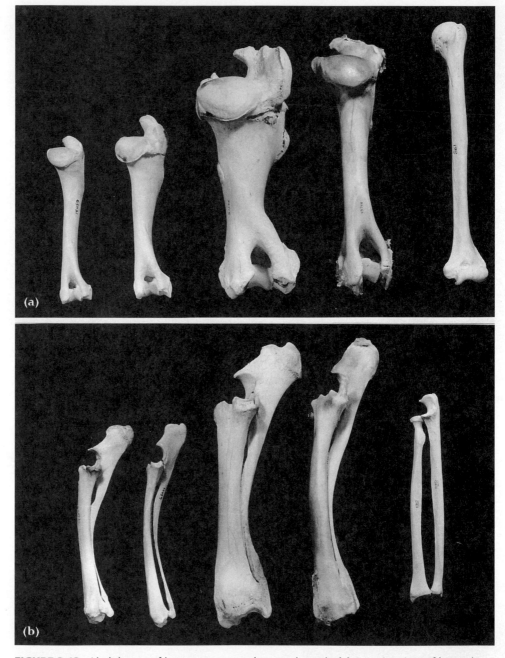

FIGURE 3.13   Limb bones of humans compared to quadrupeds. **(a)** Anterior view of humeri: from left to right, deer (*Odocoileus hemionus*), sheep (*Ovis canadensis*), cow (*Bos taurus*), elk (*Cervus elaphus*), and human (*Homo sapiens*). **(b)** Ulnae and radii, from left to right, sheep (*Ovis canadensis*), deer (*Odocoileus hemionus*), cow (*Bos taurus*), elk (*Cervus elaphus*), and human (*Homo sapiens*). (Photos by Julie R. Angel; nonhuman bones courtesy of the University of New Mexico, Museum of Southwestern Biology)

the head in this bone, while it is small and low in humans. Notice also the weak S-shape of the quadrupedal humeri (this is even more noticeable in Figure 3.2), which is missing in the more linear human equivalent. Figure 3.13b compares the radii and ulnae of a human with those of the same animals. Notice the major differences in configuration of both of these bones in the human when compared with those of the quadruped. Finally,

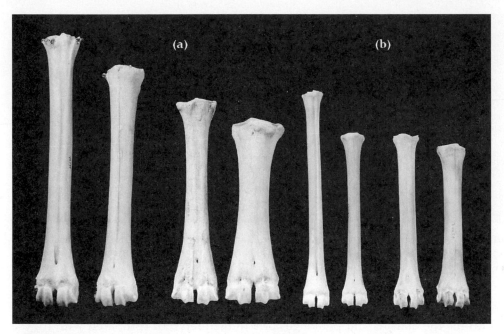

FIGURE 3.14   Front **(b)** and **(a)** back metapodials of four quadrupeds; from left to right, elk (*Cervus elaphus*), cow (*Bos taurus*), deer (*Odocoileus hemionus*), and sheep (*Ovis canadensis*). (Photo by Julie R. Angel; specimen courtesy of the University of New Mexico, Museum of Southwestern Biology)

Figure 3.14 shows the metacarpals and metatarsals (called the **metapodials**) of these four animals; since the concomitant bones in humans are so dissimilar, only a cursory examination is necessary to avoid misidentification as human.

Turning to the lower or rear limbs, Figure 3.15 presents a human os coxa alongside that of an elk, illustrating the shorter and wider configuration of the human ilium when compared to the long and narrow shape of this bone in the quadruped. Also, the difference in size and configuration of the pubis and ischium are well illustrated. Figure 3.16 depicts the assembled pelves of a cow compared to a human; the differences in the shapes of the individual bones and in the overall configuration are conspicuous. Figure 3.17a illustrates the differences between the femora of the same four ungulates and a human. Notice that the greater trochanter projects above the head in each of the quadrupeds, but not in the bipedal human. Also, the articular surface for the tibia continues higher on the shaft of the ungulates than it does on humans. Finally, Figure 3.17b illustrates the differences in the tibiae. Notice the multiple notches at the distal ends of the ungulates and the larger and more projecting tuberosity on the four quadrupeds when compared to humans.

Bear Paws and Pig's Teeth

T. Dale Stewart (1979) was one of the earliest workers to note the similarity between the hands and feet of humans and the front and hind paws of the various bears (especially the North American black bear, *Ursus americanus*). Figure 3.18a displays the left metacarpals and first two phalanges of a human versus the same bones from the right side in the black bear (Figure 3.18b). Despite the obvious similarities, the smallest digit in the human is the first (i.e., the thumb), while the last

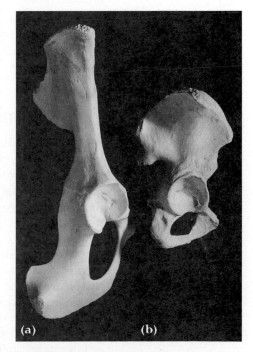

FIGURE 3.15   Os coxa of **(a)** an elk compared with that of **(b)** a human. (Photo by Julie R. Angel; elk courtesy of the University of New Mexico, Museum of Southwestern Biology)

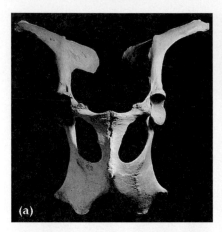 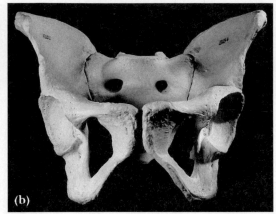

FIGURE 3.16   Assembled pelvis of **(a)** cow (*Bos taurus*) and **(b)** a human. (Photo by Julie R. Angel; cow courtesy of the University of New Mexico, Museum of Southwestern Biology)

digit is smallest in *U. americanus*. A similar situation is shown in Figure 3.19, which displays (a) the metatarsals and phalanges of a human left foot compared with (b) the same bones in the black bear. In the absence of claws, the two can be distinguished on the bases of the size of the metatarsals. The first digit of the human is considerably thicker than the remaining metatarsals; however, these bones are approximately equal in length and robustness in the bear. Finally, in both structures, the distal ends of the phalanges are more grooved in bears than they are in humans.

Less well known than bear paws is the similarity between the premolars of pigs and the molar teeth of humans (Joel Irish, personal communication). Figure 3.20a displays the palates of these two creatures. Although the differences in shape and size make it unlikely that the full jaws of these two animals would be mistaken, Figure 3.20b shows human molars adjacent to the premolars of a pig (*Sus scrofa*). Notice that they both are rectangular in outline and have low cusps in each corner. These shared features make a misidentification possible, but not probable.

CONTEMPORARY VERSUS NONCONTEMPORARY

Although the distinction between contemporary and noncontemporary is dichotomous, osteological remains can come from any place in a continuum that starts at the present and extends as far back in time as human existence. The result of this fact is that remains from the beginning of the continuum have more traits characteristic of contemporary specimens, whereas those that are older have more characteristics of noncontemporary specimens. Thus, although forensic anthropologists must make a single determination, they often need to judge the meaning of conflicting information when estimating the medicolegal significance of a specimen. This section presents a discussion of the information used to distinguish contemporary from noncontemporary remains. It is drawn partly from the descriptions of Stewart (1979) and Rhine (1998) and partly from information known to most forensic anthropologists.

Four aspects help to distinguish medicolegally significant remains from those that are not: state of preservation, body modification, personal belongings, and conditions of interment. State of preservation refers to the physical status of the bones after the loss of soft tissue (e.g., solid or broken, white or discolored). Body modification refers to changes to the normal structure of bone and teeth that is preferred or required by society (e.g., amalgams in teeth, surgical implants). Personal belongings are those

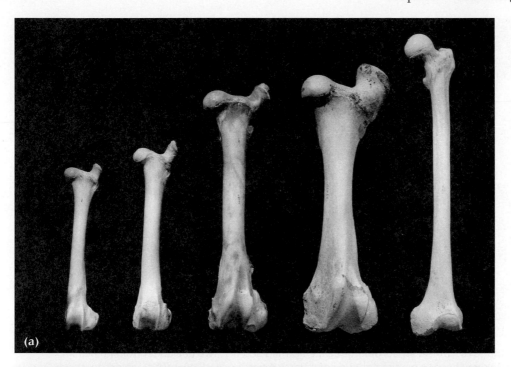

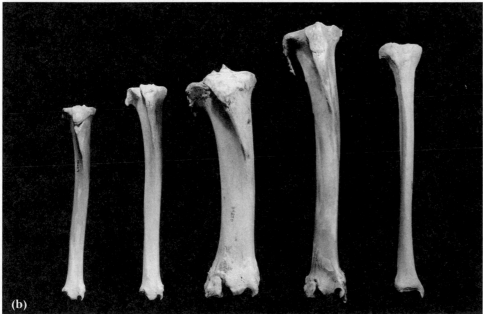

FIGURE 3.17   Limb bones of humans compared with quadrupeds. **(a)** Anterior views of femora: from left to right, deer (*Odocoileus hemionus*), sheep (*Ovis canadensis*), elk (*Cervus elaphus*), cow (*Bos taurus*), and human (*Homo sapiens*). **(b)** Anterior views of tibiae: from left to right, deer (*Odocoileus hemionus*), sheep (*Ovis canadensis*), cow (*Bos taurus*), elk (*Cervus elaphus*), and human (*Homo sapiens*).   (Photo by Julie R. Angel; nonhuman bones courtesy of the University of New Mexico, Museum of Southwestern Biology)

nonosteological items found in association with the remains that help to distinguish contemporary from noncontemporary remains (e.g., prehistoric tools, modern clothing). Conditions of interment refer to the circumstances surrounding bodies found in graves (e.g., formal burial, position of body). Each of these areas comprises considerable

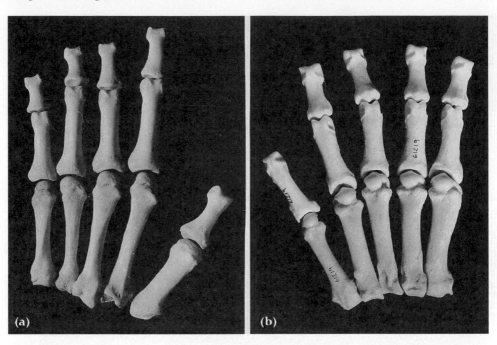

FIGURE 3.18 Dorsal aspect of left-side metacarpals and first two phalanges from **(a)** human and **(b)** same bones from the right side of a North American black bear (*Ursus americanus*). (Photos by Julie R. Angel; bear courtesy of the University of New Mexico, Museum of Southwestern Biology)

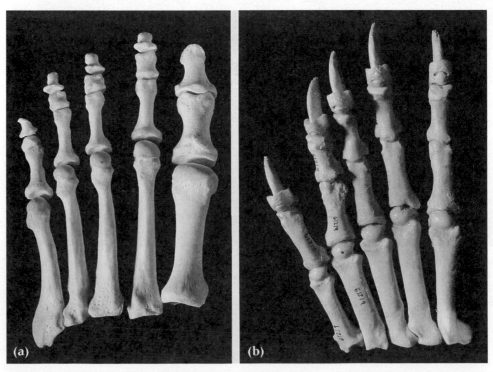

FIGURE 3.19 Dorsal aspect of metatarsals and all phalanges from **(a)** human and **(b)** North American black bear (*Ursus americanus*). (Photos by Julie R. Angel; bear courtesy of the University of New Mexico, Museum of Southwestern Biology)

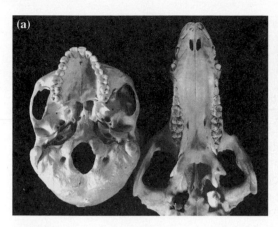 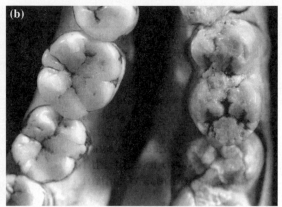

FIGURE 3.20   Comparison of human dentition with those of a pig. **(a)** Palates of human *(left)* and pig (*Sus scrofa*); **(b)** molars of human *(left)* compared with premolars of pig (*Sus scrofa*).   (Photos by Julie R. Angel; pig courtesy of the University of New Mexico, Museum of Southwestern Biology)

amounts of information related to age that, when observed together, usually allow for the identification of forensically significant remains. Each of these four factors will be discussed separately next.

State of Preservation

State of preservation refers to the visible and measurable characteristics of the bones being studied. Seven traits help to distinguish contemporary from noncontemporary remains: color, texture, hydration, weight, condition, fragility, and amount of soft tissue. Although varying according to circumstances of the environment, bone that has been exposed and/or buried for an extended period of time becomes discolored, grainy, dry, light in weight, often fragmented, fragile, and divested of any soft tissue present during life. By contrast, "fresh" bone is off-white, smooth, greasy, heavy, solid, and containing (usually) some soft tissue. Thus, because these factors can be used to estimate the forensic importance of osteological finds, each will be discussed in some detail.

COLOR   When bone is in the body, it has a yellowish-white to yellowish-brown tint due to saturation by body fats and fluids. After removal of soft tissue, it begins to dehydrate and take on the well-known ivory (i.e., off-white) color. However, over time bone may begin to change color again from exposure to environmental factors. For example, in strong sunlight, bone will turn white and then gray, even after only a few years. Also, buried bone will take on the (usually) brown color of the surrounding soil. Similarly, some prehistoric societies covered burials with red ochre, which imparts a red tint to bones. Although color changes may take only a few years, normally a considerable time is necessary before bone loses its original hue. Thus, except in special circumstances, discoloration is more indicative of age than bone that has maintained its yellowish-brown or off-white shade.

TEXTURE   The next characteristic of importance is surface texture. Generally, young bone has the same smooth surface as ivory. However, with protracted exposure, climatic factors and soil acids erode the surface, causing a loss of the original smoothness. Thus, grainy or pitted osteological material means that a considerable amount of time has passed since death. Unfortunately, several factors can affect texture in contemporary remains. First, graininess usually increases with age such that persons who are

60 years of age or older have lost the smoothness of cortical bone found in the young. Second, diseases can cause bone loss that can affect the overall texture; a common effect is raised striations along the long axes of long bones and pitting due to anemic conditions (see Chapter 15).

HYDRATION   When in the body, bone contains body fluids that give it a yellowish hue. In addition to coloration, these substances impart a greasy look and feel when soft tissue is first removed. However, with extended exposure to air, this moisture is lost and the bone appears dry and porous. Thus, hydrated and greasy bones usually indicate that little time has passed since death, while dry bone indicates greater time. As a complication, in burials, older bones will absorb groundwater, giving them a wet appearance when first excavated. However, they will not have the greasy look or feel of fresh bone; and, after exposure to air, they will lose that hydrated look within a day or so.

WEIGHT   When bone emerges from the body, the fats and fluids that are part of its makeup give it a surprising amount of weight. Generally, weight decreases as moisture evaporates and decreases still further when **decalcification** (loss of calcium and other minerals) occurs, particularly with long removal from the body and/or burial for extended periods. This loss of both fluids and calcium salts causes bone to become light in weight with the passage of time. Unfortunately, this inverse relationship between weight and age can be confounded by the accumulation of minerals in buried remains. The same groundwater that helps to leach out calcium salts (causing decalcification) can also deposit minerals that cause bone to gain weight. Thus, as with other factors, the environment in which the remains are found must be taken into account when determining the forensic significance of osteological material.

CONDITION   This factor refers to the level of fragmentation of a bone. Generally, unless exposed to excessive crushing injuries as in accidents involving aircraft and trains, contemporary bones are whole with little (if any) fragmentation. However, with time and rough handling, bones become broken and in some cases highly fragmented. Such bones may be composed of many fragments that require considerable restoration before they can be viewed in their entirety. Many burials dating from ancient times are fragmented to a degree not normally seen in fresh bone; thus, the degree of fragmentation can be used as a general indication of age.

FRAGILITY   This factor refers to the toughness of bone. Bone is a strong substance that even after some years can absorb rough handling without undue damage. However, during exposure and burial as climatic factors weather it and soil acids leach through it, bone can become fragile and friable. In some cases, it can disintegrate when it is exposed to air. Thus, generally, bones that appear as if they would fall apart just from handling indicate that the age may be beyond that of interest to forensic anthropologists while tough and strong-looking bone is more likely to be of medicolegal significance. Again, the circumstances in which the remains were found can confound this simple situation. Extremely caustic environments (see the description of the Leutgert case in Chapter 1) can cause fresh bones to disintegrate to a degree seen only in bones many decades, or even centuries, older.

SOFT TISSUE   The presence of soft tissue is one of the more important characteristics indicating age. Large amounts of soft tissue that are emanating the odor of decay normally indicate a contemporary body that is of medicolegal significance. (For an interesting exception, see Box 3.2.) However, older remains, except under unusual circumstances (e.g., freezing, mummification, embalming), rarely display soft tissue other than desiccated skin, muscle, internal organs, and so forth.

BOX 3.2
The Burial of Lt. Col. W. M. Shy

William Bass (1984) describes a case in which the factors surrounding a discovered body caused him to misjudge its forensic significance. In 1977, Bass was called to a house in Tennessee with a private cemetery where one of the graves had been disturbed. He found a body on top of an old Civil War era cast-iron coffin that had a 1-foot by 2-foot hole in its lid. The grave was marked as belonging to that of Lt. Col. W. M. Shy, killed during the battle of Nashville on December 16, 1864. The partially clothed and headless body was disarticulated, but contained soft tissue that was both recognizable and red in color. Based on this and the strong odor of decay, Bass assumed that the person had been dead approximately 6 months to 1 year. Although he discussed the possibility with the authorities that the body was that of Lt. Col. Shy, his previous experience with Civil War burials made him believe that only bones should be found in graves that old. Since he believed the body contemporary (and therefore of medicolegal significance), he brought the remains to his laboratory, where he began "cooking" them in hot water to remove the soft tissue (see Chapter 6 for a discussion of this process). During this process, he encountered a strong smell of embalming fluid. Because this was indicative of a formal burial, he began to rethink his judgment that the body was not that of Lt. Col. Shy. A revisit to the site confirmed his suspicions. The coffin contained a bodiless cranium, devoid of soft tissue, shattered by what appeared to be a large-caliber bullet. This skull combined with the lack of synthetic fibers in the attendant clothing and the presence of embalming fluid indicated that the body was that of a Civil War soldier who had been dead for over 100 years and who therefore was not of forensic significance.

Body Modifications

It is common for people in all societies to modify their bodies in some manner (Haviland, 1997). The most common modifications involve tattoos and other disfigurements of soft tissue (e.g., ear plugs, lip stretching), which will not be seen in osteological material. However, some modifications done by (especially) prehistoric societies can be preserved osteologically. Because they can help to determine the medicolegal significance of human remains, it behooves the forensic worker to be aware of such practices.

One of the most common forms of modification found in prehistoric remains is cranial deformation. Many indigenous people use cradleboards for their children's first years of life by which the infants' heads are strapped down for safety. This has the effect of deforming, to a greater or lesser degree, the pliable bones of the child's cranium. If the cradleboard is hard, this effect is amplified. Thus, skulls that have lost the normal round contour of the cranial bones usually indicate this practice. Figure 3.21 displays a line drawing of a (a) normal skull and (b) one exhibiting flattening of the occipital bone. As can be seen, the rounding that is usual for the rear bone of the right-hand skull has been reduced, causing a flattening of the back of the head.

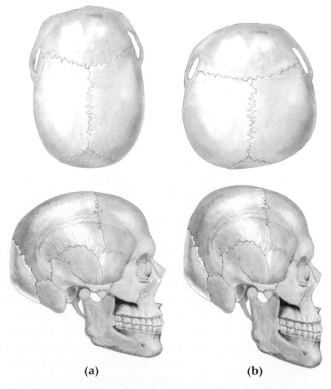

(a)   **(b)**

FIGURE 3.21   Line drawing of skulls, from superior and lateral aspects. **(a)** Skull manifesting the "normal" condition; **(b)** skull exhibiting occipital flattening. (Reprinted from W. M. Wormington: *Prehistoric Indians of the Southwest,* 1947, Figure 20. Redrawn with permission of the Denver Museum of Nature and Science. All rights reserved, Denver Museum of Nature and Science)

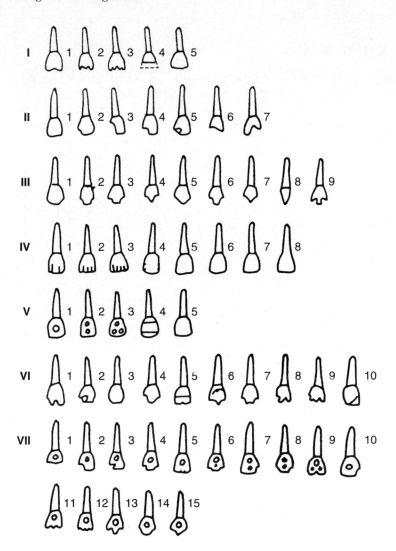

FIGURE 3.22   Varying types of dental modifications.   (After Figure 1 of Javier Romero, in *Handbook of Middle American Indians,* Robert Wauchope, General Editor, Volume 9, *Physical Anthropology,* T. Dale Stewart, Volume Editor, Copyright © 1970. By permission of the University of Texas Press)

Another common area of personal modification is the dentition. Some people in the past altered the shape of their teeth for (apparently) esthetic reasons. The wide range of variation in this practice is well illustrated in Figure 3.22. The presence of these forms usually indicates that the human remains are not of medicolegal significance. However, other dental modifications can be used to establish forensic significance. In industrialized countries, the well-known gold and silver amalgams (i.e., fillings) and other odontological prosthetics, such as bridges, caps (plastic, porcelain, or gold), implants, and dentures, are indicative of a contemporary human. Figure 3.23 illustrates an upper jaw that manifests most of these dental features.

One last attribute of teeth that can provide information on the contemporary–noncontemporary question is dental wear. Generally, persons from modern societies do not show appreciable wear even in later life. However, persons from prehistoric times (as well as those from nonindustrial societies) show so much wear that the enamel on the occlusal surface is worn away in parts, exposing the underlying dentin.

Beyond dentition, a variety of prosthetics can be found in other areas of the body, which offer information on medicolegal significance. With advances in surgery, hip replacements (see Figure 3.24a), surgical plates (Figure 3.24b), and other implants can be encountered in human remains. Their presence has a simplifying effect on establishing forensic significance; devices such as these indicate that the remains are contemporary.

Personal Belongings

It is well known that many people bury their dead with clothing, jewelry, and other items of their society (Pearson, 1999). This can leave important clues as to the age of recovered remains because of the dramatic changes in technology that have occurred over the last few hundred years. Thus, skeletal material found in association with prehistoric objects such as stone tools, pottery, or basketry is likely of prehistoric age and therefore too old to be of forensic significance. Similarly, bodies found dressed in modern clothing and accompanied by modern jewelry and other such items indicate recent remains that can be forensically meaningful. Similarly, burial in wood or metal coffins is common in industrialized countries, but absent in most prehistoric societies.

Conditions of Interment

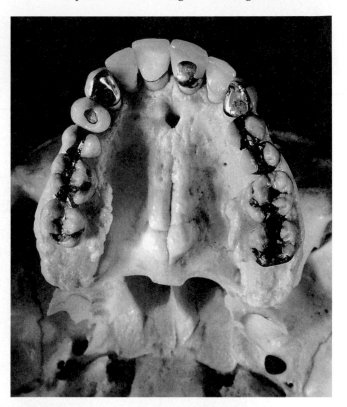

FIGURE 3.23 Upper jaw of a contemporary human showing dental prosthetics. The incisors have plastic caps, both canines have gold fillings, and all premolars and molars have silver amalgams. (Photo by Julie R. Angel; specimen courtesy of the University of New Mexico–Albuquerque, Maxwell Museum of Anthropology, #29)

For bodies recovered from graves, the last factor to consider is the conditions surrounding the burial. Several factors of interment can be used to distinguish forensically significant from nonsignificant finds. Generally, persons who have died under normal circumstances receive a formal burial that involves careful treatment of the deceased. By contrast, medicolegally significant burials are more likely to appear as though the decedents were simply thrown into a hole with no pretreatment or care. (This is a concession to expediency; generally, perpetrators burying their murder victims do not want to be in prolonged contact with the body because this increases the probability of being apprehended by law enforcement officials.) Thus, the recognition of factors that suggest formal burial is important for identifying medicolegally significant burials.

The number of burial practices surrounding formal interments is too diverse and complex to be discussed here. However, the main factors that help to identify burials of persons who have died normal deaths are arrangement, direction of face, pretreatment, and burial enclosure. Arrangement refers to how the body is laid out within the burial pit; Ubelaker (1989) summarizes the work of others when he describes four forms: tightly flexed, flexed, semiflexed, and extended. **Tightly flexed** refers to a position in which bodies are put in the fetal position as though they were inside their mother's wombs (see Figure 3.25a). Specifically, the elbows are drawn into the torso and flexed so that the hands lie against the upper thorax, close to the base of the neck. Similarly, the knees are drawn up to the abdomen, while the feet are in the proximity of the buttocks. This position, which is favored by many prehistoric societies, is found as far back in time as the Neanderthals, some 60,000 years ago. **Flexed** and **semiflexed** are relaxed

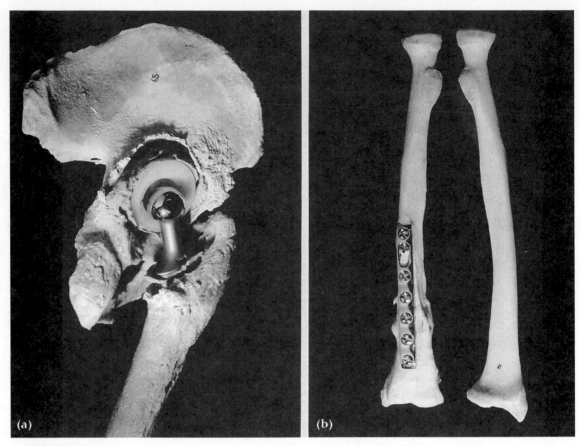

FIGURE 3.24 Prosthetics implanted in human bone. **(a)** Hip replacement; plastic insert in acetabulum with stainless steel femoral neck and head; **(b)** radius with surgical plate used to reinforce a broken wrist; pictured with normal bone. (Photo by Julie R. Angel; specimens courtesy of the University of New Mexico–Albuquerque, Maxwell Museum of Anthropology, #52)

versions of tightly flexed (see Figure 3.25b). In these positions, the elbows are not as close to the torso and the hands extend somewhat outward. Similarly, the knees extend outward close to right angles with the rest of the body, while the feet, although at the level of the buttocks, also extend somewhat away from the body. The fourth arrangement, and the most commonly recognized, is the **extended** position where bodies are laid out with their legs straight and their arms either extended at their sides or crossed over their chests (see Figure 3.25c). This is the position favored by most industrialized countries.

In any of the preceding arrangements, bodies can face either up, down, or sideways. Generally, persons buried in the tightly flexed, flexed, and semiflexed positions lie on their sides with the skull facing sideways, whereas in extended burials the usual facing is upward. Deviations from these positions do occur; in some cases, the body can be placed face down or (in rare cases) head down with the buttocks pointing to the sky. In addition to arrangement and facing, pretreatment of remains can occur. This entails both embalming, by which the body is infused with a preservative (this tradition has been practiced for over a century in Western countries), and cremation, by which all soft tissue and many osteological elements are burned away, leaving only bone fragments. Finally, placement of the body within a funerary enclosure can be favored; a coffin or mausoleum is usual in Western societies, and stone-lined pits have been used (especially) in the past.

A last aspect to consider is the recognition of long unused cemeteries. Tracy Rogers (2005) pointed out that with housing developments encroaching on rural areas and older parts of towns, there is the possibility that human remains from old and forgotten graveyards might appear to be forensic cases. She noted that before the advent of municipal cemeteries, family members were buried on private land, thereby making it likely that old family graveyards can be encountered in rural areas (especially if located on the top of a hill or overlooking water). Churchyards and land near old religious structures (e.g., churches, convents) also may have long-forgotten cemeteries. Similarly, the land near public buildings, especially if it is being used as a park or green space, can contain unknown graveyards. Forensic anthropologists must be cognizant of the possibility of encountering legitimate burials when investigating skeletal material uncovered in these areas.

Considering the preceding information, bodies recovered from coffins are not likely to be of medicolegal significance, nor are bodies that have been embalmed or treated in some way with preservatives. Similarly, bodies arranged carefully in the grave usually are from formal burials.

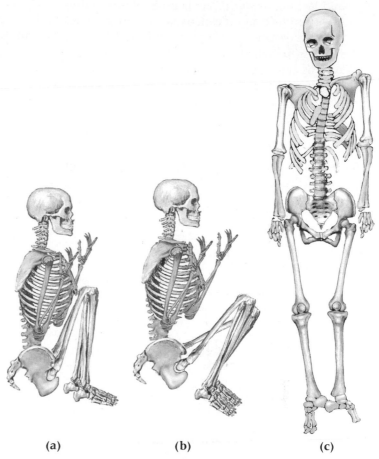

(a)   (b)   (c)

FIGURE 3.25 The three most common forms of burial: **(a)** flexed; **(b)** semiflexed; and **(c)** extended.

Conversely, untreated bodies found in a disorganized manner within a burial pit without a coffin are more likely to indicate the hasty burial typical of most forensically significant remains.

Summary

1. The important components of establishing the medicolegal significance of skeletal remains involve determining if they are human and if they are from a person who has died within the last 50 years.

2. Human bones can be distinguished from those of nonhumans by their maturity and architecture.

3. Maturity helps to distinguish humans from nonhumans by eliminating the bones of animals that are too mature to be from subadult humans and too small to be confused with adult humans.

4. Architecture distinguishes humans from nonhumans because of the functional differences required by their habitual locomotor stances.

5. Skeletal remains that have a yellowish to ivory hue, present a smooth texture, are greasy to the touch, are heavy in weight, are whole, feel solid, and contain some (or a significant amount of) soft tissue probably are of medicolegal significance (and should be treated as such).

6. Osteological material that is discolored, grainy in texture, dehydrated, light in weight, fragile,

and lacking in soft tissue is probably too old to be of forensic significance and, if corroborated by other information, can be recorded as such.

7. Human remains that manifest societal practices such as cranial flattening and tooth filing probably are too old to be of medicolegal significance.

8. Odontological remains that manifest modern societal practices such as amalgams, crowns, and bridges should be considered of forensic significance.

9. Osteological material that manifests the results of surgical procedures, such as plates and artificial joints, should be considered of medicolegal significance.

10. Bodies that appear to have been processed (e.g., embalmed), placed in a coffin, or otherwise buried in an orderly manner almost certainly represent formal burials that probably are not of medicolegal significance.

11. Remains that are buried in a haphazard manner, indicating lack of care during interment, are more likely to be forensically significant than those that are well arranged and carefully buried.

Exercises

1. If a 6-inch whole bone that appears to be a humerus is given to you for analysis, on what basis would you determine if it was human or nonhuman?

2. If a fragment of a jaw that has long and pointy teeth is brought to you for analysis, on what basis would you determine its forensic importance?

3. In the text it was stated that human skulls could be differentiated from those of nonhumans on the basis of their snouts and braincases. Looking at Figures 3.7 and 3.8, what other general characteristics can you see that distinguish human from nonhuman?

4. In the text it was noted that the nonhuman femur could be distinguished from that of humans by the height of the greater trochanter. Note other characteristics that distinguish human from nonhuman femora.

5. Compare the metapodials in Figure 3.14 with the bones of the human skeleton in Chapter 2 and determine if any human bones are likely to be mistaken for a metapodial.

6. Compare the human and nonhuman scapulae in Figure 3.12. What structure is present on the human scapula, but not on those of quadrupeds?

7. A human skull is brought to you that is dark in color, very fragmented, fragile, light in weight, and very dry, but one of its molar teeth contains a silver amalgam. Using the decision table described in Chapter 1, on what basis would you determine its forensic importance?

8. A body dressed in 19th-century clothing is discovered in a decaying wooden coffin. The skeleton is held together by a small amount of desiccated soft tissue. Determine the forensic significance of this find and state the reasoning behind your assessment. Use the decision table described in Chapter 1 to aid in your analysis.

9. A fragmented human skull is brought in for analysis. The surface of the bone is smooth, white, and very dry. The fragments are light in weight and fairly solid, but have no clinging soft tissue. On the basis of these traits, determine the skull's medicolegal significance, if any? Again use a decision table to aid you in your determination.

10. A grave is uncovered that contains three bodies; two lie next to each other in an extended position, while the third lies at an angle across the top of them. From this information alone, is it possible to determine the forensic significance of these remains, and what is the reason for your decision?

4

Recovery Scene Methods

With the publication of *Forensic Archaeology* in 1976, Dan Morse and colleagues created a new subdiscipline within the larger study of forensic anthropology. In this pioneering article, the authors suggest that methods used by archaeologists to deal with prehistoric sites are applicable to forensically significant remains. Prior to this, the recovery processes employed by forensic anthropologists varied from worker to worker; and, although most would follow a course similar to that proposed by the authors, the techniques used were not fully defined. Thus, their article and subsequent laboratory manual (Morse et al., 1983) formalized these methods for searching, mapping, and retrieving human remains already used by the most conscientious workers. Because their work is so comprehensive, this chapter summarizes their procedures, with additions from other sources as noted.

In any field operation involving human remains, four main tasks may need to be performed: location, mapping, excavation, and collection. Location refers to finding the remains, whether they are from a single individual or multiple people, whether they are visible on the surface or located belowground, and whether an informant leads investigators to the remains or a search must be instituted. After they are found, the placement of remains and associated materials must be mapped in relation to a permanent structure (set as a datum point), and their location on a larger map must be pinpointed. Next, if the remains are interred, they must be excavated following the methods of archeology. Finally, using accepted procedures, the remains must be collected and properly packed so that they can be brought to a laboratory for further analysis. These tasks are described in the middle four of the six sections of this chapter. However, before they are approached, some preliminary issues must be considered. As pointed out by many authors (Morse et al., 1976, 1983; Randall, 1991; Dirkmaat and Adovasio, 1997, to name only a few), planning the recovery process results in the gathering of the maximum amount of data pertinent to the forensic scene. This is covered in the first section of the chapter. The final section deals with mass disasters, that is, incidents involving the death of six or more individuals. Because these usually require special methods beyond those described for individuals or a small number of bodies, separate treatment is warranted.

PRELIMINARY ISSUES

A major problem surrounding the recovery of remains is the noninvolvement of forensic anthropologists. This is not due to disinterest on the part of these workers, but due to their lack of opportunity. Police, sheriffs, and other law enforcement officials, as well as medical examiners and coroners, often will not consult with these specialists when recovering partially or fully skeletonized bodies. The various bones and material evidence are simply placed in some kind of container and brought to the anthropologist for analysis.

Unfortunately, many do not use the methods of forensic archeology; thus, bones of multiple individuals are mixed, remains are not fully recovered (e.g., missing foot or hand bones), and other errors resulting in loss of information occur. Given this situation, it behooves the forensic anthropologist to work closely with local law enforcement so that police and sheriff's offices are aware of the value of these methods. Officers then can receive the training they need to understand that proper recovery is such a complex process that a specialist should be called when skeletal remains are discovered. In addition, Komar and Potter (2007) demonstrate that the rate of victim identification as well as determination of cause and manner of death is directly related to the proportion of the body that is recovered (i.e., the more of the body that is recovered, the more likely it is to be identified and the cause and manner of death determined), giving even more reason for the police to engage the services of anthropologists in this earliest stage of a forensic case.

If fortunate enough to be called to a scene, forensic anthropologists should proceed with caution. While in some cases the police are led to a scene by the perpetrator of the crime or an accomplice (thereby establishing the forensic context), in many instances remains are found by a passerby and the forensic context is not established. Thus, the area should be approached following the methods used by law enforcement when processing a crime scene.

First and foremost of these is securing the area so that outsiders cannot enter and possibly remove evidence or drop contaminating material; the agency with jurisdiction over the case usually will handle this task. Next, all investigators must be careful not to contaminate the scene by dropping items such as gum wrappers, cigarette butts, or other fresh materials. Similarly, investigators must watch where they step so that bones or other materials on the surface are not broken or pressed into the ground where they may never be recovered. Finally, any evidence of previous human intrusion into the area must not be disturbed until it has been reviewed by the investigating officer. Although some issues surrounding crime scene processing may not be important with skeletonized remains (e.g., footprints, unless the crime scene is fresh), it is axiomatic that, because the importance of findings are not known, all should be treated as equally significant.

The other preliminary issue to consider is time. Although forensic cases can be time sensitive, the urgency surrounding the recovery of remains is considerably less than that in cases involving live persons. Thus, work should be done slowly to ensure that the remains are recovered completely and accurately. As pointed out by numerous persons in anthropology and archeology, removal is a destructive process. This is particularly true with excavation, where the extraction of dirt destroys the original position of the body and accompanying items within a grave. Similarly, because evidence is taken from its original position during field recovery, part of its value is lost forever. Thus, it is best to start the process by developing a plan for searching and, after finding, for mapping (with line drawings as well as photographs) and collecting the remains. Use of the methods described here, however time consuming, is essential to prevent the loss of important information.

LOCATING REMAINS

The first task in the recovery process is determining the location of the human remains and their associated materials. To perform this task accurately and completely, a search plan should be developed that is tailored to the unique circumstances of the search area (e.g., cliffs, trees, tall grass); and, although there is no set formula, it should address several issues. The first involves determining the equipment and personnel that can be obtained within time and monetary constraints. Equipment such as a

magnetometer, ground-penetrating radar, or an **electrical resistivity kit** are used for belowground searches, while small planes and helicopters are employed for aerial surface searches. Both types are expensive and the efficacy of the equipment used for belowground searches has been questioned (Buck, 2003). Similarly, **cadaver dogs** (specially trained dogs that are sensitive to the smell of decomposition) have been used with great success, but they are both difficult to obtain quickly and require special handling. Usually, the least expensive and easiest to perform (and therefore the most feasible method) is **visual assessment.** This involves walking an area and scanning the ground for human remains and their associated materials (see Figure 4.1). Planning for this type of search involves addressing issues such as the direction of approach, the number of searchers and their spacing, and needed equipment.

After these general aspects of the plan have been determined, the number of phases in the search process needs to be considered. If their location is not known, the first phase involves finding the remains within a (sometimes large) designated area. In mass disasters or when authorities have been led to a location by an informant, this phase can be disregarded. However, even in the case of informants, this phase may be necessary because of faulty memories surrounding the deposition of a body (see Box 4.1 for an example). Once the remains have been located, the second phase of the plan must be implemented. During this phase, the area around the human remains is searched for any materials (including missing body parts) that might serve to identify the person or help in identifying the circumstances surrounding the death of the decedent.

FIGURE 4.1 Searchers scanning the ground while approaching a simulated forensic scene. (Photo by Julie R. Angel)

Searching for Human Remains

When the placement of human remains is only vaguely understood (e.g., somewhere in the forest, somewhere on the West Mesa), usually a ground search must be instituted. To ensure accuracy and completeness of coverage, systematic methods such as those employed in archeological site survey are preferred. **Site survey** involves arranging a group of searchers side by side in a line, who then walk an area while scanning the ground for any indication of previous human incursion. The use of this technique will ensure that all ground is covered completely and efficiently, thereby reducing the likelihood that important information will be overlooked.

The first step in establishing this type of search is to obtain enough helpers to adequately inspect the area being examined. Although the number needed is proportional to the amount of space to be covered, it must be remembered that too many searchers are hard to organize, whereas too few means more work for those present. Once a number of searchers have been acquired, they must be made knowledgeable in the basics involved in visual assessment. Although not absolutely necessary, this can include a discussion of human osteology. However, more importantly, these persons must be instructed in the visible signs associated with scenes involving human remains.

BOX 4.1
The Value of an Organized Ground Search

Stan Rhine (1998) describes a case in which the location of the remains of a murder victim could not be refound by one of the perpetrators. In 1987, an informant tried to lead police to the body of a woman killed 1½ years earlier in the open plains east of Albuquerque, New Mexico. Taking the police to the road traveled the night of the murder, the informant recognized two abandoned stone buildings that were "ten miles" from the site where the body was deposited. With this fact in mind, the authorities and accompanying forensic anthropologists spent an afternoon driving up and down the road, stopping and searching various locations that, according to the informant, were "definitely" the location of the body. As each stop proved fruitless, the forensic anthropologists became more and more convinced that the search should have started at the stone buildings and proceeded in the direction that the informant said that he and his accomplice were traveling on the night of the murder.

Two days after the futile search, the forensic anthropologists convinced the office of the medical investigator that, if they were allowed to organize another search, they would have better results. After receiving permission to proceed, the team arrived on the scene only to be instructed by the state police officer in charge that the search would be started at the same spot 10 miles from the stone buildings that had been examined two days previously. Although a good technique was used (e.g., a line of equally spaced searchers walking the area), again nothing of significance was found after an entire day of search.

Finally, the forensic anthropologists instigated a search starting at the stone buildings originally recognized by the informant. Because of the limited ground cover, the team of five arrayed themselves in a line with approximately 75 feet between each of them. They proceeded in the direction that the informant was driving the night of the murder and, within 10 minutes of walking, they discovered the remains.

One of the more general indicators in recently deposited remains is increased insect activity and attendant odor. As soft tissue breaks down, flies will be visible as a noisy swarm that may help in the location of remains. Similarly, the strong smell of decomposition may be evident, especially with exposed finds. Another subject that workers need to understand is the numerous colors that bone can take when found on the surface. Although usually bleached white, skeletons may darken to a tan or light brown color under the effects of wind and waterborne soil or even gray by prolonged exposure to the sun (see Chapter 3).

If an interment is being sought, helpers should know the multiple signs that indicate the presence of a grave. One of the best of these is the state of vegetation. In recent interments, the area over the burial pit may be bare, while the surrounding soil is covered by trees, bushes, grasses, and other plant growth. Additionally, the vegetation in the area immediately surrounding the interment may be bent, broken, or trampled or otherwise display the effects of human activity.

However, if the grave is a year or more older, the reverse may occur; that is, there may be more vegetation over the burial pit due to looser soil and the nutrients supplied by the decomposing body. Also, the ground over the grave may not appear uniform, because different soils from different levels may have been intermixed during excavation and refilling. Finally, surplus earth not used to bury the body may be piled near the grave perimeter.

Another visual sign involves **soil compaction** over the grave, which may create three telltale signs (see Figure 4.2). First, the dirt near the edge of the interment may pull away, forming cracks that outline the perimeter of the burial pit. Second, as the soft tissues of the body decompose and the soil compacts, a primary depression may form in

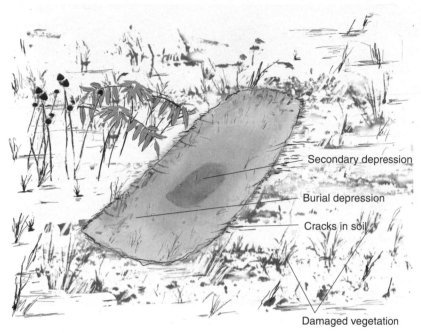

Secondary depression

Burial depression

Cracks in soil

Damaged vegetation

FIGURE 4.2 Signs of a recent human grave: cracks around the perimeter, depression sloping down from the sides, and smaller central depression.

the center that slopes up in all directions to the grave edges. Finally, a secondary (and smaller) depression may form in the middle of the primary depression, especially in shallow graves, when the abdominal cavity collapses.

After it is determined that all workers have knowledge of these signs, they are arranged side by side in a line such that their fields of view overlap by 20% to 30% (Dirkmaat and Adovasio, 1997). This overlap ensures that all ground is visible to at least one worker for the duration of the search. In open areas with little vegetation, distances between workers may be 50 feet or greater; however, in forested areas or fields of tall grass, a lesser interval is needed. Also, the search can be made only when enough daylight is available so that smaller objects (e.g., hand and foot bones) and osteological elements covered by debris (see Figure 4.3) will be visible.

Once arranged in a line, the searchers simply walk slowly over the search area, scanning the ground for human biological remains or signs of a grave. Although this may sound as if the searchers now must search an infinitely large area, logic and some data indicate that the task is not as hopeless as it appears. Because perpetrators of crimes usually wish to dispose of their victims quickly, it is generally accepted that bodies will be found in areas of easy access. Data from a study performed in Louisiana provides support for this assertion; bodies that were dumped in rural areas generally were found within one-quarter mile of the nearest road (Manheim et al., 2006). When the search commences, nonhuman bones and materials (e.g., clothes, bottles) may be encountered; however, it is best to ignore most of them at this point until the human remains have been located (shell casings or other indications of weapons might be exceptions). This is because with large search areas it is likely that a number of materials will be found that have no connection to the current case; only when the human remains have been discovered can the significance of these materials be determined. This systematic searching must be continued until the grave or (for surface finds) the main parts of the skeleton are located, or the authorities make the decision that information indicating the presence of a forensic case was faulty.

FIGURE 4.3 Ground covering obscuring osteological remains in a simulated forensic site. (Photo by Julie R. Angel)

Searching for Associated Materials

Once the human remains (e.g., body, grave) have been located, the second phase of the search is instituted. This involves finding all associated materials, such as missing body segments, clothing, weapons, shell casings, and other appropriate items. The methods for this phase are similar to those used to locate the human remains; that is, workers search the ground in an organized manner looking for indications of previous human incursion. However, because the locus of the search (e.g., the body, the grave) is known, the visual inspection involves moving outward from that center until all body parts are discovered or a point is reached beyond which it is unreasonable to expect to make relevant findings. Thus, during this phase, searchers start at the remains and search each of the cardinal directions in turn, fanning out as they go (see Figure 4.4). As in the previous phase, searchers are arranged side by side in a line as they walk slowly over the area, scanning the ground. In addition to the cardinal directions search, the area immediately surrounding the remains or grave must be inspected thoroughly because this is the area where it is most likely that relevant findings will be made. This includes not only a visual search, but also examination with a metal detector or other such instrumentation.

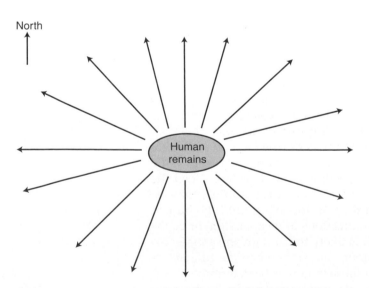

FIGURE 4.4 Pattern of search for the cardinal directions; notice that the searchers fan out as they work away from the body.

FIGURE 4.6 Flags used to mark physical evidence and human remains in a simulated forensic site. (Photo by Julie R. Angel)

FIGURE 4.5 Isolated segments removed from the main part of a body in a simulated forensic site: **(a)** human remains; **(b)** isolated item of clothing. (Photos by Julie R. Angel)

During this phase of the search, not only are any unfound human remains sought (see Figure 4.5a), but also other indications of human presence. Thus, shell casings, bludgeons, knives, or other possible weapons, as well as items of clothing (see Figure 4.5b), jewelry, personal electronic devices (e.g., beepers, cell phones), and nonhuman bones should be considered important. As these are encountered, their location should be indicated with a marker, after which the search is continued. These markers should be easily visible from a distance, but small enough not to cause undue damage to the area of placement.

With this in mind, a plastic flag on a short wooden post (see Figure 4.6) is recommended; wooden posts are preferable, because they will not confound the results of a

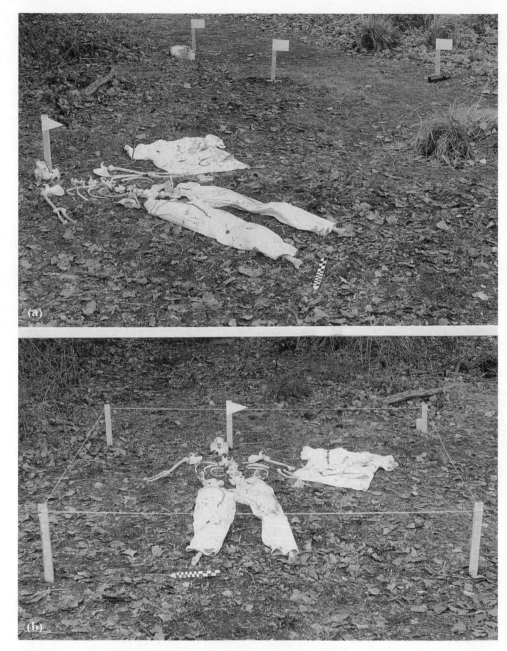

FIGURE 4.7 **(a)** Flagging of body and associated material and **(b)** placement of grid around main part of body in a simulated forensic site. (Photos by Julie R. Angel)

metal detector search. The flags can be of different colors and/or shapes to indicate the presence of either biological or material remains (e.g., the triangular flag in Figure 4.7 indicates human remains, while the square flags indicate associated material).

MAPPING REMAINS

After the remains and relevant material evidence have been located and marked, the findings must be indicated on a map of the scene. Precision in mapping is important for several reasons. First, because scattered body parts may indicate carnivore activity, the amount of this scatter can help determine time since death (see Chapter 5). Also, the relationship between body elements and physical items may hold important clues as to the cause and manner of death. Finally, precision establishes the credibility of the forensic worker. If the information gained during recovery is used to make a case against a suspected perpetrator of a crime, all persons involved (i.e., police, prosecutors, judges, and jurors) must be convinced that the evidence was gathered accurately and completely and that no pertinent evidence was either fabricated or overlooked. Finally, when drawing a map, it is best to use inches and feet, because this is the scale most known and used by police and courtroom personnel.

The first step in the mapping process is to set up a **datum point** close to the remains. This should be placed on permanent structures or objects that are not likely to be obliterated with the passage of time. In uninhabited areas, a large tree or rock can be used, while the corner of a building will suffice in populated areas. After this point has been fixed, its position on a larger map should be indicated. In towns, a city map is ideal (if it is detailed enough); outside of metropolitan areas, a **USGS quadrangle** (a map developed by the U.S. Geological Survey office that depicts geographic features in a 1-square-mile area) is preferred. When using a quadrangle, the datum point can be located by triangulation with a compass to other visible permanent structures or by using the Global Positioning System (GPS).

After the datum point is established, the area immediately surrounding the body must be marked using a **grid square** to provide a framework for mapping relevant findings. This usually entails setting up a 10- to 15-foot square, constructed of four wooden posts (one in each corner) connected with string (see Figure 4.7b). If possible, it is best to orient the sides along north–south and east–west axes for ease of understanding by law enforcement and other persons. Once established, the grid is depicted on a map, and the compass direction and distance to the datum point of its nearest corner should be noted. After this, a tape measure is used to locate bones and other items in relation to the grid square. For associated material located more than 100 feet away, pacing off distances may be sufficiently accurate. During this process, judgment must be used as to the relevance of findings; if the search covered a large area (e.g., several acres), earlier encountered material may not be important. However, as with previous steps in the forensic process, if in doubt, consider any find significant and mark its placement on the map. Also, all remains and other items should be photographed in place before collection. Finally, a hand-drawn map of the grid square must be made, indicating the location of remains and associated materials in relation to the datum point and the grid itself (see Figure 4.8).

GRAVE EXCAVATION

Retrieving all relevant information from interments requires different techniques from those described previously. After all surface findings over the grave are located, mapped, and collected (see the next section), the grave must be systematically excavated using the methods of archeology. This process cannot start until the previously mentioned datum point and grid square are established. An additional task involves attaching a line level to the grid strings so that both vertical and horizontal locations of items within the grave can be determined. Once these are established, the excavation proper can commence. This involves removal of dirt within, or immediately around, the burial pit. This process requires a number of instruments (see Table 4.1) that must be on hand before work commences.

Excavation proceeds slowly as dirt is skimmed carefully from the surface. If a large area is being excavated and the exact location of the grave(s) is not known, a backhoe may be used until the general outline of the burial pit(s) becomes visible. However,

FIGURE 4.8   Hand-drawn map of simulated forensic site in Figure 4.7. Scale: 1 square = 2 inches.

TABLE 4.1   List of Tools for Body Recovery[1]

Shovel	Square and pointed trowels
Pruning shears and saws	Screens (1/4 and 1/8 inch)
Wooden and metal stakes	Paint brushes
Toothbrushes	Dental picks
Flags on wooden posts	Wooden digging instruments
Buckets for moving dirt	Evidence bags and wrapping
Notebook and pencils	Graph paper
Protractor	String or twine
Cameras	Metal detector
Tape measure	Compass
Line level	Transit and stadia rod
Insect collection jars	Entomologist's net

[1]Compiled from Morse et al. (1983) and Table 14.1 of Burns (1999).

in most cases, dirt is skimmed with a shovel (see Figure 4.9) until human remains are encountered (most frequently the pelvis or foot). Removal of dirt proceeds in 1- to 2-inch layers at a time, with a metal detector scan made at each 2- to 4-inch level. As items are encountered, they should be fully uncovered but left in place (see Figure 4.10) for mapping, recording, and photographing.

Generally, only two people can work comfortably on a single grave. Also, when the excavation is down more than 8 inches, workers usually can no longer comfortably dig from the surface. At this point, one wall of the grave is sacrificed and a platform is excavated down alongside the burial pit to the level of the burial.

Once part of the body has been located, its orientation usually is easily determined. The task at this point is the same as when items are encountered; that is, remains are uncovered, but not removed, until they are fully exposed, mapped, and photographed. This process is best performed by two excavators, who start at either end of the body and work toward each other. For this part, small trowels or digging sticks are used to remove overlying dirt (see Figure 4.11a), with the additional use of brushes (see Figure 4.11b), except when clothing or other fibers are present.

As the soil is moved out of the grave(s), it should be placed in buckets and taken to a location where it can be sifted through a ¼-inch or finer screen (see Figure 4.12a) to recover small objects (Figure 4.12b). Although this seems tedious, the importance of this step cannot be overemphasized. Valuable information, as is well illustrated in Box 4.2, can be gained by taking the time to sift grave fill dirt. In addition to dry sifting, dirt can be washed through the screen to help to reveal fragments of evidence.

FIGURE 4.9 Skimming off dirt over a suspected grave with a shovel at a simulated forensic site. (Photo by Julie R. Angel)

FIGURE 4.10 Exposure of excavated items for mapping and final removal at a simulated forensic site. (Photo by Julie R. Angel)

FIGURE 4.11   Using **(a)** a small wooden digging instrument or **(b)** a brush to remove overlying soil at a simulated forensic site. (Photos by Julie R. Angel)

FIGURE 4.12   **(a)** Screening of fill dirt for **(b)** recovery of small item, in this case, a human phalanx from a simulated forensic site. (Photos by Julie R. Angel)

BOX 4.2
The Importance of Screening

William Maples and Michael Browning (1994) describe the murder–suicide case of Glyde Earl Meek and Page Jennings, which illustrates the importance of complete collection of remains at a scene, including the use of a screen. Two burned, commingled, and heavily fragmented skeletons were delivered to the C. A. Pound Human Identification Laboratory at the University of Florida for identification. Although an associated suicide note named the victims, authorities required proof of identity before closing the case. After hours of painstaking gluing, enough of the skeletons were reconstructed to determine that their ages, sexes, and statures matched the demographics of the

named victims. Although the identification of Page Jennings was fraught with difficulties, it was the skeleton of Glyde Meeks that proved the most difficult to identify. After a year and a half, a first rib was reconstructed enough to manifest a distinctive shape at the anterior end that matched an antemortem radiograph of his chest. Similarly, antemortem dental x-rays of Glyde Meeks matched those of teeth found at the scene. However, a gold filling was missing that Meeks's dental records noted should be found. Even after all this work, the missing gold filling prevented acceptance of the identification of Meeks by authorities. Since gold melts at temperatures in excess of those generated by the cabin fire in which the remains were found, Maples felt that the filling should have been found when the fill dirt of the cabin was originally screened through ⅛-inch mesh. Because it was not recovered, the dirt was painstakingly rescreened with ¹⁄₁₆-inch mesh. This process revealed the amalgam, which was not deformed by the fire and matched perfectly the antemortem x-ray of this appliance. With this evidence in hand, the identification was considered positive and the case subsequently closed.

COLLECTING REMAINS

After the remains have been located, marked, and mapped, they must be collected and packed for transport to the laboratory for further analysis. During this phase, all workers should be supplied with latex gloves to avoid the biohazards common to human remains (see Chapter 6). Also at this stage, three additions to the written record (beyond the drawn maps) must be started. First, an inventory of retrieved material should be made so that each item that is recovered enters the official record. Second, a log of persons who handled the evidence (crime scene investigator, medical examiner, forensic anthropologist) must be attached to this inventory to document all persons who had contact with the material after it was removed from the scene.

These two records are used to maintain the **chain of evidence** (also called the **chain of custody**), one of the most important parts of this process. For material recovered from a scene to be admissible as evidence in a court of law, it must be demonstrated that it was neither contaminated by matter not found at the scene nor lost after being removed from the recovery scene. The inventory and log are the accepted manner of ensuring that this did not happen. The last record that should be kept at this point should describe the recovery process and give the names of all participants and any other information deemed important.

FIGURE 4.13 Grocery bag of human remains at a simulated forensic site labeled, sealed, and ready for transport to a laboratory. (Photo by Julie R. Angel)

When recovery commences, each item should be placed in a suitable container (e.g., plastic bag, cardboard box), which is sealed and labeled with the date, case number, and name of the investigating officer. Thus, if a body bag is used, a seal should be placed on its zipper to ensure that its contents have not been augmented with contaminates or that body parts have not been lost. If the remains are disarticulated, they can be placed in separate bags with their tops folded over and stapled to prevent tampering (see Figure 4.13). When this is done in the field, these seals and/or stapled ends must be unbroken when received by a laboratory to ensure that contamination has not occurred and that the chain of evidence has not been compromised.

The containers used in the collection process depend on the availability of materials and the state of the remains. For bodies that are still articulated by soft tissue, a body bag is ideal for collection and transportation. For disarticulated remains, the natural body sections can be placed in simple paper grocery sacks with newspaper packing. Thus, right and left upper limbs should be placed in separate bags and labeled as such; lower limbs should be treated similarly. Vertebrae should be numbered with soft lead pencil (see Figure 4.14) for ease of rearticulation and then placed in a bag labeled as to type (i.e., cervical,

FIGURE 4.14 Marking vertebrae with a pencil for ease of reassembling the vertebral column. (Photo by Julie R. Angel)

thoracic, or lumbar). For bones that have been exposed to catastrophic trauma (e.g., large-caliber bullets, vehicular accidents), every attempt must be made to recover all pieces. Also, jaws should be examined for empty tooth sockets that indicate postmortem loss of teeth (incisors are particularly prone to this). Finally, it is important that fragile bones not be broken during recovery. Since the bones of the face are particularly susceptible to breakage, the cranium should be handled by the braincase without inserting fingers into the eye or nose orbits.

In addition to osteological material, special care should be taken to minimize loss of other information. This includes bullets inside of skulls, which usually are held in place by dirt. Similarly, items that fall off during collection should be recovered.

If multiple bodies have been discovered, skeletons found in (or nearly in) natural articulation should be kept separate from those of other individuals to ensure proper identification. Each body should be assigned a unique number (usually the case number with an alphabetic or numeric suffix), and they should be kept in separate body bags or containers. These containers should be marked as to contents and assigned a number. Good technique dictates that this separation be maintained throughout the collection and analysis process.

For interred remains, other physical findings should be collected in addition to the biological remains and items encountered during excavation. Soil from around the head should be searched for hair that can be used in laboratory analysis. Similarly, the area under the body should be examined for evidence (e.g., identifiable footprints can be seen if covered by clothing), as well as other items. Similarly, soil samples should be taken from various levels during excavation for chemical analysis. Finally, it is recommended that the first 4 inches of dirt below the body be removed for laboratory examination.

Although all human body parts must be collected, some surface finds may or may not be recovered depending on their significance. When the search encompasses a large area, many items may be encountered that may not be associated with the case at hand. During this collection stage, the significance of nonhuman findings must be judged. Generally, items found close to the remains should be considered significant and therefore collected. However, the farther that items are located from the body or its parts, the more likely it is that they are not associated with the case at hand. The only guiding principle at this juncture is the previously stated axiom: When in doubt, treat the item as though it were significant. This will reduce the likelihood that important evidence is not accidentally left at the scene.

MASS DISASTERS

The death of a large number of people, as in a commercial aircraft accident, often involves catastrophic injuries to the victims. Although these disasters fall under the purview of coroners and medical examiners, forensic anthropologists often are consulted because of their unique ability to deal with identifying disarticulated, burned, and otherwise heavily damaged bodies. When approaching such a situation, usually the previously described methods must be adjusted and supplemented for the unique circumstances of the disaster. These modifications are best articulated in a disaster preparedness plan that addresses the mapping, recovering, and identifying of human remains and their associated belongings. Randall (1991), working at the scene of the crash of Flight 232 in Sioux City, Iowa, described the major components of mass disasters, and his work forms the basis for this section.

Although all coroners' offices should have a formal disaster plan, many are unprepared to handle a situation involving multiple deaths. However, this lack of a plan should not preclude the development of one at the time of the disaster. Although it may seem callous to spend time designing the recovery and identification process after a disaster has occurred, generally it is believed that taking this time will be rewarded by a smoother operation. The following elements should be considered as minimal in dealing with a mass disaster.

Personnel

Forensic anthropologists are only one of a group of specialists who deal with matters of human death, and nowhere is this more apparent than in a mass disaster. These specialists are organized into teams that usually are assembled by the governmental agency charged with the legal responsibility of determining cause and manner of death (e.g., coroner's office or office of medical investigator). Teams are needed in these situations because of the variety of special techniques used in the identification process. Thus, medical examiners and coroners must be present to perform the legal act of documenting the deaths of victims. Similarly, pathologists should perform autopsies on remains so that not only is information on cause of death gathered, but supporting data (e.g., intoxicating chemicals in the remains of flight crews) also are obtained. In addition, forensic odontologists should be present to perform the dental exams usually necessary in these circumstances, as well as x-ray technicians who are skilled in taking dental and other radiographs. Similarly, because extensive records of victims often can be obtained, persons with expertise in taking and identifying fingerprints should be assembled. Finally, a large number of helpers are needed to move bodies through the system, get supplies, trace records, and otherwise help in the recovery and identification process.

Locating, Mapping, Collecting

Because of the special nature of mass disasters, the procedures described for locating, mapping, and collecting human remains may need to be modified. First, since the location of the scene is known, the first phase of the search can be disregarded. Although the second phase must be performed, the remains must be collected immediately (instead of locating, marking, and leaving them in place for mapping) before decomposition obscures marks that may be useful to identification (e.g., tattoos, moles, or birthmarks). Thus, a number must be assigned to each body part and associated personal effects and placed at the point of recovery for later mapping. Also, the standard grid system may be too cumbersome for large disaster areas. In these cases, measuring the distance along a central axis and the distance at right angles to that axis might be more appropriate (see Figure 4.15).

Temporary Morgue

Unlike most forensic anthropology cases in which decomposition is advanced and cleaning is necessary to start the identification process, mass disasters usually involve fresh bodies that need to be submitted to the normal process of the medical investigator.

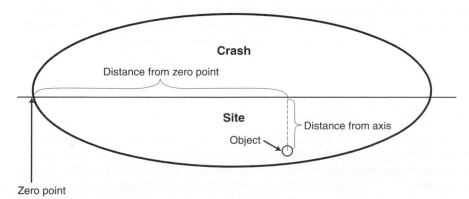

FIGURE 4.15 Elliptical search area used in the mapping of human remains and other findings from the crash of United Flight 232 in 1989 at Sioux City, Iowa. Remains were mapped by determining their distance from the central axis and by measuring the distance of that point from the zero point. (After Figure 1 of Randall [1991])

Because the location of the disaster can be some distance from a formal laboratory, the coroner or medical investigator's office must secure a building that can serve as a temporary morgue. After such a structure is located, the equipment needed to perform the necessary steps leading to identifications must be installed. These involve autopsy equipment, including stainless steel tables, receptacles for biological remains, Stryker saws, scalpels, and other hand tools used by pathologists. Also, x-ray equipment capable of doing both dental and body radiographs must be made available. Similarly, the equipment necessary to obtain and compare fingerprints should be installed. Finally, refrigeration equipment should be obtained to slow the process of putrefaction that is inevitable when the number of bodies is too great to handle in a short time. (This can be in the form of refrigeration trucks or railway cars if railroad tracks are in the immediate vicinity.)

Victim Information

Since family members of the deceased probably will be waiting for the return of the remains of their loved ones, forensic anthropologists should participate in the development of a questionnaire for relatives designed to aid in the identification process. This set of questions should include, at a minimum, name, ancestry, sex, age, and stature, as well as identifying marks, both on bone or soft tissue. Tattoos, scars, or birthmarks are very useful in the identification process, as are previously broken bones (which often display calluses; see Chapter 11), skeletal anomalies (see Chapter 15), dental appliances (e.g., false teeth, bridges), and even clothing worn on the day of the event (see Baraybar, 2008, for a discussion). Finally, the names and addresses of the victims' dentists and doctors should be obtained so that dental and medical records, which often contain information on identifying characteristics useful in positive identification (e.g., amalgam configurations, surgical scars), can be obtained (see Chapters 17 and 18 for more details). This survey should be administered by persons who are sensitive to the feelings of family members so that these other victims of the disaster do not have to endure any further pain.

DMORT

One last item to consider in mass disasters is contacting the Disaster Mortuary Operational Response Team (DMORT). This is a national organization, under the auspices of the U.S. Department of Homeland Security, designed to handle these types of tragedies. When requested by local agencies, this group can assist in all of the areas discussed above. Thus, they can provide an organizational plan, equipment (e.g., mobile morgues), and personnel to handle the tasks that are part of this type of operation (e.g., site search and recovery, forensic examination, remains identification). In addition, they can provide medical and psychological support during mass disasters (appreciated by the families) and help with record keeping, including the organization of antemortem and postmortem data. More information on this team is available on their website: www.dmort.org.

GENOCIDE INVESTIGATIONS

As mentioned in Chapter 1, forensic anthropologists have become more and more involved in genocide investigations in various parts of the world. Article 2 of the UN Convention on the Prevention and Punishment of the Crime of Genocide (1948) defines genocide as a crime ". . . committed with intent to destroy, in whole or in part, a national, ethnical, racial or religious group." At their most basic level, investigations of these types of crimes differ from other forensic cases, in that the prosecution is trying to prove that the accused not only caused the death of their victims, but also had the intent of destroying an entire group of people. Given this, the identification of the deceased as members of a particular group that were executed (i.e., did not die of natural causes or in combat) becomes central to any of these types of investigations. When the group is not necessarily identifiable by biological traits such as those described Chapter 7 for ancestral groups, forensic anthropologists must be open to new methods for determining group association. Additionally, experience has shown that methods not often used in most forensic anthropological cases become of great importance in these types of inquiries. In the following section, the work of Melanie Klinkner (2008) will be used to describe the role of forensic anthropologists in genocide investigations, with work from others where noted.

A genocide investigation generally is carried out by those prosecuting the case, and has three components: pre-forensic investigation, forensic investigation, and expert witness testimony. The pre-forensic investigation involves the identification of sites of mass murder, particularly graves. Although this would appear to be easy, the fact that this type of crime is carried out in remote areas, out of sight of the news media, makes the location of these crime scenes difficult. Eye witness accounts and aerial photography can be invaluable during this phase of activity. Once located, the site is assessed by forensic experts who help determine the best methods for excavating and exhuming the bodies.

The forensic investigation involves assembling the investigators, forensic experts, and support personnel needed to carry out the processing of the site. Four persons, supported by their respective staffs, are particularly important: investigator, chief archaeologist, chief anthropologist, and chief pathologist. The investigator is the prosecution's on-site person who ensures that the site is processed in such as way as to provide the evidence needed to convict persons accused of genocide. The chief archaeologist and anthropologist are those persons in charge of the excavation and skeletal analysis, respectively. The chief pathologist must establish the cause of death and the identity of the victims; they also are often trained to identify evidence of starvation and torture as well as perimortem trauma (in this respect, some of their responsibilities are shared with the chief anthropologist). After these persons develop a plan for excavation and exhumation, the work is performed in the orderly and systematic manner required by law. At this stage, there are two major differences between these types of investigations and mass disasters described above. First, there is a time constraint; that is, genocide investigators must do their work within a short time period because they are guided by the axiom of jurisprudence that "justice delayed is justice denied." The second is the level of briefing given the forensic experts by the investigator. Since the prosecution has access to eye witness accounts and other information prior to the excavation of mass graves, they are in a quandary as to how much information they should provide to the archaeologists, anthropologists, and pathologists. They must provide enough information for these professionals to do their work, but not so much as to bias them in their interpretation of the data. The manner in which this issue is handled is judged on a case-by-case basis.

The forensic anthropologist's role during these investigations is similar to all other forensic cases. However, several aspects become particularly important during this phase of the genocide investigation: count of minimum number of individuals (MNI), clothing as an indicator of group membership, eyewitness accounts of events, and use of population-specific methods for determining biological profile. MNI is the usual count obtained when conditions prevent the positive identification of all persons recovered from a mass grave and/or where individual bodies cannot be identified as with commingled body parts (see Chapter 6). The easiest method for determining this value is by counting the number of unique body segments found in the grave and using that segment which occurs most often. Clothing can take on extreme importance as it can be an indicator of group membership (see Baraybar, 2008; Komar and Lathrop, 2008), particularly when the group being exterminated cannot be identified by biological characteristics. Eyewitness accounts of events leading to the murder of a group of people are useful to prosecutors, particularly when corroborated by the forensic evidence. Thus, the collection of data for the purpose of supporting these accounts takes on particular importance. Finally, the use of population-specific standards are particularly important as experience has shown that defense counsel will cast doubt on expert witness testimony if the methods used are not applicable to the population being studied (Ubelaker 2008).

Conditions of Field Work

Another difference between genocide investigations and other forensic inquiries involves the organization of work in the field. Often there are no facilities or resources available at the site that allow for a temporary morgue, a place to interview family members, or a laboratory for collecting evidence and analyzing biological remains. Usually, work is done in temporary shelters such as tents, which has raised concerns among forensic workers about the quality of analyses. Also, safety is an issue in that those who perpetrated the crime may be able to threaten or even kill those doing this work. Thus, lead prosecutors may request, and receive, security from various law enforcement agencies and military groups while the investigation proceeds.

Excavating Mass Graves

The methods of excavating also should be modified for mass graves of victims of human rights abuses. Hugh Tuller and Marija Durić (2006) showed that the best way of excavating these types of interments is to use the so-called stratigraphic method. In this technique, remains are uncovered in reverse order of deposition, with no attempt to expose and photograph all individuals in situ at the same time. They show that less information is lost if the bodies are removed as they are uncovered and that a better understanding of the grave formation process is attained if each body is mapped and its strata (layer) within the grave is noted.

Summary

1. The recovery of human remains involves four steps: location, mapping, excavation (if needed), and retrieval.
2. Unless led to the scene by an informant, the methods of archeological site survey (i.e., organized walking ground search) should be employed to locate the remains.
3. Workers involved in the ground search must be well versed in the signs associated with human remains.
4. After the remains have been located, both biological and associated finds must be marked in place using flags on (preferably wooden) posts.
5. Using a permanent structure such as a building corner or large tree, a datum point must be established for mapping. This point should be located on large-scale map such as those for a city or, if in a nonmetropolitan area, a USGS quadrangle.
6. A grid square, from 10 to 15 feet on the side, should be established around the area where the major parts of the remains are located. The distance and compass direction of the datum point to the nearest corner of the grid should be determined.
7. The marked remains must be mapped in relation to the grid square and datum point.
8. The remains, both biological and nonbiological material, must be placed in a suitable container for transport to a facility where further analysis can be performed.

9. The chain of evidence must be maintained throughout the recovery process (as well as during analysis and thereafter). This involves avoiding contamination or loss of evidence through the use of sealed and marked containers to transport physical remains, and by maintaining an inventory and log of persons who were in possession of the materials.

10. Mass disasters require modification and supplementation of the methods normally used by forensic anthropologists. This includes assembling a number of other specialists, setting up a temporary morgue, and obtaining completed questionnaires from family members.

11. As with mass disasters, genocide investigations require modification and supplementation of the methods normally used by forensic anthropologists. This includes, among other things, the speedy recovery of relevant evidence and the use of population-specific standards for the biological profile.

Exercises

1. In late 1999, the Federal Bureau of Investigation (FBI) investigated a ranch in northern Mexico where it was believed that over 100 bodies of drug-related deaths were buried. Describe how you would alter or follow the methods described in this chapter to locate and excavate the human remains believed to be present.

2. A decomposed body is found on the surface in a wooded area. Within a 10-foot radius are found shotgun shell casings, the femur from a deer, items of clothing, and a beer bottle. Within 100 feet of the remains, the rest of the deer skeleton is found along with a battered cowboy hat. Of these items, which would you consider are associated with the human remains and should be mapped and collected? State your reasoning.

3. A body is believed to be lying in a very large field of mature corn (i.e., plants over 6 feet tall). Considering this, how would you go about searching for the remains? Include in your explanation the number of people that you would want, as well as their spacing and any other detail that you feel is pertinent.

4. During the excavation of a forensic burial, you find several prehistoric potsherds. Explain why you would, or would not, consider these of forensic importance and thus map and collect them.

5. A disarticulated body is found in rocky terrain characterized by crevices and other hard to reach places. How far would you extend your search for missing body parts such as hands and feet? State your reasoning.

6. A decomposed body is found at the base of a 50-foot cliff in a position, indicating the person may have fallen from the top of the cliff. You extend your search in all directions from that locus and locate most, but not all, body segments. Would you go to the top of the cliff to search for any human remains? If so, why, and if not, why not?

7. During screening, three phalanges of a human hand are found. How would you number these so that they are properly separated while being transported to the laboratory?

8. A body is found in a lightly wooded area close to a large evergreen tree (i.e., a ponderosa pine). Explain why this would be an acceptable datum point for this forensic case.

9. Suppose that three human torsos are found at a forensic site. How would you mark (i.e., with case number and the like) associated body segments found scattered within a 100-yard radius of these finds?

10. When excavating a fairly fresh body, you find several corroded and new shotgun shells, a rusty tin can, and a dirty soft drink bottle. Which of these findings are more likely to be forensically important and which are more likely to have been in the area prior to the interment? State your reasoning.

11. If an aircraft crashed in a swampy area, how would the methods for dealing with mass disasters be modified? Describe the changes within each section under the heading Mass Disasters in this chapter. How would these methods be modified for mass disasters in large bodies of water (e.g., ocean, lake)?

Estimating Postmortem Interval

With the discovery of human remains, one of the most important issues to be considered is **postmortem interval** (**PMI**). This is the amount of time that has elapsed since the death of the decedent. As described in Chapter 1, this is one of the statistics used to examine missing persons' files in search of a likely match. Therefore, its accurate determination may make the difference between an identification and a body that remains unclaimed.

In the first hours after death, medical investigators use a variety of methods to estimate PMI. These include livor mortis (settling of blood in the body), algor mortis (cooling of body temperature after death), rigor mortis (muscle stiffness), and changes in vitreous humor (changes in the fluids of the eye). However, after only 24 hours these methods become less accurate so that, by the time soft tissue has begun to decompose, they are unusable. It is at this point that the techniques used by forensic anthropologists and other specialists are employed to estimate this statistic.

After death, a number of organisms and other agents begin to break down the body, causing a general loss of skin, muscle, internal organs, and other body components. The organisms include large animals that will remove and consume much of the soft tissue. In addition, bacteria will break down internal organs, causing putrefaction. Similarly, plants will grow on, under, and between body segments, while physical factors (e.g., weather) will break up, bury, transport, and otherwise damage the remains. Studies of the rate at which these agents work have led forensic specialists in several disciplines to determine timetables for various postmortem occurrences.

One such specialty is **forensic taphonomy.** While taphonomy is the branch of science that deals with changes to biological organisms between the time of death and the time of discovery, forensic taphonomists study the stages through which the human body passes from being "fresh" to being completely skeletonized. In addition, they study the schedule by which animals eat, disarticulate, and otherwise modify biological remains. Thus, PMI is estimated by knowing the amount of time needed for bodies to reach stages of deterioration, given a particular climate and the amount of accessibility to small and large animals.

In addition to taphonomy, other fields have contributed significantly to estimating PMI. The broad area of entomology (the study of insects) includes **forensic entomology**, which is the study of insect life cycle and succession on cadavers for the purpose of determining PMI. Similarly, forensic scientists within botany (**forensic botany**) use plant growth as a method of estimating this interval. Also, various other specialists study the amount of deterioration of clothing, paper money, and other such items to yield estimates of PMI. Finally, a variety of other more complex techniques (e.g., chemical analysis of soils near bodies, amount of degeneration of DNA) can be employed when the proper equipment and personnel are available.

BOX 5.1
Using Multiple Methods for Estimating Postmortem Interval

William Bass (1987) describes a case in which a number of different methods were used to estimate PMI. In the spring of 1985, he investigated a defleshed skull in Tennessee of what turned out to be a 12-year-old girl. A nest of wasps was found inside the brain case, which helped to determine PMI. Since these insects build only in dry places, Bass reasoned that the skull was dry by the previous summer, because drying during the cool winter months would have been limited. Also his previous experience led him to believe that it would take at least another year for a skull to become dry. Thus, based on this, he determined that the child had been dead at least 2 years, or since 1983. Further searching revealed other skeletal elements of this child. A lumbar vertebra was discovered that had a tree growing through its neural arch. When cut, this tree revealed two rings, again indicating death at or before 1983. Coupled with the demographic (i.e., race, sex, age, and stature) information, police located a missing persons' file where an identification could be made.

This chapter will present four topics concerning the determination of PMI. First, the process of decomposition will be described, with an emphasis on the agents that cause the human body to break down and the factors that affect the rate with which these agents work. The second section presents the schedules by which decompositional changes occur in different geographical areas of North America and under different conditions of body deposition (e.g., surface, burial, submersion). The third section deals with timetables for determining PMI from animal scavenging, including soft tissue consumption, scattering of skeletal elements, and gnawing of bones. The last section discusses methods used by specialists in other fields; these are included here because forensic anthropologists may need to collect and preserve elements used by these specialists. This last section also illustrates the multidisciplinary nature of the forensic process. Although each technique described here can provide estimates of PMI, the use of a number of methods often results in a more accurate estimate of this statistic (see Box 5.1 for an example).

OVERVIEW OF DECOMPOSITION

When human and nonhuman animals die, a number of organisms and other natural forces begin to break down or destroy organic tissues, resulting in partial or complete loss of all components of the once living body. William Maples (Maples and Browning, 1994) describes the first two processes involved in this breakdown as autolysis and putrefaction. **Autolysis** is the term used to describe the degeneration of body tissues by the digestive fluids normally residing in the intestinal tract. Because their action is no longer controlled by the living organism, these juices digest the body just as though it was food, causing a general destruction of internal organs.

The other process, that of **putrefaction**, occurs when the microorganisms normally residing within body tissues begin to proliferate and breakdown biological components. Because, like digestive fluids, they are no longer held in check by the body's natural functions, these bacteria (particularly of the intestinal tract) begin to reproduce unhindered, eating away at muscles, internal organs, and other such tissues. (A side effect of their action is the release of gases, especially ammonia, nitrogen, carbon dioxide, and methane, which bloats the body cavity.)

While this is occurring, insects (particularly flies) will begin feeding on remains. Neal Haskell and associates (1997) summarized the activity of these animals in a review article. These authors note that within minutes of death insects (particularly flies attracted by the released gases) begin to feed on the tissues around the eyes, ears, nose, mouth, vagina, penis, and anus. As they continue to feed, these creatures deposit eggs in and around the remains, which starts a cycle of arthropod activity from the egg-laying adults through their carrion-eating offspring to a new generation of egg-laying adults. During this cycle, other arthropods are attracted to the body, where they feed not only on the human tissues, but also on the eggs and larva of other insects.

Along with microscopic organisms and arthropods, many larger animals are attracted to the decomposing remains. William Haglund has studied the effects of scavenging by these creatures, which he describes in two articles (Haglund, 1997a, b). He notes that carnivores, especially dogs and coyotes, will consume the soft tissues of the body cavity, arms, legs, and necks whenever possible. In addition, these animals will disarticulate the skeleton, pulling off arms and legs, and even break osteological remains by trampling. Finally, these meat-eating creatures (sometimes in conjunction with rodents) will gnaw bones, resulting in the loss of skeletal elements.

Although animals are responsible for the majority of tissue breakdown, plants also assist in this process by growing in, around, and through remains deposited both on the surface and in shallow graves. Roots can separate skeletal elements, causing disarticulation. Skeletal structures such as the skull can be compromised by the growth of plants through the various orifices in the structure. Even different types of molds, which grow on the skin and other tissues, slowly break down cellular matter. The activity of botanical life often is enhanced by autolysis. Since this process dissolves biotic material, the released substances can act as a fertilizer, causing faster and more aggressive growth.

One final set of forces that affects decomposition is described by Douglas Ubelaker (1997). This author notes that nonbiological agents such as soil acids, climatic forces, and other physical factors participate in the destruction of organic remains. The soil acids contained in groundwater can speed up the deterioration of both soft and hard tissues. Conversely, this same groundwater can leach through the body, causing mineralization of hard tissues, especially bone. Similarly, fire can consume body tissues, thereby speeding the decomposition process. After soft tissue has been removed, sunlight and wind can break down bone by causing weathering (i.e., cracking, flaking) or loss of cortical surfaces through peeling and sandblasting. In addition, natural interment by accumulation of sediments over the remains or burial by other forces (e.g., rock falls) can cause cracking and breaking of hard tissues. Finally, water can affect decomposition by buffeting remains against hard surfaces (e.g., river bottoms, lake shores) during transport and by causing body fats to hydrate, forming a substance called **adiopocere** (see O'Brien and Kuehner, 2007, for a detailed discussion).

Robert Mann and colleagues (1990) discuss the factors that affect the speed with which biological agents perform their actions. These authors note that the most important factors are temperature, humidity, and accessibility. Of these, temperature is the factor that is most likely to affect plant and animal activity. Remains that lie in a warm area show greater insect activity and therefore faster decomposition than those that lie in a cool area. Thus, deterioration of soft tissue is faster in geographical areas closer to the equator when compared with areas closer to the poles. Similarly, warm climates foster greater plant activity, which will be evident in and around the remains. Also, smaller temperature differences can alter rates of decomposition; studies have shown that carrion placed in the sun decompose at a faster rate than carcasses in the shade (e.g., Shean et al., 1993). Even temperature fluctuations cause tissue breakdown even in the absence of insects; studies have shown that cycles of freezing and thawing have speeded the process of decomposition by disrupting connective tissues (Ubelaker, 1997).

Humidity is the second most important factor that affects the rate at which bodies deteriorate (Mann et al., 1990). Generally, decomposition is faster in humid climates than drier areas. High humidity slows the drying of the soft tissue, which allows for ease of consumption by insects and other organisms. Conversely, arid climates cause more rapid dehydration of the skin and internal organs; this induces natural **mummification**, which acts as a barrier to these creatures.

Accessibility of the remains to scavenging is the last factor noted as affecting the activity of biological organisms (Mann et al., 1990). Since animals of all sizes (e.g., flies, beetles, rats, coyotes, bears) are the main agents of decomposition, any circumstances that make it easier for these creatures to access remains will speed this process. The two factors that increase accessibility are trauma and placement. Trauma, resulting in breaks in the skin, allows insects and other animals access to the easily consumed internal tissues of the body (Haskell et al., 1997). Thus, open wounds are often the site of greater insect activity and animal scavenging than the uninjured areas.

The factor of placement of the remains refers to the location of the body after death. Generally, bodies left outside will decompose faster than those left in an enclosed structure because of their greater availability to animals. Similarly, bodies left on the surface will decompose faster than those that are buried or immersed in water, again because of greater availability. For interred remains, burial depth also affects the speed of decay; remains close to the surface are more accessible and therefore deteriorate faster than those buried well below ground level (Rodriguez and Bass, 1985).

Mann and colleagues (1990) note that several factors appear to affect decomposition to a lesser degree than expected. Strangely, rainfall on an exposed body has little effect on decomposition despite the acceleration of decay in higher humidity. Although larva activity continues unabated, fly activity ceases during heavy rainfall, and pelting rain does not appear to accelerate the sloughing of decomposed skin. A second factor that does not affect decay is size and weight. Body fats have been observed to liquefy fairly quickly after death, thereby negating any slowing of decomposition caused by a large amount of body mass. Similarly, the bodies of infants and children do not decompose significantly faster than adults.

DECOMPOSITION AND SKELETONIZATION

The decomposition process starts with a fresh human body and proceeds until (given enough time) full skeletonization is achieved. A common device used to simplify this complex process is to divide it into identifiable stages. PMI then can be estimated by knowing the time needed by the body to reach these stages of deterioration. Unfortunately, despite its importance in the identification of decedents, little has been published quantifying this process. Although much has been written on the factors that affect decomposition, studies using large samples that calibrate PMIs with decompositional stages are rare. This section will report what has been published to date, with the hope that in the future more research on this topic will become available.

Studies of physical decomposition concentrate on describing postmortem changes in the human body (e.g., bloating of the body cavity) and the time needed for these changes to appear (e.g., 1 day to 1 week). As mentioned above, although a continuous process, research on degenerational changes usually is divided into stages characterized by visually identifiable alterations. These stages then are calibrated by observing the amount of time needed for them to appear either in samples of forensic cases (for which both the date that the victims were last seen alive and the date of discovery of their remains are known) or in experiments involving cadavers. Using this method, rough schedules of decomposition are created, which can then be used to determine PMI.

Unfortunately, a number of factors complicate the apparent simplicity of this method. First, as described previously, climatic factors affect the rate of soft tissue loss. Thus, a single schedule of decomposition for all geographic areas is difficult to attain

> ## BOX 5.2
> ### The Burial of Lt. Col. W. M. Shy, Revisited
>
> William Bass (1984) has described a Civil War burial that he initially mistook for a body that had been dead only 6 to 12 months (see Box 3.2). Given the information on determining PMI presented in this chapter, it is instructive to revisit this case to better understand how he was led to make such an incorrect assessment. The remains were found laying atop a cast-iron coffin in a private cemetery in Tennessee. The body was partially disarticulated, with the legs and arms separated from the torso. However, sections of the vertebral column were still held together, as were the segments of the arms and legs. In addition to disarticulation, a fair amount of soft tissue was present; he observed both pink flesh on the femur and the presence of the large and small intestines. Finally, he noted a strong smell of decay emanating from the remains.
>
>   A glance at his description of decomposition in Tennessee surface finds shows that the body exhibited traits expected of persons dead less than 1 year. Specifically, the odor of decay is noted as strong in the first week after death. Similarly, at least the first month after death is indicated by the body being in the decay phase and having limbs separated from the torso. Finally, because no mention is made of the characteristics in the first year (dry), an age of at least 1 month, but less than 1 year, is indicated. Continuing, using Haglund's (1997a) categories of scavenging and associated timetable, the body fits fairly well into stage 3, in which all skeletal elements are disarticulated except portions of the vertebral column. This indicates a PMI of 2 to 11 months. As can be seen, information from the state of the body indicated a fairly recent PMI. It was only when embalming fluid was smelled during preparation and the lack of synthetic fibers in the associated clothing was noted that the correct age of over 100 years was assigned.

(although see Megyesi et al., 2005, for a promising method for all climates). Second, all studies find a large range of variation in the time needed to reach the various stages of decomposition. This variation causes overlaps of time ranges between categories of deterioration, with concomitant uncertainty in PMI estimates. Third, because the process is continuous, individual bodies sometimes fit the characteristics of two (and even three) of these stages, causing some confusion as to the best estimate of PMI (see Box 5.2 for an example). Fourth, most schedules of decomposition are derived from exposed (e.g., surface) finds; this makes estimating PMI for burials and remains found in water difficult. Finally, descriptions of changes are drawn from all times of the year, thereby muddling the effects of temperature fluctuations. Considering these factors, the task of estimating PMI engenders much variation, thereby requiring the use of considerable judgment from forensic anthropologists.

The general method of determining PMI from a forensic case is to categorize the amount of decomposition seen into one of the decompositional stages. Then PMI is estimated as the observed range for that stage. However, if additional factors are known, this estimate can be refined. Although no standards exist, the best approach is to draw from either end of the time range, depending on the nature of these factors. For example, if a body discovered during the summer fits the criteria for a stage with a range of 1 to 6 months, the PMI estimate might be drawn from the lower end of the range, because decomposition is accelerated during this time of year. Conversely, if the same remains were found in winter, an estimate of PMI might be drawn from the high end of the range.

Surface Finds

Most of the studies calibrating decompositional stages and PMI have involved surface finds. Although there have been experiments involving cadavers placed in an area where soft tissue loss could be observed, most information on this process is derived from samples of forensic cases for which both the date that the victims were last seen alive and the date of discovery of their remains are known. These studies have been undertaken in various areas of the North American continent (representing various weather conditions) to account for the effects of climate. To date, research has been undertaken in the eastern, southwestern, and northwestern areas of the continent. Thus, timetables exist only for surface decomposition in warm and moist, hot and dry, and cold climates.

WARM, MOIST CLIMATES   William Bass (1997) has summarized his knowledge of the rate of decay of human remains deposited on the surface and out of doors in Tennessee. Over a 30-year period, Bass has consulted on numerous cases involving decomposed bodies for various law enforcement agencies. In addition, he observed the decay of hundreds of human remains placed in the University of Tennessee Anthropological Research Facility (ARF), an outside fenced area where body decomposition could be observed without the interference of mammalian carnivores. Bass states that most soft tissue loss was due to insects, with only a little help from birds such as crows and vultures. His timetable, based on rates in warm months, is summarized in Table 5.1. Bass notes that winter retards this schedule, but he does not provide criteria for calibrating this phenomenon.

Bass's data reveal two important points. First, notice the broad time ranges associated with the various decompositional changes. Although the first several are fairly small, the later ranges encompass long and, therefore imprecise, periods of time (e.g., first decade after the first year). This is fairly typical of the amount of precision seen in these types of studies. Second, because of these large ranges, refinements to estimates of PMI (requiring a considerable amount of judgment) may be necessary, especially for bodies in the later stages of decay. For example, fully skeletonized remains with only minor exfoliation of cortical bones are probably from individuals who died earlier in the first decade (e.g., first 2 to 5 years), while heavily weathered skeletons probably represent individuals from the later part of that time period (or, perhaps, even beyond).

HOT, DRY CLIMATES   Allison Galloway and colleagues (1989) present data on general decomposition rates in Arizona. Their study is based on 189 forensic cases gathered

TABLE 5.1   Rates of Decomposition in Warm, Moist Climates[1]

Time Period	Decompositional Changes
First day	Egg masses of insects, appearing like fine white sawdust, present; veins as seen through the skin may be blue or dark green; body fluids may be present around nose and mouth.
First week	Maggots are active on the face; bones around eyes and nose may be exposed; beetles may appear; skin and hair may be slipping from the body; remains emanate odor of decay; abdomen may be bloated; molds begin to appear on the skin; animals may be active; volatile fatty acids may have killed the vegetation in area around the body.
First month	Maggot activity less, beetles more common; no bloating; if the body was shaded, bones will be exposed; if the body was not covered, the skin exposed to sunlight will be dry and leathery because it protects the maggots from the sun; mammalian carnivores may be removing body parts; molds can be found on the soft tissue as well as bones; adipocere may be present.
First year	Skeleton fully exposed and bleached; moss and/or green algae may be growing on shaded bones; rodent gnawing may be present; animals (e.g., mice, wasps) may nest in the skull.
First decade	Exfoliation of cortical bone may be present; longitudinal cracks may occur in long bones exposed to sun; roots of plants may be growing in or through bones; rodent gnawing may be extensive.

[1]Summarized from Bass (1997).

TABLE 5.2 Categories and Stages of Decomposition (Arizona)[1]

Stage	Description
Fresh	Fresh appearance, no discoloration of skin, no insect activity.
Early decomposition	Some flesh relatively fresh; discoloration can vary from gray to green or brown to black; some skin slippage and hair loss; body bloated or deflated; skin may have leathery appearance.
Advanced decomposition	Sagging of flesh; caving of abdominal cavity; loss of internal organs; extensive maggot activity; mummification of outer tissue; less than half of the skeleton exposed; adipocere may be present.
Skeletonization	Decomposing soft tissue with possible desiccation; more than half of the skeleton exposed; some body fluids may be present; greasy to dry bones.
Extreme decomposition	Skeletonization with bleaching, exfoliation, and metaphyseal loss; cancellous bone exposed in vertebrae and long bones.

[1]Summarized from Table 1 of Galloway et al. (1989).

over a 20-year period for which the time last seen alive of decedents and the date of recovery of their remains were known. Although some were found in structures, most bodies were recovered from open areas. Thus, these data provide an indication of the rate at which bodies decompose outside in hot, arid climates.

The bodies that constituted the study sample could be grouped visually into one of five categories, each characterized by differing amounts of decomposition (Galloway et al., 1989). Table 5.2 presents a summary of the observations by category, and Figures 5.1 through 5.4 illustrate the last four of these stages (the "fresh" state is not depicted). As can be seen, categories are distinguishable on the basis of soft tissue coloration, amount of soft tissue loss, proportion of bone exposure, and other characteristics of deterioration.

FIGURE 5.1 Body in the early decomposition stage; note the bloating and skin discoloration. The extensive maggot activity is more indicative of the advanced decomposition stage.

FIGURE 5.2 Body in the advanced decomposition stage; note the exposure of less than half of the skeleton visible in the photo.

FIGURE 5.3 Body in the skeletonization stage; note the exposure of more than half (in this case, the entire) skeleton with dry looking bones.

FIGURE 5.4 Close-up of bone in the extreme decomposition stage; exfoliation of the cortex is clearly visible.

TABLE 5.3 Timetable for Stages of Decomposition in Hot, Arid Climates (Arizona)[1]

Stage	Range	Majority (66% or more)
Fresh	1 to 7 days	First day
Early decomposition	1 day to 4 months	2 to 8 days
Advanced decomposition	3 days to 3 years	10 weeks to 4 months
Skeletonization	7 days to over 3 years	3 months to over 3 years
Extreme decomposition	2 months to over 3 years	9 months to over 3 years

[1]Data compiled from Figure 1 of Galloway et al. (1989).

Accompanying these categories is a range of time needed for bodies to reach each of the stages of decomposition. The low end of the range for each category was determined from the body with the least amount of time between date last seen and date of recovery. Similarly, the maximum was determined from the body having the greatest difference between these two dates. Table 5.3 presents the ranges of time for bodies to reach each of these stages, as well as the range for the majority (at least two-thirds or, in many cases, more) of the bodies.

From Table 5.3, it can be seen that the rate of decomposition in this environment shows variability similar to that of hot, moist climates. For example, although the majority of fresh bodies had been dead only 1 day, some remained fresh for as long as 1 week. Further analysis of the data (not presented in the table) indicated that the main cause of this variability is fluctuations in temperature. Galloway and her colleagues found that the complete loss of soft tissue (i.e., skeletonization) is five times faster in the summer than in the winter months. This information can help narrow the estimate of PMI. For example, a body found in the stage of advanced decomposition (majority 10 days to 4 months) toward the end of the summer would yield an estimate of PMI from the low end of the range. Conversely, an estimate of PMI for a body found in the early part of spring would be drawn from the high end of the range.

COLD CLIMATES Debra Komar (1998) describes the relationship between amount of decomposition and PMI for bodies recovered in open or aquatic areas of western Canada. Using four categories of decay, she studied this relationship by viewing the files of 17 forensic cases of the Office of the Chief Medical Examiner in Edmonton, Alberta. Although her sample size is small, a rough correlation emerged. This is discernible in Table 5.4, which presents her definitions of stages of decomposition and the time ranges for these stages.

TABLE 5.4 Rates of Decomposition in Cold Climates[1]

Stage	Description[2]	Range
Moderate	Partial exposure of bone; loss of body parts; adipocere formation	3.5 months or less
Advanced	Loss of internal organs; moderate bone exposure; extensive adipocere	1.5 months to 2.7 years
Skeleton, with little soft tissue	Complete exposure of some bony elements; only desiccated soft tissue remaining	4 months to 3.5 years
Completely skeletonized	No soft tissue recovered	2 months to 8 years

[1]Compiled from data presented in Komar (1998).
[2]Descriptions from Komar (1998:58).

As can be seen, there is considerable overlap between the categories, causing estimates of PMI to be fairly imprecise. Notice, also, that none of her samples exhibited the early stage of decomposition; therefore, PMI for bodies manifesting small amounts of decay would not be possible. In addition, Komar's data indicate that skeletonization can occur rapidly, even in the cold climate of Alberta (i.e., in less than 2 months). However, information from her article indicates that this rate is slowed by the even colder weather of the winter months. Finally, she observed a fair degree of animal scavenging that was responsible for considerable skeletal dispersal (and, presumably, consumption of soft tissue).

Buried and Submerged Remains

William Rodriguez and William Bass (1985) provide the few data that have been published on decomposition for buried remains. They interred six White male cadavers at depths varying from 1 to 4 feet so that they could observe degenerational changes for time periods of 1 month to 1 year. Their results indicate that decomposition during burial proceeds at a much slower rate than it does on the surface. Rodriguez and Bass attribute this to the lack of carrion-feeding insects on the cadavers, which have little access to bodies buried 2 or more feet deep. The one body placed only 1 foot below the surface manifested a limited number of blowflies and their larvae, as well as beetles. Another factor that slowed decomposition was reduced temperature. Whereas surface finds are heated by sunlight, the interred bodies remained cooler because the soil insulated the body from the heating effects of sunlight. Thus, the surrounding dirt acted as a refrigerator, slowing the process of soft tissue loss.

Unfortunately, the preceding sample is too small to determine a rate of decomposition in burials. Similarly, the speed with which soft tissue is lost in bodies deposited in water is unknown due to inadequate research. However, experienced forensic anthropologists (Maples and Browning, 1994) have noticed that 1 week on the surface equals 2 weeks in water and 8 weeks underground. Thus, by knowing the rate of decomposition for surface finds for a particular climate, PMI of burials and remains immersed in water can be estimated. For example, if a body in the early stage of decomposition is recovered from a grave in a hot, dry environment, a PMI of 16 to 64 days is indicated, because this time period is eight times longer than that expected for the majority of finds recovered from the surface. Similarly, the PMI for bodies in the advanced stage of decomposition recovered from water in a cold, dry area would be considered to be 3 months to 5.4 years (i.e., twice as old as surface finds).

ANIMAL SCAVENGING

Human remains often are scavenged by carnivores and (occasionally) rodents. This is especially true of bodies deposited on the surface or interred in shallow graves. William Haglund (1997a, b) presents a review of this subject, which is summarized in this section. Haglund notes that animals consume soft tissue, scatter the skeleton, break bones, and gnaw on skeletal elements. In North America, the animals most commonly responsible for this are domestic dogs and coyotes. However, house cats, bobcats, wild or domestic pigs, raccoons, opossums, bears, birds, rodents, amphibians, and reptiles also will participate in this process. In addition, when humans encounter a body, they may remove parts for their personal collection (e.g., trophy skulls). Thus, by knowing the amount of time needed for scavenging to occur on human samples from known forensic cases, PMI can be estimated.

TABLE 5.5 Stages of Scavenging and Associated Schedule[1]

Stage	Description	Range
0	Early scavenging of soft tissue with no body unit removed	4 hours to 14 days
1	Destruction of the ventral thorax accompanied by evisceration and removal of one or both upper extremities including scapulae and partial or complete clavicles	22 days to 2.5 months
2	Lower extremities fully or partially removed	2 to 4.5 months
3	All skeletal elements disarticulated except for segments of the vertebral column	2 to 11 months
4	Total disarticulation with only cranium and other assorted skeletal elements or fragments recovered	5 to 52 months

[1]Reprinted with permission from Haglund, "Dogs and coyotes: Postmortem involvement with human remains" in *Forensic Taphonomy,* W. D. Haglund and M. H. Sorg, editors, 1997. Copyright © CRC Press, Boca Raton, Florida.

Haglund (1997a) studied 37 scavenged surface bodies recovered outside in the Pacific Northwest for which the time last seen and time of discovery were known. He categorized each body into one of five stages of tissue loss and disarticulation developed by biologists for studying nonhuman carcasses. Using the time missing for bodies within each of these categories, he was able to develop a rough schedule for each of the five stages. Table 5.5 contains both a description of his stages and the time ranges for each; and Figures 5.5 through 5.7 illustrate the last three of these stages. As can be seen, the variation of this timetable is great, rivaling that seen in the other decomposition studies described above. This variation includes overlap both between and within categories.

One possibility that should be considered when viewing skeletonized remains is scavenging by vultures. Nicole Reeves (2009) demonstrated that these birds would wait

FIGURE 5.5 Body in stage 2 of scavenging; note the lower limbs have been removed from the upper body.

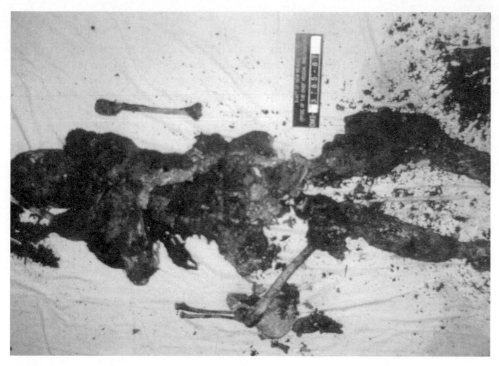

FIGURE 5.6   Body in stage 3 of scavenging; note the vertebral column is intact but other skeletal elements are disarticulated.

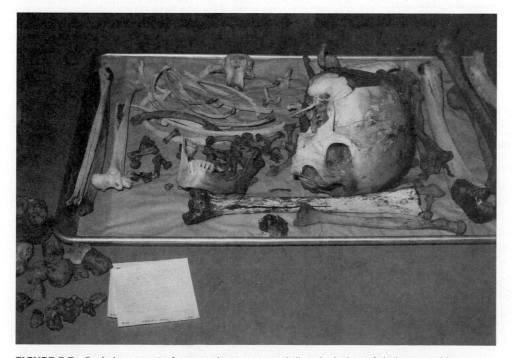

FIGURE 5.7   Body in stage 4 of scavenging; note total disarticulation of skeleton and loss of many skeletal elements.

approximately 24 hours after a pig carcass was deposited before scavenging, but then would remove most of the soft tissue from the body in another 24-hour period. Although these results must be considered preliminary due to her small sample size, forensic anthropologists must be aware of any evidence of vulture scavenging (e.g., feathers, scat, scratches on bone; see Chapter 16) as this may greatly affect an estimate of PMI.

In addition to correlating the amount of tissue consumption and disarticulation with PMI, the percentage of the skeleton recovered also is correlated (roughly) with PMI. Although based on only 11 cases, Haglund and colleagues (1988) showed that the longer the PMI, the fewer the number of bones recovered. Thus, if only 20% of a skeleton is recovered at the time of its discovery, then a PMI of 6 months to over 4 years is indicated. However, if 80% or more of the skeleton is recovered, then a PMI of less than 6 months is indicated.

One last animal type to consider when estimating PMI is the rodent. Walter Klippel and Jennifer Synstelien (2007) studied how brown rats and gray squirrels modified human bone at the University of Tennessee Anthropological Research Facility (ARF). They found that brown rats gnawed on fat-laden cancellous bone, but that gray squirrels waited for the fats to leach away before gnawing at thick cortical bone. In addition, they discovered that the earliest these latter rodents gnawed on human bones from real forensic cases was 16 months PMI, with all cases showing modifications from this rodent by the 33rd month after deposition. Their data indicate that bones containing the gnaw marks of gray squirrels are from decedents who have been dead at least a year, and more probably around 3 years.

OTHER METHODS

Numerous other methods for determining PMI have been developed by various forensic specialists. These include chemical methods for analyzing the soil under cadavers (see Vass et al., 1992) and changes in the teeth. Although these methods are useful, forensic anthropologists more commonly encounter the three specialties described previously: forensic entomology, forensic botany, and the forensic study of the deterioration of clothing and other items. Because of this, the methods of each of these will be summarized, with a general description of the postmortem events used in their techniques. In addition, methods for determining PMI from their observations will be discussed.

Forensic Entomology

Forensic entomology is the study of insects as related to the medicolegal investigation of death. In a good review article, Neal Haskell and associates (1997) outline three factors involving decedents that, under the right conditions, can be assessed from insects associated with human remains. First, by observing the different life stages of attendant insects, these workers note that PMI can be estimated (e.g., 5-day-old larvae indicate death at least 5 days prior to finding).

Similarly, since some insects are found mainly in the spring and others occur only later in the year, season during which death occurred might be determinable. Second, Haskell and his colleagues describe how the geographic location of death can be assessed if insects found on the body differ from those indigenous to the region of discovery (this would indicate movement of the remains after death). Finally, personal habits of decedents might be determinable, such as when cocaine is found in the bodies of maggots feeding on the remains. Although all these are of interest, in this section only those aspects of forensic entomology concerned with the estimation of PMI will be discussed in detail. (Readers interested in other subjects of this area of study are referred to Haskell et al., 1997, with its extensive listing of references.)

PMI can be determined by knowing several aspects of insect activity on and around human remains. These are well summarized by Haskell and associates (1997), and their article forms the bases of the following discussion. After death, a succession of insect life begins when various arthropods (especially blowflies of the taxonomic family Calliphoridae and various beetles of the order Coleoptera) begin feeding on the remains. These adults lay their eggs, which hatch into larvae that also feed. When these offspring grow to adults, they continue to eat and begin laying their own eggs, thereby starting the process again. Thus, by knowing the time needed for insects to complete a full life cycle, PMI can be determined.

In addition to life cycle, Haskell and his colleagues note that the succession of insect types can be used to determine PMI. Although blowflies begin feeding almost immediately after death, with the passage of a day or two, beetles may appear and begin feeding. Some of these consume the human remains (especially insects of the families Silphidae, and Dermestidae), while others (especially insects of the families Staphylinidae, Silphidae, Histeridae, and Hydrophilidae) eat fly eggs and larvae. As time passes, the beetles begin to outnumber flies, such that when the remains are almost devoid of soft tissue, only beetles and a few types of flies (e.g., *Piophila* "cheese skippers") remain. Thus, by knowing the ratio of flies to beetles, another estimate of PMI can be made. Although both of these methods can provide good estimates, their utility is relatively brief. Insect life cycle and succession can be used to determine only PMIs starting around several days and extending to approximately 1 year.

Haskell and associates (1997) state that the most commonly used insect to determine PMI is the blowfly. This is the brightly colored metallic blue and green fly that is commonly observed around trash areas and biological remains. This insect is useful because it is found in all parts of the country (although it is most active in warm and moist climates) and its life cycle is fairly well known. It usually appears within minutes or hours of death and, soon afterward, the females start laying eggs. These take 6 to 40 hours to hatch, after which the larvae (maggots) begin feeding. Within 3 to 10 days, they migrate off the cadaver (sometimes in a phalanx moving in one direction) and bury themselves in the ground near the remains, where they **pupate** (transform into adults) during the next 6 to 18 days. After they hatch, the new adult blowflies move back to the cadaver (if any flesh is left) and the process starts again.

This information is useful because by retrieving and identifying both the adult flies and their larvae from human remains and the surrounding soil, a determination of stages in the life cycle can be made and, from this, an estimation of PMI. Since the time needed for a complete cycle varies from 9 to 35 days for different species, identification of the adult fly and larva can lead to estimates of PMI that are accurate to within 12 hours of death.

As mentioned above, Haskell et al. (1997) note that insect succession also can be used to determine PMI. They state that the two most commonly used arthropods for this type of analysis are the fly (*Diptera*) and the beetle (*Coleoptera*). Since many beetles feed on the eggs and larva of flies, these insects appear from several days to several weeks after flies have started feeding. By knowing the various ratios in the succession of flies to beetles, PMI can be estimated. For example, studies in Tennessee by Rodriguez and Bass (1983) have shown that flies appear as early as a few minutes after death and attain their greatest frequency and numbers of types in the time period between 5 and 25 days. However, beetles usually do not appear until several days have passed and attain their greatest frequency and numbers of types between 13 and 61 days.

Again, if these insects are retrieved from the body and a determination is made as to type (fly versus beetle), the relative frequency of each can lead to estimates of PMI. Thus, if there are only flies, data from Rodriguez and Bass (1983) indicate a PMI of less than 3 days. However, if flies predominate, the estimate would be between 3 and 13 days, and if beetles and flies are approximately equal, the estimate is between 13 and 25 days. Finally, if only beetles are present, PMI is probably over 25 days.

One major problem with this technique is that some insects reoccur (e.g., show up, go away, and reappear on remains). Also, life cycle length is affected by weather, particularly heat and cold. In addition, it usually requires a specialist to identify some species of arthropod. Finally, the life cycles of beetles are not as well known as flies, rendering insect succession less useful than fly life cycle in determining PMI.

Because forensic anthropologists may not be skilled enough in entomology to determine PMI from insect activity, this work usually is left to the forensic entomologist. However, because these latter professionals may not be able to visit a recovery scene, the forensic anthropologist may have to collect the data needed for PMI estimates based on insect activity. Haskell and associates (1997) describe how flying insects are captured by sweeping an entomologist's net over the corpse six to ten times. On the last sweep, the netting material is folded over the rim, capturing the insects within its confines. The end of the net then is placed for 2 to 5 minutes in a killing jar containing cotton balls soaked with fresh ethyl acetate. The dead insects then are placed in jars containing a solution of alcohol, formalin, and glycerin for preservation. This netting technique also can be used over nearby vegetation to collect samples of adjacent insect activity. Insects remaining on the corpse can be trapped by placing the decedent in a body bag. When this bag is opened in the laboratory, several dozen specimens of adult and immature remains should be placed in jars of the previously described solution. Also, several dozen should be captured alive in plastic specimen cups with food and air holes to ensure their continued survival.

Forensic Botany

Forensic botany is the discipline concerned with the medicolegal value of plants found in association with human remains. David Hall (1997) describes how plants have four uses in this regard. First, the presence of grasses, shrubs, trees, and other such growths can be used to determine a number of factors surrounding the death of an individual. Second, Hall notes that the amount of growth into and under human remains can indicate the time of year that the death occurred. Third, previous locations of the individuals involved (e.g., victims, perpetrators) may be suggested by the presence of different plant materials in and around a crime scene. Finally, Hall notes that the amount of time that has passed since the death of decedents may be determined from aspects of plant growth. Although all these subjects are interesting, only the application of forensic botanical methods to estimating PMI will be described here.

The techniques of forensic botanists to determine PMI can be divided into two types: independent (absolute) and comparative. The independent method involves the amount of plant growth in and under human remains. P. Wiley and Alan Heilman (1987) note that PMI can be estimated by removing plant stems and roots from remains and examining their rings. Since these structures are formed during the annual cycle of growth and dormancy, each represents a year of growth. Thus, if a root exhibiting five rings is found growing into interred human remains, then a minimum of 5 years must have passed since the body was buried. In addition to observing numbers of rings, the amount of plant growth can help to indicate PMI. For example, if a body is found covered by creeping plants (e.g., vines) and the amount of time necessary for the observed growth to occur is known, then PMI can be estimated. This is useful particularly in areas characterized by heavy ground cover.

The second method involves comparing the roots from under a body, or within a grave, with those of like species in the surrounding area. Because nutrients from decomposing bodies enhance growth, roots associated with human remains may show an increase in thickness over roots from similar plants outside the area of the remains. This increase in thickness would help to indicate the amount of time that has passed since death. Thus, if the roots from a tree close to an unburied body exhibit three especially thick rings not found in similar species in the area, a PMI of at least 3 years is indicated.

The methods of forensic botany have several limitations. The first involves the accuracy of PMIs derived using independent (absolute) methods. Because plants found intermixed with human remains may have sprouted some years after the body was deposited in the area, estimates derived from this source represent a minimum PMI. Thus, if a small tree with two rings is found growing through surface remains, a minimum of PMI is 2 years. Similarly, if the body is found covered by 1 year's worth of vines, a minimal estimate of 1 year since death is indicated. However, both of these assessments can underestimate PMI to a considerable degree, because the amount of time that passed between death and the sprouting of the growth is not known. The second problem is unique to estimates derived from growth rings. Since these represent a year of growth, simple counts can be made only in annual increments. Thus, this technique cannot be used to determine PMI for persons who have been dead less than a year nor to determine weekly and monthly increments of PMI.

As with forensic entomology, the anthropologist may need to collect data needed by forensic botanists. Hall (1997) describes the methods that should be used in this process. He states that plant leaves, stems, and other parts should be preserved by placing them between pieces of paper. Color, shape, size, placement in relation to the remains, and date and time of collection also should be noted for each specimen. Although some forensic scientists collect all the plants around the remains, Hall notes that a sample of shrubs and flowers as well as grasses and trees growing near, on, or through the body is sufficient. Smaller plants can be saved in their entirety by digging them from the soil using a shovel or similar instrument. Only parts of larger plants need to be collected; for example, Hall notes that a 12- to 18-inch section of a branch or vine is sufficient. Also, the roots of plants growing through remains must be sampled by cutting at the point that they enter the body. By collecting botanical materials according to these techniques, the forensic botanist will have a reasonably complete view of the plant life associated with the remains.

Deterioration of Clothing and Other Materials

In a pioneering study, Dan Morse and associates (1983) researched the time needed for clothing and other items to deteriorate in the warm, moist weather of southern Georgia and northern Florida. Under controlled conditions, small samples of textiles and paper money were buried or scattered on the surface and their decay was monitored. The researcher's data provided an indication of how nonbiological materials could be used to determine PMI when found associated with human remains. In addition to this research, Walter Rowe (1997) has reported on studies of how synthetic fibers react when buried in well-watered soils.

The results of these researchers reveal that the same factors that cause the decay of biological remains affect the rate of decay of nonbiological materials. Their work shows that temperature has the greatest effect, because bacteria, which are largely responsible for this breakdown, live best at 70°F. Similarly, moisture, soil type, and

TABLE 5.6   Deterioration Rates of Associated Materials from Moist Areas (Time Given in Months)[1]

Material	Surface			Buried		
	Mild	Severe	Destruction	Mild	Severe	Destruction
Paper money (unprotected)	0.5	Unknown	10	0.5	1	2
Paper money (protected)	6	Unknown	36	2	6	Unknown
Cotton	1–3	Unknown	7	0.5–10	Unknown	2–10
Acetate	Unknown	Unknown	Unknown	2	3–7	8+
Rayon	2	Unknown	15	2–7	8–9	Unknown
Silk and wool	10	15	35	10	15	35

[1]Combined from data in Morse et al. (1983) and Rowe (1997).

sunlight (surface versus buried) have effects on the speed of degeneration. In addition, materials that are protected (as in a shirt pocket) decay at a slower rate than those that are not. Finally, acid soils and the presence of insects increase deterioration rates. Table 5.6 presents the combined results of their experiments on the rate of decay for various materials.

Although many materials deteriorate during the years following their deposition, this is not true of some fabrics. Acrylic, even after 2 years, either buried or on the surface, showed little destruction. Similarly, nylon showed only minor changes when buried almost a year and only mild decay after 4 years. Finally, polyester and triacetate showed no destruction after 9 months of burial in well-watered soils. Thus, these materials have little value in estimating PMI, except for very long periods (e.g., years).

Chemical Methods

Two methods for determining PMI from the chemical composition of bones or the soil below them have received some attention in the past. Arpad Vass and colleagues (1992) report on a study of the changes in the ratios of volatile fatty acids in the soil below decomposing bodies. They found that, with a general description of a body's weight and information on the temperature at the site where the decedent was found, they could determine PMI by measuring the ratio of these acids in the soil below the body. Although their findings are intriguing, their sample size is small and no further studies of this method have appeared in the literature. In a study of the levels of bone residuals (e.g., proteins, triglycerides, cholesterol), Maria Castellano and colleagues (1984) developed regression formulae predicting PMI from levels of these materials. As with the previous study, their findings are intriguing, but their small sample size and the lack of further studies have limited the popularity of these methods.

Summary

1. Decomposition is the process by which insects, large animals, plants, and physical agents (e.g., soil acids, weather) break down biological remains into their component parts.
2. Studies show that there is a correlation between amount of decomposition of human remains and PMI. Timetables correlating amount of decay and PMI have been developed only in the eastern and southwestern United States and in western Canada.
3. The amount of animal scavenging, particularly from dogs and coyotes, can be used to arrive at an estimate of the amount of time that has passed since death.

4. By knowing the life cycle and succession of insects found on decomposing remains, the PMI can be estimated.
5. Forensic botany uses plant growth found in association with human remains to help determine PMI.

6. The amount of deterioration observed in material items associated with human remains (e.g., clothing, paper money) can be used to estimate PMI.

Exercises

1. A body is discovered on the surface in the Arizona desert with most of the soft tissue present, both arms removed, and the skull and legs attached to thorax. The police think these are the remains of a person missing for over a year. Is the state of preservation consistent with that time period? Why or why not? Is the amount of scavenging consistent? Why or why not?
2. A body is found with only the skin on the arms missing; the rest of the skin is present and black in color. The bones of the arms appear greasy, and maggots are eating at remains of the internal organs. If it were found in a hot, arid place, what stage of decomposition would the remains indicate and what is the most likely PMI? If a local person matching the description of the remains has been missing 1 year, could this body be his?
3. Suppose that the body described in Exercise 2 was found in a warm, moist climate. What time period(s) would the remains indicate? Again, if a local person matching the description of the remains has been missing 1 year, could this body be his? What is the most likely PMI?
4. A body is found in a wooded area with both the adult and larval forms of flies, but only a few beetles. In addition, there are a few fly larvae in soil next to the body. What is the PMI using fly life cycle data? What is the PMI using insect successional data? Using both sets of information? Use a range chart to help you in your determination.
5. A body is found on surface of the West Mesa near Albuquerque, New Mexico. The skeleton shows some desiccated connective tissue at the joints, but is completely disarticulated. There are a few blowflies, but none of their larvae; also, a few beetles were recovered. A small tree, found growing through the obturator

foramen of an os coxa, exhibits four rings. The remains of a wallet with what looks like paper money in it, nylon stockings, and possibly a cotton blouse and skirt are found near the bones. What is the PMI based on decomposition? On carnivore scavenging? Insect life cycle? Insect succession? Plant growth? Money and clothing deterioration? Overall? Use a range chart to help you in your determination.
6. A body is found in a grave south of Chattanooga, Tennessee. It is in the postbloating stage. Plant roots in the grave show two rings. The body was found partially clothed in a silk shirt, which is in poor condition. Also, jeans found covering the legs are in poor condition. Acrylic socks found in the grave are in good condition. What is the PMI based on decomposition? Carnivore scavenging? Insect succession? Plants? Items of clothing? Overall? Again, use a range chart to help you.
7. A skull is found with a plant root in the foramen magnum that has three rings. A person matching the description obtainable from the skeleton has been missing 5 years. Could these remains be from her?
8. A body is found in a shallow grave with crumbled money in a pocket. In addition, the body is dressed in what appears to be a rayon blouse, which is now destroyed. However, the nylons are in good condition as is a wool skirt. Determine the PMI for each of these items, as well as an overall estimate of PMI. Again, a range chart should help you in your determination.
9. A body is found on the surface clad in a cotton shirt and blue jeans, both of which are in good condition. Similarly, money found in a wallet is in good condition. Using a range chart, what is the estimated PMI for each of these items, as well as an overall estimate of PMI?

6

Initial Treatment and Examination

Once human remains have been recovered from the field, they will need to be taken to a place where a complete analysis can be performed. Some sort of laboratory is necessary for this work because of the complex nature of the identification process. It is in the laboratory that the bulk of the work of forensic anthropology is performed, and it is here where problems can occur if the work area does not meet minimum standards. Thus, before any analysis can begin, a properly equipped and properly maintained laboratory must be secured.

After the remains have been moved to an appropriate work area, initial treatment and examination can commence. This part of the investigation, which can take from several days to several weeks, is divided into three main phases. First, the skeletal material must be cleaned so that any remaining soft tissue does not obscure important features of the bone that can help in the identification process. Although this is a time-consuming task, initial preparation of the body is essential to ensure accuracy throughout the analytical process. The second phase deals with reconstructing broken bones, separating bones from different individuals, and reassembling disarticulated skeletons. Although this process sounds simple, it can be very challenging with commingled, incomplete, and/or fragmented skeletal material. The last phase entails inventorying the bones that are present for each individual. During this endeavor, not only is the presence of the bones noted, but general features such as color and condition also are documented. During all these phases, notes should be made and photographs should be taken to maintain complete documentation of the examination process. This chapter first describes the components of a forensic anthropology laboratory and then each of the three main phases of initial treatment and examination.

FORENSIC ANTHROPOLOGY LABORATORY

Although the work areas of medical examiners or coroners can (and, in some cases, must) be used, laboratories specifically designed for forensic anthropology are best for skeletal analysis. Clyde Snow (1982) and Karen Burns (1999) describe much of the material needed for this laboratory, and their information will be augmented here with a description of the laboratory items used by many forensic anthropologists. The laboratory should contain at least one table that is no smaller than 3 feet wide and 7 feet long, a large sink with hot and cold water, and gas jets or electrical outlets with attached heating apparatuses (e.g., gas burner or hot plate). Also, despite the large monetary investment, every effort should be made to acquire a **fume hood** to help remove the strong odors that can be generated by decomposing bodies and the chemicals used to process them. Other tools include sliding and spreading calipers, bone board for measuring long bones, and screen drying racks, and a computer and printer. There should be plenty of room for containers holding the skeletal elements being soaked to loosen soft tissue. Similarly, there should be room for several

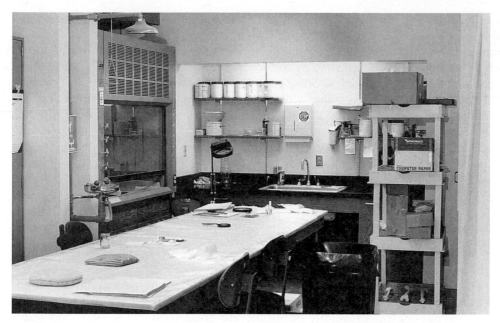

FIGURE 6.1 Laboratory facilities for forensic anthropological analysis. (Photo by Julie R. Angel)

people to work, because often the identification process includes persons other than the forensic anthropologist. Finally, cabinets are needed to store chemicals and bookshelves to hold the reference works needed for skeletal analysis. Figure 6.1 illustrates a work area that contains most of the elements just described.

In addition to the preceding physical components, at least three methodological and safety issues must be addressed. The first issue involves ensuring that the remains and attendant evidence are secure in the laboratory (Burns, 1999). Because the admissibility in a court of law of the findings of the identification process depends on the maintenance of the chain of evidence, the lab must not be accessible to outsiders. Thus, only qualified workers or visitors in the company of qualified workers should be allowed to enter and view the remains. Also, the lab should be locked whenever personnel are not present, and, ideally, it should have an alarm system. Finally, contamination of skeletal remains (and physical evidence, if present) must be avoided at all costs. The recovered remains must be kept separate from other materials in the lab so that the chain of evidence is not compromised.

The second issue involves maintaining separation between different units recovered from the scene. In the case of multiple bodies, commingling of originally separated individuals must be prevented. Similarly, material evidence (e.g., clothing) found associated with one body must not be allowed to intermingle with that from another. Although this separation should have started in the field, the importance of its maintenance in the lab cannot be overstated.

The third issue involves the safety of the work environment. Allison Galloway and J. Josh Snodgrass (1998) catalogue the biological and chemical hazards faced by forensic anthropologists. Some of these can be minimized by judicious use of the fume hood. However, to avoid infection from contaminated biological or material remains, several safeguards should be instituted. First, all personnel who handle remains should be vaccinated against all infectious diseases, including hepatitis and tetanus, and should receive periodic boosters.

Second, sterilization of all remains and their fluids should be a normal part of the treatment process. Soft tissue that has been removed can be disposed of using the procedures of the coroner's and medical investigator's offices. In addition, any remaining fluids should be cleaned up using an appropriate sterilization agent; for the most notable pathogens (i.e., human immunodeficiency virus [HIV] and hepatitis), this can be accomplished with a 1% bleach solution applied for several minutes. Finally, sterilization of the bones is accomplished by the combined effects of immersion in chemicals and boiling in water (see Residual Soft Tissue Removal in this chapter).

Third, when handling remains, workers should wear protective clothing (e.g., lab coats, latex gloves) including goggles or masks to prevent accidental splashing of fluids into the eyes. Finally, steps should be taken to reduce the probability of releasing airborne pathogens (e.g., tuberculosis). Shields should be placed over remains being processed by electrical equipment (e.g., oscillating **Stryker saw**), and breathing apparatuses should be considered when the likelihood of this type of infection is high.

PREPARATION OF REMAINS

Before the examination of bones can begin, all remaining soft tissue must be removed from the skeleton. Although a seemingly tediously unimportant task, T. Dale Stewart (1979) and many other workers warn about the danger of missing potentially important skeletal features hidden by pieces of fresh or desiccated skin, muscle, tendon, cartilage, or even internal organs. Especially important are areas such as the skull and pubic bones, which provide considerable information about the demographics of a person. These must be viewed grossly, as radiographs do not give the detail needed for accurate identification of the features used in assigning ancestry, sex, age, and stature. Similarly, soft tissue might obscure scars on bone from antemortem surgeries that may provide a means of personal identification (see Chapter 18). Finally, fresh bone is not ideal for handling, because usually at least some soft tissue remains attached to it, and because it has a greasy look and feel as well as an odd color (i.e., yellowish to brownish white). Thus, cleaning and degreasing with a bleaching agent and stabilization with an appropriate chemical should be performed before forensic anthropological analyses start.

The preparation of remains is a five-step process. First, the remains should be examined for any evidence of trauma or postmortem modification that might be removed when the bones are cleaned. Second, the bulk of the soft tissue is removed from the body with just enough care that the bone is not damaged. Third, the remains are disarticulated for further processing. Fourth, the remaining soft tissues, such as tendons and cartilage, are softened and then removed, and fifth, the bones are stabilized so that they can be handled without fear of damage or discoloration. Each of these steps, as they apply to adult and adolescent remains, is discussed in the following paragraphs. (Methods for treating fetal or infant remains are described by Snyder et al., 1975.)

Initial Examination

Due to the intense nature of the cleaning process, forensic anthropologists should be aware that some evidence of trauma and postmortem damage can be removed along with the unwanted soft tissue. Thus, it is imperative that the soft tissue and bone be examined for this type of evidence before continuing to the next step. One indication of trauma that may be removed is bone staining. Norman Sauer (1984) describes a wound to a rib that displayed a "dark stain" that he felt was indicative of a vital reaction (in this case, bleeding) that occurred due to trauma; this type of evidence would be easily washed away during the preparation of remains. Similarly, Nicole Reeves (2009) notes that superficial scratches on bone left by vulture scavenging may be washed away during the cleaning process. Thus, forensic anthropologists must examine the bone closely for these and similar features before proceeding to the next step.

Bulk Soft Tissue Removal

Removal of the bulk of soft tissue is the next step accomplished by forensic anthropologists after receiving a body for analysis. (If the medical examiner or coroner has not already done so, it might be wise to radiograph the remains for metal objects such as bullets when dealing with suspected cases of trauma.) Generally, a scalpel or tissue scissors are used for the removal of the majority of this tissue. If a large amount is present (e.g., the cadaver is nearly fresh), only minimal care need be taken to remove the bulk of this tissue (Snyder et al., 1975). However, as the bone is approached during cutting, the work should become more controlled to avoid causing nicks that might latter be mistaken for trauma that occurred around the time of death. (If any such damage does occur, it should be documented as a further precaution against being mistaken for trauma.)

Also, parts of the soft tissue should be retained for further forensic analysis. For example, any skin adhering to the fingertips should be placed in a sealed container that is labeled with the side (right or left) and number of the digit (one through five starting at the thumb). In addition, other tissues can be retained for DNA analysis using the methods described by H. C. Lee and colleagues (1998). Unfortunately, as discussed by Parsons and Weedn (1997), DNA chains begin to degrade after death such that they become unusable after a time. For example, DNA in the liver generally will degrade within 2 days of death, other internal organs within 1 week, and the brain within 1 month (and occasionally more). Therefore, the remains most often analyzed by forensic anthropologists (e.g., persons dead for several months or years) usually will not provide soft tissue samples with useful DNA. However, if it is desirable to harvest such tissues, it is recommended that these be removed first from the brain, followed by muscle and blood, and finally internal organs (except the liver). It is also advisable to remove bone samples at this point because several studies (Arismendi et al., 2004; Steadman et al., 2006) have shown that the techniques for soft tissue removal described further in this chapter may damage DNA, making positive identification from this biochemical difficult or impossible.

A useful starting point in the bulk removal of soft tissue is the large muscle masses of the torso and limbs. Even if skin is present, only a superficial knowledge of anatomy is necessary to guide the worker during this phase. The process is to start at one end of a muscle and cut at the level of the tendon(s) where it attaches to the body, peel the tissue away from the bone, and then cut at the remaining tendon(s). In this manner, the muscles of the neck and shoulders can be removed, followed by the biceps and triceps of the upper arm and the muscles surrounding the ulna and radius. A similar procedure will remove the muscles of the legs by starting at the pelvis and peeling back the tissue so that they can be cut at their tendons. After removal of the muscles of the limbs, the body cavity can be opened and the internal organs can be cut away from their connective tissues. (This process can be difficult because of the confining nature of the thorax.)

Another approach to bulk soft tissue removal is to use **dermestid beetles** (Knudson, 1972). The larva of these insects will eat skin, internal organs, muscle, and even tendons and cartilage (if given enough time). Therefore, the remains can be placed in a container inhabited by these insects, where they will consume the remaining soft tissue. When they have finished, the skeleton generally is so clean that the next two steps in the treatment process (**disarticulation** and **residual soft tissue removal**) can be omitted.

Unfortunately, there are several drawbacks to using these insects. First, the amount of time necessary for them to do their work can be as great as a month; thus, if the body represents a recent and highly publicized case, time constraints may prevent their usage. Also, the smells generated by the decomposing tissues can be intense and, because of the time involved, enduring. A second drawback is that a colony must be maintained between cleanings. This can be done using a large container (e.g., 5-gallon bucket) with a closely fitting lid that allows both for air circulation and access for feeding (usually with dog biscuits or other dried meat products). A last problem is that the beetles are most active in warm, dry climates; therefore, the container in which they work must be maintained at a temperature that promotes their rapid consumption of soft tissue. Also, it must be sealed reasonably tightly, because some insects will attempt to leave the container in search of other food.

Disarticulation

Once the muscle and internal organs are removed, the articulated bones usually must be separated for further processing. This is necessary because of the difficulty in securing vats large enough to hold an entire body for the **maceration** (softening) of the remaining tissues. Thus, the skull must be removed from the spine, the arms from the torso, the pelvis from the vertebral column, and the legs from the pelvis. Similarly, the arms may need to be separated into two segments at the elbow, and the legs at the knee. Depending on the condition of the remaining cartilage and the surrounding capsules, all these separations can be difficult. However, the fibrous tissue of the capsule can be cut with an appropriate instrument, after which the blade of a scalpel can be inserted between the cartilaginous pads of the joints and any tendons holding them together can be cut. Care must be taken that the bone is not damaged during this process (Stephens, 1979), because this might lead to a false assertion of perimortem trauma.

Decapitation should be carried out between the second and third (or lower) cervical vertebrae to avoid damage to the foramen magnum (Stephens, 1979). Once the head is removed, the pelvis can be separated from the fifth lumbar vertebrae. The spinal column can be left as a unit for the next stage, because this structure is notoriously difficult to disassemble without softening its connective tissue (Stan Rhine, personal communication). Removal of the arms requires separating the scapula from the clavicle where they join at the acromion and cutting the tissues holding the shoulder blade to the ribs. Detachment of the femur from the pelvis can be difficult, even after initial cutting of the capsule enclosing the joint, due to the ligament that connects the head of the femur to the acetabulum. This ligament (*ligamentum capitis*) must be cut by twisting the femur down such that it is exposed superiorly. The ligaments of the knee must be separated in a manner similar to that described for removal of the femur from the pelvis. There are no internal ligaments in the arms paralleling those of the leg, making their disarticulation somewhat easier.

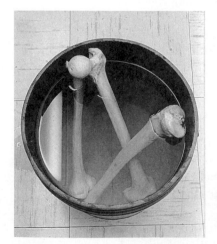

FIGURE 6.2 Bucket for maceration of soft tissue from bone. (Photo by Julie R. Angel)

Residual Soft Tissue Removal

The next step in the preparation process is to soften any clinging muscles, tendons, and cartilage so that they can be removed from the bone. The most common method for accomplishing this task is maceration in water, with or without an enzymatic additive. Stan Rhine (1998) presents a good description of this process, which will be summarized here, with additions from others where noted. The first step is to submerge the bones in room temperature water using 5-gallon plastic containers (Figure 6.2). During this step, much of the remaining muscle and other such tissues soften, forming strings of decomposing matter. The process can be accelerated by periodically renewing the water to remove the tissue that already has liquefied. Since maceration generates smells that are both intense and offensive, it is best to perform this operation in a room with direct outside venting (the fume hood mentioned before is ideal). After several days or weeks, much of the soft tissue will be dissolved and only the bone with attached cartilage and tendons will remain. These latter tissues usually are tender enough to be safely removed without harming the bone's cortical surfaces.

After this initial maceration, the remains are transferred to metal vessels containing water (and laundry detergent, if desired), which is heated and simmered for several days. Todd Fenton and colleagues (2003) state that the use of detergent can be supplemented by sodium carbonate to speed up this process.

The water or detergent solution works best if it is replaced several times over the next days. As before with simple soaking maceration, this "cooking" gives off strong odors (in this case, it is similar to a rich beef stew); thus, again a room with outside venting and/or hood is recommended. After several days, the bones are removed and allowed to air dry. This "cooking" not only removes the remaining soft tissue, but also degreases and bleaches the skeleton in preparation for further treatment. Fenton et al. (2003) recommend that the last cooking solution be made up of sudsy ammonia to facilitate the bleaching process.

Stephens (1979) presents a process that is faster than the one just described. He recommends simmering the bones in a solution of tap water and household bleach for 3 to 4 hours. After the bones are removed, the remaining soft tissue is cut or scraped away. The remains then are reimmersed in a new solution of water and bleach. If the tissues are unusually resistant, the amount of detergent can be increased. This process is repeated several times over a 2- to 3-day period until all remaining soft tissue is removed. Once this process is completed, degreasing is accomplished by immersing the remains in a solution of acetone overnight, after which they are air dried (preferably in a fume hood).

A last method, proposed by Snyder et al. (1975), is faster than either of those described previously because it uses an **antiformalin solution** (chemicals that break down formalin, the most common preservative used with biological samples) for cleaning. This solution is prepared by mixing sodium carbonate, bleaching powder, sodium hydroxide, and water. The remains are immersed in this mixture and "cooked" at a temperature just below boiling for anywhere from a few minutes to less than an hour. The remaining soft tissue either dissolves into the solution or becomes soft enough to be removable by a brush. Care must be taken during this process, because overuse of this formula can cause the bone to disintegrate.

After denuding the bones of cartilage and tendons, the remains are washed under water and then air dried. Degreasing is accomplished by soaking in benzol for 1 to 2 days, after which the remains are rinsed with water and dried. The bones then are bleached by soaking in a solution of either hydrogen peroxide or potassium hydroxide for 8 to 20 hours. Once the bleaching is complete, the bones should be rinsed under water and allowed to air dry.

A side benefit of using heat and chemicals to remove the remaining soft tissue and to degrease bones is the inactivation and destruction of many of the biological hazards found in human remains. As described earlier, Galloway and Snodgrass (1998) warn of infection from HIV, hepatitis, tuberculosis, and other pathogens. However, since HIV is inactivated by the chemicals just discussed and hepatitis B by a 1% bleach solution, the probability of infection after the remains have been cleaned is very low. Similarly, heating to temperatures as low as 133°F for as little as 10 minutes will inactivate HIV. (The time and temperature for destroying tuberculosis in human tissue are not known, so care must be taken with remains infected with this pathogen.)

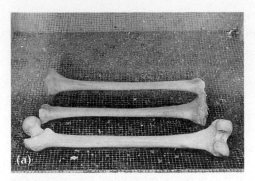 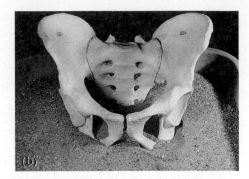

FIGURE 6.3 Treatment of bones in the laboratory: **(a)** bones drying after immersion in a stabilizing agent; **(b)** drying a glued reassembled pelvis with the help of a sandbox. (Photos by Julie R. Angel)

Stabilizing Remains

The last step in the preparation process is to treat the bones with a stabilizing agent, particularly if there is reason to believe that the individual will not be identified soon, if ever. Stabilization allows the bones to be handled without undue fear of breakage or loss of dimensions; also, discoloration due to handling will be avoided.

Although materials such as hot wax and shellac have been used in the past, one of the most favored chemicals for preservation is Alvar® (Rhine, 1998). Flakes of this substance (approximately 500 ml) are stirred into 1 gallon of acetone until they dissolve. Individual bones then are immersed in this solution for 24 hours or until bubbles stop rising from the remains. The bones then are placed on a wire mesh drying rack (Figure 6.3a), where they are turned regularly until the solution dries. This substance permeates the bone, providing a tough surface that does not obliterate features or add significantly to bone dimensions.

RECONSTRUCTION, SORTING, AND REASSEMBLY

After the initial treatment, up to three steps may need to be performed as dictated by the state of the remains. First, damaged bones must be reconstructed; usually, this only involves gluing together broken segments to achieve a complete bone. Second, commingled remains must be sorted into separate individuals. Since a personal identification is the desired result of forensic anthropological analysis, this step is particularly important. Third, the skeletons of each person should be reassembled. This will aid not only in the process of achieving an accurate inventory of the bones, but also in checking the internal consistency of bones attributed to a single skeleton. Each of these steps requires further description.

Reconstruction

As pointed out by T. Dale Stewart (1979) and others, broken bones should be reconstructed whenever possible. Reconstruction involves gluing together bones broken by any number of forces, such as colliding vehicles, large-caliber firearms, and extreme bludgeoning. In these cases, reconstruction can be a tedious and difficult task that must be accomplished to ensure the accuracy of further analyses. Also, precision is important at this stage. Thus, if pieces are incorrectly joined, they should be taken apart and their proper mates should be located. Finally, recovery of all bone segments is crucial to this phase, because missing parts will be glaringly obvious in the subsequent reassembled bones or structures.

BOX 6.1
Death in 10,000 Fragments

William Maples and Michael Browning (1994) describe the Meek–Jennings case, in which commingling and fragmentation occurred to such a degree that identification of the individuals seemed impossible. This involved a murder–suicide between an older man and a young woman, which was followed by an intense cabin fire that burned both bodies to calcined bone. When the police arrived, they gathered all the remains into a single body bag, which they treated fairly roughly while delivering them to the C. A. Pound Human Identification Laboratory for analysis. To quote Maples, "Inside, totally commingled and crushed, were approximately ten thousand bone fragments, not counting bone that had been reduced to ash and particles of sand" (Maples and Browning, 1994:151).

Although the task was daunting, Maples and his students began the laborious process of reassembling the burned, fragmented, and intermixed remains. Using large photographs of the scene taken before the skeletons were moved, they were able to determine that only two individuals were present. From the thickness of the bone fragments, they were able to divide the larger ones from those that were more gracile to tentatively separate the male from the female. Bit by bit, the bones were reconstructed using plastic cement. Some fragments were so fragile that they had to be splinted after gluing. To sum up his work in his own words:

> We looked for fragments that could be identified as coming from particular bones. We carefully gauged the thickness of the bone walls. We closely measured the curvature of fragments, which indicated the circumference of a certain bone shaft. We looked carefully at the size of the cavity within the shaft as opposed to the thickness of the walls of the shaft. We scrutinized the shapes of joint surfaces and kept an eye out for the special protuberances that indicate muscle attachment.*

The diligence of Dr. Maples and his students was rewarded by a positive identification of both Glyde Meek and Page Jennings after over a year of painstaking work.

---

*From W. R. Maples and M. Browning, *Dead Men Do Tell Tales*, Doubleday, New York, 1994, pp. 178–179, with permission.

Mating of pieces of broken bones spans the range from the easy to the difficult (see Box 6.1 for an extreme example). Fragmented skulls usually are the most challenging, while long limb bones normally are fairly straightforward. When fragments are found that fit together, they should be joined with glue that is not water soluble (such as Duco® cement) and placed in a specially made sandbox (see Figure 6.3b) until strong enough to handle. Improperly glued segments can be separated with acetone before being reglued to their proper mates. Finally, in some cases reinforcing tape, small wooden sticks (Figure 6.4), and even steel rods may be necessary to maintain the reconstruction.

Sorting

After fragmented bones are reconstructed, sorting into separate individuals must be approached. This can be easy with skeletons that were found still articulated by their soft tissue and that were properly recovered and treated. Thus, multiple bodies interred in a single grave or multiple surface remains found in, or nearly in, natural articulation can be sorted readily. Also, skeletal elements from a single individual that were found scattered on the surface may be easily reassembled. However, in a number of situations this process is more difficult. For example, in accidents causing catastrophic injuries to multiple individuals, separation is not readily accomplished, because parts of multiple persons may be fragmented, scattered, incomplete, and **commingled** (intermixed). Also, incomplete

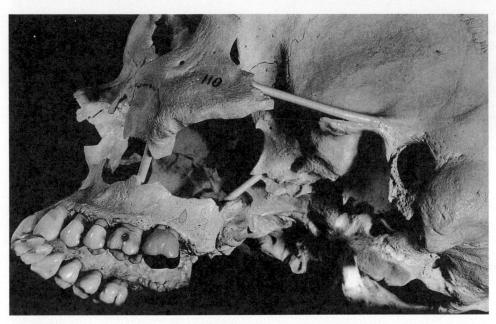

FIGURE 6.4 Reinforcing a reconstructed skull with small sticks. (Photo by Julie R. Angel)

skeletons for which bones cannot be rearticulated make the process less straightforward. Finally, if the remains are incomplete, individual persons might not be evident.

When body parts become commingled as in a mass disaster such as an aircraft crash or explosion (e.g., terrorist attack), the process of rearticulating bodies is more difficult, and in some cases impossible, without using DNA. This is due to the fact that associations between different bones in the body (even joined bones) are not exact. T. Dale Stewart (1979) recommends starting the process by first separating the bones by type and side, after which the demographic characteristics of ancestry, sex, and age are applied (see Chapters 7, 8, and 9 for a discussion of these). In this manner, the bones of large males would not be mixed easily with those of small females. Similarly, bones showing unfused or newly fused epiphyses would not go with those of adults for which epiphyseal lines were obliterated. Also, bones with arthritic lipping or osteophytic development (see Chapter 15 for a description of these) would not be associated in the same body with osteological elements that lack these features (Snow, 1948). To associate left- and right-sided bones, similar weights, lengths, widths, and muscle markings can be used because of the high correlation between sides for all long bone measurements (see Trotter and Gleser, 1952). Even associated body hair and skin color (if present) as well as clothing are useful at this stage (Owsley et al., 1995). Also, similarity of taphonomic alterations may aid in the process of rejoining the remains of individuals (Byrd and Adams, 2009).

Unfortunately, apart from those just mentioned, there are few other methods for sorting commingled remains, and some that do exist are both complex and costly (see Stewart, 1979, for a discussion; see also Fulton et al., 1986; London and Hunt, 1998, Schaefer and Black 2007). In addition, all of these techniques have high error rates, thereby limiting their usefulness. However, two studies use regression to sort commingled remains that, while not perfect for matching bones that belong together, should be useful for identifying bones that do not belong to the same individual. Paul Baker and Russell Newman (1957) present formulae associating the weights of long bones with each other, while John Byrd and Bradley Adams (2003) use the regression of bone length and width measurements. Both of their methods use formulae, generated from a reference sample (e.g., Hamann-Todd collection, Terry collection), to predict the measurement, or a set of measurements, of one bone from another. For example, if it is desired to match a femur with any one of several humeri, the femoral measurement(s) are entered into a regression formula that predicts humeral measurement(s), and a prediction interval is computed from the standard error of the equation. If the resultant humeral measurement(s) falls within the expected range, then it is possible that the bone associated with the femur. However, if the humeral measurement(s) are larger or smaller than predicted, then the bone can be eliminated as a possible match with the femur. Although Stewart (1979) expresses doubts that the Baker and Newman formulae (which remain untested) are any better than the eye for associating commingled remains, and Byrd and Adams feel that their method is only one of many that should be employed when the untangling disassociated skeletons, the elimination of potential matches is probably the most useful result of these researchers' work.

From these results, sorting becomes as much a matter of judgment as a science, and forensic anthropologists must make decisions as to the suitability of associating skeletal elements with one another. When only a few individuals are concerned, this sorting may be fairly accurate. In mass disasters involving hundreds of individuals, this process may be impossible.

Given the inaccuracy of sorting techniques, it is unlikely that severely commingled individuals can be sorted and complete skeletons from multiple persons reassembled. In these instances, the only alternative is to search for characteristics within the remains that might be able to be associated with an individual person (see Chapter 18). Thus, distinctive osteological traits (e.g., oddly shaped bones that may appear on antemortem radiographs) and odontological features (e.g., distinctive dental work) may yield, by themselves, an identification. Using this method, the end result is not a skeleton to be inventoried and analyzed. Rather, the forensic anthropologist performs as many of the analyses described in subsequent chapters as possible and then tries to identify only a single structure that goes with a known victim. Bones and/or teeth distinguished in this manner can be returned to the family for reburial with the knowledge that, even though the remains are woefully incomplete, the decedent has been identified.

Reassembly

After reconstruction and sorting, the individual should be reassembled into a complete skeleton. This involves placing the bones of each person in the anatomical position (Figure 6.5). In this position, as described in Chapter 2, the skeleton is placed as though the person were lying on his or her back on a flat surface. The arms are arranged straight along the sides with the palms of the hands facing upward and the legs are extended with the feet flat. Although this can be time consuming, it is a crucial step, because gathering further information from the 206 bones of the skeleton is difficult if they are simply placed in a disorganized pile.

Once the bones are reassembled, consistency within the skeleton should be checked to ensure that all osteological elements belong to the same individual. Although remains that were still joined by soft tissue when recovered do not need to be examined in this manner, this task is necessary in cases involving any disarticulation. Also, this step is especially important in mass graves where skeletons appear in natural articulation, but minor commingling can occur. This process must be performed so that forensic anthropologists are reasonably sure that the bones that they assign to an individual come from that individual (this is a matter of ethics; see Chapter 19). Thus, after skeletons are arranged in the anatomical position, remains should be checked for three aspects of consistency: duplication, size, and joint surface concurrence.

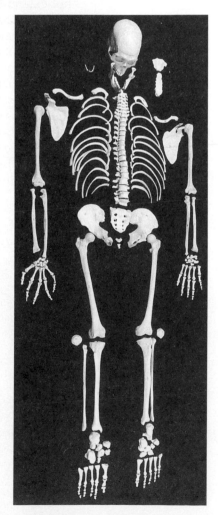

FIGURE 6.5 Skeleton in the anatomical position. (Photo by Julie R. Angel)

Duplication involves ensuring that no two bones of the same type and side are present in the skeleton. Thus, no matter how consistent other aspects of the remains are, two right femora (or other like bone) indicate that the articulation is faulty, in that there are no less than two individuals represented by the osteological remains. Similarly, if a fragment (no matter how small) of an extra bone is found in association with a complete and undamaged skeleton, duplication is present and the commingled remains must be further analyzed.

Consistency in size refers to ensuring that bones within individuals are of similar proportions. The guiding criterion in this analysis is ensuring that a person represented by a skeleton would appear "normal." Although there are a number of genetic conditions in which body segments are not in balance with each other (e.g., certain forms of dwarfism), most people have body portions that "seem right" for their size (see Box 6.2 for an exception). Thus, torsos should not appear out of proportion with their limbs, while feet and hands should appear in balance with their respective legs and arms.

Three aspects of bone aid in determining consistency in size: length, robusticity, and rugosity. Consistency of length refers to ensuring that the long limb bones, as well as bones of the axial skeleton, are similarly proportioned. Thus, long arms are associated with long legs and torso; also, arms are of such length that the tips of the fingers do not extend further than mid-thigh. These types of similarities should be evident in all bones of the skeleton. Robusticity means that thick leg bones are not associated with gracile arms; and, similarly, light bones of the torso should not be associated with robust limbs. Finally, consistency in rugosity must be considered; persons with large muscle markings on the arms generally have large muscle markings on the legs.

Unfortunately, determining association from size is hampered by inconsistencies. For example, some women have large heads that make the skeleton appear as though the skull is male and the postcranial skeleton is female. Similarly, a small skull can go with a tall, robust, and otherwise "male-looking" skeleton. Because imbalances such as these do occur, only experience and persistence can ensure accuracy in this process.

The last aspect of consistency is determining **joint surface concurrence**, that is, ensuring that the articular surfaces of the bones match. This can be accomplished after

BOX 6.2
Male Bones But Female Mandible?

Kathleen Reichs (1989) describes a case in which using sex criteria to relate scattered osteological remains brought up the possibility of the commingling of two individuals. In 1986, Reichs was given a skull missing the face, a mandible, several vertebrae and long bones, and both os coxae for analysis. Her examination revealed that the robust nature of the long bones was almost certainly indicative of a male, as were characteristics of the os coxae and skull. However, the small size and narrow dimensions of the mandible caused her to question its association with the other remains. This bone was gracile by comparison with the skull and long bones; also, when placed in position, it did not articulate well with the cranium. Thus, preliminary sorting of remains indicated that two individuals were present, one male and one female.

Further analysis revealed that only one person was present and that the mandible did belong with the other osteological remains. By measuring other "fits" of mandible to skull, she determined that the case in question fell within the range of variation expected of this articulation. She thus came to the conclusion that the bones represented one individual who had a moderate cranial deformity, probably caused by premature closure of his cranial sutures. With her demographic information in hand, the police found a record of a missing person who fit the profile developed by Reichs; and, using dental x-rays, a positive identification was made. Analysis of a photo of the identified person revealed the same narrow head and jaw exhibited by the skull and mandible.

the body is laid out in the anatomical position so that the areas of articulation are in proximity. Although a far-from-perfect technique, the use of this process will help ensure that (at least) extremely dissimilar bones can be prevented from being considered as belonging to a single person.

Starting with the skull, two articulations are possible: that of the jaw with the mandibular fossa (called the temporomandibular joint or TMJ) and that of the atlas with the occipital condyles. The mandibular condyles of the lower jaw should fit well into both mandibular fossa of the temporals, with only a small space for their cartilaginous pads, and the teeth of the mandible should align with those of the upper jaw with (in some groups) a slight overbite (see Figure 6.6). The atlas usually does not join well with the occipital unless it is pushed forward (see Figure 6.7a); however, the distance between the condyles and the supe-

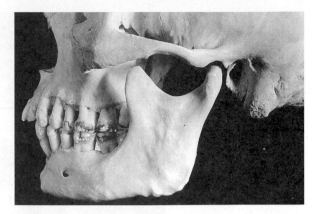

FIGURE 6.6 Articulation of the lower jaw with the skull. (Photo by Julie R. Angel)

rior articular surfaces of the atlas should match fairly well. Similarly, both sets of structures should be the same size. Continuing downward, the inferior articular facets of the atlas should articulate well with the superior facets on the axis (see Figure 6.7b).

This process of articulating each vertebra with that above and below it should be continued down the spinal column to the sacrum and coccyx. The cervical vertebrae usually articulate fairly well with only small gaps between the adjoining surfaces of the vertebral bodies (see Figure 6.8). Similarly, the articular facets of the thoracic (Figure 6.9a) and lumbar vertebrae (Figure 6.9b) usually align well, but gaps often appear between the body surfaces.

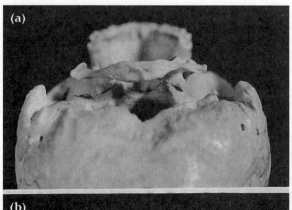

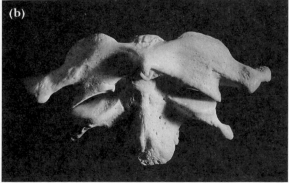

FIGURE 6.7 Articulation of the atlas with **(a)** the occipital bone and **(b)** the axis. (Photos by Julie R. Angel)

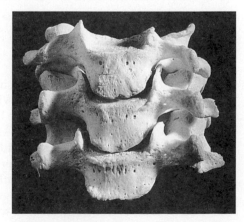

FIGURE 6.8 Expected dry articulation of cervical vertebrae. (Photo by Julie R. Angel)

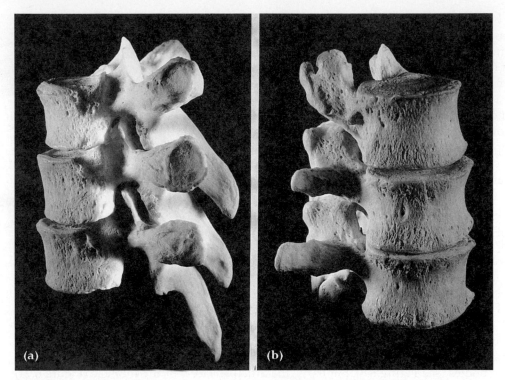

FIGURE 6.9 Expected dry articulation of **(a)** thoracic vertebrae and **(b)** lumbar vertebrae. (Photos by Julie R. Angel)

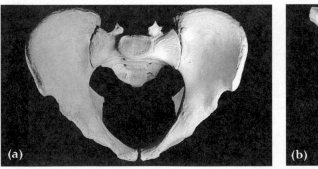
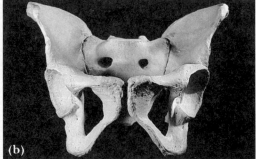

FIGURE 6.10 Natural articulation of the pelvis: **(a)** superior view showing both sacroiliac joints and gap between pubic bones; **(b)** anterior view showing the gap between pubic bones. (Photo by Julie R. Angel)

Next the sacroiliac joints should be reunited to ensure a good fit of the os coxae with the sacrum (Figure 6.10). When this is accomplished, the pubic faces should be in proximity, but not touching (see Figure 6.10a and b), because in life a fibrocartilaginous pad separates these two bones. Also, their superior surfaces should be at the same level.

Articulation of the ribs with their respective vertebrae is difficult to accomplish. However, as pointed out by Owers and Pastor (2005), among others, it is a necessary task so that any fracture patterns would become evident (see Chapter 13) and so that the correct ribs are used in estimating age at death (see Chapter 9). It is best to lay out the ribs in size order; that is, from smallest to largest going down the body (except for the two floating ribs). The increasing distance of the angle of the rib from the head can be used to arrange these bones from top to bottom (again, except for the two floating ribs). If more involved methods are desired, Hoppa and Saunders (1998) and Owers and Pastor (2005) provide useful quantitative techniques for this process, whereas Dudar (1993) and Mann (1993) provide qualitative methods.

Next, the elements of the appendicular skeleton should be checked for consistency. Although the head of the humerus does not fit well into the glenoid cavity of the scapula (Figure 6.11), other elements of the arms fit together in a fairly precise manner. The olecranon process of the ulna should articulate with the trochlea of the humerus (Figure 6.12a), and the head of the radius will fit into the radial notch of the ulna simultaneously when the head of the ulna fits into the ulnar notch of the radius (Figure 6.12b).

The leg elements should be similarly examined. The head of the femur will fit into the hip socket (see Figure 6.13) with enough, but not too much, space for the cartilage lining the inside of the acetabulum. Elements of the knee joint will be consistent only in width and size, because the condyles of the femur contact only the top of the tibia and the

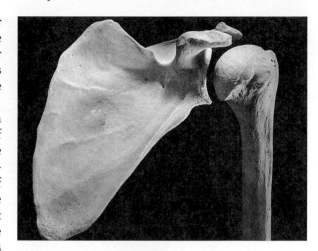

FIGURE 6.11 Scapula and humerus in proximity, showing the nature of the shoulder joint. (Photo by Julie R. Angel)

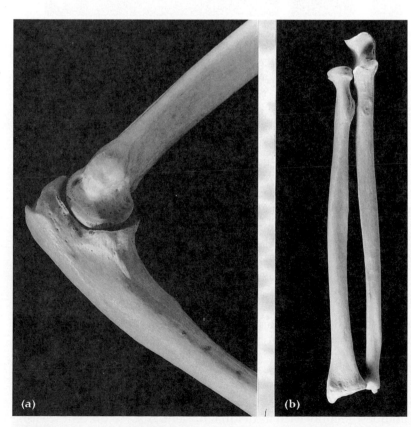

(a)

(b)

FIGURE 6.12 Articulations of the arm: **(a)** humerus and ulna at the elbow; **(b)** ulna and radius in natural articulation. (Photos by Julie R. Angel)

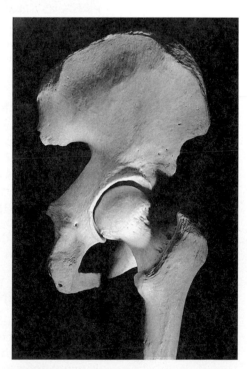

FIGURE 6.13 The hip socket joint, showing the space between the head of the femur and the acetabulum. (Photo by Julie R. Angel)

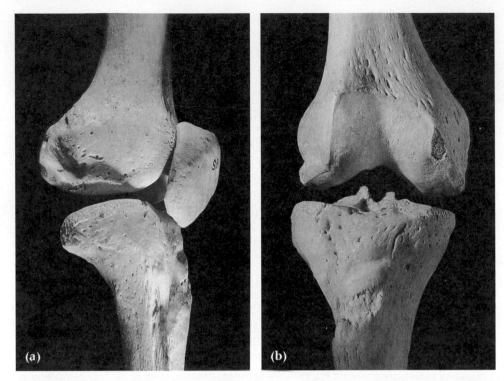

FIGURE 6.14 Articulations of the knee: **(a)** lateral view showing the femur, tibia, and patella in articulation; **(b)** relationship between the eminence of the tibia and the fossa of the femur. (Photos by Julie R. Angel)

patella simply lays on the ventral surface of the joint (Figure 6.14a). However, there should be enough space in the intercondyloid fossa of the femur to accept the intercondyloid eminence of the tibia when the two bones are properly spaced (see Figure 6.14b). The articulation of the fibula with the tibia usually is very good, with the base of the maleolus of the former fitting well into the lateral surface on the distal end of the tibia (see Figure 6.15a). Notice that the fibular maleolus projects more inferiorly than its counterpart on the tibia. Also, the talus should fit well into the ankle joint, with enough space for its cartilaginous lining (see Figure 6.15b). Finally, checking the articulation of the bones of the hands and feet, as well as their placement at the ends of the arms and legs, will determine congruence between these body segments.

INVENTORYING REMAINS

Once individuals are sorted and rearticulated, the bones within each person should be marked and then inventoried. Marking involves placing the case number on each bone (Rhine, 1998). This is a lengthy but necessary process to ensure that the chain of evidence is maintained. A razor-point felt-tipped pen with permanent black ink can be used for this procedure (see Figure 6.16); however, many people still use a quill pen with India ink. If multiple burials are being processed, a number or letter suffix can be appended to the case number to uniquely identify each individual present. Also, to prevent wearing during handling, a preservative can be painted over the number after marking.

Once the case number has been placed on the bones, the remains must be inventoried. Unfortunately, most of the methods suggested for this process were derived from archeological studies, which have different goals than forensic anthropology. This

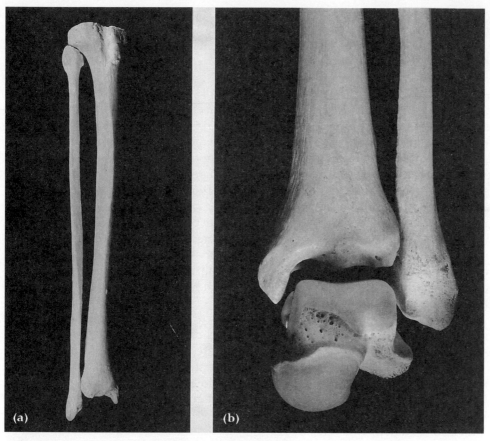

FIGURE 6.15 Articulations of the lower leg bones: **(a)** the tibia and fibula; **(b)** talus in articulation with the tibia and fibula. (Photos by Julie R. Angel)

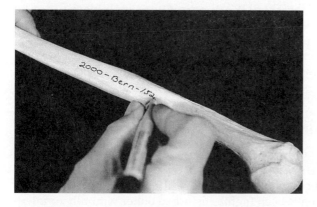

FIGURE 6.16 Marking bones with the case number using permanent ink.
(Photo by Julie R. Angel)

situation is made more complex due to the lack of a standard within the discipline. Although statements such as "the skeleton is complete except for the bones of the right hand, which were not recovered" are sufficient for complete or nearly complete remains, usually more detail is necessary (Stan Rhine, personal communication). Given this, any method that involves tabulating all the bones or structures that are present, with statements as to their general condition, probably is acceptable. When doing this, it is best to divide the skeleton into the traditional segments of cranial, axial, and appendicular. Another method involves using line drawings of skeletal elements, such as those pictured in Attachments 3a through 10b of Buikstra and Ubelaker (1994). When used, missing elements can be darkened with a pencil or pen to indicate that they were not recovered.

Subadults pose special problems because the epiphyses and growth centers appear as extra bones. As discussed in Chapter 2, ossification of the human skeleton is a complex process by which bone forms within a cartilaginous precursor that provides the structure for the deposition of bone matrix. Because this process occurs at different times in different bones, the inventory expectations of subadult skeletons depend on the age at death of the individual being analyzed. Thus, if a newborn is the object of study, an inventory of the skeletal remains would not include the carpals, because they do not begin to ossify until after birth. Similarly, there is no expectation of osseous epiphyses of most of the long bones unless the remains represent an individual over 5 years of age. Finally, some bones have complex ossification schemes in which several centers unite to form a single epiphysis before it fuses to its parent bone (e.g., proximal end of humerus). For these reasons, providing a method for inventorying all subadults is not possible within the confines of this text. The reader is referred to Fazekas and Kosa (1978), which has information on the skeletons of young individuals.

When inventorying bones, usually it is best to start at the skull and proceed down the axial skeleton; then move to the appendices, starting first with the upper limbs and followed by the bones of the legs. The presence of each bone or epiphysis should be indicated by the percentage of bone present. Simple anthroposcopic estimation is sufficient (e.g., 90%), with a "Comments" field being used for notes about missing segments. If less precision is desired, the categories of Buikstra and Ubelaker (1994) can be used; that is, 1 for when 75% or more of bone is present, 2 for 25% to 75%, and 3 for less than 25%. The state of preservation of the remains also should be noted. The categories should include good (G), fair (F), poor (P), and absent (A); not applicable (N) is used with subadults. Similarly, the color of the bones should be noted as well as any weathering. For bones exhibiting cracking and flaking of the cortex, the categories of Buikstra and Ubelaker (1994), reproduced in Table 6.1, can be used. Any inventory or conditions not covered by these categories can be noted in a "Comments" field, which can be very helpful for jogging one's memory at a later date. Finally, during this procedure it is best to refrain from analyzing defects for perimortem trauma and other such conditions; this is best accomplished later in the analytical process.

HIGHLY FRAGMENTED REMAINS

Occasionally, forensic anthropologists must deal with human remains from multiple individuals that are so fragmented and comingled that many of the methods described above are of limited, or no, value. The most common causes of this situation are extreme cremation, explosions, or mass graves that have been highly disturbed either naturally or intentionally. In cases where fragmentation is so great that only small but identifiable segments of bones remain, a first step in the identification process is the calculation of **Minimum Number of Individuals (MNI)**. This is accomplished by sorting bones by side and type, then counting that bone fragment that occurs most often. Thus, if there are 30 fragments of the right eye orbit of the frontal, 20 segments of the proximal left femur, 15 fragments of the right distal tibia, as well as smaller numbers of elements from other bones, the MNI would be 30 individuals. Although this appears to be a poor representation of the people who were recovered, this may be the only statistic that can be generated from these types of assemblages unless the resources are available for identification through DNA (see

TABLE 6.1   Bone Weathering Stages[1]

Stage 0: Bone surface shows no sign of cracking or flaking due to weathering.

Stage 1: Bone shows cracking, normally parallel to the fiber structure (e.g., longitudinal in long bones). Articular surfaces may show mosaic cracking.

Stage 2: Outermost concentric thin layers of bone show flaking, usually associated with cracks, in that the bone edges along the cracks tend to separate and flake first. Long thin flakes, with one or more sides still attached to the bone, are common in the initial part of Stage 2. Deeper and more extensive flaking follows, until most of the outermost bone is gone. Crack edges are usually angular in cross section.

Stage 3: Bone surface is characterized by patches of rough, homogeneously weathered compact bone, resulting in a fibrous texture. In these patches, all the external, concentric layers of bone have been removed. Gradually the patches extend to cover the entire bone surface. Weathering does not penetrate deeper than 1.0–1.5 mm at this stage, and bone fibers are still firmly attached to each other. Crack edges usually are rounded in cross section.

Stage 4: The bone surface is coarsely fibrous and rough in texture; large and small splinters occur and may be loose enough to fall away from the bone if it is moved. Weathering penetrates into inner cavities. Cracks are open and have splintered or rounded edges.

Stage 5: Bone is falling apart, with large splinters. Bone easily broken by moving. Original bone shape may be difficult to determine. Cancellous bone usually exposed, when present, and may outlast all traces of the former, more compact, outer parts of the bones.

[1]Reprinted with permission from Table 5 of J. E. Buikstra and D. H. Ubelaker, *Standards for Data Collection from Human Skeletal Remains* (1994). Fayetteville, AR: Arkansas Archeological Survey Publications.

Miscellaneous Techniques in Chapter 18). As mentioned earlier, this statistic is of particular importance to genocide investigations where personal identifications may not be possible.

Despite its apparent logic and simplicity, errors of considerable magnitude can occur in the calculation of MNI with this method (see Hermann and Devlin, 2008, for an example). A more accurate although more time-consuming method involves the use of a **Geographic Information System (GIS)**-based approach. Nicholas Hermann and Joanne Bennett Devlin (2008) provide a good description of this method which will be summarized here. The first step in the GIS process is to identify the most recognizable bone fragments that appear with the most frequency in the assemblage being studied. In the paper of Hermann and Devlin, these were the frontal, zygomatic, maxilla, and mandible; however, any bone or bones are usable if their segments are recognizable and are found in abundance. Thus, the femur with its distinguishable linea aspera on the shaft or the humerus with its recognizable deltoid tuberosity would be good candidates for this type of study because of their likelihood of survival even with the most destructive forces. Conversely, bones such as the parietal with few identifiable features would be avoided in this type of study. Once the bones have be chosen, the next step is to create shapefile templates that contain images of the complete chosen bone, which will serve as models against which bone fragments are compared. This comparison is achieved by digitizing these fragments, and fitting them into their proper place on the bone template. In this manner, all recognizable bone fragments can be identified as to their location within a bone. From here, the last step is to identify the MNI represented on the templates.

Although Hermann and Devlin state that GIS-based methods result in better estimates of MNI than standard methods, they also note several drawbacks. First, there is a considerable investment in time needed to develop the shapefile templates, and even more in digitizing recognizable bone fragments. Second, the system requires the use of elements that have identifiable features (e.g., eye orbit of the frontal); although these are usually present in even the most fragmented remains, their absence would make it impossible to use this method. (However, no other method could be used to estimate MNI either.) Third, only the most skilled and experienced osteologists can employ this method effectively. Because of the fragmentation and the skill required to digitize, this method is not usable by persons new to the field of forensic anthropology.

Summary

1. A forensic anthropology laboratory, containing tables and drying racks, as well as a fume hood and sink, is the preferred environment in which to perform the analysis of human remains.

2. Before beginning the examination of bones for features relevant to identification, a thorough removal of soft tissue is necessary so that any remaining skin, muscle, tendon, or cartilage does not obscure those features needed in further analyses.

3. The initial treatment is a four-step process involving the removal of bulk soft tissue, disarticulation, softening and removal of residual soft tissue, and stabilization.

4. After the removal of soft tissue has been accomplished, broken and otherwise fragmented bones must be repaired.

5. In cases of commingling of multiple bodies, sorting of individuals must be performed before analysis can continue.

6. When individuals have been sorted, bodies should be arranged in the anatomical position and the bones should be checked for internal consistency to ensure the accuracy of body reconstruction.

7. Individual bones should be marked with a case and (if appropriate) individual number with permanent ink to ensure the maintenance of the chain of evidence.

8. A complete inventory of bones within all represented individuals must be accomplished before moving to the next stage of analysis. Included in this step are notations on the amount of each bone present (complete or incomplete), as well as general condition and any other noteworthy characteristics.

Exercises

1. Using your own body as an example, describe where you would cut and how you would remove the skin and large muscle masses of the arms, legs, torso, and neck.

2. A desiccated body (e.g., bones with dried soft tissue still attached) is brought to you for analysis. Describe how you would go about performing the initial treatment. Would you follow the same steps outlined in the text, or would you deviate from that step-by-step procedure?

3. A series of heavily fragmented bones are brought to you for reconstruction. Ignoring sorting by individual, describe how you would go about the initial sorting of bone fragments to help you in the process of reconstruction.

4. Three bones are brought to you: a robust right humerus with heavy muscle markings, a large left os coxa, and a gracile right femur whose head fits easily into the acetabulum. Describe how you would determine if this assemblage represents one, two, or three individuals.

5. Suppose that a right femur and left tibia, a right humerus and radius, and a left ulna are brought to you for analysis. Could the methods described in the reassembly section be useful for determining if these bones are from the same individual?

6. If a complete skeleton is brought in for analysis that has an unusually large skull and upper limbs, can you ensure that all bones are from the same individual and how would you attempt to prove that?

Attribution of Ancestry

The major function of forensic anthropology is to provide law enforcement officials with enough information about human remains so they can be matched with a missing persons file, leading to a positive identification. The first data that should be discerned from the skeleton to aid this process are the demographic characteristics of ancestry (race or ethnicity), sex, age, and stature. Knowledge of these attributes helps to limit the search for a possible match, thereby hastening the identification. Thus, the assessment of these four traits of personal information constitutes the critical first steps in forensic anthropological analysis.

Since these characteristics are so critical, the methods for assessing each of them will be given in separate chapters. This chapter will deal with the techniques by which forensic anthropologists attempt to discern the genetic background of individuals represented by their skeletons. Chapter 8 will deal with methods for attributing sex, and Chapter 9 will deal with methods for estimating age. Finally, Chapter 10 will present techniques for calculating the living height (stature) of persons represented by skeletal remains.

Presently, there is a debate within anthropology concerning the nonexistence of race. Some researchers feel that only individual traits should be studied, while ignoring the natural groupings formed by persons who have similar skin color, nose form, and other characteristics. Anthropologists adhering to this belief prefer the term *ethnicity* or *cultural affiliation.* Other researchers feel that, because these groupings can be identified, they should be recognized as natural biological entities. These anthropologists prefer the term *race* to describe these groupings. Whichever argument prevails in the long term, forensic anthropologists do not have the luxury of debating this issue; rather, they must arrive at an assessment of this demographic characteristic to aid the police in their identification process. However, in deference to the debate and to avoid controversy, the terms race and ethnicity will be avoided in favor of the term *ancestry* to describe the genetic background of persons. Also, because forensic anthropologists work closely with law enforcement officials in their work, this chapter will use the ancestral groupings familiar to these officials, which are derived from the U.S. Bureau of the Census. Thus, *White* will be used to describe persons of mainly European descent, *Black* will be used for persons of African descent, and *Asian* for persons whose ancestors originated in the Orient. In addition, *Native American* will be used instead of the more common *American Indian*, and *Hispanic* will describe persons of mixed European and Native American heritage.

Table 7.1 lists the ancestral groups in the United States along with percentages of each as of the 2009. Several points must be made concerning these groups. First, as has long been pointed out by numerous workers, there is no such thing as a pure ethnic group, race, or ancestral group. Because of admixture (i.e., intergroup matings), there is considerable overlap between the traits that characterize the different categories appearing in Table 7.1. This overlap causes an ambiguity that makes the attribution of ancestral group one of the most

TABLE 7.1 United States Bureau of the Census Ethnic Groups and Their Frequencies (2009 estimates)

Ethnic Groups	Frequency (%)
Whites (non-Hispanic)	66.3
Blacks	12.5
Hispanics	15.8
Asian	4.5
Native Americans	0.8
Other	0.2

difficult assessments to be made during osteological analysis. Therefore, this demographic factor is best left to an experienced forensic anthropologist (as evidenced by the poor assessment by a physician described in Box 7.1). Second, remains that exhibit ambiguous ancestral grouping should be assigned to the group that is considered the minority (e.g., a skeleton that exhibits part White and part Black features would be considered Black). This is because in life, with soft tissue present, these persons would have been classified as such by their fellow humans (Stewart, 1979). A last point is that the majority of characteristics that help assess ancestry apply only to adults. The exceptions

BOX 7.1
The White Native American

Stan Rhine (1998) describes a case in which a physician overstepped the boundaries of his knowledge when he offered an opinion on human bones that he discovered while picnicking with his family on the Navajo Reservation in New Mexico. The description of what happened follows:

> Finishing their isolated midday repast, the physician and his family started off on a hike around the base of craggy Ship Rock. They had not gone far before they bumped into some bones lying in the sand amid scattered basaltic fragments from the towering landmark. They gathered up the bones—a human skull, part of a pelvis, and some leg bones—and took them to the San Juan County Sheriff. Most physicians are happy to offer opinions, and this one was no exception. With the skull present, most people would have felt competent to venture a guess that the bones were human, but he went on—so far as to say that they were Indian, and female. One problem in any sort of analysis is that observers may be moved by a logic that

grows out of context. Out here, on the red desert steppes of the Navajo Reservation where green is an abstract concept, it is reasonable to assume that these skeletal remains were Indian.

But they were not. The facial skeleton exhibited the features more likely to be found in the faces of most residents of nearby Farmington, an Anglo trade and tourist center, than in the Navajo town of Ship Rock. In the latter population, the face is flatter and smoother featured. The features of this skull were so classically white that a first-year forensic anthropology student could have made the correct diagnosis. Moreover, the physician's guess about sex was wrong. No measurements were required to see that the pelvis, the skull, and the other bones found were all obviously "textbook" male. But, after all, it is the job of the anthropologist rather than the physician to analyze bones.*

_____
*From S. Rhine, *Bone Voyage,* University of New Mexico Press, Albuquerque, 1998, pp. 92–93, with permission.

to this rule are the features of the dentition, which can be used in persons who have not achieved sexual maturity.

As discussed in Chapter 1, two basic methods are used by forensic anthropologists in osteological analysis: anthroposcopy and osteometry. Anthroposcopy, as it applies to attributing ancestry, deals with observing visually discernible differences between Whites, Blacks, Asians, and other groups. This is the subject of the first section in this chapter. The second section deals with metric methods for assessing ancestry. Metric assessment is possible because research in osteometry has yielded a number of measurements that help quantify the anthroposcopic characteristics described in the first section. Finally, miscellaneous characteristics of ancestral groups will be discussed in the last section of this chapter.

ANTHROPOSCOPIC TRAITS

The visual identification of traits that differ among the ancestral groups remains the main method for assessing ancestry. Unfortunately, the subjective nature of these traits makes them difficult to utilize. Because they are not measured on a continuous scale (e.g., millimeters, centimeters), their expression is divided into discrete categories, which also can be difficult to identify. For example, the projection of the nasal bridge can be used to distinguish ancestral group, with Blacks and Asians having nonprojecting bridges, while those of Whites jut forward to a considerable degree. Recognizing this characteristic requires knowledge of where the nasal bridge starts and ends, as well as what constitutes "projecting" versus "nonprojecting." Also, despite the discreteness of categories, these traits are characterized by gradations, particularly in individuals whose ancestry is mixed. Thus, a person may have a medium "projecting" bridge or a bridge that juts "somewhat" forward. These ambiguities make the identification of ancestral group the most difficult attribution to be made by forensic anthropologists.

Anthroposcopic characteristics that can be used to assess ancestry are found mainly in the cranial skeleton. Thus, these will be discussed in the first part of this section. The second part deals with those few anthroposcopic characteristics of the postcranium that also can be used for this purpose. Unfortunately, this information is only well documented for three of the ancestral groups in the United States: White, Black, and Asian. Little has been written about the characteristics that distinguish Hispanics and Native Americans from these first three. However, characteristics of Asians can also be used to describe Native Americans (within limits), while Hispanics generally have characteristics of both Whites and Asians.

Cranial Skeleton

Figure 7.1 presents examples of the skulls of the three main groups in front and side views. In his classic work *The Human Skeleton in Forensic Medicine,* Wilton Krogman (1962) lists the basic features of the cranium by which these three ancestral groups can be distinguished from each other. A summary of these features, with additions from Brues (1977) and Rhine (1990b), is presented in Table 7.2. This table is divided into four sections: nose, face, vault, and jaws and teeth.

NOSE   Of all the cranial features for differentiating ancestral group, the nose is the most useful. This structure contains five observable features that vary in a fairly distinct manner among the three main groups. These features are root (arrow a, Figure 7.2), bridge (arrow b, Figure 7.2), spine (arrow c, Figure 7.2), lower border, and opening. The **root** is that area of the nose where the nasals meet the frontal (i.e., nasion). It varies from projecting forward from the plane of the face to being so flat that it does not obstruct the

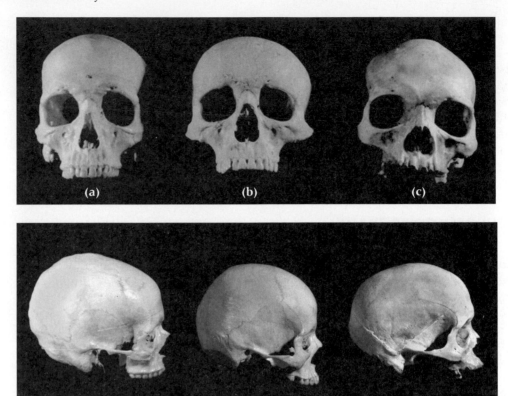

FIGURE 7.1 Skulls of three main ancestral groups: **(a)** White; **(b)** Asian; **(c)** Black. (Photos by Julie R. Angel; White and Asian skulls courtesy of the University of New Mexico–Albuquerque, Maxwell Museum of Anthropology, #176 and #55; Black skull courtesy of the University of Tennessee, Knoxville, #19-94)

view of both eye orbits when observing the skull from the side. The **bridge** is the ridge of bone formed by the nasals; it extends from the root to the ends of these bones. The **spine** is a projection of bone emanating from both the floor of the nasal aperture and the anterior part of the maxillae; when it is present, it appears as if the bone were pinched (like clay between the fingertips) into a pointy projection. The lower border of the nose also varies; it can be flat, such that the floor of the nose merges with the anterior maxilla, or it can be raised into a distinct **sill**, forming a sharp wall. The last feature is the shape of the nasal opening; this can range from an isosceles triangle with a narrow base to a roughly shaped equilateral triangle.

As can be seen in Table 7.2, Whites have a high nasal root, whereas this structure in the other two groups is low. The terms "high" and "low" are best understood as projecting and nonprojecting; that is, the nasal root of whites projects forward from the face, while those of Blacks and Asians are more flat (do not project). This is most easily seen in relation to the lower border of the eye when viewed from the side. Distance 1 of Figure 7.3a shows how the root of the nose of a White projects well in front of the lower border of the eye; Figures 7.3b and c show how much closer this structure is to the plane of the eye orbit in Asians and Blacks, respectively. Figure 7.4 shows the widths of the roots of the three ancestral groups; notice how narrow this structure is in the White (7.4a), while it is wide in Blacks (7.4c) and intermediate in Asians (7.4b).

As seen in Table 7.2, the bridge also varies among groups. According to Alice Brues (1977), the high nasal bridge of Whites causes the nose to assume the shape of an A-frame house, while the low and broad nasal bridge of Blacks gives this structure a

TABLE 7.2   Anthroposcopic Characteristics of the Skull of the Three Main Ancestral Groups in the United States[1]

Structure	Whites	Blacks	Asians
Nose			
Root	High, narrow	Low, rounded	Low, ridged
Bridge	High	Low	Low
Spine	Pronounced	Small	Small
Lower border	Sharp (sill)	Guttered	Flat, sharp
Width	Narrow	Wide	Medium
Face			
Profile	Straight	Projecting	Intermediate
Shape	Narrow	Narrow	Wide
Eye orbits	Angular	Rectangular	Rounded
Lower eye border	Receding	Receding	Projecting
Vault			
Browridges	Heavy	Small	Small
Muscle marks	Rugged	Smooth	Smooth
Vault sutures	Simple	Simple	Complex
Postbregma	Straight	Depressed	Straight
Jaws and teeth			
Jaws	Small	Large	Large
Palatal shape	Parabolic	Hyperbolic	Elliptical
Upper incisors	Spatulate	Spatulate	Shoveled

[1]Combined from information in Krogman (1962), Brues (1977), and Rhine (1990b).

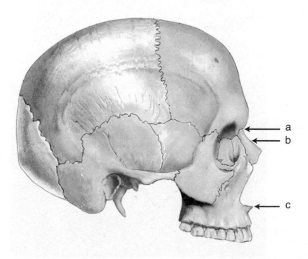

FIGURE 7.2   Side view of human nose showing three of five features useful in assessing ancestry: root (*arrow a*); bridge (*arrow b*); spine (*arrow c*).

Quonset-hut shape, and the thin, low bones of Asians make this structure appear as a "sagging tent." (These traits are not visible in Figure 7.4.)

   The spine also varies by group (arrows 2 in Figure 7.3). In Whites, it can be pronounced (i.e., very large and projecting, see Figure 7.3a), whereas it is fairly small in Asians (Figure 7.3b) and almost nonexistent in Blacks (Figure 7.3c).

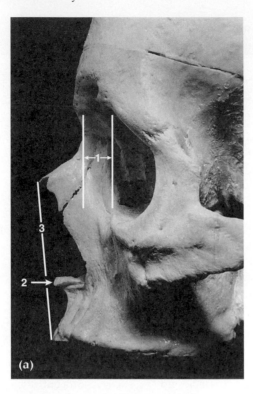

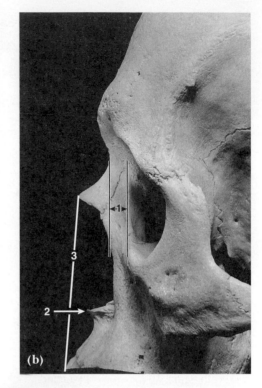

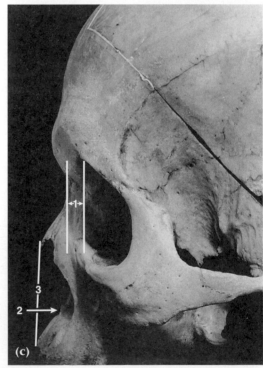

FIGURE 7.3 Side views of the noses of the three main ancestral groups: **(a)** White; **(b)** Asian; and **(c)** Black. Distance 1 shows the span between the plane of the lower eye orbit and the nasal root; arrow 2 points to the nasal spine; line 3 connects the tips of the nasals with the most forward projection of the upper jaw. (Photos by Julie R. Angel; White and Asian skulls courtesy of the University of New Mexico–Albuquerque, Maxwell Museum of Anthropology #176 and #55; Black skull courtesy of the University of Tennessee, Knoxville, #19-94)

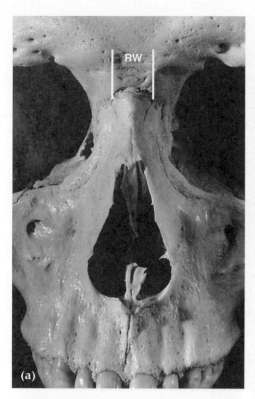

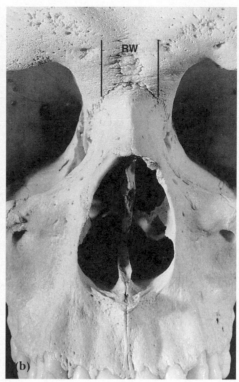

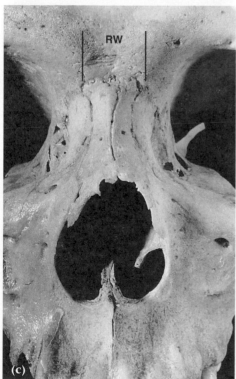

FIGURE 7.4   Front view of the nose in the three main ancestral groups. **(a)** Notice how both the root (RW) and nasal opening are narrow in Whites, with the latter structure forming an isosceles triangle. **(b)** These features are intermediate in Asians. **(c)** In Blacks, the root and opening are wider and the nasal aperture forms a rough equilateral triangle. (Photos by Julie R. Angel; White and Asian skulls courtesy of the University of New Mexico–Albuquerque, Maxwell Museum of Anthropology, #176 and #55; Black skull courtesy of the University of Tennessee, Knoxville, #8-91)

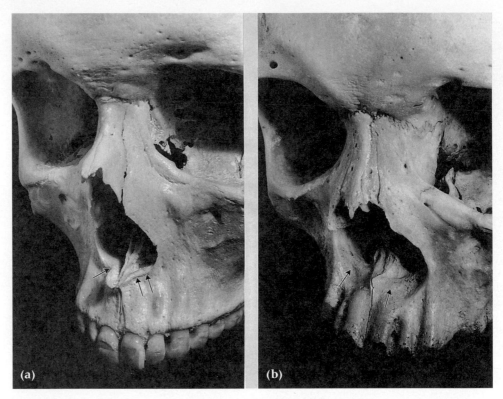

FIGURE 7.5 Variations in the lower border of the nose: **(a)** distinct sill (*arrows*) in Whites; **(b)** indistinct lower border with guttering (*arrows*) on either side of the midline in Blacks.
(Photos by Julie R. Angel; White skull courtesy of the University of New Mexico–Albuquerque, Maxwell Museum of Anthropology, #176; Black skull courtesy of the University of Tennessee, Knoxville, #19-94)

Similarly, the lower border of the nose is distinct in Whites, in many cases forming a sill (Figure 7.5a), while it is less sharp in Asians. In Blacks, this feature can be so indistinct that the floor of the nose merges into the anterior bone of the maxilla, causing a gutter on either side of the midline (Figure 7.5b).

Finally, the nasal opening is wide and shaped like an equilateral triangle in Blacks (Figure 7.4c), while it is a narrow and more of an isosceles triangle in Whites (Figure 7.4a); in Asians, this feature is intermediate (Figure 7.4b).

FACE Several characteristics of the face, other than the nose (see Table 7.2), also can be used to distinguish the three main groups. Of these, the most important is facial profile. Because of the differences in the size of the jaws between the groups, the faces differ by the amount of projection. In Blacks, the face projects forward because the jaws in this group are larger than those of the other two groups. Whites have a more vertical (even receding) face due to their smaller jaws; in Asians the amount of projection is intermediate. This is easiest to visualize by drawing a line connecting the tip of the nasals with the forwardmost point on the upper jaw (lines 3 in Figure 7.3). Notice how the line is slanted forward in Blacks (Figure 7.3c), while it slants backward in Whites (Figure 7.3a). Although the Asian in Figure 7.3b is fairly slanted, this group is usually intermediate for this characteristic.

Another aspect of the face that can be used to differentiate the three groups is its shape. In Whites and Blacks, the face is narrow; in Asians, it is wide. This is easiest to observe by noting that the heights of the faces in Figure 7.1 are approximately the same; however, notice that the width of the Asian is much greater than that of the White. In addition,

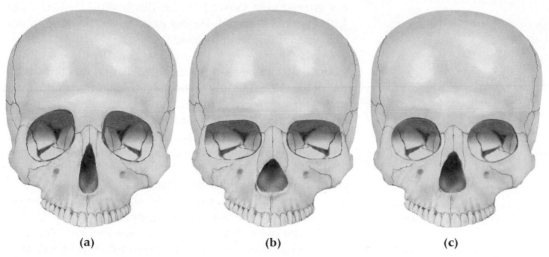

FIGURE 7.6   Different shapes of eye orbits for ancestral groups: **(a)** angular of Whites,
(b) rectangular of Blacks, and **(c)** round of Asians.

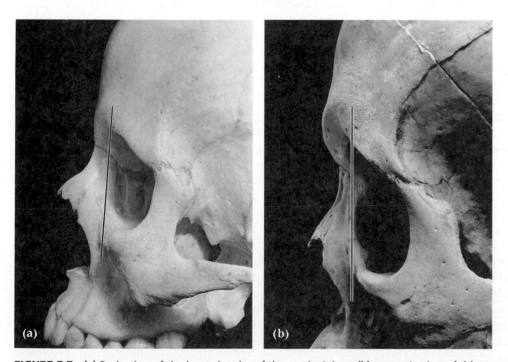

FIGURE 7.7   **(a)** Projection of the lower border of the eye in Asians; **(b)** nonprojection of this structure
in Blacks (Whites not pictured).   (Photos by Julie R. Angel; Asian skull courtesy of the New Mexico, Office of the
Medical Investigator; Black skull courtesy of the University of Tennessee, Knoxville, #19-94)

the shape of the eye orbits also varies among the three main groups. Whites generally manifest angular eye orbits (Figure 7.6a), while those of Blacks are rectangular (Figure 7.6b) and
Asians are round (Figure 7.6c). One last characteristic of the face is useful for distinguishing Asians from the other two groups; this is the projection of the lower border of the eye.
In Asians, this structure projects forward of the upper border when viewed from the side;
however, this border does not project in Whites and Blacks. This is easily seen when a line
is drawn between the upper and lower borders of the eye orbit when the skull is held in the
Frankfort plane (see Figure 7.7). Notice how this line slants forward in Asians (Figure 7.7a),

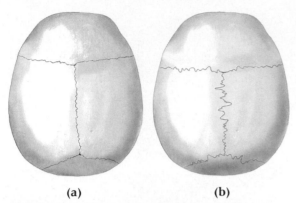

(a)   **(b)**

FIGURE 7.8 Variations in the complexity of cranial vault sutures: **(a)** simple in Whites; **(b)** complex in Asians.

but is relatively vertical in the Black skull (Figure 7.7b). Although not depicted, Whites have a similar configuration as Blacks for this characteristic.

VAULT As can be seen from Table 7.2, several characteristics of the cranial vault can be used to distinguish the three major groups: browridges, muscle markings, sutures, sagittal contour, and postcoronal area. Generally, the browridges and muscle markings of Whites are more pronounced than in either of the other two groups. The skulls of Blacks and especially Asians are not noted for their rugosity and browridge development.

The complexity of the vault sutures also can be used to distinguish the ancestral groups. Generally, Asians exhibit the most complex sutures (see Figure 7.8b), with moderate to pronounced undulations from side to side (sometimes referred to as "tortuous"), while those of Whites and Blacks are more simple (Figure 7.8a). Also, **Wormian bones** (accessory bones in the lambdoid suture) are more common in people of Asian origin (see Chapter 15 for a discussion of these bones).

The last vault characteristic of value is the shape of the area behind bregma. Blacks often are characterized by a slight concavity in this area that is easily seen in profile. However, this area is relatively flat or slightly convex in Whites and Asians. This also affects the sagittal contour of the groups; generally, the vault of Blacks is somewhat flattened when compared to Whites or Asians.

JAWS AND TEETH The size of the jaws and teeth differ between Whites and the other two groups. Often the teeth in Whites are too large for their jaws, causing crowding that is rare in Blacks and Asians. These latter groups have both large teeth and concomitantly large jaws; this is carried to an extreme in Blacks, for whom the maxilla is so large that enough extra bone appears behind the third molar to accommodate another entire tooth. Additionally, the dental arch of the upper jaw differs among the three groups. In Whites, the arch is parabolic (Figure 7.9a), in Blacks it is hyperbolic or U-shaped (Figure 7.9c), and in Asians it is rounded (Figure 7.9b).

Finally, a feature of the teeth can be used to distinguish Asians from the other two groups. This is the **shovel-shaped incisor**, which is formed by raised edges on the lingual side of these teeth (Figure 7.10b). This variation stands in marked contrast to the flat lingual surface of the incisors of other groups (Figure 7.10a). Shoveling is particularly common on the upper central incisors; however, all other anterior teeth (including occasionally the canines) can exhibit this trait, although usually to a lesser degree. In some cases, the ridges can be so well developed that the tooth is barrel shaped; in other cases, the labial side can exhibit raised edges. This trait appears in approximately 90% of Asians and Native Americans, but occurs only in low frequency in Whites and Blacks (i.e., less than 15%).

Joseph Hefner (2009) studied the frequency of a subset of the above traits (in addition to a few not mentioned here) to determine which of them could be considered "characteristic" of an ancestral group. What he discovered is that no one trait is useful for identifying Whites, Blacks, or Asian (including Native American). For example, his data show that there is a 85.4% likelihood that a skull with a "narrow" nose is White, which is a reasonably high probability. However, a skull with a "wide" nose is only 68.7% likely to be Black, which by itself is too low of a probability to be useful. All of the other traits that he explored showed similar results, which led him to state that the

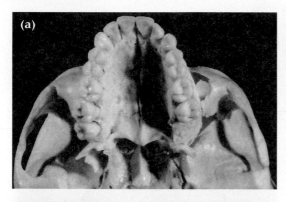

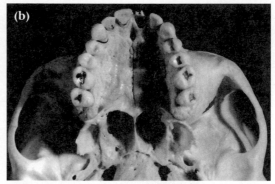

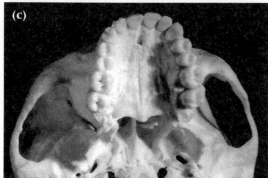

FIGURE 7.9   Variation in the dental arch:
(a) parabolic in Whites; **(b)** rounded in Asians;
(c) hyperbolic (rectangular) in Blacks. (Photo by
Julie R. Angel; specimens courtesy of the New Mexico,
Office of the Medical Investigator)

ability of forensic anthropologists to determine ancestral group was not based on the identification of individual traits within the skull, but by viewing the skull in its entirety.

Postcranial Skeleton

Anthroposcopically, little is known about using the postcranium to assess ancestry. Several bones that have been extensively studied in this context (e.g., pelvis, scapula) yield results that are too variable to be of much value. Also, some groups (e.g., Hispanics) have not been studied at all in this context. Therefore, the use of postcranial bones to distinguish ancestral group is limited.

One bone that has been studied is the femur (Stewart, 1962). Generally, Blacks are characterized by straight femoral shafts (Figure 7.11b). However, with the exception of some Native Americans from South America (see Gilbert , 1976), all Asians and Whites are characterized by femora that exhibit anterior curvature (Figure 7.11a). Similarly, in Blacks and Whites the axis of the head and neck of the femur tends to be horizontal when this bone is laid on a flat surface with its posterior side down. However, among Native Americans, the femur exhibits torsion; that is, the axis of the femoral head and neck has a

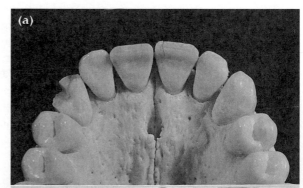

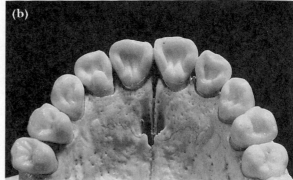

FIGURE 7.10   Variation of the lingual surface of the
incisors: **(a)** spatulate in Whites and Blacks; **(b)** shovel-
shaped incisors in Asians. (Photos by Julie R. Angel; specimens
courtesy of the New Mexico, Office of the Medical Investigator)

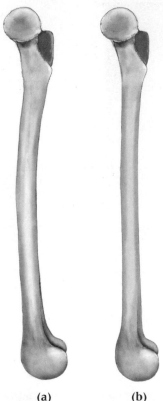

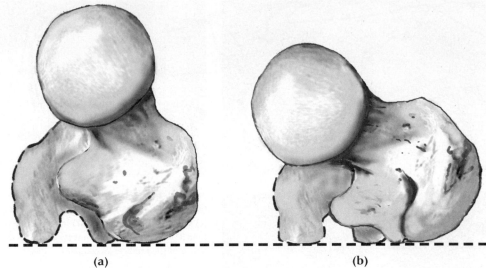

FIGURE 7.12   Torsion in the femoral neck: **(a)** strong torsion typical of Native Americans, **(b)** mild torsion typical of Whites and Blacks. (From Figure 2 of Stewart, 1962)

(a)   **(b)**

FIGURE 7.11   Line drawing of the anterior curvature of the femoral diaphysis: **(a)** curved as in Whites and Asians; **(b)** straight as in Blacks.

tendency to angle up when the posterior side of the bone is laid on a flat surface (Figure 7.12).

The venerable anthropologist Ernest Hooton (1947) lists several other postcranial features that help to distinguish only Blacks from Whites. Blacks are characterized by light and thin postcranial bones with slight muscle markings. Also, the long bones are slender, with small articular heads and joint surfaces. Furthermore, their pelvises have a tendency to be high and narrow; and the lumbar curve of the vertebral column of this group is fairly deep. By contrast, the bones of Whites are heavy, thick, and massive, with large joint surfaces and heavy muscle markings (particularly among males). In addition, the pelvis is wide and rugged, and the lumbar curve is fairly shallow.

METRIC METHODS

Metric methods have been used for distinguishing ancestry since the early part of the 1900s (see Krogman, 1962, for a summary). Although these generally provide a single most probable group for a skeleton of unknown ancestry, the results from metric techniques are deceptive in their apparent accuracy. This is because the distributions of measurements used in these methods are based on samples not necessarily representative of the modern population of the United States. Much of this research is based on the Hamann–Todd and Terry collections as described in Chapter 1, which were accumulated in the midwestern United States in the early and middle parts of the 1900s. Since skeletal changes have been documented over the last 50 years, the usefulness of these collections is diminishing. Also, the measurements are sometimes ambiguous; thus, they are not necessarily easy to take or replicate. Finally, these methods fail most when they are needed most. Because they quantify what is visually observable, it is unlikely that, if ancestry cannot be attributed by anthroposcopy, an unequivocal determination will be made through metric methods.

The general technique in metric methods involves measuring individuals of known ancestry and calculating the distribution of the measured dimensions in the various groups. Thus, measuring the width of the nose in a series of known Whites and

Blacks would reveal the narrow nature of this dimension in the former and its wide character in the latter. Other measurements could be used to quantify the projection of the jaws, the shape of the face, and any other of the features described previously. Measurements such as these are used in three different procedures: direct measurements, indexes, and discriminant functions. Direct measurements involve comparing an unknown specimen with the known values of different groups. As described in Chapter 1, indexes involve dividing one measurement by another (to standardize for size) and multiplying the result by 100 (to calculate a percentage). The distributions of these values then are assessed for the various ancestral groups and the placement of an unknown specimen's index within these distributions determines its ancestry. Discriminant functions are more involved statistical techniques that use multiple measurements to assess ancestry. The application of these methods to the problem of determining ancestry is described next.

Direct Measurements

A femoral measurement that appears able to attribute ancestry has been researched by Emily Craig (1995). She studied the angle of the intercondlyar shelf of the distal femur on over 400 Black and White individuals of either sex. This feature is formed by the angle between the roof of the intercondylar notch and the long axis of that bone (see Figure 7.13). When x-rayed, the shelf appears as a radiopaque line on radiographs. Its angle with the femoral axis is easily measured using a simple protractor after a line is drawn parallel to the long axis of the bone with a grease pencil. Craig showed Whites had a higher angle than Blacks, with the sectioning point between the two being 141° (i.e., values higher than 141° are more likely White, while angles below that are more likely Black). Since only 18% of the sample overlapped for this feature, there is an over 80% chance that ancestral group will be correctly attributed from this trait. However, since the distribution of this feature is known only for Blacks and Whites, this method should be used only when there is good evidence that an unknown decedent is from one of these ancestral groups. Also, Gregory Berg and colleagues (2007) found considerable inter- and intra-observer error when testing this method, indicating a need for a more refined measurement technique that will reduce these types of errors.

Indexes

In the past, indexes figured prominently in the attribution of ancestry. Although there were a number of these, their usefulness was limited by a fairly high failure rate. Also, with the increased availability of computers, they were superseded by the more complex and usually more accurate discriminant functions. However, some indexes have withstood the test of time.

George Gill and B. Miles Gilbert (1990) describe three indexes of the nose that distinguish Whites from both Blacks and Native Americans; these are the maxillofrontal, zygoorbital, and alpha indexes. Each of these employs two measurements, width (Figure 7.14a) and height (Figure 7.14b). The widths are taken at three different locations on the face, and the heights are taken as the least forward projection of the nasals from the line drawn across the two width points. Both widths and heights need to be taken with a special kind of sliding caliper called a **simometer** (see Figure 7.15).

Once taken, the height is divided by the width and multiplied by 100 to calculate the percentage. (In Figure 7.14, height 1 is divided by width 1,

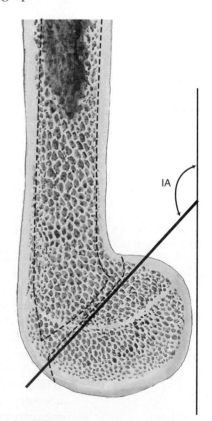

FIGURE 7.13 Intercondylar shelf at the distal femur. Shelf angle with long axis of bone (IA) can be used to attribute ancestral group. (From Figure 1 of Craig, 1995. Copyright ASTM International. Reprinted with permission)

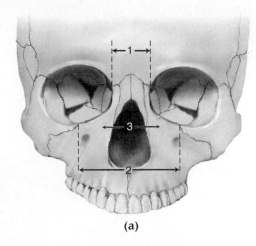

(a)

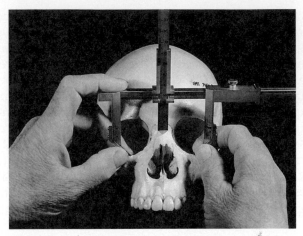

FIGURE 7.15 Simometer used to take measurements in Figure 7.14. (Photo by Julie R. Angel)

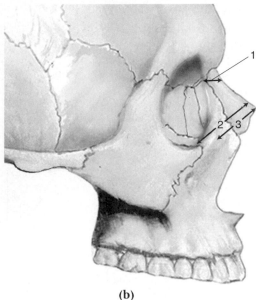

(b)

FIGURE 7.14 Six measurements of the nose: **(a)** three widths; **(b)** three heights.

height 2 by width 2, and height 3 by width 3.) This percentage then is compared with the known distribution of the index within each of the three groups to determine the most likely affiliation. Figure 7.16 displays these distributions of the three indexes for several hundred Whites and Blacks, as well as for Whites and Native Americans. In these graphs, the height of the bars represents the number of individuals; thus, there are a small number of Whites with a maxillofrontal index of 65, while there are a larger number with index values from 40 to 47. Notice that the majority of Whites have index values falling to the right of the vertical dotted line, whereas values falling to the left of that line are more likely to be Black or Native American. Considering that these indexes measure the proportion of nasal projection and that Whites have the greatest projection of these three groups (see Table 7.2), this finding is not surprising. Tests of Gill's method indicate an accuracy of 80% or more (Gill and Gilbert, 1990; Curran, 1990).

As an example of how these indexes would be used, suppose that the distance across the points labeled 1 in Figure 7.14a in a skull is 13 mm and the forward projection (line 1 in Figure 7.14b) is 7 mm. The maxillofrontal index would be 53.8%. This value falls above the dotted line in the graph in Figure 7.16, indicating that the individual measured is most likely to be White. Similarly, a skull yielding values of 20 and 6 mm would have a value of 30%, which is well within the range of the maxillofrontal index for Blacks and Native Americans.

A number of researchers (Gilbert and Gill, 1990; Gill and Rhine, 1990; Wescott, 2005) use the shape of the femur immediately distal to the lesser trochanter to attribute ancestry. These authors use the anterior–posterior (A–P) and medial–lateral (M–L) measurements from this area as a means of quantifying the observation that Native American femurs are flatter front-to-back than Blacks and Whites (i.e., the femoral shaft is more round in these latter groups). These measurements can be combined into the Platymeric index (PI), which is given by the following formula:

$$PI = (A - P)/(M - L) \times 100$$

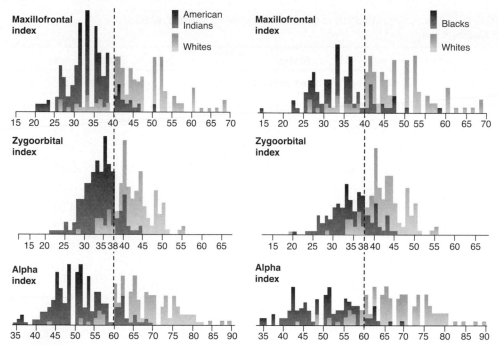

FIGURE 7.16 Graph of indices for Whites, Blacks, and Native Americans. (Reprinted with permission from George W. Gill)

The midpoint of this index is 84.3 (Daniel Wescott, personal communication) so that values below this point are more likely Native American, while values above are White or Black (the latter two groups cannot be distinguished from each other using this method).

Discriminant Functions

With their pioneering article, Eugene Giles and Orville Elliot (1962) popularized the use of discriminant functions to assess ancestry on the basis of cranial measurements. Unlike indexes, this statistical procedure uses any number of measurements to distinguish two or more predetermined groups. Thus, these authors employed nine measurements to distinguish Whites and Blacks from the Terry Collection and Native Americans from the prehistoric site of Indian Knoll. Since their original article, research has shown that the Terry sample is not necessarily representative of modern peoples in the present-day United States. Thus, the Forensic Data Bank is continuing to gather data to improve on their original work (see Chapter 1).

The discriminant functions that can be used to distinguish the three ancestral groups are presented in Table 7.3. The measurements listed in the first column are illustrated in Figures 7.17 and 7.18. Several points must be made about these formulas. First, notice that the functions are divided by sex within each group, because Giles and Elliot determined that discrimination occurred best when sex was known. (This is an exception to an earlier statement that ancestry needs to be assessed before sex.) Second, the formulas for Native Americans are based on prehistoric skulls from Indian Knoll, which are not necessarily representative of Asians in general; consequently, these have been shown to be less valuable than formulas for distinguishing Whites from Blacks. Last, the sectioning point is used to separate Whites from either of the other two groups; values below these points represent this group while values

TABLE 7.3 Discriminant Functions for Distinguishing Whites, Blacks, and Native Americans[1]

| | Males | | Females | |
| | Whites versus: | | Whites versus: | |
Cranial Measurement	Blacks	Native Americans	Blacks	Native Americans
BaPr	3.06	0.10	1.74	3.05
Maximum length (ML)	1.60	−0.25	1.28	−1.04
Maximum breadth (MB)	−1.90	−1.56	−1.18	−5.41
BaBr	−1.79	0.73	−0.14	4.29
BaNa	−4.41	−0.29	−2.34	−4.02
Bizygomatic Br (BB)	−0.10	1.75	0.38	5.62
NaPr	2.59	−0.16	−0.01	−1.00
Nasal breadth (NB)	10.56	−0.88	2.45	−2.19
Sectioning points	62.89[2]	22.28	92.20	130.10

[1]After Table 26 of Ubelaker (1999). Courtesy of Taraxacum Press.
[2]From text on page 121 of Ubelaker (1999).

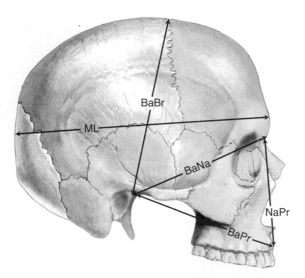

FIGURE 7.17 Measurements used in the calculation of discriminant functions.

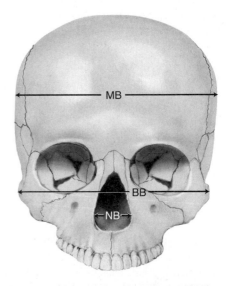

FIGURE 7.18 Measurements used in the calculation of discriminant functions.

above represent Black or Native American, whichever is appropriate (see Giles and Elliot, 1962).

As an example of how to use these functions, consider the following situation. The skull of a male is measured for the dimensions presented in Table 7.3. These are entered in the formula for Whites versus Blacks (column 1 of Table 7.3) and calculated as such:

$$
\begin{aligned}
\text{Value} &= 3.06(87) + 1.6(178) - 1.9(155) - 1.79(142) - 4.41(102) - 0.1(120) \\
&\quad + 2.59(109) + 10.56(20) \\
&= 266.2 + 284.8 - 294.5 - 254.2 - 449.8 - 12 + 282.3 + 211.2 \\
&= 34.8
\end{aligned}
$$

Because the person falls below the sectioning point for these two ancestral groups (i.e., 62.89), the skull probably represents a White person. However, to ensure that the person is not Native American, the formulas in column 2 of Table 7.3 are applied with the following results:

$$
\begin{aligned}
\text{Value} &= 0.1(87) - 0.25(178) - 1.56(140) + 0.73(142) - 0.29(102) \\
&\quad + 1.75(120) - 0.16(109) - 0.88(20) \\
&= 8.7 - 44.5 - 218.4 + 103.66 - 29.58 + 210 - 17.44 - 17.6 \\
&= -5.16
\end{aligned}
$$

Because this value also falls below the sectioning point separating Whites from Native Americans (i.e., 22.28), the assessment of this person as White is supported further.

Table 7.4 contains the rules for determining ancestral group from the results of both formulas for all possible outcomes. Notice if both formulas indicate White, as in the example above, then White is the group to which the individual should be assigned. However, if the White versus Black formula indicates White while the White versus Native American formula indicates Native American, then the individual should be assigned to the latter group (i.e., Native American). The reverse is true if the White versus Native American formula indicates White but the other formula indicates Black; in these cases Black group association is indicated. The only difficulty arises when both formulas do not indicate White. In these cases, males must be considered differently from females because the sectioning points between the ancestral groups are different between the sexes. For males, if the result of the White versus Black formula is greater than 3.99 times the value of the White versus Native American formula, then the individual should be assigned Black, otherwise the person is Native American. In females, if the result of the White versus Native American formula is greater than 37.9 added to the value of the White versus Black formula, then the individual should be assigned Native American, otherwise the person is Black. As an example, suppose for the above formulas, the values were 102.3 and 35.7, respectively. Since neither are below the sectioning points, ancestral group is Native American, because 102.3 is less than 3.99×35.7 (=142.4).

TABLE 7.4   Rules for the Application of Discriminant Functions

Result of White versus Black	Result of White versus Native American	Ancestral Group
Males		
White	White	White
White	Native American	Native American
Black	White	Black
Black	Native American	Black if W − B>(3.99 × W − NA) else Native American
Females		
White	White	White
White	Native American	Native American
Black	White	Black
Black	Native American	Native American if W − NA>(37.9 + W − B) else Black

Over the years, data has been accumulating in the Forensic Data Bank (see Chapter 1) that has been used to calculate new discriminant functions for assessing ancestry. These new functions, which are part of FORDISC, calculate most ancestral groups with great accuracy. (FORDISC is available for purchase by contacting the Department of Anthropology at the University of Tennessee, Knoxville.) However, using these newer data, the author noted an accuracy of only around 60% for the above formulas, which is a considerable drop from the 80% to 95% reported by Giles and Elliot. Similar disheartening results were obtained by Katherine Spradley and colleagues (2008) who used the Forensic Data Bank to calculate discriminant functions for attributing ancestry to Hispanics. Their findings indicate that, given the samples currently available, this group could not be determined with any great accuracy using this statistical procedure.

Discriminant functions can be used for a variety of other skeletal measurements. For example, the following formula from the previously described PI can be used to determine ancestral group:

$$F = 0.139 \times (PI) - 11.738$$

The sectioning point for this function is zero (0), with positive values indicating White or Black and negative values Native American. Wescott (personal communication) has said that this function correctly identifies ancestral group 76.9% of the time and that the flattened shape of the proximal Native American femur appears by 5 years of age (Wescott, 2006). Unfortunately, this index is of little value in attributing ancestry to Hispanic femora (see Wescott, 2005 and Spradley et al., 2008).

Other discriminant functions have been calculated for measurements of both the lengths and breadths of the long bones, and measurements of the pelvis and foot bones. Although an accuracy of close to 90% and above is stated for these functions, they are based on small sample sizes. Also, they involve measurements that are too complex to describe here.

MISCELLANEOUS ANCESTRAL CHARACTERISTICS

Although Table 7.2 presents the most useful anthroposcopic characteristics for distinguishing the three main ancestral groups, a number of other traits also can lend weight to this assessment (a complete set of these are presented by Rhine, 1990b). For example, Asians have a more vertically oriented ascending ramus of the mandible than the other two groups. Also, the chins of Whites (Figure 7.19a) are more pointed, those of Blacks are blunted (Figure 7.19b), and those of Asians are more rounded (Figure 7.19c). Finally, extensions of the enamel beyond the molar crown onto the neck are more

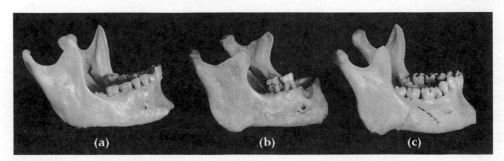

FIGURE 7.19 Side view of mandibles: **(a)** pointed chin of Whites, **(b)** the blunt chin of Blacks, and **(c)** the rounded chin of Asians. (Photo by Julie R. Angel)

BOX 7.2
Ancestry of a "Trophy" Skull

Michael Charney (1974) describes a case in which a single ossicle helped to assess the ancestry of a skull. The ossicle, called *os japonicum,* is formed when the zygomatic bone separates into two segments (see Figure 15.18a). Because of its prevalence in Japanese skulls, its presence can help refine an attribution of ancestry, as shown by the following:

Dr. Alice Brues of the Faculty of Anthropology, University of Colorado, Boulder, tells of a fascinating case (all are interesting; some more so than others) when she was Professor of Anatomy at the University of Oklahoma Medical School. The police brought her a skull in a paper bag. It had been found in an attic by new tenants of the house. The *owner* of the skull had obviously been *done in,* as evidenced by a large, irregular hole on the side, a hole with sharp, jagged edges. Dr. Brues had already determined that the skull was Mongoloid, and then noticed the extra malar sutures. A Japanese skull? It all fell into place; there could be but one explanation, admittedly a bit crude and unusual.

[T]he skull was a *trophy* of the fighting in Guadalcanal. Killed and allowed to lie where he fell, the body of the Japanese soldier was soon reduced to skeleton by the jungle. A Leatherneck or G. I. took it home as a souvenir. The family moved and his wife put her foot down—"That bloody head is NOT going with us!" So it was put in a paper sack and left in the attic to be found, with suitable gasps and gulps, by the new tenants.*

---

*From Michael Charney, Chapter 13, in C. G. Wilbur, *Forensic Biology for the Law Enforcement Officer,* 1974, p. 310. Courtesy of Charles C. Thomas Publisher, Ltd., Springfield, IL.

common in Asians than in Whites and Blacks. Although this is only a partial list, knowledge that miscellaneous characteristics do exist is essential to forensic anthropologists, because it can never be predicted when they will be needed to assist in an identification (see Box 7.2 for an example).

Another structure that can be used (cautiously) to help assess ancestry is hair. Brues (1977) describes the well-known differences in hair form and color between the three main groups. In Whites, it is straight to slightly wavy with dark to light color (e.g., blond or red). Blacks have a naturally curled (and in some cases tightly curled) form and black or dark brown color. In Asians (including Native Americans and Hispanics), hair is black (with occasional red highlights), coarse, and straight (i.e., little or no wave). One characteristic of hair that makes it particularly useful to forensic anthropology is its resilience. This structure does not easily break down either when buried or on the surface (although birds may use it for nesting material). Thus, the presence of hair may provide valuable additional information concerning the ancestry of decedents. However, extreme caution must be exercised because of cultural practices. For example, many persons of Black ancestry remove the curl from their hair, giving it a straight or slight wavy appearance. In addition, dyeing hair is not uncommon in all ancestral groups, particularly in females.

The last trait to consider is skin color. Although one of the major characteristics for attributing ancestry in life (Coon, 1969; Brues, 1977), this feature is not particularly useful for those individuals usually examined by forensic anthropologists. For the most part, skin exposed to air turns a dark color that would obscure any light coloration seen in life. In addition, dark skin will bleach white if lying on damp ground for any length of time. Thus, unless a body is fairly fresh, skin color is of very limited value in estimating ancestry.

Summary

1. When possible, forensic anthropologists should provide an assessment of ancestry from skeletal remains. When attributing this demographic characteristic, the categories of White, Black, Asian, Native American, and Hispanic should be used, because these are the categories utilized by most law enforcement agencies.

2. The skull exhibits the greatest number of traits that can be used in discerning the ancestry of an individual.

3. Generally, Whites are distinguished from others by their narrow noses that project forward from the plane of the eye, prominent nasal spine, narrow face, and angular eye orbits.

4. Blacks are distinguished by their wide and low nasal bones, wide nasal aperture, large jaws and teeth that cause a forward projection of the face, and rectangular eye orbits.

5. Asians are distinguished by their nonprojecting nose, flat face formed by forward projecting cheekbones, round eye orbits, shovel-shaped incisors, and complex cranial sutures.

6. Only a limited number of characteristics of the postcranial skeleton can be used to assess ancestral group.

7. Three facial indexes have proved to be of value in distinguishing Whites from Blacks and Native Americans.

8. A number of discriminant functions can be used to assess ancestry based on metric measurements of a human skull.

9. If present, hair can be used to distinguish ancestry on the basis of its form and color.

10. Skin color is of little utility in forensic cases because of its propensity to change hue when exposed to sun or moisture.

Exercises

1. Suppose that a skull is brought in for analysis that manifests a projecting nasal root and bridge with a prominent nasal spine and sharp lower border. Additionally, the face is nonprojecting, while the muscle markings are heavy and the browridges are large. The police believe that it is from a Black woman who recently disappeared from the area in which it was found. Does this seem likely? If not, why not? If so, why?

2. A skull exhibiting a wide nose with guttered lower border is found in the same area as the skull described in Exercise 1. It has a projecting face with rectangular eye orbits and a depression behind bregma. Could this be from the missing Black woman?

3. Suppose that a skull is brought in for analysis that manifests a projecting nasal root and bridge, but wide nasal opening and guttered lower border of the nose. In which ancestral group would you place this skull and why?

4. A femur, found outside a small New Mexico town, exhibiting strong anterior curvature is believed to be that of a Native American who has been missing from the area. Is it likely that this bone could belong to that person? Why?

5. Measurements from a skull entered into the Giles and Elliot formulas for males result in a value of 52 and 15. What is the most likely ancestral group of the individual represented by this cranium? If the nose exhibits a large nasal spine and sharp lower border, would this change your decision?

6. A skull is found with an even number of Black and White characteristics. In addition, a small amount of hair is tightly curled and dark brown in color. What is the most likely ancestral group of this person and why?

7. Several long bones are brought in for analysis. They are large, with heavy muscle markings and large articular surfaces. The police believe that they belong to a missing Native American from the area. Is it possible to confirm or deny their suspicion from these bones? How would you proceed?

8. A lower and upper jaw are discovered and brought in for analysis. The teeth are large, the dental arcade is gently curved, and the incisors manifest shoveling. Could these remains belong to a White person who has been missing from the area? If so, why? If not, why not?

9. A skull is brought in with a narrow nose and nonprojecting root and bridge. The cheekbones are prominent, the incisors are shovel shaped, and vault sutures are simple. What is the most likely group that this individual would have been classified in life and why?

10. Remains are brought in for analysis with a small amount of black skin and curly brown hair. The nose is wide and nonprojecting, and the skull has simple sutures, with small muscle markings and browridges. The police believe that the remains are from a Black person missing from the area. Could they be right? If so, why? If not, why not?

8

Attribution of Sex

The attribution of sex is another demographic feature needed by law enforcement officials when searching their missing persons' files. Methods for identifying this characteristic in skeletal remains are based on the two primary biological differences between male and female: size and architecture. A casual observance of men and women reveals that males on the average are larger and more strongly built than females. This difference has been widely stated to be approximately 8%; that is, on the average females are about 92% the size of males. This basic difference leads to male skeletons that are more robust, taller, wider, and more rugged than those of females. Architectural differences also distinguish the sexes. Since females carry and give birth to children, their pelvises are designed to accommodate the passage of infants. Thus, these structures are wider than those of males of comparable size. Concomitantly, the pelvic differences require different angles among other bones, such as those that make up the elbow (angled to prevent hitting the arm on the pelvis while walking) and knee (the femur angles inward more on females than males so that the knees are still under the body).

The above discussion indicates that sexing can be done on human bones by knowing how to interpret size and architectural differences. Data from forensic anthropologists (Krogman, 1962; Stewart, 1979; Krogman and Iscan, 1986) report 90% to 100% accuracy in assessing this trait when using the entire skeleton. However, with only the pelvis, this accuracy drops to 90% to 95%, and, with only the skull, an accuracy of only 80% to 90% is reported. Finally, with only long bones, an accuracy of only 80% has been noted. Knowledge of these differences in probability helps forensic anthropologists to untangle conflicting information when confronted with a skeleton displaying both male and female traits (see Box 8.1 for an example).

This chapter details the means by which the sexes are differentiated using the skeleton. Because the sex of subadults is not easily distinguished (the primary sexual differences have not yet appeared), the first three sections deal with determining this demographic characteristic on adults. Thus, the anthroposcopic and metric characteristics of the adult pelvis are described first because this structure contains the most amount of information for this task. Next, visual and metric methods for sexing from the skull are discussed, and in the following section miscellaneous methods for determining sex from various postcranial bones are presented. Finally, in the last section the thorny issue of sexing subadults is discussed.

SEXING THE PELVIS

The pelvis contains the greatest number of characteristics useful for determining sex because it is the part of the skeleton that is most affected by birthing. As described in Chapter 2, this structure is composed of three bones: right and left os coxa and the sacrum. Similarly, each os

BOX 8.1
Male and Female Characteristics in a Skeleton

Stan Rhine (1998) describes the case of a decomposed body that arrived for his analysis that manifested conflicting information on sex. Luckily, he remembered the accuracies afforded the various parts of the skeleton, which helped him to interpret the enigmatic data presented by the case. His description follows:

> The body in question was received in an advanced state of decomposition, the circumstances suggesting that the person had left a western New Mexico bar after a somewhat longer than advisable stay. The individual's physical abilities being somewhat impaired by spirituous excess, the reveler must have stumbled into an arroyo and lapsed into a sleep that proved to be permanent…
>
> At autopsy the sex was not immediately obvious, due to the decomposed state of the body. However, those in attendance took the very short hair, the flannel shirt, Levi's, and work boots as a reasonable indication that the body was male. Hence the consternation when, upon removing the shirt, the pathologists found a bra. This confusion was compounded by the jockey shorts that popped into view as the Levi's were stripped off…
>
> The skull proved to be heavily built and thick, with a large browridge and showing prominent markings indicating the origin and insertion of large muscles. This is what one would expect to see on a male skull. Nevertheless, the pelvis was very clearly female. Anthropologists have contended that the probability of making the correct assessment of sex from the skull alone is only about 90%. The pelvis is generally less enigmatic and delivers its secret with less reluctance, rendering a correct reading about 95% of the time… There are many traits that betray the truth to the observant, but the tighter genetic control of the pelvis makes it more trustworthy than the skull for determination of sex. This initially puzzling decomposed body was female."*

*From S. Rhine, *Bone Voyage,* University of New Mexico Press, Albuquerque, 1998, pp. 77–78, with permission.

coxa is composed of three bones (the ilium, ischium, and pubis) that fuse sometime after the twelfth year of life. By viewing the configuration of these bones, the pelvis can be sexed anthroposcopically. Similarly, by measuring various dimensions of this structure, male pelvises can be distinguished from those of females.

Anthroposcopic Traits

Table 8.1, modified from information provided in Krogman (1962), presents the classic attributes of the pelvis that distinguish males from females. As with any anthroposcopically identifiable characteristic, these traits show a large amount of variation. For example, although the pelvis is larger and more rugged in males than females, there exist an almost infinite number of gradations between the extremes in size of this structure. Within this continuum, although males are more often found at the high end and females at the low end, there is considerable overlap between the pelvises of lightly built males and strongly built females. Thus, although the following discussion will focus on the stereotypic differences between the sexes, it must be remembered that this determination often is not as easy as described and, as with all other aspects of skeletal analysis, it requires much practice to perfect.

In addition to size differences, a number of variations in shape can be used to distinguish the sexes. As illustrated in Figure 8.1, the male pelvis is taller and narrower than the shorter and wider female. This is caused by the more vertical orientation of the ilium in the former as opposed to the flatter, less vertical orientation of these bones in females. In addition, the **pelvic inlet** (the area enclosed by the os coxae and sacrum when viewed superiorly) is heart shaped in males, but more oval in females (see

TABLE 8.1   Classic Traits of the Male Versus Female Pelvis[1]

Trait	Males	Females
Size	Large and rugged	Small and gracile
Ilium	High and vertical	Low and flat
Pelvic inlet	Heart shaped	Circular or elliptical
Pubic shape	Narrow and rectangular	Broad and square
Subpubic angle	V-shaped	U-shaped
Obturator foramen	Large and ovoid	Small and triangular
Greater sciatic notch	Narrow	Wide
Preauricular sulcus	Rare	Well developed
Shape of sacrum	Long and narrow	Short and broad

[1]After Table 37 of Krogman (1962).

Figure 8.2). The wider configuration in females is almost certainly attributable to the need for greater space when giving birth.

In addition to overall differences, individual bones and features of the pelvis differentiate the sexes. Starting with the pubic bone, two characteristics can help in this matter: shape and subpubic angle. The shape differences are illustrated by Figure 8.1a; notice that a box drawn adjacent to the edges of this bone would form a rectangle in males, while it is more square in females. Also, notice that the female pubis appears "stretched" by comparison to the male, as though the bone were made of rubber and pulled away from the rest of the pelvis. The sex differences in the **subpubic angle** are illustrated in Figure 8.1; notice how the male angle (Figure 8.1b) is V-shaped and less than 90°, while it is more rounded (said by some to be U-shaped) in females (Figure 8.1a). In addition, lines drawn adjacent to the medial parts of the female pubic bones form an angle over 90°. This configuration also appears to be directly related to child-bearing, in that it allows more space for the head of infants during birth.

Along with the pubis, other individual bones and structures differentiate the sexes. Differences in the shape of the obturator foramen (the opening encircled by the ilium, ischium, and pubis) are visible in Figure 8.1. In males, it is oval in outline or assumes the configuration of a flattened isosceles triangle (see Figure 8.1b, particularly

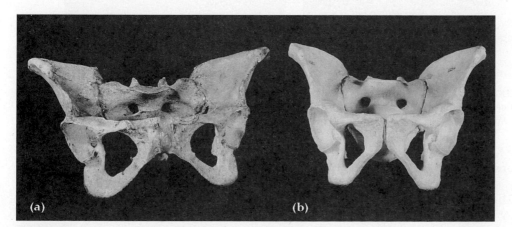

FIGURE 8.1   (a) Female and **(b)** male pelvis showing wider and lower construction of female over the male. (Photo by Julie R. Angel; female pelvis courtesy of the University of New Mexico, Osteology Lab, specimen #51)

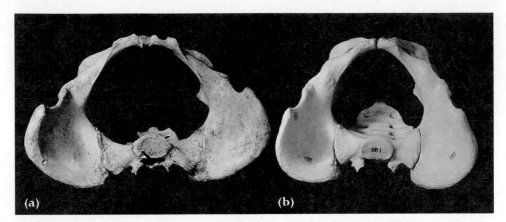

FIGURE 8.2 Top view of male and female pelvis showing the pelvic inlet: **(a)** oval in females; **(b)** heart-shaped in males. (Photo by Julie R. Angel; female pelvis courtesy of the University of New Mexico, Osteology Lab, specimen #51)

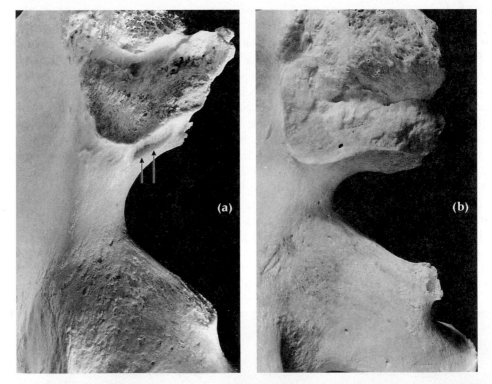

FIGURE 8.3 Variations of the greater sciatic notch: **(a)** wide in females; **(b)** narrow in males. Notice the preauricular sulcus (*arrows*) in the female. (Photos by Julie R. Angel; specimens courtesy of the University of New Mexico–Albuquerque, Maxwell Museum of Anthropology, #51 and #6)

the foramen on the reader's left), while its shape in females is more of an equilateral triangle (see Figure 8.1a, particularly the one on the reader's left). Using fourier analysis as a means of describing these shapes objectively, Guillaume Bierry and colleagues (2010) showed that this feature can be used to arrive at a correct sex determination 84.6% of the time (at least in their sample of 104 known sex individuals).

Another feature that differs between the sexes is the greater sciatic notch, which varies in a manner similar to that of the subpubic angle. Female notches are wide and spacious (Figure 8.3a), while males exhibit narrow, constricted notches (Figure 8.3b).

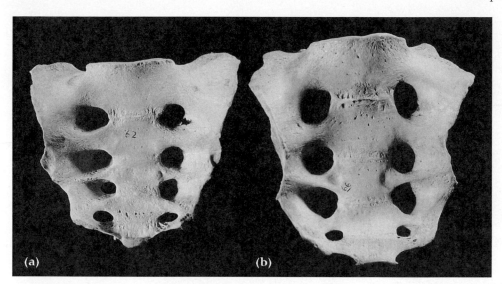

FIGURE 8.4   Variation in the shape of the sacrum: **(a)** short and broad in females; **(b)** long and narrow in males. Although both bones are approximately the same width, the right bone is 25% longer than the left.   (Photo by Julie R. Angel; specimens courtesy of the University of New Mexico–Albuquerque, Maxwell Museum of Anthropology, #66 and #62)

Similarly, the preauricular sulcus is wide and well developed in females (see arrows in Figure 8.3a), while it is narrow or absent in males. Finally, Figure 8.4 illustrates the differences between the shape of the sacrum in the sexes; males have longer and narrower bones (Figure 8.4b), while those of females are wider and shorter (Figure 8.4a). In addition, the male sacrum is more evenly curved when viewed laterally, while in females this bone often exhibits a marked angle between segments two and three.

In addition to the classic traits of the entire pelvis, T. W. Phenice (1969) observed three characteristics of the pubic bone that he claimed were over 95% accurate in differentiating males from females. Phenice stated that the method requires little training, making it easier to use than the classical traits. Although some have challenged his published accuracy (MacLaughlin and Bruce, 1990), others have shown that his method is both sound and highly accurate (Lovell, 1989; Sutherland and Suchey, 1991; Ubelaker and Volk, 2002). The three characteristics are described in Table 8.2 and the first two are illustrated in Figure 8.5. Figure 8.5a depicts the manifestation of the **ventral arc** in females (arrow 1); notice how this raised ridge of bone gently curves from the superior-medial corner of the anterior pubis, down and laterally, to where it merges into the inferior part (called the **ramus**) of this bone. This gentle curve leaves the inferior-medial corner of the pubis untouched by the ventral arc (see arrow 2 in Figure 8.5a). In males, this structure is small to nonexistent (left bone in Figure 8.5a); when present, it follows

TABLE 8.2   The Three Traits of Phenice for Sexing the Pelvis[1]

Ventral arc	Ridge of bone beginning at the superior-medial corner on the anterior surface of the pubis and curving down to the ischiopubic ramus
Subpubic concavity	Concavity of ischiopubic ramus starting below the pubic faces; best viewed from posterior side
Medial aspect of the ischiopubic ramus	Area of the medial part of the ischiopubic ramus just below the pubic face

[1]After Phenice (1969).

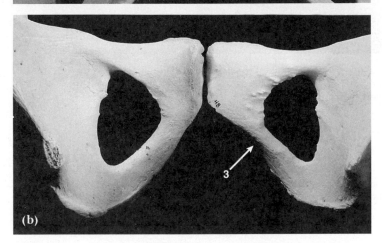

FIGURE 8.5 Male versus female expression of two of Phenice's three characteristics: **(a)** the ventral arc (*arrow 1*) in females (notice large triangular area medial to that structure; *arrow 2*); **(b)** subpubic concavity in females (*arrow 3*). Both of these structures are absent or less distinct in males. (Photos by Julie R. Angel; specimens courtesy of the University of New Mexico–Albuquerque, Maxwell Museum of Anthropology, #148, #66, #69, and #48)

the edge of the pubic bone so closely that it occupies the inferior-medial corner of the pubis. The ventral arc is visible in females as young as 14 years (called a precursor arc), but most easily recognized in women from the mid-twenties on (Sutherland and Suchey, 1991).

The second structure observed by Phenice is the subpubic concavity of the **ischiopubic ramus.** This structure is composed of the lower parts of the pubis and ischium, where it forms the subpubic angle discussed previously. In females, the ramus is concave (i.e., curves superiorly), while it is straight or slightly convex in males. This is easiest to see from the posterior surface (see Figure 8.5b), where the eversion of the sub-pubic bone does not obscure the configuration of this feature. Finally, the medial edge of the pubic bone just below the pubic face is relatively wide and dull in males, while it is narrow and sharp in females. This latter trait is considered to be the least reliable of the three characteristics.

Two studies have attempted to determine the accuracy of the classic traits of the pelvis for attributing sex. Tracy Rogers and Shelley Saunders (1994) studied 17 traits of the pelvises (all of those from Tables 8.1 and 8.2, as well as others) of 49 known sex

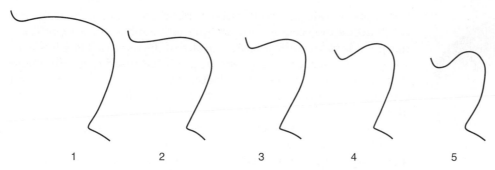

FIGURE 8.6   Variations in the size of the sciatic notch: **(1)** female, **(2)** indeterminate, **(3)** and **(4)** probable male, and **(5)** male. (From Figure 2 of Buikstra, J. E., Ubelaker, D. H. [1994] *Standards for Data Collection from Human Skeletal Remains,* Fayetteville, AR: Arkansas Archeological Survey Research Series 44; with permission.)

individuals from a 19th-century Canadian cemetery. Their data indicate that the individual traits in Tables 8.1 and 8.2 could be used to attribute sex with varying degrees of accuracy, from a low of 80% to a high of 93.8%. They also found that all traits had intra-observer error rates below 10%, except the preauricular sulcus and the medial aspect of the ischiopubic ramus. Genesse Listi and Elizabeth Bassett (2006) studied 876 left os coxae from American Whites and Blacks, whose sex was known at death. They chose eight traits of the 12 traits listed in Tables 8.1 and 8.2 and found an overall accuracy rate between 95% and 96% and a near-zero inter-observer error rate. Both of these studies indicate that the classic traits of the pelvis can be used with great accuracy to attribute the sex of an individual.

Unfortunately, the preceding discussion masks the variability of these pelvic traits. By way of demonstrating this, Figure 8.6 illustrates variations in the form of the sciatic notch that can be seen in the os coxa. Phillip Walker (2005) studied the probability of correct sex identification using this scale of variation on almost 300 known sex individuals of White and Black ancestry. His data show that a pelvis with a wide notch (i.e., category 1) is 88% likely to be female, while scores greater than 2 are 91% likely to be male. In addition, his study revealed that inter- and intra-observer errors occurred mainly in the intermediate categories, especially between 2 and 3, while there was near perfect agreement between and within observers for notches placed in category 1. Since all of the traits presented in Table 8.1 vary in a manner similar to that of the greater sciatic notch, each of them need to be studied in a manner similar to this structure to increase the precision of accuracy statistics, which would bring anthroposcopic pelvic traits closer to the requirements of *Daubert*.

Metric Methods

Because of the difficulty in measuring this bone, there are few methods for distinguishing males and females from metric dimensions of the pelvis. The only technique that has wide acceptance is the **ischium–pubic index**, popularized by Sherwood Washburn (1948, 1949). This index was developed as a way of quantifying the longer, more stretched character of the pubic bone in females when compared to males.

Although the ischium–pubic index is fairly accurate for determining sex, the two measurements needed for its calculation can be difficult to obtain. Figure 8.7 illustrates the method for taking these measurements. The base point inside the acetabulum (hip socket) is the place where the ilium, ischium, and pubis fuse. Although difficult to see,

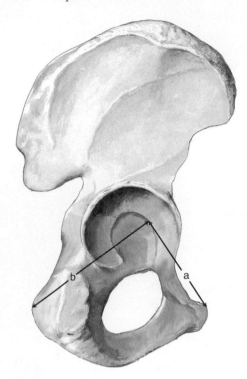

FIGURE 8.7 Two measurements used for the ischiopubic index: length of the pubis (*line a*), length of the ischium (*line b*).

this point is represented either by a raised area, an irregularity, or a notch inside the acetabulum. An alternative method for identifying this point is to view the internal surface of the os coxa. Here it is usually easy to observe a scar where the pubis has fused to the ilium and ischium (see Figure 8.8). By placing the thumb on this area and pinching the bone with the index finger, the point inside the acetabulum can be obtained. The two measurements then can be taken by holding the tip of a sliding caliper on this point in the hip socket and swinging it first to the end of the pubic bone (line a in Figure 8.7) and then to the bottom of the ischium (line b in Figure 8.7). The index is obtained by dividing the pubic length by the ischium length and multiplying by 100 to obtain a percentage.

The distribution of this index has been determined on over 500 skeletons in the Terry Collection (100 White males, 100 White females, 150 Black males, and 150 Black females). If ancestral group is not known, index values below 84% are in the male range, while values above 94% are in the female range. The area of overlap represents approximately 32% of the sample; therefore, this method is likely to be correct only around 68% of the time. However, if ancestral group is known, accuracy increases. For Whites, values under 91% are male, while any index over 95% is female; the area of overlap encompassed 9% of the sample, giving this technique a 91% accuracy. Finally, in Blacks, values under 83% are male, while indexes over 88% are female. In this ancestral group, the area of overlap encompasses 17% of the sample (83% accuracy).

Since this work, there has been considerable research into the value of pelvic measurements (either by themselves or in conjunction with other postcranial bones) in attributing sex. All of these are too complex for a book of this nature.

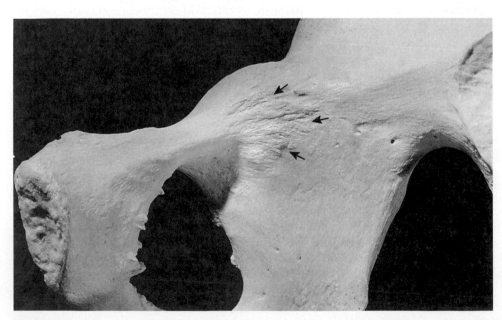

FIGURE 8.8 Scar (*arrows*) from the fusion of the pubis to the ilium and ischium, seen on the medial side of the os coxa. (Photo by Julie R. Angel; specimen courtesy of the University of New Mexico–Albuquerque, Maxwell Museum of Anthropology, #58)

However, the interested reader should consult the works of John Albanese and colleagues (2003, 2008), who developed methods with very high accuracy rates and low inter-observer error rates.

SEXING THE SKULL

The skull is the second most useful structure for determining sex. Unfortunately, some of the characteristics helpful in this decision vary among ancestral groups. For example, generally, females have higher foreheads than males; however, males from Asian populations are more likely to manifest this feature than White males. Similarly, on the average, female skulls are smaller than males, but the skulls of males from Asian populations are closer to White females in size than to White males. Complications such as these make it advisable to assess race before attempting sex.

As with the pelvis, the skull can be sexed either anthroposcopically or metrically. However, because the skull is less useful than the pelvis for this task, the expression of visually identifiable traits that distinguish males from females exhibits more overlap. Thus, proper assignment of sex for this structure requires more experience than when using the pelvis. Also, the accuracy of the metric methods has been questioned recently (due to the realization that the samples on which they are based may not reflect modern populations), making assessment of sex from measurements more doubtful. These points must be kept in mind when reading the following sections.

Anthroposcopic Traits

Table 8.3 presents the visual traits, given by Wilton Krogman (1962) and Diane France (1998), by which male skulls are distinguished from female. The most basic difference, well illustrated in Figure 8.9, is size and rugosity; notice the larger and more rugged appearance of the male (Figure 8.9a) when compared with the smaller and more gracile female (Figure 8.9b). After overall size and roughness, the mastoid process is the next most favored trait for determining the sexes. The arrows in Figure 8.9 show the typical male mastoid process as being larger and more projecting than the female. Another characteristic of value involves the frontal bone (forehead). This bone is more sloping, with larger browridges, in the males (Figure 8.10a) when compared with the more vertical and smaller browridged female (Figure 8.10b). A fourth feature of value is the **nuchal** area of the occipital (the area where the neck muscles attach to this bone); the more rugged appearance and pronounced protuberances in the male (Figure 8.11a) contrast with the smoother appearance of this area in females (Figure 8.11b). Although not

TABLE 8.3   Characteristics of Male and Female Skulls[1]

Traits	Males	Females
Size	Large and rugged	Small and smooth
Mastoid	Large, projecting	Small, nonprojecting
Browridges	Large	Small, none
Frontal	Slanted	High, rounded
Nuchal area	Rugged with hook	Smooth, hook uncommon
Supraorbital margin	Rounded	Sharp
Chin	Broad	Pointed

[1]Summarized from Krogman (1962) and France (1998).

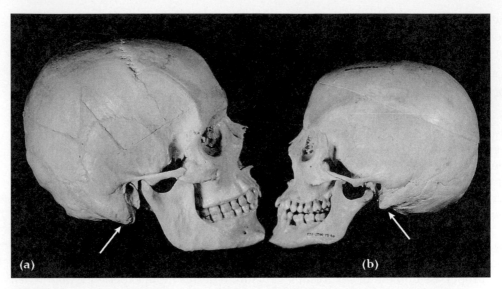

FIGURE 8.9 Lateral view of **(a)** male and **(b)** female skulls showing basic size and rugosity differences. Notice the larger mastoid process in the male as opposed to the female (*arrows*). Both skulls bear autopsy scars. (Photo by Julie R. Angel; specimens courtesy of the University of New Mexico–Albuquerque, Maxwell Museum of Anthropology, #176 and #29)

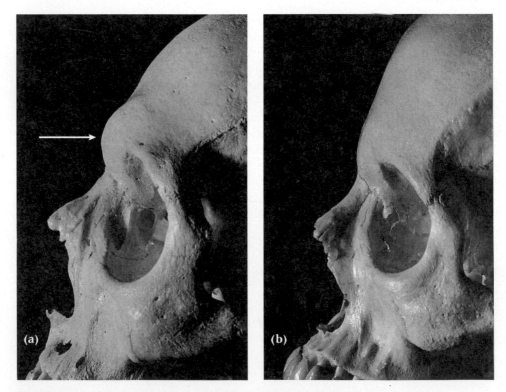

FIGURE 8.10 Differences in the frontal: **(a)** slanted with large browridges (*arrow*) in males; **(b)** high and rounded without browridges in females. (Photos by Julie R. Angel; specimens courtesy of the University of New Mexico–Albuquerque, Maxwell Museum of Anthropology, #6 and #29)

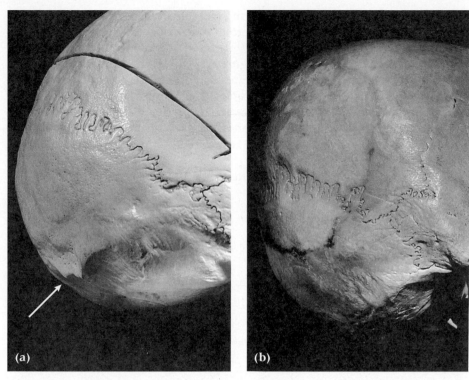

FIGURE 8.11   The nuchal area in males and females: **(a)** rugged with inion hook (*arrow*) in males; **(b)** smooth in females without hook. The male specimen has an autopsy cut.
(Photos by Julie R. Angel; male courtesy of the University of New Mexico–Albuquerque, Maxwell Museum of Anthropology, #97; female courtesy of the New Mexico Office of the Medical Investigator)

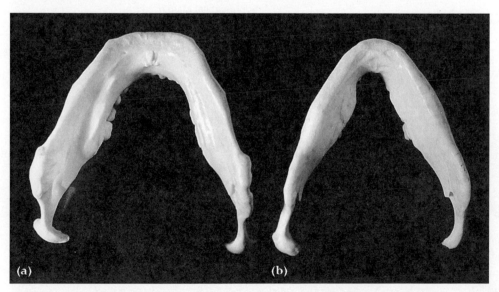

FIGURE 8.12   The chin viewed from below: **(a)** broad in males; **(b)** narrow in females.
(Photo by Julie R. Angel; specimens courtesy of the University of New Mexico–Albuquerque, Maxwell Museum of Anthropology, #17 and #29)

pictured, the superior-lateral corners of the eye orbits also are of value, with males having relatively rounded margins, while this is sharp in females. Finally, males are characterized by broad and almost square chins, as seen from below (see Figure 8.12a), while this structure in females is more pointed (see Figure 8.12b).

Although these characteristics may seem straightforward, the descriptions in Table 8.3 mask variability in a manner similar to that described for the pelvis. For this reason, Jane Buikstra and Doublas Ubelaker (1994) present drawings that help to show the variation within each of these traits (see Figure 8.13). In their scheme, traits that appear as category 1 would be classified as female, while those category 5 as male. Categories 2 and 4 would be probable female and male, respectively, while category 3 would be considered indeterminate. Of the characteristics listed, only the mental eminence needs explanation. This is an anterior protrusion in the chin region that can be best seen by holding the mandible by the chin using the forefinger and thumb of both

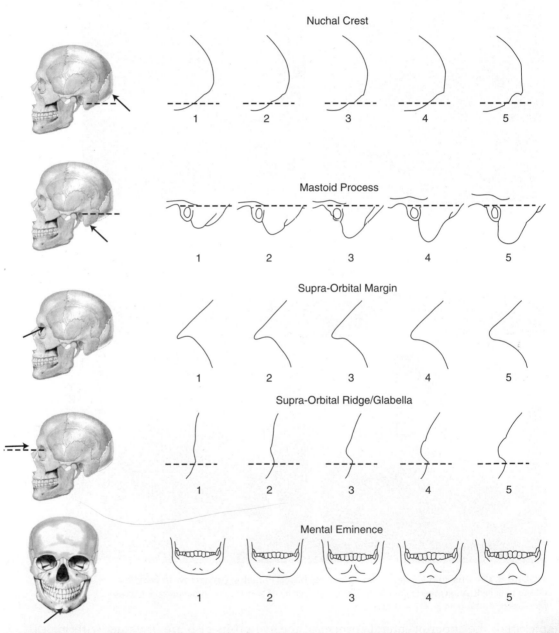

FIGURE 8.13   Variations on cranial characteristics used to attribute sex: **(1)** female, **(2)** probable female, **(3)** indeterminate, **(4)** probable male, and **(5)** male. (From Figure 4 of Buikstra, J. E., Ubelaker, D. H. [1994] *Standards for Data Collection from Human Skeletal Remains.* Fayetteville, AR: Arkansas Archeological Survey Research Series, 44; with permission.)

TABLE 8.4 Logistic Discriminant Functions for Predicting Sex of Skulls[1]	
Modern Populations	**% Correctly Classified**
Y = 9.128 − 1.375(Glabella) − 1.185(Mastoid) − 1.151(Mental)	87.4
Y = 7.434 − 1.568(Glabella) − 1.459(Mastoid)	84.2
Y = 7.372 − 1.525(Glabella) − 1.485(Mental)	84.4
Y = 7.382 − 1,629(Mental) − 1.415(Mastoid)	81.8
Y = 6.018 − 1.007(Orbital Margin) − 1.850(Mental)	78.0
Y = 5.329 − 0.7(Nuchal) − 1.559(Mastoid)	79.9
Native Americans	
Y = 3.414 − 0.499(Orbital Margin) − 0.606(Mental)	78.0
Y = 4.765 − 0.576(Mental) − 1.136(Mastoid)	73.4
Y = 5.025 − 0.797(Glabella) − 1.085(Mastoid)	76.2

[1]From Table 9 of Walker (2008).

hands. If there is little or no projection between the thumbs, a category of 1 is assigned while a projection that encompasses most of the chin region would receive a category 5.

The value of these traits for determining sex has been tested by Phillip Walker (2008). He assigned a score for each of the five traits on a total of 304 individuals of known sex, age, and population affinity (European American, African American, English) at death. In addition, he scored almost 150 prehistoric Native Americans from California whose sex could be determined from accompanying pelves. Although he did not find significant age differences, population differences in the expression of traits were obtained between the sexes. He used a type of discriminant function (see Chapter 1 for discussion of this statistical technique) called logistic discriminant function as a way of combining the trait scores for the determination of sex. His equations are presented in Table 8.4; the top half contains equations for the modern groups while the bottom half contains equations for Native Americans. Values derived from the equations that are less than zero should be considered male while those over zero are female.

As an example of how these can be used, suppose a fragmented skull from a European American is found and that a score of "2" is assigned to Glabella and "1" to the Mastoid Process. The second formula in Table 8.4 can be used to calculate sex in the following manner:

$$Y = 7.434 − 1.568(2) − 1.459(1) = 7.434 − 3.136 − 1.459 = 2.839$$

Since the value is over 0, then there is an 84.2% likelihood that the skull comes from a female. The other formulas can be used in a like manner when more than two cranial traits can be scored.

Metric Methods

In 1963, Eugene Giles and Orville Elliot followed their article using discriminant functions to estimate ancestral group with another article using this statistical method to assess sex (Giles and Elliot, 1963). Using the measurements of over 400 skulls from the Terry and Hamann–Todd collections, the authors demonstrated that sex could be determined correctly around 85% of the time by taking 11 measurements of the skull.

TABLE 8.5   Definition of Measurements Used in Cranial Discriminant Functions[1]

Identifier	Definition
ML	Maximum length of the skull (Figure 8.14)
MB	Maximum breadth of the skull above the supramastoid crest (Figure 8.15)
BaBr	Basion to bregma (Figure 8.14)
BaNa	Basion to nasion (Figure 8.14)
BB	Maximum width across the zygomatic arches (Figure 8.15)
BaPr	Basion to prosthion (Figure 8.16)
NaAl	Nasion to lowest point on the alveolar border between the central incisors (Figure 8.14)
PB	Maximum breadth of the palate (Figure 8.16)
LM	Length of the mastoid process while orienting the skull in the Frankfort plane; place the upper arm of the caliper in line with the upper border of the external auditory meatus, while the lower arm is brought in line with the lowest point on the process while holding the caliper vertically (Figure 8.17)

[1]After Appendix to Giles (1970).

Although further study has shown less accuracy when applying these functions to modern populations, their method still is considered sound and their equations are widely used.

Table 8.5 presents descriptions of the measurements that Giles and Elliot found effective in determining sex from the crania; and Figures 8.14, 8.15, and 8.16 present a graphical representation of these dimensions. As can be seen, most measurements are straight distances between two points. However, the last measurement requires further explanation. This dimension is an attempt to estimate the height of the mastoid process, which is a good visual indicator of sex. Unfortunately, the points used cannot be touched directly by the tips of the sliding caliper. Instead, the instrument is placed alongside the skull, and its jaws are adjusted as in Figure 8.17 while the cranium is held

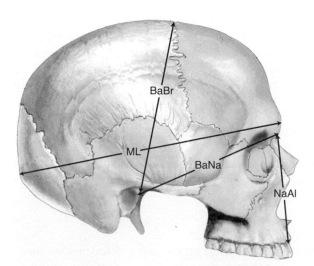

FIGURE 8.14   Lateral view of the skull showing measurements used in discriminant functions.

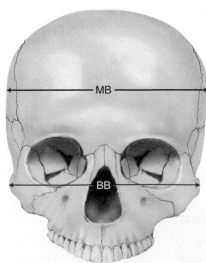

FIGURE 8.15   Anterior view of the skull showing measurements used in discriminant functions.

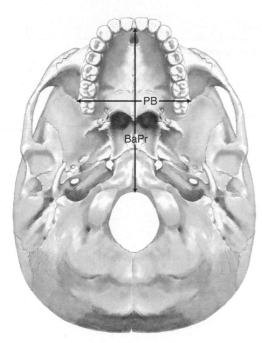

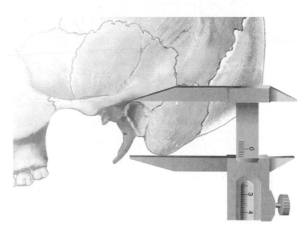

FIGURE 8.17   Method for measuring the length of the mastoid process (LM). (From Figure 2, Sex determination by discriminant function analysis of crania, Giles and Elliot, 1963, *American Journal of Physical Anthropology.* Reprinted by permission of Wiley-Liss, Inc., a subsidiary of John Wiley & Sons, Inc.)

FIGURE 8.16   Basal view of the skull showing measurements used in discriminant functions.

in the Frankfort plane (see Chapter 2). Unfortunately, this measurement is prone to considerable error in the hands of inexperienced persons.

Once taken, these dimensions are entered into the discriminant functions presented in Tables 8.6, 8.7, and 8.8 for White, Black, and Asian skulls, respectively. Three points should be made about these equations. First, notice that the functions use different sets of measurements. This is to accommodate incomplete crania, a situation not unknown in forensic anthropology. Thus, function 4, which does not include dimensions of the braincase, is usable with cranial remains represented only by the face. Conversely, function 3 uses only dimensions of the braincase to determine sex. Second, the percentages of correct classification using these formulas are not as high as those attained through anthroposcopy by experienced forensic anthropologists. Although this seems to reduce the value of this method, discriminant functions enjoy wide popularity because they require less training to apply properly. Third, the percentages of correct classification were determined from the samples on which these equations were calculated. Because it is becoming increasingly apparent that the skeletons from the Terry and Hamann–Todd collections from which these functions were derived do not adequately represent modern populations, the classification rate with forensic cases usually is lower than the published rates. However, there is reason to believe that the loss in accuracy is not that great. The author used three of these formulas (one from each ancestral group) on data from the Forensic Database, and found only a small decrease in the percentage of individuals correctly sexed. Thus, it FORDISC is not available, forensic anthropologists can use the above formulas and be reasonably confident in their resultant classification.

MISCELLANEOUS METHODS

In addition to the pelvis and skull, a number of other bones have been studied for their usability in attributing sex (Stewart, 1979). Earliest research centered on the sternum, clavicle, and humerus without much success (but see the following section on the

TABLE 8.6 Discriminant Functions for Determining Sex of White Crania[1]

Measurement	Discriminant Function Number					
	1	2	3	4	5	6
ML	3.107	3.400	1.800		1.236	9.875
MB	−4.643	−3.833	−1.783		−1.000	
BaBr	5.786	5.433	2.767			
BaNa		−0.167	−0.100	10.714		7.062
BB	14.821	12.200	6.300	16.381	3.291	19.062
BaPr	1.000	−0.100		−1.000		−1.000
NaAl	2.714	2.200		4.333		4.375
PB	−5.179			−6.571		
LM	6.071	5.367	2.833	14.810	1.528	
Section point	2672.39	2592.32	1296.20	3348.27	536.93	5066.69
Percent correct	86.6	86.4	86.4	84.5	85.5	84.9

[1]Taken from Table LI in Giles (1970), functions 1 through 6. Values above sectioning points indicate male.

TABLE 8.7 Discriminant Functions for Determining Sex of Black Crania[1]

Measurement	Discriminant Function Number					
	7	8	9	10	11	12
ML	9.222	3.895	3.533		2.111	2.867
MB	7.000	3.632	1.667		1.000	
BaBr	1.000	1.000	0.867			
BaNa		−2.053	0.100	1.000		−0.100
BB	31.111	12.947	8.700	19.389	4.936	12.367
BaPr	5.889	1.368		2.778		−0.233
NaAl	20.222	8.158		11.778		6.900
PB	−30.556			−14.333		
LM	47.111	19.947	14.367	23.667	8.037	
Section point	8171.53	4079.12	2515.91	3461.46	1387.72	2568.97
Percent correct	87.6	86.6	86.5	87.5	85.3	85.0

[1]Taken from Table LI in Giles (1970), functions 7 through 12. Values above sectioning points indicate male.

humerus for an exception). Similarly, early attempts to differentiate males from females based on anthroposcopic characteristics of postcranial bones other than the skull and pelvis were unsuccessful. This leaves a number of methods that use either a single dimension of a bone (e.g., the height of the scapula) or a number of measurements that are combined in discriminant functions. Generally, all these methods use the size differences between the sexes to arrive at a determination of male or female and can be useful when remains are incomplete or as supporting data for the methods previously described.

TABLE 8.8   Discriminant Functions for
Determining Sex of Asian Crania[1]

Measurement	Discriminant Function Number	
	13	14
ML	1.000	1.000
MB	−0.062	0.221
BaBr	1.865	
BB	1.257	1.095
NaAl		0.504
Sectioning point	579.96	380.84
Percent correct	86.4	83.1

[1]Taken from Table LI of Giles (1970) for Japanese, functions
13 and 14. Values above sectioning points indicate male.

Multiple Postcranial Bones

Starting in the 1950s, discriminant functions and regression equations for determining sex from postcranial bones (including the pelvis) were developed by numerous researchers. Virtually all long bones, the pelvis, foot bones, some vertebrae, and even sternal rib ends have been measured for this purpose. Much of this research produced methods for different ancestral groups (especially White and Black). In addition, most of these studies show that sex determination from multiple postcranial bones yields a higher probability of accuracy than sex determination from the skull. (The reason for this phenomenon might be that cranial measurements may be confounded by traits indicative of ancestral group differences more so than measurements of the postcranium.) Unfortunately, because of the large amount of research published in this area, these functions will not be discussed further; interested readers should consult Giles (1970) and Bennett (1993) for summaries of these functions.

Scapula

The scapula has been studied by several researchers over time and has been shown to be of some value in attributing sex. Stewart (1979) studied 50 males and 40 females by taking two measurements: maximum length (actually height) of the scapula and height of the glenoid fossa. The maximum height of the bone is measured between the superior and inferior borders (Figure 8.18a), with values less than 14 cm indicating female, while values of 17 cm and above indicate males. Measurements falling in between these two numbers cannot be used to distinguish the sexes without resorting to methods not covered in a book of this nature. These cutoff points were mostly confirmed by Gretchen Dabbs (2009), who studied 495 males and 308 females of White and Black ancestry. Although she feels strongly that this dimension should not be used to determine sex, her data show that 141 of 149 (94.6%) scapulas with a height less than 14 cm are female, and all scapulas greater than 17 cm are male. Thus, if this is the only bone available for analysis and its height falls above or below one of these cutoff points, sex can be determined with considerable accuracy. The second dimension that can be used is the height of the glenoid cavity (Figure 8.18b). Although there is some overlap between the sexes, measurements above 36 mm generally are male (due to the larger size of the humeral head),

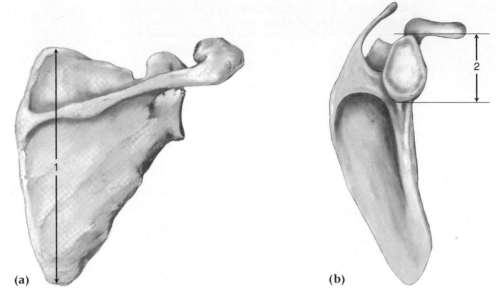

(a)   (b)

FIGURE 8.18   Measurements of the scapula used to estimate sex: **(a)** height of the scapula (*line 1*); **(b)** height of the glenoid cavity (*line 2*).

while those below are female. (For a more complex method that uses discriminant functions to attribute sex from this bone, see Dabbs and Moore-Jansen, 2010).

Humerus

T. Dale Stewart (1979) has shown that one measurement on the humerus that is particularly good for differentiating males from females is the vertical head diameter (Figure 8.19). This value varies from below 43 to over 55 mm, with females having a greater probability of coming from the lower end of the range. Using information on this measurement, the sex of humeri can be determined from the vertical head diameter in the following manner. Values below 43 mm almost certainly represent a female, while measurements from 43 to 44 are probably of a female. Measurements from 46 to 47 are probably male, while measurements over 47 mm are almost certainly male. Information from a study by Katherine Spradley and colleagues (2008) indicates that this measurement does not discriminate Hispanic males and females. However, since their research was based on a small sample (n=44), this result may change in the future.

Radius

Emily Berrizbeeitia (1989) has shown that two measurements on the head of the radius, the maximum and minimum diameters as shown in Figure 8.20, are particularly good for differentiating males from females. The values for these measurements vary from 13 to 30 mm, with females having a greater probability of coming from the lower end of the range. Radii that have a maximum diameter of 21 mm or under are likely to be female, whereas male diameters are greater than or equal to 24 mm. For the minimum diameters, these values are 20 mm and 23 mm. Interestingly, when the measurements from both sides are used in tandem, the accuracy of the attribution of sex increases from around 92% to approximately 96%. Although it is tempting to consider measurements of the radius to be the most accurate of all the postcranial bones, it must be remembered that

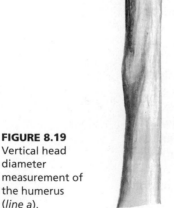

FIGURE 8.19
Vertical head diameter measurement of the humerus (*line a*).

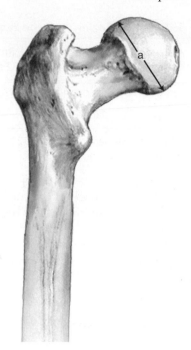

FIGURE 8.20 Measurement of the radial head. The maximum diameter is the greatest value of distance "a" when rotating the radius 360°. The minimum diameter is the least value of "a" when the bone is rotated.

FIGURE 8.21 Measurement of the femoral head (*line a*) used to attribute sex.

these standards were developed on Blacks and Whites in the Terry Collection; thus, the accuracy would not be this high with modern populations.

Femur

As pointed out by William Bass (1995), the femur is one of the more studied postcranial bones, with much of this research centering on its utility in sexing. T. Dale Stewart (1979) summarizes the information on the best single measurement, the head diameter (Figure 8.21), for the different sexes in Whites, while Bass (1995) cites information on this distance in Blacks. The results from both of these authors are summarized in Table 8.9. As can be seen, the differences due to sex between the ancestral groups are relatively minor, with Black females appearing somewhat smaller than White females. For example, a femoral head of over 47.5 mm would indicate almost certain male, whether White or Black. Conversely, a measurement less than 40 mm would indicate female, irrespective of ancestry. Again, the results of Spradley et al. (2008) indicate that this measurement is not particularly useful for determining sex of femora from Hispanics.

SEXING SUBADULTS

Methods for determining sex on the osteological remains of subadults have a long history, frequently filled with hope, but usually ending in discouragement. Because most differences in shape and size emerge at puberty, it has been problematic to sex individuals who do not fully express the adult characteristics described previously. This is despite the fact that methods for determining sex in infants and children have an accuracy of 70% or more. Most forensic anthropologists prefer not to provide this demographic characteristic on subadults because of the possibility of misleading investigators. They feel that the 30% probability of error is likely to be ignored by law enforcement officials in their search of missing persons files.

TABLE 8.9 Sexing from the Femoral Head Diameter[1]

Ancestral Group	Female	Probable Female	Indeterminate Sex	Probable Male	Male
White[1]	Under 42.5	42.5–43.5	43.5–46.5	46.5–47.5	Over 47.5
Black[2]	Under 40	40–43	43–44	44–47	Over 47

[1]From data in Stewart (1979), page 120.
[2]From data in Bass (1995), Table 3-30.

Although none of the methods has high accuracy, several features have received considerable attention in this regard. First, sex differences in the auricular surface of the ilium have been researched. In females, this structure is more likely to be raised above the plane of the rest of the bone, while in males it is not raised. Second, the configuration of the greater sciatic notch has been considered; although not as distinct as in adults, subadults vary in a similar manner in the shape of this feature. Finally, there are several miscellaneous methods.

Auricular Surface

Researchers (Weaver, 1980; Mittler and Sheridan, 1992; Sutter, 2003) of the auricular surface of subadults have determined that sex differences exist for this structure. Generally, females exhibit surfaces with the entire edge of the surface raised above the plane of the ilium, while males display surfaces with all or some of the surface edges in line with this plane (Figure 8.22). The subadults used in this research were of mixed ancestry and

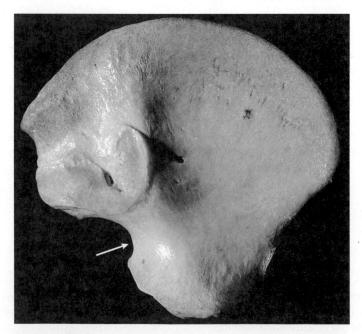

FIGURE 8.22 Ilium of a subadult male. Notice that the auricular surface is not raised above the plane of the bone except on the anterior edge; this surface on females is raised along its entire perimeter. Notice the greater sciatic notch (*arrow*). (Photo by Julie R. Angel; specimen courtesy of the University of New Mexico–Albuquerque, Maxwell Museum of Anthropology, #1)

TABLE 8.10 Percentages of Elevated Versus Nonelevated Auricular Surfaces in Subadults Separated by Sex[1]

	Elevated	Nonelevated
Male	27.4	72.2
Female	72.6	27.8

[1]Combined from data given by Weaver, 1980; Mittler and Sheridan, 1992; and Sutter, 2003.

known sex; and although they ranged in age from the sixth fetal month to around 18 years, the majority (83%) were less than 10 years old at the time of death. Percentages calculated from data combined from the studies cited are presented in Table 8.10. Notice that there is a slightly better than 70% chance that the presence of an elevated auricular surface indicates female and that a nonelevated surface indicates male. Although these percentages are well above the 50% probability expected by chance, they are not so impressive as to persuade the majority of forensic anthropologists that this characteristic should be used regularly.

Greater Sciatic Notch

Three studies, each using different methods, have explored the utility of the depth of the greater sciatic notch (see arrow, Figure 8.22) to determine sex. Barbara Boucher (1957) found that the depth of this feature had some utility in determining this demographic characteristic. Using a sample of children of known age and sex from different ancestral groups, the value of an index relating the depth of the notch to its width could be used to correctly determine sex anywhere from 57.8% to as high as 95.1% of the time. (The accuracy varied depending on the ancestral group represented by the sample.) However, a second study by David Weaver (1980), using ilia of known sex and age from a sample of 153 fetuses and infants of mixed ancestry, found no relationship between sex and the value of an index relating the depth of the notch to its width. Finally, H. Schutkowski (1993) and Richard Sutter (2003) showed that anthroposcopic evaluation of this structure as "deep" would yield a correct determination of sex as male approximately 83.3% of the time. Conversely, an evaluation of "shallow" would yield a correct determination of female around 76.5% of the time. From these studies, it can be seen that the depth of the greater sciatic notch holds some promise for being able to determine sex in subadults. However, a standard method for using this structure that gives accurate results has not been developed as of this writing.

Other Methods

One method, proposed by Edward E. Hunt and I. Gleiser (1955), that held promise for distinguishing the sex of subadults involved comparing dental age with skeletal age. Because the skeletons of boys mature more slowly than those of girls, differences between ages derived from various skeletal structures (see Chapter 9, for a description of these techniques) were more likely to indicate male than female. The Hunt and Gleiser method involved comparing age derived from dental development or eruption with skeletal maturation derived from ossification of wrist bones. Unfortunately, although teeth usually are available in forensic situations, the difficulty in finding all the bones of the wrist from skeletonized remains renders this method relatively unusable in forensic anthropology.

Another promising technique for determining sex of subadults used measurements of the deciduous dentition. Since the teeth of boys generally are larger than those of girls, two studies attempted to develop discriminant functions from tooth widths and lengths to determine sex. Unfortunately, the results were mixed. The study of T. K. Black (1978) yielded functions that discriminated sex correctly only 64% to 68% of the time. However, the study of Carol De Vito and Shelley Saunders (1990) was more promising in that it generated formulas that were correct 76% to 90% of the time. Unfortunately, these latter authors note that their sample is biased, in that it showed the greatest difference between male and female deciduous dental measurements when compared with six other sample groups. Thus, it is not surprising that their functions, which are based on tooth size differences, performed so well. Considering this information, the use of deciduous dental measurements to determine the sex of subadults probably is not warranted as of this writing.

One last study that deserves mention is that of Laura Wilson and colleagues (2008), who used Eigenshape analysis to discriminate sex on 25 ilia of known sexed individuals from a late historic cemetery in England. They found that the shape of the greater sciatic notch could correctly identify sex 96% of the time, while auricular surface morphology was correct 84% of the time. Although these results are very promising, the sample size is too small and too narrow (e.g., "White" children) to definitively state that their method has solved the problem of sexing subadults. However, further study may well show that this method has great utility for sex discrimination in all ancestral groups.

Summary

1. Because males generally are larger and more robust than females, the skeletons of the sexes can be distinguished by simply observing size and rugosity.
2. There are a number of shape characteristics of the female pelvis, related to childbirth, that differentiate it from the pelvis of males.
3. The ischium–pubic index, which quantifies the longer pubic bone of females when compared to males, is the only commonly used metric method for distinguishing the sexes from the pelvis.
4. The skulls of males generally are larger and more rugged, with larger mastoid processes and browridges, than the skulls of females.
5. A number of metric measurements of the skull can be used with discriminant functions to differentiate the sexes.
6. A number of measurements of the postcranial bones can be used to separate males from females.
7. Generally, methods for sexing individuals under 18 years of age are not accurate enough to be usable in forensic situations.

Exercises

1. An assemblage of bones is brought in for analysis. If both the skull and pelvis, as well as the bones of the lower limbs, are present, which should be used to determine sex anthroposcopically and why?
2. Using the decision table method of Chapter 1, determine the sex of a pelvis with the following characteristics: wide subpubic angle, ovoid obturator foramen, wide greater sciatic notch, deep and wide preauricular sulcus, high and vertical ilium, and wide sacrum.
3. Suppose that the pubic bone of Exercise 2 displays a prominent and curving ventral arc, a deep subpubic concavity, and a wide medial border. Does this change the determination of sex? If so, why? If not, why not?
4. A braincase is found without any facial bones below the frontal. If the mastoids are large, the nuchal area smooth, and the frontal sloping with large browridges, what is the most likely sex of this individual? Why?

5. A pelvis is found with an ischial length of 7.9 cm and a pubic length of 6.0 cm. Calculate the ischium–pubic index. What is the most likely sex of this individual? If the ancestral group is known to be White for this person, does this change your decision?

6. If a female-looking skull is found with the pelvis in Exercise 5, does this change the sex designation? If so, why? If not, why not?

7. A Black skull is found with the following measurements: cranial length = 175 mm, cranial width = 125 mm, bizygomatic width = 128 mm, mastoid length = 26 mm, and basion–bregma =130 mm. What is the most likely sex of this individual?

8. An assemblage of bones yields the following measurements: height of the scapula = 13.8 cm, glenoid fossa height = 34 mm, vertical head diameter of humerus = 41 mm, and ischium–pubic index = 72. What is the most likely sex of this individual?

9. The head of a humerus, which has a vertical head diameter of 45 mm, is brought in for analysis. Considering the information provided in this chapter, would it be advisable to provide law enforcement officials an estimate as to sex? Why or why not?

9

Estimation of Age at Death

The estimation of age at death is the third demographic characteristic that aids law enforcement officials in narrowing their search of missing persons files for a match with human remains. Although roughly determinable from fully fleshed bodies using amount of skin wrinkling and hair graying, in the absence of written documentation, the most reliable methods for determining age at death from the human body rely on bone changes. As seen in Chapter 2, bones are not static during life but constantly changing, albeit slowly and in tiny increments. Since these alterations follow a rough schedule, observance of characteristics known to change through time can be used to determine the age at death of deceased (and of living) persons.

Methods for determining age at death can be divided into those that are based on the growing skeleton and dentition, and those based on the deteriorating skeleton. The first, which deal with events such as ossification and fusion, are applicable to subadults, from fetuses to older adolescents and even young adults. These yield relatively accurate estimates of age, usually in the range of 1 to 3 years. However, starting in the time period between 18 and 25 years of age, the skeleton finishes maturation and begins a process of slow deterioration that continues throughout adulthood. Estimates of age based on these changes are not as accurate or as easy to apply as are those for subadults. Thus, this chapter is divided into two main sections. The first deals with assigning age to the skeletons of persons approximately 18 years of age or younger using features of the growing skeleton and dentition. The second section deals with methods for estimating the age of adults from the deterioration associated with aging in the skeleton.

SUBADULTS

The growth of the human skeleton is a complex process that is not understood fully. Available information indicates that bones form within cartilaginous precursors by the deposition of calcium salts. This occurs initially in multiple areas, called primary and secondary areas of ossification, which eventually grow together forming larger segments (e.g., diaphyses, epiphyses). When these areas of ossification unite, bone growth proceeds in earnest. Long bones grow to their adult length by deposition of osseous material at their ends under the epiphyseal caps. At a mostly genetically predetermined time, the epiphyses fuse to the diaphyses (at the metaphyses), causing growth to cease. Other bones grow by apposition over all surfaces (e.g., those of the wrist and ankles), while the skull grows along the edges of its bones at the suture lines.

BOX 9.1
The Estimation of Age of an Adolescent Female

Anthony Perzigian and Paul Jolly (1984) present a case in which multiple indicators were used to determine the age at death of a skeletonized body recovered in 1977 from rural Ohio. The complete skeleton was present, so the sex of the person could be determined to be female from the configuration of the pelvis and skull. In addition, the presence of long, straight brown hair indicated a person of White ancestry; and the long bones (see Chapter 10) provided a measurement of stature of around 5 feet, 3 to 4 inches. In addition to these demographic characteristics, Perzigian and Jolly wished to develop as precise an approximation of age as possible from the osteological evidence.

The estimation of age at death could be derived from the sources discussed in this chapter. First, all adult teeth, except the third molar, were fully erupted and in their final place, indicating an age of over 12 years. Second, all three bones of each os coxa were fused, indicating an age over 13. Similarly, the epiphyses of the elbow (i.e., distal humerus, medial epicondyle, proximal radius, and ulna) and knee (i.e., distal femur, proximal tibia, and fibula) also were fully fused, indicating an age of 14 to 17. Conversely, only partial fusion was seen in the distal radius and ulna, the femoral head, the distal tibia, and the acromion and coracoid process of the scapula; these indicated an age over 13 but less than 17. Other epiphyses showing partial union also indicated an age less than 17. Finally, no suture closure was seen in the skull, corroborating the previous indications that the person had not reached adulthood (i.e., was less than 18 years of age).

By using several decision tables, Perzigian and Jolly were able to narrow the age down to between 16 and 17 years at death. When the remains were finally identified, it was determined that the girl had just missed reaching her seventeenth birthday when she was strangled by a convicted murderer. This case is a fine example of how the use of multiple indicators increases the accuracy of estimates of age at death.

In addition to bone, teeth also grow by deposition of hard tissue in open areas called crypts. This process starts at the tips of the cusps and proceeds toward the roots. When the crown is formed fully and the root is approximately half of its final length, the continuous deposition of material to the tips of the roots causes the tooth to push its way out of its crypt, through the bone nearest its occlusal surface and through the gum. The root continues to grow until the tooth is fully erupted and settled into its natural position within the jaw.

Knowledge of these events and the schedule by which they occur has been used by anthropologists for many decades to determine the age at death of subadults from their skeletons and teeth. Also, because multiple structures can be used for this purpose, this demographic characteristic can be roughly estimated if only one structure is present or precisely estimated if the entire skeleton is present (see Box 9.1 for an example of the accuracy possible from multiple indicators). To elucidate these methods, this section is divided into five parts. The first part deals with determining age from the lengths of long bones. Because size differences between the sexes and ancestral groups are less in subadults than in adults, this method is useful with infants and young children (i.e., age 10 and under). The second part deals with determining age from the union between primary and secondary centers of ossification. Although there are a large number of these, only those most likely to be found in a forensic situation will be discussed. The third part outlines the stages of tooth formation within the crypts, and the fourth part presents the timetable by which teeth erupt from the jaws. Finally, the last part deals with the schedule for the union of epiphyses with their associated bones.

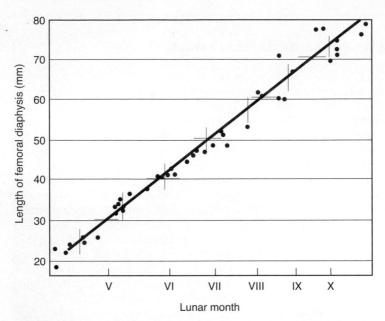

FIGURE 9.1 Chart showing relationship between femoral shaft length and fetal age. (Modified from Figure 31, Chapter 9, *Gradwohl's Legal Medicine* [1976], p. 117)

Long Bone Lengths

The remains from prenatal, natal, and early postnatal infants can be determined from the lengths of their long bones (Stewart, 1979). Although differences in size exist between subadults from different ancestral groups and sexes, fetal size up to the time of birth shows less variation among groups than do their adult counterparts. Because divergence in size accelerates postnatally, the lengths of fetal, infant, and child long bones are only reasonably accurate indicators of age until around 10 years.

From the time of their first appearance and up to birth, the relationship between age and long bone length appears linear. Measurements of the femoral shaft (without the epiphyseal ends) on three separate populations (American, French, Hungarian) all yield a graph similar to that presented in Figure 9.1. Notice that the line drawn on the chart is straight (indicating the linear relationship just mentioned). This chart can be used to determine the age of fetal and infant remains up to 1 month after birth by finding the lunar month that corresponds to the length of a femur from an individual of unknown age. For example, a femur of 50 mm indicates that the fetus was in its seventh month of development. If only other long limb bones are present, age can be estimated by knowing their relationship with the femur; these relationships, given in Table 9.1, can be used to determine the probable femoral length, which then can be used in Figure 9.1 to determine age. For example, if a tibia is discovered that is 63 mm in length, its associated femur would have been approximately 70 mm (63/0.899 = 70.1), which indicates an age between 9 and 10 months.

After birth, long limb bone length becomes a less reliable estimator of age. Data gathered by J. M. Hoffman (1979) on Whites and Blacks of known age and on Native Americans of

TABLE 9.1 Lengths of Long Bones in Terms of Percentage of Femur[1]

Bone	Percentage of Femur
Tibia	89.9
Fibula	84.6
Humerus	88.6
Ulna	84.6
Radius	73.8

[1]Calculated from data presented in Figures 37 and 38 of Stewart (1979).

inferred age show that bone growth decelerates after birth, causing the graph of this dimension against the number of post-partum years to climb at an ever-decreasing rate. Conversely, the amount of variation increases, causing the graph of points to form a cornucopia shape (i.e., the band formed by the points is narrow at birth and widens as time goes on). These two factors cause estimates of age to have ever-widening ranges through time. For example, 95% of femora that are 140 mm long come from children who are 6 months to 1.5 years old; however, 95% of 260 mm femora come from children who are 4.5 to 7 years of age (see Figure 9.2).

The best data for determining age at death of both males and females are those of Hoffman from measurements of bone radiographs of White females. This is because x-raying adds 2% to 3% to the lengths of long bones due to parallax distortion. Thus, these lengths are too long for females and too short for males, thereby providing a reasonable "middle ground." Figures 9.2 through 9.7 display the relationship between length and age for each of the six major long limb bones. All of these illustrate the two factors of deceleration and ever-increasing variation discussed above. Thus, estimates using these graphs would be relatively accurate in the early years. However, as bones reach the upper limits of the chart(s), the amount of variation in length increases to such an extent that age can be determined only within a range of 5 to 6 years.

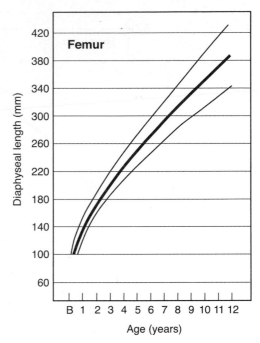

FIGURE 9.2 Chart showing the relationship between age and femoral length in subadults birth to age 10. (Taken from Figure 6 of Hoffman [1979]. Copyright ASTM International. Reprinted with permission)

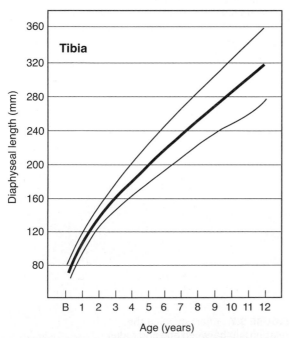

FIGURE 9.3 Chart showing the relationship between age and tibial length in subadults birth to age 10. (Taken from Figure 7 of Hoffman [1979]. Copyright ASTM International. Reprinted with permission)

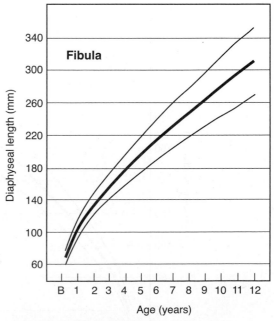

FIGURE 9.4 Chart showing the relationship between age and fibular length in subadults birth to age 10. (Taken from Figure 8 of Hoffman [1979]. Copyright ASTM International. Reprinted with permission)

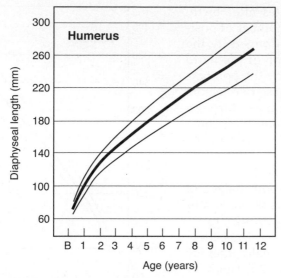

FIGURE 9.5 Chart showing the relationship between age and humeral length in subadults birth to age 10. (Taken from Figure 3 of Hoffman [1979]. Copyright ASTM International. Reprinted with permission)

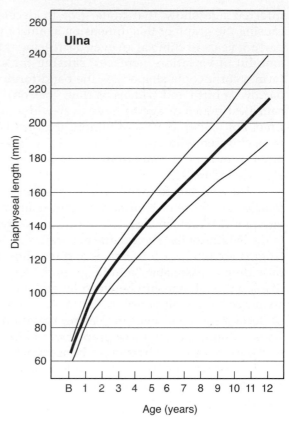

FIGURE 9.6 Chart showing the relationship between age and ulnar length in subadults birth to age 10. (Taken from Figure 5 of Hoffman [1979]. Copyright ASTM International. Reprinted with permission)

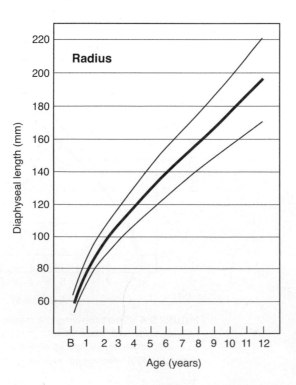

FIGURE 9.7 Chart showing the relationship between age and radial length in subadults birth to age 10. (Taken from Figure 4 of Hoffman [1979]. Copyright ASTM International. Reprinted with permission)

Union of Primary Ossification Centers

The time of appearance of primary and secondary centers of ossification is potentially valuable in the forensic situation (Stewart, 1979). Bone is deposited in these centers according to a rough schedule, so the amount of their development in a skeleton indicates an approximate age at death. Additionally, the union of secondary centers to their associated primary centers also follows a rough schedule that can be utilized in a similar manner. Unfortunately, the small size and fragility of these bony structures make their recovery unlikely. Therefore, the timing of these events is rarely applicable in forensic anthropology.

Although the appearance and ossification of centers have little utility in forensic anthropology, the joining of the primary centers to each other occasionally can be used, because these structures are more likely to be recovered (Stewart, 1979). The main skeletal elements that can be used for this function are the skull, mandible, atlas, and axis. In the skull, two types of unions occur. First, newborns exhibit gaps, called **fontanelles**, in the areas of bregma (the frontal fontanelle), pterion (the sphenoid fontanelle), asterion (the mastoid fontanelle), and lambda (the posterior fontanelle).

In addition to these gaps closing during life, the ossification centers of a number of cranial bones unite during growth. This is true of the right and left halves of the frontal bone, which are divided from each other by the **metopic suture** at birth. Similarly, the four parts of the occipital, illustrated in Figure 9.9, fuse during development. Additional fusions occur between the left and right halves of the mandible (divided during gestation), as well as

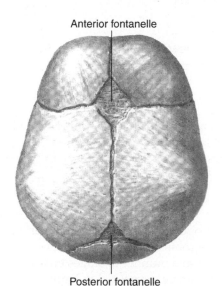

Anterior fontanelle

Posterior fontanelle

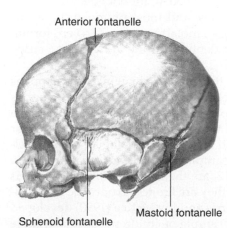

Anterior fontanelle

Sphenoid fontanelle

Mastoid fontanelle

FIGURE 9.8 Placement of fontanelles in the infant skull.

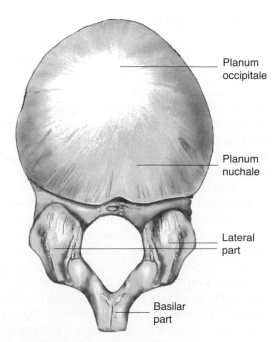

Planum occipitale

Planum nuchale

Lateral part

Basilar part

FIGURE 9.9 Primary centers of ossification seen in the occipital.

TABLE 9.2   Fusion of Primary Centers of Ossification[1]

	Time of Closure
Fontanelles	
Sphenoid and mastoid	Soon after birth
Occipital	During first year
Frontal	During second year
Mandible	
Right and left halves	Completed by second year
Frontal	
Right and left halves	In second year (remains open in as many as 10% of people)
Atlas	
Union of halves (posteriorly)	In third year
Union of halves (anteriorly)	In sixth year
Axis	
Dens, body, and both arches	In third and fourth years
Occipital	
Squamous with lateral parts	In fifth year
Lateral and basilar parts	In sixth year

[1]Taken from data presented on pages 139 and 140 of Stewart (1979).

in the atlas. Finally, the axis is composed of four elements: the body, dens, and right and left halves of the arch. The schedule by which these primary centers unite during growth is presented in Table 9.2. As can be seen, these fusions are useful only for persons under 10 years of age.

Tooth Formation

The process by which teeth grow is that of deposition of enamel and osseous material, starting at the tips of the cusps and proceeding to the roots. Although this process is continuous, it is convenient to divide tooth formation into a number of stages based on the amount of calcification. The most commonly used scheme, presented in Figure 9.10, was developed by Coenraad Moorees and colleagues (1963a, b) for both deciduous and permanent single-rooted teeth (i.e., incisors, canines, and most premolars) and for deciduous and permanent multiple-rooted teeth (i.e., molars). As can be seen, formation occurs by apposition of first enamel and then dentin, starting at the crown cusps and working toward the root.

Although all teeth pass through these stages, the timetable by which this happens is different for different types of teeth. Thus, the deciduous dentition calcifies before its permanent counterpart, the incisors before the molars, and so forth. Because humans have two sets of teeth, there are two schedules of tooth formation. The timetables for deciduous teeth that are used by most forensic (and other) anthropologists were developed by Moorees et al. (1963a) based on a small sample of White males and females. These schedules, presented in Figures 9.11 and 9.12, are the standards by which age is estimated for young children, despite the fact that they are limited to only the lower canine and molars. For permanent teeth, Edward Harris and Joy McKee (1990) developed a timetable from a large (almost 1000) multiracial sample of children from the middle southern United States; their chronology, which contains information on all teeth, is presented in Tables 9.3 and 9.4.

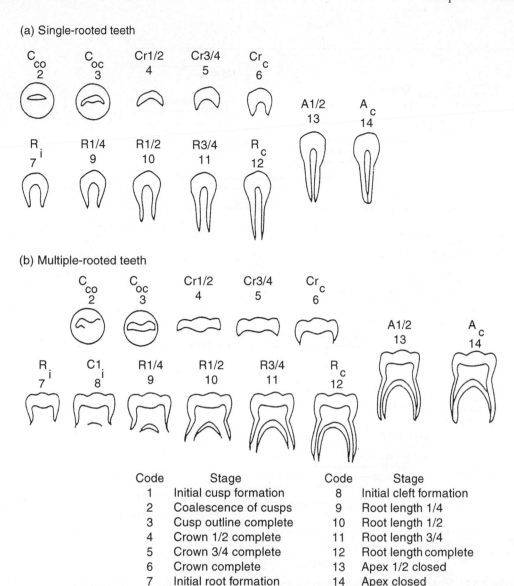

FIGURE 9.10 Tooth formation stages: **(a)** single-rooted teeth; **(b)** multiple-rooted teeth. (Some of these stages are not known for deciduous teeth.) (Reprinted from Moorrees et al. [1963b], Age variation of formation stages for ten permanent teeth, *Journal of Dental Research*, 42:1490–1502. Reprinted with permission from *Journal of Dental Research*)

The method for determining age from these schedules is fairly straightforward. After radiographs of the dental arcades of a forensic case are obtained, the amount of calcification for each tooth is matched with the appropriate stage pictured in Figure 9.10 which is matched with the time range from Figures 9.11 and 9.12 or Tables 9.3 and 9.4, whichever is appropriate. Using the 95% ranges from these data, a range chart then can be produced according to the method described in Chapter 1 for each of the teeth that is present. In this manner, the most likely age of the dentition, and therefore the decedent, will be evident.

Although relatively minor, there are problems with using tooth calcification information. First, the amount of dental formation generally is visible only in x-ray; therefore, radiographic equipment and qualified technicians must be available for

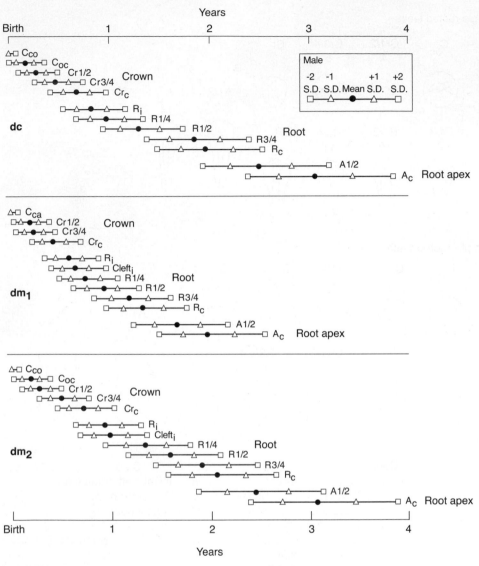

FIGURE 9.11   Schedule of tooth formation for the male deciduous dentition. (Reprinted from Moorrees et al. [1963a], Formation and resorption of three deciduous teeth, *American Journal of Physical Anthropology*. Copyright © 1963, John Wiley & Sons. Reprinted with permission of Wiley-Liss, Inc., a Subsidiary of John Wiley & Sons, Inc.)

this technique to be utilized. Second, information on the deciduous dentition is restricted to the lower canines and molars; because the relationship between upper and lower dental development is unknown, these schedules must be used with considerable caution when only the maxillary dental arcade is present. Also, if only the deciduous incisors are present (an unlikely situation), the method is unusable. Third, the schedules are divided by sex for deciduous teeth and by sex and ancestral group for the permanent dentition. As seen in previous chapters, these characteristics cannot be told with any reliability in subadults. Therefore, with remains of unknown demographic affiliation, age is estimated best by averaging the results from the applicable figures and tables. Finally, research has shown that workers often disagree with each other as to the amount of development visible in x-rays (Fanning, 1961);

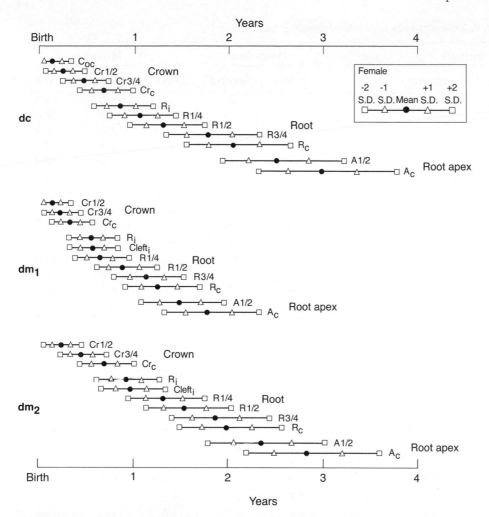

FIGURE 9.12 Schedule of tooth formation for the female deciduous dentition. (Reprinted from Moorrees et al. [1963a], Formation and resorption of three deciduous teeth, *American Journal of Physical Anthropology*. Copyright © 1963, John Wiley & Sons. Reprinted with permission of Wiley-Liss, Inc., a Subsidiary of John Wiley & Sons, Inc.)

however, since these disagreements rarely exceed more than one stage, this problem is relatively minor.

Tooth Eruption

When the roots reach approximately one-half to three-quarters of their final length, the teeth emerge from their crypts into the mouth. The time of this emergence, which varies within the dentition, has been documented by many researchers. However, the methods employed and terminology used differ to such an extent that arriving at a single standard based on the multitude of studies is difficult. Given this situation, the most often used schedule is that devised by Schour and Massler (1941) and periodically revised by the American Dental Association. This chronology, presented in Figure 9.13, pictures both stages of tooth emergence and formation for given ages, as well as the ranges for these stages. To use this chart, the forensic anthropologist needs only to match the dentition of a case with that of one of these stages to arrive at an estimate of age.

TABLE 9.3   Schedule of Tooth Calcification for Maxillary Permanent Dentition[1]

Stage	Subjects	Incisors		Canine	Premolars		Molars		
		Central	Lateral		First	Second	First	Second	Third
1	WM	—	—	—	—	—	—	3.9	9.3
	BM	—	—	—	—	—	—	4.3	8.6
	WF	—	—	—	—	—	—	4.0	8.9
	BF	—	—	—	—	—	—	3.3	9.2
	(SD)	—	—	—	—	—	—	(0.49)	(0.99)
2	WM	—	—	—	—	4.0	—	4.5	9.7
	BM	—	—	—	—	4.3	—	4.0	9.2
	WF	—	—	—	—	4.6	—	4.4	10.0
	BF	—	—	—	—	3.9	—	3.6	9.0
	(SD)	—	—	—	—	(0.83)	—	(0.55)	(1.32)
3	WM	—	—	—	4.1	4.8	—	4.8	10.8
	BM	—	—	—	3.3	4.2	—	4.4	9.9
	WF	—	—	—	3.9	4.4	—	5.1	10.7
	BF	—	—	—	3.3	4.7	—	4.6	9.2
	(SD)	—	—	—	(0.70)	(0.67)	—	(0.77)	(1.06)
4	WM	—	3.6	3.8	4.7	5.6	—	5.7	11.5
	BM	—	3.5	3.6	4.2	5.0	—	5.3	9.9
	WF	—	4.3	4.2	4.7	5.8	—	5.6	10.6
	BF	—	3.8	3.5	4.2	5.3	—	4.8	9.7
	(SD)	—	(0.70)	(0.80)	(0.79)	(0.78)	—	(0.65)	(1.03)
5	WM	3.6	4.5	4.8	5.8	6.4	3.4	6.7	11.9
	BM	3.7	4.6	4.1	5.7	6.7	2.7	6.3	11.1
	WF	4.3	4.5	4.6	6.0	6.4	3.5	6.5	11.9
	BF	3.8	3.8	4.1	5.2	6.0	3.0	6.0	9.9
	(SD)	(0.77)	(0.78)	(0.83)	(0.77)	(0.92)	(0.53)	(0.93)	(1.17)
6	WM	4.3	5.3	6.0	7.3	7.7	4.0	7.4	12.4
	BM	3.9	4.2	5.5	6.8	7.9	3.4	7.3	10.8
	WF	4.6	4.9	5.6	6.5	7.3	3.8	7.2	11.6
	BF	4.1	4.8	4.7	6.2	7.0	3.7	6.8	11.3
	(SD)	(0.79)	(0.90)	(0.93)	(1.14)	(1.04)	(0.71)	(0.99)	(0.70)
7	WM	5.3	6.5	6.7	8.0	8.5	4.6	8.5	13.2
	BM	5.4	5.8	6.1	8.2	8.4	4.2	8.6	13.1
	WF	5.4	5.9	6.1	7.7	8.4	4.3	8.4	13.4
	BF	5.1	5.4	5.9	7.2	8.2	4.3	7.9	12.1
	(SD)	(0.90)	(1.22)	(1.14)	(0.90)	(0.98)	(0.87)	(0.99)	(1.37)
8	WM	6.3	7.1	7.8	9.0	9.4	4.3	9.7	—
	BM	5.9	7.0	7.9	8.6	9.5	3.9	9.1	—
	WF	6.1	6.7	7.3	8.7	9.0	4.7	9.1	—
	BF	6.0	6.4	6.9	7.9	9.1	4.2	8.9	—
	(SD)	(0.75)	(0.83)	(0.90)	(0.95)	(0.98)	(0.58)	(1.13)	—
9	WM	7.5	8.1	8.9	9.2	10.1	5.3	10.5	—
	BM	7.2	7.8	8.3	9.7	9.9	5.3	9.7	—
	WF	6.9	7.4	8.1	9.5	10.1	5.5	10.0	—
	BF	6.4	6.9	7.9	8.9	9.3	4.8	9.5	—
	(SD)	(0.82)	(0.90)	(0.88)	(0.85)	(1.12)	(0.78)	(0.81)	—

(Continued)

TABLE 9.3   Schedule of Tooth Calcification for Maxillary Permanent Dentition[1] (Continued)

Stage	Subjects	Incisors		Canine	Premolars		Molars		
		Central	Lateral		First	Second	First	Second	Third
10	WM	8.1	8.5	10.2	10.7	11.4	6.4	11.8	—
	BM	7.6	8.3	9.7	9.7	10.4	6.9	11.5	—
	WF	7.5	8.2	9.4	10.0	10.5	6.3	11.3	—
	BF	7.1	8.5	9.1	10.3	10.0	6.0	10.8	—
	(SD)	(1.04)	(0.75)	(0.92)	(0.96)	(1.06)	(0.74)	(1.10)	—
11	WM	8.8	9.6	11.9	12.3	12.6	7.5	12.6	—
	BM	8.9	9.7	11.3	12.1	12.3	7.5	12.5	—
	WF	8.1	9.1	11.0	11.2	11.2	7.3	11.5	—
	BF	8.5	9.1	10.1	10.5	11.4	6.6	11.4	—
	(SD)	(0.86)	(0.84)	(1.07)	(1.02)	(0.81)	(1.03)	(0.93)	
12	WM	9.7	10.5	12.5	12.7	12.3	8.5	12.4	—
	BM	9.3	9.6	12.7	11.9	12.8	8.5	12.8	—
	WF	9.1	9.7	11.8	11.6	12.0	8.0	12.1	—
	BF	8.8	9.6	11.5	11.1	12.2	8.4	12.2	—
	(SD)	(0.91)	(1.00)	(0.95)	(0.85)	(0.77)	(1.05)	(1.06)	—
13	WM	—	—	—	—	—	9.5	12.5	—
	BM	—	—	—	—	—	9.3	13.0	—
	WF	—	—	—	—	—	9.2	12.9	—
	BF	—	—	—	—	—	8.8	11.8	—
	(SD)	—	—	—	—	—	(1.07)	(1.43)	—

[1]Reproduced from Table 2 of Harris and McKee (1990). Copyright ASTM International. Reprinted with permission. WM = White male, BM = Black male, WF = White female, BF = Black female, SD = standard deviation.

Unfortunately, this chart was developed on White children, and there are no similar standards for Blacks and Asians. However, for Native Americans, the chronology developed by Ubelaker (1999) is accepted by most forensic (and other) anthropologists as the best method for determining age in this ancestral group. His schedule, presented in Figure 9.14, also gives average ages and ranges for each stage of development.

Since its inception, the Schour and Massler chart has been criticized because it is based on a small sample of diseased children. However, research has shown that it is more accurate than its critics believe, and that its precision can be increased with only minimal modification (Ciapparelli, 1992). The first modification is to the average ages. Although these are relatively accurate for males, females are more precocious in their dental development. Thus, if a skeleton of this sex is being evaluated, the estimated age should be reduced by 3 to 6 months. The other modification involves the range. This statistic is relatively accurate for the lower ages, up to around 4 years. However, as time progresses, the ranges increase such that, by the twelfth year, they are double those shown in the chart. Similarly, by the year 16, the ranges have tripled. Therefore, the ranges of a determined estimate should be expanded in proportion to the estimated age.

Epiphyseal Union

As described earlier, bones grow by the deposition of osseous material on their ends. This process starts after the primary centers of ossification have fused with each other and the entire cartilaginous precursor has transformed into bone. At this point, their ends do not exhibit bony joint surfaces (see Figure 9.15a); rather, they are covered by

TABLE 9.4 Schedule of Tooth Calcification for Mandibular Permanent Dentition[1]

		Incisors		Canine	Premolars		Molars		
Stage	Subjects	Central	Lateral		First	Second	First	Second	Third
1	WM	—	—	—	—	3.9	—	4.1	9.0
	BM	—	—	—	—	3.2	—	3.7	8.2
	WF	—	—	—	—	5.0	—	3.6	9.6
	BF	—	—	—	—	3.7	—	3.5	8.4
	(SD)	—	—	—	—	(1.17)	—	(0.51)	(1.23)
2	WM	—	—	—	—	4.6	—	4.2	9.9
	BM	—	—	—	—	3.8	—	3.9	9.0
	WF	—	—	—	—	4.3	—	4.7	10.0
	BF	—	—	—	—	3.6	—	3.6	9.0
	(SD)	—	—	—	—	(1.02)	—	(0.58)	(1.21)
3	WM	—	—	—	4.0	5.3	—	5.0	11.0
	BM	—	—	—	3.4	4.4	—	4.7	9.6
	WF	—	—	—	4.0	4.8	—	5.2	10.6
	BF	—	—	—	3.4	4.8	—	4.5	9.4
	(SD)	—	—	—	(0.63)	(0.94)	—	(0.81)	(1.10)
4	WM	—	—	3.5	4.5	5.4	—	5.9	11.5
	BM	—	—	3.7	4.3	5.1	—	5.5	10.4
	WF	—	—	4.2	4.6	5.7	—	5.6	11.2
	BF	—	—	3.2	4.2	4.9	—	5.2	9.8
	(SD)	—	—	(0.62)	(0.63)	(0.73)	—	(0.74)	(1.03)
5	WM	—	3.8	4.3	5.8	6.1	—	6.3	12.5
	BM	—	3.6	4.2	5.8	6.7	—	6.4	11.3
	WF	—	4.1	4.2	5.5	6.4	—	6.4	12.0
	BF	—	3.5	4.4	5.2	5.7	—	6.0	10.7
	(SD)	—	(0.79)	(0.64)	(0.73)	(0.90)	—	(1.03)	(1.22)
6	WM	3.7	4.1	5.6	6.8	7.6	3.5	8.0	12.6
	BM	4.0	4.4	5.5	6.3	7.2	3.0	7.3	12.2
	WF	3.9	4.5	5.0	6.4	7.3	3.5	7.4	11.7
	BF	3.4	4.1	4.9	6.2	6.6	3.2	6.8	12.2
	(SD)	(0.57)	(0.73)	(0.75)	(1.14)	(1.12)	(0.29)	(1.04)	(0.74)
7	WM	4.7	5.3	6.4	7.7	8.6	4.3	8.1	13.0
	BM	4.1	4.9	6.6	7.8	8.5	4.0	8.7	13.2
	WF	4.4	4.7	5.8	7.3	8.0	4.2	8.1	13.5
	BF	4.0	5.1	6.1	7.0	7.6	3.5	7.6	12.6
	(SD)	(0.75)	(0.77)	(1.21)	(0.84)	(0.89)	(0.64)	(0.95)	(1.34)
8	WM	5.5	6.1	7.6	9.0	9.8	4.3	9.0	—
	BM	5.4	6.0	8.3	9.0	9.4	4.0	8.7	—
	WF	5.2	5.8	6.9	8.5	8.8	4.5	8.9	—
	BF	5.4	5.7	6.8	8.4	8.9	4.1	8.6	—
	(SD)	(0.70)	(0.76)	(0.94)	(0.86)	(0.96)	(0.68)	(0.92)	—
9	WM	6.4	6.9	8.8	9.4	10.2	5.2	10.2	—
	BM	5.8	6.7	8.8	9.7	10.0	5.2	9.7	—
	WF	6.2	6.3	8.0	9.0	9.7	5.2	9.8	—
	BF	5.5	5.9	7.7	9.0	9.5	4.8	9.5	—
	(SD)	(0.72)	(0.73)	(0.99)	(0.90)	(1.16)	(0.70)	(1.03)	—

(Continued)

TABLE 9.4   Schedule of Tooth Calcification for Mandibular Permanent Dentition[1] (*Continued*)

		Incisors		Canine	Premolars		Molars		
Stage	Subjects	Central	Lateral		First	Second	First	Second	Third
10	WM	6.6	7.7	9.7	10.8	11.3	6.1	11.5	—
	BM	6.5	7.7	9.9	9.8	10.7	6.6	11.2	—
	WF	6.3	7.3	9.1	10.0	10.7	6.3	10.8	—
	BF	5.9	6.9	9.3	9.6	9.7	5.8	10.7	—
	(SD)	(0.74)	(0.86)	(0.95)	(0.91)	(1.03)	(0.71)	(1.02)	—
11	WM	8.0	8.2	11.5	11.7	12.4	7.5	12.2	—
	BM	7.4	8.4	11.3	11.4	11.9	7.4	12.1	—
	WF	7.4	8.0	10.1	11.1	11.7	7.0	11.6	—
	BF	6.5	8.0	9.4	11.2	11.7	6.6	12.0	—
	(SD)	(0.85)	(0.99)	(1.04)	(1.00)	(0.99)	(1.05)	(0.93)	—
12	WM	8.6	9.2	12.4	12.5	12.5	8.4	12.6	—
	BM	8.6	9.4	11.6	12.0	12.8	8.4	12.5	—
	WF	8.3	8.9	11.3	11.5	11.8	8.1	12.2	—
	BF	7.8	8.6	10.7	11.7	11.4	7.8	11.5	—
	(SD)	(0.97)	(1.01)	(0.91)	(0.95)	(0.97)	(0.87)	(1.01)	—
13	WM	—	—	—	—	—	9.2	12.8	—
	BM	—	—	—	—	—	9.5	13.0	—
	WF	—	—	—	—	—	9.0	13.2	—
	BF	—	—	—	—	—	8.4	13.2	—
	(SD)	—	—	—	—	—	(1.01)	(1.21)	—

[1]Reproduced from Table 3 of Harris and McKee (1990). Copyright ASTM International. Reprinted with permission. WM = White male, BM = Black male, WF = White female, BF = Black female, SD = standard deviation.

cartilage that will eventually ossify. As time progresses, epiphyses ossify within the cartilaginous joint area, where they conform closely to the bone ends (see Figure 9.15b). With the further passage of time, growth ceases, and the epiphyseal caps unite to their diaphyses, leaving a temporarily visible line where the two structures once were separated (Figure 9.15c). Finally, this line becomes completely obliterated (Figure 9.15d) by the mechanisms of bone remodeling as people age.

There are numerous epiphyses in the human skeleton. All long limb bones have at least two (one on each end) and often more (e.g., the femur has four). Similarly, the first 10 ribs have two, one on the head and the other on the articular surface of the tubercle. By contrast, each metacarpal and metatarsal exhibits only one. Also, the bottom 22 vertebrae have at least five epiphyses: one on the superior and inferior surfaces of the body, one on each transverse process, and one on the tip of the spinous process. In addition, the lumbar vertebrae have two more, one on each **mammillary process** (projection of bone containing the superior articular facet).

One of the more accepted schedules of epiphyseal union, derived from Buikstra and Ubelaker (1994), is presented in Figure 9.16. As can be seen, this information is most useful for estimating the age at death of individuals between 10 and 25 years, because very few epiphyses fuse before this time and the majority of epiphyses have fused by the end of this time. Also, notice that there is a range within which fusion occurs. Generally, bones from the early part of this range are recognizable by the presence of clearly visible lines that appear to cut deeply into the bone (similar to Figure 9.15b), whereas those that have less visible and/or almost obliterated lines are more often from the end of these ranges (Figure 9.15c). A last feature of Figure 9.16 is that some of the

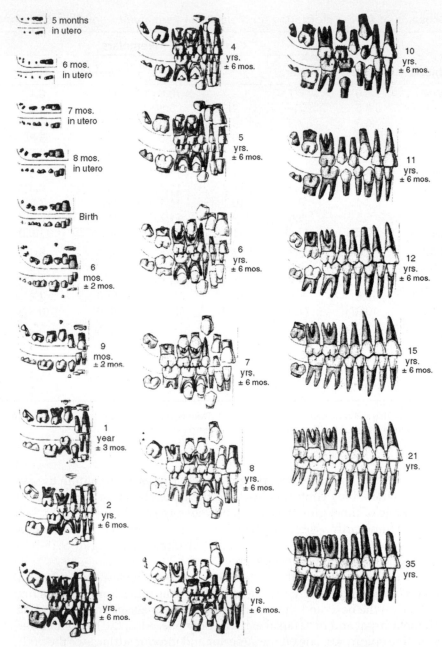

FIGURE 9.13 Chart of tooth formation and emergence for White children. (Adapted from Schour, I., and Massler, M. [1941], The development of human dentition, *JADA,* 28:1153. Copyright © 1941 American Dental Association. Reprinted by permission of ADA Publishing, a Division of ADA Business Enterprises, Inc.)

fusions are divided by sex. Thus, to get age estimations, either the difficult decision as to the sex of the deceased subadult must be made or the ranges of the two sexes must be combined.

The estimation of age using Figure 9.16 involves noting the amount of epiphyseal union in each bone of the skeleton. Because this is the classic problem of combining information from several sources, a range chart can be produced using the method described in Chapter 1. For bones that do not display union, a line can be extended

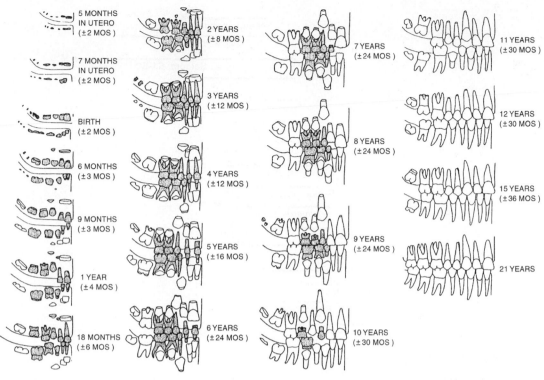

FIGURE 9.14   Chart of tooth formation and emergence for Native American children.   (Reprinted from Figure 71, Ubelaker [1999]; courtesy of Taraxacum Press)

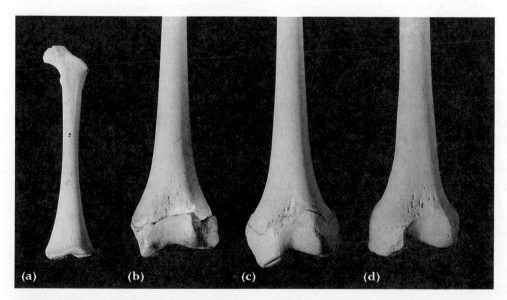

FIGURE 9.15   Stages of epiphyseal union of the distal femur: **(a)** no union (missing epiphysis); **(b)** unfused; **(c)** fused; **(d)** obliterated.   (Photo by Julie R. Angel; specimens courtesy of the University of New Mexico–Albuquerque, Maxwell Museum of Anthropology, #1, #12, #71)

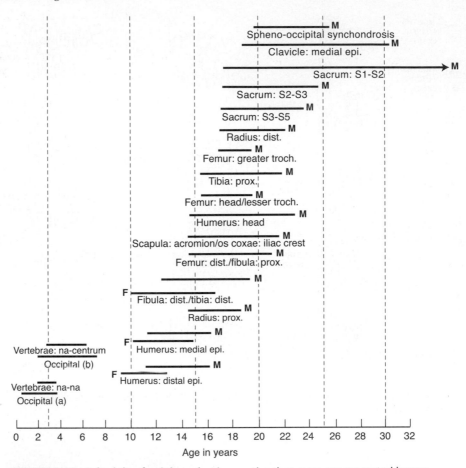

FIGURE 9.16 Schedule of epiphyseal union; notice that some are separated by sex. (Reprinted from J. E. Buikstra and D. H. Ubelaker [1994], *Standards for Data Collection from Human Skeletal Remains*, Figure 20; courtesy of Arkansas Archeological Survey Publications; distal fibula and tibia lines from Crowder and Austin, 2005)

backward from the time of initial fusion. Similarly, bones that are fused fully can be represented by a line extending forward in time, starting at the end of the range of union. From a chart so constructed, the most likely age of decedents should become obvious. Generally, most chart lines will be only 2 or 3 years in length, but for some this will extend to as much as 5 years.

Unfortunately, the timetables by which these epiphyses unite to their associated bones are known only partially. As can be seen in Figure 9.16, information on the ribs and most vertebrae, as well as on metacarpals and metatarsals, is lacking. If these bones are present, the time of fusion can be obtained from any standard human anatomy reference (e.g., *Gray's Anatomy*). However, because the information in these works is usually from small samples of anatomical specimens, the accuracy of the ages determined from these sources must be considered as unknown.

ADULTS

After the dentition is fully emerged and growth has ceased, other methods must be employed to determine age. Although tooth loss and other such events may be used as an indication of age (see Box 9.2 for an example of the dangers of believing the obvious), several structures in the skeleton undergo changes over time that follow a rough

BOX 9.2
The Young "Old Codger"

Stan Rhine (1998) describes a case in which a pathologist mistook missing teeth as an indicator of advanced age at death for an autopsy specimen, a man named Llewelen Gumm. Rhine's description of this misinterpretation of information follows:

> Forensic odontologist Homer Campbell and I were once called in to assist in identifying the decomposed body of an "old codger" on whom the autopsy was winding up. The pathologist snapped the skull x-ray smartly into the viewer and stepped back. We advanced to the plate, and looked at it and then at each other. We both laughed. The pathologist looked puzzled. He was, we explained, not particularly old at all. "But," the pathologist said, "he must be old. His mouth doesn't contain a single tooth!" We pointed to the deep alveoli (the area of the jaws that hold the teeth) and noted several other features of the skull that seemed inconsistent with great age...
>
> In our usual frame of reference, a person does not lose all of his teeth until considerably later in life. Llewelen Gumm probably had the bad luck of being born with a lousy set of choppers and opted for their complete extraction.... His driver's license photo portrayed him with that sort of collapsed-mouth look that accompanies the extraction of all teeth. The obvious conclusion that Mr. Gumm had accumulated an impressive number of years prior to his demise was wrong...*

_____

*From S. Rhine, *Bone Voyage,* University of New Mexico Press, Albuquerque, 1998, pp. 81–82, with permission.

timetable. Although these alterations are much more subtle (and therefore difficult to use) than those of subadults, they have considerable value in determining this demographic characteristic. Thus, the age at death of adults can be determined by comparing the status of these structures in skeletons with accepted schedules of these changes.

Four osteological features alter during adulthood: pubic symphyses, auricular surfaces, sternal rib ends, and cranial sutures. The pubic symphysis changes from an area covered with ridges of fine-grained bone to a flat area with porous, rough, and otherwise "old-looking" bone. Similar transformations occur on the auricular surface of the ilium and on the sternal ends of ribs; these areas are composed originally of smooth and youthful-looking bone that eventually becomes old and pitted with osteophytic development. The fourth structure that changes through time involves the cranial sutures. These lines separating the bones of the skull (including the palate) close with age until they fuse and may eventually obliterate. In addition to these four features, there are two methods that take advantage of histologic (microscopic) changes that occur during the aging process. Thus, the rest of this chapter will deal with methods for estimating age at death from the various changes in the adult skeleton that take place through time.

Pubic Symphyses

In his pioneering article, T. Wingate Todd (1920) described the alterations that occur in the pubic symphysis over time and how these can be used to estimate age at death. Todd described 10 stages of changes to this structure that occur during aging, with time ranges of uneven lengths (e.g., 18 to 19, 30 to 35, 50+) for each stage. Since his initial research, the value of using pubic face changes to evaluate age at death has received much attention. In 1955, Sheila Brooks, feeling that the age ranges for each stage were too high, modified Todd's time ranges down by several years in each category. Similarly, Thomas McKern and T. Dale Stewart (1957), using data on the Korean War dead, developed a numerical method of determining age from stages of change that are similar to those of Todd. Also, studies by Judy Suchey and D. Katz (1986) and by

Sheila Brooks and Judy Suchey (1990) were able to demonstrate sex, but not ancestral group, differences for changes in the pubic symphysis. Finally, Richard Meindl and colleagues (1985), when modifying the original Todd method, showed that changes in this structure provide the best estimates of age at death for adults of any method developed to date.

Although the schedules and stages vary, all the above-mentioned techniques look at the same features originally described by Todd: the bone of the pubic face, the ventral and dorsal margins, the upper and lower extremities, and ossific nodules. The bone of the pubic face undergoes several changes with age. When young, it exhibits **ridges** separated by **furrows** that run transversely across the surface (see Figure 9.17a); over time, the

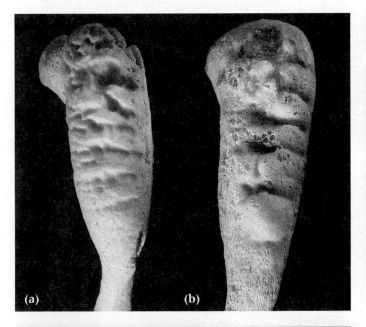

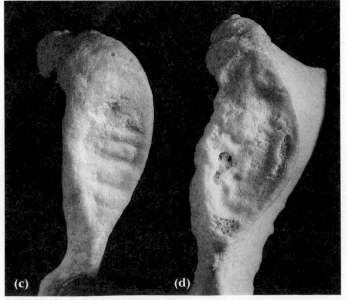

FIGURE 9.17 Age changes in the pubic surface from young to old: **(a)** ridges and furrows; **(b)** furrows filling in; **(c)** furrows almost gone; **(d)** flat with fine-textured bone; **(e)** pitted and eroded. (Photo by Julie R. Angel; specimens courtesy of the University of New Mexico–Albuquerque, Maxwell Museum of Anthropology, #71, #97, #89, #19, #145)

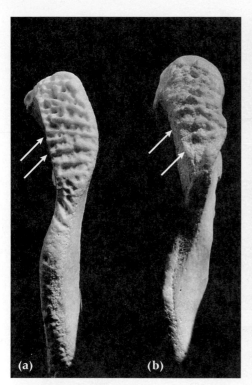
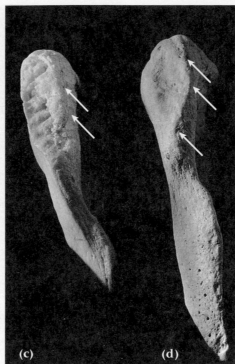

FIGURE 9.18 Changes in the ventral margin (*arrows*) from young to old: **(a)** right angle with the pubic face; **(b)** ventral bevel; **(c)** rampart; **(d)** fully developed ventral margin. (Photos by Julie R. Angel; specimens courtesy of the University of New Mexico–Albuquerque, Maxwell Museum of Anthropology, #197, #49, #49, #120)

furrows fill in, usually starting posteriorly and proceeding anteriorly (see Figure 9.17b). Eventually, the face becomes flat with a granular look to the bone, which is replaced with fine-textured bone (see Figure 9.17c), which again becomes more granular (see Figure 9.17d). Finally, in old age the face becomes pitted and eroded (see Figure 9.17e).

The ventral (anterior) margin of the pubic face exhibits two characteristics that develop over time: a bevel and a rampart. In youth, the ventral margin forms a right angle with the pubic face (see arrows in Figure 9.18a). However, during the second decade of life as the above-described ridges degenerate and the furrows fill in, the cortical bone of the ventral surface begins to invade the pubic face. This causes the sharp corner between the ventral margin and pubic surface to become blunted, until the margin bevels from the anterior surface of the pubis onto the pubic face (see arrows in Figure 9.18b). As time progresses, bone is deposited on the ventral bevel, forming what Todd called a **rampart**. This new bone causes the ventral margin to take the form of a right angle again between the anterior surface of the pubis and the pubic face (see arrows in Figure 9.18c). This feature usually starts inferiorly and begins to grow upward; at a slightly later time, it starts superiorly and moves downward. Eventually, the two ramparts grow together, forming a single well-defined structure (see arrows in Figure 9.18d).

In addition to ventral changes, the dorsal margin similarly alters over time. Initially, the pubic surface is slightly curved from front to back (see Figure 9.19a [1]). As the ridges break down and the furrows fill in, the bone of the ventral pubic face builds up; this causes the surface to extend backward, forming a **plateau** (see arrow in Figure 9.19a [2]). This margin usually extends farther backward than the posterior surface of the pubic bone, causing its dorsal edge to be fairly sharp.

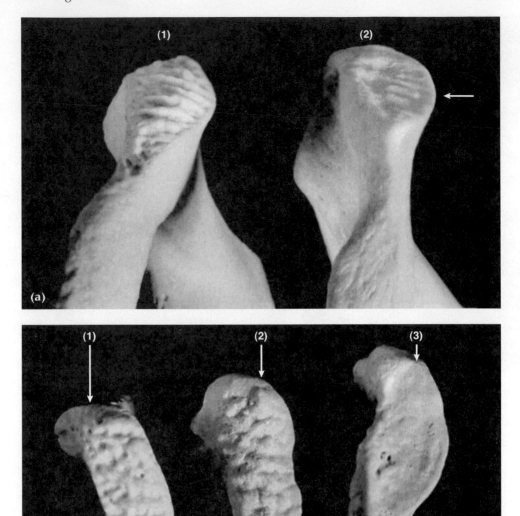

FIGURE 9.19 Development of two aspects of the pubic symphysis. **(a)** The dorsal plateau from young (1) without a plateau to old (2) with a plateau (*arrow*). **(b)** The extremeties: no extremeties (1), extremities forming (2), extremities fully formed (3). (Photos by Julie R. Angel; specimens courtesy of the University of New Mexico–Albuquerque, Maxwell Museum of Anthropology, #197, #89, #49, #19)

The upper and lower margins of the pubic face, called **extremities** by Todd, also undergo changes. During youth, the extremities are not easily distinguished, because the bone of the pubic face blends with both the inferior and superior surfaces of the pubis (see arrows in Figure 9.19b [1]). With aging, these margins become more defined, starting first with the lower extremity (see arrow in Figure 9.19b [2]). Eventually, the upper extremity also becomes defined (albeit not as distinctly as the lower), and both extremities are distinguished easily by viewing the pubic face (see arrows in Figure 9.19b [3]).

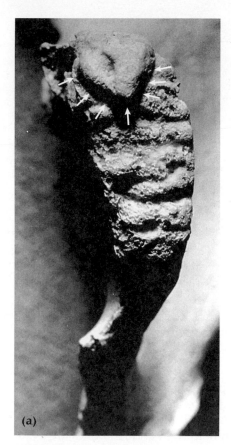
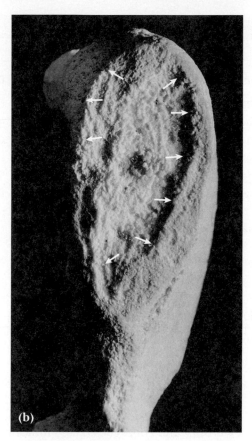

(a)

(b)

FIGURE 9.20 Miscellaneous changes in the pubic symphysis: **(a)** ossific nodule (*surrounded by arrows*) on the superior portion of pubic face; **(b)** rim (*arrows*) around the pubic face.
(Photos by Julie R. Angel; specimens courtesy of the University of New Mexico–Albuquerque, Maxwell Museum of Anthropology, #163)

Three last osteological features that appear with increasing age are ossific nodules, the rim, and lipping. **Ossific nodules** are "blobs" of bone (see Figure 9.20a) that can be seen in early adulthood. These appear to aid in the formation of both the upper extremity and the superior part of the ventral rampart. The **rim** is formed by the appearance of both the upper and lower extremities, as well as ventral and dorsal margins. This rim, which can be very distinct, usually is composed of cortical bone surrounding the more rough bone of the surface (see Figure 9.20b). The last feature is **lipping**. As age progresses, both the ventral and dorsal margins begin to curl outward, forming distinct lips. These structures are more visible on the dorsal surface, where they extend and thicken the edge already formed by the dorsal plateau.

The timetable of these events, derived from Meindl et al. (1985), is presented in Table 9.5. As can be seen, this schedule is tailor-made for use as a decision table (although rotated 90° to that described in Chapter 1). As each feature is assessed, the appropriate stage of modification can be circled; and, after all stages have been determined, the most likely age range will be the row with the most circles. In some instances, the stage for a feature may span two or more divisions; in these cases, those features that fit into only one stage can be given greater weight in estimating age.

Although the times given for the changes in the pubic face are in 5-year increments, other research has shown that these are too narrow. One such study by Judy Suchy and D. Katz (1986) shows 95% ranges that span four or more decades. Although there is anecdotal evidence that Meindl et al.'s (1985) modifications to the Todd method are useful

TABLE 9.5 Schedule of Changes in the Pubic Face[1]

Age Range	Pubic Surface	Margins		Extremities	
		Ventral	Dorsal	Upper	Lower
<20	Ridges and furrows	No bevel	Undefined	Undefined	Undefined
20–24	Ridges and furrows filling	No bevel	Begins definition	Undefined	Undefined
25–29	Ridges and furrows reduced	Bevel present	Plateau complete	Undefined	Partially defined
30–34	Granular appearance	Rampart complete	Plateau complete	Starts forming	Continues forming
35–39	Texture finer	Rampart complete	Plateau complete	Continues forming	Continues forming
40–44	Surface smooth	Rampart complete	No lipping	Fully formed	Fully formed
45–49	Rim around face	Irregular lipping	Uniform lipping	Fully formed	Fully formed
50+	Erosion and erratic ossification ⟶				

[1]Summarized from Meindl et al. (1985) and Table 22 of Krogman (1962).

as presented, age ranges derived from pubic faces probably should be increased somewhat over those given in Table 9.5. Also, if sex differences are desired, the above-mentioned study of Suchy and Katz should be consulted. Finally, a study by Rebecca Overbury and colleagues (2009) indicate that, when both right and left bones are available, better age estimates are derived from the pubic face that shows the greatest age.

Auricular Surface of the Os Coxa

While trying to improve methods of human osteology, Owen Lovejoy and colleagues (1985) discovered that the bones of the sacroiliac joint changed with time. They observed that the area of the auricular surface of the ilium underwent alterations that were similar to those seen in the pubic face. By correlating these changes to a timetable, they developed a new method for determining age at death from the skeleton. Although these alterations are subtle and therefore difficult to identify, their method is exceedingly useful, because this area of the os coxa often will survive cataclysmic events that destroy other skeletal structures. Also, the original study by Lovejoy et al. (1985) and a later one by Katherine and Tracy Murray (1991) show that the method works regardless of sex. The Murrays similarly demonstrated that it was equally applicable to Whites and Blacks.

Three parts of the posterior ilium (Figure 9.21) figure in this method of estimating age: the auricular surface, its apex, and the retroauricular area. The auricular surface is the L-shaped region where the sacrum and ilium articulate; it is easily recognized not only because of its shape, but also because it is a roughened area that stands in sharp contrast to the surrounding region. The **apex** is the anterior-superior

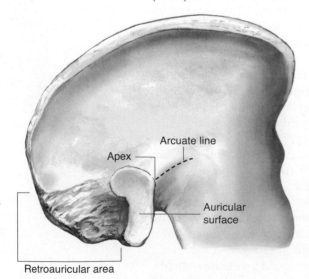

FIGURE 9.21 Major components of the posterior ilium used in aging: auricular surface; apex; retroauricular area.

corner of the auricular surface; it is located where the **arcuate line** intersects the auricular surface. The **retroauricular area** is that section of the ilium that lies behind the auricular surface; this oddly shaped region varies in contour from flat to fairly wavy.

Within these three parts, five features change with age. The first feature is the **transverse organization** of the auricular surface; this refers to the manner in which the bone appears to be arranged across the joint. In youth, this organization takes the form of **billows** (see [1] Figure 9.22a) that are similar to, but not as distinct as, the ridges on the pubic face. These too begin to fill in over time, becoming less well defined, and eventually they are replaced by **striae** (see [2] Figure 9.22a). Finally, all transverse organization, including striae, is lost (see [3] Figure 9.22a).

The second feature that changes with time is the **texture** of the bone of the auricular surface. This bone starts out granular in youth (see [2] Figure 9.22b), but becomes more coarse (see [1] Figure 9.22b) with age (this coarse bone is described by Lovejoy et al., 1985, as having the same roughness as fine sandpaper). As time passes, this gives

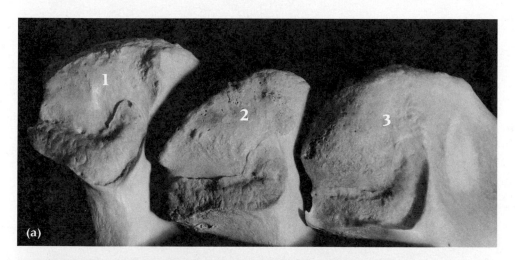

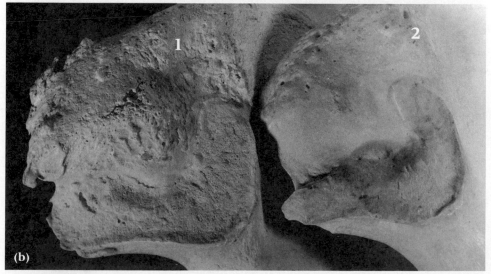

FIGURE 9.22   Changes to the auricular surface. **(a)** Aspects of the transverse organization: billows (1), striations (2), and no transverse organization (3). **(b)** Surface bone: coarse grained (1) and fine grained (2). (Photos by Julie R. Angel; specimens courtesy of the University of New Mexico–Albuquerque, Maxwell Museum of Anthropology, #49, #69, #55, #163)

way to dense bone that is similar to, but not as smooth as, compact bone of the diaphyses. Eventually, this smoothness is lost as the bone degenerates. The third feature, an increase in **porosity** of the auricular surface, is affected by this degeneration. Initially, perforations in this surface are small, called **microporosity** (see [1] Figure 9.23a), but they become larger, called **macroporosity,** over time (see [2] Figure 9.23a). These latter openings can be as much as 10 mm in diameter, although, generally, they are much smaller.

The fourth feature to change with age is the retroauricular area. The bone of this region starts out smooth and youthful looking (see [1] Figure 9.23b), becomes more coarse with time (see [2] Figure 9.23b), and eventually exhibits osteophytes and other outgrowths (see [3] Figure 9.23b). The final structure to undergo changes with time is

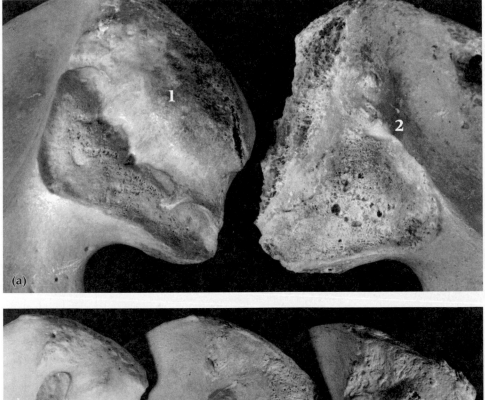

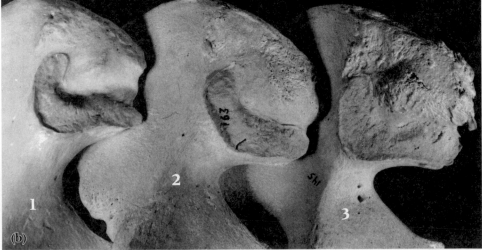

FIGURE 9.23   Changes to the auricular area. **(a)** Porosity: small (1) versus large (2). **(b)** Retroauricular area of ilium: smooth (1), coarse (2), rugged with ossifications (3).   (Photos by Julie R. Angel; specimens courtesy of the University of New Mexico–Albuquerque, Maxwell Museum of Anthropology, #103, #41, #49, #19, #145)

the apex; this begins in youth as a thin crescent border (Figure 9.24a) that thickens with age (Figure 9.24b).

The information on changes to the auricular surface and associated structures can be used to determine age. Table 9.6 displays the condition of each of the five features described previously in predetermined age ranges. This table can be used in the same manner as the decision table of Chapter 1. By assessing each feature and circling its condition on the table, age can be estimated from the row with the most circles. For example, suppose that an os coxa is found with reduced billows and striae composed of coarse bone over the enire auricular surface and accompanied by some microporosity, no apical activity and slight coarsening of the bone in the retroauricular area. Comparison with Table 9.6 would show that three of the five features fall into the 35 to 39 age range, while the other two fall into the 25 to 34 range. Therefore, the best estimate of age at death for this individual would be the late thirties, because the majority of the features fall into the 35 to 39 row.

Since the original work by Lovejoy and colleagues, the auricular surface has been the subject of considerable study. Osborne and colleagues (2004) noted that the age ranges given for the auricular surface changes were too small and needed to be expanded from 5 to 15 years. They also found that the method worked equally well in both sexes and ancestral groups (Black and White). Using a method that appears easier than the original technique, J. L. Buckberry and A. T. Chamberlain (2002) assigned a score based on the degree of development of each of the characteristics except for changes in the retroauricular area. Their findings, and that of two other studies of their method (Mulhern and Jones, 2005; Falys et al., 2006), indicate that scores can predict age at least as well as the Lovejoy et al. technique. Also, the method is equally applicable to males and females (Buckberry and Chamberlain, 2002; Mulhern and Jones, 2005) and to Blacks and Whites (Mulhern and Jones, 2005).

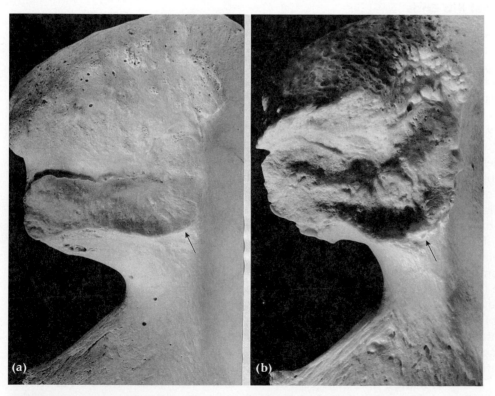

FIGURE 9.24 Apical activity: **(a)** thin (*arrow*); **(b)** thick (*arrow*). (Photos by Julie R. Angel; specimens courtesy of the University of New Mexico–Albuquerque, Maxwell Museum of Anthropology, #69, #19)

TABLE 9.6   Changes in the Auricular Surface of the Os Coxa by Age Range[1]

Age Range	Transverse Organization	Granularity	Apical Activity	Retroauricular	Porosity
20–24	Billowing	Very fine	None	None	None
25–29	Billows being replaced by striae	Slightly coarser	None	None	None
30–34	Less billowing, more striae	Distinctly coarser	None	Slight may be present	Some micro
35–39	Marked fewer billows and striae	Uniformly coarse	Slight activity	Slight	Slight micro
40–44	No billows; vague striae	Transition from granular to dense	Slight	Slight to moderate	Micro, maybe macro
45–49	None	Dense bone	Slight to moderate	Moderate	Little or no macro
50–60	None (surface irregular)	Dense bone	Marked	Moderate to marked	Macro present
60+	None	Destruction of bone	Marked	Marked with osteophytes	Macro

[1]Summarized from data in Lovejoy et al. (1985).

Sternal Rib Ends

In a pair of pioneering articles, M. Yasar Işçan and colleagues (1984, 1985) showed that the ends of the ribs that join with the sternum (via the **costal cartilage**) experience changes through time. Their work added yet another method for estimating age at death of adults from their skeletons. As mentioned previously, at birth and through infancy, the cartilaginous precursors of bone ossify into the hard tissues that are maintained throughout adulthood. However, as age increases, there is a tendency for the cartilage that joins bone also to ossify. This tissue appears to provide a framework for the deposition of calcium salts that produce bonelike structures within and around the cartilage. Many areas exhibit this phenomenon, including the thyroid cartilage of the throat and xiphoid process on the inferior end of the sternal body, as well as the costal cartilage. The outer surface of this latter cartilage ossifies and joins to the bone, causing the changes seen in the rib ends. Although only the right fourth rib has been studied, the changes discussed next appear to occur on either side of any of the ribs from three through ten (Dudar, 1993; Yoder et al., 2001).

Four features of rib ends change over time according to a varied but discernable timetable: surface bone, surface contour, rim edge, rim contour. The **surface bone** of the rib end begins as smooth cortical bone (see [1] Figure 9.25a), becomes granular over time (see [2] Figure 9.25a), and eventually becomes porous (see [3] Figure 9.25a). As these changes occur, the **surface contour** of the rib end transforms. This feature starts out billowy (see [1] Figure 9.25b), but, as time goes on, this becomes less noticeable and eventually the end becomes more flat (see [2] Figure 9.25b). With increasing time, the surface contour becomes indented, starting first as V-shaped (see [3] Figure 9.25b) and eventually becoming U-shaped (see [4] Figure 9.25b).

The next feature that changes with time is the **rim** around the sternal end. In youth, the end does not display this structure; however, as time goes on, a rim with a rounded edge begins to form as the costal cartilage starts to ossify (see [1] Figure 9.25c).

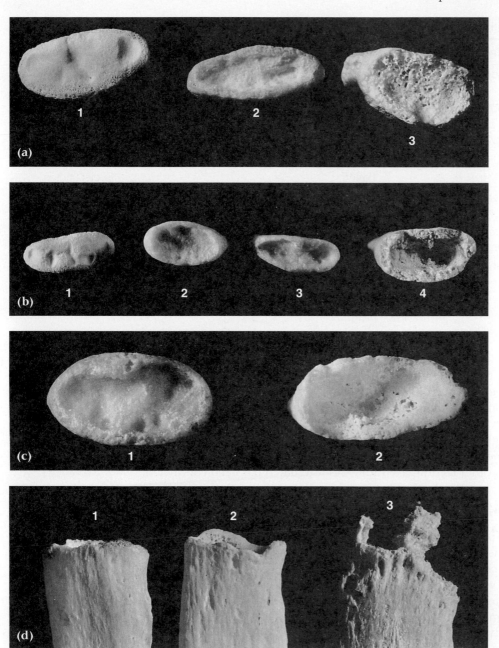

FIGURE 9.25 Sternal rib changes. **(a)** Surface bone from young to old: smooth (1), granular (2), porous (3). **(b)** Sternal rib end surface contour from young to old: flat with billowing (1), indented (2), V-shape (3), U-shaped (4). **(c)** Sternal rib end rim edge from young to old: rounded (1), sharp (2). **(d)** Sternal rib end rim contour from young to old: straight (1), undulating (2), projecting with fingers of bone (3). (Photos by Julie R. Angel; specimens courtesy of the University of New Mexico–Albuquerque, Maxwell Museum of Anthropology, #197, #49, #69, #176, #48, #179)

As more times passes, this rim becomes thinner and assumes a jagged edge (see [2] Figure 9.25c). The final feature of the rib end that changes with time is the **rim contour**. In youth, this feature is fairly straight, with contour only supplied by the coarseness of the bone (see [1] Figure 9.25d). As time passes, this structure becomes more wavy (see [2] Figure 9.25d) until, in advanced age, the rim begins to send fingers of bone medially toward the sternum (see [3] Figure 9.25d).

TABLE 9.7 Age Changes in the Sternal Rib Ends (White Males and Females)[1]

Age Range	Surface Bone	Surface Contour	Rim Edge	Rim Contour
19 and under	Smooth	Flat/indented with billows	Rounded	Regular to slightly wavy
20–29	Smooth	Indented; U- to V-shaped	Rounded	Wavy to irregular
30–39	More porous	V- to U-shaped	Sharp	Irregular
40–49	More porous	U-shaped with flaring	Sharp	Irregular with projections
50–59	Light and porous	U-shaped and deeper	Sharp	Irregular with projections
60–69	Lighter and more porous	U-shaped and deeper	Sharp	Irregular with projections
70+	Deteriorating	U-shaped	Sharp with thin walls	Same but with "windows"

[1]Condensed from data in Isçan et al. (1984, 1985).

The method developed by Iscan and his colleagues is too complex for a book of this nature. However, his major findings have been condensed into the schedule presented in Table 9.7, by which the above-described changes occur in White males and females. Again, the age of an individual can be determined by comparing the characteristics of the four features from a rib with those in the table. Notice that the age ranges are greater than those given in studies of other areas used for age determination (e.g., pubic face, auricular surface). Thus, this method probably will remain less accurate than other techniques until further research has been conducted.

Cranial Suture Closure

The use of cranial suture closure for estimating age has a long and controversial history. In the mid-1920s, T. Wingate Todd and D. W. Lyon published a series of articles describing changes in the cranial vault sutures related to age (Todd and Lyon, 1924, 1925a, b, and c). They discovered that these lines were open in young people but had a tendency to close through time until, by old age, they were completely obliterated. Despite this promising start, their research was flawed because they discarded specimens from their study that exhibited anomalous closures. Over 13% of Whites and 34% of Blacks that were originally part of their sample were excluded during analysis. Although these attempts to choose only specimens that fit a preconceived notion of "normal" were well intentioned, modern scientific theory renders this unacceptable. In addition, even though they culled their sample to obtain more homogeneous results, Todd and Lyon still encountered a high amount of variability, which made age estimates based on their method prone to considerable error. Thus, as time passed, many forensic (and other) anthropologists simply did not use this method.

In 1985, Richard Meindl and Owen Lovejoy published a restudy of the validity of determining age from cranial suture closure. Although they also encountered considerable variation, the method that they developed has been received more favorably because they used acceptable research procedures. In addition to their work, Robert Mann and colleagues (1987) have shown that changes to the sutures of the palate also can be used to estimate this demographic characteristic. Thus, because of the efforts of many workers, the use of cranial suture closure to estimate age at death has become more common. Unfortunately, despite this ample research, age estimates based on this phenomenon still are fairly inaccurate.

There are three areas of the skull whose sutures close according to a rough timetable (Buikstra and Ubelaker, 1994): the ectocranium, the endocranium, and the palate. The **ectocranium**, or outside of the skull, exhibits numerous sutures that close and obliterate through time; however, because the schedule of fusion is too irregular for many sutures, only those of the vault are useful in estimating age at death. The **endocranium**, or inside of the skull, manifests three sutures in its superior half that fuse over time. Although Todd and Lyon originally felt that these lines gave more accurate age estimates than those from the ectocranium (see Galera et al., 1998, for a recent treatment of this topic), Buikstra and Ubelaker (1994) feel that endocranial sutures provide only a rough indication of age at death. Finally, the **palate** also contains sutures that close and obliterate through the years; four sites on this structure can be either measured or observed for determining age at death.

ECTOCRANIAL SUTURES   As stated in Chapter 2, the human skull is composed of 22 easily visible bones, most of which are divided from each other by sutures (see Figures 2.6 through 2.9). Five of these have special names: coronal (dividing the frontal from the parietals), sagittal (separating the right from the left parietal), squamosal (dividing the temporal from the parietal), lambdoid (separating the occipital from the parietals), and basilar (dividing the occipital and sphenoid). All other sutures are named after the bones that they separate. For example, the sphenotemporal suture divides the sphenoid from the temporal bone; similarly, the sphenofrontal divides the greater wing of the sphenoid from the frontal. Thus, by knowing the names of the bones that they separate, all other sutures can be named.

Buikstra and Ubelaker (1994) recognize four stages of closure: open, minimal, significant, and obliteration. **Open** refers to sutures where there is no evidence of closure (Figure 9.26a). The gap between the bones is easily discernable and appears as a "bottomless" groove separating the bones. **Minimal** is characterized by the closing of these gaps by bridges of bone that vary from a single connection to bridges that encompass less than 50% of the entire suture (Figure 9.26b). **Significant** closure means that there is more than 50% fusion between the bones, but with some parts still open (Figure 9.26c). Finally, **obliteration** refers to complete fusion between bones with no discernible gap; the sutures either appear as lines drawn on the bones or are no longer visible (Figure 9.26d). Although these stages can be somewhat ambiguous, research has shown that rarely do workers deviate from each other's estimates by more than one category (Meindl and Lovejoy, 1985).

Meindl and Lovejoy (1985) found 10 locations on the cranial vault to be particularly useful for determining age. These are listed in Table 9.8 and illustrated in Figure 9.27. Furthermore, they found that the accuracy of the technique could be enhanced by dividing the sites into two groups. The vault locations consist of the midlambdoid, lambda, obelion, anterior sagittal, bregma, and midcoronal sites. The locations on the lateral-anterior cranium are the midcoronal, pterion, sphenofrontal, inferior sphenotemporal, and superior sphenotemporal sites; age estimates from these sites are considered more accurate than those from the vault locations.

Scoring at each of the previous sites is accomplished by assigning a numeric value to the amount of closure observed in the 1-cm area surrounding each point (i.e., half of a centimeter to either side of the site centers). For each category of closure described, these values are 0 for none, 1 for minimal, 2 for significant, and 3 for obliteration. After each site is scored, the resultant numbers are added together to determine the appropriate stage of closure depicted in Table 9.9. Using this stage, the age is determined by

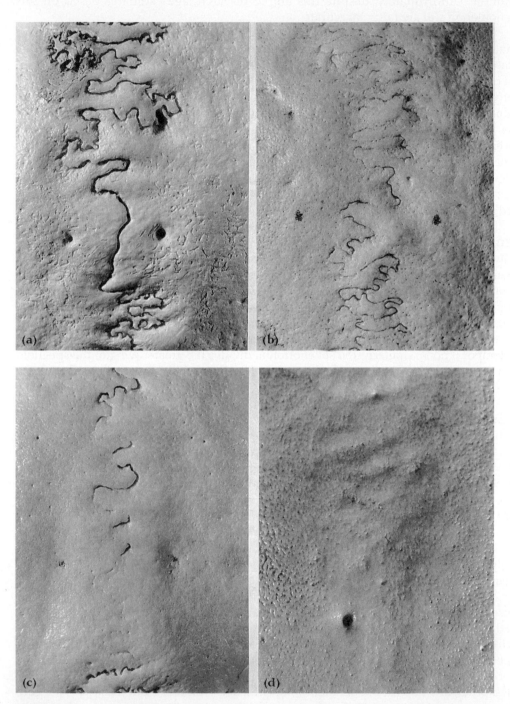

FIGURE 9.26 Suture closure at obelion (see text): **(a)** open; **(b)** partial; **(c)** significant; **(d)** obliterated. (The locations of the parietal foramen on b and c are darkened by pencil marks.) (Photos by Julie R. Angel; specimens courtesy of the University of New Mexico–Albuquerque, Maxwell Museum of Anthropology, #103, # 176; and of the State of New Mexico, Office of the Medical Investigator)

TABLE 9.8   Sites on the Ectocranium Used for Age Determination[1]

Site		Definition
1	Midlambdoid	Midpoint on lambdoid suture (usually observed on left side)
2	Lambda	Area around lambda
3	Obelion	Area between the parietal foramen
4	Anterior sagittal	Area at vertex of skull when held in Frankfort horizon; usually one-third the distance from bregma to lambda
5	Bregma	Area around bregma
6	Midcoronal	Area approximately two-thirds of the distance from bregma to Pterion
7	Pterion	Meeting of the sphenoid with the frontal and parietal
8	Sphenofrontal	Area between greater wing of the sphenoid and frontal
9	Inferior sphenotemporal	Area opposite the glenoid fossa on the sphenotemporal suture
10	Superior sphenotemporal	Area on the sphenotemporal suture superior to the zygomatic arch

[1]Summarized from Table 1 of Meindl and Lovejoy (1985).

matching with the information provided in Figure 9.28. Thus, an added score of 8 for the vault sutures would correspond to stage three in Table 9.9, which translates to an age of late twenties to mid-forties in Figure 9.28. As can be seen, there is considerable variability in the ages determined by this method; therefore, forensic anthropologists must be prepared to consider a large number of missing persons as possible matches with any human remains that are aged by only this technique.

ENDOCRANIAL SUTURES   A second set of sutures that can be used to determine age at death are found in the superior portion of the endocranial area (Buikstra and Ubelaker, 1994). Observed either through the foramen magnum or directly on the top of the skull that has been removed during autopsy, the amount of fusion in these sutures is considered to be only a general indicator of this demographic characteristic. Thus, age at death usually is assigned as only one of three broad categories of adulthood: early (between 20 and 34 years of age), middle (from 35 to 49), and late (50 years and over). Fusion at three sites on the three superior endocranial sutures (see Figure 9.29) has been shown to be roughly correlated with age. The site on the coronal suture is partway from bregma but not quite as far as pterion; it usually is taken on the left side (letter a of Figure 9.29). Closure of the sagittal suture is observed for the entire length of this feature (letter b of Figure 9.29), while only the segment from lambda to asterion on the lambdoid suture is observed, again on the left side (letter c of Figure 9.29). The amount of closure follows the four categories described previously for ectocranial sutures (i.e., 0 through 3). Minimal (or less) closure at all these sites indicates young adulthood, while significant closure is typical of middle adulthood; suture obliteration is found in the later years (50 and over).

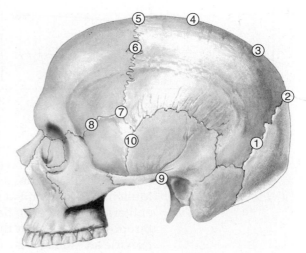

FIGURE 9.27   Vault sites used in determining age from ectocranial suture closure.

TABLE 9.9   Composite Scores of Vault and Lateral-Anterior Sutures[1]

Composite Score (vault)	Stage	Composite (lateral-anterior)	Stage
1–2	S1	1	S1
3–6	S2	2	S2
7–11	S3	3–5	S3
12–15	S4	6	S4
16–18	S5	7–8	S5
19–20	S6	9–10	S6
		11–14	S7

[1]From Ubelaker and Buikstra (1994).

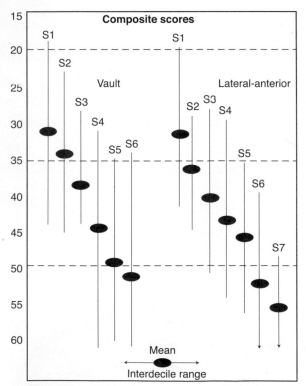

FIGURE 9.28   Chart showing relationship between closure scores and age.

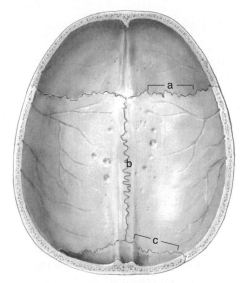

FIGURE 9.29   Endocranial suture locations: **(a)** area between bregma and pterion; **(b)** sagittal suture; **(c)** segment from lambda to asterion on the lambdoid suture.

PALATAL SUTURES   The final set of sutures that can be used to estimate age at death are those of the palate. Workers studying these lines (Mann et al., 1987; Gruspier and Mullen, 1991) attempted to predict age to the nearest year from the amount of suture obliteration. However, despite these efforts, most forensic (and other biological) anthropologists feel that the relationship between these two factors is too variable to provide an estimate any finer than one of the three categories of adulthood described previously. Therefore, as with endocranial sutures, the age of a person at death can only be estimated as young, middle, or late adulthood by observing the palate.

Three sutures in the palatal area are used in this method: incisive, median palatine, and transverse palatine (TP) (see Figure 9.30). The **incisive suture** separates the part of the palate containing the upper incisors from the rest of the maxilla. This area, sometimes called the **premaxilla**, is seen in infants and children; however, by adulthood it is usually obliterated. The **median palatine suture** separates the right from the left maxillary and palatine bones, while the **transverse palatine suture** separates the maxillae from the palatines. On these sutures, the amount of closure is recorded at four sites (Figure 9.30): the incisive suture (IN) described previously, the anterior part of the median palatine (AMP), the posterior part of the median palatine (PMP) suture, and the TP suture (observed on the left side). Buikstra and Ubelaker (1994) indicate that complete closure of the incisive suture (IN) and partial closure of the PMP and TP areas are indicative of young adulthood. They go on to state that middle adulthood is characterized by complete closure of these same three areas, with the anterior part of the AMP partially open; and complete obliteration of all sutures is indicative of advanced age.

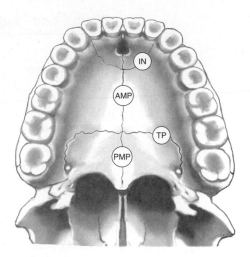

FIGURE 9.30 Sutures and sites of the palate used for determining age: incisive suture (IN), median palatine (AMP, PMP), transverse palatine (TP).

Histological Methods

There are a number of systems for determining age at death using microstructures of bone and teeth. These so-called histological methods require special instrumentation (e.g., microscope, microtome) to see the structures, as well as special training to use them. The two most common methods of this type involve cortical bone remodeling and the dental changes. Because each of these is labor-intensive, most forensic anthropologists are reluctant to use them. However, if only a single bone or tooth is available, or if multiple sources of information for determining this parameter are desired, estimates of age at death can be made.

CORTICAL BONE REMODELING Ellis Kerely (1965) is credited with the first attempt to use cortical bone remodeling to predict age at death. He employed quantitative measurements of four histological structures within a circular field of view encompassing 2.06 mm^2; these structures are number of whole secondary osteons (the Haversian systems [HS] described above), number of secondary osteon fragments (HS encroached by other HS), percentage of primary lamellar bone remaining, and non-Haversian canals (HCs) (primary vascular canals). These statistics are summed from four circular fields at mid-shaft of the femur, tibia, or fibula. The fields are located on the anterior, posterior, medial, and lateral quadrants of the bone cross section, tangent to the periosteal surface (see Figure 9.31). When the sums are entered into the formulae in Table 9.10, an estimate of age at death results.

Other researchers have developed similar methods either on the femur, tibia, and fibula or on the clavicle, rib, and the iliac crest. All of these methods result in estimates with similar (or slightly better) accuracy as other techniques described in this chapter. Although particularly useful in cases of fragmentary remains or those so severely damaged that histology is the only option, they have not gained popularity probably because of the special training and equipment required. In addition, there are several difficulties involved in their use. To view and count the osteons and other structures, thin sections of bone must be cut from the mid-shafts of one or more bones. These sections must be

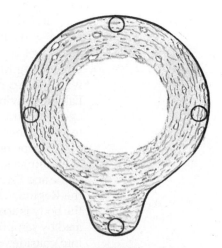

FIGURE 9.31 Sampling sites for counting histological structures. (From Figure 105 of Ubelaker [1999]. Courtesy of Taraxacum Press.)

TABLE 9.10 Regression Formulae for Calculating Age at Death from Histological Data[1]

Factor	Predicting Equation	SEE
Femoral osteons	$Y = 2.278 + 0.187X + 0.00226X^2$	9.19
Femoral fragments	$Y = 5.241 + 0.509X + 0.017X^2 - 0.00015X^3$	6.89
Femoral lamellar	$Y = 75.017 - 1.79X + 0.0114X^2$	12.52
Femoral non-Haversian	$Y = 58.39 - 3.184X + 0.0628X^2 - 0.00036X^3$	12.12
Tibial osteons	$Y = -13.4218 + 0.66X$	10.53
Tibial fragments	$Y = -26.997 + 2.5X + 0.014X^2$	8.42
Tibial lamellar	$Y = 80.943 - 2.281X + 0.019X^2$	14.28
Tibial non-Haversian	$Y = 67.872 - 9.07X + 0.044X^2 - 0.0062X^3$	10.19
Fibular osteons	$Y = -23.59 + 0.74511X$	8.33
Fibular fragments	$Y = -9.89 + 1.064X$	3.66
Fibular lamellar	$Y = 124.09 - 10.92X + 0.3723X^2 - 0.00412X^3$	10.74
Fibular non-Haversian	$Y = 62.33 - 9.776X + 0.5502X^2 - 0.00704X^3$	14.62

[1]From Table 1 of Kerley, E. R., Ubelaker, D. H. (1978). Revisions in the microscopic method of estimating age at death in human cortical bone. *American Journal of Physical Anthropology*, 49:545–546. Copyright © 1978 American Journal of Physical Anthropology.

ground to a thickness ranging from 100 μm to 10 μm (1 μm = one-millionth of a meter), sometimes stained, and then viewed under a 100-power microscope. These activities are both difficult and labor-intensive, especially considering the breakage that can occur with such delicate pieces of osseous tissue, and because multiple samples should be taken to arrive at precise estimations. In addition, accurately locating sites on the bone for counting histological structures is not easy, and the observation (count) error rate can be great especially near the edges of the fields of view. Finally, many researchers are unwilling to sacrifice a complete bone to arrive at an estimate of time since death. (This latter problem has been alleviated with the use of wedge and core samples.)

In addition to the difficulties just described, there are a number of factors that affect the rate of cortical bone remodeling through time, thereby adding to the difficulty in correctly applying this method. Although not unequivocal, some studies have noted differences in the remodeling rate between the sexes. Similarly, variations due to ancestry have been noted, with Whites having a higher rate of change in histological structures than Blacks, and Eskimos having an even higher rate. (This has led to the development of population-specific age-estimation regression formulae; see Cho et al., 2002.) Physical activity also appears to affect remodeling rates, with populations engaging in strenuous activity having an accelerated rate of bone removal and replacement. Even location of sample sites in the bone may affect age estimates (see Cho et al., 2006) as do pathological conditions, nutrition (see especially Paine and Brenton, 2006), and various drugs. Finally, many environmental factors can trigger the **Regional Acceleratory Phenomena** (an occurrence in which metabolism in a region of the body is accelerated), causing greater bone turnover in the area affected (this can be alleviated by sampling from more than one section of a bone). All of these factors need to be taken into consideration when employing histology as they can have a profound effect on age at death estimates. Thus, more than most methods, only persons who have received special training should attempt to determine age from these methods.

DENTAL CHANGES   A number of histological changes have been observed in the teeth of aging adults. Gustav Gustafson (1950) is credited as being the first researcher to develop a method for using these to determine age at death. His technique is well described by Karen Burns and William Maples (1976) who tested it on a large sample of teeth from persons of known age. Their article is used as the basis for the following discussion, with additions from others where noted. The Gustafson method involves using a 4-point scale (i.e., 0 to 3) to measure the amount of change through time of six dental characteristics: attrition, deposition of secondary dentin, changes in the paradentium, cementum apposition, root transparency, and root resorption. **Attrition** refers to the wear that occurs to the cusps and (later) crown of teeth over time; a value of 0 (A_0 in Figure 9.32) represents no wear while a 3 (A_3 in Figure 9.32) represents such severe wear that the pulp cavity is exposed. Secondary dentin, which is similar to the dentin that composes the tooth root and interior of the crown, is deposited into the pulp cavity during aging. It (usually) is not present when the tooth erupts (S_0 in Figure 9.32) but becomes more pronounced through time and even accumulates in the root canal (S_3 in Figure 9.32). The paradentium refers to the area on the root where the periodontal ligament attaches the tooth to its socket. At eruption, this level is located at the cemento-enamel junction (P_0 in Figure 9.32) but recedes with age (P_3 in Figure 9.32); this feature is affected heavily by periodontal disease (i.e., recession of the alveolar margin of the jaw). Cementum apposition refers to the accumulation of cementum on the roots of teeth; C_0 denotes little or no apposition while C_3 indicates cementum that almost doubles the thickness of the tip of the root. Root transparency refers to the increasing propensity through time for light to pass through more and more of the roots when the tooth is held up to a light source (T_0 to T_3 of Figure 9.32). This appears to be due to the accumulation of minerals in dentinal tubules that honeycomb the dentin of the tooth roots; these minerals allow for the passage of light, making the tips of the

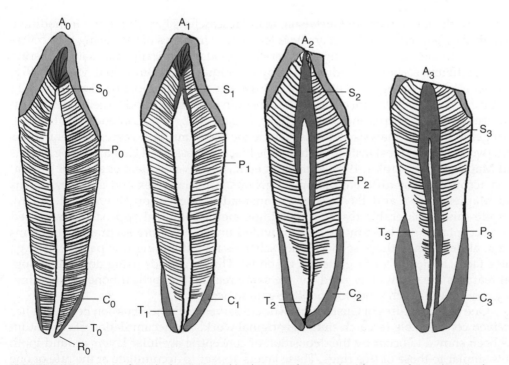

FIGURE 9.32   Stages of tooth changes used in the Gustafson method (see text for explanation). (From Figure 3 of Burns and Maples [1976]. Copyright ASTM International. Reprinted with permission.)

roots more transparent. This subject has received considerable attention through the years (see Drusini et al., 1991, for a list of sources); and there is even evidence that the amount of change through time differs between ancestral groups (Whittaker and Bakri, 1996). The final characteristic of Gustafson, root resorption, refers to the loss of the tips of the roots during aging in a manner opposite their formation. When fully developed, the root tip appears as R_0 in Figure 9.32; however, with age, this structure shows root resorption only on small isolated spots. With the greater passage of time, there is a greater loss of substance, and finally there are great areas of both cementum and dentin greatly affected.

To obtain the scores for each of these characteristics, the tooth must be cut into 300 μm (or thicker) sections. Gustafson (1950) favored longitudinal slices such as those in Figure 9.32; however, Burns and Maples (1976) point out the advantages of serial (multiple) cross sections, particularly in multi-rooted teeth. Also, any tooth can be used; however, some researchers feel that the anterior teeth yield better results than the molars. Once scores are obtained for each characteristic, they are summed and entered into a regression equation (see Chapter 1 for discussion of regression) to estimate age at death. Gustafson's original formula is as follows:

$$\text{Age at death} = 11.43 + 4.56 \text{ (sum of scores)} \tag{1}$$

Thus, if a tooth shows A_1, S_0, P_1, T_2, C_2, R_0, equation (1) would be given as follows:

$$
\begin{aligned}
\text{Age at death} &= 11.43 + 4.56 \ (1 + 0 + 1 + 2 + 2 + 0) \tag{2}\\
&= 11.43 + 4.56 \times 6 \\
&= 11.43 + 27.36 \\
&= 38.79 \text{ years}
\end{aligned}
$$

Since the initial work of Gustafson, many researchers have built on, or modified, both his data gathering and data analysis techniques in hopes of increasing the accuracy of his estimates or simplifying the overall method. Modifications to data gathering include different sectioning and microscopy techniques (e.g., Burns and Maples, 1976; Metzger et al., 1980; Sognnaes et al., 1985; Drusini et al., 1991), more precise scales (e.g., Sognnaes et al., 1985; Drusini et al., 1991; Lamendin et al., 1992), and larger and more diverse samples (e.g., Burns and Maples, 1976; Drusini et al., 1991; Lamendin et al., 1992). Changes to the data analysis methods include the use of multiple regression (equations with two or more slopes) instead of the single linear regression of Gustafson (e.g., Burns and Maples, 1976; Maples, 1978; Lamendin et al., 1992; Valenzuela et al., 2002), equations accounting for different biological groups, especially sex and ancestry (Burns and Maples, 1976), and Bayes theorem instead of regression (Lucy et al., 1996). Despite this considerable research, no single methodological approach has gained wide acceptance nor has any method provided unusually more accurate estimations of age at death than those seen in other schemes for estimating this parameter (e.g., pubic faces, auricular surface, sternal rib ends). Thus, methods using dental histological features are not widely used for the same reasons as cortical bone remodeling: they require too much work for too little gain in accuracy.

One of the features of Gustafson's work deserves further discussion because it has received considerable research since his original work. The accumulation of cementum has been shown to occur by the deposition of concentric acellular layers around tooth roots similar to those of tree rings. These layers appear to accumulate at the rate of one for each year of life after the tooth has fully erupted and formed. Thus, by taking the average age of eruption of a tooth and adding the number of these annulations appearing on the tooth, age at death can be estimated (Kagerer and Grupe, 2001). Although the possible precision of this is extremely attractive, research has shown that the scheme does not provide any greater accuracy than other methods (Jankauskas et al., 2001), apparently due to health and other factors that affect the rate of deposition and due to the difficulty in obtaining an accurate count of lines.

Other Methods

There are a number of other methods, not already described, that are less often used to determine age at death. Robert Walker and Owen Lovejoy (1985) studied the loss of proximal femur and clavicle cortical bone to see if it could be used to estimate age at death. They found that this **cortical bone involution** correlated with age at death, but was so variable that its use was limited. In addition, Stewart (1979) and Snodgrass (2004) cite the association between the development of osteophytes (see Chapter 15) and increasing age; the 4-point scale of osteophytic development used by them shows a definite but highly variable association with age. Also, Ubelaker (1989) describes a number of similar changes in joints of the body that are indicative of advanced age; and, he also calls attention to degeneration of joints and other structures (e.g., braincase) that indicate advanced age at death. All of these have their uses in forensic anthropology; however, most can be employed properly only by experienced forensic anthropologists.

A final method of estimating age at death involves aspartic acid racemization. A review by Susumu Ohtani and Toshiharu Yamamoto (2005) of numerous articles shows that considerable data supports the accurate estimation of age at death using this method. Racemization is a process by which one chemical converts (at least partially) to another. In the case of aspartic acid, the L-form of this amino acid converts to the D-form according to a relatively reliable timetable. (The L and D refer to different configurations of the atoms within the aspartic acid molecule.) By determining this relationship, a regression equation (see Chapter 1) can be calculated between the ratio of D- to L-form and age; thus, by knowing the ratio in an unknown specimen, the age of the individual can be calculated. Ohtani and Yamamoto recommend using the dentin of teeth (see Chapter 2) to determine the amounts of D-form and L-form of aspartic acid, but bone (especially from the skull and femur) also can be used. They note that a standard error of ±3 years is possible from this method.

Summary

1. The age at death of persons can be estimated from the human skeleton by knowing changes that occur in both the growing and deteriorating skeleton.
2. The age of fetuses and neonates can be approximated from the lengths of their long bones.
3. The age of children 12 and under can be estimated from the lengths of their long bones, the development and eruption of their teeth, and the fusion of their primary and secondary ossification centers.
4. The age of adolescents can be approximated from the amount of union in their various epiphyses.
5. Adults can be aged by observing changes in the pubic face, the auricular surface, the sternal ends of ribs, and the amount of suture closure observed in the skull.
6. Generally, the bone of the pubic face changes over time, from an undulating surface covered by youthful-looking cortical bone to a flat area covered by pitted and old-looking bone.
7. The aging bone of the auricular surface changes in a manner similar to that seen on the pubic face.
8. Changes to the sternal ends of the fourth (and other) ribs include loss of smooth bone, development of a rim, and medial growth of fingers of bone along the costal cartilage.

9. The amount of fusion of the palatal as well as cranial sutures (observed both inside and outside the skull) can yield a rough estimate of age at death.

10. Changes in the number and construction of microscopically visible structures in cortical bone can be used to estimate age at death.

11. The Gustafson method uses histological structures of the teeth to estimate the age of persons when they died.

12. Several less popular methods used to determine age at death include cortical bone loss, and the development of vertebral osteophytes.

Exercises

1. A femur is found that measures 75 mm in length. What is the approximate age of the infant represented by this bone?

2. A tibia measuring 250 mm is found with a radius that measures 140 mm. What is the approximate age of the infant represented by these bones?

3. A subadult skull with partial mandible is brought in for analysis. After x-raying, it is revealed that the crown of the lower right deciduous canine is fully formed, but the root has not yet developed. What was the approximate age of the person represented by this mandible?

4. The same person described in Exercise 3 has a lower left deciduous first molar whose crown is fully formed with a partially developed root. What is the age of the person from this source? Is there a conflict between these two sources of information?

5. A child's skull is found with no deciduous dentition; however, all permanent teeth, except the third molar, have erupted, but have not yet reached their final placement. What is the age of this person using the standards for Whites? For Native Americans?

6. A subadult skeleton is found with its permanent teeth (except the third molar) fully erupted and in their final place. In addition, none of the epiphyses on the femur, tibia, and fibula has begun to fuse with its respective diaphyses. What was the approximate age of this individual at the time of death?

7. An adult os coxa is found with a pubic face with smooth surface bone surrounded by a rim. What is the approximate age at death of this individual?

8. Suppose the posterior ilium of the person described in Exercise 7 exhibited an auricular surface with no transverse organization, microporosity, slight apical activity, and slight activity in the retroauricular. What is the approximate age at death from this information? Is there a conflict with the data provided by the pubic face?

9. Suppose that a skull is found with the remains of the person described in Exercises 7 and 8. The palatal and endocranial sutures are fully fused. In addition, the summed score for the lateral-anterior ectocranial sutures is 6. What is the approximate age at death of this individual based on this information?

10. Using a range chart, determine the best estimate of age at death for the person described in Exercises 7, 8, and 9.

10

Calculation of Stature

An estimation of stature is the final demographic characteristic that aids law enforcement officials in their search for a match between skeletal remains and their missing persons files. Early methods promoted rearticulating the skeleton and measuring the resultant length to arrive at this estimate. (See Box 10.1 for an example of how this can go astray.) However, later work showed that there was a strong correlation between living height and bones and/or skeletal segment lengths. This led to the development of formulas and tables that allow for the estimation of stature from measurements of these elements. For example, it was found that the humerus was approximately 20% of total height, leading to a well-known (albeit imprecise) method of multiplying the length of that bone by 5 to arrive at an estimate of stature. Many other bones, skeletal structures (e.g., the vertebral column), and even body segments have been studied in this manner, making stature reconstruction one of the more heavily researched areas in forensic anthropology.

In the following seven sections, the subject of estimating stature from skeletal remains of adults will be examined. (Height estimation in subadults is of limited utility because the rapid growth of young persons renders stature records quickly out of date; Ruff, 2007, presents formulas for this purpose if desired.) First, the basics of stature reconstruction are discussed, with a description of the principal methodological errors. Second, the calculation of stature from the full, or nearly full, skeleton will be presented. Third, the more common technique of using long limb bone measurements to determine this parameter will be described. Fourth, the use of other skeletal elements for this task will be presented, followed by a discussion of using fleshed body segments to reconstruct stature. The sixth section involves the use of fragmented long bones to calculate this demographic characteristic, while the final section deals with adjustments due to age, bone shrinkage, and discrepancies between reported and measured height.

BASICS OF STATURE RECONSTRUCTION

From a logical standpoint, stature is composed of the heights and lengths of five skeletal structures: skull, vertebral column, pelvis, lower limbs, and ankles. Knowing this obvious fact lead Thomas Dwight to develop a method of determining stature by direct measurement of a rearticulated skeleton. He did this by propping up bones in modeling clay, with proper spacing between skeletal elements for tissues lining the joints, to simulate their positions in life (see Stewart, 1979). Others have advocated that, if all connective tissue is present, the remains can be hung from probes placed in the ears and the body can be simply measured. Although it is tempting to use such methods, there are a number of difficulties with these techniques (Stan Rhine, personal communication). First, all the bones that compose stature must be present (i.e., skull, all 24 vertebrae, sacrum, leg bones, and feet); this is

BOX 10.1
Full Skeleton Versus Stature Formulas

Michael Charney (1974) describes a case in which the measurement of a cadaver would have ended in a poor measurement of stature that may have prevented an ultimate identification. The case involved human remains found in a reservoir in Idaho. The partially skeletonized body was taken to a funeral home, where a pathologist and funeral home director did a preliminary analysis before calling Charney for assistance. His examination revealed that the skeleton was that of a Native American woman who was approximately 25 to 35 years old at the time of her death. Although these conclusions were fairly straightforward, the estimation of stature was more problematic.

In their preliminary analysis, the pathologist and funeral home director had measured the supine remains from head to foot, resulting in a stature of 4'11". However, when Charney observed the cadaver, he noted that the vertebral column was no longer a single articulated structure. Rather, it consisted of two halves, which overlapped each other to a considerable extent. Noting that, he proceeded to use the methods of forensic anthropology to determine stature. After cleaning the remaining soft tissue from the skeleton, he used information provided by Santiago Genovese for Mesoamerican Indians since these were the only data available that are specific to Native Americans. Noting that the combined lengths of the left femur and tibia were 78.75 cm, he determined that the individual was around 5'2.5" tall. When he reported his findings to the police, they located a missing persons file that matched his demographic profile, including stature. When it was proved from rehydrated fingerprints that the skeleton was that of the missing person, Charney was gratified to see that his estimation of stature was off by only ½". The woman was 5'3", not the 4'11" height estimated by the pathologist and funeral director.

not common in the forensic situation. Second, the logistical problems of laying out a disarticulated skeleton in the living position are many. For example, connecting the vertebral column to the skull requires that the atlas, axis, and other cervical vertebrae be raised off the surface on which they lie. Also, holding all the vertebrae in the position normal in life (i.e., with the three curves) is difficult in the absence of soft tissue. Similar problems exist when the lower limbs and feet are rearticulated. Third, reassembling a skeleton in such a manner as to reproduce the spacing of bone in life is difficult. As discussed in Chapter 2, cartilage lines the joints between the bones, and this adds to the measurement of height. Because few standards exist for these thicknesses, reassembled skeletons may underestimate or overestimate these amounts. Finally, for articulated remains, the soft tissues dry and shrink unevenly; this causes skeletal elements, particularly the vertebral column, to assume positions not normal in life. Thus, despite their apparent logic, these methods have little utility in real life.

The basic approach to stature reconstruction has been to measure the bones from skeletons of persons whose stature in life was known. This information has then been used to develop tables or formulas relating stature to bone lengths and heights for use with bones from persons of unknown living height. The Terry and Hamann–Todd collections have been employed extensively for these types of studies. Similarly, this is one of the goals of the Forensic Anthropology Data Bank being maintained by the University of Tennessee (see Chapter 1).

As with full skeleton techniques, a number of problems are engendered by this method. In a fine review article, Stephen Ousley (1995) outlines the majority of these difficulties, and his article is summarized here. One major difficulty in these types of studies involves the mismeasurement of statures on the living. There are examples of heights taken on the same person that vary by as much as 5 inches. Similarly, statures measured on the cadavers of the Terry and Hamann–Todd collections have problems of accuracy, because hanging a body by probes placed in the ears (the usual method) adds as much as 2 inches to this estimate. Another problem is that stature varies with time of day; measurements taken in the morning, or after a reclining rest, are almost 1 inch greater than those taken after 6 or more hours without lying down. Presumably, this phenomenon is due to compression of disks of cartilage between the vertebrae and the tissues of the heel pad.

A third problem involves **secular changes** that have occurred in stature over the last century. For example, it has been shown that the relationship between bone length and living height in contemporary persons is different from that in bodies of the Hamann–Todd and Terry collections. This makes tables and formulas developed from these latter collections less valuable. A fourth problem is that there is a consistent bias associated with reported stature (as stated on driver's licenses and similar documents) and measured stature. Generally, males tend to overestimate their heights, whereas women estimate this measurement more accurately. Finally, there are problems with taking bone measurements. In the past, there have been conflicting definitions of how bones (especially the tibia) should be measured. Similarly, there is an inter-observer error (albeit small) associated with even properly measured bones.

All these problems must be kept in mind while considering the contents of the following sections. Although a single estimate of height is the result of all stature reconstruction methods, the error engendered in the research leading to these methods and the error surrounding these estimates make the calculation of living height subject to considerable variability.

FULL SKELETON METHODS

Although only rarely used, the most common method for reconstructing stature from the complete skeleton is that of Georges Fully, described by Stewart (1979) and later revised by Michelle Raxter and colleagues (2006). This technique estimates height from the summed heights and lengths of the body segments that make up stature, with a correction factor for soft tissue. The body dimensions (taken in centimeters) are skull height, the heights of the vertebra, the lengths of the femur and tibia, and the ankle height (AH). Skull height is the distance from basion to bregma, which is taken with a spreading caliper (see Figure 10.1). The vertebral heights are taken from the superior to the inferior surfaces of the bodies (see Figure 10.2); except for the atlas all cervical, thoracic, and lumbar vertebrae are measured as well as the height of the first segment of the sacrum. The measurement of the femur is its bicondylar length (Figure 10.3), and the length

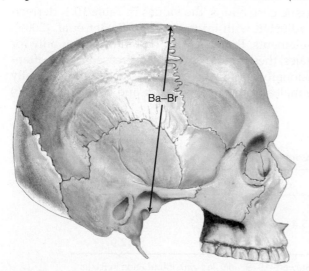

FIGURE 10.1 Basion–bregma (Ba–Br) height of skull.

FIGURE 10.2 Thickness (T) of the vertebral body.

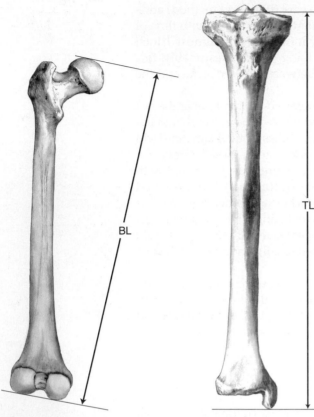

FIGURE 10.3 Bicondylar length (BL) of the femur.

FIGURE 10.4 Length (TL) of the tibia.

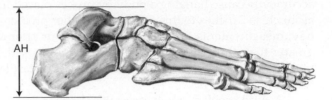

FIGURE 10.5 Ankle height (AH) from the talus and calcaneous.

of the tibia excludes the spines (Figure 10.4). Finally, AH (Figure 10.5) is the distance from the superior surface of the talus to the inferior surface of the calcaneous when they are held in natural articulation. (See Raxter et al., 2006, for more complete instructions on how each of these measurements is taken.) Stature can be obtained either by summing of all these measurements and adding a correction factor for soft tissue thicknesses or by using the following regression formula provided by Raxter and colleagues (2006):

Stature = 11.7 + 0.996 (sum of skeletal elements) **(1)**

If age can be estimated from the remains, Raxter and colleagues (2007) provide a modified version of the above formula that they show increases its accuracy. They include an age factor in their regression equation, which can be the actual age in years, or the middle of the age decade in which the remains lie (e.g., 25 for individuals judged to be in their twenties):

$$\text{Stature} = 12.1 + 1.009 \times (\text{sum of skeletal elements}) - 0.0426 \times (\text{age}) \qquad \textbf{(2)}$$

For those wishing to use soft tissue corrections, the values in Table 10.1, derived by Fully on males from France and adjusted with information in Raxter et al. (2006), are added to the sum of the skeletal elements. Because Fully had information only for males, to apply this technique to females, these amounts can be decreased by the often-stated statistic that this sex is dimensionally about 92% of males. Also, although Fully developed this method using White males from France, Raxter and colleagues (2006)

TABLE 10.1 Soft Tissue Correction Factors for the Fully Method[1]

Calculated Height (cm)	Male (cm)	Female (cm)
153.5 or less	12.2	11.2
Over 153.5 and less than 165.4	12.8	11.8
165.5 or above	14.0	12.9

[1]Male data from Fully quoted by Stewart (1979) adjusted with information in Raxter et al. (2006); female values 92% of male values.

BOX 10.2
A Sixth Lumbar Vertebra and the Fully Method

John Lundy (1988) encountered an anomalous situation when using the Fully method to calculate stature. While examining the skeleton of a naval aviator shot down during the Vietnam War, he discovered that the sacrum contained an extra element. Instead of S1 (the first sacral element) being the first member in this structure, a lumbar vertebra was found fused to its top. On further examination, it was discovered that this individual had five normal lumbar vertebrae. Therefore, not only was this lumbar vertebra fused to the sacrum, but also it was an extra one at that! Since the living height of this person was known from his naval personnel records, Lundy saw this as an opportunity to determine the effect of supernumerary vertebrae on the anatomical method.

Lundy proceeded to determine stature using the method of Fully (1956). First, he measured and summed all the bones and structures required by this technique. For the first segment of the sacrum, he used the height of the fused sixth lumbar vertebra. This process resulted in a stature of 5'10", approximately 1½" shorter than the measured height. Although this was a fairly good estimate, Lundy then added the height of S1, because it was reasonable to assume that this element also added to the height of the person in life. The inclusion of this bone in the reconstructed stature resulted in an estimate that was equal to that listed in the personnel records.

From his experience, Lundy feels that the inclusion of the fused lumbar vertebra in the reconstruction of stature is warranted in most cases. He feels that if the pelvis is rearticulated and held in the normal anatomical position, the fused lumbar vertebra should be included in the calculation of stature if both the lumbar vertebra and the first sacral vertebra lie above the upper border of the hip socket.

have shown that the factors are applicable to Blacks; and although there is no direct evidence, there is no reason to believe that they are not also directly applicable to Asians and Hispanics. This method is considered to be very accurate (although, as seen in Box 10.2, the presence of extraneous factors sometimes must be taken into account) because Fully estimated that his method comes within 1 cm (i.e., approximately one-half inch) of the true stature. However, when Raxter et al. (2006) found that his method underestimated true stature in their sample by approximately 2.5 cm, they calculated the preceding regression equation and adjusted his soft tissue corrections (see Table 10.1) to arrive at estimations of living stature that were within 4.5 cm in 95% of the individuals they studied. Addition of the age factor in their formula led to no significant difference between actual stature and predicted stature (Raxter et al., 2007).

LONG LIMB BONES

Although full skeleton techniques are more accurate, the most popular methods for determining height from the skeleton use long limb bones. Employment of these bones is based on the recognition that tall people have long arms and legs, while short people have short limbs. This correlation between body segments has led to the development of tables showing statures for corresponding bone lengths and regression formulas that give the relationship between limb bone lengths and living height (see Chapter 1 for a discussion of regression formulas).

Mildred Trotter, with the help of Goldine C. Gleser (1952, 1958), is credited with collecting and analyzing the earliest and best data on correlations between known stature and lengths of long limb bones for the U.S. population. Her studies include over 5000 males and females of White and Black ancestry from both the Terry collection and American servicemen killed in World War II and the Korean War. The Korean War sample included males not only of White and Black ancestry, but also Asians (she used the term *Mongoloid*), Hispanics (she used the term *Mexican*), and Puerto Ricans. Stature was available from the documentation of the Terry collection, and from records of the Armed Forces on the heights of the servicemen at the time of their enlistment and afterward. She used this measurement in correlation with the total lengths (TLs) of the humerus, radius, ulna, femur, tibia, and fibula (although there is some confusion as to how she measured the tibia; see Jantz et al., 1995) to develop tables and formulas that use bone length to estimate stature. For a summary of their work, including formulas for calculating stature from various long bones, see Trotter (1970).

Unfortunately, data has been accumulating that the relationship between bone length and stature changes through time. Individuals in the Terry collection represent persons born from the mid-1800s to the early 1900s, while American servicemen were born mainly in the early 1900s and modern forensic skeletal collections contain people usually born in the middle 1900s and later. Comparison of stature-bone relationships between these groups showed that they differed significantly (Meadows and Jantz, 1995), indicating a need for newer formulas based on modern populations. Rebecca Wilson and colleagues (2010) have calculated these formulas based on 242 individuals born after 1944 using data in the National Institute of Justice Database and the Forensic Anthropology Databank. Unfortunately, there is enough data to create formulas only for Whites and Blacks of both sexes, making it necessary to continue to use the formulas of Trotter and Gleser for Asians and Hispanics (Trotter's Mexican; Trotter and Gleser, 1958, indicate that the stature of Puerto Rican males are best estimated from the formulas for Blacks).

The analysis of stature-long bone data discloses several important points. First, there is a fairly strong relationship between lengths of long bones and stature. Although this relationship is not perfect, the bones of the arms and legs can be used to predict the living height of a person within a reasonable margin of error. Regression formulas with attendant standard errors (SEs) proved the best for making this prediction. Second, the correlation between right and left bones is very strong; thus, since asymmetry between sides is relatively minor, it is irrelevant which bone (right or left) is used in any stature calculation. Third, there is a strong correlation between the lengths of different bones within the same individual. Thus, analysis showed that long humeri are found in persons with long radii and ulnae; similarly, short femora are found in persons with short tibiae and fibulae. Fourth, dividing the sample by sex and ancestral group results in a more accurate estimate of stature. Therefore, it appears that various groups differ proportionally in trunk length, head height, AH, and other unmeasured features. Fifth, lower limb bones correlate more strongly with stature than those of the upper limb. Thus, using the femur, tibia, and fibula in the calculation of living height yields more accurate estimates of this parameter than the humerus, ulna, and radius. Finally, the accuracy of the estimate of stature increases with the number of bones used. Usually, regression formulas employing multiple long limb bones have the smallest SEs, whereas those using only one bone have the largest errors.

Table 10.2 presents the Wilson et al. and Trotter and Gleser formulas, separated by ancestral group and sex, for determining stature from long limb bones. These equations use the maximum lengths of the humerus (see Figure 10.6), ulna (see Figure 10.7), radius (see Figure 10.8), fibula (see Figure 10.9), femur (see Figure 10.10), and tibia (see Figure 10.4), and are presented with their respective SEs. Although there are no equations for Asian and Hispanic females, the male formulas can be used and their results can be multiplied by 0.92 to arrive at an approximation of feminine stature. Also note that these two groups do not have formulas for the tibia; this is due to problems with the Trotter and Gleser measurement of this bone alluded to earlier.

Unfortunately, to use the formulas of Table 10.2, ancestry and sex must be known. Because this is not always possible (particularly in mass disasters where body parts may be scattered over a large area), the absence of the skull and pelvis makes the application

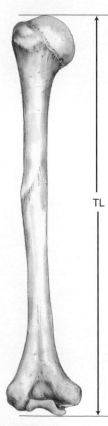

TL

FIGURE 10.6 Total length (TL) of the humerus.

TABLE 10.2 Stature Reconstruction Formulas Using Long Limb Bones, Separated by Ancestral Group and Sex[1]

Formula	SE	Formula	SE
White Males		**Black Males**	
St = 3.574*Hum + 57.21	5.71	St = 3.277 * Hum + 65.46	5.72
St = 4.525 * Rad + 61.22	5.70	St = 4.235 * Rad + 63.46	5.07
St = 4.534 * Uln + 53.33	5.66	St = 3.979 * Uln + 62.95	5.79
St = 2.701 * Fem + 48.10	5.12	St = 2.455 * Fem + 56.66	4.84
St = 2.891 * Tib + 62.95	5.06	St = 2.455 * Tib + 75.48	5.03
St = 2.832 * Fib + 66.96	5.15	St = 2.665 * Fib + 69.39	4.53
St = 1.728 * (Hum + Fem) + 36.76	5.16	St = 1.522 * (Hum + Fem) + 50.69	4.83
St = 1.525 * (Fem + Tib) + 44.19	4.81	St = 1.295 * (Fem + Tib) + 60.18	4.73
St = 1.556 * (Fem + Fib) + 42.77	4.90	St = 1.341 * (Fem + Fib) + 57.18	4.28
White Females		**Black Females**	
St = 2.534 * Hum + 86.62	5.32	St = 3.785 * Hum + 47.35	4.56
St = 3.530 * Rad + 83.29	4.81	St = 3.781 * Rad + 75.20	5.01
St = 3.346 * Uln + 82.82	4.51	St = 3.285 * Uln + 80.70	4.18
St = 2.624 * Fem + 49.26	3.58	St = 2.449 * Fem + 54.86	4.34
St = 2.351 * Tib + 80.11	4.26	St = 2.855 * Tib + 58.20	3.83
St = 2.487 * Fib + 76.51	4.16	St = 2.993 * Fib + 55.83	4.29
St = 1.656 * (Hum + Fem) + 46.71	3.72	St = 1.566 * (Hum + Fem) + 46.12	4.12
St = 1.330 * (Fem + Tib) + 58.37	4.01	St = 1.340 * (Fem + Tib) + 54.75	3.50
St = 1.382 * (Fem + Fib) + 54.89	3.85	St = 1.365 * (Fem + Fib) + 54.28	3.87
Asian Males		**Hispanic Males**	
St = 2.68 * Hum + 83.19	4.25	St = 2.92 * Hum + 73.94	4.24
St = 3.54 * Rad + 82.00	4.60	St = 3.55 * Rad + 80.71	4.04
St = 3.48 * Uln + 77.45	4.66	St = 3.56 * Uln + 74.56	4.05
St = 2.15 * Fem + 72.57	3.80	St = 2.44 * Fem + 58.67	2.99
St = 2.40 * Fib + 80.56	3.24	St = 2.50 * Fib + 75.44	3.52

[1]Data for White and Black, males and females from Table 2 of Wilson et al. (2010), data for Asian and Hispanic males taken from Trotter (1970).

of formulas in Table 10.2 impossible. In these cases, general formulas for stature are needed irrespective of ancestral group or sex. Unfortunately, although such equations can be calculated, the amount of imprecision would be so great as to render them value-less. For example, from the Trotter and Gleser data for males and females of all ancestral groups, the 95% confidence interval (CI) for statures from skeletons with femurs of average length (approximately 45 cm) extends from 155.6 to 177 cm. This corresponds to heights of 5 feet, 1 inch, to 5 feet, 10 inches. Thus, the variation of stature from femora of this length would encompass a huge proportion of persons in the United States. Because this is not very informative, general equations for stature in the absence of demographic group probably are not accurate enough to be useful.

As an example of how to calculate stature, given the information provided above, suppose that an ulna is measured at 31 cm. If there are no data on ancestry and sex, the

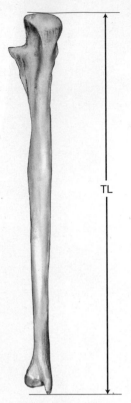

FIGURE 10.7 Total length (TL) of the ulna.

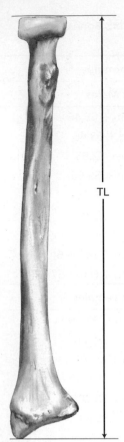

FIGURE 10.8 Total length (TL) of the radius.

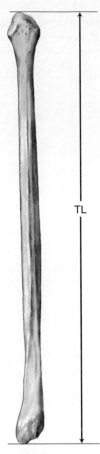

FIGURE 10.9 Total length (TL) of the fibula.

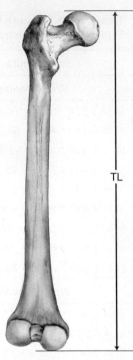

FIGURE 10.10 Total length (TL) of the femur.

most that can be said is that the person probably was about average in height (this value is close to the average of all ulnae). Suppose, however, that a skull is found with this bone and its characteristics indicate that it is a Black male. The appropriate formula from Table 10.2 is

$$\text{Stature(St)} = 3.979(31) + 62.95 \approx 186.3 \tag{3}$$

Because law enforcement agencies use standard American measurements, this figure should be converted into inches and feet. Some calculators have a button for making this conversion. However, in their absence, the method for conversion given below for this example can be used:

$$\frac{186.3}{2.54} \approx 73 \text{ inches} \tag{4}$$

$$\frac{73}{12} = 6 \text{ feet (plus a remainder)} \tag{5}$$

$$73 - (6 * 12) = 73 - (72) = 1 \text{ inches} \tag{6}$$

$$\begin{aligned}\text{St} = {}&6 \text{ feet from calculation (5) and (approximately)} \\ &1 \text{ inches from calculation (6)}\end{aligned} \tag{7}$$

When reporting the range within which the actual stature could fall, the SE can be employed. As discussed in Chapter 1, the general (and erroneous) approach has been to multiply this number by 2 and both add and subtract that amount from the calculated stature to give the 95% CI. For the example in equation (3), the SE for the formula using the ulna of Black males is 5.79 cm. Thus,

High end of range: 186.3 + (5.79 × 2) = 197.88 (or 6 feet, 6 inches)   **(8)**

Low end of range: 186.3 − (5.79 × 2) = 174.72 (or 5 feet, 9 inches)   **(9)**

Unfortunately, although this method is in common use, the resultant limits, as discussed under Regression Equations in Chapter 1, do not account for the greater deviation of the estimates at the ends of the ranges. Again the reader is referred to any text on statistics for a discussion of the proper method for determining the 95% CI of an estimate derived from regression.

OTHER SKELETAL ELEMENTS

In addition to long limb bones, stature can be calculated from other bones and bony structures. The three that have been studied as of this writing are the metacarpals, metatarsals, and the vertebral column. Of these, only the studies involving metacarpals and the vertebral column use adequate sample sizes and persons drawn from diverse populations. Although none of these results in formulas with accuracies of the order seen in Table 10.2, they can be used when the long bones are missing.

Two studies have explored the relationship between metacarpal length and stature; however, the research of Lee Meadows and Richard Jantz (1992) employs the largest and most diverse sample, so only their findings will be discussed here. These researchers used recorded stature and measured the lengths, to the nearest millimeter, of the five metacarpals. This measurement was taken from the middle of the proximal articular surface to the middle of the distal tip. Table 10.3 presents their formulas for

TABLE 10.3   Stature Reconstruction Formulas Using Right Metacarpals Separated by Ancestral Group and Sex[1]

Formula	SE	Formula	SE
White Males		**Black Males**	
St = 1.659 * Met1 + 91.77	5.52	St = 1.659 * Met1 + 89.15	5.52
St = 1.261 * Met2 + 85.51	5.15	St = 1.261 * Met2 + 81.60	5.15
St = 1.279 * Met3 + 85.98	5.36	St = 1.279 * Met3 + 81.61	5.36
St = 1.375 * Met4 + 89.54	5.33	St = 1.375 * Met4 + 85.44	5.33
St = 1.443 * Met5 + 93.16	5.67	St = 1.443 * Met5 + 89.35	5.67
White Females		**Black Females**	
St = 1.659 * Met1 + 90.02	5.52	St = 1.659 * Met1 + 85.45	5.52
St = 1.261 * Met2 + 82.52	5.15	St = 1.261 * Met2 + 76.11	5.15
St = 1.279 * Met3 + 83.44	5.36	St = 1.279 * Met3 + 76.80	5.36
St = 1.375 * Met4 + 86.44	5.33	St = 1.375 * Met4 + 81.07	5.33
St = 1.443 * Met5 + 89.95	5.67	St = 1.443 * Met5 + 84.41	5.67

[1]Taken from Meadows and Jantz (1992); metacarpal measurements in mm, stature in cm.

TABLE 10.4 Stature Reconstruction Formulas Using Right Metatarsals Separated by Ancestral Group and Sex[1] (All Measurements in mm)

Formula	SE	Formula	SE
White Males		**Black Males**	
St = 15.2 * Met1 + 76.8	6.32	St = 17.6 * Met1 + 55.6	5.10
St = 11.3 * Met2 + 86.8	7.01	St = 14.0 * Met2 + 60.5	5.68
St = 12.0 * Met3 + 86.2	6.89	St = 13.3 * Met3 + 70.6	4.22
St = 12.3 * Met4 + 86.3	6.85	St = 13.0 * Met4 + 75.9	4.65
St = 12.8 * Met5 + 93.8	7.22	St = 14.7 * Met5 + 76.1	6.80
St = 11.2 * Met5$_m$ + 91.2	7.03	St = 11.5 * Met5$_m$ + 84.6	6.42
White Females		**Black Females**	
St = 16.3 * Met1 + 65.6	4.96	St = 12.8 * Met1 + 79.6	5.08
St = 12.8 * Met2 + 71.2	5.20	St = 10.9 * Met2 + 78.3	3.99
St = 13.3 * Met3 + 73.2	5.76	St = 9.9 * Met3 + 90.4	4.49
St = 13.8 * Met4 + 71.9	5.75	St = 9.3 * Met4 + 96.1	4.65
St = 12.3 * Met5 + 90.0	6.63	St = 10.2 * Met5 + 97.9	4.74
St = 10.6 * Met5$_m$ + 90.5	6.49	St = 10.2 * Met5$_m$ + 89.1	4.52

[1]Met5$_m$ indicates morphological length. From Byers, S. N., Churchill, S., Curran, B. (1989). Determination of stature from metacarpals. *American Journal of Physical Anthropology*, 79: 275–279. Copyright © 1989 John Wiley & Sons, Inc. Reprinted by permission of Wiley-Liss, Inc., a Subsidiary of John Wiley & Sons, Inc.

White and Black males and females calculated on the right bones only. As can be seen, their SEs are larger than those in Table 10.2, indicating that metacarpals should not be used when long limb bones are present.

The author of this textbook with the help of several friends performed a similar study in which they used the lengths of foot bones, specifically the five metatarsals, to calculate stature (see Byers et al., 1989). Their sample consisted of 130 individuals: 57 White males, 51 White females, 13 Black males and 9 Black females. Although Blacks are woefully underrepresented, the results of their analysis are presented because they are the only formulas associating metatarsal length and stature. The authors regressed stature recorded during life against the (total) lengths of each of the five metatarsals (the straight distance from the head to the center of the articular surface) and the morphological length of the fifth metatarsal (the distance from the tip of the head to the tip of the tuberosity). Table 10.4 presents their resultant formulas with the attendant SEs. As with the metacarpals, these formulas have such large SEs that they should only be used when long limb bones are not present.

Donald Jason and Kathy Taylor (1995) studied the relationship between vertebral column length and stature among Whites and Blacks of both sexes. They used crown–heel measurements of cadavers as an estimate of living height, and they measured the lengths of the cervical, thoracic, and lumbar segments of the vertebral column while the bones were still articulated by soft tissue. Table 10.5 presents their equations for reconstructing stature from the lengths of the various vertebral column segments. As can be seen, some segments have fairly sizable SEs (e.g., the cervical segments of females), making them less useful in stature calculation than other segments. As with

TABLE 10.5 Stature Reconstruction Formulas Using the Vertebral Column (All Measurements in cm)[1]

Formula	SE	Formula	SE
White Males		**White Females**	
St = 5.40 * C + 103.7	6.45	St = 5.19 * C + 101.4	7.11
St = 3.60 * T + 69.6	5.91	St = 3.92 * T + 57.1	6.08
St = 4.06 * L + 95.6	6.66	St = 4.38 * L + 82.4	6.87
St = 2.39(TL) + 58.6	6.03	St = 2.65(TL) + 42.9	5.72
St = 2.07 * (CTL) + 47.3	5.29	St = 2.33 * (CTL) + 29.7	5.32
Black Males		**Black Females**	
St = 8.92 * C + 62.3	5.94	St = 2.50 * C + 134.1	5.41
St = 4.07 * T + 59.3	6.09	St = 3.02 * T + 84.2	3.58
St = 4.70 * L + 85.7	6.74	St = 3.93 * L + 91.5	4.32
St = 2.79(TL) + 42.7	5.82	St = 1.98(TL) + 75.2	2.60
St = 2.42 * (CTL) + 29.4	5.09	St = 1.66 * (CTL) + 70.3	3.62

[1]C = cervical, T = thoracic, L = lumbar; taken from Jason and Taylor (1995).

metacarpals and metatarsals, these formulas should be used only in the absence of long limb bones.

FLESHED BODY SEGMENTS

Bradley Adams and Nicholas Herrmann (2009) studied the relationship between fleshed body segments and stature using two very large samples from the National Health and Nutrition Examination Survey (NHANES) and the U.S. Army Anthropometric Survey (ANSUR). Not unexpectedly, they discovered medium to high correlations between various body segments and stature, thereby generating useful regression equations when forensic anthropologists are confronted with a situation when the removal of soft tissue from decedents is not desirable or possible. Table 10.6 lists the measurements used in their study while Tables 10.7 and 10.8 present their stature reconstruction formulas. One particularly useful result of their research is that the large sample sizes mean that 95% CIs can be obtained directly from the SE; thus, the multiplication of SE by 1.96 and its subtraction and addition to the stature estimate is a very accurate estimation of this interval (see discussion in Chapter 1, Data Analysis Methods).

PARTIAL LONG LIMB BONES

Bones submitted for osteological analysis often have been damaged by physical, biological, or chemical forces. Injury by impact with hard surfaces, gnawing by carnivores, and erosion by caustic substances is not unknown in forensic cases. In some instances, this damage is sufficient enough that the length of a bone cannot be measured reliably. Faced with this situation, forensic anthropologists must either guess the length of the bone before it was damaged or not provide an estimate of stature. Because the latter option is not favored, several researchers have attempted to provide information on the

TABLE 10.6 Measurement Definitions on Fleshed Bodies[1]

Measurement	Definition
UPARMLTH	Taken with the right arm flexed 90° at the elbow and the palm facing up. On the right scapula, locate and *mark with a horizontal line* the uppermost edge of the *posterior* border of the acromion process. . . . Hold the zero end of the measuring tape at this mark and extend the tape down the posterior surface of the arm to the tip of the olecranon process (the bony part of the mid-elbow).
UPLEGLTH	Taken with the upper leg at right angles to the body, and the knee bent at 90°. Position the small sliding caliper as if you were measuring the breadth of the patella. Position the caliper blades against the distal end of the femur on either side of the patella. The horizontal bar of the caliper should be touching, or close to the anterior surface of the thigh, proximal to the patella. Using the superior edge of the horizontal bar of the caliper as a guide, mark a line with a wax-based cosmetic pencil on the anterior surface of the thigh. Place the zero end of the steel measuring tape at the inguinal crease, just below the anterior superior iliac spine (this is easily located if the hips are in a sitting position). Do not apply pressure at the inguinal crease. . . . Extend the tape down the anterior midline of the thigh to the mark that was previously made proximal to the patella.
BUTTKLTH	The horizontal distance between the most posterior point on the buttock and the anterior point of the knee measured while the knee is flexed 90°. Measured along the lateral thigh with an anthropometer rod.
FOOTLGTH	The maximum length of the foot from the heel to the tip of the longest toe measured with calipers.
FORHDLG	The horizontal distance between the posterior surface of the elbow and the tip of the middle finger taken while the elbow is flexed 90°. Measured with a caliper.
HANDLGTH	The distance from the tip of the styloid process of the radius to the tip of the middle finger. Measured with a caliper.
KNEEHTSI	The vertical distance between the bottom of the foot and the suprapatellar landmark (point on the superior surface of the patella when standing). Measured with an anthropometer rod with the knee flexed 90°.
LATFEMEP	The vertical distance between the bottom of the foot and the lateral femoral epicondyle. Measured with an anthropometer rod and lower leg in vertical position.
SHOUELLT	The distance between the superior tip of the acromial process of the scapula and the bottom of the elbow. Measured with a caliper with the upper arm vertical and the elbow flexed 90°.
SPAN	The distance between the tips of the middle fingers when the arms are horizontally outstretched.

[1]UPARMLTH and UPLEGLTH taken from Anthropometry and Physical Activity Monitor Procedures Manual of the National Health and Nutrition Examination Survey; all others taken from Gordon et al. (1989).

relationship between fragmentary long bones and their TLs. Of these studies, the work of Gentry Steele (1970), supplemented by Müller quoted by Wilton Krogman (1962), will be discussed because it is the most widely accepted.

Stature determination from fragmented bones takes advantage of correlations between bone segments and total bone lengths. By obtaining the length of a segment of a known portion, the undamaged length of the bone can be determined. Although all bones can be analyzed in this manner, only segments for the femur, tibia, humerus,

TABLE 10.7 Stature Reconstruction Formulas Using Fleshed Body Segments[1]

Group	Formula	SE
All	St = 61.27 * 2.88 (UPARMLTH)	6.04
Male	St = 83.25 * 2.38 (UPARMLTH)	5.56
Female	St = 88.8 * 2.05 (UPARMLTH)	5.2
White	St = 65.68 * 2.81 (UPARMLTH)	5.84
Black	St = 66.84 * 2.72 (UPARMLTH)	6.36
Hispanic	St = 60.26 * 2.87 (UPARMLTH)	5.53
White male	St = 95.87 * 2.1 (UPARMLTH)	5.3
White female	St = 97.02 * 1.88 (UPARMLTH)	4.91
Black male	St = 98.48 * 2 (UPARMLTH)	5.34
Black female	St = 100.65 * 1.72 (UPARMLTH)	5.01
Hispanic male	St = 83.71 * 2.31 (UPARMLTH)	5.13
Hispanic female	St = 84.91 * 2.11 (UPARMLTH)	4.74
All	St = 85.56 * 2.02 (UPLEGLTH)	6.51
Male	St = 103.77 * 1.67 (UPLEGLTH)	5.77
Female	St = 109.85 * 1.34 (UPLEGLTH)	5.45
White	St = 86.03 * 2.05 (UPLEGLTH)	6.37
Black	St = 84.18 * 2.02 (UPLEGLTH)	6.58
Hispanic	St = 87.74 * 1.94 (UPLEGLTH)	6.04
White male	St = 115.26 * 1.45 (UPLEGLTH)	5.55
White female	St = 114.02 * 1.28 (UPLEGLTH)	5.19
Black male	St = 105.83 * 1.61 (UPLEGLTH)	5.35
Black female	St = 118.24 * 1.11 (UPLEGLTH)	5.26
Hispanic male	St = 105.58 * 1.57 (UPLEGLTH)	5.41
Hispanic female	St = 109.88 * 1.28 (UPLEGLTH)	5.03

[1]Taken from Adams and Herrmann (2009); measurements in mm, stature in cm.

TABLE 10.8 Stature Reconstruction Formulas Using Fleshed Body Segments[1]

Formula	SE	Formula	SE
Males		**Females**	
St = 1.80 * BUTTKLTH + 64.94	3.99	St = 1.60 * BUTTKLTH + 68.91	4.25
St = 3.57 * FOOTLGTH + 79.24	4.77	St = 3.50 * FOOTLGTH + 77.40	4.71
St = 2.15 * FORHDLG + 71.70	4.43	St = 1.94 * FORHDLG + 77.14	4.47
St = 4.44 * HANDLGTH + 89.58	5.08	St = 4.18 * HANDLGTH + 87.58	4.91
St = 2.12 * KNEEHTSI + 57.17	3.11	St = 2.07 * KNEEHTSI + 56.23	3.28
St = 2.21 * LATFEMEP + 64.69	3.30	St = 2.18 * LATFEMEP + 62.36	3.37
St = 3.05 * SHOUELLT + 63.10	3.84	St = 2.92 * SHOUELLT + 64.97	3.83
St = 0.66 * SPAN + 54.45	3.37	St = 0.62 * SPAN + 59.92	3.92

[1]Taken from Adams and Herrmann (2009); measurements in mm, stature in cm.

and radius have been studied in this regard. The sections of these bones are depicted in Figure 10.11, and their definitions are given in Table 10.9. Finally, Table 10.10 presents the percentage of each bone that the various segments comprise of the total.

The method for using this information is to determine the length of a segment of a bone that can be accurately measured. Then, using the percentages in Table 10.10, the total bone length can be calculated and this value can be entered into one of the formulas presented in Table 10.2. For example, suppose that a proximal portion of a male tibia is found such that only segments 1 to 2 and 2 to 3 can be accurately measured. If this section is 9.1 cm, then, using the percentages for males, the length of the tibia is

$$\text{tibia length} = \frac{9.1 * 100}{8.19 + 17.22} = \frac{910}{25.41} = 35.8\,\text{cm} \tag{10}$$

Similarly, if the head of a female humerus is discovered and the length of segment 1 to 2 is 32 mm, the TL of the bone would be (from the female formula)

$$\text{humerus length} = \frac{3.2 * 100}{10.77} = \frac{320}{10.77} = 29.7\,\text{cm} \tag{11}$$

Unfortunately, the SEs of statures derived from fragmented long bones are larger than those derived from both metacarpals and the vertebral column. Therefore, estimation

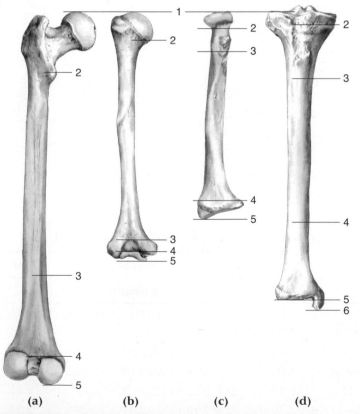

(a)   (b)   (c)   (d)

FIGURE 10.11 Segments of bone used to determine total bone length for **(a)** femur; **(b)** humerus; **(c)** radius; and **(d)** tibia. (Drawing of radius from Figure 46 of Krogman (1962); remaining bones from T. Dale Stewart, Figure 63 of *Essentials of Forensic Anthropology* (1979). Courtesy of Charles C. Thomas Publisher, Ltd., Springfield, IL.)

TABLE 10.9 Definitions of Long Limb Bone Segments[1]

	Femur
1 to 2	Distance from the most proximal point on head to the middle of the lesser trochanter
2 to 3	Distance from the middle of the lesser trochanter to confluence of the medial and lateral supracondylar lines on the popliteal surface
3 to 4	Distance from the confluence of the supracondylar lines to the most proximal point of the intercondylar fossa
4 to 5	Distance from the most proximal point of the intercondylar fossa to the most distal point on the medial condyle

	Tibia
1 to 2	Distance from the most proximal point on the lateral half of the lateral condyle to the most proximal point on the tibial tuberosity
2 to 3	Distance from the most proximal point on the tibial tuberosity to the confluence of the lines extending from the lower end of the tuberosity
3 to 4	Distance from the confluence of the lines extending from the lower end of the tuberosity to the point where the anterior crest crosses over the medial border of the shaft
4 to 5	Distance from the point where the anterior crest crosses over the medial border of the shaft to the proximal margin of the lateral part of the inferior articular surface
5 to 6	Distance from the lateral part of the inferior articular surface to the most distal point on the medial malleolus

	Humerus
1 to 2	Distance from the most proximal point of the head to the most distal point of the head
2 to 3	Distance from the most distal point of the head to the proximal margin of the olecranon fossa
3 to 4	Distance from the proximal to the distal margin of the olecranon fossa
4 to 5	Distance from the distal margin of the olecranon fossa to the most distal point on the trochlea

	Radius
1 to 2	Distance from the top of the head to the distal margin of the head
2 to 3	Distance from the distal margin of the head to the middle of the radial tuberosity
3 to 4	Distance from the middle of the radial tuberosity to the distal epiphyseal line
4 to 5	Distance from the distal epiphyseal line to the tip of the styloid process

[1]Definitions for the femur, tibia, and humerus compiled from information in Steele (1970); definitions for the radius from information of Müller quoted by Krogman (1962).

TABLE 10.10 Percentage of Total Bone Length for Segments Described in Table 10.9[1]

Segment	Femur		Tibia		Humerus		Radius
	Male	Female	Male	Female	Male	Female	
1 to 2	17.16	16.48	8.19	7.80	11.29	10.77	5.35
2 to 3	58.97	59.73	17.22	16.85	77.51	78.22	8.96
3 to 4	15.55	15.48	43.85	46.46	6.00	5.92	78.72
4 to 5	8.32	8.41	27.06	25.16	5.21	5.10	7.46
5 to 6	N/A	N/A	3.58	3.73	N/A	N/A	N/A

[1]Percentages for the femur, tibia, and humerus calculated from information in Steele (1970); percentages for the radius from Müller quoted by Krogman (1962).

of the length of incomplete long bones for use in the formulas for calculating stature should be avoided unless they are the only osteological material available.

ADJUSTMENTS TO STATURE

Several adjustments to stature can be made if other characteristics of decedents are known. First, as has often been observed, people lose stature with increasing age. This is due (presumably) to compression of the cartilage between bone joints and the collapsing of vertebral bodies due to fatigue fractures especially prevalent in osteoporosis. Second, bone shrinkage due to drying results not only in lighter weight (as discussed in Chapter 3), but also in smaller size. Thus, shrinkage must be considered before bone lengths are entered into regression equations. Third, studies have shown that reported stature often deviates from measured stature. Because drivers' license heights often are the source of height in a missing persons file, any bias due to this factor needs to be considered. Since each of these affects the final outcome of estimated height, each will be discussed in detail next.

Age of Individual

People lose stature with increasing age due to compression of the cartilage between bone joints. Although the tissues of the ankle, knee, and hip play a role, the cartilaginous pads between the vertebrae probably are responsible for the greatest part of this phenomenon. Generally, reduction starts around 45 years of age and accelerates over time (especially in females). To quantify this phenomenon, several formulas have been offered over the years (Trotter and Gleser, 1951; Galloway, 1988). However, work by Eugene Giles (1991), quoting large sample sizes, has shown that these formulas either overestimate or underestimate this effect. Therefore, only his work will be discussed here.

Using information on over 1000 Whites of each sex, Giles presented stature reductions by year starting with age 46. Unfortunately, as seen in Chapter 9, usually forensic anthropologists only have an estimate of age within 5- and 10-year increments. Thus, rather than provide his data in total, Table 10.11 presents a summary by the age groups most likely encountered in the forensic anthropology situation. As can be seen, the loss in height is not great, particularly in persons in their forties and fifties. However, when providing an estimate of this statistic on an unidentified person, all possible adjustments should be made in order to provide the most accurate approximation possible.

Bone Shrinkage

As described in Chapter 3, when in the body, bones contain various liquids (e.g., blood, lymph fluid) that hydrate these hard tissues, causing them to enlarge in all dimensions. With decomposition and exposure (as well as burning), bone loses these fluids, resulting in a concomitant shrinkage in length and width. This shrinkage affects stature calculations because the loss of several millimeters is amplified by the slope of the regression equation. Therefore, once bone lengths have been measured, this loss of dimensions should be accounted for when stature is calculated.

The amount of shrinkage due to desiccation is related to the length of time that the bones were exposed and the relative humidity of the environment in which the remains decayed. Rollet, working in the late 1800s, found a 2-mm shrinkage over a 10-month period

TABLE 10.11 Average Amount of Decrease in Stature (in mm) by Age Group for Males and Females[1]

Age Category	Males	Females
46–49	3.1	0.1
50–59	7.2	2.8
60–69	16.0	12.5
70+	32.3	33.9

[1]Summarized from data in Giles (1991).

in male and female long limb bones from French cadavers (Krogman, 1962). In a later study using a larger sample both of Whites and Blacks, N. William Ingalls (1927) found 1.5% shrinkage in the femur. Because his figure takes into account differences in bone length and since it is logical that other long bones shrink with a similar proportion, it is reasonable to apply this correction factor to desiccated bones.

The application of a correction factor is relatively simple at the extremes of bone moisture. For remains where there is abundant soft tissue, the correction factor most likely does not need to be applied. Conversely, when the bone is dry with no soft tissue, the full correction factor probably applies. However, for bones that exhibit some hydration, it becomes a matter of judgment as to how much correction should be applied. In these cases, only experience can guide the forensic anthropologist.

Fire can also affect both bone size and shape. Exposure to heat will result in a loss in all bone dimensions; thus, both widths and lengths are affected. In addition, heat can cause warping such that bones may bend along their long axes, making the measurement of length problematic. This subject is discussed in detail in Chapter 16; the reader should consult this chapter for further information.

Reported Versus Measured Stature

Several studies, summarized by Ousley (1995), have shown that there is bias between a person's reported height and his or her actual height as measured in a controlled manner (e.g., a doctor's office). On the average, males overreport their statures by ½ inch on documents such as drivers' licenses, whereas females generally only overreport this dimension by ¼ inch. Also, reported stature may not be updated as persons get older. Since it is known that stature at 16 (the legal driving age in most states) can be less than that after full growth (18 and above) and that stature begins to decrease after 45 years of age, heights on drivers' licenses can be fairly imprecise. The 95% range for this statistic from this source has been reported to be between 2 inches less and 3 inches greater than measured stature. One final bias is determined by the person's height; generally, taller persons estimate stature more correctly than shorter persons, who often overestimate their heights.

Summary

1. Stature is composed of the combined measurements of many bones in the skeleton: height of the skull, combined heights of the vertebrae, lengths of the femur and tibia, and height of the articulated talus and calcaneous.

2. One of the most accurate methods for estimating living stature from the skeleton is to measure these elements and apply a correction factor for soft tissue.

3. Despite its lesser accuracy, the most common method for calculating stature is to use the lengths of the long limb bones: humerus, ulna, radius, femur, tibia, and fibula.

4. A number of other bones can be used to estimate living height; those particularly useful are the length of the metacarpals and the height of the vertebral column.

5. If no complete limb bones (including hands and feet) are available, fragments of the femur, tibia, humerus, and radius can be used to reconstruct the total length of the bone. This length can then be entered into a stature reconstruction formula to estimate living height.

6. Because it has been documented that persons lose stature with age, estimates of living heights among persons determined to be 45 years or older at death need to be adjusted downward.

7. Fresh bones are approximately 1.5% larger than bones that have dried. Thus, the lengths of dry bones should be corrected upward by this amount before stature is calculated.

8. Reported stature is usually greater than actual stature; thus, calculated height may need to be adjusted downward.

Exercises

1. What is the stature of a White female with a 35-cm tibia? Give the answer in both metric (centimeters) and American (inches and feet) measure.

2. What is the stature of the same female with a 40-cm femur? Give the answer in both centimeters and inches and feet.

3. Which of the estimates in Exercises 1 and 2 is most accurate? Why?

4. The following series of bones are presented for stature estimation: skull, all vertebrae (including sacrum), humerus, ulna, tibia, femur, and the bones of the left foot. What is the best method for determining stature from this assemblage? Why?

5. A 4.2 cm fragment of a radius, composed of segments 1 to 2 and 2 to 3, is presented for analysis. What is the best estimate of the length of the complete radius before fragmentation?

6. Suppose that a humeral head is 5.2 cm. What is the stature of the person represented by the partial bone? What formula was used and why?

7. The following assemblage of bones from a Black male is presented for stature estimation: femur, left first metacarpal, thoracic and lumbar segments of the vertebral column (still articulated), and segments 1 to 2 of a tibia. What is the best bone for use in height reconstruction? What is his stature?

8. The calculated stature of a 60-year-old person is 168 cm. By what amount should this estimate be decreased? What is the best estimate of his stature?

9. A fully dried and desiccated tibia, measuring 35 cm long, is recovered in a forensic situation. What was the most likely length of this bone when in the body?

11

Death, Trauma, and the Skeleton

As outlined in Chapter 1, the last two topics of the forensic anthropology protocol involve the cause and manner of death. Although it is not their legal responsibility, forensic anthropologists should provide information that medical examiners or coroners can use to make these determinations. Logically, from skeletal remains, the only source of data on these two issues involves trauma to bone. Thus, to meet the expectation of helping to determine cause and manner of death from skeletonized remains, forensic anthropologists must be knowledgeable of the characteristics of trauma on human bone.

Trauma is a pathological category defined as injury caused to living tissue by an outside force. Outside forces include a variety of objects normally associated with violent deaths, such as bludgeons (e.g., clubs), projectiles (e.g., bullets), and cutting (e.g., knives) or chopping (e.g., axes) instruments. However, any hard surface can cause trauma, including the ground (during a fall) or large moving objects such as cars, trucks, and trains, as well as bulkheads during an aircraft accident. Another source of trauma is any chemical (e.g., acids) that may have a deleterious effect on the human body. Finally, extremes of heat (usually caused by fire) or cold can damage living tissue. Although these forces affect all tissues, forensic anthropologists are interested mainly in how they affect bone.

The early texts on forensic anthropology did not emphasize the analysis of trauma in the human skeleton. Wilton Krogman, who felt that this was not in the purview of the anthropologist, did not discuss the subject at all in the first edition of his classic *The Human Skeleton in Forensic Medicine* (1962). Similarly, T. Dale Stewart only briefly considers trauma in his *Essentials of Forensic Anthropology* (1979). However, emphasis on this type of analysis is increasing as forensic anthropologists become more involved in the criminal justice process (e.g., providing expert testimony in court). Thus, edited volumes by Ted Rathbun and Jane Buikstra (1984) and Kathleen Reichs (1986, 1998b) contain a number of chapters dealing with this subject.

In any analysis of trauma to human bone, the major issues that are important to law enforcement agencies must be kept in mind. These persons are interested in any specifics that can help them in their investigation of a medicolegally significant death. Generally, this involves five aspects of this subject. First, and probably most important, they are interested in any trauma that occurred at the time of death because this may provide evidence as to the cause and manner of death. Trauma occurring before death or postmortem damage to bone may be of interest for other reasons (see Box 11.1), but generally they do not speak to the circumstances of death. Second, the force that caused the trauma is of interest. If it was a weapon (e.g., club, knife), its size, construction, shape, and other characteristics will be of

BOX 11.1
Example of Antemortem Injury

Healed skeletal trauma is common in forensic cases. Usually, this takes the form of a broken wrist or simple fracture to the lower leg. However, Douglas Ubelaker and Henry Scammell (1992) describe the remains of a White female in her early twenties, who manifested multiple antemortem injuries that would have influenced the way she appeared in life. The accompanying police report mentioned three objects found in association with the remains: an unidentified metal device, a glass eye, and a silicone implant. Their description is given in full below.

One important key to identity lay in the old injury to her skull, which included evidence of massive trauma to the right frontal and right facial region. There was an immense hole in the forehead, an old compression fracture which had healed but not closed, traversing some 65 mm from the eye orbit to a place above the likely hairline. The right upper jaw just below the eye socket also had been fractured with a 3 mm displacement on the outside of that socket, so that one eye was lower than the other. A small wire (the unidentified metal device in the police report) extended through two natural canals in the right nasal bone. The glass eye, the wire insert, and the implant were almost certainly part of the surgical attempt to restore the face after that old trauma, which I estimated had taken place at least two years earlier.*

*From *Bones: A Forensic Detective's Casebook*, Copyright © 1992, by Douglas Ubelaker and Henry Scammell. Published by M. Evans and Company, New York.

interest. Third, the number of wounds are important; single wounds or multiple traumas speak to the manner of death (e.g., single gunshot wounds are more indicative of suicide; multiple wounds of homicide). Fourth, with multiple traumas, the sequence of wounds may yield information on circumstances surrounding the death. Finally, the placements of wounds are significant because they can help to determine the manner of death and the location of an attacker in homicides. Thus, trauma to the front and side can be associated with any manner of death; however, trauma to the back during an attack is more indicative of homicide.

If the trauma appears to be the result of an attack, the preceding topics may help law enforcement officials to determine characteristics of the attacker(s). Traits such as height may be suggested from the placement of wounds (e.g., wounds on top of the head are more likely to be delivered by a tall person). Also, sex may be suggested from the severity of wounds; for example, crushing trauma caused by a club is more indicative of a male, because females on the average are not strong enough to deliver such injuries. Even handedness might be able to be guessed by the placement of wounds (e.g., front trauma to the left side of the body is more indicative of a right-handed attacker). Because it is difficult to predict the use of any information gathered on trauma, forensic anthropologists are enjoined to describe all injuries in as much detail as possible.

All these issues of interest to law enforcement will be addressed in the following chapters. However, to understand how to interpret injuries, several topics surrounding bone trauma must be understood. First, the cause and manner of death will be defined and discussed, followed by a discussion of how they relate to bone injury. Next, the characteristics of the forces causing trauma will be presented; the emphasis will be on how moving objects cause injury to bone since damage caused by heat and cold as well as chemicals is less informative and more difficult to analyze. Third, the four types of trauma will be described: projectile, blunt, sharp, and miscellaneous; and the basic characteristics of each will be elucidated. Finally, the timing of bone injury in relation to death (i.e., before, around, or after) will be discussed with an emphasis on the traits that characterize each.

CAUSE AND MANNER OF DEATH

Several authors (Snow, 1982; Morse et al., 1983; Sauer, 1984; Sauer and Simson, 1984) have discussed the concepts of cause and manner of death as they relate to forensic anthropology. Because their work is so comprehensive, this section is based on their discussions, with observations from others. Although it seems flippant to state, the **cause of death** in all humans is the same; that is, the person stops breathing and his or her heart stops beating. This rather simple observation is of little use in forensics (as well as to the medical profession), so the cause of death here will refer to those factors that prompt these two events to occur. As is well known, there are any number of such factors. Diseases, such as cancer or heart disease, are major causes of death in industrialized countries. Additionally, accidental or intentional trauma causes the untimely end of people in both developed and undeveloped countries. Similarly, malnutrition causes many deaths, particularly in undeveloped countries. Finally, simple old age is a cause of death (although usually a single factor, such as heart failure, is given as the cause). Of all these, forensic anthropologists are most interested in death by trauma because this is most likely to be expressed in bone.

Bone trauma is usually the only source of information about cause of death available from skeletal remains. Unfortunately, with present methods it is rare that an actual determination of the factors that bring about death can be assessed simply by examining injuries to bone (Stewart, 1979). This is because there are too many unknowns surrounding this type of trauma. Most forensic anthropologists acknowledge this ambiguity by stating that observed trauma is "consistent" with a certain cause of death (see Ethical Responsibilities in Chapter 19). Thus, a gunshot wound to the head may have been the cause of death; however, because the existence of this type of wound in a skull does not prove it (e.g., the person was dead from other causes before being shot in the head), forensic anthropologists will list such cases as "consistent with death by gunshot." Although it constricts the meaning, statements such as this used (in conjunction with other associated evidence) usually will result in a determination of cause of death that is acceptable to the medicolegal community.

Manner of death refers to the way a person died, that is, by violence, from natural causes, or for other reasons. For forensic purposes, five manners have long been recognized: homicide, suicide, accident, natural, and unknown. For these, bone usually only exhibits clues concerning violent deaths, that is, deaths by homicide, suicide, or accident. These manners of death are most likely to result in skeletal trauma that can be interpreted by forensic anthropologists. However, occasionally some natural deaths leave bone markers. For example, some diseases leave skeletal lesions that may help to indicate a natural manner of death. Also, some deaths by natural causes may be the result of trauma to bone weakened by disease. Finally, many deaths by homicide, suicide, accident, disease, or natural causes leave indications only in the soft tissues. Because this leaves no imprints on the bones, forensic anthropologists generally state that there is no trauma to the skeleton; the medical examiner then may have to list the cause of death as unknown.

Although more possible to be assessed from bone than the cause of death (Sauer and Simson, 1984), recognizing the manner of death even when there is evidence of violence may not be as straightforward as it seems (see Box 11.2 for an exception). For example, a skeleton exhibiting multiple fractures resulting from what looks like a fall

BOX 11.2
Cause of Death in Mr. Miracle

Stan Rhine (1998) describes the case of a person that he refers to as Mr. Miracle. Not only did the skeleton of this individual manifest multiple healed fractures to the nose and humerus, as well as side of the face, but there were also numerous perimortem traumas. Rhine's description of the injuries to the head, spinal column, rib cage, arm, and pelvis is too long to quote in full. However, his account of what these injuries tell concerning the circumstances surrounding the death of Mr. Miracle is an excellent example of the information concerning cause of death that can be determined from bones.

This is what an analysis of the skeleton told us, and on the basis of this information, it was possible to say that about the time he died Miracle had been hit in the left side of the head, shot in the arm, kicked in the chest, and kicked or hit on the back. He was stabbed at least eight times: once in the right chest, twice in the neck, three times in the front of his chest, in his arm, and in his groin. The stab to the neck and at least one to the chest entered on his left side, suggesting that the knife blade was probably more like six to eight inches long...

What can one conclude about the cause and manner of death when essentially all of the information comes from the skeleton? First, given the nature of the defects that can be seen on the skeleton, it is clear that nothing succeeds like excess. The large number and types of defects on Miracle's skeleton, for example, made it easy to determine that his death was not a natural one. Nor was it suicide or accidental. All that is left is homicide.*

*From S. Rhine, *Bone Voyage*, University of New Mexico Press, Albuquerque, 1998, pp. 212–214, with permission.

from a high place probably indicates accidental death, but could be the result of homicide (e.g., the victim was pushed) or suicide (e.g., the victim jumped). Similarly, a gunshot wound to the back of the head usually indicates homicide, but some suicides have been documented with this type of wound (Eisele et al., 1981). Finally, there are any number of ways of dying by violence that leave no indication in the skeleton (e.g., quick poisoning). Such complicating factors only make the job of forensic anthropologists more difficult.

BASICS OF BONE TRAUMA

Donald Ortner and Walter Putschar (1981) present a readable account of the affects of traumatic-causing force on human bone, and their work is summarized here. When sufficient force is applied to bone, a discontinuity (i.e., break) will occur. If this discontinuity travels completely through the bone, it is called a **fracture** (see Figure 11.1a); if it is incomplete (see Figure 11.2a), the term **infraction** is used.

Although discontinuity refers to any break in bone, distinguishing between two types is useful in studying trauma: displacements and lines. **Displacement** occurs when surfaces that once were continuous no longer meet or meet at an unnatural angle. Examples of these include **complete fractures** of long bones where broken ends are separated from each other (Figure 11.1a). In cases of infraction where part of the fractured area is still attached to its original bone, the surfaces meet at an unnatural angle, forming a **hinge fracture** (see Figure 11.2b).

Other infractions include **green stick fractures**; these are breaks in bones where separation between the broken ends does not occur. They are most commonly seen in subadults when trauma occurs to a long bone, especially the clavicle. When a single

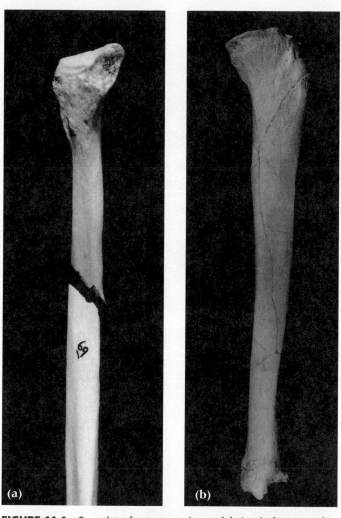

FIGURE 11.1 Complete fractures to bone: **(a)** simple fracture of the proximal fibula and **(b)** comminuted fracture to the tibia with multiple fragmentation of bone. (Photos by Julie R. Angel; specimens courtesy of the University of New Mexico–Albuquerque, Maxwell Museum of Anthropology, #69, #30)

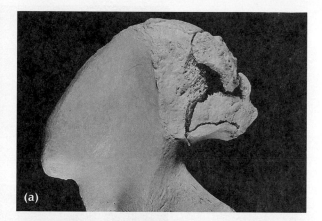

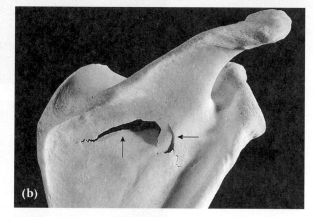

FIGURE 11.2 Two types of infractions: **(a)** incomplete fracture to the os coxa and **(b)** infraction resulting in hinge fractures (*arrows*) to the scapula. (Photos by Julie R. Angel; specimens courtesy of the University of New Mexico–Albuquerque, Maxwell Museum of Anthropology, #30, #58)

discontinuity results in a bone broken into two segments, it is referred to as a **simple fracture** (see Figure 11.1a); these are common in breaks resulting from falls (e.g., broken arm). **Comminuted fracture** refers to breaks that result in the production of multiple fragments of bone (see Figures 11.1b and 11.3a). These are more common in death by violence, including homicide (e.g., bludgeoning of the skull), suicide (e.g., jumping from a high place or in front of a speeding vehicle), and accident (e.g., automobile accident).

The other type of discontinuity involves **fracture lines**. These usually originate near the point of impact, where they help dissipate the contacting force across the bone surface. These lines usually are described as taking two forms: radiating and concentric. **Radiating lines** are the most common form of fracture lines; these disperse outward, like an irregular sunburst, from the area of applied force (see Figure 11.3b). Generally, because of their pattern, their center of radiation indicates the point of impact of the causative force. The other type of fracture line, most common in high-velocity projectile

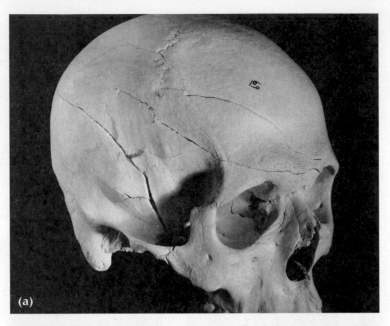

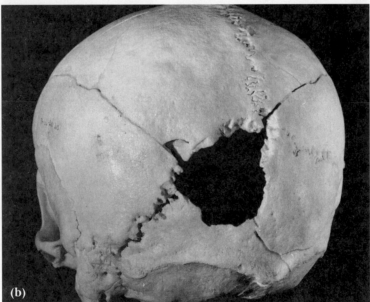

FIGURE 11.3   Results of trauma to the skull: **(a)** comminuted fracture
with multiple fragmentation of bone and **(b)** radiating fracture lines.
(Photos by Julie R. Angel; **(a)** courtesy of the University of New Mexico–Albuquerque,
Maxwell Museum of Anthropology, #69; **(b)** courtesy of the State of New Mexico,
Office of the Medical Investigator)

wounds, forms concentric rings around the area of impact (see Figure 11.4). These are
called **hoop fractures**, which are caused by the inward and outward bending of the
surface of bone. Because fracture lines dissipate force, generally they will not cross pre-
existing fracture lines or, in the skull, suture lines. This is because, when the force causing a line hits a preexisting discontinuity, its energy is lost, causing no more fractures
(see Figure 11.5). As will be described in future chapters, this fact helps to determine the
timing of breaks in bones that exhibit multiple fractures. One last point needs to be

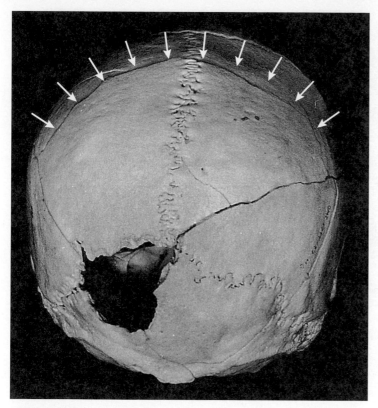

FIGURE 11.4 Concentric (hoop) fracture (*arrows*) from gunshot
wound. (Photo by Julie R. Angel; specimen courtesy of the State of New Mexico,
Office of the Medical Investigator)

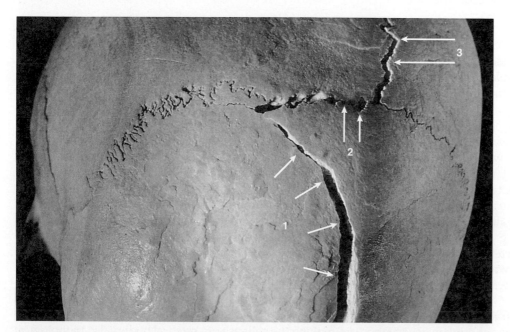

FIGURE 11.5 Fracture line through the frontal (*arrows 1*) that ends at the coronal suture, and
dissipates its force by separating both the coronal (*arrows 2*) and sagittal sutures (*arrows 3*).
(Photo by Julie R. Angel; specimen courtesy of the University of New Mexico–Albuquerque, Maxwell Museum
of Anthropology, #110)

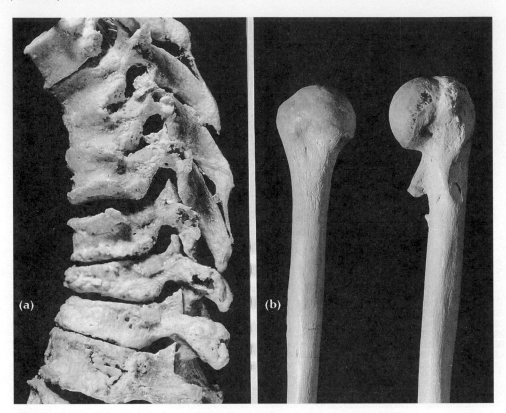

FIGURE 11.6   Healed fractures: **(a)** stress fractures of vertebrae weakened by osteoporosis, and **(b)** callus with irregular outline and uneven surface formed on proximal humerus (right bone).
(Photos by Julie R. Angel; specimens courtesy of the University of New Mexico–Albuquerque, Maxwell Museum of Anthropology, #186, #62)

made about fracture lines. Although they usually radiate from and around the point of impact, they can appear at the opposite side of the structure receiving the force. For example, in some cases of skull fracture, force applied to the left side will result in lines occurring on the right side.

Traumatic fractures resulting in discontinuities and lines are the breaks that usually come to mind when considering bone trauma. However, several other types of fractures can be distinguished. **Pathological fractures** are breaks that occur in bones that are weakened by disease. Thus, skeletons affected by *osteogenesis imperfecta* (a disease that makes bone weak and brittle) usually exhibit pathological fractures. **Stress fractures** are breaks caused from overuse; athletes can suffer from these types of injuries, especially in their heels and legs due to repeated strain on these structures. Finally, **fatigue fractures** occur in bones that are exposed to intermittent stress over a long period of time. The most common example of this injury is stress fractures of the vertebrae in older persons (see Figure 11.6a); this is the ailment that causes the **dowager's hump**, a condition where the spinal column is angled so prominently forward as to appear to form a hump on the back.

In some cases, nontraumatic injuries are attributable to more than one of these types of fractures. Thus, the stress fracture causing "dowager's hump" is most common in persons suffering from osteoporosis, making the collapse of vertebral bodies also pathological fractures. Although forensic anthropologists generally are interested mostly in traumatic fractures, all these are caused by outside forces and all may provide information concerning the cause of death, as well as information on individualization (see Chapter 15).

After a discontinuity occurs, the injured bone responds in several different ways. First, the veins and arteries that are inevitably ruptured by the break leak blood, which forms a pool over the damaged area. This pool, termed a **hematoma**, helps to stabilize the broken pieces, especially after it coagulates. Trauma also stimulates the osteogenic properties of the periosteum that is responsible for forming new bone (see Chapter 2). The first action of this osteogenic layer is to produce connective fibers that span between the broken surfaces. This flexible tissue can infiltrate the hematoma to bridge the gap formed by the discontinuity. These fibers form the framework for the second action, which is the development of a **callus** composed of fibrous bone. If the break is sufficiently immobilized, this initial callus develops within the connective fibers as calcium matrix is deposited. Although composed of true bone, it does not have the strength of ordinary bone because it is not well organized and its matrix is not dense. The last stage in healing involves the replacement of fibrous bone with lamellar bone that is much stronger due to its greater organization and denser structure.

Calluses formed during the last two phases are visible as raised and somewhat irregular areas over and around discontinuities (see Figure 11.6b). Under normal circumstances, calluses begin to form by the sixth week after injury, where they can remain visible for years after complete healing. In some cases, with enough time, all traces of fracture and callus can be resorbed, leaving no indication of a previous break.

Sometime early during the above-described process, remodeling of the fracture edges occurs. The bone near the break begins to resorb, rounding the otherwise sharp borders of the break. Whereas new fractures have edges that can easily cut people handling defleshed bone, the borders of healing breaks are less likely to cause such injuries. In addition to rounding, occasional pores develop in the area of the break. This porosity contrasts sharply with the smooth surface of the cortex. Forensic anthropologists usually look for these early signs on broken edges because it indicates that the fracture occurred before death; and, although it could be a contributing factor, it probably was not the cause of death.

CHARACTERISTICS OF FORCES CAUSING TRAUMA

To identify the types of trauma, three characteristics of forces that cause bone injury need to be understood: direction, speed, and focus. **Direction** refers to the direction from which the force contacts the bone; that is, does the force originate from the side, top, bottom, or some combination? **Speed** is distinguished as either dynamic (i.e., sudden impact) or static (slow buildup). Finally, **focus** refers to the size of the surface on which the force impacts (i.e., wide or narrow). Understanding the intricacies of these characteristics is necessary in interpreting bone trauma.

Direction of Force

The nature of a break depends on the direction from which a force impacts a bone. Ortner and Putschar (1981) distinguish five directions, illustrated in Figure 11.7, that can cause discontinuities: (a) tension, (b) compression, (c) torsion, (d) bending, and (e) shearing. Since these directions

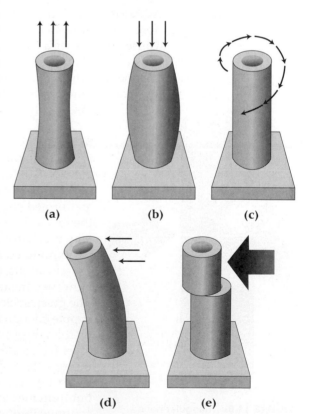

(a)   **(b)**   **(c)**

(d)   **(e)**

FIGURE 11.7 The five directions of force that can cause bone fractures; **(a)** tension; **(b)** comprehension; **(c)** torsion; **(d)** bending; **(e)** shearing. (After Figure 51 of Ortner and Putschar, 1981)

cause different types of breaks with different attributes, understanding the effect of these forces on bone is paramount to performing trauma analysis.

TENSION Tension refers to force that pulls on bone, usually along its long axis, with sufficient energy to cause a break. Tension forces are most common in dislocations where the pulling force is applied to a bony process (such as a tubercle) by way of a tendon. If the force is sufficient, the process breaks away from the main part of the bone, displacing it some distance from its point of attachment. Discontinuities caused by tension forces usually exhibit few fracture lines. Although they do occur in the forensic context, these types of breaks are more common in accidents than deaths from other types of violence.

COMPRESSION Compression forces push down on bone, causing discontinuities and/or fracture lines. Discontinuities can be either complete or incomplete; fracture lines, which often radiate from the point of impact, can be numerous and wide reaching. Fractures caused by such forces are most commonly found on the skull; however, compressed fractures can be seen on any bone where the cortical surface is displaced inward. Often the shape of the displaced bone follows the configuration of the fracturing instrument. This has led some forensic anthropologists to go to great lengths in identifying the causative implement (e.g., William Maples describes searching the local Sears store in search of a tool shaped like a particularly distinctive fracture).

TORSION Torsion (twisting) forces are most common in accidents. With this type of force, one end of a bone usually is held stationary while the other end is twisted. This causes both the fracture surfaces and their concomitant lines to spiral down the long axis of bones. Injuries from torsion forces are most common in long bones where the manner of death is accident (e.g., skiing accidents, falls from bicycles). Conversely, they are not common in homicides or suicides (unless the suicide is by falling), except in cases of child abuse (Walker et al., 1997).

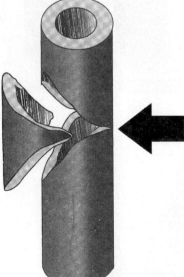

FIGURE 11.8 Triangular bone fragment broken away from area at the point of impact (*arrow*). (After Figure 49 of Ortner and Putschar, 1981)

BENDING Of all the forces causing breaks, bending is the most common force. This force impacts the side of a structure at approximately right angles to its long axis, causing a break through its cross section. Although misalignments and discontinuities are common, usually few fracture lines are formed either at the point of impact or on the side opposite the area of the break. However, sometimes the force is so great that a triangle of bone may break from the surface at the point of impact (Figure 11.8), producing a comminuted fracture.

In adults, the discontinuities from bending forces usually are complete. However, in subadults, infractions are more common. These latter breaks (the green stick fractures described previously) occur because young bone is supple enough to bend under the force of impact. This causes breakage only on the side opposite from where the force contacts the bone. The bending allows for dissipation of the force such that the fracture does not continue through the entire cross section. Thus, the discontinuity resembles the breaking of a fresh piece of wood (i.e., a green stick, where fibers of the wood stick out from the side facing away from the force, but the discontinuity does not continue through the wood).

One break that occurs from a bending force is so common that it has a special name. The **parry fracture** of the ulna (Figure 11.9a) is caused when persons hold their arms up, bent at the elbow, as a form of self-defense (e.g., to ward off a blow). This causes the ulna to absorb the force, resulting in a fracture and inward displacement of the broken surfaces. Usually, parry fractures occur at the distal segment of this bone; however, fractures near the elbow have been observed. This type of traumatic injury is common in many deaths by violence.

SHEARING   The last force is similar to bending, but it involves the immobilization of one segment of the bone. When a force is applied from the side under these conditions, a shearing of the bone can occur. Colles's fracture is the most common injury due to this type of force. This is found in the distal radius (see Figure 11.9b) and results in a fall forward when victims attempt to catch themselves. In this case, the ground immobilizes the bone while the weight of the body delivers the side force. As with twisting, injuries due to shearing force are not common in homicides and suicides, but are more consistent with accidents.

Another example of shearing is cutting of bone by a toothed instrument (e.g., saw). These injuries are associated with dismemberments, when a body is deliberately separated into segments usually in an attempt to conceal a crime (see Dismemberments in Chapter 16). In these cases, bone is held immobile while a side force shears out small sections of tissue across the width of the instrument. With thin-bladed saws (e.g., hack saw, butcher's saw), the amount of bone that is removed is fairly small; in the case of a carpenter's saw, the amount may be several times larger.

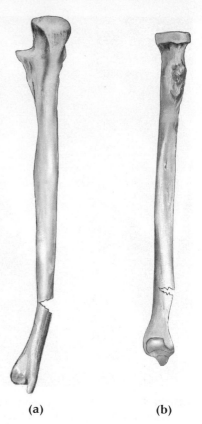

(a)   **(b)**

FIGURE 11.9   Fractures with special names: **(a)** parry fracture to the ulna, and **(b)** Colles's fracture to the radius.

Speed of Force

The next factor to consider when analyzing force is its speed. Ortner and Putschar (1981) recognize two speeds, at the extremes of the wide range of possibilities: dynamic and static. **Dynamic force** refers to sudden stress, that is, force that is delivered powerfully and at high speed. This is the most common form of fracturing force and the one that causes most of the discontinuities and fracture lines seen in violent deaths. Generally, force delivered by a bludgeon, knife, or projectile is dynamic in nature.

The reverse of dynamic is **static force**; this refers to stress that is applied slowly. Typically, this force starts low and builds to the point where the bone breaks. This usually results only in displacement of bones, with few, if any, fracture lines. In the forensic context, the most common injury caused by static force is breaking of the hyoid bone during manual strangulation (see Chapter 14).

Focus of Force

Focus refers to the size of the area impacted by a force. Generally, the focus of a force can be divided into two types: narrow and wide. **Narrow focus** means that the force is applied to a single point or a thin line. Any pointed or sharp-edged instrument will deliver force to a narrow focus. Thus, ice picks, knives, axes, meat cleavers, machetes, or swords are classic instruments for delivering narrowly focused forces.

Wide focus indicates that the force is delivered over a large area of bone. Instead of small indentations, the indications of wide focus trauma generally are breaks over a considerable percentage of the bone area. In some cases, the focus is fairly small (e.g., an inch or so); in other cases, areas of several inches (sometimes as high as 6 inches) result. Generally, an injury caused by any mechanism other than a cutting or chopping instrument is considered to have a wide focus.

TYPES OF TRAUMA

Most modern texts dealing with forensic anthropology (Morse et al., 1983; Reichs, 1986, 1998a; Burns, 1999) divide trauma into four categories: blunt, sharp, projectile, and miscellaneous. **Blunt trauma** is any injury resulting from a blow from wide instruments that have either a flat or a round surface. **Sharp trauma** generally is caused by an implement with a point or edge. **Projectile traumas**, which have characteristics of both blunt and sharp trauma, are considered as causing a third type of trauma. Finally, several miscellaneous forces can cause injury to bone. Although each of these is the subject of separate chapters, it is instructive to consider them first in general terms.

Blunt Force Trauma

Blunt force trauma refers to any injury caused by a force that has a wide area of impact on bone (see Figure 11.3a). Generally, these are the result of compression, bending, and (occasionally) shearing forces that are applied dynamically over a wide focus. Bones with blunt traumatic injuries usually exhibit both discontinuities and fracture lines. Typically, these forces cause at least simple fracture wounds. However, comminuted fractures also are common, particularly when the bone is shattered by the application of excessive force. Although many instruments wielded as clubs result in blunt force trauma, any hard surface can cause this type of injury. Thus, impact of the body on the ground after falling generally results in crushed and shattered bone, as does impact during automotive, train, and airplane accidents.

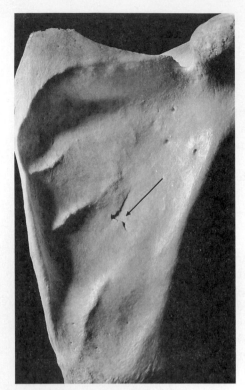

FIGURE 11.10 Puncture wound (*arrow*) to the scapula. (Photo by Julie R. Angel; specimen courtesy of the State of New Mexico, Office of the Medical Investigator)

Sharp Force Trauma

Sharp force trauma usually results from either compression or shearing forces applied dynamically over a narrow focus. When the force is applied perpendicularly and down onto the surface, punctures (see Figure 11.10) or chop marks result. However, when the force grazes the cortex, incisions are the usual manifestation (see Figure 11.11). Complete discontinuities occur with chopping instruments, while cutting instruments more often cause infractions. Usually, these are in the form of discontinuities and displacements, rather than fracture lines. The instruments typically associated with this type of force are knives, axes, or any instrument with a sharp edge or point.

Projectile Trauma

Projectiles have such distinct wounding characteristics that they constitute a separate category of trauma. The results of projectiles impacting on bone generally are complete discontinuities with both displacement and fracture lines. The direction of the force usually is compressive; however, some projectiles deliver bending force. The speed is dynamic and the focus, which starts out small, generally becomes wide as the projectile passes through

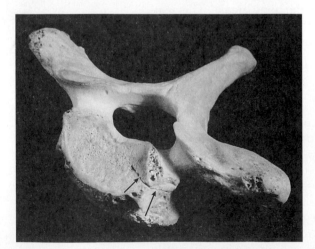

FIGURE 11.11 Incision (*arrows*) on a vertebra. (Photo by Julie R. Angel; specimen courtesy of the State of New Mexico, Office of the Medical Investigator)

the bone. The most common projectiles that cause this type of trauma are bullets from firearms; however, any object that travels through the air that impacts with enough energy (e.g., arrows, spears) can cause bone trauma.

Miscellaneous Trauma

Forces that do not fit into one of the preceding types usually are placed in a miscellaneous category. These include trauma caused by static pressure (the most common of which is strangulation), generalized dynamic pressures (i.e., explosions), sawing, and trauma due to chemicals and heat. Generally, only the first three result in complete discontinuities with displacement of bone; and they usually do not exhibit a large number of fracture lines. Also, the focus can be small or large and the direction can be compressive, bending, or shearing. Finally, although the traumas caused by heat are not dynamic in nature, they can exhibit both discontinuities and fracture lines (e.g., crosshatching from burning; see Chapter 16).

TIMING OF BONE INJURY

One of the most important issues surrounding bone injury is its relationship to time of death. Norman Sauer (1998) provides a good discussion of the characteristics associated with timing of bone injury and his work forms the basis for the following discussion. In forensics, three such timings are recognized: antemortem (premortem), perimortem, and postmortem. **Antemortem trauma** refers to trauma that occurred before death such that there is partial or complete healing of the injury. Although it does not give information about the cause of death, it can provide clues that help in positive identification (see Chapter 15). **Perimortem trauma** refers to injuries that occurred around the time of death; because of its timing, this type of trauma is of paramount interest to law enforcement officials. Finally, **postmortem damage** refers to injury that occurs after death. When this happens soon after death and the bone is still fresh, it takes on the characteristics of perimortem trauma. However, when the bone is dry, specific traits emerge. Since a clear understanding of the different characteristics of these types of injuries is important in relation to cause of death, each will be described in more detail.

Antemortem Trauma

Since the process of healing has distinctive characteristics, injuries that occur antemortem usually can be distinguished from those that occur at the time of, or after, death. The description given previously under **Basics of Bone Trauma** presented several changes that can aid in the recognition of antemortem trauma. The first characteristic is the porosity near the breaks that indicates bone activity and resorption. These pores contrast with the otherwise smooth cortical surface. The second feature is the rounding of the edges of the break (Sauer, 1998); the remodeling of tissues cause the borders of broken surfaces and the edges of fracture lines to become blunt, losing their sharpness. This blunting can begin as early as 1 week after the break (Sauer, 1998) and, over time, causes the fracture lines to appear as V-shaped grooves (see Figure 11.12a) or to disappear entirely. The last characteristic of antemortem trauma is the presence of a callus. This structure, which usually begins to develop by the sixth week after injury, not only covers the broken bone ends, but also extends some distance from the area of the break. The callus has three fairly distinctive characteristics. It is irregular in shape, exhibits a disorganized surface (particularly when it is newly formed), and is raised above the surrounding area. The presence of these three features usually allows for the easy recognition of calluses when they are present on bone (Figures 11.6b and 11.13), meaning that such traumas cannot have occurred at the time of death.

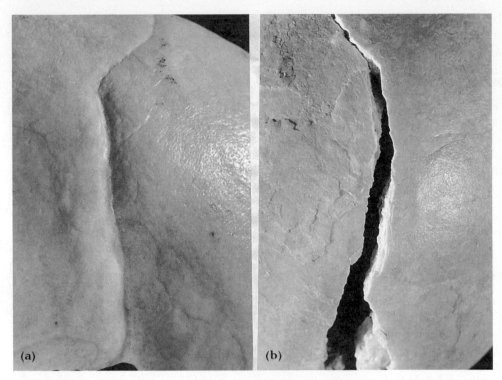

FIGURE 11.12   Differences between antemortem and perimortem fractures: **(a)** healed fracture line showing rounding of edges and **(b)** sharp edge of perimortem fracture to the skull. (Photos by Julie R. Angel; antemortem fracture courtesy of the State of New Mexico, Office of the Medical Investigator; perimortem courtesy of the University of New Mexico–Albuquerque, Maxwell Museum of Anthropology, #110)

Perimortem Trauma

Injuries that occur close to the time of death will not exhibit the signs of healing seen in antemortem trauma (Sauer, 1998). Thus, their characteristics are different enough to be distinguished from the trauma that occurred before death. Perimortem trauma is recognizable by what is called *green bone* response; this is the type of response that is seen when bone is injured while it is still covered with soft tissue and still contains the fluids present in life. Generally, green bone will bend and snap back into place more often than bone that is damaged postmortem.

Five characteristics of fractures indicate perimortem trauma. The first, and most common, is sharp edges (see Figure 11.12b); this applies both to the borders of the broken bone surfaces and to the fracture lines. The edges of the breaks are sharp and somewhat irregular, exhibiting no rounding due to the remodeling concurrent with healing. The second feature is hinging; this occurs when a section of a bone is bent away from the direction of a blow (see Figure 11.2b). Its usual manifestation is an inward bending with separation at the end opposite the hinge, where continuity is maintained. This can only occur if the bone is moist, because dry bone usually will snap off when acted on by a force sufficient to cause a break (Sauer, 1998). The third feature of perimortem trauma is the formation of fracture lines. These lines most often radiate from the point of impact in an irregular sunburst shape (see Figure 11.3b), or they can form concentric breaks around the point of impact (see Figure 11.4). Since fracture lines generally will not occur in dried bone, their presence can be used to distinguish perimortem from postmortem injuries. The fourth feature of breaks to fresh bone is the shape of the broken ends; these are usually angled with a jagged surface (see Figure 11.14a). Fresh bones usually do not fracture at right angles to their long axes, nor do they have flat broken surfaces. The last characteristic that can occur in some instances of perimortem trauma is staining from the hematoma (Sauer, 1984). Sometimes dried bone will exhibit discoloration near and around the break where this pool of fluid would have been found. All these features should be noted when present because they can provide evidence on the cause and manner of death.

Although the length of time that encompasses perimortem is imprecise, two studies help to quantify this time range. Lenore Barbian and Paul Sledzik (2008) studied cranial wounds of 127 civil war soldiers who died within the first eight weeks of the traumatic incident. They found that osteoclastic (bone resorption) activity was visible in a small percentage of individuals within the first week after trauma, but became more common as time progressed such that it was present in almost all individuals by the eighth week. Osteoblastic (bone formation) activity followed a similar course, although it was first visible in the second week. (Two other aspects of healing, demarcation line and sequestration, showed progressions that were too variable to be of value.) Their data indicate that traumatic injuries that show these two types of bony responses associated with healing could have contributed to the cause of death, thereby moving the perimortem interval to as much as 2 months prior to death.

The study by Danielle Wieberg and Daniel Wescott (2008) helps to quantify the length of the perimortem time range after the time of death. These researchers studied the affect of fracturing on pig (*Sus scrofa*) bones at regular intervals while drying outside during the summer and fall in Missouri. They discovered that those bones intentionally fractured at death had the characteristics of perimortem

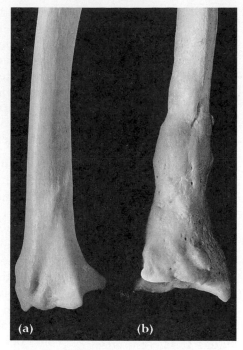

FIGURE 11.13 Normal distal radius (a) shown alongside of radius with well-healed callus (b) from Colles's Fracture. (Photo by Julie R. Angel; specimens courtesy of the University of New Mexico–Albuquerque, Maxwell Museum of Anthropology, #52)

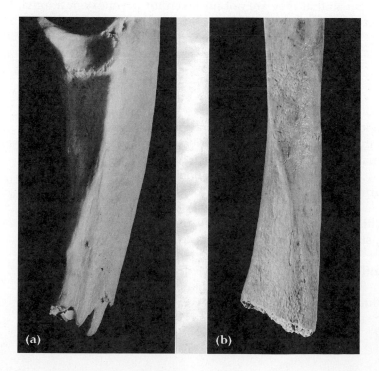

FIGURE 11.14 Differences between perimortem fracture and postmortem damage: **(a)** perimortem fracture to the ulna showing irregular end with jagged surface, and **(b)** postmortem break to the distal end of the fibula showing a relatively flat plane. (Photos by Julie R. Angel; perimortem fracture courtesy of the University of New Mexico–Albuquerque, Maxwell Museum of Anthropology, #71; postmortem break courtesy of the State of New Mexico, Office of the Medical Investigator)

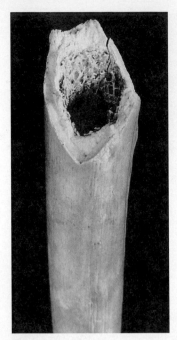

FIGURE 11.15 Postmortem break showing lighter color of broken surface when compared with rest of bone. (Photo by Julie R. Angel; specimen courtesy of the New Mexico, Office of the Medical Investigator)

fracture described above, and that the bones broken after 141 days (approximately 5 months) had the characteristics of postmortem damage described in the next section. However, those bones broken during this interval had combinations of the characteristics of both time periods, with a small percentage of bones fractured after the first month of exposure already displaying features of postmortem damage. Thus, their findings push the perimortem timeframe to around 1 month postmortem.

Postmortem Damage

Although not strictly trauma, recognizing damage to bone after death is an important part of the forensic anthropology process. Between the time of death and the discovery of remains, many forces can cause significant changes to the skeleton. Similarly, damage to remains can occur during body recovery and transport. This is the subject of forensic taphonomy. Although any number of forces can damage bones postmortem, this section will describe the results of those forces that cause breakage.

In the same manner that fracture of wet bone is recognizable by certain characteristics, fracture to dry bone also exhibits distinctive characteristics. Breaks in dry bone rarely exhibit radiating fracture lines. Because the bone is not hydrated, it is more likely to snap like a dry twig when impacted by a (especially bending and shearing) force. Also, green stick fractures and hinging are rare for the same reason. Similarly, long bones usually break nearly at right angles, with ends that are almost flat (see Figure 11.14b). Finally, the color of the break is usually different from the rest of the bone (Buikstra and Ubelaker, 1994). The broken surface normally will be lighter in color than the other bone surfaces (see Figure 11.15); this is due to the uncovering of the original off-white color that contrasts with the outer surface that has been discolored by outside forces (e.g., soil color, sunlight; see Chapter 3). Breaks with light-colored ends indicate fracturing near the time of recovery or during transport. All these characteristics should be noted when present so that they are not mistaken for perimortem trauma, leading to false information concerning the cause and manner of death.

Summary

1. Trauma to bone is studied by forensic anthropologists because it is one of the few subjects that can provide information on the cause and manner of death from skeletal remains.
2. Cause of death refers to the forces that bring about the death of an individual.
3. Manner of death refers to the manner in which persons die; five are recognized: homicide, suicide, accident, natural, or unknown.
4. The direction, speed, and focus of impact influence the production of trauma.
5. Four types of bone trauma are recognized: blunt, sharp, projectile, and miscellaneous.
6. The timing of trauma to bone is important in identifying injuries that might relate to cause and manner of death.
7. Three timings of bone injury are recognized: antemortem trauma (trauma occurring during life), perimortem trauma (trauma occurring around the time of death), and postmortem damage (injuries occurring after death).
8. Injuries occurring at the different times in relation to death have distinctive characteristics that allow for their identification.

Exercises

1. A skeleton is found that has a healed fracture to the left femur, broken tibia exhibiting an irregular break surface, and a fractured humerus whose ends are light in color, while the rest of the bone is dark. Which of these injuries most likely provides information on the cause of death? Why?

2. Skeletonized remains are found at the bottom of a cliff on top of jagged rocks. Of the four types of trauma (i.e., blunt, sharp, projectile, miscellaneous), which are most likely to be visible on the skeleton? Explain your answer.

3. What can be said about the manner of death of the specimen described in Exercise 2? Explain.

4. One of the most common defects seen on the human skull is a healed fracture to the nose. Describe the characteristics (direction, speed, focus) of the force that probably causes such injuries.

5. In some parts of the world, fights between males usually escalate from fists to machetes. Describe the types of bone injuries most likely to be caused by both instruments.

6. A skeleton is found lying on railroad tracks with multiple traumas. All long bones, the ribs, and most short bones exhibit simple and comminuted fractures. The skull is smashed and the pelvis is broken in several places. Describe as many causes and manners of death that you can think of that would result in these types of injuries.

7. A skull is discovered that exhibits a golf ball-sized hole in the braincase. There are no radiating or hoop fracture lines, and the edges of this hole are rounded. Does this represent a perimortem fracture that could be the cause of death? Why or why not?

8. What direction, speed, and focus of force would most likely cause a break in the wrist when falling off a bicycle?

9. The ulnae of victims of the Colorado cannibal, Alferd Packer, exhibited perimortem cuts on their outer surfaces. Does this agree with Packer's story that these persons died of natural causes before he butchered their bodies for food? Explain your answer.

10. What is the most likely direction, speed, and focus of the force causing the wounds described in Exercise 9?

12

Projectile Trauma

Projectiles have such distinctive wounding characteristics that they deserve a separate category of trauma. Projectiles that impact bone with enough force to penetrate its surface generally will result in complete discontinuities, with both displacement and (usually) fracture lines. Some projectile trauma is so devastating that entire structures (e.g., skull) are shattered, requiring considerable reconstruction before analysis can begin. Although bullets are the projectiles most commonly causing this type of injury, pellets (from shotguns), shrapnel, arrows, spears, or any flying objects that impact bone with enough force can cause the types of trauma described in this chapter.

When faced with a skeleton containing projectile wounds, forensic anthropologists should aim to supply as much information concerning the causative weapon as possible to law enforcement officials. Ideally, this information should include type of firearm, characteristics of the projectile, placement of the weapon in relation to the victim, sequence of wounds (if multiple), and any individual traits of the assailant (e.g., handedness, height) that can be estimated. Although not all this information can be discerned from all wounds, projectiles leave marks on bone that provide important clues to their characteristics and the weapons discharging them.

Firearms are a preferred method of killing in murder and suicide because of their lethality. Generally, these weapons can be divided into three basic types: handguns, rifles, and shotguns (see Figure 12.1a). For the most part, the first two expel single projectiles (bullets) when discharged, while the latter eject multiple projectiles (pellets). Thus, the first section of this chapter deals with firearms and ammunition to help provide the basic concepts needed by forensic anthropologists to perform projectile wound analysis. Next, because of the difference in wounding characteristics between bullets and pellets and because wounds caused by the former contain the most information, the effects of bullets on bone and the analysis of bullet wounds will be treated in some detail. Afterward, the effects of shotgun wounds will be discussed, followed by a final section on injuries caused by miscellaneous projectiles.

BASICS OF AMMUNITION AND FIREARMS

Eric Barach and associates (1986a, b) provide a readable summary of the basics of firearms, and their work forms the basis of the following discussion. Because of the wide variety presently available, ammunition and firearms constitute a highly complex subject. Both come in various sizes and powers, and each has noticeable wounding characteristics. However, despite this complexity, three main aspects of these devices most directly determine effects on bone: size, construction, and velocity. Size refers to the diameter of a projectile and/or barrel of a weapon; this can be as small as 0.05 of an inch to almost a 0.5 inch in diameter. Construction refers to projectile shape, internal composition, and covering (jacketing), while velocity refers to the

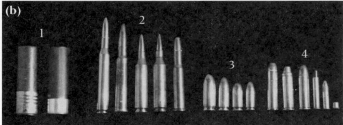

FIGURE 12.1   Aspects of modern firearms: **(a)** various rifles, shotguns, and handguns available in the United States, and **(b)** various types of ammunition: shotgun shells (1), rifle ammunition (2), handgun ammunition (3, 4).   (Photos by Julie R. Angel)

speed at which the projectile hits its target. The basics of each of these concepts for the most commonly found ammunition and firearms are treated separately next.

Size

The size of a projectile and/or weapon barrel is measured in terms of caliber, gauge, or number. **Caliber** refers to the diameter of a bullet and/or barrel of a handgun or rifle. This size is usually given in hundredths of an inch; however, in recent years, metric calibers have become popular (i.e., millimeters). Table 12.1 gives a listing of the most popular calibers. Notice that the determination of caliber is complicated by the fact that the actual diameter of bullets is sometimes less or greater than that advertised by their manufacturers.

In contrast to rifles and handguns, shotguns are more complicated because their barrel diameters are measured in gauges, while the pellets that they expel are measured by number. **Gauge** refers to the maximum weight of a lead ball that would fit down the barrel of the weapon. Thus, a 10-gauge shotgun would allow a ball weighing one-tenth of a pound down its barrel, while a 12-gauge shotgun would admit a lead ball weighing one-twelfth of a pound. The most common gauges of shotguns are 10, 12, 16, 20, 28, and 410; the last number refers to tenths of inches rather than gauge (i.e., 0.410 inches).

Pellets are merely solid balls made of lead and, in some cases, steel. Pellet size is denoted by birdshot or buckshot number. The relation between birdshot number and pellet size is linear; that is, #12 shot is 0.05 inch in diameter, #11 shot is 0.06, #10 is 0.07, and so forth to #2 shot, which is 0.15 inch. Buckshot numbers range from 4 to 0 and 00 (double-0 buck); however, the relationship between pellet size and buckshot number is

TABLE 12.1 Common Bullet Calibers for Handguns and Rifles[1]

Type of Weapon	Caliber of Bullet	Actual Bullet Size
Handguns	0.22	0.222–0.224
	0.25	
	0.32	
	9 mm	0.354
	0.357 magnum	0.358
	0.38	0.358
	0.38 special	
	0.44	0.423
	0.45	0.451
Rifles	0.22 long rifle	0.222–0.224
	0.30–30	0.300–0.323
	0.30–'06	0.300–0.3231
	0.308	

[1]Summarized from data supplied by Barach et al. (1986a), Di Maio (1993), and Berryman et al. (1995).

not linear. Thus, #4 buck denotes a pellet of 0.24 inch, #3 buck indicates 0.25, and #1 buck is 0.30; double-0 buck is the largest commercially available pellet and measures approximately 0.33 inch. Generally, shotgun ammunition is designed to expel 1 ounce of pellets independent of their size; therefore, a shell containing double-0 buck would contain nine pellets that sum to 1 ounce in weight, and a shell containing #6 birdshot would contain 225 pellets, also totaling 1 ounce.

Bullet Construction

As mentioned above, bullet construction refers to profile, internal composition, and jacketing. There are three basic bullet profiles: sharp, blunt, and hollow-point (see Figure 12.1b). The sharp profile is most commonly seen in rifle ammunition (e.g., 0.30–'06), while blunt (either flat or round tips) and **hollow-points** (bullets with indentations on their tips) are more common in handguns. Blunt and hollow-point bullets are most likely to deform on impact and therefore would be expected to cause larger (especially exit) wounds in bone. This is particularly true of hollow-points, which are designed to expand when hitting and traveling through a target.

The internal composition of a bullet is of two basic types. In most cases, the bullet is constructed of solid lead (this metal is chosen because it is heavy and deforms more than iron or steel). However, some bullets are constructed to fragment or explode on contact. Fragmenting bullets encase pellets that scatter throughout the target when the bullet hits and the casing ruptures. The profile of these is usually round or, in some cases, flat.

The final factor of bullet construction is the presence or absence of a **jacket**. This refers to a thin copper (or other metal) coating on the bullet. Some such coatings cover the entire projectile (**full-metal jacket**), while others only cover part of the bullet (**semijacket**). Jacketing reduces deformation and fragmentation of the projectile during passage through the body. Thus, nonjacketed bullets are more likely to deform while passing through tissue because they lack the reinforcing afforded by a covering (these types of bullets are usually termed soft tipped).

Projectile Velocity

Although caliber is a factor, the velocity of a projectile has the greatest effect on its wounding power. This is due to the fact that the kinetic energy (i.e., power) of a projectile has a linear relationship with its weight, but is a function of the square of its velocity. Thus, doubling the weight of a projectile doubles its kinetic energy; however, doubling the velocity quadruples that energy (Morse et al., 1983). Considering this, wounds of a catastrophic nature (e.g., blowing apart of the skull) are more indicative of high-, rather than low-, velocity projectiles. This gives an important clue as to the type of weapon. Rifles generally produce higher velocity bullets than regular handguns, while magnum-powered handguns have velocities at the low end of the range of rifles.

BASICS OF BULLET TRAVEL

When expelled from most modern firearms, a bullet is pointed toward the target while spinning around its long axis. Spiral grooves (called **rifling**) cut into the internal surface of barrels and, running from one end to the other, impart a spin so that the bullet will go straighter for a longer period of time. Thus, at the beginning of its flight the long axis of the bullet is parallel to its flight path (trajectory). However, after a bullet has traveled some distance, it is likely to start to tumble. This is simply due to the dynamics of bullet travel; however, this effect is seen most often in bullets discharged from inexpensive or improperly maintained weapons. The net effect is that the bullet's long axis will no longer be parallel to its trajectory. Thus, when it reaches a target, instead of presenting a circular outline, the bullet may impact on its side, causing a noncircular wound. Another factor that may cause a noncircular wound is the angle of trajectory. This is the angle between the target's surface and the weapon discharging the projectile. If the weapon is perpendicular to the target (and the bullet is not tumbling), a circular outline is presented; if the weapon is not oriented at a right angle, a noncircular outline results.

When a bullet strikes a target, if it has enough energy, it will cause a perforating wound. Where it enters a target, it causes a **penetrating (entry) wound**; where it leaves the target (if it has enough energy), it will cause an **exit wound**. If it enters intact, its original characteristics will be imparted directly to the target. However, if it has struck an intermediate object (ricochets), it usually deforms and perhaps fragments, particularly if it is of nonjacketed construction (Burke and Rowe, 1992); the same is true of bullets that travel through a significant amount of tissue. Splinters from fragmented bullets may embed in any type of tissue or cause chipping of hard tissue (e.g., bone). These can be discerned either visually or radiographically.

EFFECTS OF BULLETS ON BONE

Hugh Berryman and Steve Symes (1998) describe what happens when a bullet strikes osteological material. First, a wound is formed in, and sometimes through, the bone. In addition, fracture lines radiate out from, and in some cases encircle, the point of impact. Finally, the bone can fracture so severely as to shatter into a number of small pieces, presenting the appearance of having exploded. All the aspects of ammunition and firearms described, as well as bullet angles and types of wounds (i.e., entry, exit), help to determine the characteristics of wounds. To describe these effects systematically, the features of bullet wounds to bone are divided into four subjects: wound beveling, wound shape, wound size, and fracture lines.

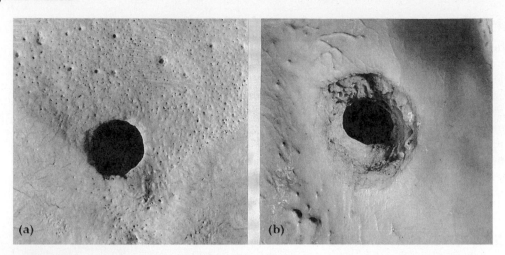

FIGURE 12.2 Close-up of entry wound to rear of skull: **(a)** view from outside and **(b)** view from inside showing internal beveling. (Photos by Julie R. Angel; specimen courtesy of the State of New Mexico, Office of the Medical Investigator)

Wound Beveling

When a projectile perforates bone, it deforms to one extent or another, depending on the factors of bullet construction discussed previously. This deformation causes the hole where the bullet exits to be larger than where it entered. Thus, the entire wound has a funnel shape, with the smaller end at the site of bullet entry (Berryman and Symes, 1998). This funnel effect is called **beveling** and can be categorized into three types: inward, outward, and reverse.

Inward beveling is seen in bone wounds at the site of a bullet's entry into the body. The outer hole on the bone's surface is smaller than the inner hole, which can be quite large. Figure 12.2a illustrates an entry wound on the rear of a skull as viewed from the outside. Figure 12.2b shows this same wound when viewed from inside the skull with inward beveling. **Outward beveling** is seen in wounds at the site of a bullet's exit from the body. In this case, the inner hole is smaller than the outer hole, in direct contrast to entry wounds. Figure 12.3a shows an exit wound on the left frontal, and Figure 12.3b shows a close-up of that same wound with the outward bevel typical of this type of wound. In addition to inward and outward, there are instances of **reverse beveling**. This can be seen as beveling in the opposite direction of the entrance (Peterson, 1991) or exit wounds already described. Figure 12.4 illustrates such a case; as can be seen, this skull manifests a relatively round entry wound (with a large area broken out below it) that has a small amount of outward bevel (see arrows). This is fairly typical; reverse beveling usually is considerably smaller than the beveling that it opposes.

Wound Shape

Generally, bullet wounds to bone can be categorized into one of four shapes: round, oval, keyhole, or irregular. **Round** and **oval wounds**, as indicated by their names, are circular and elliptical in outline, respectively. **Keyhole wounds** have the appearance of old-fashioned keyholes; that is, they are circular on one end and triangular on the other. Finally, **irregular wounds** are those that do not show any general pattern. The shape that a bullet produces depends on four factors: its construction, its angle of trajectory, its

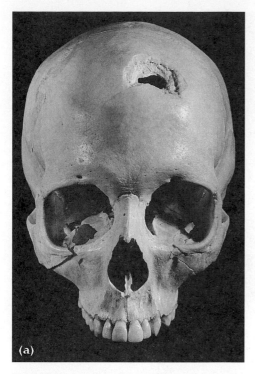

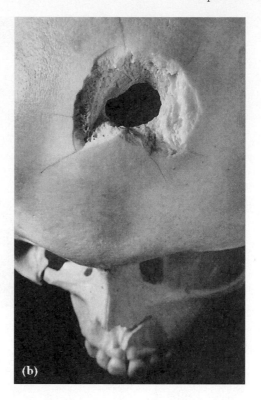

FIGURE 12.3 Views of an exit wound to a frontal: **(a)** full skull showing minimal fracture lines and **(b)** close-up showing external beveling. (Photos by Julie R. Angel; specimen courtesy of the State of New Mexico, Office of the Medical Investigator)

angle of axis, and the type of wound (entry or exit) that it forms. The effect of these factors in relation to each of the different shapes bears further discussion.

Round wounds are most likely to occur when both the angle of trajectory and the angle of bullet axis are perpendicular to the bone's surface. Also, they are more likely to be seen in entry, rather than exit, wounds and in the smaller opening of the wound's bevel (see the preceding section on wound beveling). Finally, although any bullet construction normally will cause a round entry wound, a round exit wound is more likely to be caused by jacketed projectiles because of their nondeforming nature. Figures 12.2a and b show a typical round entry wound, both on the outside and inside of the skull. Notice that the smaller end of the bevel forms an almost perfect circle even though the larger end is more irregular.

Oval shapes are more likely to occur when either the angle of trajectory is not perpendicular to the bone's surface or when the bullet is tumbling when it strikes. The net effect of both of these factors is that the angle between the bullet axis and the bone's surface is less than 90°, causing an elliptical defect. As in round wounds discussed previously, these shapes are more likely to occur with entry wounds and to be seen on the smaller opening of the bevel. Jacketed projectiles are more likely

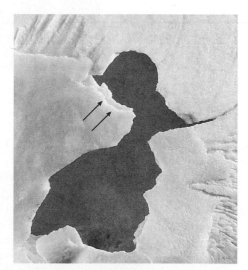

FIGURE 12.4 Reverse beveling (*arrows*) on an entry wound. (Photo by Julie R. Angel; specimen courtesy of the State of New Mexico, Office of the Medical Investigator)

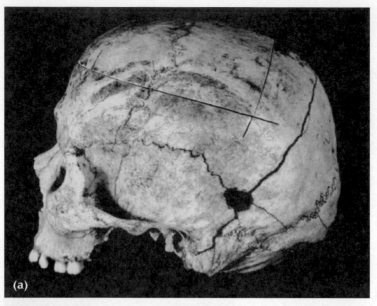

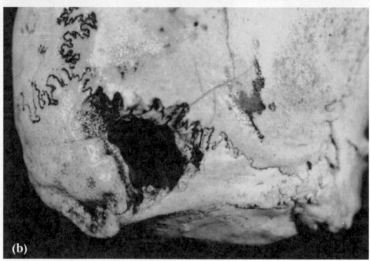

FIGURE 12.5 Shapes of skull wounds: **(a)** oval entry wound and **(b)** irregular exit wound. (Photos by Julie R. Angel; specimens courtesy of the State of New Mexico, Office of the Medical Investigator)

to cause oval entry or exit wounds, while any bullet construction can cause this type of entry wound. Figure 12.5a illustrates a typical oval entry wound on a skull, and Figure 12.6 shows a similar defect on a humerus.

Although occasionally occurring in exit wounds, keyhole wounds usually are caused by bullets that graze bone (i.e., the angle of trajectory is acute in the extreme), with little penetration (Dixon, 1982). Because of this, they constitute both entry and exit wounds. Thus, there is a fairly round entrance defect with inward beveling and, connected to it, is a splayed out triangular exit wound with outward beveling (Figure 12.7). Found most often in the cranial vault, keyhole shapes can originate from any type of bullet.

The last shape that a bullet wound can take is called irregular because of its lack of uniformity in outline. These types of wounds can take on a variety of configurations,

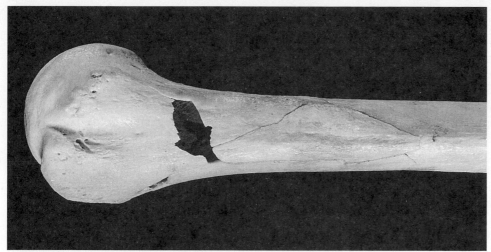

FIGURE 12.6   Oval entry wound to humerus; notice butterfly fracture lines leading down from lower border of wound. (Photo by Julie R. Angel; specimen courtesy of the State of New Mexico, Office of the Medical Investigator)

from jagged circular to asymmetric stellar to irregular rectangular. They normally are the result of shattering that gives the appearance of a bone that has exploded. Although entry wounds occasionally manifest this type of outline, irregular shapes are more characteristic of exit wounds (Huelke and Darling, 1964; Stewart, 1979). Also, since blunt and hollow-point bullets are more likely to deform during passage through tissue, it is reasonable to conclude that these types of defects are more common with soft-tipped projectiles. Figure 12.5b shows a typical irregular exit wound on a skull.

Wound Size

Many factors affect the size of wounds that projectiles cause in bone. The most important of these are wound type (i.e., entry versus exit) and bullet characteristics (i.e., caliber, construction, and velocity). Generally, exit wounds are larger than entry wounds (Rhine and Curran, 1990). Also, larger-caliber ammunition causes larger wounds, as do soft-tipped and hollow-point bullets. To simplify this discussion, only round or oval entry wounds will be discussed because these are the least variable of all wound types.

Ann Ross (1996) researched the correlation between cranial gunshot entrance wounds and the caliber of the causative projectile. All defects she studied were located on the bones of the vault (i.e., frontal, parietals, temporals, and occipital) and all were measured across their narrowest point. Two aspects of her work are important. First, larger calibers create on the average larger entry wounds. Although intuitively obvious, there is an exception to this finding. The 0.22 has an average wound that is larger than those caused by a 0.25-caliber bullet. This anomalous result appears to be due to the greater propensity for 0.25-caliber ammunition to be jacketed (Berryman et al., 1995) and therefore less likely to deform on impact. Another possible cause is greater flattening of the 0.22 bullet because of its smaller size when impacting the relatively thick bones of the cranial vault.

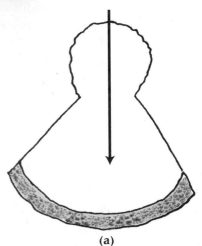

(a)

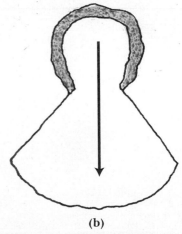

(b)

FIGURE 12.7   Keyhole wound to the skull. The arrows represent the direction of bullet flight. Stippled areas indicates exposed diploe; **(a)** external view, **(b)** internal view. (From Figure 13 of Dixon, 1982. Copyright ASTM International. Reprinted with permission)

The second important aspect of her work is the considerable overlap between wounds caused by all calibers. Occasionally a 0.22 projectile can cause an entrance wound that appears to be 0.45 in caliber, and a 0.32-caliber bullet can cause a wound that would appear as though it were caused by a 0.25 projectile. Larger-than-caliber entrance wounds appear to be related to bone thickness; thicker bones cause bullets to deform more on contact and therefore cause larger entry wounds (Ross, 1996). Smaller-than-caliber entry wounds may be due to several factors. First, in young individuals, bones may be pliable enough to bend in slightly at bullet impact; this would cause a smaller hole when the bone snaps back into place. (Similar effects are seen in soft tissue such as skin.) Another factor that could affect size is collision of the projectile with an intermediate object before striking the victim. This ricochet may cause fragmenting of the bullet, and this fragment would be smaller than that of the original caliber. Finally, passage of a bullet through a suture or pre-existing fracture line can cause smaller-than-caliber entry wounds (Berryman et al., 1995).

Fracture Lines

In addition to the subjects discussed above, the impact of bullets on bone may cause fracture lines to form. Generally, more powerful weapons cause more extensive fracturing. Currently, there is information on fracturing for the skull vault, bones of the thorax, and long limb bones. Thus, the effect of projectiles on other bones of the skeleton must be extrapolated from the following discussion. Also, because the lines that form on the skull vault are somewhat different than those formed on long limb bones and ribs, they will be discussed separately.

The two types of fracture lines, described in Chapter 11, are distinguishable on the cranial vault: radiating and concentric. **Radiating fracture lines** originate from the site of impact where they move outward in any direction (this is seen especially in entrance wounds). These lines follow the (usually invisible) areas of weakness in the vault bones. Also, when they encounter a foramen or another fracture line, their power can dissipate, causing them to stop (Rhine and Curran, 1990). Similarly, when they encounter a suture line, they can stop, or they can follow the suture for a while before continuing in their original direction. Figures 12.5a and 12.8 illustrate radiating fracture lines from an entry wound and an exit wound, respectively. Notice the propensity for some of the lines to follow the lambdoid suture for a while before continuing on their way.

Concentric fracturing also can occur in the skull through a process well described by O'Brian Smith and colleagues (1987). These authors note that concentric lines appear as part (or all) of a circle whose center is at the point of bullet impact. Thus, similar to a paper target, a series of concentric circles (or, more normally, parts of a circle) may appear at various intervals away from the entry or exit wound. Smith and his associates state that concentric lines are caused by intracranial pressure created by the bullet as it passes through the skull and compresses soft tissue in front of it. Because they occur later in the fracturing sequence, their power can be dissipated when they encounter radiating lines, causing them to stop. Also, their production depends on the power of the weapon; powerful weapons (e.g., rifles) are more likely to cause these types of fractures.

One last feature of these fractures has been described by Gina Hart (2005). She noted that concentric fractures due to projectiles are externally beveled; that is, the fracture occurs from the inner table to the outer table, angling away from the point of impact. (This is important when distinguishing between projectile and blunt trauma in cases of extreme skull fragmentation.)

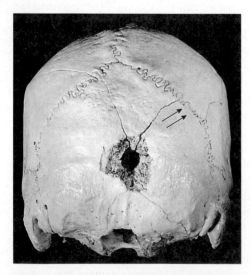

FIGURE 12.8 Classic radiating fracture lines from exit wound. Notice line following lambdoid suture (*arrows*) before continuing forward. (Photo by Julie R. Angel; specimen courtesy of the State of New Mexico, Office of the Medical Investigator)

Figure 12.9 illustrates a concentric line connecting two fractures radiating from an entry wound on the left side of the skull.

On long bones, Huelke and Darling (1964) note that two different types of fracture lines occur: butterfly and irregular. **Butterfly fractures** occur around the site of bullet impact on the diaphyses, appearing as lozenge-shaped lines extending along the long axis of the bone. When the bullet strikes near the center of the bone (either mediolaterally or anteroposteriorly), these fractures are bilateral (i.e., extend up and down from the site of bullet impact). If the bullet strikes away from the center, these fractures may be only unilateral; Figure 12.6 illustrates just such a defect on a proximal humerus. Notice the lozenge-shaped fracture extending down from the site of bullet impact. The second type of fracturing in long bones occurs when a bullet exits. Generally, this causes shattering of the bone outward such that no pattern can be discerned (i.e., *irregular* wound shape). Natalie Langley (2007) notes this same type of injury in gunshot wounds to the ribs.

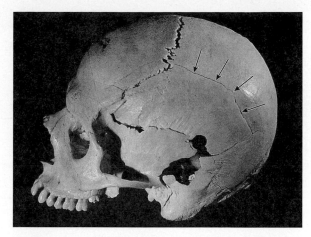

FIGURE 12.9   Concentric fracture line (*arrows*). (Photo by Julie R. Angel; specimen courtesy of the State of New Mexico, Office of the Medical Investigator)

BULLET WOUND ANALYSIS

Using the preceding information, bullet wounds can be analyzed to determine as much information about the weapon and its relation to the victim as possible. Unfortunately, because of variability in ammunition and firearms and in their effect on bone, any information developed from this type of analysis should be phrased carefully and in general terms. However, a description of the wound should always be made and, when possible, estimations of caliber, bullet construction, velocity, direction of fire, and sequence of wounds (if multiple) should be attempted.

Description of Wound(s)

The first task in any analysis of trauma is to describe the wound(s). This includes placement, size, shape, fracture lines, and any other relevant characteristics. In describing placement, the bone exhibiting the defect should be named as well as its side (if applicable). In addition, where the injury appears on the bone (i.e., proximal, middle or distal, medial/lateral, anterior/posterior) should be noted. Next, size should be measured, especially of injuries that have regular and well-defined margins (e.g., circular or oval entry wounds). After size has been determined, a basic description of the shape (e.g., circular, oval, irregular) should be documented, as well as a description of any radiating or hoop fracture lines. Finally, the presence of beveling should be documented.

Estimation of Caliber

Estimation of caliber usually is only necessary when the bullet cannot be found with the human remains (e.g., it exited the body). In these cases, the size of the entrance wound can be an indicator of the projectile, and therefore weapon, size. Using a caliper that is accurate to a hundredth of an inch, measure the wound hole in several directions to determine the smallest diameter. It is best to use only round or oval holes that are not located in sutures or fracture lines when performing this analysis. As noted by Ross (1996), this measurement can lead to an estimation of caliber in relative

TABLE 12.2 Relationship between Caliber and Minimum Wound Size in the Human Skull[1]

Caliber of Bullet	Sample Size	Average Size of Wounds	Range of Wound Sizes!	
			Minimum	Maximum
0.22	37	0.27	0.22	0.45
0.25	5	0.26	0.24	0.30
0.32	6	0.34	0.26	0.43
0.38	25	0.43	0.34	0.69

[1]From data in A. H. Ross: "Caliber estimation from cranial entrance defect measurements," *Journal of Forensic Science,* Vol. 41, pp. 629–633; her wound measurements converted to caliber.

terms, that is, small versus large. Small caliber would refer to 0.22-, 0.25-, 0.30-, and 0.32-inch projectiles; large caliber would refer to any weapon with a larger diameter. The information in Table 12.2 shows that holes of less than 0.34 inch are more likely to originate from small-caliber weapons, and holes greater than 0.43 inch are more likely to be caused by large-caliber weapons. Unfortunately, entrance wounds of the size between these values can be caused by any weapon. Also, despite the apparent precision of the data, when such determinations are made, it should be explained that in some cases smaller-caliber projectiles can cause larger wounds, especially if the bullet is hollow-point in construction or the bone at the point of impact is thick. Conversely, in rare cases, larger calibers could cause small wounds (especially after collision with an intermediate object).

Using this information, the entry wound in Figure 12.10, which is 0.22 inch at its smallest point, would most likely be caused by a small-caliber bullet. By contrast, the size of the weapon causing the wound seen in Figure 12.9 is more problematic. This defect, which is 0.41 inch at its smallest point (measured on the round part), falls in the overlap range of the data presented in Table 12.2. Although it is risky to estimate diameter in this case, a caliper estimation of large is likely, because the wound's size is at the high end of the overlap range and because the bones in this area of the skull are relatively thin.

Estimation of Bullet Construction

Unfortunately, as of this writing, there are no studies linking bone wound characteristics and bullet construction. Therefore, hypothesizing traits of a projectile by examining osteological defects caused by gunshots is only speculative at present. However, logic may shed light on this speculation. Because the bullet deforms and enlarges while traveling through the body, it is reasonable to assume that blunt and hollow-point ammunition are likely to cause shattering of bone at the site of exit. By contrast, because jacketed bullets are less likely to deform, exit wounds caused by these projectiles are less likely to shatter the impacted surface. Unfortunately, despite this logic, it must be remembered that high-powered (especially high-velocity) weapons are likely to cause bone shattering (Berryman and Symes, 1998).

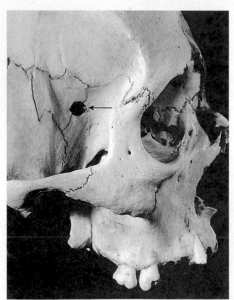

FIGURE 12.10 Small-caliber bullet entry wound (*arrow*) to right greater wing of the sphenoid. (Photo by Julie R. Angel; courtesy of the State of New Mexico, Office of the Medical Investigator)

Therefore, a large and irregular exit wound with accompanying outward breakage of bone and multiple fractures (see Figure 12.5b) may indicate a soft-tipped projectile or merely a high-velocity bullet. By contrast, an exit wound that does not exhibit shattering (Figure 12.3) is more likely to be caused by a jacketed bullet because this type of projectile does not deform as easily as it passes through bodily tissues. Given the preceding information, any statements as to bullet construction in the absence of the causative projectile must be made with extreme caution.

Estimation of Velocity

The velocity of a bullet can be told only within relative limits (e.g., low versus high). Low velocity is indicative of regular handguns, whereas rifles and handguns using magnum ammunition are more likely to expel high-velocity projectiles. High-velocity bullets are more likely to cause exit wounds because their kinetic energy is more likely to be great enough to carry them through and out of the body.

Figure 12.11 shows probes passed through the entry and exit wounds on a human cranium; these wounds are more likely to have been caused by a rifle rather than a handgun. Also, high-velocity bullets impacting the cranial vault are more likely to cause radiating and concentric fractures (Berryman and Symes, 1998), as well as catastrophic shattering of the skull (Rhine and Curran, 1990).

Figure 12.9 illustrates large fractures radiating from an entrance wound with concentric fracturing; thus, it is more likely that this wound was caused by a rifle or magnum handgun than by a regular handgun. Conversely, Figures 12.3a and b illustrate an exit wound with few radial or no concentric fracturing; based on this information, it is reasonable to hypothesize that this wound was more likely the result of a handgun.

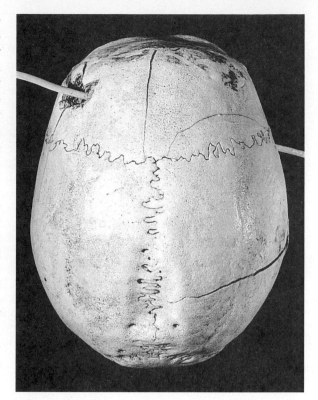

FIGURE 12.11 Probe passed through entry *(right)* and exit *(left)* wounds. (Photo by Julie R. Angel; specimen courtesy of the State of New Mexico, Office of the Medical Investigator)

Estimation of Direction of Fire

The shapes and alignments of the wounds can provide clues as to the direction from which a bullet was fired into a body. Round-shaped wounds indicate that the bullet axis (and therefore placement of the weapon) was at a near right angle to the bone surface. Figure 12.2a illustrates an entry wound to the skull that is nearly round and places the weapon to the back of the victim's head. Figure 12.5a illustrates an oval entry wound that indicates the placement of the weapon at an angle to the victim.

The alignment of entrance and exit wounds also provides a clue to the placement of the weapon (see Box 12.1 for a complex example). Figure 12.11 shows a probe passed into the entry and out the exit wounds of a skull; the placement of these injuries indicates that the weapon was discharged from the side of the skull. Estimating direction of fire from a keyhole wound also takes advantage of shape. The round part of the defect that exhibits inward beveling (see Figure 12.7) points to the placement of the weapon at the time of discharge (Dixon, 1982). It is important to note that, when direction of fire analysis is performed, careful examination should be made of both the skeleton and the bullet (if present) for ricochet marks.

BOX 12.1
The Skeleton of Carl Weiss

Douglas Ubelaker and Henry Scammell (1992) describe the analysis of the skeleton of Carl Weiss, the putative assassin of Senator Huey P. Long. Senator Long was a popular politician from the state of Louisiana where he served both as governor and later as senator. He was very controversial in both elected positions, so it was not surprising that he would be the target of an assassination attempt. On September 8, 1935, Weiss met Long in the capitol building in Baton Rouge where he reportedly shot the senator with a 0.32 caliber pistol. Long's bodyguards responded by shooting Weiss numerous times, killing him at the scene. Senator Long died 30 hours later.

Because the handling of the case was considered inadequate, many questions concerning the assassination have been circulated through the years. Thus, Ubelaker was asked to review the skeletal remains of Weiss in 1991 to help answer some of these questions. When the skeleton was delivered to his office at the Smithsonian, Ubelaker reassembled it and placed probes to indicate the direction of gunshot wounds. There were no less than 23 trajectories, and a possible twenty fourth, indicated by this action. Half of these entered from the back, seven from the front, and five from the sides. One small-caliber projectile entered the lower left eye orbit from below, but did not exit the braincase. Similarly, another bullet entered under the chin without shattering the cranium or causing an exit wound. In sum, the angles of the bullets' trajectories indicate that they entered Weiss's body while he was either standing or lying on the ground. This is consistent with the original version of the events, which states that Weiss was shot by Long's bodyguards numerous times, first as he stood and moments later after he was felled by the first bullets.

Estimation of Sequence

Determining the sequence of wounds when multiple injuries are discovered can be a tricky and complex business. To simplify the process, Stan Rhine and Bryan Curran (1990) present guidelines for performing this analysis. Using an example crania to illustrate their method, these authors note that the first steps involve locating the defects and distinguishing the entrance from the exit wounds. The information on beveling will aid in performing this step. The second step is to distinguish radiating from concentric fracture lines; again the information presented previously will help in this process. After fracture lines are identified, the next step is to follow the radiating fracture lines from their origin to their terminus. If that terminus is at another fracture line, it can be said that it is later in sequence than the line at which it stops. By identifying the entrance wound whose radiating fractures do not end at another line, the first wound in the sequence can be determined.

After the first in the sequence is identified, the process continues with the next entrance wound whose radiating fracture lines end only in the radiating lines caused by the predetermined first entrance wound. This process continues until all wounds are accounted for. In some cases, the number of wounds is so great that the fracture lines become too jumbled to determine their termini. Additionally, in some cases the radiating lines miss each other and go to their natural terminus at a suture or where they simply run out of energy. In both of these cases, this type of analysis may not be able to be performed.

Miscellaneous Estimations

Miscellaneous features concerning the death of the victim and characteristics of the assailant sometimes can be determined from the placement of wounds. For example, a wound located near the top of the skull would indicate that the weapon and therefore assailant were above the victim at the time of firing, by standing on an elevated area, by forcing the victim to kneel, or by the supine position of the victim. Also, the alignment of the entrance to the exit wound may give a clue as to the handedness of the attacker. Thus, a skull with an entrance wound on the left side of the forehead with an exit wound on the right side of the rear of the skull may indicate a right-handed assailant and vice versa. However, despite the seeming logic of these observations, it is important to note that these same effects can be caused by any number of other circumstances. Finally, Fenton and colleagues (2005) described symmetric and specific types of fracturing that occur in midline contact gunshot wounds to the skull. Knowledge of their findings can help in the determination of manner of death because almost half of suicides by firearms are from these types of wounds. Therefore, hypotheses about assailant characteristics and other estimations must be undertaken with extreme caution, and only by experienced forensic anthropologists.

PELLET WOUND ANALYSIS

Only two aspects of shotgun wounds usually can be determined: direction of fire and range of fire. Unfortunately, no published information is available linking wound size with pellet size. However, because it is unlikely that all pellets would exit the body after impact (except at very close ranges), retrieval of pellets from the area around the remains may be possible due to the usually large number of these expelled by shotguns. (This underscores the importance of careful retrieval of physical evidence when recovering human remains, as discussed in Chapter 4.)

The direction of fire can be told from the placement of pellet wounds on the bones. This is a relatively straightforward part of the analysis of such wounds. Pellets usually cause indentations (Stewart, 1979) in thick bones and perforations in thin bones, depending on the range of fire. Therefore, pellet indentations to the posterior side of the ribs, os coxae, sacrum, vertebrae, and skull indicate that the weapon was behind the victim at the time of discharge. Pellet wounds to the front or sides of these same bones naturally would indicate placement of the weapon to the front or side of the victim, respectively.

The range of fire (i.e., the distance from weapon to victim) can be estimated within limits due to the propensity of pellets to disperse during flight. Generally, pellets are bunched in a size matching the weapon's barrel diameter at the time of discharge. However, as they travel through the air, they begin to disperse into an ever-widening pattern. Thus, although pellets may leave a 12-gauge shotgun in a bunch that is no more than 0.73 inch in diameter, by the time they have traveled 35 feet, their spread is up to 9.5 inches (Horvath et al., 1993). Unfortunately, since many factors affect the spread of pellets (e.g., pellet size, barrel choke, and shell temperature), the calculation of range of fire is best left to ballistics experts. However, forensic anthropologists can help these specialists by locating all pellet wounds to bone and by determining their spread. This is done by laying the skeletal remains in the anatomical position (see Chapter 6), with spaces between skeletal elements closely approximating their distances in the living. This allows for reasonably accurate measurements of the distance between pellet wounds.

MISCELLANEOUS PROJECTILES

Any device that throws a projectile with as little as 66 foot-pounds of kinetic energy potentially can be deadly to humans. Since this amount of energy can be delivered by a 2-ounce projectile traveling at 184 feet per second, forensic anthropologists may encounter wounds to bone that do not fit any of the patterns described previously. Figure 12.12 illustrates an entry wound of a tear gas canister fired at close range into the left frontal of a skull; notice the large, oval hole caused by this unorthodox

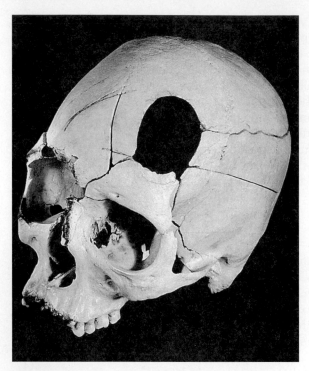

FIGURE 12.12   Entry wound caused by a tear gas canister fired at close range. (Photo by Julie R. Angel; specimen courtesy of the State of New Mexico, Office of the Medical Investigator)

projectile. Thus, when confronted with wounds of unknown nature, it is up to forensic anthropologists to use whatever resources are at their disposal to determine the characteristics of the wounding device.

Although there is a wide variety of other weapons, the most likely instruments to be encountered that can expel a lethal projectile are bows and crossbows. Unfortunately, little is known about the fracturing of bone by these projectiles; however, James Downs and associates (1994) present a description of the wounding characteristics of these types of weapons that is summarized here. The projectiles from bows and crossbows typically have one of two types of heads: field tips and broadheads. Field tips are reminiscent of round-tipped bullets that have been fashioned with a slight point. Because of their similarity of form, they can inflict wounds on bone that are analogous to low-velocity jacketed bullets. Thus, the inward bevelings of an entrance wound and outward bevelings of an exit wound can be encountered, but extensive fracturing is not common (Downs et al., 1994). Broadheads are arrow points that have anywhere from two to five triangular vanes attached to them. These vanes can cause radial fracturing in the tabular bones of the skull that closely approximates their pattern on the arrow or bolt point. Thus, a broadhead with four equally spaced vanes that penetrate the cranial vault would leave a round wound with four fractures radiating outward in the form of a plus sign. Again, extensive shattering of bone is not expected from this type of projectile.

DETERMINING CAUSE AND MANNER OF DEATH

As stated in the Forensic Anthropology Protocol in Chapter 1, information concerning the cause and manner of death should be gathered from the skeleton if there are osteological indicators that concern these subjects. However, also stated earlier, the forensic anthropologist is not legally responsible to make such determinations. In addition, they can cause serious harm if they make statements concerning the cause and manner of death but the person legally tasked with this responsibility (i.e., medical examiner, coroner) arrives at a different conclusion. These conflicting opinions, which could easily occur if one of the specialists has knowledge concerning the death that is unknown to the other, might make the prosecution of a criminal case more difficult. Also, determining these two matters in unexplained deaths is not as straightforward as it may appear.

When attempting to determine cause of death, the only evidence regularly available to forensic anthropologists is the location and severity of wounds. (Interestingly, Geoffroy de la Grandmaison and colleagues (2001) found that bone lesions were absent in approximately 11% of 130 gunshot fatalities that they studied, indicating that the absence of bone trauma does not rule out gunshot wounds as a cause of death.) With a perimortem gunshot wound to a vital spot (e.g., braincase), the low likelihood of survival might tempt them to argue that as cause of death. Conversely, a wound to a part of the body that is not vital (e.g., hand) might bring a judgment of not causing death. Similarly, a small wound with little bone shattering is less likely to be mortal than one involving catastrophic bone fragmentation, again leading to inferences concerning cause of death. However, such interpretations are misleading in their simplicity due to the complicated nature of death due to gunshot wounds. A perimortem catastrophic gunshot wound to the head that entails fragmentation of the skull into numerous pieces certainly points toward projectile trauma as a cause of death; however, one must be certain that this is perimortem trauma and not postmortem damage. Conversely, gunshot wounds to seemingly nonvital spots can easily cause death by exsanguination (bleeding to death) in the absence of proper medical care.

There are similar potentials and (even greater) pitfalls when determining manner of death using perimortem projectile trauma. Information such as location of wound, bullet travel, type of weapon, and number of wounds gleaned from skeletal remains surely provides vital evidence as to this issue. However, the interpretation of this information again is not necessarily straightforward. A common belief is that the location of a gunshot wound can be an indicator of manner of death. A projectile wound to the back of the body or back of the head would rule out suicide because of the difficulty of inflicting an injury on oneself in such an inaccessible location. Such a belief obscures the (albeit rare) instances when persons do commit suicide by shooting themselves in these locations. Also, knowledge of common sites of suicide can lead forensic anthropologists astray for similar reasons. There are several classic methods of suicide by firearms: into the mouth, under the chin, and through the temple. In the first of these, the muzzle of a weapon (handgun, rifle, or shotgun) is placed in the mouth so that when the trigger is pulled, the projectile(s) enters the skull through its base and exits (if the weapon is powerful enough) through the occipital (e.g., Figure 12.8). When placed under the chin, the path of a projectile will be through the palate and rear of the nasal passages, with an exit wound (if any) through the superior part of the frontal (e.g., Figure 12.3). Finally, suicide in the temple causes the projectile to enter near or through the greater wing of the sphenoid (e.g., Figure 12.10) with an exit wound (if any) through the opposite side of the skull (e.g., Figure 12.11). However, the presence of any of these wounds on a skull does not necessarily indicate suicide. It is easy to imagine an assailant placing a gun in any one of these locations before discharging the weapon, thereby committing murder. Similarly, accidental firing of a weapon into any of these locations could occur, indicating accident as manner of death.

Even the path of the bullet is not necessarily useful in this determination. Although bullets that travel forward (toward the frontal) from the temple during suicide or bullets that travel downward in self-inflicted gunshots through the mouth are rare, their presence in documented cases of suicide makes the ruling of manner of death from this information tenuous. Using the type of weapon in these analyses can cause similar problems. Although it seems more likely that persons would commit suicide with a handgun, a surprising number choose a rifle or shotgun for this purpose. In the absence of a weapon, determining the type from wound characteristics is not as clearcut as one might hope. For example, as stated in this chapter, projectile wounds with large, radiating fracture lines and shattering of bone are indicative of a high-velocity bullet, such as from a rifle. If these criteria are used in the analysis of the skull pictured on the front cover of this book, an estimation of this type of weapon as causing the injury would seem appropriate. However, the injury pictured there is a contact wound from a handgun (Stan Rhine, personal communication). Finally, the number of injuries is not indicative of manner of death despite the logic that a single gunshot wound is all that is necessary to commit suicide. There are documented cases of persons inflicting a second, third, or more projectile injuries on themselves after surviving the first wound.

The circumstances surrounding the recovery of the decedent provide some of the most important clues for determining manner of death. Although it may be obvious that the causative weapon should be recovered near the body in suicides and self-inflicted accidents, the presence of a weapon does not rule out either homicide (as the murderer may leave the weapon) or accident (as the shooter may drop the weapon and leave the scene simply out of fear and horror of what had happened). Conversely, the absence of a weapon does not rule out suicide as there are documented instances where suicide victims set up a situation such that the weapon becomes hidden after their deaths. There are even cases when another person finds a body before the authorities and removes the weapon for his or her own use.

If forensic anthropologists are present when the body is recovered, the circumstances of the recovery might bias the analysis by predisposing them toward conclusions not necessarily supported by the evidence. The presence of a handgun or rifle at the recovery scene might incline forensic anthropologists to interpret any perimortem trauma encountered as due to projectile trauma. Also, forensic anthropologists might be disposed to give an opinion on the cause and manner of death because they observed the circumstances surrounding the body. This all-too-human propensity must be avoided because, as stated earlier (but deserving reiteration), it is not within the purview of forensic anthropologists to state either of these matters.

Even when knowledgeable of the recovery scene, forensic anthropologists would need to know other aspects of the case to render a determination of manner of death. For example, a suicide note found at the scene would certainly speak to manner of death. Similarly, the psychological state of victims and their actions just prior to their deaths are important factors to consider. Persons exhibiting fear of another person during their final days indicates a greater possibility of homicide as a manner of death than persons either expressing a lack of interest in living or making threats of suicide. Conversely, the process of "setting their affairs in order" before their death indicates suicide more than activities that concern the future (e.g., buying a house, planning a wedding).

Although much of what was just described represents unlikely circumstances, the importance of determining the correct manner of death makes it imperative that it is accurate. Ruling a homicide to be a suicide allows a murderer to go free (where he or she may murder again). The converse can have similarly disastrous effects, in that the police may arrest a person for murder when the manner of death is actually suicide or accident.

These examples show the difficulties surrounding these types of analyses, in that multiple scenarios are possible even with the most simple of situations. Thus, considering the complexity of the circumstances surrounding an unexplained death, the safest course of action for the forensic anthropologist is to describe the perimortem skeletal injuries in minute detail. In this manner, the authorities with the legal responsibility to declare these aspects of unexplained deaths will have as much information as possible to help them in their determinations. It also can be stated that, as a general rule, forensic anthropologists should not attempt to provide cause and manner of death. The only exception to this is when their opinion is sought by persons legally responsible for determining these matters. In these cases, only experienced forensic anthropologists should provide that opinion, and only if they are in receipt of all of the information surrounding the recovery of the body and the decedent's last days.

Summary

1. To perform correct projectile wound analysis, forensic anthropologists should understand a number of characteristics of firearms and ammunition, such as size (e.g., caliber, gauge), velocity, and bullet construction.

2. When analyzing gunshot wounds to bone, forensic anthropologists should attempt to provide law enforcement officials with as much information as possible about the causative weapon, the placement of the firearm, and any other information that can be accurately determined.

3. Generally, by measuring round entrance wounds in bones, the size of the bullet causing the defect can be estimated in terms of small or large caliber.

4. Extensive fracturing resulting in shattering of the bone at an exit site is more indicative of a soft-tipped bullet or high-velocity projectile than of a jacketed or low-velocity bullet.

5. The direction from which a bullet entered a bone can be determined by observing the shape (round, oval, keyhole, irregular) and beveling (inward, outward, reverse) of the resultant wound.

6. The sequence with which multiple wounds were delivered can be determined by identifying the entrance wound(s) with radial fracture lines that do not stop at other fracture lines.

7. Usually, only two aspects of shotgun wounds can be told from bone: direction of fire and range of fire. Forensic anthropologists generally can only determine the former characteristics; the latter trait is estimated by a ballistics expert.

8. Generally, arrows and bolts from bows and crossbows cause wounds similar to those caused by bullets. However, due to their low velocity, extensive fracturing and shattering are not expected.

9. Any device that launches a projectile at a fast enough rate is potentially lethal to humans. It is up to the imagination and ability of forensic anthropologists to distinguish their effects on bone.

Exercises

1. A skull is brought in for projectile analysis, which exhibits a single clean, round wound measuring one-quarter of an inch in the center of the occipital bone. Given these data, provide as much information as possible on this apparent gunshot wound.

2. The shattered remains of a cranium are brought in for analysis. The braincase is broken into approximately 25 pieces. After reconstruction, three entrance wounds can be distinguished, each approximately three-eighths of an inch in diameter. However, exit wounds are virtually impossible to reconstruct. What can be said about the weapon causing these injuries?

3. A skull exhibits a round entrance wound to the left temporal and an outwardly beveled exit wound to the right temporal. No fracture lines emanate from the entrance wound, but several large lines radiate from the exit wound. Hypothesize as to the placement and type of weapon used to cause these injuries.

4. Two projectile wounds are found on a skull. One entered the right temporal and exited through the left half of the frontal. The other entered through the occipital and exited through the center of the frontal. No radiating fracture lines were found emanating from the entrance wounds, but the exit wound in the center of the frontal exhibited a line that passed laterally to the other exit wound. The wound on the left half of the frontal exhibited lines that curved over the cranium stopping at various sutures. What is the sequence of these wounds?

5. A femur exhibits a clean, round entrance wound to the popliteal surface that measures approximately one-quarter of an inch; however, there is no exit wound. What can be said of the power, size, and placement of the weapon causing this wound? If there had been an exit wound, where would it have been located and what types of fracture lines would have radiated from it?

6. A skeleton exhibits two wounds in the thoracic area. One wound, showing internal beveling, is found near the sternal end of the left third rib. The other, exhibiting an outward bevel, is found on right fourth rib. From these data, provide as much information as possible on the gunshot wound.

7. An oval entrance wound is found in the right temporal of a skull. The face has been shattered, and several radiating fracture lines traverse the braincase. Describe the causative weapon and its placement in relation to the victim.

8. A circular entrance wound, measuring approximately one-half of an inch across, is found in the palate of a skull. The exit wound, measuring almost three-quarters of an inch across, is found on the frontal, near bregma. Few fracture lines radiate from either wound. Describe the placement of the weapon and any other of its characteristics that can be determined.

13

Blunt Trauma

A second type of skeletal trauma that forensic anthropologists must be able to recognize is caused by blunt force. As discussed in Chapter 11, injuries of this type result when a force impacts bone over a relatively wide area, causing discontinuities and fracture lines. Implements such as a club swung by hand, and hard surfaces such as the ground in a fall, can be the causative factors in these types of injuries. In addition, the fronts of automobiles in collisions and parts of airplanes and trains (e.g., bulkheads, seats) in a crash can produce blunt traumas in the human skeleton. Thus, because of the variety of instruments and surfaces that can produce this type of injury, assessing the specific characteristics of the causative instruments in blunt trauma is difficult, if not impossible.

This chapter will cover similar topical areas as those presented in the discussion of projectile trauma. First, the general attributes of instruments and surfaces that can cause blunt trauma will be described, including a discussion of their size, shape, and weight. Second, a typology of fractures is presented. Third, the effects of instruments on bone will be presented, starting first with injuries to the cranium followed by discussions of the effects of blunt trauma to the postcranial skeleton. Finally, the elements germane to wound analysis will be presented, with an emphasis on estimating the characteristics of causative implements and/or surfaces.

CHARACTERISTICS OF INSTRUMENTS

Any number of instruments can cause blunt trauma to the human skeleton. These include objects wielded as bludgeons, such as baseball bats, pieces of wood, crowbars and other metal objects, and rocks. In addition, any hard surface can also cause this type of injury. This includes stationary objects such as the ground during a fall, exterior parts of automobiles during pedestrian–automobile collisions, and the interior components of moving vehicles (e.g., dashboards in automobiles, seats and bulkheads in airplanes and trains). Given the wide variety of objects that can deliver blunt force, a description of their basic characteristics must, by necessity, be general. Therefore, this section will focus on three traits of objects that can cause blunt trauma: size, shape, and weight.

Size

The size of an object causing blunt trauma includes its length and width. Length, which refers to the long dimension (axis), is relatively easy to describe for bludgeons such as baseball bats, glass bottles, and other such instruments wielded as clubs. However, unless the long axis of an instrument is clearly imprinted in the bone(s), this dimension usually cannot be estimated on an objective scale (i.e., in terms of centimeters or inches); rather, only words such as long or short can be used to describe the causative instrument. Width, the dimension at right angles to length, presents similar problems during analysis. Although narrow versus wide may be evident from a wound, determining the actual width in inches or centimeters from its imprint on bone again is unlikely except under the most optimal of conditions. Considering this, a large percentage of blunt trauma may only be visible as focused versus diffused. Thus, an injury to the skull where the area of impact is clear, but the imprint of the causative instrument is not visible, would indicate that the causative force was focused. By contrast, diffused forces would cause blunt traumas that would not exhibit a distinct area of impact.

Unfortunately, not all objects causing blunt trauma have long and short axes that allow for length and width estimates. For example, a person impacting level ground after a fall would exhibit a blunt injury that would not necessarily be characterized by long and short axes. Similarly, an injury caused by a skull striking the windshield (or windshield striking a skull) during an automobile collision may show a diffuse, rather than a narrowly focused, area of injury. However, as with much of forensic anthropology, the determination of bludgeon versus collision can be complicated by many factors. For example, a fall onto an uneven surface (e.g., onto rocks) may cause traumatic injuries that appear as though they were delivered by a bludgeon with distinct long and short axes. Similarly, a club with a circular outline on the impacting surface (e.g., a hammer) may inflict an injury mimicking a wound from a fall. Thus, in cases of blunt force trauma more than in any other type of trauma, it is important that forensic anthropologists be aware of the circumstances under which the remains were recovered.

Despite the preceding limitations, some aspects of the circumstances surrounding death can be assessed even with only rough estimates of width. For example, objects with small widths need less force to cause fractures than wide instruments. This can be seen in Table 13.1, where the amount of force necessary to cause a skull fracture on the frontal bone is presented for various radii of curvature of the impacting instrument. Notice that the amount of energy (in terms of pounds) needed by a 3.1 inch object to fracture a human frontal bone is only two-thirds of that with an instrument that is 20 inches. This information may provide clues as to the strength of an assailant in cases of bludgeoning. For example, injuries that appear to be the result of a narrow instrument indicate that law enforcement officials need not search only for strong males; a weak person could also have delivered this type of blow.

Shape

The shape of an instrument causing blunt trauma refers to both its cross-sectional outline and its longitudinal configuration. Generally, two cross-sectional shapes are recognized: round and angular. Round outlines are common in many tools and other objects

TABLE 13.1 Diameter of Weapon Causing
Frontal Fracture of the Skull[1]

Force (lbs)	Radius of Curvature (in.)
1590	20.0
1500	12.5
1400	8.0
1100	3.6
1040	3.1

[1]From C. G. Wilber: *Forensic Biology for the Law Enforcement Officer* (1974). Courtesy of Charles C. Thomas Publisher, Ltd., Springfield, IL.

used as clubs, such as baseball bats, glass bottles, tree branches, and some crowbars. Angular outlines similarly are common in bludgeons such as lumber (e.g., two-by-fours), some crowbars, and pieces of metal (e.g., angle iron). Generally, an object with an angular outline will be more likely to inflict an injury with distinct, almost incisive edges with fewer fracture lines than objects with circular or oval cross sections. In addition, these types of objects are the most likely to leave an imprint of their shape at the site of impact.

Many longitudinal configurations of instruments can deliver blunt trauma. Some objects have a straight long axis (e.g., baseball bat), while others exhibit a curve, angle, or other kind of bend (e.g., crowbar). Injuries that exhibit a straight long axis usually are the result of an object with a straight longitudinal configuration. However, only under optimal circumstances will the angle of a curved instrument be determinable from a blunt force injury because of the nearly infinite number of degrees of curvature and angle of striking that is possible in these types of objects (see Box 13.1).

On rare occasions, **patterned injuries** occur that specifically identify the causative instrument. In this type of trauma, the imprint of the impacting instrument or surface is clearly visible on the affected tissue (Spitz, 1980). These are most easily seen on soft tissue, such as when a belt buckle is used as a striking instrument or a tool with an unusually distinct contacting surface impacts living tissue. Unfortunately for identification, these types of injuries are rare on bone. The only osteological area prone to such wounds is the cranial vault, where the bony expanse is large and relatively unprotected by muscle or other soft tissues. Despite its rarity, forensic anthropologists must be aware that such injuries can occur so that they will be recognized during osteological examination.

Weight

The weight of a blunt object usually can only be estimated from the resultant injury into categories such as heavy or light. Generally, light objects will cause smaller injuries with fewer fracture lines than those that are heavier. For example, a 2-pound crowbar will cause less damage than a 4-pound baseball bat when delivered with the same force on the same surface. Conversely, heavy objects swung with determination can cause

---

BOX 13.1
Causative Instrument from Wound Shape

William Maples and Michael Browning (1994) describe a case where an angular wound could be used to estimate the causative instrument. The case involved a White male who exhibited several instances of blunt trauma to the cranium. One of the injuries, located on the back of the skull, was too amorphous in shape to aid in determining the causative instrument. However, one injury to the anterior part of the right parietal and another on the frontal were sufficiently unique to help identify the source of the wound.

The shape of these two injuries was distinctive. Although one was larger than the other, both exhibited angulation of approximately two-thirds along their lengths. The odd configuration of these wounds caused Maples to search the local hardware stores for an instrument that exhibited the bend inscribed in the wound. Unfortunately, none of the tools manifested the precise shape needed to cause the fractures seen on the skull. After contemplating this situation, Maples hit on the idea of estimating the effect of an angled instrument when not delivered straight down on the cranial surface. With this in mind, he purchased a crowbar with a bent end for extracting nails. By changing the angle of impact on the cranium, he was able to demonstrate that this tool could have been the causative instrument. The dramatic recreation illustrated in his book confirms that he almost certainly was right in his conclusion.

catastrophic injuries to bone, resulting in large wounds with extensive fracture lines, as well as crushing and fragmentation.

Unfortunately, the concept of weight is not applicable with some blunt force injuries. In collisions involving humans and a moving vehicle, weight is irrelevant. Similarly, with injuries caused by falls from high places, the concept of weight does not apply. Therefore, caution must be exercised with estimating this characteristic from bone injuries. If wounds are encountered with well-defined axes (both long and short) and catastrophic fracturing, an estimation that they were caused by a heavy blunt object may be warranted. Conversely, diffuse fracturing of the skeleton would make an assessment of object weight risky at best.

TYPES OF FRACTURES

Alison Galloway (1999) provides a fine summary of the types of fractures that can result in blunt trauma to the human skeleton, especially to long bones. She recommends utilizing these descriptions in forensic situations to standardize the multitude of injuries possible due to this type of force. Her descriptions divide these fractures into the two basic types, discussed in Chapter 11: incomplete (infractions) and complete fractures. Incomplete fractures take seven forms:

1. Bow fracture or plastic deformation
2. Bone bruise or occult intraosseous fracture
3. Torus or buckling fracture
4. Greenstick fracture
5. Toddler's fracture
6. Vertical fracture
7. Depressed fracture

Bow fracture or **plastic deformation** is an infraction caused by compression along the long axis of a bone (most commonly the forearm of children). Macroscopically, they cause the bone to bend to an unnatural degree; microscopically, they appear as a series of miniature fractures running obliquely across the long axis. **Bone bruise** or **occult intraosseous fracture** is mainly visible in radiographs or MRI images. Not often seen in the forensic context, they appear to be microfractures to trabecular bone due to compression forces. **Torus** or **buckling fracture** is the result of compressive forces that cause an outward buckling of the cortex around the circumference of a bone. Most of these are seen at the juncture between metaphyses and their respective epiphyses. **Greenstick fracture** was discussed in Chapter 11; it is an incomplete, transverse fracture (see discussion later) to long bones, which results in the diaphyses being bent at an abnormal angle. **Toddler's fracture** is an oblique or spiral fracture (see discussion later) where the ends do not separate. Seen most often in the lower limbs (especially the tibia) of infants and toddlers, this type of injury is not common in the forensic situation. **Vertical fracture** is due to compressive forces which split the bone along its long axis. The final type of infraction is the **depressed fracture**. This break is identifiable as segments of bone that point inwardly toward the bone's center. Seen most often in the skull due to compressive forces, it may also occur at the end of long bones.

Complete fractures take five forms:

1. Transverse fracture
2. Oblique fracture
3. Spiral fracture
4. Comminuted fracture
5. Epiphyseal fracture

Transverse fracture crosses the diaphysis at right angles to the long axis of the bone. This type, which is most common in long bones, is due to bending (and possibly shearing) forces. **Oblique fracture** passes through the shaft of the bone at an angle approximating 45°. This is the result of bending and compression forces that cause the bone to fail transversely (following the bending force) but also linearly (following the compression force).**Spiral fracture** results when excessive torsion is applied to a bone. The resulting fracture spirals along the long axis of the bone, producing an oblique-like break around the bone axis. **Comminuted fracture**, as described Chapter 11, is a break that results in the production of more than two pieces. Galloway distinguishes two special types of this fracture: butterfly and segmental. The **butterfly fracture** occurs when a wedge of bone separates from the other two bone pieces on the side where the fracturing force impacts the bone (see Figure 11.8). These, seen most often in the legs of pedestrians struck by automobiles, appear to be due to the same forces that cause oblique fractures (compression and bending). **Segmental fracture** is distinguished by three segments of bone: a medial and a lateral piece, which are separated by a section between their two ends. These may result when two separate forces are applied to the bone simultaneously or when the bone impacts a large surface. The last complete fracture type, **epiphyseal fracture**, occurs to the ends of long limb bones. This type of break can separate the epiphyses from their respective metaphyses and divide either of these structures into two or more pieces. Such fractures are seen mainly in subadults as these two bone segments are fused in adulthood. All of these can be caused by forces of a static or dynamic nature.

EFFECTS OF BLUNT INSTRUMENTS

The general effects of blunt objects on human bone are known relatively well. Simple and comminuted fractures, as described in Chapter 11, are commonsense results of this type of force. However, the characteristics of wounds caused by blunt surfaces depend on the skeletal structure or individual bone being impacted. Thus, the skull reacts differently to blunt force than long bones and ribs. Similarly, thick bones respond somewhat differently to this type of force than thin bones. Considering this, it is convenient to recognize three skeletal structures in the following discussion: skull, long bones, and other bones (especially elements of the thorax).

Skull

Hugh Berryman and Steven Symes (1998) provide a readable account of the effect of blunt trauma on the human skull. These authors state that when a blunt force of sufficient magnitude to cause fracturing is applied to the skull vault, the bone passes through several phases. First there is inbending at the site of impact, with concomitant outbending surrounding the impact site (see Figure 13.1). With sufficient force, fracture lines begin at various points on the outbent surface and progress both inward to the impact site and outward, where they form radiating fracture lines. If the force has not been dissipated by these events, the lines continue outwardly, causing the formation of wedge-shaped pieces of bone. Finally, if the force is sufficient to penetrate the vault, concentric fractures occur around the area of impact as the tips of the wedge-shaped pieces are forced inward. Gina Hart (2005) has demonstrated that these fractures are internally beveled, in a manner opposite that seen in projectile trauma. In this case, the fracture occurs from the outer table to the inner table, angling away from the point of impact. These *hoop fractures,* which can occur separately or in groups of two or more, either partially or completely encircle the point of impact.

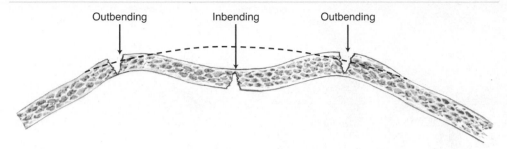

Outbending   Inbending   Outbending

FIGURE 13.1 Inbending at the point of impact with concomitant outbending at some distance from this point. The dashed line indicates the original contour of the bone.

Hugh Berryman and Steven Symes (1998) note that elastic bone deforms inwardly at the point of impact, causing the outer table to be under compression while the inner table is under tension. Because bone fails more readily under tension, fracture lines start on the inner surface of the point of impact and then progress outward (Figure 13.2a). However, brittle bone (as with older persons) is affected differently. If the force is sufficient, it drives through both tables, resulting in a plug of bone being pushed into the cranial vault (Figure 13.2b). In other instances, when the trabecular bone is brittle and weak, the diploe crushes under the force, causing a depressed fracture at the point of impact (Figure 13.2c). Finally, if the inner table is more brittle or weaker than the outer table, the tensional forces will cause the inner table to divide into a number of segments (see Figure 13.2d). Considering this information, it is important that the inner surface of the cranial vault be inspected for fracturing in any forensic case, because this area may present information on the degree of force and on the health of the individual.

Berryman and Symes (1998), in describing fractures to the face, note that blunt forces are guided by the three paired areas of buttressing depicted in Figure 13.3: the **alveolar ridge**, the **malar eminences**, and the

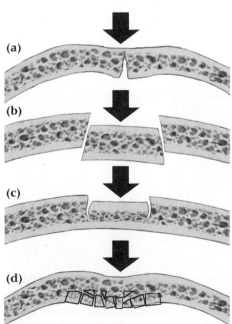

(a)

(b)

(c)

(d)

FIGURE 13.2 Fractures characteristic of blunt trauma to the skull: **(a)** inbending at the impact site with concomitant fracturing on the inner table; **(b)** formation of a plug in brittle bone; **(c)** crushing of the diploe; **(d)** crushing of the inner table.

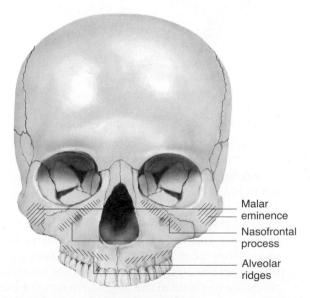

Malar eminence

Nasofrontal process

Alveolar ridges

FIGURE 13.3 Buttresses of the face.

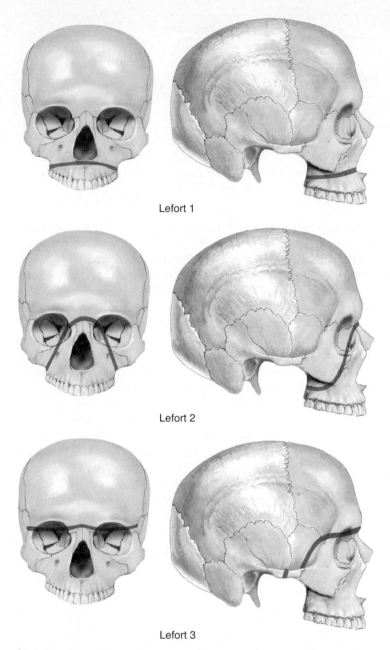

Lefort 1

Lefort 2

Lefort 3

FIGURE 13.4   LeFort fractures of the face.

nasofrontal processes of the maxillae. These buttresses guide the dissipation of force when blunt force is applied to the face, resulting in **LeFort fractures** (see Figure 13.4). There are three expressions of these types of breaks. **LeFort 1** involves separation of the alveolar part of the maxilla from the rest of the face in the area between the alveolar ridges and the nasofrontal processes. It results when a blow impacts the lower face, either from the front or side. **LeFort 2** involves separation of the mid-face from the rest of the cranium. It results from an anterior blow to the mid-face, which causes fractures to occur in the areas between the buttresses formed by the malar eminence and the nasofrontal processes. Finally, **LeFort 3** occurs when the entire face is separated from the braincase, caused by a centrally focused blow to the upper part of this structure. The fracture lines formed by this force are guided into the area between the malar eminence buttress, the frontal buttress, and the anterior temporal buttress (see Figure 13.5). Although these types appear straight-forward, as with other aspects of forensic anthropology, fractures rarely occur in such neat categories. Generally, LeForts 2 and 3 co-occur, muddling the issue as to type of break; in addition, sufficient force applied to the face can cause such crushing as to confound any attempts at classification. Therefore, it is important that facial fractures not be forced into the categories when they are too complex to fit a single type.

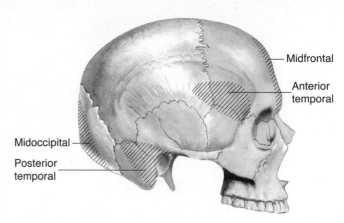

FIGURE 13.5 Buttresses of the cranial vault.

Blunt forces to the cranial vault are guided between the four areas of buttressing depicted in Figure 13.5: **midfrontal, midoccipital, posterior temporal**, and **anterior temporal** (Berryman and Symes, 1998). Although vault fractures do not have a classificatory scheme, blunt force applied to the braincase generally will guide between these areas in a manner similar to that seen in facial fractures. Thus, a blow to the middle of the parietal may send radiating fracture lines between the midfrontal and anterior temporal buttresses, sparing the area of the forehead at midline. Similarly, a blow to the top of the squamous suture generally will result in fracture lines that guided between the anterior and posterior temporal buttresses.

The speed with which blunt force impacts the cranium can affect the type of fracture. If the force is relatively slow, the bone may bend, producing a complete fracture on one side, but an infraction on the other. These hinge fractures are usually inwardly bent and remain in that position without returning to their normal configuration. By contrast, force delivered swiftly will normally result in complete fracture and (with sufficient force) fragmentation.

Berryman and Symes (1998) describe a special type of break that occurs on the base of the skull called a **ring fracture** (Figure 13.6). This is caused by the skull being forced down onto the vertebral column (as in a headlong fall or a feet-first fall) or by the skull being pulled away from the column. The direction of the force can be determined by the bevel of the fracture; if it bevels inwardly (Figure 13.7b), the force will most likely drive the skull and vertebral column toward each other. However, an outward bevel (Figure 13.7a) indicates a pulling apart of these two elements. This type of fracture starts at the posterior part of the occipital and progresses anteriorly. Thus, relatively mild forces will only affect the occipital, and the resultant fracture will only partially encircle the foramen magnum. If the force is sufficient, fracturing continues into the petrous part of the temporals and terminates in the foramen of the middle fossa. Finally, with severe examples of these fractures, the fracture completely encircles the foramen magnum, ending at the *sella turcica* (an osseous structure near where the occipital meets the sphenoid).

Other types of common fractures affect the mandible (Figure 13.8) and the zygomatic bone (Figure 13.9). Blows to the lower jaw can result in fractures first to the body, followed by the angle, then the condyles, the symphysis, the ascending

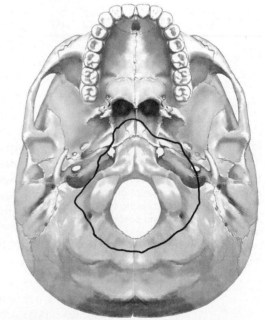

FIGURE 13.6 Ring fracture to the base of the skull.

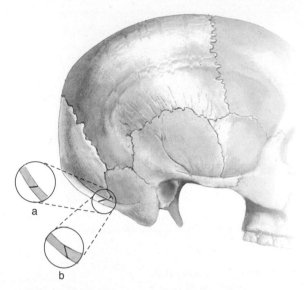

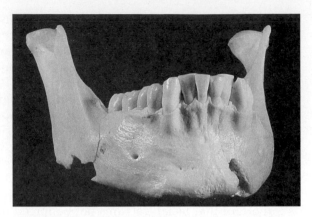

FIGURE 13.8 Fracture to the mandibular body, the most frequent type of blunt force injury to this bone. (Photo by Julie R. Angel; specimen courtesy of the State of New Mexico, Office of the Medical Investigator)

FIGURE 13.7 Bevel of base skull ring fractures: **(a)** outward, implying tension force; **(b)** inward, implying compression force.

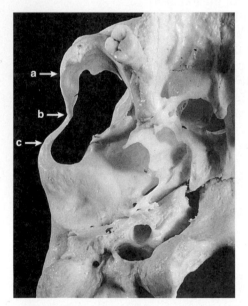

FIGURE 13.9 Healed fracture to the right zygomatic bone. The point of impact was in the center (*arrow b*), causing fractures both anteriorly (*arrow a*) and posteriorly (*arrow c*). (Photo by Julie R. Angel; specimen courtesy of the State of New Mexico, Office of the Medical Investigator)

ramus, and finally the coronoid process (Berryman and Symes, 1998). In some cases, enough energy is applied through the condyles that the temporal bone also will exhibit fractures.

The zygomatic area can exhibit several types of fractures. First, the sutures that attach this bone to the maxillae, frontal, and temporals can give way, especially when a blow is delivered off center to the mid-face. A second type occurs when the zygomatic arch is traumatized. Generally, in these cases, three fractures occur: one anterior to the focus of the blow (Figure 13.9, arrow a), one at the focus (Figure 13.9, arrow b), and one posterior to the focus of the blow (Figure 13.9, arrow c).

Long Bones

Blunt instruments applied to long bones usually deliver compression and bending forces that result in complete, simple fractures without fracture lines. Complete fractures are more common than infractions because the amount of force necessary to cause a displacement generally is the same as that needed to traverse the long axis of the bone, thereby entirely separating the two segments. The exception is the green stick fractures described in Chapter 11, seen in subadults. However, comminuted fractures with fracture lines can result from blunt forces when they are delivered with sufficient energy to shatter the thick cortex of these bones (see Figure 13.10).

Other Bones

Other bones are affected by blunt traumas in special ways. David Daegling and colleagues (2008) submitted adult ribs to experimental fracturing and found that these bones generally break toward their anterior end. Additionally, complete and incomplete fractures were observed, and the type of breakage varied from buckle,

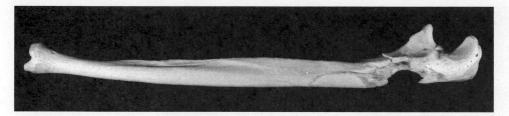

FIGURE 13.10 Complete and comminuted fracture to a long bone, in this case an ulna.
(Photo by Julie R. Angel; specimen courtesy of the State of New Mexico, Office of the Medical Investigator)

transverse, spiral, and even butterfly fractures (see Figure 13.14). Vertebrae can manifest simple fractures at any of the transverse or spinous processes. Also, the pelvis can be affected in many ways by blunt trauma, including breakage of the pubis and the iliac crest. Finally, blunt trauma to the scapula can result in separation of the glenoid, as well as part or all coronoid and corocoid processes, from the body of the bone.

WOUND ANALYSIS

When confronted with a skeleton exhibiting blunt trauma wounds, forensic anthropologists must provide a complete description of the injuries and the characteristics of the possible causative instruments to law enforcement officials. When possible this information should include data on the type and extent of the wounds, as well as aspects of the assailant (in cases of bludgeoning). The process of wound analysis can be broken down into eight steps: description of wound(s); estimation of size, shape, direction, energy, number, and sequence; and miscellaneous estimations.

Description of Wound(s)

As with any analysis of trauma, the first characteristics to be noted for blunt injuries are the placement within the skeleton. This is most important because it can help to determine the manner of death. For example, blunt force attacks in homicide generally are to the head, resulting in injuries to that structure or to bones of the upper body (as in parry fracture). However, accident or suicide can produce an injury to any part of the skeleton, as in a fall from a high place (e.g., a person fell accidentally or purposely jumped) or collision with a moving object (e.g., a person stepped accidentally or intentionally in front of an automobile). Thus, a complete description of injury(s) is the first step in this (or any similar) analysis.

The description of a wound should include naming the bone affected, the location of the injury, and the type of fractures. If multiple injuries are present, these characteristics should be described for each. Naming of the bone affected should include the side, if paired (e.g., right ulna). Similarly, the location of the injury within the bone or structure should include the position in relation to the center of the body (i.e., proximal, distal, or middle) and the surface affected (e.g., anterior or posterior, medial or lateral). Finally, a full description of the injury should be undertaken; this should include the amount of displacement (complete or incomplete), number of displacements (simple and comminuted), and the presence and types (radiating or concentric) of fracture lines.

As an example, the injury depicted in Figure 13.11a would be described as an infraction to the right frontal with radiating fracture lines. This is accompanied by a complete fracture of the right nasal area, with concomitant loss of parts of the right maxilla, lacrymal, and nasal bones, as well as loss of the right incisors and the bone overlying their roots.

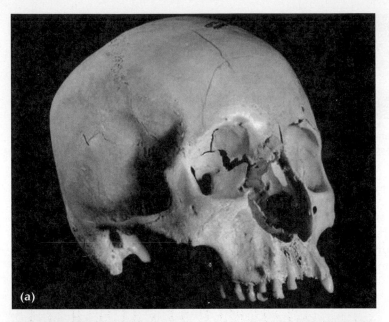

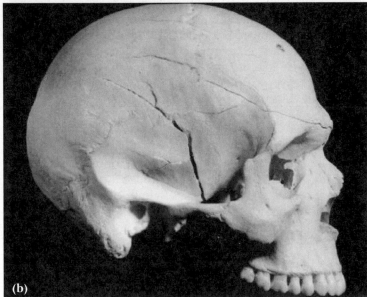

FIGURE 13.11 Fractures to the head: **(a)** right side of the forehead and face and **(b)** blunt trauma to the right side of the skull, indicating that the force was delivered from that direction. (Photos by Julie R. Angel; **(a)** courtesy of the State of New Mexico, Office of the Medical Investigator; **(b)** courtesy of the University of New Mexico–Albuquerque, Maxwell Museum of Anthropology, #69)

Estimation of Size

Estimating the size of an instrument causing blunt trauma varies from the relatively easy to the virtually impossible. This is due to the large variety of objects that can cause this type of trauma. Usually, only in wounds where the extent of the defect is easily determined can the size of the causative instrument be estimated. For example, a round compressed fracture to the cranial vault that has easily visible edges can be measured to

BOX 13.2
Causative Instrument from Wound Shape: Another Example

William Maples and Michael Browning (1994) discuss a case where the shape of a wound was so reminiscent of a hammerhead that it was almost certain that this was the causative instrument, despite the confession of the person who caused the trauma. The case involved a headless and handless body of a female retrieved from the waters of the Santa Fe River in Florida. Apparently, alligators had devoured the missing parts except for the top of the skull, which was retrieved by divers while searching for more remains of the woman. The skullcap had a high forehead, sharp upper borders of the eye orbits, and smooth muscle markings that were consistent with a female. In addition, the amount of suture closure also coincided with the age of the headless, handless body. Therefore, because the skullcap was found in the same river and near the same place as the body, it was considered to be part of the missing woman.

The frontal bone manifested a depressed fracture that was circular in outline. Part of the bone was hinged inward, indicating that the injury occurred around the time of death. A similar wound with similar characteristics was found further back on the cranial vault. With this information, Maples felt confident that the woman had been hit at least twice on the head by a hammer or similarly shaped instrument. Unfortunately, when the accused murderer confessed to the crime, he stated that he had used a hatchet to kill the decedent. Because this was at odds with the osteological findings, Maples was unsure how the wounds could take on the characteristics that he observed. It was only later that he learned that the hatchet was of the type used by carpenters; that is, it had a blade on one side and a hammerhead on the other, which accounted for the shape of the wounds. Maples still puzzled as to why the murderer had not used the blade end when he attacked the woman. It was only through later experience that he learned that the hammerhead is more favored in murder because of the lesser splattering of blood that occurs than when a hatchet blade is used during an attack.

determine the size of the instrument's impacting surface. Similarly, long compressed fractures would indicate that an object of at least the length of the fracture was the causative instrument.

Estimation of Shape

As with size, estimating the shape of an instrument causing blunt trauma varies from the relatively easy to the virtually impossible. When the extent of the wound is determinable, two aspects of shape should be described: cross-sectional outline and axial configuration. Cross-sectional outline refers to the shape of the instrument across its long axis. This outline can vary from circular (e.g., baseball bat) or other rounded shape to angular (e.g., two-by-four wood). If the object is more round in cross section, the resultant wound generally will be more amorphous than with angular instruments.

The configuration of the axis occasionally can be determined from wounds that manifest distinct outlines. Round injuries that lack a long axis indicate that the causative instrument had a circular impacting surface (see Box 13.2). Figure 13.12 illustrates such an injury; notice that the round shape of the depressed fracture almost certainly was caused by a hammer or similar instrument that had a round, flat outline. Similarly, injuries that change direction indicate that the causative instrument had a bent long axis. This bend can vary by any degree from an acute through a right (i.e., 90°) to an obtuse angle. Because of the wide variety of such bends, determining the actual instrument is possible only in rare instances (see Box 13.1). Figure 13.13 illustrates such a wound; as can be seen, the causative instrument would have had an angled impacting surface.

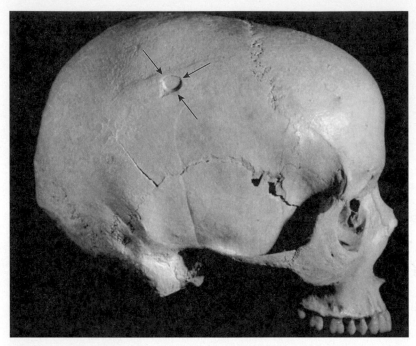

FIGURE 13.12   Circular depressed fracture (*arrow*) to the right parietal bone almost certainly caused by a small hammer. (Photo by Julie R. Angel; specimen courtesy of the State of New Mexico, Office of the Medical Investigator)

Estimation of Direction

Estimating the direction from which the force impacted the bone is another component that should be provided to law enforcement officials. In most cases, the location of the injury in terms of bone and side should be sufficient to describe this characteristic. Figure 13.11b illustrates blunt trauma to the right side of the skull, indicating that the blow was delivered from the right side at an angle perpendicular to the surface of the braincase. Similarly, Figure 13.14 depicts blunt trauma to the left ribs, indicating that the blow impacted the middle of the left side of the thorax.

Estimation of Energy

The amount of energy with which force impacts a body can be determined only within broad limits. This characteristic is composed of two aspects: speed and weight. Generally, low speed results in an infraction, and high speed results in a complete fracture. Similarly, light-weight objects are more likely to result in infractions, and heavy objects usually cause complete fractures. However, these two characteristics interplay in a complex manner. For example, skull fractures in automobile collisions usually result in infractions unless the car is traveling at least 50 miles per hour (Shkrum et al., 1994). Although there is the potential for high energy because of the weight of the object (i.e., around one ton), the low speed of such vehicles (especially by comparison with a bludgeon) translates to an energy that usually is too low to completely fracture bone.

FIGURE 13.13   Oddly shaped injuries to the skull (*arrows*), probably caused by an instrument with an angled cross section. (Photo by Julie R. Angel; specimen courtesy of the State of New Mexico, Office of the Medical Investigator)

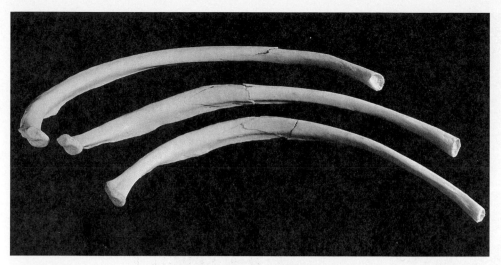

FIGURE 13.14 Fractured left ribs, indicating that a blunt force impacted the middle rib cage on the left side. (Photo by Julie R. Angel; specimens courtesy of the State of New Mexico, Office of the Medical Investigator)

Unfortunately, there are other complications in this interplay between weight and size. First, a low-energy impact to a bone may result in a complete fracture if the causative instrument is narrow in cross section. Similarly, high energy impacting across a broad area may only result in an infraction. Thus, a fall from a high place onto a flat surface such as a paved road or sidewalk may only result in an incomplete, rather than a complete, fracture. Another complicating factor is the thickness of the affected bone. Generally, the thick cranial bones of mature males do not fracture as easily as those of females. This requires forensic anthropologists to look at the bone thicknesses to properly interpret the amount of energy.

Figure 13.15a and 13.16 depict high-energy blunt force traumas to the skull. Figure 13.15a illustrates an amorphous comminuted fracture to the rear of the skull with radiating fracture lines and loss of bone fragments. Figure 13.16 depicts complete,

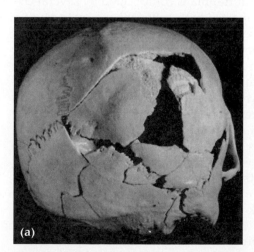

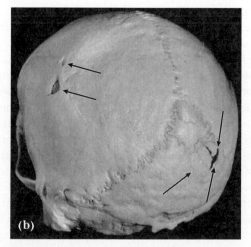

FIGURE 13.15 Blunt trauma to the skull: **(a)** massive blunt trauma to the rear and **(b)** trauma indicating two or three points of impact (*arrows*). (Photos by Julie R. Angel; specimens courtesy of the State of New Mexico, Office of the Medical Investigator)

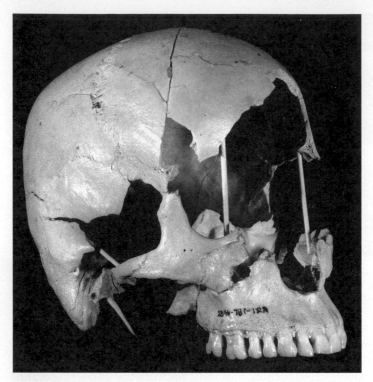

FIGURE 13.16   Massive blunt trauma to the face. (Photo by Julie
R. Angel; specimen courtesy of the State of New Mexico, Office of the
Medical Investigator)

comminuted fracture to the face of an adult male that was delivered with a force great
enough to shatter the upper-facial skeleton.

Estimation of Number

Estimation of the number of blows causing blunt trauma is complicated by several circumstances. First, some forces may not have impacted with sufficient energy to cause a
fracture. Although these would manifest themselves as contusions in soft tissue and occasionally as discoloration on the underlying bone (Berryman and Symes, 1998), breaks
or lines would be absent. Similarly, blows to areas lacking osteological structures (e.g.,
anterior abdomen) also would not leave imprints in the skeleton. A second complication involves multiple blows to the same location. These may be hidden by previous
fractures that merely deform inward with no new bone breaks.

The process of estimating the number of blows to the skull or other structure is
similar to that described for projectile wounds. First, the identifiable points of impact
are determined by noting areas of fracture with surrounding (hoop) or radiating
fracture lines. The resultant figure represents the minimum number of blows that
could have caused the injuries. Figure 13.15b exhibits a skull with three points of impact, indicating that the decedent was struck at least two or three times. Once this
count is obtained, the broken ends within the fractures are examined for signs of repeated impact. Multiple blows to the same point may be evident from the presence of
knapping or flaking along the edges of fractures that are caused by rubbing of the
broken bone fragments during repeat blows (Berryman and Symes, 1998).

Figure 13.17 presents an example of this type of flaking. Although the presence of these features indicates multiple blows, an actual count is not possible with present methods.

In cases where there are rib fractures, some information bearing on the manner of death may be possible. Love and Symes (2004) studied decedents with fractures to their rib cages due to falling, collision with a motor vehicle, or beating by a person. Statistical tests calculated from their results indicated that the number of fractures per rib did not differ by sex, age, and ancestry but did differ for the various causes of these breaks. Not unexpectedly, falling and collision with motor vehicles caused a greater number of fractures per rib (approximately 1.5 for each rib with a facture), whereas beating resulted in fewer breaks per rib (approximately 1 for each rib with a fracture). Also, the maximum number of ribs with fractures due to beating ranged to about half those due to the other causes (i.e., the number of fractured ribs in beating ranged from 3 to 13, while it ranged from 1 to 24 for falling and motor vehicles). Although the small sample size ($n = 43$) of their study makes these results preliminary, it is reasonable to conclude that a decedent with many fractured ribs (i.e., greater than 15) is unlikely to have received these due to beating by another person. Rather, it is more likely that the decedent experienced a high-speed collision with a large object (e.g., the ground after a fall, a traveling motor vehicle).

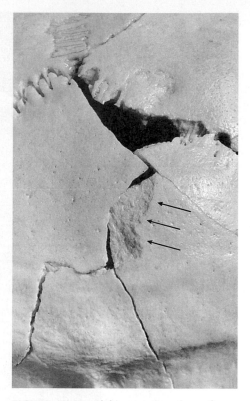

FIGURE 13.17 Flaking on the edges of fractures, indicating rubbing with other broken ends during repeated blows to the same area. (Photo by Julie R. Angel; specimen courtesy of the State of New Mexico, Office of the Medical Investigator)

Estimation of Sequence

Determining the sequence of blows caused by blunt instruments uses the same method as that for projectiles. That is, fracture lines are traced from the impact sites to determine which lines end naturally and which end at another fracture. Since this process has been described, the reader should consult the section "Estimation of Sequence" in Chapter 12 for further details.

Miscellaneous Estimations

Under some circumstances, other information concerning blunt trauma can be gathered from the skeleton. In auto accidents the placement of injuries can determine various aspects of the accident, such as bumper height and stance of victim (see Spitz, 1980, for further details).

Similarly, the placement of wounds resulting from a human attack might indicate characteristics of the assailant. Thus, fractures to the left side of the face may indicate attack by a right-handed person (Maples, 1986). Although opportunities for such determinations are rare, forensic anthropologists must be cognizant of such possibilities whenever performing this type of examination.

Some injuries involving blunt force can be so catastrophic as to prevent any of the preceding analyses. These usually involve collisions with large moving objects that impart massive force to the stationary or moving human body. Figure 13.18 illustrates such an injury. This victim of a homicide was thrown onto railroad tracks after first being stabbed; his body then was rolled by an oncoming train. Over half of the bones exhibited fractures, both simple and comminuted, with radiating fracture lines and crushing of skeletal elements. Considering the state of this body, it was extraordinary

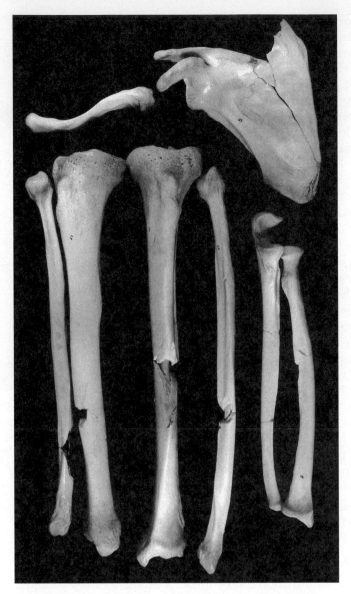

FIGURE 13.18 Bones from person thrown on railroad tracks and rolled by an oncoming train. Many of the ribs also exhibited fractures, as did a number of vertebrae. (Photo by Julie R. Angel; specimen courtesy of the State of New Mexico, Office of the Medical Investigator)

that the forensic anthropologist (Stanley Rhine) was able to identify a sharp force injury to one of the ribs, indicating stabbing prior to deposition of the body on the railroad tracks.

DETERMINING CAUSE AND MANNER OF DEATH

As with projectile wounds, perimortem blunt trauma to the skeleton contains vital clues concerning the cause of death of deceased persons. And, as with projectile wounds, there are many pitfalls awaiting forensic anthropologists who offer opinions on this subject. Although crushed skulls exhibiting extreme fragmentation would appear to offer a straightforward interpretation concerning this issue, determining cause of death is not a simple matter. Postmortem damage to a body that occurs shortly after death can masquerade as perimortem trauma, thereby leading to an erroneous conclusion. This can occur when a person dies of unrelated reasons before the traumatizing event. Also, other causes of death may be concealed by (especially extensive) blunt trauma. The case illustrated in Figure 13.18 is an excellent example of this. Although a cause of death by blunt trauma may seem warranted, the true cause was very different. These circumstances should make the forensic anthropologist wary of offering an opinion on this matter.

On the subject of determining manner of death, the admonitions from Chapter 12 also hold. Although persons rarely commit suicide by hitting themselves on the skull with a bludgeon, landing on the top of the head during a suicidal jump from a high place is not unknown. Similarly, plunging headfirst through a car windshield or against a bulkhead during a train or aircraft accident also can cause massive head trauma. In addition to these large items, small objects found near a body assume great importance when this issue is considered. For example, a skeleton exhibiting blunt injuries to the skull found in the presence of a piece of two-by-four wood stained with blood is more indicative of homicide than suicide or accidental death. Thus, as with projectile trauma, information surrounding the recovery of the body provides vital clues for determining manner of death beyond those offered by the nature of the skeletal traumata. Since forensic anthropologists may not be present during this part of the investigation, their ability to offer an opinion on this subject is severely limited. Similarly, as discussed in Chapter 12, forensic anthropologists usually do not have information concerning the psychological state of victims during their last days. Since this is very important information in an investigation of unexplained death, any forensic specialist who is unaware of these facts is severely hampered in his or her ability to offer an opinion as to manner of death.

Thus, as in Chapter 12, the complexity of the circumstances surrounding skeletons exhibiting blunt traumata militates against forensic anthropologists offering judgments concerning cause and manner of death. The best action they can take is to describe any perimortem skeletal injuries caused by blunt instruments in minute detail so that those responsible for this task will have as much information as possible to help them in their decisions. Again, forensic anthropologists may offer an opinion when it is requested, but they should only do so when they are very experienced and they are knowledgeable of all of the information surrounding the recovery of the body and the decedent's last days.

Summary

1. When analyzing blunt trauma, forensic anthropologists should attempt to determine the size, shape, and weight of the causative instrument.
2. Bludgeons wielded by assailants are not the only causes of blunt trauma; impact with the ground after a fall and collision with objects outside and inside vehicles will produce these types of injuries.
3. Any analysis of blunt force trauma must start with a complete description of the injury, including type (fracture or infraction), bone affected, side, and placement in the bone.
4. Only in rare instances can the shape of a blunt instrument be determined from the shape of an injury.
5. An estimation of the direction of the force usually can be made from the placement of the injuries on the body and within the affected bone.
6. Any estimation of the number of blows causing multiple wounds due to blunt force must be considered a minimum count, because some impacts may not be recorded in the bone.

7. Estimation of the sequence of blunt force injuries follows the method given in Chapter 12.
8. Because the variety of objects and the manner in which they are delivered is so great, forensic anthropologists must use the knowledge gained from experience when analyzing blunt force injuries.

Exercises

1. Considering the effect of blunt trauma on bones of the skull vault, what is the most likely source of hoop fractures surrounding the injury: the inbending at the point of impact or the outbending that occurs some distance away?
2. Describe the injury depicted in Figure 13.10. Be sure to note the name of the bone affected, the side from which it comes, the placement of the wound, and any other characteristics that you can see.
3. Describe the injuries depicted in Figure 13.11a. Note as many characteristics as can be seen in the photo.
4. Suppose that a blunt force wound is found on the occipital of a 20-year-old White female. The long axis of the injury is perpendicular to the sagittal plane, and fracture lines radiate outward in all directions. A baseball bat was found in the vicinity of the body. Describe how this weapon could have been used to produce the injury seen on the occipital.

5. A 1-inch-diameter galvanized water pipe and a wooden baseball bat are found next to a body with multiple blunt force injuries to the forehead of the skull. Considering the data presented in Table 13.1, which of these objects could have most easily caused these injuries and why?
6. Analyze the injury depicted in Figure 13.16. What type(s) of LeFort fracture is seen in the facial skeleton? Support your answer.
7. Analyze the injuries seen in the mandible depicted in Figure 13.8. From what direction(s) did the force impact the bone? Was the impacting object most likely heavy or light? What type of break(s) (i.e., fracture or infraction) can be seen?
8. Describe the rib fractures depicted in Figure 13.14. What types of fractures are present? What can be said about the number of blows that caused them? Was the causative instrument light or heavy? Did it have a wide or narrow cross section?

14

Sharp and Miscellaneous Trauma

Along with projectile and blunt traumata, two other types of bone injuries can be encountered by forensic anthropologists in their analysis of skeletal remains. The first involves wounds due to sharp instruments. Although these injuries can be more subtle than those previously described, they represent a separate class of trauma that deserves specific discussion. A second type of injury is fracture to the hyoid bone. The most common cause of breaks in this small bone of the throat is static pressure during strangulation. In addition to these two, trauma due to chemical agents can be encountered during forensic analysis. Although not caused by a physical force, these agents can be detected in human bone and other tissues. Because these topics have not been previously covered, the purpose of this chapter is to review the manifestations of sharp trauma to the skeleton, as well as evidence of strangulation and chemical injury.

SHARP TRAUMA

Sharp trauma is the result of narrowly focused, dynamic compression forces applied to the surface of a bone. The result of such force is a discontinuity, such as a puncture, incision, or cleft. Additional discontinuities include fracture lines, hinge fractures, and chips of bone (called **wastage**). Any number of instruments can cause these types of injuries (Figure 14.1), including ice picks, knives, machetes, hatchets, and axes. (Because persons usually are not "sawed to death," the effects of saws will be discussed in Chapter 16.)

This section deals with sharp trauma to the skeleton. First, the effects of sharp instruments on bone will be discussed, with an emphasis on the characteristics of the wounds resulting from these types of implements. Next, the expression of these characteristics in each of the three types of wounds (i.e., punctures, incisions, and clefts) will be described. Finally, a section will be presented on using features of wounds to identify causative instruments and to provide other information concerning sharp trauma events.

Effects of Sharp Instruments

When enough compressive force is applied by a sharp instrument to bone, a number of events occur. The primary result is the formation of a wound at the point of impact. These are discontinuities in the skeleton that take different forms, depending on the direction, focus, and energy of the causative force. If the direction is vertical (or nearly vertical) to the bone surface and its focus is cone shaped (Morse et al., 1983), a **puncture** results. Such injuries are typical of stabbing by an ice pick or other instrument that ends in a point. **Incisions**, defects that are longer than they are wide, result from forces applied across the surface of bone with an implement having a long, sharp edge. These cut marks can be

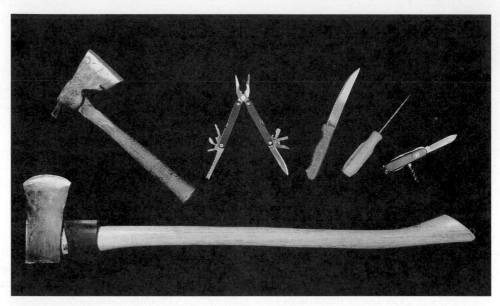

FIGURE 14.1 Common instruments causing sharp trauma to bone (starting at bottom and proceeding counter-clockwise): axe, hatchet, multi-purpose tool, kitchen knife, ice pick, and pocketknife. (Photos by Julie R. Angel)

caused by slashing actions or stabbings that graze cortical surfaces. Finally, vertically applied dynamic force, with an instrument having a long, sharp edge, results in the formation of a **cleft** or **notch**. These types of injuries usually are caused by hacking actions with such implements as axes, meat cleavers, and machetes.

In addition to these basic injuries, other events occur when enough sharp force is applied to bone. One of these is fracture lines. Although hoop fractures are unlikely, lines have been observed radiating from punctures and clefts. These lines are governed by the same rules that apply to those resulting from projectile and blunt trauma; that is, they spread outward from the point of impact, and they usually stop at previously existing lines (including other fractures as well as sutures).

In addition to lines, hinge fractures can result from sharp traumas. Because the bone is fresh, a fragment of bone may bend away from the primary injury in the same manner as in blunt trauma. These hinged segments can be large when accompanying a cleft caused by a heavy chopping instrument (e.g., axe) or small when resulting from a puncture caused by a pointed implement (e.g., knife).

In addition to hinge fractures, another effect of sharp force on fresh bone is compression followed by expansion of hard tissue around the point of impact. This is because living bone is somewhat plastic. The outcome is that bone first bends away from the force and then snaps back close to its original position (Maples, 1986). Because of this, the resultant wound can be smaller than the instrument causing it.

Another effect of sharp trauma is the occurrence of **striations** on the walls of the primary injury. These lines, etched into the bone by the passage of the causative implement, run parallel to the direction of the applied force. These are small when the instrument is finely honed, but large with dull or serrated blades (Reichs, 1998b).

A final effect is **wastage**; this refers to fragments separated from the main section of the bone (Reichs, 1998b). Although they can occur with all types of sharp force injuries, they are most commonly found associated with clefts from heavy chopping instruments.

Considering this information, there are eight characteristics of sharp trauma that can help to determine attributes of the causative instrument: cross-sectional shape,

TABLE 14.1   Characteristics of the Different Wounds Resulting from Sharp Trauma[1]

Characteristic	Punctures	Incisions	Clefts
Cross section	V-shaped	V-shaped	V-shaped
Width	Narrow/wide	Narrow/wide	Wide
Depth	Shallow/medium	Shallow/deep	Medium/deep
Length	Same as width	Short/long	Short/long
Striations	Vertical	Horizontal	Vertical
Fracture lines	May be present	Usually absent	May be present
Hinge fracture	May be present	Usually absent	May be present
Wastage	Minimal	Minimal	Significant

[1]Taken partly from K. J. Reichs: *Forensic Osteology,* 2/e; 1998b; p. 359. Courtesy of Charles C. Thomas Publisher, Ltd., Springfield, IL.

width, depth, length, striations, fracture lines, hinge fractures, and wastage. The first five are all characteristics of the primary injury; the remaining three occur in the area immediately surrounding it. Also, most of these are visible through anthroposcopic examination; however, magnification is useful for identifying some of their finer details (especially striations). Table 14.1 presents the manifestations of these eight characteristics as they apply to each of the three wound types, which are discussed in detail next.

PUNCTURES   Puncture wounds are created by forces delivered by a pointed instrument (e.g., ice pick, knife) directed vertically (or nearly vertically) to a bone surface. The form of the wound is an indentation at the point of contact, usually accompanied by small sections of bone breaking inward (Figure 14.2a). In cross section, these injuries generally are shaped like a cone; they range from circular to somewhat oblong pits with pointed floors. The depth of the wound depends on the energy of the causative force and the nature of the instrument. Light force will produce barely discernible punctures; heavy forces may penetrate the cortical bone and into the medullary cavity and, in some cases, out the side opposite the point of contact. Striations in wounds from vertically applied forces are usually only visible with magnification, where they will appear perpendicular to the surface of the bone. With heavy force, both fracture lines and large hinge fractures may occur; however, wastage is rare.

INCISIONS   Although incisions can result from a forceful stabbing action (Figure 14.2b), these types of injuries usually are caused by sharp forces drawn across the cortical surface of bone. Cuts can be so thin in cross section that they appear only as lines (Figure 14.3a), or they can be strongly V-shaped, similar to clefts (Figure 14.3b). The length, width, and depth of these wounds depend on many factors, including the size of the causative implement, the amount of energy delivering it (Morse et al., 1983), and the dimensions of the bone impacted. Generally, long instruments that contact bone over a large area will cause long incisions, whereas short instruments contacting a small section of bone will cause short incisions. Similarly, the width of incisions depends on the thickness of the causative instrument; however, measurements of this dimension are largely uninstructive because of the reexpansion of bone after withdrawal of the incising implement (Maples, 1986) and wiggling of the object during cutting. Finally, the depth of the incision depends on the energy by which the force was delivered and the strength of the impacted bone. Logically, instruments delivered forcefully will cause deep incisions.

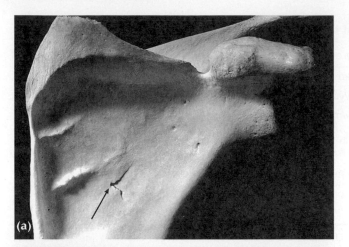

FIGURE 14.2 Results of stabbing action: **(a)** puncture wound to scapula (*arrow*); the instrument entered through the chest and impacted the shoulder blade, causing a puncture accompanied by a hinge fracture; **(b)** stab wound to the manubrium (upper part of the breastbone) causing an incision (*arrows*). (Photos by Julie R. Angel; specimens courtesy of the State of New Mexico, Office of the Medical Investigator)

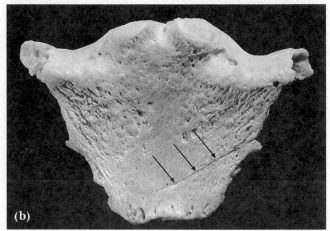

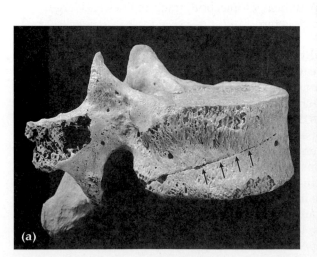

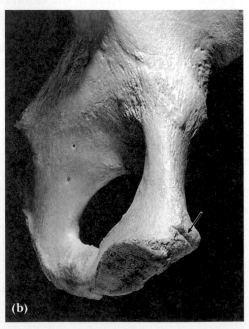

FIGURE 14.3 Variations on incisions: **(a)** thin line of an incision (*arrows*) on the body of a thoracic vertebrae; **(b)** V-shaped incision (*arrow*) on the superior surface of the pubis. (Photos by Julie R. Angel; specimens courtesy of the State of New Mexico, Office of the Medical Investigator)

Fracture lines are rare with these types of wounds because the main energy of the force is directed across, rather than down onto, the bone's surface. Similarly, wastage only results when the instrument is of such width and the incision of such depth that the bone is stressed beyond its limit (Figure 14.4a). However, hinge fractures, in the form of peeled away bone (Figure 14.4b), have been known to occur. Finally, striations generally appear parallel to the long axis of the cut.

CLEFTS   Clefts or notches are caused by vertical (or near vertical) forces applied by heavy instruments with long, sharp edges. The resultant wound usually is a V-shaped notch, which can penetrate the interior of the bone or structure (Figure 14.5). Because of the power required to cause these types of wounds and the heaviness of the instruments producing them, clefts can be accompanied by extensive fracture lines radiating from any part of the primary injury. In addition, hinged segments may be formed and, if enough force is applied, sections may break off from the impacted bone, resulting in wastage. Cleft wounds can be short, as in a notch at right angles to the long axis of a bone, or long, as in a cleft halfway through the cranial vault. Their depth depends on the force applied and, because the force generally is downward, striations will appear vertical to the surface of the bone.

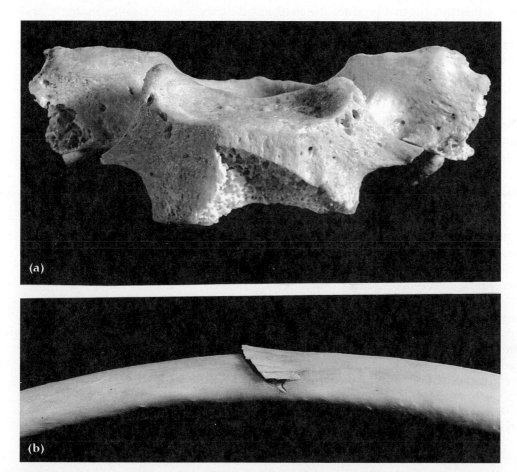

(a)

(b)

FIGURE 14.4   Various forms of wastage: **(a)** loss of bone caused by a deep incision to the body of a thoracic vertebra; **(b)** hinge fracture from an incision with peeling of part of the bone. (Photos by Julie R. Angel; specimens courtesy of the State of New Mexico, Office of the Medical Investigator)

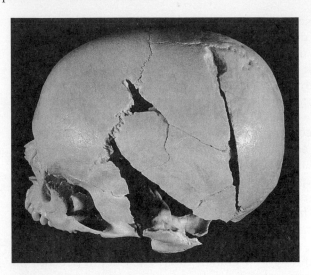

FIGURE 14.5 Multiple clefts (notches) caused by a chopping instrument. (Photo by Julie R. Angel; specimen courtesy of the State of New Mexico, Office of the Medical Investigator)

In a pair of papers on what the authors termed "hacking trauma" (Humphrey and Hutchinson, 2001; Tucker et al., 2001), a group of researchers studied the effects of three types of instruments that produce the clefts just described: meat cleaver, machete, and ax. The researchers discovered that, due to differences in weight and blade configuration of these implements, the resultant wounds showed characteristics distinct enough that the causative instrument could be identified. Using the limbs of pigs (chosen for their similarity in thickness to human bone), the authors were able to document aspects of the wounds caused by these hacking instruments at the entry and exit sites (if any). These included clean cuts, chattering (small chips of bone broken off during the traumatic event), crushing (bones pushed into the entry site), fractures (medium to large fragments broken off during the event), and striations. The results of their observations are summarized in Table 14.2.

Macroscopic and microscopic features of wounds resulting from the three instruments are fairly distinct. A well-trained forensic anthropologist may be able to determine the type of weapon that caused a cleft in a bone by analyzing the wound's characteristics. Thus, wounds with clearly recognizable, clean, and narrow entry sites exhibiting no fractures, no exit site, and fine, parallel-sided striations would indicate a cleaver as the causative implement. Conversely, wounds with no clearly visible entry sites, which may be clean or exhibit chattering, medium wide, with fractures emanating from the kerf floor, and clearly recognizable exit sites are more likely to be caused by machetes.

The above findings are largely confirmed, and expanded, by Kalan Lynn and Scott Fairgrieve (2009). However, in their study of the effects of axes and hatchets on pig (*Sus scrofa*) limb bones, they observed that chattering occurred less often than reported by Humphrey and Hutchinson. In addition, they found that the angle with which one of these instruments impacted the bone could be determined by the side where flakes were detached; bone would flake off on the side where the blade formed an acute angle with the bone. They also found that the length of the wounds depended on the blade width and force used, such that this characteristic did not provide information on the type of weapon.

Alexandra Croft and Roxanna Ferllini (2007) discovered somewhat different results of sharp trauma on ribs. Using flat-tipped and cross-tipped (i.e., Phillips head) screwdrivers, they had volunteers stab pig torsos and analyzed the resulting trauma. They discovered a high degree of complete and incomplete fractures to the ribs, as well as the production of wastage and bony protrusions (wastage still connected to bone).

TABLE 14.2   Summary of Macroscopic and Microscopic Characteristics of Hacking Trauma[1]

Characteristic	Cleaver	Machete	Ax
Entry site recognition	Clearly recognizable	Less clearly recognizable	Sometimes clearly recognizable
Entry site appearance	Clean	Clean, chattering	Clean, chattering, crushing, fracture
Width of entry site	Narrow (approx. 1.5 mm)	Medium (approx. 3.5 mm)	Medium to large (approx. 4 mm to 5 mm)
Entry site fracture lines	Never	Emanate from kerf floor	At entry site; bone pushed into entry site
Depth of penetration	Never through entire bone	Rarely through entire bone	Rarely through entire bone
Exit site	None	Clearly recognizable	Clearly recognizable
Exit site fractures	None	Small to medium fragments	Large triangular bones
Striation	Fine, well-defined edges, parallel sided	Coarse, thick, rounded edges	None

[1]Taken from Humphrey and Hutchinson (2001) and Tucker et al. (2001). Copyright ASTM International. Reprinted with permission.

They also discovered that the cross- and flat pattern of the screwdriver head sometimes was discerned on the surfaces of the ribs.

One last study dealing with sharp trauma concerns the differences between the microscopic characteristics of wounds caused by a hatchet and a knife (Alunni-Perret et al., 2005). The hatchet was used to hack at a bone while the knife was used both in a hacking and a stabbing manner. The authors showed that the macroscopic characteristics of the clefts and the punctures were, for the most part, indistinguishable. However, they showed that the three types of wounds had different features when viewed using scanning electron microscopy (SEM). They demonstrated that the hacking wounds caused by a knife had straight edges, with one side exhibiting flaking and raising, whereas the edges were uneven with pushing back (compression of bone away from the wound) on both sides of the clefts caused by the hatchet. The puncture wounds caused by the knife differed from the other two by exhibiting a triangular-shaped wound outline when viewed from above. Studies such as these last three are making the analysis of bone trauma more detailed, thereby aiding law enforcement personnel in their tasks of apprehending perpetrators of crime.

Despite the promise of the above findings, forensic anthropologists must be wary of going beyond what is supported by the data. Eric Bartelink and colleagues (2001) analyzed the striations produced by a scalpel, paring knife, and kitchen knife using SEM. They discovered that the same instrument produced different arrangements of striations during different cutting episodes. Even more disturbing, these differences overlapped between weapons (i.e., striations from the paring knife and scalpel were similar). Their results indicate that weapon identification can only be determined in general (e.g., knife versus axe) rather than specific terms (e.g., this particular knife produced this wound).

Wound Analysis

As with projectile and blunt trauma, the needs of law enforcement officials must be kept in mind when analyzing wounds resulting from sharp instruments. Again, forensic anthropologists are enjoined to provide as much information as possible on the causative implement and its method of delivery, without exceeding that allowed by the data. Therefore, the result of any analysis of sharp traumatic injuries is a description of the wound, determination of the characteristics of the sharp implement, the direction from which it contacted the bone, the number of injuries, and sequence of injuries (if multiple).

DESCRIPTION OF WOUND(S)   As discussed in Chapters 12 and 13, a description of the wound(s) is the first task in any trauma analysis. This should start by noting the type (i.e., puncture, incision, cleft) of wound(s) and any associated fracture lines and segments of peeled bone. In addition, the location of the injury(s) should be described in terms of the bone(s) affected and the side(s) and the location within the bone. Also, the size in terms of length, width, and depth should be noted. Finally, any other characteristics of interest should be noted. Statements such as "There is an incision on the left side of the sternum between the attachments for the third and fourth rib that penetrates 5 millimeters toward the midline" may be all that is necessary to depict a sharp force injury. However, more involved descriptions may be necessary with larger and more complex wounds.

INSTRUMENT CHARACTERISTICS   When analyzing sharp force trauma wounds, two main aspects of causative instruments may be determinable: type and size. There are three basic types of implements, which are defined by their method of delivery: stabbing, cutting, or chopping. Size refers to blade characteristics, such as length, width, surface contour (serrated or smooth), and sharpness. These two aspects can be determined in general terms from the resultant wound.

   The main clue for determining the type of instrument is to identify the primary injury visible on the bone. Using the information given previously, punctures are easily distinguished from the other two types of sharp trauma by the presence of a point of focus (rather than a line) that is recognizable as an inward bending of bone with (occasional) radiating fractures. Any number of implements can cause these injuries, including ice picks, awls, and even knives. By contrast, because incisions are lines or V-shaped depressions on bone, the presence of these types of wounds indicates that an instrument with a long, thin cutting edge (i.e., not merely a pointed implement) came in contact with the bone. In these cases, ice picks and awls can be excluded in favor of knives and other comparable implements. Finally, clefts, especially when accompanied by bone fragments chipped from the cortical surface, are indicative of a chopping instrument, such as an ax, hatchet, meat cleaver, or machete.

   In addition to indicating a stabbing instrument, the size and placement of punctures might indicate characteristics of the causative instrument. Deep but small wounds may be indicative of an ice pick or awl, whereas larger wounds would suggest a bigger implement, such as a hunting knife. Also, punctures on inaccessible parts of the skeleton may indicate length characteristics. For example, a puncture on the scapula (Figure 14.6a), delivered anteriorly, would indicate that the instrument was long enough to pass through part of the chest to impact this bone. In cases such as these, reassembly of the affected skeletal elements can allow for a determination of the minimal length of the causative implement (see Walsh-Haney, 1999, for an example).

   The size of instruments causing incisions may also be evident from characteristics of the wound. Unfortunately, because of the plastic characteristics of living bone, the

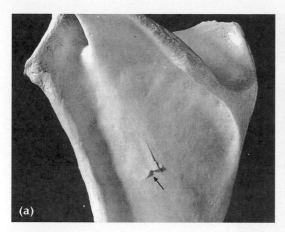
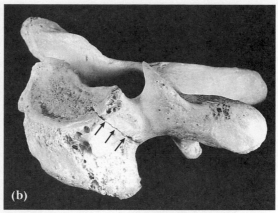

FIGURE 14.6   Using placement to determine length of weapon. **(a)** Posterior side of the wound depicted in Figure 14.2a; because the instrument entered through the chest and punctured the scapula (*arrow*), its length must have been close to 6 inches. **(b)** Incision (*arrows*) on an upper thoracic vertebrae; because the cut indicated that the instrument passed through part of the neck and thorax to impact this bone, it is reasonable to conclude that a long implement was used to cause this injury. (Photos by Julie R. Angel; specimen courtesy of the State of New Mexico, Office of the Medical Investigator)

width of the causative implement usually cannot be determined from the width of the incision. However, as with punctures, blade length might be determined from the placement of the wound. Although incisions found on only one outer part of the skeleton are of little value in this regard (Figure 14.7), cuts on both front and back parts of the same or adjoining structures (such as ribs) would indicate that the causative instrument could not have been short. Similarly, an incision to an inaccessible part of the skeleton (Figure 14.6b) also would help determine blade length. Finally, the presence of striations indicates that the blade had a serrated (toothed) edge.

Generally, size characteristics of the instruments causing clefts are least likely to be determined from this type of trauma. Unless a wound has distinct ends (showing that it stopped at the ends of the impacting blade), the length of the chopping instrument cannot be estimated. However, occasionally the width of the wound can indicate the width of the instrument; thin clefts generally are caused by thin-bladed chopping tools (e.g., meat cleavers, machetes), whereas wide notches indicate thicker-edged tools, such as axes and hatchets.

DIRECTION OF FORCE   The direction from which the force was applied to bone(s) may be determined from characteristics of the resultant wounds. Injuries to the front of the skeleton without associated wounds toward the back would indicate a frontal delivery. Concomitantly, wounds to the back but not the front would indicate rear delivery. Unfortunately, the direction of penetration may not be determined when pairs of wounds are found on opposite sides of the skeleton. In these cases, the only guiding principle is that the entry wound of sharp trauma usually is larger than the exit wound (the reverse of that seen in projectile trauma). Therefore, a large wound to the anterior skeleton with a paired smaller wound to the posterior side would indicate frontal entry. However, this is complicated by the fact that such injuries could be due to two different wounding episodes.

From this information, the placement of an attacker may be determined in rare instances. For example, if all punctures and incisions are to the back of the skeleton, it is not unreasonable to postulate that the decedent was assaulted from behind. Similar

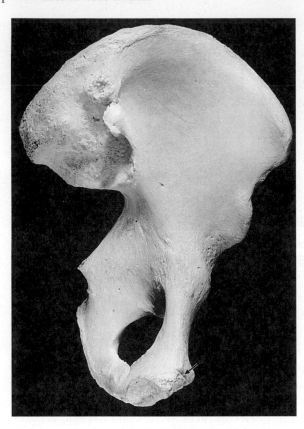

FIGURE 14.7 Incision on the pubic bone (*arrow*). Because the sacrum was not affected, the length of the causative instrument cannot be determined from this wound. (Photo by Julie R. Angel; specimen courtesy of the State of New Mexico, Office of the Medical Investigator)

statements can be made if there is clear evidence of sharp trauma only to the front or side. However, these types of assessments are tricky, because victims usually move to avoid blows. Thus, what may start as an attack from the front that leaves no marks in bone may end in an attack from the rear as the victim tries to flee the assailant or is knocked to the ground and assaulted while lying face down.

NUMBER OF TRAUMATIC EVENTS   The number of traumatic events (if multiple) can be estimated by counting the number of separate primary injuries. The first step in assessing this is to count the points of impact. With punctures and incisions, usually this is fairly straightforward. However, with clefts, the number of distinct surfaces within a notch may only indicate the minimal number of blows causing the wounds. This is because with each impact the signs of a previous blow may be obliterated as bone is chipped from the notch surface.

Although the number of points of impact can be enumerated, the count may either overestimate or underestimate the number of wounds sustained by the decedent (see Box 14.1 for an example). Overestimation can result because a single traumatic event may cause two or more wounds on bones (see Figure 14.8a). Similarly, injuries caused by the decedent falling on a sharp object may masquerade as a separate blow. The best protection against this type of error is to recreate the action that caused the injuries (see Figure 14.8b). Underestimation can result because sharp forces may also have occurred to soft tissue without leaving marks on bone. These could be to the abdomen or fleshy parts of the arms, legs, and neck. Therefore, the total number of blows would be more than the number of traumatic events recorded on the skeleton.

BOX 14.1
The Perils of Discerning Number of Blows from Number of Injuries

Norman Sauer (1984) presents an example of sharp trauma, accompanied by an injury caused by a blunt instrument, that reveals the perils of equating the number of injuries to the number of traumatic events and the importance of recreating these events. The case involved a young adult male whose skeleton was recovered from a wooded area in 1979. The skull exhibited a crushing wound to the tip of the mastoid process that appeared to be caused by a blow delivered to the side of the head. In addition, there was a peeled back section of bone on the inferior border of the second rib, apparently due to sharp trauma. Finally, there was a flattened section of bone opposite the one just described on the superior surface of the third rib.

A simple count of injuries resulted in a minimum number of three impacts causing these wounds. However, reenactment of the wounds to the ribs revealed that they probably were both caused by the same event, in this case, a knife with one sharpened edge and one flattened edge. The instrument entered with the sharpened edge up, where it peeled away part of the second rib. At the same time, the other edge caused the opposite third rib to compress, forming a flattened area. This realization dropped the number of traumatic events to two.

Further information revealed that the original count was correct, albeit for reasons that could not have been known to Sauer. One of the perpetrators of the crime confessed to taking the victim to the wooded area, where he was struck on the side of the head by a tree branch. After he had fallen, he then was stabbed twice, once in the chest and another time in the throat. Thus, the actual number of events was three, with one not leaving a bone signature.

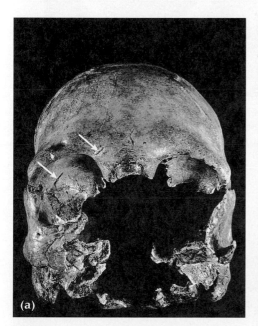
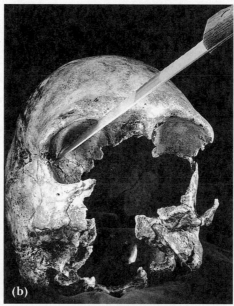

FIGURE 14.8 Determining number of traumatic events: **(a)** multiple injuries (*arrows*); **(b)** recreation of the event to confirm the hypothesis that the injuries to the upper eye orbit were caused by a single stabbing action. (Photos by Julie R. Angel; specimen courtesy of the State of New Mexico, Office of the Medical Investigator)

SEQUENCE OF EVENTS   The sequence of sharp force wounds probably cannot be determined, because these types of injuries generally do not manifest lengthy fracture lines. However, in the case of extensive fracturing, the method outlined in Chapter 12 can be used to determine this characteristic.

STRANGULATION

In a fine summary article, Douglas Ubelaker (1992) discusses the osteological effects of death by strangulation. In this work, Ubelaker notes that this type of death takes three forms: hanging, ligature, and manual. Death by **hanging** refers to strangulation that occurs when the body is suspended by its neck using flexible cordage. As is well known, this has been a form of execution in a number of countries, and it is a common form of suicide (Ubelaker, 1992). By contrast, **ligature** occurs when cordage of some kind is placed around the neck, tightened, and held in place by a force. Although accidental deaths by ligature occur, this form of strangulation is more common in murder. Finally, **manual strangulation** occurs when the throat is squeezed by human hands until death occurs. Because this position must be held for approximately 4 minutes, homicide is indicated in this type of death.

As pointed out by many researchers (Stewart, 1979; Angel and Caldwell, 1984; Ubelaker, 1992), the hyoid (see Figure 14.9) is the main bone to manifest the osteological consequences of strangulation (see Box 14.2 for an exception). As described in Chapter 2,

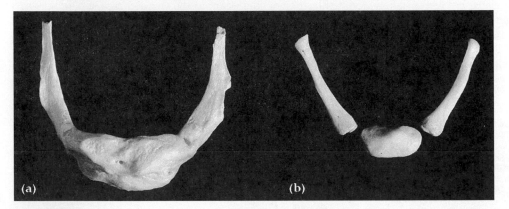

FIGURE 14.9 Two hyoid bones: **(a)** mature and **(b)** immature. Note the three segments of the immature bone: body and right and left cornua (the lesser cornuae are not easily discernible on these specimens). (Photo by Julie R. Angel; mature specimen courtesy of the University of New Mexico–Albuquerque, Maxwell Museum of Anthropology, #53)

BOX 14.2
Death by Strangulation

Lawrence Angel and Peggy Caldwell (1984) present an interesting example of death by a special kind of ligature called the "Spanish Windlass" that resulted in the fracturing of a bone other than the hyoid. The case involved a young adult female whose remains were discovered near the eighteenth hole of a golf course. Although a perimortem fracture was found to the mandible, the most interesting trauma was located on a vertebra.

The sixth cervical vertebra displayed perimortem fractures to the laminae (the bone connecting the body to the neural arch) of the left side. Both the anterior and posterior sections displayed breaks, indicating that a strong force compressed the side of the neural arch. Because this force would also have to compress soft tissues of the neck, which would have resulted in death, it was reasonable to assume that the young woman died from strangulation. The body was found with a ligature around the neck composed of wire with a wooden handle. When the handle was twisted, the wire would have tightened in such a manner as to cause the fractures seen in the vertebra. This is one of the few examples where forensic anthropologists were able to state that ligature was the probable cause of death in the absence of fracturing of the hyoid bone.

TABLE 14.3   Fusion of Hyoid Segments[1]

Age	Percent Fused
<20	7.1
20–29	35.9
30–39	68.5
40–49	67.02[2]
50–59	65.62[2]
60–69	81.7
70+	73.22

[1]From O'Halloran and Lundy (1987); combined unilateral and bilateral fusions and averages of both sexes.
[2]Lower percentages in these groups are due to sampling error.

this is a free-floating bone that envelops the larynx (windpipe) just superior to the thyroid cartilage. It is composed of a central part, called the body, right and left lesser horns (cornuae), and right and left greater horns (Ubelaker, 1992). The lesser horn is a small projection on the superior end of either side of the body; the greater horns are long projections on the posterior side of the body. The central part of this bone ossifies before birth, and the horns appear in the first year. All components are joined according to the schedule in Table 14.3. In life, the greater horns are attached to the styloid processes of the temporal bones via the stylohyoid ligaments; this bone can be felt in the neck by (gently) squeezing the larynx below the lower margin of the mandible.

In deaths by strangulation, fracture of this bone in the young is unlikely because the horns have not yet fused with the body (Ubelaker, 1992); thus, pressure on the throat would cause the horns merely to fold inward. However, Michael Pollanen and David Chiasson (1996) noted that, with age, the probability of fracture increases, because the percentage of persons with fused hyoids also increases (see Table 14.3). Other work by Pollanen (Pollanen et al., 1995) revealed that when fractures occur they are generally unilateral (i.e., occur only on one side), with bilateral breaks being rare. Also, fractures are most common in the middle and rear of the greater horns, but rare in the area where these structures join the body.

Research on the hyoid in cases of strangulation reveals that this bone stands up well to neck pressure. This is particularly apparent from the percentages of fracture, given by Ubelaker (1992), related to this form of death. For example, Ubelaker notes that only 8% of hangings result in a fracture of the hyoid. (A study by Sharma et al., 2005, had a 7% rate.) Given this, there is a low expectation of breakage in suicide (as well as in accident and homicide) by this method. Similarly, he notes that ligature results in only 11% of hyoids breaking; this probably is due to the fact that most of these deaths result from some sort of cord held around the neck at levels below this bone. Finally, Ubelaker states that only in manual strangulation is there a substantial percentage (34%) of hyoid fracture. This information indicates that the lack of hyoid fracture does not rule out death by strangulation. However, the presence of a broken hyoid is a strong indicator that strangulation figured into the circumstances surrounding the death of the decedent.

Several problems can lead to a misdiagnosis of hyoid fracture and, consequently, death by strangulation. First, rough postmortem treatment can break the bone due to its small size (Ubelaker, 1992). Both poor excavation methods and rough treatment during removal of remaining soft tissue can cause this breakage. The second problem is incomplete ossification (Ubelaker 1992); because the greater horns never fuse to the hyoid bodies in a substantial proportion of people, their separation may appear to be due to a fracture. However, the smooth end of the body and horns would indicate incomplete ossification, whereas fracture would be indicated by jagged ends of both structures.

CHEMICAL TRAUMA

Many causes of death do not leave signatures in bone. For example, numerous diseases are evident only in soft tissue. Similarly, some deaths by violence (e.g., drowning) also are not recorded in the skeleton. However, there is one violent death that has not been discussed that leaves a bone signature in some cases. This is death by slow poisoning (e.g., over a period of days and weeks). When the victim lives for several days after ingestion of a toxic substance, the poison is deposited in body tissues such as hair, fingernails, toenails, and occasionally bone (Maples and Browning, 1994). These substances, particularly heavy metals (e.g., arsenic, lead, and uranium), can be detected postmortem through laboratory testing. Although some amounts of these elements occur normally in humans, excess quantities of these substances detected in remaining tissue are strong evidence of poisoning contributing to the cause of death.

DETERMINING CAUSE AND MANNER OF DEATH

In a manner similar to that discussed in Chapters 12 and 13, sharp traumatic injuries to the skeleton hold vital clues as to cause and manner of death. And again, forensic anthropologists must take care not to offer an opinion on these matters unless specifically asked, and then only when they are knowledgeable of all of the facts of an unexplained death. The location and severity of wounds caused by a sharp instrument are not enough to establish cause of death, due to the large number of people who survive these types of injuries, even injuries to vital spots. Similarly, there are many wounds that can cause death by exsanguination which do not leave evidence on the bone.

Assessments of manner of death in cases of sharp trauma are similarly complex. Although most people associate this type of trauma with murder (or accident) rather than suicide, it is surprising how many people take their own lives by stabbing themselves to death. Thus, the presence of sharp trauma does not in itself establish manner of death as murder or accident. Also, as pointed out in Chapter 12, the number of traumatic events may help establish manner of death, but this information by itself is not unequivocal. Again, objects at the recovery scene and the state of mind of victims in their last days all play a part in determining this matter.

Summary

1. Sharp trauma is the result of narrowly focused, dynamic compression forces applied to the surface of a bone.
2. Forces from sharp instruments result in three distinct injuries: punctures, incisions, and clefts.
3. Punctures, caused by pointed instruments such as ice picks and knives, can be distinguished as pointed indentations that penetrate the surface of cortical bone.
4. Incisions, caused by knives and other sharp instruments with long cutting surfaces, are visible as cuts across the surface of the cortex.
5. Clefts appear as V-shaped depressions in bone that usually are accompanied by wastage

(i.e., chips of removed bone); these types of wounds generally are caused by chopping instruments.
6. Death by strangulation can occur due to hanging, ligature, and manual strangulation.

7. Fracturing of the hyoid bone is the main osteological consequence of death by strangulation.
8. Death by poisoning that occurs over several days or weeks can be determined by examining hair, nails (both finger and toe), and bone for toxic substances.

Exercises

1. A perimortem puncture wound is found to the posterior of the sternal body. What can be estimated about the type and size of the instrument that caused this wound?
2. If an incision is found on the inner face of the ilium, what can be determined about the type and size of the causative implement and the direction from which it entered the body?
3. What can be said about the instrument that caused the hinge fracture and peeling seen in the rib pictured in Figure 14.4b?
4. What is the minimum number of blows from a chopping instrument necessary to cause the defects depicted in Figure 14.5?

5. From the photo in Figure 14.5, which blow was probably delivered first, the one causing the long and thin cleft toward the rear of the skull or the one that resulted in the large triangular defect toward the front of the skull?
6. A bilateral fracture of the hyoid bone is found associated with skeletonized remains. In the absence of other information, what can the forensic anthropologist tell law enforcement about the possible cause of death?
7. A skeleton is found with a ligature surrounding the neck. There are no visible fractures either to the cervical vertebrae or to the hyoid bone. Lacking any osteological evidence of strangulation, what inferences can be made about a possible cause of death of this individual?

15

Antemortem Skeletal Conditions

As described in many texts on human anatomy, the normal adult human skeleton is composed of 206 bones, which have macroscopically similar shape and structure in all individuals. However, upon closer examination, almost all skeletons exhibit some deviation from the norms developed from the study of anatomy. One such form occurs when bones fail to ossify where and when they should, leaving an opening in an unexpected area. Another is the **accessory ossicle** (small extra bone), formed when a single bone is divided into two or more segments. Similarly, sometimes bone parts do not join at the time expected for fusion during growth. Finally, a number of pathological conditions and other anomalies can appear in any part of the skeleton, which represent deviations from the norm.

These conditions are caused by the interplay between genetics and the environment within the setting of the incredible complexity of the human body. The unpredictability of this interplay has several repercussions for forensic anthropologists. First, deviations from the norm can be mistaken for perimortem trauma by the inexperienced. Because the nonfusion of bone segments and accessory ossicles could be misdiagnosed as fractures, forensic anthropologists must possess a broad breadth of knowledge of the variety that these deviations can take. Similarly, nontraumatic pathological conditions can expose the internal components of bone, which also could be misinterpreted as trauma.

Second, these deviations could be mistaken for postmortem damage. Bone that has been eroded by disease might be confused with damage due to water, wind-carried sediments (e.g., sandblasting), or other environmental forces. In a like manner, warping during life due to a mineral deficiency (e.g., calcium) could be mistaken for burial distortion. Thus, a thorough familiarity with anomalous and pathological conditions is necessary to avoid improper taphonomic analysis.

A third repercussion is that the presence of bony deviations from the norm may provide more information on decedents, thereby aiding law enforcement officials in their search for a match with a missing persons file. For example, conditions that indicate the occupation of decedents might narrow the search to members of a general or specific socioeconomic class. Similarly, the relative health of the deceased before death may further expand the information on decedents.

The last repercussion to forensic anthropologists involves the *positive* identification of individuals. Because they may be documented in medical records or remembered by friends and relatives, any atypical skeletal condition that would appear on radiographs, or that could be observed in the living, has the potential to provide information on identification. Persons with these defects may have sought medical help for some problem, and the anomalies are discovered in x-ray. Similarly, a pathological condition severe enough to have osteological manifestations may also be documented in the medical records of persons.

BOX 15.1
An Identifying Pathological Condition

William Maples (1984) describes a pathological condition that he feels was so distinct that it led to positive identification in a forensic case. An almost complete skeleton, believed to be that of an old man from the area, was recovered without evidence of foul play from a peat bog in the Florida panhandle. The skull indicated both White ancestry and male sex, and the pelvis also indicated male. The individual was so advanced in years that features of the pubic bone could not be used to determine age at death, and all cranial sutures were fused and obliterated except a portion of the squamous suture. The calculation of stature indicated a height of around 5 feet, 8 inches. Unfortunately, the teeth had been missing antemortem for many years, making an odontological identification impossible. In addition, although there were a number of healed antemortem injuries, none were distinct enough to determine the identity of the deceased.

The skull did exhibit one feature that was relatively unique. Instead of a right ear orbit, there was a large cavitating lesion that exposed much of the inner ear and mastoid process. The shape and location of this condition were consistent with a diagnosis of cholesteatoma, a disease apparently initiated by an upper respiratory infection that causes the destruction of temporal bone. The two major symptoms are loss of hearing and the production of foul-smelling drainage. However, because the onset of the disease may be slow and without pain, patients may not seek medical treatment. The person thought to be represented by the skeleton did not have a medical history of treatment for the disease, but had been seen for over 20 years by the local social services department. Their records indicated that, starting in the early 1950s, he had complained of hearing loss in the affected ear that was not corrected after receiving a hearing aid. In addition, acquaintances complained of a bad smell from a drainage oozing from his right ear. Since the missing person matched the demographic profile of the skeleton and the information concerning his auditory problems coincided with his known history, the police considered the identification as positive and the case was closed.

Therefore, the presence of the anomalies and bone disease may make the difference between an unresolved case and a positive identification. (See Box 15.1 for an example.)

This chapter will present information on three types of deviations from the norm: pathological conditions, skeletal anomalies, and markers of occupational stress. **Pathological conditions** vary by causative factors, from endocrine disturbances and nutritional deficiencies to congenital deformities and infectious diseases. Although there are a large number of these, this discussion will concentrate on only those diseases that are most likely to appear in persons from industrialized countries. **Skeletal anomalies** can be divided into four categories: accessory ossicles, nonfusion anomalies, accessory foramina, and miscellaneous anomalies. Because they may be misconceived as fractures and puncture wounds by the unwary, it is useful to discuss the characteristics of these anomalies to reduce the likelihood of their being mistaken for trauma. Finally, **markers of occupational stress** are those bone conditions that appear to be caused by atypical body movements. These include facets, hypertrophies, lytic lesions, and other such defects.

PATHOLOGICAL CONDITIONS

Although few diseases cause osteological changes, some pathological conditions might be mistaken for trauma or taphonomic damage because of their effect on the overall appearance of bone. Donald Ortner and Walter Putschar (1981) provide a complete

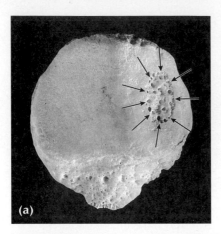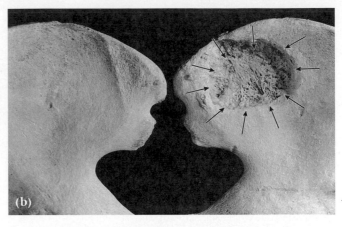

FIGURE 15.1 Manifestations of osteolytic disease: **(a)** pores (*arrows*) on the posterior side of a patella; **(b)** cavitation on the lateral side of the ilium (*arrows*) caused by a severe osteolytic disease. A normal ilium is included for comparison on the left. (Photo by Julie R. Angel; ilia courtesy of the University of New Mexico–Albuquerque, Maxwell Museum of Anthropology, #125)

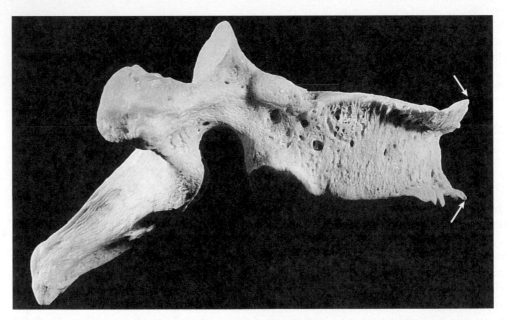

FIGURE 15.2 An example of a small osteoproliferative lesion; osteophytosis of a thoracic vertebra (*arrows*). (Photo by Julie R. Angel; courtesy of the State of New Mexico, Office of the Medical Investigator)

discussion of bone disease seen in the human skeleton and the following discussion is based on their work. These authors divide pathological conditions into three basic types, which can be termed lytic, proliferative, and deformative. **Lytic lesions** are those that involve an abnormal loss of bone, that is, erosion and/or destruction of cortical or trabecular bone. This loss varies in size from small pores (see Figure 15.1a) to large cavitations (see Figure 15.1b). **Proliferative lesions** take the form of excess bone being deposited at various locations throughout the skeleton. These also vary in size from small exostoses (see Figure 15.2) to large outgrowths (see Figure 15.3). Finally, **deformative lesions** involve abnormal contours or shapes; **rickets** (insufficient vitamin D in children) is the most well known of this type of lesion (see Figure 15.4). Because all three of these

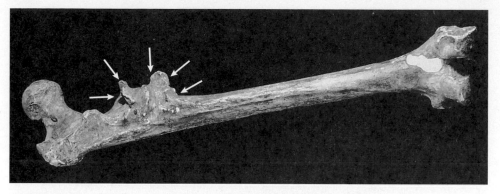

FIGURE 15.3 Osteoproliferative lesion (*arrows*) on the femur of an early human (*Homo erectus*) from Java. (Photo by Julie R. Angel)

types mimic (albeit slightly) the effects perimortem trauma and postmortem damage, an abbreviated description of the most common forms of pathological conditions is warranted.

Lytic Lesions

A widespread disease that causes lytic bone changes, if untreated, is **anemia**. Ortner and Putschar (1981) describe this illness as being due to low levels of iron in the hemoglobin molecules located on the red blood cells. This lack of adequate iron causes the cells to become distorted from their original round shape, which causes them to break as they flow through capillaries and other blood vessels. Once broken, these cells must be eliminated from the body and replaced. The normal response to both low levels of iron and accelerated loss of cells is to increase the production of red blood cells. This causes the structure largely responsible for this task, the diploe of the skull, to expand to meet the greater demand. This expansion can result in the pushing of the diploe through the outer table of the bones of the cranial vault and occasionally the face. The result of this pushing is the formation of pores and (sometimes) outgrowth of the diploe.

In dried bone, this condition (termed **porotic hyperostosis**) usually is found on the occipital, but can be located on the parietals (particularly near the sagittal suture), frontal (near bregma), or any other bone of the vault or face. The pores come in varying sizes, from small pinpricks to larger openings that can be as much as 3 mm in diameter. Although found more often in prehistoric than contemporary individuals, this condition may appear in persons suffering from general malnutrition (a possibility among people from the lower socioeconomic classes) or from an inherited anemia, such as sickle cell anemia, seen most often in persons of Black ancestry. Figure 15.5a illustrates an example of these lesions on the occipital of a modern human.

A second common lytic defect seen in bone is caused by localized bone death (**necrosis**). Ortner and Putschar (1981) note that these injuries can be produced by any factor that reduces or completely stops blood flow to part of a bone. The result is death of the bone, which leaves a cavity and occasionally a free-floating osteological fragment. Figure 15.5b illustrates such a necrotic lesion. Another

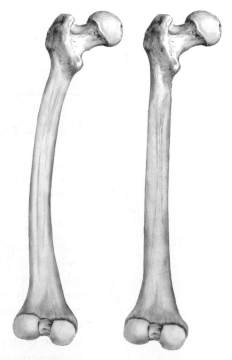

FIGURE 15.4 Line drawing of a femur (left bone) typical of rickets or osteomalacia. A normal femur (right bone) is included for comparison.

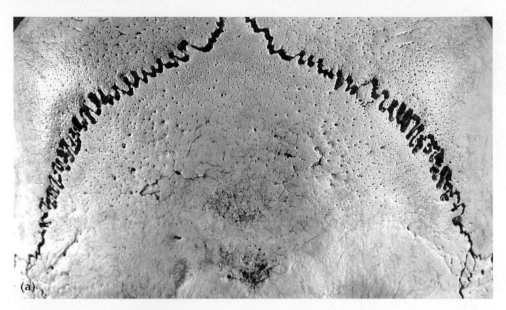

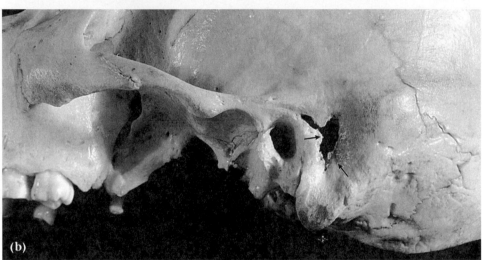

FIGURE 15.5   More osteolytic diseases: **(a)** porosity (porotic hyperostosis) in the occipital and parietals; **(b)** necrotic lesion at the base of the mastoid process of the temporal bone (*arrows*). (Photos by Julie R. Angel; courtesy of the State of New Mexico, Office of the Medical Investigator)

common expression of this type of defect takes the form of cavitary lesions on the superior and inferior surfaces of the vertebral bodies. Although the etiology of these **Schmorl's nodes** (see Figure 15.6) is unknown, they are not uncommon findings, particularly in prehistoric specimens. Similarly, Ortner and Putschar (1981) note that untreated infections of the teeth can result in abscesses (cavitary lesions) that may form a vent in the alveolar part of the jaws (see Figure 15.7). Finally, amputations will be both evident in the skeleton and documented in hospital medical records. These procedures reveal a shortened bone with a healed end. In cases of long life after the event, the affected bone will atrophy, as will other bones on the side of the amputation (Stewart, 1979).

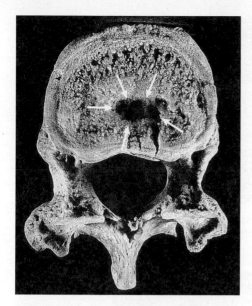

FIGURE 15.6 Schmorl's node (*arrows*) on the superior surface of the body of a lower thoracic vertebra. (Photo by Julie R. Angel; specimen courtesy of the State of New Mexico, Office of the Medical Investigator)

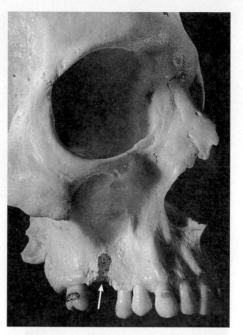

FIGURE 15.7 Vent (*arrow*) for abscess of the upper first molar. (Photo by Julie R. Angel; specimen courtesy of the University of New Mexico–Albuquerque, Maxwell Museum of Anthropology, #31)

Proliferative Lesions

The most common proliferative pathological conditions occur on vertebral bodies (Figure 15.2). These spurs of bone, called **osteophytes**, have been linked to osteoarthritis as well as to general deterioration due to age (Stewart, 1979). In the past, anyone over the age of 40 would possess these lesions (visible in x-ray); however, due to the less stressful conditions of modern life, their development in all present-day persons is not necessarily assured.

Debra Martin and colleagues (1990) describe another common proliferative condition that takes the form of striations on the otherwise smooth cortical surface of long bones, particularly the tibia. Because their cause is still debated, the term **generalized bone disease** is used to describe these lesions. As with anemia, this condition is not seen as often in contemporary peoples as in past populations; however, it may be present in forensic specimens from persons of poor economic circumstances. Figure 15.8 illustrates its appearance on the distal portion of a tibia.

A third source of proliferative lesions can be found around healing or healed antemortem breaks. As described in Chapter 11, a bony callus at the site of the fracture forms to reinforce the compromised bone until the broken surfaces can fully reunite. In addition to the callus, deformation of the bone may occur when repair therapies are faulty or in cases where perfect alignment is not possible (Figure 15.9a).

Surgical procedures can cause proliferative lesions, especially around implanted orthopedic appliances. If patients live for several years after a procedure, reactive bone will form around and sometimes over these appliances (see Figure 15.9b; also see Figure 3.24a and b).

One last common proliferative lesion is the **button osteoma**. This nonmalignant neoplasm can be found on the skull (Ortner and Putschar, 1981) and, if located on a

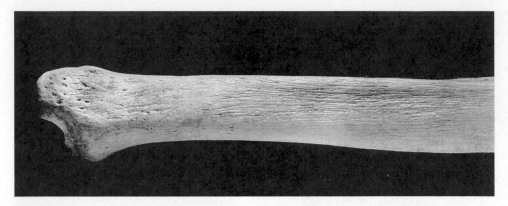

FIGURE 15.8 Striations termed *generalized bone disease* on the distal tibia. (Photo by Julie R. Angel; specimen courtesy of the State of New Mexico, Office of the Medical Investigator)

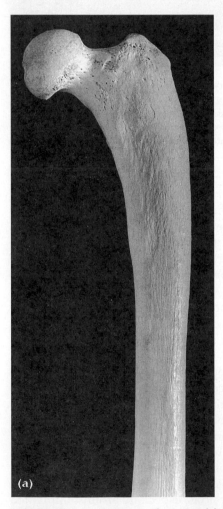

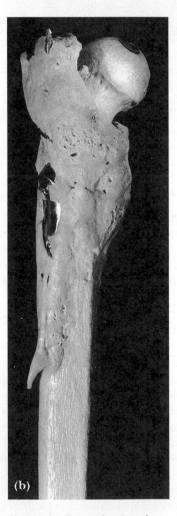

FIGURE 15.9 Antemortem fractures. **(a)** Deformation and callus at the site of a fracture to the proximal femur; the spasm caused by the muscles in this area makes proper alignment after this type of break difficult. **(b)** Reactive bone growth over an orthopedic appliance on the proximal femur. (Photos by Julie R. Angel; specimens courtesy of the State of New Mexico, Office of the Medical Investigator and the University of New Mexico–Albuquerque, Maxwell Museum of Anthropology, #3)

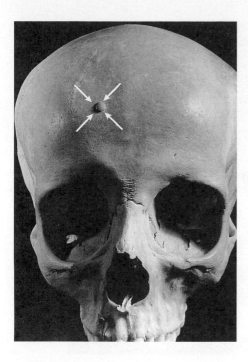

FIGURE 15.10   Button osteoma (*arrows*) on the frontal. This defect would be clearly visible on the forehead of the live individual, lending support to a positive identification. (Photo by Julie R. Angel; specimen courtesy of the State of New Mexico, Office of the Medical Investigator)

visible part of the cranial vault, such as the frontal (see Figure 15.10) or parietals and occipital of bald persons, it can be used to help develop a positive identification.

Deformative Lesions

The two major types of deformative lesions are those of environmental origin and those that are congenital. Of the environmentally caused deformities, the most common is **wedging** of the vertebrae seen in many older persons. This condition, which can appear anywhere in the spine, is due to microfractures occurring over time that cause the anterior part of the bodies to reduce in height (see Figure 15.11a). Similarly, these microfractures can occur lateral to the midline, causing the spine to lean to one side (see Figure 15.11b). Osteoporosis and occupations involving heavy lifting are contributing factors to both of these deformities.

In addition to fractures, nutritional diseases can cause skeletal deformities. The best known of these is vitamin D deficiency, which causes rickets in children and **osteomalacia** in adults. In this pathological condition, the long bones bow either anteroposteriorly or mediolaterally (see Figure 15.4) to a noticeable extent. Although malnutrition is rare in industrialized countries, the immigration of persons from the third world makes it possible that skeletons exhibiting nutritional deficiency conditions will appear in forensic situations.

Ortner and Putschar (1981) describe a wide variety of congenital deformities that have skeletal manifestations. **Kyphosis** of the spine is a condition in which the vertebral column curves forward to a degree greater than normal. Congenitally, this condition is caused by a hemivertebra (half of a vertebra) located in the posterior half in the spine. Similarly, **scoliosis** is a disease in which the vertebral column exhibits a lateral curvature. This condition can be caused by hemivertebrae located lateral to the sagittal plane in the spine. Both of these pathological conditions are rare in industrial populations.

SKELETAL ANOMALIES

In a now famous article, Berry and Berry (1967) described nonmetric variations seen in the human cranium that appear to be of epigenetic origin (i.e., under both genetic and environmental control). These variations include accessory ossicles, nonfusion of bony

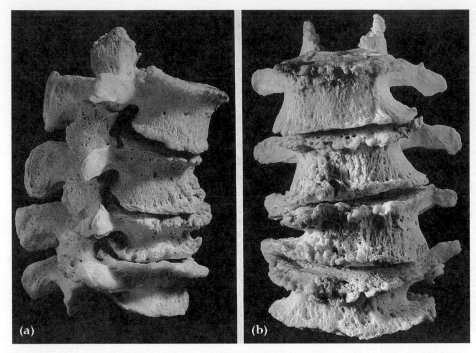

FIGURE 15.11   Effects of vertebral wedging: **(a)** kyphosis caused by anterior wedging of the lumbar spine caused by microfractures over time; **(b)** scoliosis of the lumbar spine caused by microfractures over time. (Photos by Julie R. Angel; specimen courtesy of the University of New Mexico–Albuquerque, Maxwell Museum of Anthropology, #7)

segments, and extra foramen as well as a number of other miscellaneous anomalies. Work by other researchers demonstrated the existence of similar variations in the postcranial skeleton (Anderson, 1963; Finnegan, 1978). Although they normally are used to show genetic relationships between populations, these anomalies may confound osteological analysis due to their superficial similarity to perimortem trauma. Thus, forensic anthropologists must be cognizant of the existence of such conditions and of their manifestations in the human skeleton. Buikstra and Ubelaker (1994) describe the most common forms of these nonmetric variations, which will be summarized here. For ease of understanding in the following discussion, these are divided into four different types: accessory bones, nonfusion anomalies, accessory foramen, and miscellaneous anomalies.

Accessory Bones

Accessory bones are extra ossicles that occur in various parts of the skeleton. In the skull, they occur in or adjacent to suture lines, where they appear to be the result of improper ossification of cranial bones. Of all the anomalous conditions, these are the most likely to be mistaken for perimortem trauma for several reasons. First, because they are separate ossicles within larger bones, they can appear to be the result of blunt trauma that disconnected a section of bone from its source bone. Also, because they can be lost after death, the opening left by their absence may be mistaken for a gunshot or other type of wound. For these reasons, the differences between accessory bones and traumatic injuries deserve further discussion.

Examination of cranial anomalies in light of the characteristics of trauma reveals five important differences. First, as illustrated in Figure 15.12, the outline of these ossicles are too irregular; that is, they are wavy instead of straight or angular

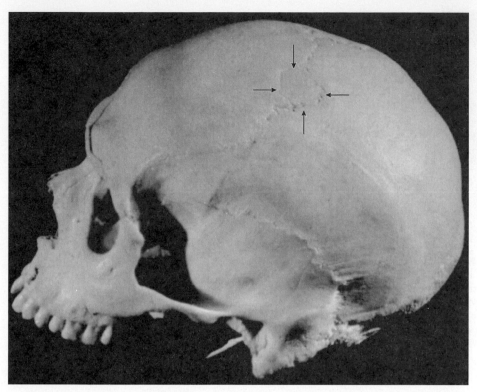

FIGURE 15.12 Accessory ossicle in a skull, in this case a coronal ossicle, (*arrows*) showing a wavy outline and the lack of both a traversing suture and radiating fracture lines. (Photo by Julie R. Angel; specimen courtesy of the State of New Mexico, Office of the Medical Investigator)

as seen in perimortem trauma. Second, as also illustrated in Figure 15.12, suture lines do not continue through these types of defects. Where the bone fragments at the site of perimortem trauma to the skull would manifest the presence of a suture, in these anomalies, sutures end at the ossicle and then continue on the other side. Third, there are no fracture lines either radiating outward from them or surrounding these defects (see Figure 15.12). Fourth, if the ossicles are missing, cortical bone usually can be seen on the inside edges of the resultant opening (Figure 15.13) where the diploe should be visible. Finally, these anomalies and other conditions show rounded edges (Figure 15.13) instead of the sharp edges found in perimortem fractures.

Accessory bones come in many forms and locations. Figures 15.14 through 15.16 show the various positions of these ossicles on the human skull. The most common site is the lambdoid suture, where they are called **wormian bones** (Figure 15.16; see also Figure 15.17). These very common bones occur in 20% to over 80% of skulls, depending on the geographic area of origin. Other common sites are in the sagittal (Figure 15.14), coronal (Figure 15.14), and the squamosal sutures (Figure 15.15); this last variant, called the parietal notch bone, can be seen in 3% to over 30% of skulls. Ossicles can also occur at landmarks, such as lambda (Figure 15.16), bregma (Figure 15.14), and pterion (Figure 15.15); this last ossicle, called an **epipteric bone**, occurs in 5% to as many as 20% of skulls. Finally, an ossicle that occurs on the inferior border of the zygomatic bone (see Figure 15.18a) is called **os japonium** (sometimes spelled **os japonicum**), because it is seen most frequently among Japanese people.

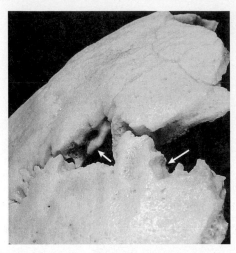

FIGURE 15.13 Face of the edge of the openings caused by missing ossicles (*arrows*) showing the presence of cortical bone. Also note rounded edges. (Photo by Julie R. Angel; specimen courtesy of the State of New Mexico, Office of the Medical Investigator)

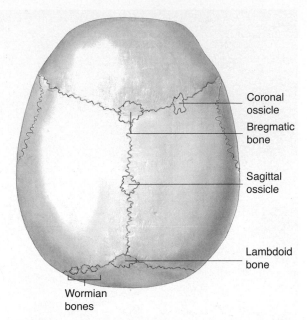

Coronal ossicle

Bregmatic bone

Sagittal ossicle

Lambdoid bone

Wormian bones

FIGURE 15.14 Sites of accessory bones on the human skull (superior view).

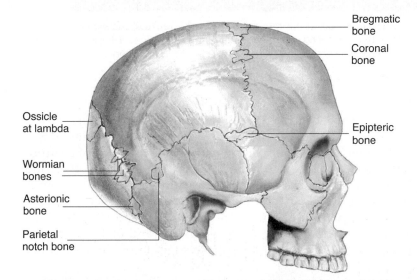

Bregmatic bone

Coronal bone

Ossicle at lambda

Epipteric bone

Wormian bones

Asterionic bone

Parietal notch bone

FIGURE 15.15 Sites of accessory bones on the human skull (lateral view).

Nonfusion Anomalies

Another common occurrence within the human skeleton that could be mistaken for trauma is the nonfusion of ossification centers that normally unite with age. Theoretically, there are four areas where nonfusion can occur: between two primary ossification centers, between a primary and a secondary center, between primary and accessory centers, and between secondary and accessory centers. Therefore, to prevent the misidentification of these as trauma, forensic anthropologists must be aware of the centers of ossification in

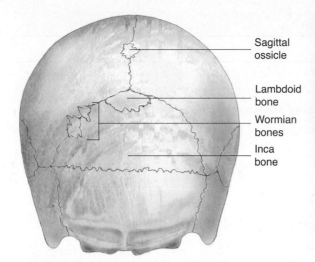

FIGURE 15.16   Sites of accessory bones on the human skull (posterior view).

FIGURE 15.17   Lambdoid bone with paired wormian bones in the lambdoid suture.
(Photo by Julie R. Angel; specimen courtesy of the State of New Mexico, Office of the Medical Investigator)

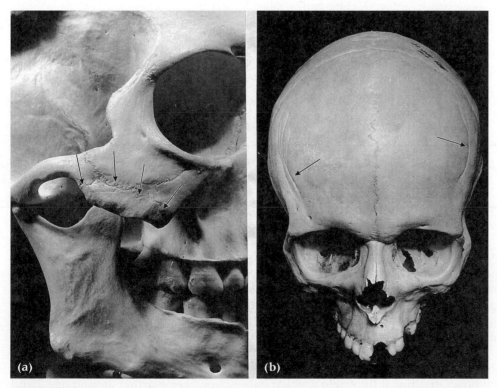

FIGURE 15.18   Nonfusion anomalies of the skull: **(a)** Os japonium, an ossicle of the zygomatic bone (*arrows*) that occurs most often in persons of Japanese ancestry; **(b)** retention of the metopic suture (metopism) separating the left and right halves of the frontal in an adult; notice also the grooves (*arrows*) on either side of the frontal bone. (Photos by Julie R. Angel; os japonium courtesy of University of New Mexico, Osteology Lab; metopism courtesy of the State of New Mexico, Office of the Medical Investigator)

TABLE 15.1 Nonfusion Anomalies of the Postcranial Skeleton[1]

Bone	Anomaly
Axial skeleton	
Axis	Unfused odontoid process
Vertebral body	Nonfusion of right and left halves; nonfusion of anterior and posterior halves
Vertebral arch	Spondylolysis, hypoplasia, and agenesis of the pedicle; persistent neurocentral synchondrosis
Sacrum	Spina bifida
Thorax	
First rib	Congential synchondrosis at the angle
Sternum	Congenital perforation, nonfusion of right and left sides (cleft sternum)
Appendicular skeleton	
Upper limbs	
Clavicle	Nonfusion of left and right halves (congential synchondrosis)
Scapula	Nonfusions of the acromion and coracoid process
Humerus, ulna, radius	Nonfusion of proximal and distal halves (congenital synchondrosis)
Ulna	Nonfusion of the styloid process (os triangulare)
Carpals, metacarpals	Various nonfusions of the bodies, tubercles, and other structures
Lower limbs	
Os coxa	Persistent os acetabuli (accessory bone in hip socket), congenital synchondrosis of the ischopubic junction
Femur, tibia, fibula	Nonfusion of proximal and distal halves (congenital synchondrosis)
Tibia, fibula	Nonfusion of malleolus
Tarsals, metatarsals	Various nonfusions of the bodies, tubercles, and other structures (especially os trigonum)

[1]From Byers (1984).

the various bones of the human body. (A good source of this information is the osteology section of *Gray's Anatomy*.)

There are a large number of anomalies of the human skeleton in which segments that usually fuse early in life remain open in adulthood (see Table 15.1). Similarly, bones that normally develop from one center of ossification can have two parts that never grow together. These nonfusion anomalies can be mistaken for perimortem trauma or postmortem damage. However, they are distinguishable from either of these conditions by the presence of cortical bone on what would appear to be the "broken" surfaces. Similarly, they lack splintering common in taphonomic changes and the fracture lines seen in trauma.

The only common nonfusion anomaly of the cranium is retention of the metopic suture, a condition called **metopism**. At birth, this suture runs vertically through the frontal bone, dividing it into right and left halves; however, starting around age 2 and ending around age 8 years, the two sections usually fuse and the line obliterates. Although it is fairly common for a small section to remain visible just superior to glabella, worldwide between 1% and 10% of adults maintain the entire metopic suture throughout life. Figure 15.18b illustrates an example of metopism; although reminiscent of a fracture line, the straight course and wavy line, as well as rounded edges, make a misdiagnosis of trauma unlikely.

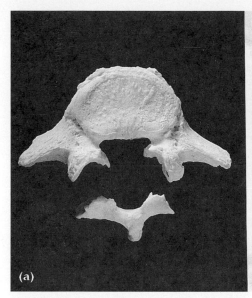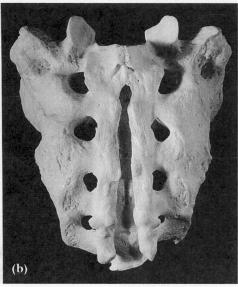

FIGURE 15.19   Nonfusion anomalies of the vertebral column: **(a)** spondylolysis of a lumbar vertebra; **(b)** severe case of spina bifida seen in the human sacrum; only the superior neural arch is unaffected by this condition. (Photos by Julie R. Angel; spondylolysis courtesy of the University of New Mexico–Albuquerque, Maxwell Museum of Anthropology, #40; spina bifida courtesy of the State of New Mexico, Office of the Medical Investigator)

In the axial skeleton, there are a number of nonfusion anomalies. The most common vertebral anomaly is **spondylolysis**; this occurs when there is separation of the neural arch from the body of a vertebra (see Figure 15.19a). Because it is seen most often in the lumbar area, many researchers believe that this is not the result of nonfusion, but is due to stress fracturing related to strenuous occupations that caused separation of originally fused components (see Markers of Occupational Stress in this chapter). In most cases, the defect is unilateral (i.e., it affects only one side of the arch); however, many cases are bilateral in expression.

Similar to the vertebrae, the sacrum can exhibit separation between the right and left halves of what would be the neural arch in this structure. This condition, called **spina bifida**, is a congenital anomaly that had a high mortality rate in the past before advances in medicine gave persons stricken with the disease a longer life. Nonfusion of neural arch halves in the sacral vertebrae (Figure 15.19b) varies in expression from one arch not fused to all five arches not fused. Although the sternum is prone to several nonfusion anomalies, the most common is a perforation through the body (see Figure 15.20) that has been mistaken by many osteological students as a projectile wound because of its usually circular outline.

In the appendicular skeleton, there are a number of nonfusions which vary from being rare to fairly common (e.g., seen in as many as 10% of skeletons). In the scapula, the most prevalent occurs in the acromion at the tip, the segment just distal to the angle, and the segment just proximal to the angle (Figure 15.21). These nonfusions are visible in 1% to 8% of human populations.

In the limb bones, several nonfusions have been recorded. The kneecap exhibits the most common of these conditions, called a **bipartite patella**. This condition most usually manifests as a notch in the superiolateral corner; however, these notches can occur in the upper medial corner as well as the tip (see Figure 15.22). Bipartite patellae occur in about 3% of the population. The clavicle can also manifest a nonfusion in the form of **congenital pseudarthrosis**; this occurs when medial and lateral sides of

FIGURE 15.20   Congenital perforation of the sternum; this defect has been mistaken for a projectile wound by many first-year osteology students. Compare with Figure 2.13. (Photo by Julie R. Angel; specimen courtesy of the State of New Mexico, Office of the Medical Investigator)

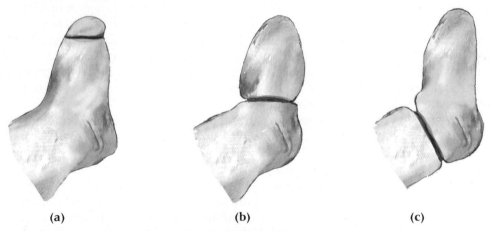

(a)   (b)   (c)

FIGURE 15.21   Common sites of nonfusion of the acromiom of the scapula: **(a)** tip, **(b)** segment just distal to angle, **(c)** segment just proximal to angle.

FIGURE 15.22   Common nonfusions of the patella.

FIGURE 15.23 Nonfusion of the styloid process of the ulna (os triangulare).

this bone fail to unite. Generally, the lateral portion is only one-third of the bone's length and the medial section comprises the remaining two-thirds. The majority of these occur on the right side; however, bilateral expression has been seen.

The ulna can exhibit an **os triangulare**, which is formed by nonfusion of the styloid process (Figure 15.23). Similarly in the lower leg, the malleoli of both the tibia and the fibula can remain unfused into adulthood; this is seen in about 4% of people with ankle problems. Also, the talus can exhibit an **os trigonum**, which is the nonfusion of the posterior process of this bone (Figure 15.24). Finally, both hand and foot bones exhibit a number of nonfusion anomalies; however, these are too rare to be discussed here.

Accessory Foramen

Another variation that might be mistaken for perimortem trauma and postmortem damage is the accessory foramen. These foramina in bones where they "don't belong" might be mistaken for punctures or pitting except for their rounded edges and lack of fracture lines. Figure 15.25 shows the location of accessory foramen on the facial skeleton; these generally are relatively small openings, which also makes their misdiagnosis unlikely. Another common location is at obelion on the parietal close to where the right and left parietal foramen normally appear; the existence of a third foramen in this area may mislead the inexperienced investigator. A final foramen that occurs occasionally is located on the floor of the ear canal (Figure 15.26). This opening, called the **foramen of Huschke**, is visible at birth, but usually closes by 5 years of age. However, in a small number of adults, it remains open into adulthood.

In the postcranium, the most common variation that could be misdiagnosed is the **septal aperture**. This is a somewhat irregular hole through the olecranon fossa of the humerus (see Figure 15.27a) that is reminiscent of a bullet hole. However, like most of the defects described in this section, it lacks the fracturing found in projectile and blunt traumas.

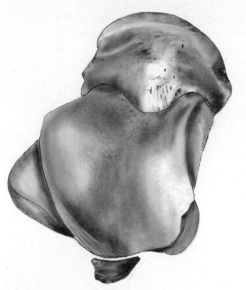

FIGURE 15.24 Nonfusion of the posterior process of the talus (os trigonium).

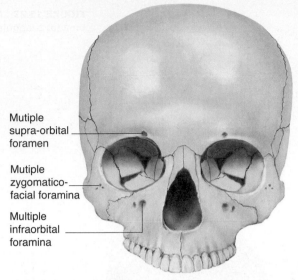

Mutiple supra-orbital foramen

Mutiple zygomatico-facial foramina

Multiple infraorbital foramina

FIGURE 15.25 Sites of accessory foramen on the human facial skeleton.

FIGURE 15.26 Huschke's foramen (*arrows*) seen on the inferior part of the ear canal. (Photo by Julie R. Angel; specimen courtesy of the State of New Mexico, Office of the Medical Investigator)

Miscellaneous Anomalies

A number of other anomalous conditions appearing in the human skeleton can be mistaken for perimortem trauma or postmortem damage. One such deviation that occurs antemortem is **trephination** (sometimes spelled **trepination**). These are small to large (Figure 15.28) holes in the braincase that are the result of a surgery. Because they normally exhibit some healing (i.e., persons are not usually released from the hospital for some time after such a surgery), their misdiagnosis is unlikely. Similar to trephination are amputations where bone segments are missing; again the presence of healing would indicate an antemortem, rather than perimortem or postmortem, condition.

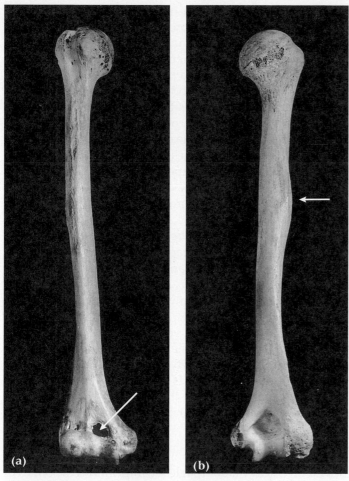

FIGURE 15.27   Two variations of the humerus: **(a)** foramen through the olecranon fossa (*arrow*); **(b)** enlarged deltoid tuberosity (*arrow*) indicating long-term heavy use of this muscle. (Photos by Julie R. Angel; specimens courtesy of the State of New Mexico, Office of the Medical Investigator)

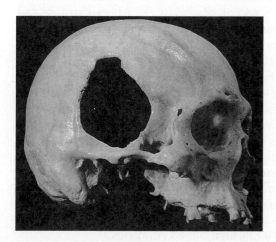

FIGURE 15.28   Large trephination due to surgical removal of part of the braincase. (Photo by Julie R. Angel; specimen courtesy of the State of New Mexico, Office of the Medical Investigator)

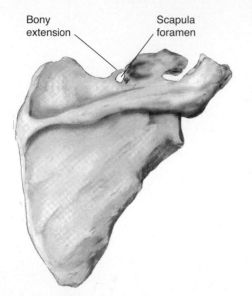

Bony extension

Scapula foramen

FIGURE 15.29 Foramen at the site of the scapular notch.

Another anomaly is the **trauma-induced pseudarthrosis**; this is similar to the congenital expression of this condition described previously, in that a single bone is divided into two segments joined by a fibrous tissue. These occur when broken bone ends are not immobilized during healing (as when persons refuse medical treatment) or when fractures do not respond to traditional therapy. What appears to happen is that the fibrous tissue that initially joins the broken halves during the healing process does not calcify either with fibrous or with lamellar bone, leaving a pseudarthrosis composed of this initial tissue. These bones remain permanently in two sections, the ends of which usually taper. This tapering, in conjunction with the presence of cortical bone on the broken ends, makes it unlikely that these joints would be mistaken for anything but an anomalous condition.

Epiphyseal areas also could be mistaken for trauma. As already seen, epiphyses attach to metaphyses of bone shafts in children and adolescents, which forensic anthropologists might mistake as broken bones. Since these are seen in all long bones (including metacarpals and metatarsals), a knowledge of skeletal growth is essential to avoid this type of mistake.

Two final anomalies seen in the skeleton are blood vessel grooves and a foramen at the scapular notch. The first of these are furrows in bone apparently caused by blood vessels pulsing against the cortical surface; a particularly common location is on the frontal bone of the skull (see Figure 15.18b). The other is a foramen at the site of the scapular notch (Figure 15.29) on the superior edge of the scapula. This appears to be due to bridging between the superior corners of this structure.

OCCUPATIONAL STRESS MARKERS

Many occupations and activities involve heavy labor that leave imprints on the bones of the persons engaged in them. Enlarged areas of muscle attachment, regions of erosion, and ossifications of soft tissue can be indicative of concentrated use. The presence of these lesions is important because they can help complete the profile of the person represented by the remains. (See Box 15.2 for a good example.) Although most of the markers of occupational stress are likely to be seen only in third-world countries, there are a number of activities even in industrialized societies that are so strenuous that it is believed they can modify living bones. (A recent study by F. Alves Cardos and C. Y. Henderson, 2010, challenged this assumption when they showed that areas of enlarged muscle attachment on the humerus are mainly due to advanced age.)

In a fine review article, Wilczak and Kennedy (1998) divide markers of occupational stress into four types: modifications to areas of insertion, osteophytosis, discrete markers, and stress fractures. Modifications to areas of insertion involve the attachment of soft tissues such as tendons or ligaments. These are visible as either **hypertrophy**, where the area of attachment is enlarged and rugged, or lytic lesions where the bone has resorbed. The etiology of these changes has been attributed to mechanical loading (i.e., strenuous activity) or microfractures due to this type of loading. One of the most common areas exhibiting a hypertrophic lesion is the tuberosity for the insertion of the deltoid muscle onto the humerus (see Figure 15.27b). Conversely, an area where lytic-type lesions are common is the radial tuberosity (see Figure 15.30). Table 15.2 provides information on the major lesions at points of insertion for occupations and activities normally found in the United States and other industrialized countries.

BOX 15.2
Death by Strangulation (Revisited)

In Box 14.2 in Chapter 14, a case involving a special kind of ligature called the "Spanish Windlass" was described from an article by Lawrence Angel and Peggy Caldwell (1984). This case involved a young adult female whose remains exhibited a perimortem fracture to the mandible as well as fracture lines on the left neural arch of the sixth cervical vertebra. Since a compressive force strong enough to cause these latter breaks would have had to compress the soft tissues of the neck, it was reasonable to conclude that the young woman died from strangulation. However, two areas of the skeleton exhibited activity-related stress markers that helped to complete her personal profile.

The first area was the pelvis. In this structure, both acetabula showed hypertrophic bone growth that extended the weight-bearing part of these structures medially. In addition, both sacroiliatic joints (area of articulation between the sacrum and the ilia) showed bony

extensions posteriorly and the areas of ligamentous attachments showed "spikes," indicating that the attaching soft tissues had ossified and become part of the bone. These features suggested that the victim had participated in strenuous activities; and given the age of the woman, it was reasonable to conclude that this involved school sports. In addition to the pelvis, the lower jaw (mandible) exhibited anomalous features. The anterior surface of the condyles had bony extensions both medially and laterally; these indicated that the victim had engaged in an activity that required thrusting the jaw forward, as when playing a wind musical instrument. Lawrence Angel later confirmed both these deductions with the mother of the victim. When he asked her what wind instrument the victim had played, the surprised parent responded that her daughter had played the clarinet since she was eleven. In addition, the mother confirmed that the victim was active in school sports.

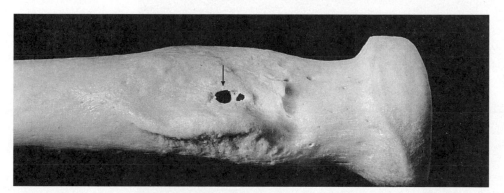

FIGURE 15.30   Lytic lesion (*arrow*) of the radial tuberosity.   (Photo by Julie R. Angel; specimen courtesy of the State of New Mexico, Office of the Medical Investigator)

Osteophytosis is a condition in which small spurs or ridges of bone project from an area that is normally smooth or flat. These occur around articular surfaces, especially in the vertebrae and the diarthrodial joints (e.g., shoulder, knee, elbow). Vertebral osteophytes can be anywhere from small (see Figure 15.2) to large spicules of bone that, over time, can join to form ridges. Unfortunately, these are age-related markers (so much so that T. Dale Stewart proposed estimating age at death from their size); therefore, the age of an individual at death must be taken into account when reporting these lesions as being caused by occupation or strenuous activity. Diarthrodial joints most commonly exhibit ridging rather than spicules of bone. Common areas manifesting these lesions include the glenoid cavity of the scapula (see Figure 15.31) and the bones of the knee.

TABLE 15.2 Lesions of Insertion Areas from Occupations and Activities of Industrialized Countries[1]

Bone or Structure	Muscle or Structure	Occupation or Activity
Mandible	Lateral pterygoid (sharp tubercles on condyles)	Clarinet or other woodwind playing
Humerus	Pectoralis major and deltoid Medial epicondyle	Kayaking Golfing
Radius	Tuberosity	Masons and bakers
Ulna	Supinator crest Triceps brachii exostosis	Fruit picking, iron workers Baseball playing
Hands	Palmar insertions of proximal phalanges	Grasping writing tool, holding paddle or oar
Femur	Gluteal tuberosity, linea aspera	Football players, horseback riders
Calcaneous	Achilles tendon, adductor hallicus	Joggers
	Plantar fascia (bony spurs)	Police officers, floorwalkers

[1]Reduced from Table 1 of Wilczak and Kennedy (1998).

FIGURE 15.31 Ridging around the glenoid cavity of the scapula. (Photo by Julie R. Angel; specimen courtesy of the University of New Mexico–Albuquerque, Maxwell Museum of Anthropology, #18)

TABLE 15.3   Osteophytosis from Occupations and Activities of Industrialized Countries[1]

Bone or Structure	Affected Area	Occupation or Activity
Vertebrae	Bodies of C4, C5 and C6, C7	Fruit pickers
Shoulder	Glenoid cavity with wrist affected	Pneumatic drill
Elbow	Primary capitulum and radial head	Kayak paddling
	Lateral epicondyle of humerus	Tugging on extended arm (e.g., dog walking)
Knee	Lateral and medial surfaces of femur, tibia, and patella	Martial arts, walking in deep snow
Foot	First and fifth metatarsal	Walking over rough terrain
	First metatarsal	Golfing

[1]Reduced from Table 2 of Wilczak and Kennedy (1998).

Table 15.3 provides information on osteophytosis for occupations and activities normally found in industrialized countries.

As used by Wilczak and Kennedy (1998), discrete markers of activity can take many different forms in the skeleton: facets, grooves, deformations, tori, and accessory bones. **Facets** occur where two bones collide near a joint surface; the classic example of this type of lesion is the facets that occur on the anterior part of the distal tibia where it contacts the neck of the talus during squatting (Figure 15.32). In a similar manner, **grooves** can occur in areas characterized by smooth surfaces. A common location is on the occlusal areas of teeth when objects are held in the mouth (e.g., nails by carpenters). **Deformations** appear when a segment of bone is placed under repeated and (usually) high stress. An example is the slight flattening of the humeral head seen in persons who often raise their arms above their heads (e.g., citrus fruit pickers). Other such changes include **tori** (raised area of a bone) and **accessory bones**. These markers are found in most areas of the skeleton (further emphasizing the need to inspect all bones during a forensic examination). Because these types of markers can have a genetic component,

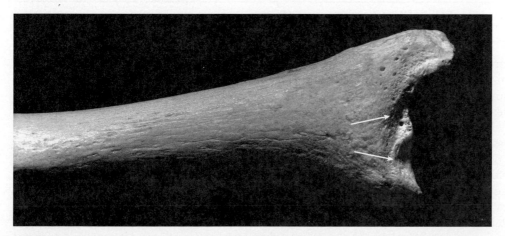

FIGURE 15.32   Squatting facets (*arrows*) on the distal tibia; a similar defect can be seen on the superior surface of the talar neck. (Photo by Julie R. Angel; specimen courtesy of University of New Mexico, Osteology Lab)

TABLE 15.4 Discrete Markers of Occupations and Activities of Industrialized Countries[1]

Bone or Structure	Affected Area	Occupation or Activity
Ear	Auditory exostoses	Divers
Vertebrae	Kyphosis of spine	Tailors, weavers, shoemakers, factory workers
	Scoliosis of spine	Carrying burdens on one shoulder
	Schmorl's node	Heavy labor
Chest	Fusion between manubrium and body with concavity of sternum and ossification of first rib	Shoemaker
	Flattened ribs with flattened spines in T5 through L5	Wearing back brace
Clavicle	Robusticity at acromial end	Milkmen
	Robusticity at sternal end	Hand sewing
Glenoid	Superior facet with slight humeral head flattening and deltoid hypertrophy	Fruit pickers
Acromion	Bipartite	Fruit pickers
Ulna	Hypertrophy of proximal half	Rodeo cowboys
Ankle	Facets on the anterior of the distal tibia and superior surface of the neck of the talus	Squatting
Ischium	Craggy tuberosity	Sitting for long periods
Foot	Extension of metatarsal–phalangeal articulation	Canoeing and other activities with kneeling
Incisors	Dented edges	Holding things in teeth (e.g., nails)
Premolars	Ellipsoid aperture	Pipe smoking

[1]Reduced from Table 3 of Wilczak and Kennedy (1998).

determination of their relation to activity depends on knowledge of the population from which the forensic skeletons were derived. Table 15.4 provides information on the major discrete markers for occupations and activities normally found in the United States and other industrialized countries.

The final category of Wilczak and Kennedy (1998) involves fractures caused by stress, from repeated and strenuous activities. Common examples include separation of the neural arch from the body of lumbar vertebrae (Figure 15.19a) and compression fractures to the anterior part of vertebral bodies (see Figure 15.11a). Unfortunately, like osteophytosis, these fractures can occur in aging persons, especially those suffering from osteoporosis. This is particularly true for compression fractures of the thoracic vertebrae (see Pathological Conditions in this chapter). Therefore, the age at death of a person must be taken into account when evaluating these lesions as potential occupation-related markers. Table 15.5 provides information on those stress fractures for occupations and activities normally found in industrialized countries.

TABLE 15.5 Fractures Associated with Occupations and Activities of Industrialized Countries[1]

Bone	Condition	Occupation or Activity
Vertebrae (middle and lower)	Separation of neural arch from vertebral body	Heavy lifting
	Anterior wedging	Travel in vehicles with poor shock absorption, parachuting
Radius	Bilateral stress fracture	Bakers, masons
Ulna	Chipping at notch with exostoses on medial surface	Baseball pitchers
Thumb	Transverse fracture	Rodeo or mechanical bull-riding
Calcaneous	Exostoses and fractures	Impact of heel on ground (e.g., dismounting after riding)

[1]Reduced from Table 4 of Wilczak and Kennedy (1998).

Summary

1. There are a number of pathological conditions, anomalies, and markers of occupational stress appearing in the human skeleton that might be mistaken for perimortem trauma and postmortem (taphonomic) damage or that could be used to support an identification of deceased persons.
2. Pathological conditions in bone take three different forms: lytic, proliferative, and deformative.
3. Porosity due to anemia and areas of local bone death (necrosis) are the most common forms of lytic lesions of bone.
4. Striations on bone, called generalized bone disease, and calluses surrounding healed fractures are the most common forms of proliferative lesions.
5. Deformed bone can be due to deficiency diseases or congenital conditions.
6. Skeletal anomalies take four forms: accessory ossicles, nonfusion anomalies, accessory formaina, and miscellaneous anomalies.
7. Accessory ossicles have been mistaken for trauma by the inexperienced.
8. The nonfusion of normally complete bones, which appear in any part of the skeleton, can confuse trauma and taphonomic analyses.
9. There are four types of lesions due to occupational stress: modifications to areas of insertion, osteophytosis, discrete markers, and stress fractures.
10. Markers of occupational stress expand the demographic profile of decedents, thereby aiding law enforcement officials in their search for a missing person.
11. Generally, markers of occupational stress take the form of increased height or cavitating lesions at the sites of tendon and ligament insertions, osteophytosis, stress fractures, and assorted other conditions.

Exercises

1. A hole is found in the center of the left parietal bone. Is it likely that this is an accessory bone, and how would you determine that it is more likely to be due to trauma?
2. Small indentations are found in the occipital bone of a skull that is of forensic significance. Describe how these lesions could be determined to be either due to pellets from a shotgun or due to the anemic condition described in this chapter.
3. A number of small holes are found in the facial skeleton of a forensic case. Describe how these could be determined to be either puncture wounds or the accessory foramen described in the text.

4. Describe the differences between the epipteric bone in Figure 15.15 and the projectile wound displayed in Figure 12.10.

5. Four striations parallel and equidistant from each other are found on the shaft of the femur. Describe why these are more likely indicators of generalized bone disease, rather than incisions due to sharp forces.

6. Describe the similarities and differences between the coronal bone pictured in Figure 15.12 and the blunt force trauma injury pictured in Figure 13.11b.

7. A line dividing the right and left halves of the frontal bone is found in a forensic setting. Describe how to distinguish trauma from metopism in this defect.

8. Describe how the blood vessel grooves pictured in Figure 15.18b could be caused by sharp trauma. Does the description seem reasonable? Why or why not?

16

Postmortem Changes to Bone

In Chapter 5, forensic taphonomy was introduced as it relates to judging the amount of time that has passed between the death of persons and the discovery of their remains. In addition to the changes that can be used to estimate this parameter, a large number of other modifications to bone also can occur postmortem, which provide information on other circumstances surrounding the deaths of decedents. These changes include loss of bones or their segments, cracks and marks of various kinds (e.g., pits, grooves), and modifications in shape. These are caused by a diverse number of natural and artificial forces that can have major effects on the skeleton. Since these forces begin acting immediately after death, postmortem changes of all varieties are encountered in human remains. Thus, forensic taphonomy is an important subject for all forensic anthropologists.

Postmortem bone damage is studied for reasons similar to those given for antemortem skeletal conditions in the previous chapter. First, taphonomic damage to bone may manifest some of the characteristics of perimortem trauma (Maples, 1986), especially if it occurred shortly after death. For example, breakage due to carnivore trampling during disarticulation and consumption can appear as blunt trauma to the inexperienced forensic worker. Similarly, long-term burial often causes cracking that can be mistaken by the unwary for fracture lines. A second reason for studying postmortem damage is that it may be misidentified as an indicator of health. This could distort the personal profile to such an extent that law enforcement officials might overlook a potential match because the missing person was not reported with a noticeable antemortem condition. Third, taphonomic changes may obscure important aspects of the circumstances surrounding death, such as perimortem trauma. A final reason is that taphonomic changes may provide indications of circumstances surrounding the death of decedents and the events occurring to the body afterward. This information may lead investigators to search areas other than where the remains were found, because postmortem damage has indicated that the remains were moved from the original area of deposition. Similarly, taphonomic changes caused by humans might provide investigators with information on perpetrators (e.g., choice of tools used in dismemberments) that may lead to their apprehension.

Although the number of forces that cause taphonomic changes is almost endless, six sources produce the greatest amount of postmortem damage. First, humans disfigure dead bodies (usually their murder victims) either to prevent identification or to show their lack of respect for, or hatred of, decedents (Reichs, 1998b). The most common form of human-caused changes involves dismemberment. Second, nonhuman animals cause taphonomic changes by consuming soft tissues, gnawing bones, and scattering skeletal elements (Ubelaker, 1997). Although any animal can produce these, domestic dogs and coyotes are the most common creatures responsible for this type of damage (Haglund, 1997a). Third, fire causes a number of changes in human bone, including shrinking, cracking, and discoloration (Correia, 1997).

By careful examination of these alterations, information concerning the source and temperature of the causative heat source can be determined. Fourth, weather (especially sunlight) has a distinctive effect on bone that is recognizable by the configuration of cracks, flaking of the cortex, and overall discoloration (e.g., graying). Fifth, burial can deform bone by the application of differential pressure and the presence of erosive soil acids. Finally, water causes damage during transportation as bone is abraded while being pushed along the bottom or sides of a watercourse. Because all these subjects are important in taphonomic analysis, this chapter presents a discussion of the types of changes to skeletal remains caused by each of these forces.

DISMEMBERMENTS

Dismemberment, the intentional separation of body segments, is the major post-mortem change brought about by humans on the remains of other humans. Although many societies perform this activity on their dead with no ill intentions, dismemberment and disfigurement have been used by criminals for centuries to prevent the identification of their victims. When body parts are simply separated but left in a single area, reassembly may not be a particularly difficult task. However, in some cases the separation and removal of segments is so extensive that osteological analysis is severely limited. For this reason, some forensic anthropologists feel that dismemberments pose the greatest challenge to workers in the field (Maples and Browning, 1994). Kathleen Reichs (1998b) presents a fine overview of this subject concerning the means and methods used by persons to separate body segments. Her article forms the basis of the discussion that follows.

Dismemberments provide a unique opportunity in forensic anthropology for the development of information concerning the circumstances surrounding the deaths of decedents. For example, because this activity almost always is carried out by murderers on their victims, the manner of death can be accepted with little doubt as homicide. Given this, the examination of dismemberments has the greatest potential of any osteological analysis to provide data on perpetrators of this crime. For example, localized dismemberments involve the separation of only parts of the body (e.g., head, hands, fingertips) to hinder identification, or the removal of the limbs (especially the legs) to ease transportation and/or disposal of the body. However, generalized dismemberment involves cuts to all areas of the skeleton, usually clustering near or within the joint areas. This type of dismemberment is more indicative of a disregard for the victim than the expediency of body transport and/or hindering of identification. Thus, characteristics of dismemberments suggest the state of mind of murderers. Similarly, precise and well-chosen cuts around the joints may indicate that the perpetrator has knowledge of anatomy, or experience with the methods of butchery. Finally, similarities between different dismemberment cases may indicate that they share a common perpetrator (i.e., a serial killer). All this information assists law enforcement officials when investigating these deaths and when prosecuting those accused of such crimes.

According to Reichs (1998b), analyzing dismemberments is a five-step process. First, each cut bone end should be photographed, in black and white as well as in color, before soft tissue is removed. This will ensure that any residual information contained in the skin, muscle, fat, and other tissues will be documented. Second, if remains must be returned to family members for reburial, at least 3 inches of bone adjacent to any cuts should be removed and preserved for further analysis. Where the cuts completely bisect the bone, the segment removed should include both ends of the cut so that any false starts, which provide valuable information on the nature of the tool(s) used and the anatomical knowledge of the perpetrator, will be preserved. Third, when segments are removed from bone, a notch should be incised into the autopsy surface so that this cut is not mistaken for dismemberment. Fourth, all remaining soft tissue should be removed so that the evidence of postmortem changes will be clearly visible (see Chapter 6). Fifth, if desired, a mold and cast of the incisions should be made so that the floors of deep cuts are more easily visible. Vinyl polysiloxane is a favored substance for this process because it provides good detail for both the mold and the cast.

Generally, injuries due to dismemberments are caused by cutting (e.g., knives), chopping (e.g., axes), and chiseling (e.g., saws) implements. The types of damage caused by cutting and chopping instruments already have been described; because dismemberments usually occur shortly after death, the reader is referred to Chapter 14 for information on the appearance of these types of injuries during dismemberments. The effects of toothed instruments that chisel bone during dismemberments have been described well in an article by Steven Symes and colleagues (1998); thus, the rest of this section will summarize their discussion of saws and the taphonomic changes due to these types of instruments, with additions from other authors as noted.

Basics of Saws and Saw Damage

A wide variety of handsaws (see Figure 16.1) and power saws (with either straight or circular blades) can be used for dismemberment. Despite this variety, all saws generally can be divided into two types based on their function: crosscut and rip. **Crosscut saws** are designed to cut across the grain of the material being worked. To accomplish this, the edges of the teeth angle approximately 70° to the long axis of the saw. (Most meat and hacksaws and a large number of carpenter's saws are of this type.) The edges of the teeth of **rip saws** form a right angle (i.e., 90°) with the long axis; since these types of saws are designed to cut along the grain, this arrangement allows them to chisel their way through the material being cut. On both of these types of saws, the teeth are bent laterally from the main axis of the blade; this **tooth set** causes the groove formed by the saw action (called a **kerf**) to be wider than the blade, preventing binding while sawing.

The number of teeth (points) per inch in straight-bladed saws, whether hand or powered, varies considerably (Symes et al., 1998). Generally, ripsaws have three and a half to seven points per inch, while crosscut saws have between five and twelve per inch. The teeth of all saws form triangles that do not have equal sides. Usually, the front side is more vertical so that it can cut during the push stroke, while the backside slants more to allow easy movement during the pull stroke. Thus, most modern handsaws are designed to cut on the push, rather than pull, stroke. Similarly, straight-bladed power saws (e.g., band saw, jig saw) cut on the downstroke. Power saws, with circular blades, turn in such a manner that cutting is done with the vertical face of the teeth turning toward the table or platter.

Three types of marks are caused by saws on bone: superficial false start scratches, false start kerfs, and sectioned bone cuts (Symes et al., 1998). **Superficial false start scratches** are caused when the blade of a saw is drawn across a bone (usually on the pull stroke) without much pressure. These types of injuries can be mistaken easily for cuts from other sharp instruments; however, their location near a true kerf usually will prevent such misdiagnosis. **False start kerfs** (arrows 1 in Figure 16.2a) are caused by bouncing of the saw blade off the bone during a push stroke; these types of grooves are common with handsaws because it is difficult to control the blade until an adequate kerf has been created. **Sectioned bone cuts** (arrow 2 in Figure 16.2a) generally are deep kerfs that indicate that a number of strokes have been executed within the same groove. Sectioned bone cuts are of the most use in determining blade construction and therefore saw type.

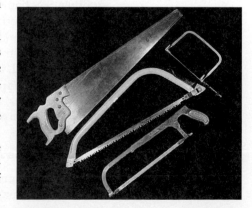

FIGURE 16.1 Various types of handsaws available for purchase. (Photo by Julie R. Angel)

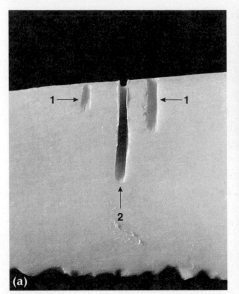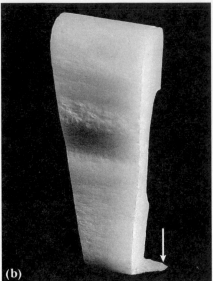

FIGURE 16.2 Effects of dismemberment by sawing: **(a)** false starts (*arrows 1*) and cut (*arrow 2*) on a sawed bone; **(b)** breakaway spur (*arrow*) caused by the emersion of a saw at the end of a cut; the presence of this feature indicates that the saw proceeded from the top of the bone toward the bottom. (Photos by Julie R. Angel)

When a saw cuts through a material, the kerf it produces can reveal characteristics of the cutting instrument. During cutting, striae are formed by the uneven action of the teeth on the wall of the cut; generally, power saws with small teeth create the finest striations, while those that are powered by hand with few teeth per inch cause the most prominent striae. In addition, the floor of the kerf can display characteristics of the teeth; a rough floor would indicate a coarse saw, and a smooth floor would indicate a saw with many teeth per inch. Unfortunately, the kerf floor is usually destroyed when a bone is traversed completely. However, traits of this kerf component often will be visible on a residual spur. This structure, called a **breakaway spur** (Figure 16.2b), is almost always present in complete cross sections because of breakage during the final cutting stroke.

The above features would appear to be permanent as they are imbedded in bone; however, other taphonomic processes may modify some, or all, of them to one degree or another. Stephanie-Marie Marciniak (2009) studied the effects of burning on the walls and floors of saw kerfs. Using the bones of pigs (*Sus scrofa*), she examined cut marks before, and after, burning to assess any loss of information due to this taphonomic process. She found that the striae left by some types of saws became difficult to identify after the burning process and, in some cases, were completely destroyed. By contrast, false starts and kerf floor were unaffected by burning. Thus, when forensic anthropologists encounter burned remains, they must be extra cautious when examining the ends of incomplete bones as evidence of dismemberment may have been diminished or completely removed.

Analysis of Saw Marks

As with any injury to bone, law enforcement officials want to know as much information on the damage, as well as the causative agent, as can be reliably determined from the human remains. When possible, three subjects should be addressed when dismemberments are analyzed. First, the cuts should be fully described, including information on the location of injuries and the number of cuts and false starts. Second, the direction of the saw cuts should be determined so that an assessment of the position of the body (i.e., on its back or face) during dismemberment or characteristics of the perpetrator (e.g., handedness) can be made. Third, information on the type of tool should be estimated from characteristics of the kerf when possible; this should include number of points, width of blade, shape of blade, and source of energy.

BASIC DESCRIPTION   Any analysis of saw damage should start with a thorough description of the cuts seen. Minimally, this should include the number of cuts and any attendant false starts or superficial false start scratches. The widths of incomplete cuts or sectioned bones with breakaway spurs should be measured with a caliper. In addition, the affected bone and the location of the cut on that bone (anterior or posterior, medial or lateral, proximal or distal) should be noted.

DIRECTION OF SAW CUT   Direction of cut involves two separate characteristics: the direction of saw progress and the direction of the saw stroke. The direction of saw progress can be determined from the location of false starts (see Figure 16.2a) and breakaway spurs (see Figure 16.2b). Thus, false starts located on the anterior surface of a bone with a breakaway spur on its posterior side would indicate that the saw operator started at front of the bone (probably with the victim lying on his or her back) and cut down through the bone until it was sectioned. The other component of direction deals with the saw stroke. The direction of this stroke can be told from exit chipping. When a saw cuts through material, the surface that is first encountered during the push stroke usually will be sharp and well defined. However, the surface through which the teeth emerge during the push stroke will exhibit small-to-large (depending on tooth size) spalls. These structures are prominent especially in power circular saws.

NUMBER OF TEETH   Unfortunately, with present technology, the number of saw teeth per inch cannot be determined precisely from characteristics of the kerf. However, the roughness of the kerf walls may be an indication of general tooth size. Rough gouges, such as caused by chain saws, would indicate a saw blade with few points, whereas thin striations on the kerf walls would indicate finer teeth (see Figure 16.3). Therefore, coarse versus fine probably is the only determination that can be made as to number of saw teeth.

BLADE WIDTH   Since the thickness of the saw blade cannot exceed the width of the kerf, an intact saw cut as illustrated in Figure 16.4 can be measured for an approximation of blade width. However, this saw characteristic is less than the distance across the teeth, due to the tooth set. Therefore, blade width generally is less than kerf width. As a general rule, the set of teeth does not exceed one and a half times the width of the blade (any greater ratio would cause the teeth to leave an uncut segment in the floor of the kerf, causing difficulty during cutting). Therefore, blade width can be estimated by dividing the breadth of a measurable kerf by one and a half.

BLADE SHAPE   When saws move through bone, they leave residual striae that approximate the shape (i.e., straight or curved) of the blade causing the cut. Generally, two types of striae are visible: fixed radius and nonfixed radius. Usually, fixed-radius striae, which indicate circular blades from power saws, appear as semicircular lines on the kerf walls of the cut material (see Figure 16.5a). These lines generally are the same shape throughout the entire surface of the cut, forming concentric arched lines. Although this sounds straightforward, differences in blade diameters (e.g., 6 to over 10 inches) and bone widths often make the determination of fixed-radius cuts difficult. Nonfixed-radius striae are formed from straight, rigid, and nonrigid blades. Rigid straight blades

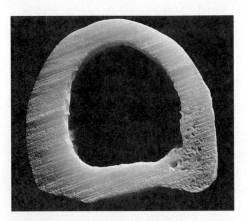

FIGURE 16.3 Fine lines (striae) caused by a fine toothed saw, in this case a hacksaw. (Photo by Julie R. Angel)

FIGURE 16.4 Vertical cut that could be measured to estimate the width of the saw blade. (Photo by Julie R. Angel)

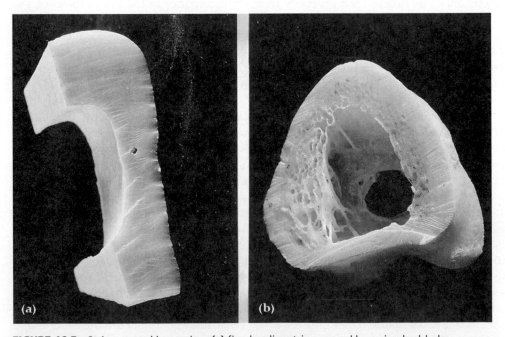

FIGURE 16.5 Striae caused by sawing: **(a)** fixed-radius striae caused by a circular blade; **(b)** slightly upwardly curving lines caused by changing the angle of attack during cutting. (Photos by Julie R. Angel)

form relatively linear lines that may or may not be parallel (see Figure 16.3); the occasions when the lines are not parallel indicate alterations in the angle of cutting (see Figure 16.5b) that can occur with, especially, hand-powered saws and chain saws. Nonrigid straight blades may bend around the object being cut, causing the striae to curve slightly.

SOURCE OF ENERGY   There are two sources of energy by which saws cut through materials: hand and power. Hand energy is the usual source of power with straight-bladed saws that work by reciprocation (i.e., back and forth movement). This movement, coupled with the inherent unsteadiness of human-powered motion, causes the kerf walls to be uneven both in flatness and in direction (saw progress). Handsaws generally produce groove walls that have more striae than power saws. In addition, they may change direction while cutting both in the vertical and in the horizontal planes. Thus, cuts that appear to be beveled at the edges or do not move straight through the material are more likely to have been made by a handsaw. By contrast, because of their faster speed and greater energy, power saws are more likely to leave cuts with smooth, almost polished walls. In addition, they have a tendency to be straighter in both planes because of their inherent steadiness.

ANIMAL SCAVENGING

Human bodies deposited on the surface outdoors or in shallow graves are prone to scavenging by animals. As pointed out by Douglas Ubelaker (1997) and William Haglund (1997a), animals have three major effects on human skeletons: scattering of bones, breakage through trampling, and removal by chewing of bony elements. (See Box 16.1 for a good example of this latter effect.) Although there are a number of animals that produce postmortem changes to bone, carnivores (especially dogs and coyotes) are responsible for the majority of them (Haglund, 1997a). This section presents a description of the effects of scavenging by these types of animals, focusing on the types of bone changes from chewing. Afterward, the less commonly seen effects caused by rodents will be described.

Carnivores

The changes to bone caused by carnivores are well presented by Haglund (1997a) in his review of this subject; his article forms the basis of this discussion. Four different types of primary postmortem injuries are attributed to these animals: punctures, pits, scoring, and furrows.

   Punctures are areas of bone that have collapsed under the force of carnivore tooth pressure. These appear most often as holes through thin sections of bone (e.g., the blade of the scapula where they superficially resemble projectile wounds) or on the ends of long bones. Although punctures share some characteristics with perimortem trauma, their lack of fracture lines and the presence of the other three injuries (i.e., pits, scoring, and furrows) prevent a misdiagnosis.

   Pits are similar to punctures except that they fail to penetrate through the cortical surface of bone (see Figure 16.6a). These injuries are similar to those caused by sharp instruments with conical points (e.g., ice pick), as during a stabbing action. Pits can be found on any skeletal element that a carnivore can encompass within its jaws.

   Scoring are scratches across the cortical surface of bones that usually occur as a group of parallel lines (arrow 1 of Figure 16.6b). These appear most often on the shafts of long bones where the animal's teeth contacted the cortex during soft tissue consumption. Even vultures may leave these types of taphonomic changes; see Nicole Reeves (2009). **Furrows** are similar to scoring except that they are deeper (arrow 2 of Figure 16.6b) and occur at the

> ## BOX 16.1
> ### Attack and Consumption by a Bear
>
> Turhon Murad and Margie Boddy (1987) describe taphonomic changes to human remains that appeared to result from an unlikely source. The case involved the skeleton of a man, discovered in early July, that had been severely scavenged by a large animal. Found near a car abandoned along a logging road in northern California, the remains consisted of a skullcap, several teeth in portions of the maxillae, and an almost complete lower jaw. In addition, incomplete diaphyses of both femora and tibiae, both humeri and the right radius, and a portion of the left os coxa were recovered from the area around the car. Analysis of these remains indicated that the person was a White male who was between 45 and 55 when he died. In addition, his height was calculated to be between 5 feet, 8 inches, and 6 feet, 2 inches. All these parameters agreed closely with the decedent's demographic profile when an identification was secured. Although a fine example of skeletal identification from fragmentary remains, the indications of scavenging made this case even more interesting.
>
> Many of the ends of the long bones exhibited spiral fractures and other evidence of gnawing by a large carnivore. Although not stated in their article, the missing facial elements of the skull almost certainly were the result of this same animal. In addition, one example of feces that was found in the vicinity of the car contained the remains of the fourth digit of a left human hand with the nail in place. All of this pointed to the possibility of a life and death struggle between the man and a large carnivore, most likely a bear (*Ursus americanus*), with the bear ultimately prevailing and consuming its adversary.
>
> Although a tempting scenario (as well as entertaining in a macabre sort of way), other evidence militated against this interpretation. First, information on the last sighting of the man and the first sighting (although not recovery) of the automobile indicated that the decedent had died sometime during the winter prior to the recovery of the remains. However, animal tracks were discovered in mud around the car, indicating that the carnivore had consumed the body during springtime, rather than winter when the ground would have been frozen. Additionally, analysis of the feces indicated that the bear had consumed foods available only in the spring. Finally, scavenging behavior is common among bears after first emerging from hibernation, whereas bear attacks on humans are rare at any time. Thus, the more likely situation was that the decedent was caught unprepared for the cold while traveling on the logging road during the late fall or early winter, where he perished from exposure. His body remained inside the car during the winter months, after which it was extensively scavenged by a passing bear or bears the following spring.

ends of bone. These grooves would rarely be misidentified as perimortem trauma because they almost always are accompanied by considerable bone end destruction (Figure 16.7).

In addition to the primary damage, carnivore scavenging can produce at least three types of secondary injury: fracture lines, splintering, and depressed fractures. Fracture lines are similar to the radiating lines seen in blunt and projectile trauma; they are due to the relatively static force imparted on the bones by the jaws of the carnivore. If this force is excessive, the second type of injury, splintering, can result. This takes the form of fingers of bone separated by fracture lines that radiate longitudinally (e.g., parallel to the long axis of a bone) from the area of contact. Finally, depressed fractures, with or without pointed floors, can be caused by animal chewing, especially if the posterior teeth are being used. These are different from pits, in that they are larger and have hinge fractures.

When carnivores (especially canids) scavenge human remains, they generally follow a rough pattern (Haglund, 1997a). Knowledge of this pattern, in conjunction with other information, lowers the probability that disarticulation due to animals will be mistaken for postmortem dismemberment. This sequence is best visualized as a five-step

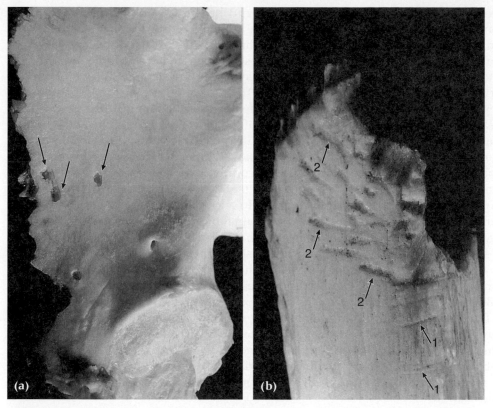

FIGURE 16.6   Effects of carnivore scavenging: **(a)** punctures (*arrows*) caused by carnivores during scavenging of an os coxa; **(b)** close-up of chewed bone ends showing scoring (*arrows 1*) and furrows (*arrows 2*) caused by carnivore teeth. (Photos by Julie R. Angel; specimens courtesy of the State of New Mexico, Office of the Medical Investigator)

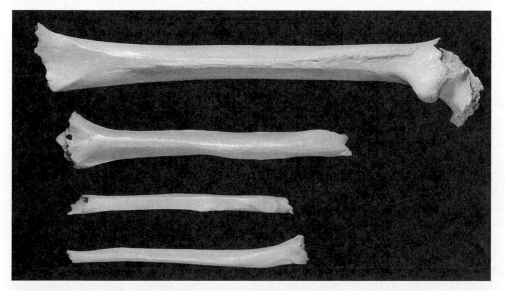

FIGURE 16.7   Removal of bone ends by carnivores. (Photo by Julie R. Angel; specimens courtesy of the State of New Mexico, Office of the Medical Investigator)

process. First, the soft tissues of the neck and head are removed and consumed. Second, the ventral thorax is opened and the contents of the abdomen and chest are eaten, and then the sternum is chewed from the ends of the ribs and eaten. This continues until the muscles of the pelvis and thighs are consumed. Third, the upper limbs, including the scapulae and all or part of the clavicles, are separated from the thorax. Fourth, the lower limbs are removed from the pelvis. Often this only includes the lower leg (tibia, fibula, and foot); however, removal of the femur at the pelvis is not unheard of. Also, this may involve removal of the pelvis from the spine at the lumbar or lower thoracic vertebrae. Fifth, although the major elements of the axial skeleton may remain articulated, usually these are removed from the area where the body was deposited. Thus, elements of the vertebral column may remain articulated, but the spine may be separated into several pieces (e.g., cervical vertebrae articulated but disconnected from the thoracic vertebrae). In addition, the long bones can become separated from each other (humerus from ulna and radius, ulna from radius), and their ends may exhibit damage from gnawing. Finally, if scavenging continues, all bones are disarticulated, scattered, and extensively chewed.

Comparison of this sequence with that of human-caused dismemberment described previously reveals basic differences. First, the pattern described by Reichs (1998b) does not include removal of the scapula and clavicle as in carnivore scattering. This is because, during dismemberment, the humerus usually is the only bone of the upper limb where detachment is attempted. Similarly, removal of the femur from the hip socket is rare; if the leg is removed, the proximal femur usually is cut (Reichs, 1998b). Finally, rarely are the anterior portions of the chest (i.e., anterior ends of ribs, sternum) removed during dismemberments; the thorax usually remains as a whole unit.

Marks from carnivore scavenging can occur on any bone small enough for the jaws of an animal to encompass. This usually entails the ends of long limb bones, ribs, and the edges of the os coxae. In addition, any osteological element small enough to be swallowed whole (e.g., bones of the hand) or delicate enough to be crushed and then swallowed (e.g., sternum) will exhibit taphonomic change (when recovered from animal feces). Similarly, small projections (e.g., transverse and spinous processes of the vertebrae) are common targets of carnivore chewing (Haglund, 1997a). Finally, although adult crania generally exhibit few scavenging marks due to their size, the mastoid processes and areas around the nose can manifest this type of damage.

Rodents

In a good review article, William Haglund (1997b) describes taphonomic aspects of rodents in relation to human bone, which are summarized here. Rodents occasionally will chew on bones with the apparent purpose of keeping their incisor teeth worn down or of obtaining supplementary calcium in their diet. The animals that usually cause this type of damage vary from voles and mice (which leave chew marks less than 1 mm wide), to rats and squirrels (whose marks are 1 mm to 2 mm wide), to marmots, beavers, and porcupines (with 2- to 5-mm marks). Generally, these animals do not contribute significantly to the consumption of soft tissue or the removal of body segments. Rodent chew marks usually are easily distinguished from those caused by carnivores because they leave straight grooves with relatively flat floors (rather than the sharp V-shaped floors of carnivore marks), and they usually come in pairs that meet to form a tip. Because the edges of the incisors are rounded, the width of the grooves may be smaller than the causative tooth. In some examples of rodent damage, the upper incisors embed in the bone and only the lower incisors cause parallel grooves. This type of damage generally is found only on the cortex of large bones; smaller tubular bones, such as metatarsals and metacarpals, normally will not manifest these types of defects.

FIRE DAMAGE

Because burning is a favored manner of disposing of the bodies of victims (especially murder), bones damaged by fire are not uncommon in forensic anthropology. (However, as seen in Box 16.2, identification can be done even when fire damage is extensive.) Heat and/or exposure to fire causes a number of distinct changes in bone beyond the charring and discoloration normally associated with this event. Pamela Correia (1997) presents a good description of what is known about the effect of heat on skeletal elements, and the reader is referred to her article for further details and references. This section summarizes her discussion and includes information from T. Dale Stewart (1979) and William Maples and Michael Browning (1994).

BOX 16.2
Identification of Cremains

William Maples and Michael Browning (1994) tell of a case in which cremated remains (called *cremains*), found along a highway, were thought to be those of a woman by her family. The woman in question had died after a long fight with cancer; her cremated remains were placed in a cardboard box in which they were transported to a cemetery and placed in a burial niche. The evening of the interment, a person traveling on a nearby highway found a cardboard box, marked with the decedent's name, containing ashes. The police then returned the box and its contents to the family, who immediately accused the funeral home of negligence. The outraged family asked for $10 million in compensation.

Maples was hired by the insurance company to determine if the ashes in the cemetery urn were those of the woman and that those found along the highway were not. Because of the difficulty inherent in examining cremains, he put together a team of forensic anthropologists to investigate. The process of cremation involves prolonged burning in a fire that reaches temperatures in excess of 900°C. Although this removes all soft tissue, the skeleton is left intact, albeit much reduced in size. After burning, the remains are ground up and pulverized such that little is recognizable as human bone. Although the skeleton does not survive in any form other than ashes and small chips of bone and teeth, prosthetic devices often are discernible even after this rough treatment.

Because the woman was old at the time of her death, it was reasonable to assume that she might have had such devices implanted during life. A search of her medical records indicated that she had had surgery that involved the use of hemaclips (small clamps used to close off blood vessels) and that those used in her surgery were made of tantalum, a rare metal for this purpose. Maples counted 29 hemaclips on her radiographs taken while she was alive and found 18 in the cremains from the cemetery; however, the remains found on the highway did not contain any such clips, tantalum, or otherwise.

Similarly, a search of the woman's dental records revealed a procedure that involved the placement of a post. Again a post was found in the cemetery remains, while no such prosthetic was recovered from the highway remains. In addition, the recovered post matched, thread by thread, those from radiographs taken by the woman's dentist.

Given this and other evidence, there was no reason to believe that the remains from the highway represented the woman in question or that the cremains from the cemetery did not. After the initial testimony by the first team member called to the witness stand, the family settled out of court for an undisclosed sum of money. However, Maples states that, judging from the smiles and handshakes of the insurance personnel, the settlement was for a sum well below the original $10 million.

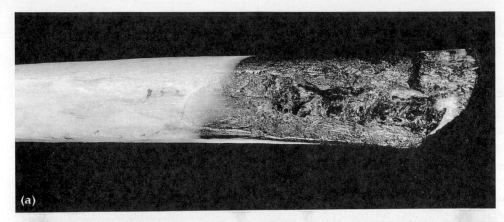

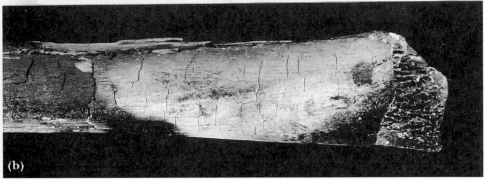

FIGURE 16.8 Effects of burning: **(a)** black discoloration of bone indicative of being subjected to heat of at least 700°C; **(b)** fire-caused checkerboard cracking of the distal diaphysis of a long bone. (Photos by Julie R. Angel; specimens courtesy of the State of New Mexico, Office of the Medical Investigator)

When bone is subjected to fire, it undergoes a series of changes in color that follows a predictable pattern. First it maintains the yellowish-brown color that it is while inside the body. As temperature rises and heat is applied over time, the color changes to a darker yellow or brown and then to black (see Figure 16.8a) as natural oils burn away and the organic substances within the bone are fully carbonized (Maples and Browning, 1994). With further heating, these compounds burn away and the bone changes to a dark gray, which becomes a lighter gray (with occasional blue) and finally a pure white composed only of the calcium salts deposited in the bone during growth. This last color indicates a state of complete **calcination,** which is characterized by light weight and brittle fragility, making the bones easily broken by even the slightest ill treatment.

In addition to color changes, bone tends to crack, warp, and distort when exposed to flame. Some research into bone burning has pointed to different expressions of these effects when bone was burned while fleshed, defleshed but green, or defleshed but dried; however, the review by Correia (1997) does not bear out these conclusions. Warping includes bending and twisting that make it appear as though a bone was made of rubber that was deformed intentionally by a person set on preventing recognition by shape. In addition to deformation, the cortex will exhibit cracks (Stewart, 1979) when the temperature and duration of burning are sufficient. Long bones will exhibit either a checkerboard pattern (see Figure 16.8b) or a series of crescents, depending on the thickness of the

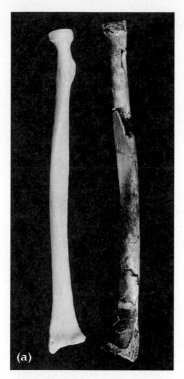

FIGURE 16.9   Further effects of burning: **(a)** concentric fracturing of a radius (right bone); **(b)** longitudinal fracturing of a distal humerus. (Photos by Julie R. Angel; specimens courtesy of the State of New Mexico, Office of the Medical Investigator)

cortical tissue. In addition, transverse or oblique ring fractures may be seen encircling the shaft (see Figure 16.9a), as well as longitudinal breaks (Figure 16.9b). The flat bones of the cranial vault and the blade of the ilium similarly will exhibit fire cracking. (In earlier editions of this book, Rhine [1998] was cited as saying that the skull also would explode from the buildup of steam inside the cranial vault. However, Pope and Smith [2004] did not observe this when they experimentally burned fleshed cadaver heads. Their findings indicated that braincase fragmentation is due to collapsed debris, recovery methods, and other such external forces.)

One final effect of burning is shrinkage. Inside the body, the oils and fats that saturate bone cause it to be larger through hydration than it would be in the absence of these substances. As these burn away or evaporate during heating, the entire structure decreases in size. This decrease is greatest in those areas that are composed only of cortical bone (i.e., tubular segments such as the diaphysis), while affecting areas enclosing trabecular bone less (i.e., articular ends). Studies of shrinkage indicate that there are three stages through which bone passes during burning. In the early stage of heating to temperatures of less than 700°C, bone shrinkage is minimal, ranging from being immeasurable to around 2%. During the second stage, with temperatures from approximately 700° to 800°C, 1% to 2% shrinkage is almost always present. Finally, in the over 800°C range, shrinkage averages between 10% and 15% (however, a value as high as 25% has been documented by Maples and Browning, 1994). Because these amounts may affect the calculation of stature or even attribution of sex, an estimation of the amount of probable shrinkage should be made by observing coloration changes.

TABLE 16.1   Correlation of Color, Temperature, and Bone Shrinkage Due to Heat[1]

Temperature (°C)	Color Change	Shrinkage (%)
Under 700	White, yellow, brown, gray, black	0 to 2
700 to 800	White, gray, blue	1 to 3
Over 800	White	5 to 25 (average 9.5%)

[1]Combined from data in Stewart (1979), Maples and Browning (1994), Correia (1997) and Thompson (2005).

The correlations among color changes, temperature, and probable shrinkage are presented in Table 16.1. Notice that colors of yellow and yellowish brown indicate little or no shrinkage, while black indicates a 1% to 2% loss in dimensions and gray to white color indicates significant shrinkage. Unfortunately, this information is so variable that a good reduction factor for gray to white bone is difficult to assign; given this, the best method with this type of bone is to assume a shrinkage of around 10% and adjust bone dimensions accordingly.

WEATHERING

Although rain can cause hydration of dried bone and wind can have a sandblasting effect on cortical surfaces, the weathering force that causes the greatest postmortem changes to the skeleton is sunlight. These changes usually occur after the soft tissue is lost and the bony elements have been exposed to the sun for an extended period of time. This type of weathering has two results. First, as the natural oils evaporate, bone begins to shrink in a manner similar to that seen with burning. All dimensions decrease in size to the same amount as bone exposed to temperatures of less than 700°C. Additionally, as drying continues, the cortex loses so much moisture that the top part of that surface shrinks to a greater extent than the underlying bone. This causes tension between the two layers that is relieved by the formation of cracks. Although these can take several forms, the most commonly encountered are mosaic or parallel-sided cracks seen over the bone's surface (Figure 16.10a). If this process continues, the topmost layer will begin to separate (Figure 16.10b), eventually flaking off and exposing the underlying cortex. With extended weathering, the bone eventually will disintegrate entirely by losing successive layers of these flakes. In addition to causing tension between layers of bone, drying can cause cracks to form along the long axes of bones (Figure 16.11a). In this case, tension develops between two or more segments of the skeletal element as one loses more moisture than the other(s). This tension is relieved by longitudinal cracking that allows the drier segment to shorten by the amount needed.

The second effect of weathering is warping (Figure 16.11b) due to uneven drying. If the bone is thin and pliable enough, the tension between two or more segments that are drying at different rates is relieved by a bending of the long axis toward the side that has lost the most moisture. This warping can be so dramatic that length measurements may not be possible even with complete bones. Similarly, warping can take the form of twisting about the long axis, thereby causing further distortion of the bone shape. In this respect, warping due to weathering is similar to that seen in burning.

Teeth also react to weathering forces. Cris Hughes and Crystal White (2009) studied the effects of high (e.g., summer) temperature on crack propagation in pig teeth. They found that cracks started in the pulp cavity and proceeded outward until it contacted the dentin-enamel junction. At that point it could stop because of the strength of this junction; however, if it had enough force, it could either continue along the junction

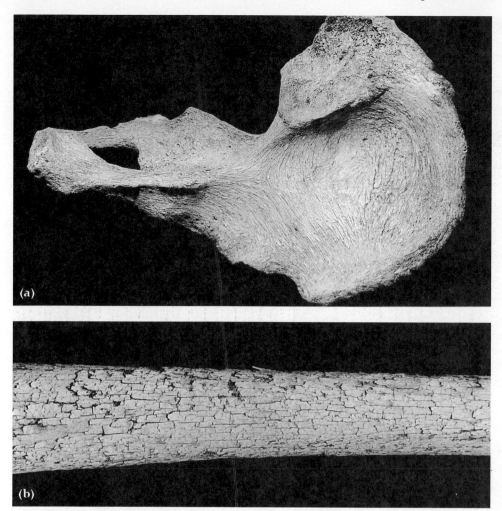

FIGURE 16.10 Effects of weathering: **(a)** cracking due to weathering on an os coxa; in this case, the cracks swirl along the grain of bone; **(b)** flaking of cortical bone due to severe exposure to sunlight. (Photos by Julie R. Angel; specimens courtesy of the State of New Mexico, Office of the Medical Investigator)

and then out through the enamel or simply propagate through the enamel. Of great importance is their finding that the cracks move from inside to the outer surface; this is in direct contrast to cracks due to trauma, which travel from the enamel surface toward the pulp cavity. Thus, forensic anthropologists who observe cracks in burned teeth must be careful to observe the direction of travel before making a judgment of perimortem trauma. Cracks on the surface that do not penetrate the pulp cavity probably are due to trauma, while those that do may indicate heat cause cracks.

Weathering also can obscure evidence of perimortem events. Stephanie Calce and Tracy Rogers (2007) demonstrated that bone submitted to freezing and thawing (e.g., bone deposited outside for an extended period) could both mimic the effects of blunt force trauma and obscure its presence. Additionally, they found that rain and/or snow could cause inward displacement of bone at a fracture site. Conversely, they found that soil erosion did not obscure evidence of perimortem fracture and that bleaching due to sunlight could accentuate it when bones were also stained by soil or surrounding vegetation.

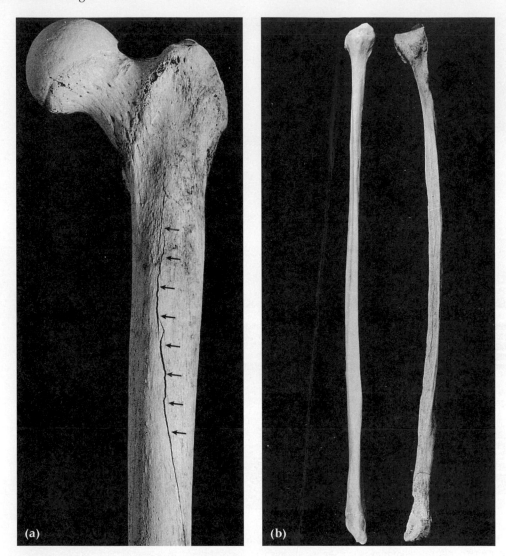

FIGURE 16.11   Effects of differential drying when exposed to the sun: **(a)** longitudinal cracking in a femur (*arrows*); **(b)** warping of a fibula (*right*) compared with a normal bone.   (Photos by Julie R. Angel; specimens courtesy of the State of New Mexico, Office of the Medical Investigator)

BURIAL DAMAGE

Burial has two primary effects on bone. First, mild to extreme cracking and warping of skeletal elements can occur, which takes the same forms already described for burning and weathering. Cracking in buried remains is distinguishable from those due to trauma by the lack of a point of impact (Figure 16.12a). The second effect of burial is erosion of cortical bone. This usually occurs only with long-term burial or interment in acidic soils; however, the resultant pitting of the normally smooth cortex can appear similar to a disease condition or old-age coarsening. One last effect of burial is not due to the soil, but due to the method of excavation. Unfortunately, damage during recovery (Figure 16.12b) can leave prominent injuries that may confuse subsequent osteological analysis.

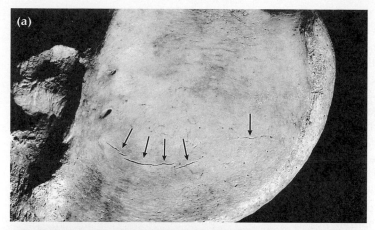

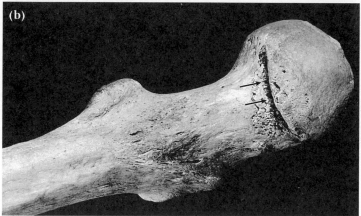

FIGURE 16.12 Effects of burial: **(a)** minor cracking (*arrows*) due to burial pressure (or simply dehydration); **(b)** excavation damage (*arrows*) due to a shovel during recovery of an interred body. (Photos by Julie R. Angel; specimens courtesy of the State of New Mexico, Office of the Medical Investigator)

WATER TRANSPORT DAMAGE

Damage due to water transport is well summarized by Nawrocki and colleagues (1996). In their article, which is condensed here, they describe three phases of fluvial transport. During the first phase, the body is moved as a unit from its point of initial insertion. The amount of this movement is affected by the currents that occur in streams or from eddies formed by the mixture of warm and cold water in lakes and seas. During this phase, all air escapes from the lungs and the body normally sinks to the bottom, where it can be damaged by scraping across objects and the components of stream beds or lake bottoms (i.e., gravel, sand).

Second, as the bacteria in the intestines begin to multiply and release gas, the body bloats and rises to the surface, where it can be moved farther by currents. This second phase of transport involves movement of separate body segments. Usually, the skull and mandible and the hands are the first elements to be separated from the rest of the body, followed by the feet, lower limbs, and the remainders of the arms. In cases of extreme decomposition, the torso and pelvis with attached thighs (which usually remain articulated) will separate. During this phase, the amount of transport depends on the type of body part. Generally, limbs will travel less on the surface than torsos distended by bowel gases. Similarly, some components will be more likely to catch on the various snags that are part of the fluvial environment.

The last phase of water transport concerns the movement of individual bones. The amount of mixing of skeletal elements and the differential transport of various bones make generalization of this phase difficult. However, round segments such as the cranium are most likely to be moved long distances, whereas flat elements are more likely to stay closer to their points of insertion in the water. In all these phases, the distance of transport can be great; movements of 50 or more miles have been reported in the forensic taphonomic literature.

Nawrocki and associates (1996) document two types of indicators of fluvial transport on the human skull: damage and modifications. Damage can include perforation or complete destruction of thin bones, such as those of the face. In addition, abrasion (including pitting, scratching, and gouging) of various projecting anatomical features occurs as the skull impacts objects on the bottom, or shore, of a body of water. Modification includes the loss of articulating bones (e.g., mandible from skull), staining from algae, hardening of silt in various orifices and the forming of a crust on the surface, and finally the deposition of aquatic insect egg casings. Although these modifications have been studied only on the cranium, other skeletal elements almost certainly are affected in a similar manner.

MISCELLANEOUS

Douglas Ubelaker (1997) lists a number of other forces that can both disperse and modify bone: wind (i.e., sandblasting), diagenic (geologic) movements, volcanic shock wave, release and breakup by ice and other forms of **cryoturbation**, acid attack by plant roots, mineralization by groundwater, and exposure to chemicals. The first four involve physical movement that can bend, break, disperse, or abrade skeletal elements. In this respect, modifications due to these forces may be indistinguishable from those caused by burial and water transport. Acid attack by plant roots generally will result in curved, crossing, and intersecting lines on cortical bone (Figure 16.13a), which eventually can

FIGURE 16.13 Miscellaneous postmortem damage: **(a)** root damage (lines at right angles to the long axis of the bone) to the cortical surface of a long bone; **(b)** deposition of minerals carried by groundwater to the distal end of a femur. (Photos by Julie R. Angel; specimens courtesy of the State of New Mexico, Office of the Medical Investigator)

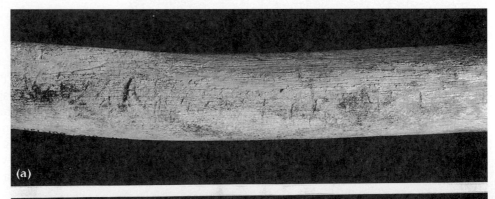

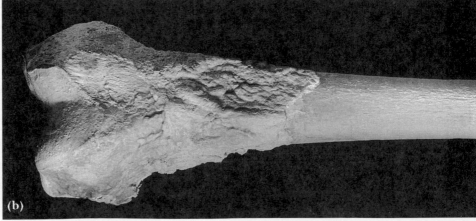

FIGURE 16.14 Cortical bone loss on a cranial vault due to a chloride bleaching agent.
(Photo by Julie R. Angel; specimen courtesy of the State of New Mexico, Office of the Medical Investigator)

lead to cortical flaking and disintegration of bony elements. **Mineralization** is caused by groundwater leaching through skeletal elements and depositing various salts into the bone matrix. The main effect of this process is to increase the weight to an amount unexpected of otherwise dry bone. Additionally, deposits of minerals may be visible on the surface of skeletal elements (Figure 16.13b). Finally, exposure to chemicals can result in cortical flaking (Figure 16.14) or even dissolution of bony segments.

Summary

1. Postmortem damage can be caused by any number of sources, including humans, nonhuman animals, heat (e.g., fire), weathering, burial, and water.

2. Dismemberment to prevent identification or to show disregard for victims is the most common form of human-caused postmortem changes to the skeleton.

3. A number of characteristics of dismemberments should be assessed from traits visible in bone; these include number of cuts, type of saw, and direction of cut.

4. Carnivores and other animals can cause splintering and bone loss by gnawing on osteological elements and by scattering skeletal segments.

5. The postmortem effect of burning includes charring, cracking, discoloration, warping, and shrinkage. These last two changes can affect the calculation of stature and the attribution of sex.

6. Weathering, mainly due to sunlight, has two manifestations on human bone: cracking and warping. Either cracks can be mosaic in form or they can run along the long axis of the bone; warping usually is manifested as bending and twisting around the bone axis.

7. Burial damage is similar to that seen in weathering and low-temperature burning, that is, cracking of the cortex and changing of the overall configuration of bone (warping).

8. Water transport damage includes abrading and scattering of skeletal elements.

9. There are a number of less common physical and chemical forces that also can affect human bone.

Exercises

1. Considering the marks visible in Figure 16.2a, was the saw most likely powered by hand or some other force? Support your answer.

2. A dismemberment is discovered, which consists only of the torso of the decedent. After cleaning, it is revealed that the legs were cut off at the proximal femur and the arms were removed at the proximal humerus. In addition, only the sixth and seventh cervical vertebrae are present. Describe what you would look for on the cut ends of the femora and humeri that would help you to assess the causative instrument.

3. From the torso described in Exercise 2, what is the likely motivation of the dismemberer? Support your answer.

4. A skeleton with clinging charred flesh is discovered in the ruins of a burned-out house. The color of the bone is yellowish brown to brown. Using the information in Table 16.1, what is the most likely temperature of the fire that caused this discoloration? What is the most likely percentage of shrinkage?

5. Skeletal remains that appear to be many years old are recovered from a grave. The long bones exhibit longitudinal cracks as well as abnormal bowing. The skull exhibits a series of fracture lines radiating from a single point on the occipital. From this information, describe why it is likely that the long bones exhibit burial damage, whereas the skull probably contains a perimortem fracture.

6. If the cut pictured in Figure 16.4 was measured to be ⅛ inch, what is the best estimation of the width of the saw blade that caused this cut? Is it likely to have been caused by a handsaw or power saw? Support your answer.

7. From the fire damage pictured in Figure 16.8a, what are the possible explanations for the differences in color between the burned end and the rest of the bone shaft? Give as many as you can think of.

8. Suppose that the bone displayed in Figure 16.10b was recovered from South Carolina. Given the data provided in Table 5.1, what is the most likely estimation of time since death for the individual represented by this bone? Support your answer.

9. Consider the saws exhibited in Figure 16.1. Knowing what you know of the hardness of bone, which of these instruments is the least likely to be chosen for dismemberment? Support your answer.

Additional Aspects of Individualization

In previous chapters, a variety of methods were described for determining characteristics of persons from their skeletal remains. Although the number of these methods already is impressive, there are other osteological examinations that can determine further characteristics of an individual. These other aspects of **individualization** increase the likelihood of a match between human remains and a missing persons file. In addition, they can provide corroborative evidence in a positive identification. Whatever the eventual use of the generated data, it is appropriate to describe the techniques that extend the biographical profile of decedents.

This chapter deals with three methods available to, although not widely used by, forensic anthropologists. First, the technique of facial reproduction is described. This procedure involves developing a face from the skull, which can be released to the news media in the hope that it will be recognized by a friend or a loved one who will provide information leading to an identification. Second, the issue of assessing handedness from the skeleton is discussed, despite the disappointing results of current studies. Third, methods for determining body weight from the skeleton are presented. This information can be used not only in the search of missing persons files, but also to aid in the production of facial likenesses.

FACIAL REPRODUCTION

Many times a search of missing persons files will not result in a potential match. In these cases, law enforcement authorities may attempt to elicit the public's help by asking that a likeness of the person's face be developed from the skull of the decedent. This is done either by sculpting clay to the appropriate soft tissue thicknesses directly on a skull (or a reproduction of it) or by drawing these soft tissues on a picture of the skull. The resultant representation of the appearance of the person in life is called a facial reproduction (Rhine, 1990a). (The terms *facial representation*, *facial restoration*, and even *facial reconstruction* also have been used.) This reproduction then is publicized using mass media such as television or newspaper. The hope is that both the facial likeness and a description of the decedent (e.g., White female between 25 and 30 years old, approximately 5 feet, 3 inches tall) will jog the memory of persons missing a friend or family member, who then will contact law enforcement officials with information leading to a positive identification.

Andrew Tyrrell and colleagues (1997) provide a useful summary of facial reproduction, including its history and methods, that will be condensed here. First introduced in the late 1800s, this technique was developed as a means of reproducing the face of historical persons from their skulls. Although a scientific curiosity for almost half a century, its true value was not realized until Wilton Krogman proposed its application to forensics. Krogman had a sculptress layer clay on the skull of a known Black man using commonly accepted facial tissue thicknesses. Once completed, he felt that the reproduction was easily recognizable. Unfortunately, he was criticized strongly for proposing the use of this technique. M. F. Ashley Montagu (1947) was particularly pessimistic when he stated that accurate reproductions are improbable, especially in Whites for whom the soft elements, such as hair, eyebrows, nose, lips, and subcutaneous fat, vary considerably. Because of this and similar criticisms, the method was not widely used over the next 20 years.

Since this early time, research into facial reproduction vindicated Krogman's belief in the usefulness of the method. When Clyde Snow and colleagues (1970) published a reevaluation, they stated that 80% of their reproductions elicited information that lead to a positive identification. Although this percentage is considered to be too high, most workers still report that approximately 50% of their likenesses produce favorable results. Thus, forensic anthropologists are almost unanimous in believing that the technique is useful in jogging the memory of friends or relatives, thus leading them to contact law enforcement officials about a missing person. However, the method has its limitations. Although some workers feel that it can go beyond simple jogging of memory into providing a positive identification, Rhine (1984) voices the majority opinion when he states that facial reproduction can never by itself establish a positive identification.

The method of facial reproduction is based on the realization that the face is composed of tissues, both muscles and skin as well as fat, that lie atop the bones of the facial skeleton. Further consideration of this fact reveals that these tissues are thick in some places and thin in others. Therefore, placing thick and thin simulated tissues correctly on a skull will result in an estimate of facial contour. To best place these simulated tissues, points have been chosen on the face that are based loosely on the position of underlying muscles and fat deposits, as well as on their importance in outlining the basic shape of the face. The number of points chosen for measurement varies from as few as 9 to as many as 32, although the 17 points in Figure 17.1 are sufficient for most purposes.

Once chosen, standards of thickness at these sites must be obtained on fleshed faces using any number of methods. The older and more popular technique involves direct measurement of cadavers using a thin blade or needle. In this method, an instrument is inserted into the skin and pressed inward until it contacts bone; the depth of penetration then is measured. This action is repeated at all the predetermined sites on

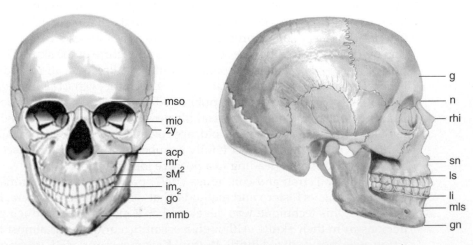

FIGURE 17.1 Location of points used in facial reproduction. (Abridged from Figure 6 of Stephan and Simpson, 2008a)/Illustration by Jay R. Alexander, I-hua Graphics.

as many subjects as can be found. The measurement of a large enough number of individuals will lead to average thicknesses for each of the facial locations.

Unfortunately, there are several problems with this technique. First, positioning the blade or needle at the correct location can be difficult. Although the sites for measurement are chosen for their importance in defining the limits of the face, their exact locations are not as straightforward as they appear. Second, inward deformation of tissue at the point of insertion has been encountered, reducing the accuracy of the resultant measurements. Third, differences between thicknesses of dead versus living tissue lead to further imprecision of tissue depths unless the measurements are taken immediately after death. As discussed in Chapter 5, the human body undergoes many postmortem changes, the most important of which for facial measurement are desiccation and bloating. Although faster in some climates than others, desiccation starts immediately at death and causes tissues to be thinner than in life. Bloating, occurring early in the decomposition process, can cause an extreme increase in thickness. Both of these changes can add to the inaccuracy of tissue depth measurements.

Newer methods employ ultrasound, computed tomography (CT), and magnetic resonance imaging (MRI) to determine tissue amounts. Although still plagued by the problem of locating the sites for measurement, these methods are more accurate than the blade or needle technique for two reasons. First, the machines used for this purpose have greater precision when estimating dimensions. Whereas inward deformation of tissues adds to the imprecision inherent in caliperlike measurements (particularly), CT and MRI instruments do not press in on soft tissues of the face. In addition, these devices measure dimensions more accurately than those obtained by physical measurement. Second, the tissue depths can be taken on the living. This eliminates the distortions caused by bloating and desiccation. Thus, although more expensive than the older technique, these methods probably will be used more in future studies.

Earlier research into observations of facial tissue thicknesses indicated that there were three sources of variation: ancestry, sex, and body type. However, an investigation by Stephan and Simpson (2008a) of 66 studies on diverse samples demonstrated that differences between the first two groups (ancestry and sex) were too small to have a significant effect on a facial reproduction. Thus, only tissue depths varying by body type should be considered when approaching this task, with obese persons being given greater thicknesses than those who are emaciated, while persons of "medium" weight have depths that are in between.

The process of facial reproduction is well described by John Prag and Richard Neave (1997), and their method will be summarized here. The first step is to reassemble fragmented skulls to arrive at as close an approximation of the original bone as possible. Not only is this necessary for the steps involving the application of clay onto the skull, but it has the added benefit of revealing any healed trauma that could have changed the contour of a person's face (see Box 17.1). After this (sometimes daunting) task is completed, a mold and cast of the decedent's skull are created. Using a cast for the reproduction has several purposes. First, it both maintains the chain of evidence and makes the original skull available for further study when a possible match with a missing person is made. Second, in some cases, casting may be necessary for crania that are too traumatized from blunt forces or ballistics to withstand the rigors of the reproduction process. Finally, skulls that are incomplete may have to be cast so that missing parts can be added without damaging the original material. These reconstructions are possible only when there is sufficient bone in both vertical and horizontal dimensions to allow for a good approximation of the original structure. Because the human face (as well as most of the human body) is bilaterally symmetrical, a missing facial side can be mirror-imaged from the side that is present.

> ## BOX 17.1
> ### Facial Asymmetry That Affected Facial Reproduction
>
> Douglas Ubelaker and Henry Scammell (1992) describe a case of a woman who sustained antemortem facial injuries that would have affected her overall appearance. The woman was represented by a complete skeleton, which was found near a major highway in Georgia. In association with the osteological remains were an artificial eye, a silicon breast implant, and an unidentified metal object. After examination by several workers, including Ubelaker, it was concluded that the person was a female in her early to middle twenties of White and Black ancestry who was around 5 feet, 3 inches tall when she died. What was most important from the standpoint of appearance was a massive healed trauma to the face.
>
> The right side of the frontal manifested a large hole from a poorly healed compression fracture of that bone. In addition, the lower border of the right eye also exhibited a poorly healed fracture that caused this structure to be noticeably lower than the left orbit. Also, the metal object was shown to be a surgical appliance for supporting a previously fractured right nasal bone. This information and the presence of the artificial eye and breast implant indicated that the person represented by the remains had suffered a severe blow to the right side of the face that required medical attention several years before death. Despite the efforts of the attending surgeon, the trauma would have left permanent scars and disfigurement. Because of the almost certain uniqueness of this person's appearance, a sketch was made for publication in the towns and countryside surrounding the discovery site. However, despite these efforts and the singular countenance of the decedent, the person was unidentified as of publication of this case.

After molding has resulted in a usable cast, the process can begin by obtaining information on body build so that the best tissue depths can be determined. The methods described in the Estimating Body Weight section of this chapter or from available clothing (i.e., dress or shirt size) and other associated items (belt sizes for estimates of girth) can help determine if the person was unusually thin or heavy in life, or if an average body build is appropriate. This information can be used to determine the best tissue depths from the means and standard deviations in Table 17.1 (for subadult see Stephan and Simpson, 2008b). Although no standards exist, it is reasonable to subtract one or two standard deviations from the mean of a measurement for thin persons, while adding that same amount to persons who were obese in life. Persons with an average build would be given the mean value from Table 17.1

Once it has been determined which tissue depths should be used, the next step in the process is to implant or affix spacers on the face of the cast that correspond to these thicknesses. This is done by first cutting 1/8-inch wooden dowels (many sculptors use pencil erasers) to the proper length for each of the predetermined facial locations. These can be affixed either by gluing them on the cast at the points of measurement (see Figure 17.2a) or by making them a little longer and inserting them in holes drilled for this purpose.

Next, artificial eyes are placed in the ocular orbits using clay for proper orientation (see Figure 17.2b); dark eyes should be used in Blacks and Asians, while light eyes may be appropriate with Whites. The protrusion (anterior position) of the glob within the eye orbit has received considerable attention over the years. As of this writing, the most recent is that of Carl Stephan and colleagues (2009), who present data that this structure should protrude approximately 16 mm from the deepest point on the lateral orbital margin. These same authors present findings of their study of the medial-lateral and superior-inferior placement of the eye glob such that the pupil is slightly superior and lateral to the center of the eye orbit. (More specifically, the pupil is inferior 46.6% of the

TABLE 17.1   **Adult Standards of Facial Tissue Thicknesses for All Groups[1]**

Site Number	Location – Definition	Mean (mm)	Standard Deviation (mm)
Median points			
G	Glabella – see Chapter 2	5.5	1.0
N	Nasion – see Chapter 2	6.0	1.5
rhi	Rhinion – most inferior point on the internasal suture	3.0	1.0
Sn	Subnasal – see Chapter 2	12.5	3.0
1s	Labrale superius – see prosthion in Chapter 2	11.5	3.0
Li	Labrale inferius – most anterior point between the medial lower incisors	13.0	2.5
mls	Mentolabial sulcus – deepest point on the mandible above the mental eminence	11.0	2.0
Gn	Gnathion – see Chapter 2	8.5	3.0
Lateral points			
mso	Mid-supraorbital – point on the superorbital rim at the mid-sagittal plane of the orbit	6.0	1.5
mio	Mid-infraorbital – point on the infraorbital rim at the mid-sagittal plane of the orbit	7.0	3.5
zy	Zygion – most lateral point on the zygomatic arch	6.0	1.0
acp	Alare curvature point – point ca. 3 mm lateral to the nasal aperture	9.3	2.0
mr	Mid-ramus – point on the center of the ascending ramus	17.5	4.0
sM^2	Supra-M^2 – point on the maxillary alveolar ridge superior to the second molar	26.0	5.5
iM_2	Infra-M_2 – point on the mandibular alveolar ridge inferior to the second molar	19.5	4.5
go	Gonion – see Chapter 2	10.0	6.0
mmb	Mid-mandibular border – the mid-point on the inferior margin of the mandible	10.5	4.5

[1]Abridged from Tables 5 and 6 of Stephan and Simpson (2008a); means and standard deviations (Std Dev) from columns 5 and 6 of Table 6

total distance between the superior and inferior orbital margins, and lateral 42.6% of the distance between the lateral and orbital margins.) T. Dale Stewart (1983) notes that the corners of the eyelids (canthi) should be in line with the malar tubercle (a small bulge medially on the inferiolateral border of the eye) on the lateral side and the lacrimal fossa (a furrow on the lacrimal bone) on the medial side. Carl Stephan and Paavi Davidson (2008) present two final statistics when they note that the distance between the canthi should be 75% of the distance between the lateral and medial orbital margins, and that

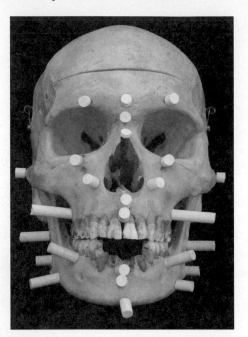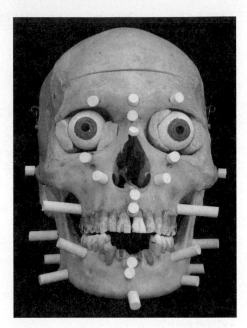

FIGURE 17.2 Reproduction of a face: **(a)** dowel (eraser) spacers; **(b)** placement of glass eyes to simulate these structures in life. (Photos by Steven N. Byers)

the distance between the orbital margins and the canthi should be approximately the same on the medial and lateral sides.

After these preliminaries have been completed, slabs of clay or Plastocene® are applied in the proper thicknesses to simulate skin and underlying fat, muscle, and other tissues (see Figure 17.3a). These slabs bridge the areas between the spacers to give fullness to the face. In addition to the spacers, muscle markings on the skull may help in thickness estimates not available from tables (e.g., thickness of neck muscles).

Reproduction of the nose in life requires special attention. Bonnie Hoffman and colleagues (1991) studied the relationship between width of the nasal opening and width across the "living" nose. Using cadavers of Whites and Blacks, they measured the widths of both the fleshed nose and (after removal of soft tissue) the nasal opening. It was discovered that the relationships between these were constant in Whites; that is, the living width is 12.2 mm wider than the nasal opening. This relationship is expressed in the following formula:

$$\text{living width} = \text{opening width} + 12.2 \tag{1}$$

However, in Blacks the relationship between the widths increases with the breadth of the nose; this is best expressed in the following equation:

$$\text{living width} = \text{opening width} \times 1.63 \tag{2}$$

Unfortunately, as with all such formulas, there is an illusion of accuracy. Hoffman and colleagues showed that there could be great differences between predicted and actual living widths. In Whites, 95% of actual living breadths fall within 5 mm on either side of the predicted breadths. This makes a difference of approximately 3/16 inch in facial reproduction. In Blacks, this amount is higher; 95% of actual living widths fall within 7½ mm to either side of predicted widths. This is a difference of around 5/16 of an inch.

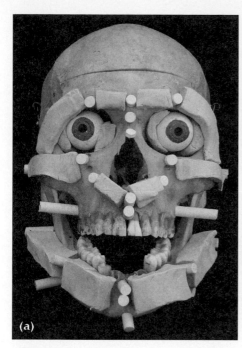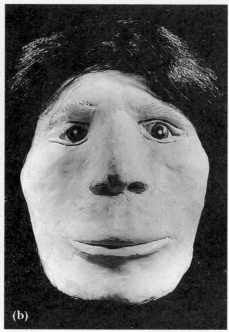

FIGURE 17.3 Reproduction of a face: **(a)** first layers of Plastocene® applied to the face to simulate muscle and fat tissues; **(b)** final layer of thin Plastocene to simulate skin in life with wig to give realism. (Photo "a" by Steven N. Byers, "b" by Julie R. Angel)

In addition to nasal width, attainment of a good approximation of the nose depends on two measurements of the nasal tip (called **pronasale**): projection and position. Carl Stephan and associates (2003) present a review of four methods commonly used in facial reproduction as well as a new method developed by themselves on a sample of 59 Australians of European decent. Although their technique is too complex for a book of this nature, the vertical position of pronasale (line PH in Figure 17.4) is approximately one-fifth of the way up a line connecting nasion and a point approximated by subnasale (line Na–S in Figure 17.4); that is, PH = 0.2 × Na–S. Using the method of George (1987), maximum projection of pronasale (line PP in Figure 17.4) anterior to a line connecting nasion and the most posterior point on the maxilla below the nasal aperture (line Na–M in Figure 17.4) is approximately 60.5% of that length in males (PP = 0.605 × Na–M) and 56% in females (PP = 0.56 × Na–M).

After formation of the nose, the mouth should be approached. Although several techniques have been offered for determining the width of this structure from various measurements of the face, the easiest method that has reasonable accuracy is that proposed by Carl Stephan and Maciej Henneberg (2003). They recommend setting the mouth width at 133% of the distance between the lateral borders of the canines. This is particularly attractive not only because it is easier than other methods presented in the literature, but also because it has an acceptable error rate. Thus, when forming this structure, keep track of the lateral borders of the canines and fashion the corners of the mouth approximately 1/3 wider (i.e., approximately 16% on either side) than these borders.

Once the preceding steps are performed, the process becomes a mixture of art and science. This is particularly true when the last layer, simulating the skin, is added over the preceding clay (see Figure 17.3b). Generally, this layer conforms to the underlying soft and hard tissues, but lessens their harshness and gives humanity to the face. Using information on ancestral groups provided by Carleton Coon (1969) and Alice Brues

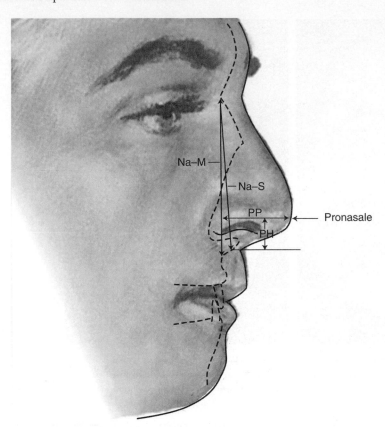

FIGURE 17.4 Lines and measurements used to determine the placement of pronasale (the most forward point on the nose).

(1977), the configuration of various aspects of the human head can be predicted with caution. For example, eye shape, such as the presence of an **epicanthic fold** (the fold of skin over the superior and lateral parts of the eyes) in Asians, would be modeled. In cases where little admixture is suspected (e.g., native-born Japanese and Chinese), the folds would be more developed; in cases of Native Americans these structures would have a lesser expression. Similarly, persons suspected to be of Chinese ancestry may be given **fat pads** under the eyes. Both of these structures would be absent in most reproductions of Whites and Blacks. In addition to the eyes, the shape of the lips and mouth can be affected by ancestral group membership. Blacks and some Asians have thick, **everted** (outwardly turned) lips, whereas Whites and most Asians and Native Americans exhibit thin lips.

In addition to ancestral group, age can play a part in the ultimate appearance of the skin. Older persons are more likely to show wrinkles, especially around the eyes (more pronounced after 30) and mouth, as well as on the forehead. Similarly, in older adults (e.g., over 50), the lateral edges of the eyelids droop, partly obscuring the pupil of the eye.

Finally, the shape of the ears would be determined by the sculptor because the configuration of this body part cannot be estimated from characteristics of the temporal bone. (This is unfortunate because these can protrude outward or fold inward, as well as having lobes that attach or hang free.)

Once the skin layer has been sculpted, a wig usually is placed on the head to add realism to the reproduction (Figure 17.3b). Given the differences between ancestral groups for this trait, there are some guidelines for the type of hair used in this addition. Generally, Asians have straight black hair while, in Whites, it is slight to medium wavy and light (blond or red) to dark in color. In Blacks, curled to strongly curled dark hair can be seen, except where the cultural practice of straightening is prevalent. Also, facial hair among males may be found, particularly with Whites because this group has the most body hair. In the areas of hairline and cut or style, there are no guidelines, leaving the configuration of these up to the forensic sculptor.

Other hair characteristics include graying for persons over 50 years (except for artificial coloring in some females and males), as well as balding in Whites and Blacks (but rarely in Asians). Finally, there are no guidelines for eyebrows except that some women pluck these hairs to the point that they are thin lines above the eyes, and in males these structures can bristle with older age.

The desired result of the application of these and the previously described methods is a reproduction that is average in appearance (Stanley Rhine, personal communication). By avoiding extremes, recognition by a wide variety of people is possible, thereby increasing the chance of a personal identification. Through the years three persons have gained prominence as being particularly skilled in bringing facial reproductions to life. Betty Pat Gatliff is a retired medical illustrator whose interest and ability in facial reproduction have earned her an international reputation for her work in this area. Mary Manheim is director of the Forensic Anthropology and Computer Enhancement Services (FACES) laboratory at Louisiana State University where she uses facial reproduction as an aid for solving unusually intractable cases. Karen Taylor is a forensic portrait artist who has turned her talents to making faces on skulls. All of these individuals teach their art/craft to others, including to members of (some prominent) law enforcement organizations.

Although the method described provides for a useful likeness that can be publicized by law enforcement authorities, it is relatively slow and expensive and requires specialized skills to be performed. Two alternatives combat these problems. First, using the given tissue thicknesses, a face can be drawn on a picture of the skull. Although this decreases the time needed to arrive at a completed reproduction, it suffers from the dual problems of requiring special skills to actualize and of resulting in a two-dimensional image that cannot be photographed from any angle, as can a clay model. The other method uses a computer to generate a picture on the skull employing, again, the facial tissue thicknesses (see Ubelaker and O'Donnell, 1992, for a description). Although this method requires special software, it is less expensive after the initial investment and is faster and requires less skill to use than the other two methods.

ASSESSING HANDEDNESS

In earlier editions of this textbook, the method of T. D. Stewart (1979) was described as a means of estimating the handedness of decedents. Stewart based his system on the belief that this characteristic could be determined from the skeleton by identifying the side with the largest and most modified arm bones. Because (especially heavy) use will add bone mass and reshape contours, he reasoned that the most modified side would indicate handedness (i.e., larger and more modified right arm bones would come from a right-handed person). Unfortunately, several studies have not supported this belief. Amanda Blackburn and Christopher Knüsel (2006) found that the width of the distal humerus (epicondylar breadth) was only correlated with handedness in 68% of 50 living persons of known handedness. Marie Danforth and Andrew Thompson (2008) tested the value of dimensions of arm bones on a series of 137 decedents of known handedness and did not find any measurements that were of value for assessing this characteristic. Thus, given the state of knowledge as of this writing, handedness cannot be determined with any accuracy from the skeleton.

ESTIMATING BODY WEIGHT

Several attempts have been made to determine body weight from characteristics of the skeleton. Some forensic anthropologists (Michael Charney, quoted by Jackson, 1996) believe that a reasonably precise estimate of this statistic can be made from four factors: sex, muscle markings, height, and skeletal robusticity. This belief is based on observations in the living. Because they usually exhibit more muscle mass, males are expected to be heavier than females of approximately the same size. Similarly, because larger muscle markings indicate greater weight (muscle weighs more than fat tissues), skeletons with well-defined markings would weigh more than persons with light markings of approximately the same size. Also, skeletal robusticity would indicate greater living weight because thick bones not only are heavier than thin bones, but also indicate greater weight due to bone mass increase under stress. Finally, because taller people usually weigh more than shorter people, greater skeletal stature would indicate greater weight.

The process by which body weight is determined from these characteristics is as follows (see Box 17.2 for an example case). First, a determination of sex and stature should be performed using the methods described in Chapters 8 and 10. Next, height–weight charts, such as those published by the National Institutes of Health, can be consulted, which correlate body weight with these two characteristics. Then, accounting should be made for skeletal robusticity, with thin and light bones indicating weight from the lower end of the range provided by the chart and robust and heavy bones indicating weight from the upper range of the chart. Similarly, heavy muscle markings would indicate that again the upper range of the chart should be used, whereas slight muscle markings would indicate that the lower end should be used. Finally, the presence of clothing can provide information on body build (e.g., small dress sizes and narrow-waist trousers would indicate thin and therefore light people), thereby increasing the precision of the estimate.

Although such estimates are possible when supplementary evidence is available (e.g., clothing), the determination of body weight directly from the skeleton is more

---

BOX 17.2
Determining Body Weight from a Skeleton in Missouri

Donna Jackson (1996) describes a case investigated by Michael Charney in which he developed an estimation of body weight from osteological remains. The case involved a partial skeleton recovered from a Boy Scout ranch in Missouri. The remains consisted of seven ribs, a nearly complete skull, four long limb bones (most with the ends removed, presumably by carnivores), a right os coxa, and a number of foot bones. His demographic analysis indicated that the person was a short, approximately 5-foot female of Asian ancestry who was in her mid-twenties when she died. To further describe the individual, Charney attempted an estimate of body weight.

The data on sex and height already had been developed, which allowed the use of a medical height–weight chart. However, to further refine this statistic, the sizes of the muscle markings were examined to assess if the person was engaged in strenuous activity while alive. If the woman was particularly athletic or was employed in a physically demanding job, these would have been more developed than the smooth areas visible on the skeleton. In addition, the overall thicknesses of the bones were relatively small for their lengths, indicating a person of slight build. All this information suggested that the weight of this person would be best estimated from low values presented in the height–weight chart. By using this approach, Charney estimated that the woman was around 110 pounds. When an identification was finally made, the person was a 5-foot, 33-year-old woman born in Thailand living with her American husband in Missouri. The estimate of weight was vindicated when she was described as "petite" and not carrying excess body fat.

TABLE 17.2 **Determination of Living Weight of Males from Skeletal Weight[1]**

Regression Equations	Standard Error
Whites	
Living wt = 0.024 (dry skeletal wt) + 50.593	20.1
Living wt = 0.233 (dry femur wt) + 57.385	22.2
Blacks	
Living wt = 0.013 (dry skeletal wt) + 85.406	13.7
Living wt = 0.163 (dry femur wt) + 76.962	13.3

[1]Taken from Baker and Newman (1957).

desirable because of its wider applicability. Paul Sciulli and Richard Pfau (1994) researched the value of predicting living weight from age and femur diameter in children. Although there was a strong correlation between these characteristics, they found that body weight estimates could vary by as much as 200%. Paul Baker and Russell Newman (1957) sampled the skeletons of 115 White and Black male soldiers who died during the Korean War in an attempt to determine body weight from bone weight. Their findings are summarized in the four regression equations given in Table 17.2; in these formulas, skeletal weight is provided in grams and living weight is given in pounds. As can be seen, the standard errors of the estimates are fairly high, indicating a wide 95% confidence interval (CI) for body weight estimates. (The smaller size of the standard error for Blacks almost certainly is due to the smaller number of persons from this group in the sample, some 20 individuals, than Whites.)

Unfortunately, all these techniques are riddled with problems of precision. Despite the apparent simplicity of the method involving demographic characteristics and skeletal observations, extremely wide variations can exist between these factors and living body weight. Similarly, the variation seen in the methods using bone characteristics is also great. For example, the determination of a White male as weighing 180 pounds in life from a 526-gram femur, provides a 95% CI of 136 to 224 pounds; such estimates are so imprecise as to be unusable. The situation with both of these methods is so unfavorable that most forensic anthropologists will not attempt to determine this parameter from the skeleton. Therefore, without supporting information from other items such as clothing, living weight should not be estimated from the skeleton except by the most experienced workers.

Summary

1. Facial reproduction can be used as a last resort if a search of missing persons files has not revealed a possible match.
2. The general approach in facial reproduction is to mold and cast the original skull, apply spacers that indicate the amount of tissue thickness at various places on the facial skeleton, and fill in the area between and around these spacers with clay to mimic the look of human tissue.
3. More modern methods for reproducing facial likenesses use computer software to produce faces on images of the skull.
4. Current research indicates that handedness cannot be estimated by comparing differences between the dimensions of right and left upper limb bones.
5. Body weight can be determined, only within a broad range, by observations, as well as by measurements and weights of specific bones within the skeleton.

Exercises

1. Considering the variability in the tissue depths used in developing facial reproductions, is it reasonable that this technique is not accepted as a form of positive identification by the legal community? Support your answer.

2. If a skeleton was found without a scapula and the bones of the right side were larger (both in thickness and in length) than the left, would it be reasonable to state that the person was right-handed and why?

3. A skull is found that is considered to have belonged to a female of White ancestry. Using the information given in Table 17.1, what would be the most likely thickness for the forehead in midline, nasion, and the tips of the nasal bones and chin?

4. Suppose that the skull in Exercise 3 is from a female of Asian ancestry. What are the measurements for the points listed?

5. What is the most likely weight of a White male whose femur is 180 grams? What is the 95% CI for that weight? Suppose that the remains are found in association with a pair of pants with a 42-inch waist; how would the estimate of body weight be affected?

6. If the entire weight of the skeleton of the person described in Exercise 5 is 1750 grams, is the resultant estimation of weight reasonable when compared with the estimate derived from the femur?

7. What are the main features of a facial reproduction that are affected by membership in the three main ancestral groups discussed in this book?

18

Obtaining an Identification

The terminus of forensic anthropological analysis is the attainment of an identification of osteological remains. Although the determination of circumstances surrounding the death of decedents is important, no further investigation of medicolegally significant skeletal material can be performed until the remains have been matched with a missing person. This not only allows for the continuance of the investigation of a suspicious death, but also provides closure to the family of the deceased, a service that forensic anthropologists describe as one of the greatest rewards for their work (Stan Rhine, personal communication; Ubelaker and Scammell, 1992; Manhein, 1999).

Currently, there are two types of identifications: **positive** and **probable. Positive** (sometimes called **personal**) **identification** involves the use of antemortem information that is so unique that, when an exact match is made with postmortem data, the remains are determined to be associated with one person *to the exclusion of all others*. This is the type of identification that is normally associated with forensic work; that is, human remains are identified as those of one and only one person. Probable identification involves determining the identity of remains by using the point-by-point comparison of multiple sources of antemortem and postmortem data. As the number of matches between these two sources increases, the probability that the remains are associated with the person represented by the antemortem data becomes so large as to be considered proof of identity Although it appears inaccurate, this type of identification can be just as compelling, and ultimately acceptable in a court of law, as positive identification.

This chapter is divided into four parts. The first deals with those methods used to obtain a positive identification, while the second part deals with probable identification. The third part deals with Forensic Odontology (the use of teeth in forensics); this subject deserves a separate section since it has applications to both positive and probable identifications. Finally, a section on miscellaneous methods is presented.

POSITIVE IDENTIFICATION

In previous chapters, methods were presented for gathering information on individuals from only their skeletal remains. Demographic characteristics, evidence of trauma, preexisting osteological conditions, and even reproduction of facial form can be determined by applying the proper methods to human bones. However, once a tentative match with a missing person has been made, a new set of techniques must be employed to yield the positive identification. The most frequently used of these are the techniques of forensic odontologists, who compare pre- and postmortem tooth restorations (see Forensic Odontology section of this chapter) to determine identity. In addition, forensic anthropologists also have methods for this purpose such as comparing antemortem radiographs with x-rays from forensic cases, matching medical records with unique surgical and osteological features, and so forth. Despite the divergence in particulars of these techniques, all rely on matching the (normally small) unusual traits that exist within the skeleton and teeth of each person with antemortem medical and dental records. For this reason, any characteristic proved to vary among persons can serve to uniquely identify decedents from their skeletal and odontological remains.

Radiography

The basic method of obtaining a positive identification through radiography involves comparing antemortem radiographs of a missing person with those obtained from a decedent's skeletal remains. This involves both a point-by-point visual comparison between osteological structures and a match between measurements taken on the two radiographs (Krogman, 1962). When all attributes are in agreement, a positive identification is concluded. An especially favored feature for this type of analysis is the frontal sinus, because extensive study has demonstrated that these structures are unique to individuals and therefore can be used for this purpose (Ubelaker, 1984). In the past, any trait of a nature pictured in an antemortem radiograph has been used. This has included the unique shape of a first rib (Maples and Browning, 1994), an odd contour of the proximal edge of a scapula (Ubelaker and Scammell, 1992), and a defect on the dorsal side of a patella (Riddick et al., 1983), to name only a few. However, with the greater and greater emphasis on *Daubert*, forensic anthropologists have begun to develop standard methods for gathering radiographic data, and testing its reliability and replicability before using in a forensic context. In the following section, the formal method for comparing the radiographs of the frontal sinus will be presented. Afterward, the more general methods for obtaining identifications from other bony structures will be summarized.

FRONTAL SINUSES   As described in Chapter 2, the frontal sinus is an open area between the inner and outer table of the frontal bone just above the eye orbits (see Figure 18.1). Estimates range from as few as 5% to as high as 27% of adults lack this structure. However, when present, this sinus usually is composed of right and left sides, divided by an either complete or partial **septum**. The right and left sides (called **cells**) vary in size and shape. Especially important is the distinctive configuration of the upper border

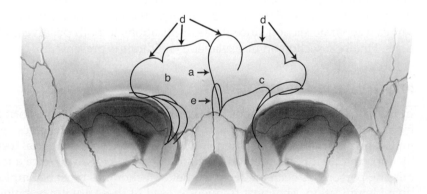

FIGURE 18.1   Line drawing of the frontal sinus showing its component parts:
(a) septum, **(b)** right and **(c)** left halves, **(d)** scalloping on superior border, and
(e) medial cells. (From W. Krogman Figure 82 *The Human Skeleton in Forensic Medicine*,
1st ed., 1962. Courtesy of Charles C. Thomas, Publisher Ltd., Springfield, IL)

of these cells; referred to as **scalloping**, this characteristic is believed to be unique to each individual person Additionally, the lower part of the sinus halves can exhibit other cells that appear to be extensions of those of the ethmoid sinus.

In previous editions of this textbook, the method of Wilton Krogman (1962) for obtaining identifications involving frontal sinuses was discussed in some detail. In recent years, more complex methods have been developed and tested for accuracy in the spirit of *Daubert*. Christensen (2005) studied the configuration of the upper border of the sinuses by describing it as a series of overlapping ellipses. She found an acceptably low probability of false positives in the radiographs of 503 persons from documented and archaeological skeletons. Similarly, Roberto Cameriere and colleagues (2005, 2008) modified an earlier method developed by Yoshino et al. (1987), where aspects of the frontal sinuses (e.g., area, symmetry, upper border outline, septa) were described using a series of ordinal scales (see Chapter 1 for discussion of ordinal and other scales of measurement). They also found a low probability of false positives in their two studies of almost 200 persons. Although both of these methods are too complex for a book of this nature, these workers have helped to ensure that the use of frontal sinuses for identification meets the guidelines described in *Daubert*.

When there is concordance between pre- and postmortem features, an identification is considered complete. Unfortunately, for observations and measurements to be accurate, the postmortem radiographs must be taken using the same technique as that for antemortem film (Ubelaker, 1984). This requires that the distance of the x-ray tube to the skull and the space between the subject and the film match these same distances in the antemortem radiograph (otherwise, divergence of the beam may cause magnification of the sinuses). Additionally, both the side-to-side and top-to-bottom angles must match. The effects of these problems can be mitigated by taking postmortem radiographs as many times as necessary to match the above features. One last problem in this analysis is the clarity of the antemortem radiograph. Unfortunately, this film can be somewhat blurry, making comparison difficult; in these cases, the forensic anthropologist must work carefully to ensure that all observations and measurements match properly.

OTHER STRUCTURES   In addition to those of the frontal, the sinuses of the ethmoid, maxillae, sphenoid, and mastoid processes can be used to obtain a personal identification if antemortem radiographs of these features are available. Stan Rhine and Kris Sperry (1991) positively identified a person using radiographs of the temporal bone near the ear opening. They compared pre- and postmortem radiographs looking for concordance between the cell configurations of the mastoid sinus and for the general shape of the mastoid process. In addition, the arterial pattern on the inside of the skull was similar in both radiographs. When these characteristics matched perfectly, the identification was considered positive.

In addition to sinuses, the pattern of trabecular bone and cranial sutures has been used for personal identification. As described in Chapter 2, the metaphyses of long bones are reinforced by a special kind of bone that is laid out in a crisscross pattern that has the appearance of a sponge. Because this pattern is complex and affected by the stresses applied to the bone, it is considered unique to each person. Therefore, an antemortem radiograph of one of the long bone ends can be compared to its postmortem counterpart to develop an identification. Tracy Rogers and Travis Allard (2004) discussed the validity of using cranial suture patterns, visible in antemortem and postmortem radiographs or computed tomography (CT) scans, for positive identification. They feel that these structures have been shown to be sufficiently individualistic to use for this purpose.

Finally, any antemortem pathological condition or anomaly (see Figure 18.2) that could be visible radiographically can be used for identification purposes (see Murphy

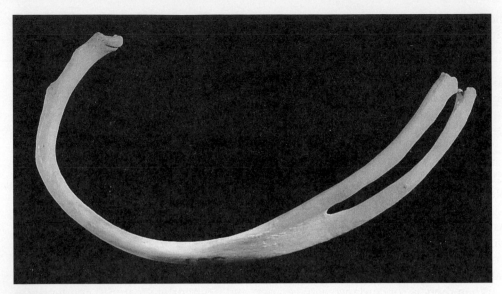

FIGURE 18.2 Bifid rib; if found in an antemortem radiograph, this feature could provide support for a positive identification. (Photo by Julie R. Angel)

and Gantner, 1982, for multiple examples). In addition, rare enough antemortem conditions that are only textually documented can serve this purpose. An example of this is the case of a femur manifesting an unnatural angulation due to the imperfect setting of a fracture. The antemortem records of a missing person described a break to the proximal femur that agreed closely with this angled bone. Because all demographic characteristics matched and the placement of the fracture and its deviation are so rare, a positive identification was obtained (Rhine, 1998).

Surgical/Dental Devices

Surgically or dentally implanted devices or medical supplies can be used to determine the identity of skeletonized remains (see Shepherd et al., 2010 for an example). Devices and prosthetics such as those pictured in Figures 3.23, 3.24, 15.9(b), and 18.8 have value for this purpose because they contain a unique number assigned by the manufacturer. Often this number can be traced to the surgeon or dentist who implanted them, thereby resulting in an identification. Thus, any appliance found with the remains of a decedent should be studied in case it can help provide an identification.

PROBABLE IDENTIFICATION

As described above, a probable identification can be made by combining the results of the previous methods to the point where it is highly probable that the decedent is the person represented by the antemortem records. Since these methods have already received considerable attention, their use in the identification process will be discussed only briefly. A method that has not been described, photographic superimposition, will receive more attention.

Combining Information

The Scientific Working Group for Anthropology (SWGANTH) is proposing that five factors be combined, when available, to develop a probable identification. First, forensic anthropologists should consider the aspects of the biological profile: ancestry, sex, age, and stature. When these match with antemortem records, the case for an identification is supported; when one or more of these do not match (particularly a firm characteristic such as multiple unfused epiphyses which cannot occur in an old adult), the decedent is excluded. Second, medical/dental charts and notes should be compared with the postmortem remains for similarities. As with the biological profile, when a decedent displays a medical condition that matches this information, the identification is supported; conversely, an obvious problem that is noted in medical records but is not seen in the decedent argues for exclusion. Even if not noted in medical/dental records, various anomalies and pathologies that could be seen in a person when alive (e.g., dwarfism) can be valuable. Finally, personal effects and other material evidence gathered at the recovery scene can be used by forensic anthropologists to support a probable identification.

When combining the results of multiple sources of information, **Bayesian statistics**, including the likelihood ratio, are useful as a means of identifying a decedent. Bayesian statistics use known probabilities to help in the determination of the probability of an event (see any basic textbook on probability and statistics for a discussion of Bayes' Theorem and any of the textbooks that deal exclusively with this subject). Dawnie Steadman and colleagues (2006) present a discussion of how this type of statistic can provide an identification by combining the probabilities of obtaining each of the biological characteristics of sex, age, stature, and pathology in a skeleton. In their case of "Mr. Johnson," they calculate the probability of obtaining the visually assessed pelvic traits in a male, given that Mr. Johnson was male. (As pointed out in earlier chapters, there is overlap between the males and females for the characteristics used by forensic anthropologists to attribute sex; Steadman and colleagues go beyond the mere mention of this overlap by calculating a probability of sex given this overlap.) After calculating similar probabilities for the biological traits available, they combine these to obtain a probability that it is 3 million times more likely that the skeleton they analyzed is "Mr. Johnson" than it is not. Although some object to their method (see Anderson, 2007), the use of probability and statistics will continue to expand in future forensic anthropological research and case work.

Photographic Superimposition

One of the earliest methods developed in forensic identification involved superimposing pictures of skeletal remains onto photographs or portraits of persons when they were alive (see a description of the Ruxton case in Chapter 1; see Maples and Browning, 1994, for further details). The two images are compared, point by point, both qualitatively and quantitatively for agreement or disagreement. Although it can be used with "normal"-looking people, this method is useful particularly with people who have distinctive facial and other characteristics (e.g., oddly spaced, chipped, rotated, or missing teeth visible in a smile). If, after the analysis, there is significant nonconcordance, then the method provides positive evidence of exclusion (i.e., the remains cannot be from the person represented in the antemortem picture.) However, if there is significant agreement, an identification is only supported, not concluded (see Box 18.1 for an exception). This is due to a small but significant number of times that false positives result during this type of analysis (Austin-Smith and Maples, 1994).

As described by Dana Austin-Smith and William Maples (1994), one method of superimposing antemortem and postmortem images is to place a negative of a skull over the photograph of a person so that osteological points can be compared to areas of the face. Pictures of the skull and face can be treated similarly, see Figure 18.3. This method is relatively difficult because the negative and photograph must be the same size. To combat this problem, the images can be made into photographic slides and the

> ## BOX 18.1
> ### Positive Identification from a Face–Skull Superimposition
>
> Douglas Ubelaker and Henry Scammell (1992) describe a case in which it was reasonable to conclude a positive identification from the superimposition of a skull with the picture of a woman when she was alive. The case involved the skeleton of a young adult black woman recovered from an agricultural field in Ohio. Evidence indicated that the remains were those of a missing woman from the area; however, because there were no dental or medical records, the only means of providing a positive identification was through a photograph sent along with the skeleton. Faced with this information, Ubelaker performed the following analysis to show why he believed that the skeleton was that of the missing woman.
>
> First, he compared the photograph with the skull and the mandible (when held in articulation); this revealed an exact match between the two. However, because of the nature of such comparisons, this was not considered proof of identity. Therefore, he decided to see how many of the 33,000 specimens in the Smithsonian's collection of human remains could be matched to the photograph. He first compared the demographics of the individual to find skeletons that approximately matched the ancestral group, sex, and age of the osteological remains. This process uncovered 52 specimens from the Terry collection that were relatively good matches. Next, he calculated the ratio between the heights of the upper and lower face of the specimen to compare them with the same ratios developed from the 52 matches. This yielded a figure of 0.69 for the forensic case, while the Terry Collection individuals ranged from 0.48 to 0.84, with 18 of them being only a single point off from the forensic case. Ubelaker then calculated a similar ratio between the width and the height of the faces of the forensic case and these 18 specimens. None of the Terry Collection skulls exactly matched the value of 0.49 obtained in the forensic case. He then chose the four skulls whose values most closely approximated this figure for comparison to the photograph. Using computerized superimposition, none of these exactly matched the photograph of the person sent with the forensic case. Therefore, by showing that not one of the 33,000 specimens in the Smithsonian collections matched the photograph sent with the skull and that the skull and photograph matched each other perfectly, he felt that the evidence was conclusive that the photograph and forensic case were the same person.

superimposition can be performed by dual slide projectors (Michael Charney, personal communication). Although both of these methods are effective, recent technology has allowed for the development of newer and more accurate methods. One involves using two or more video cameras focused on the photograph and skull while a video mixer combines the pre- and postmortem figures. Another involves digitizing the two images so that computer software can compare the two likenesses (Ubelaker et al., 1992).

Whichever method is used for superimposition, the basic analysis is the same. This involves searching for points of concordance between the bony landmarks of the skull with those parts of a portrait where there is little soft tissue to obscure these landmarks. Thus, the position of the eye orbits, nasal aperture, and ear openings and the spacing and configuration of the dentition (McKenna et al., 1984) are compared for agreement. In addition, the general size and shape of the skull (Nickerson et al., 1991), especially the length and width of the face and height of the forehead, are compared.

In the more complex digital method, the comparison is performed using four landmarks on each digitized image: glabella, nasion, subnasal, and ectocanthion (Nickerson et al., 1991). Computer software then manipulates the images to obtain the correct orientation of the three-dimensional skull map to two-dimensional photograph by centering both on a usable landmark (an anchor point), after which the size of the skull and the size of the face from the anchor point to all other landmarks are computed. The images then are compared for points of concordance. Generally, the same traits are

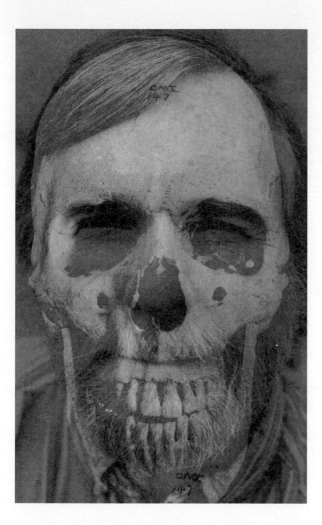

FIGURE 18.3 Positioning of a picture of a skull over that of a person to search for points of concordance. The poor agreement between the two images indicates that the skull does not belong to the person in the photograph. (Photo by Julie R. Angel)

used as with the less technical method described previously. Thus, the widths of face and placement of the features (e.g., eyes, nose) and the height of face (e.g., forehead to chin) are compared for correspondence.

In addition to the skull, Murray Marks and colleagues (1997) have shown that distinctive characteristics of the teeth can be used in the superimposition method. This is especially true when high- (or enhanced low-) quality photographs or even videos are available. Despite the different subject being investigated, the analysis is still the same; i.e., points of concordance between the images are sought. These points usually include spacing of the dentition, rotation of one or more teeth, amount of dental tipping, and general size and shape. In one case, Marks and colleagues used a video of the suspected victim that provided an image of the front teeth, which was matched with the dentition in the skull. The concordance between the two was so great that Marks considered the possibility of a misidentification as remote. (Some forensic odontologists would disagree with his finding.)

Several problems plague all methods of superimposition. First, as described by Ubelaker and colleagues (1992), the photographic plane of the two images must be the same; this means that both the vertical and the horizontal angles must match. In addition, the sizes of the two images must be equal. Problems with differences in the figures usually can be solved by taking numerous postmortem photos of the skeletal or odontological structure or by manipulating their digitized images until the angles and sizes match. In addition, the sizing problem can be solved by using background information from the antemortem photograph to calibrate the two likenesses. Thus, skeletal dimensions can be derived from pictured items such as clothing (e.g., buttons, ties) and furniture, as well as doors and windows, thus giving useful information for determining the necessary size of the postmortem photograph.

The other problem with the superimposition method involves obtaining good-quality antemortem photographs or videos. Unfortunately, these images can be affected by numerous commonly occurring conditions, such as poor camera optics, low-quality film, or poor developing. Fortunately, this problem can be somewhat alleviated by using computer software to clean up the image.

FORENSIC ODONTOLOGY

Forensic odontology is a specialty within dentistry in which the method and theory of dental examination are applied to medicolegal problems. The examination of teeth has three areas of use in the forensic situation: formulation of a positive identification, analysis of bite marks on persons or associated evidence, and interpretation of injuries and other changes to oral tissue (Levine, 1972). Although interesting in some circumstances, the analysis of bite marks will not be discussed here because it usually is not required in the cases of extreme decomposition encountered by forensic anthropologists. However, a summary of methods used in achieving the other two goals is necessary because of the frequency with which forensic anthropologists encounter dental remains in their work.

Forensic odontologists have similar goals to those outlined in this book, and they follow a protocol that parallels that developed by Snow (1982) (see Chapter 1). The questions of the odontological process are stated well by R. M. S. Taylor (1978):

1. Is it a human tooth?
2. What class of tooth is it?
3. Is it upper or lower?
4. Is it first or second?
5. Is it from the right or left side?
6. To what race did the person belong?
7. What was the person's age?
8. Was the person male or female?
9. How long is it since death took place?
10. Is it a "civilized" tooth or not?
11. What was the cause of death?
12. Was the person in good health at the time of death? (p. 109)*

One last question can be asked when a tentative match is made with a missing person: Are these the teeth from this individual? If this question can be answered in the affirmative, an identification is considered positive.

The first five questions apply only to loose teeth, because dentition implanted in jaws generally is easily identified as to human or nonhuman, class (incisor, canine, premolar, or molar), side (right or left), and location (first, second or third, upper or lower). For information concerning these topics, the reader is referred to Chapter 2.

Question 9 cannot be answered with any accuracy from the teeth as of this writing. However, the remaining questions can be answered, at least partially, when the amount and condition of dental remains are sufficient. Therefore, each of these will be examined in turn, because they replicate much of the forensic anthropology protocol.

Also, it is useful to see what teeth can tell forensic workers about the persons represented by odontological remains.

Race (Ancestry)

Ancestral group (race) can be deduced from the teeth only when a few conditions, more prevalent in one group than others, are present. The most useful of these are shovel-shaped incisors, Bushman canine, and cusp 7. As discussed in Chapter 7, shoveling is the term used when incisors exhibit thickening along their perpendicular (i.e., mesial and distal) edges (see Figure 7.10b). Because frequencies of this trait approach 100% in Asian populations (closer to 85% in Native Americans), most forensic anthropologists look for this characteristic when skull features indicate Asian ancestry. Black ancestry sometimes can be inferred from the other two characteristics. **Cusp 7** is located between the lingual cusps of the lower molar teeth (see Figure 18.4a). Because over one-third of Blacks manifest this condition, while it is rare in Whites and Asians (see Table 18.1), the presence of this feature supports an attribution of a skull to this ancestral group. The **Bushman canine** also is useful for this purpose. In this trait, an additional cusp appears on the lingual side of the crown of the maxillary canine, making this tooth similar in configuration to a lower first premolar (Figure 18.4b). Again, because its frequency is high in Blacks and low in other ancestral groups, the presence of this trait in the dentition of forensic remains generally implies Black ancestry. (See Edgar, 2005, for a more in-depth study.)

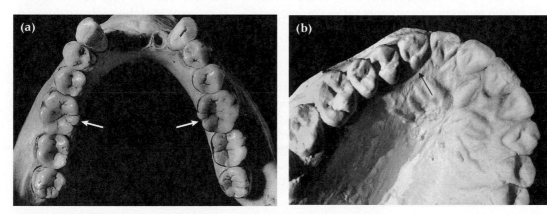

FIGURE 18.4   Dental variations: **(a)** cusp 7 (*arrows*) on the lower first molar common in persons of Black ancestry; **(b)** Bushman canine common in persons of Black ancestry; (arrow points to lingual cusp).   (a: Photo by Julie R. Angel; b: photo courtesy of Joel Irish)

TABLE 18.1   Frequencies of Dental Traits in Various Ancestral Groups[1]

Ancestral Group	Shovel-Shaped Incisors[1] (%)	Cusp 7[2] (%)	Bushman Canine[2] (%)
Whites	8.4	5.8	4.8
Blacks	12.1	38.5	18.1
Asians	92.4	9.8	1.2

[1]From Hinkes (1990); Asian percentage from Hrdlicka for Chinese.
[2]From Irish (1997); White percentages those of Europeans, Blacks those of sub-Saharan Africans, and Asians from Northeast Asia, including Native Americans.

Age

As discussed in Chapter 9, age at death can be estimated from the teeth using information on tooth calcification, emergence, and histological traits. In addition to these, there are several other traits that can be used with adult teeth. As described in the Gustafson method, secondary dentin is deposited through time in the pulp cavity of permanent teeth. However, **pulp stones** also develop within this same structure. The exterior of the crown manifests two additional features with advancing age not already described: staining and tartar. **Staining** involves discoloration of the enamel, and **tartar** is the chalky substance that forms on teeth from **plaque**. Finally, the openings at the tips of roots begin to close as persons get older, forming smaller areas for the passage of nerves and blood vessels. Although no standards exist for approximating years of age from these four characteristics, their presence is indicative of an older adult (or, in the case of staining and plaque, inadequate dental care).

Sex

As of this writing, there are no known qualitative differences between male and female teeth. However, quantitative differences have been documented between the sexes by several researchers (Garn et al., 1967; Anderson and Thompson, 1973; Black, 1978). Once these size differences were recognized, two attempts were made to determine sex from measurements of the teeth using discriminant function analysis (Ditch and Rose, 1972; De Vito and Saunders, 1990). Unfortunately, the resultant functions were too inaccurate (Owsely and Webb, 1983) to gain wide acceptance. Also, the area of overlap between tooth measurements for males and females is so great that these dimensions are of little value for determining sex.

"Civilized" Teeth

The differentiation of civilized from uncivilized teeth refers to dental remains from industrialized versus third-world countries. Generally, the dentition of persons from these latter areas exhibits heavy dental wear, whereas minimal wear is characteristic of persons from Europe, North America, and other technologically advanced countries. Thus, the finding of unworn dentition would indicate a modern person from an industrialized country, rather than a person from a nation characterized by a rural economy. (Additionally, as described in Chapter 3, heavy wear also might indicate prehistoric persons of no medicolegal significance.)

Cause of Death

Although it is rare that the teeth will provide a cause of death, forensic odontologists must be open to any information that can help untangle this factor. Generally, the dentition will supply only an indication of perimortem trauma, such as breakage (see Figure 18.5) or shattering due to some outside force. When this breakage is sufficient to indicate a severe blow that likely caused damage beyond the dental area, forensic odontologists may be in a position to provide information concerning the cause (and perhaps manner) of death.

Antemortem Health

Generally, the teeth can provide very little information on the antemortem health of deceased persons. Although the developing dentition can be affected by systemic pathological conditions (Suckling et al., 1987, among others), the manifestations of these in the teeth usually are too limited to make statements other than that the

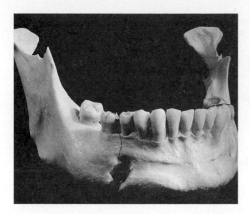

FIGURE 18.5 Damage to the dentition indicating a perimortem blow to the lower jaw. (Photo by Julie R. Angel; specimen courtesy of the State of New Mexico, Office of the Medical Investigator)

deceased endured an acute stress episode during growth. Conversely, diseases of the mouth (e.g., dental decay, recession of the alveolar bone, traumatic alteration) usually do not indicate a condition that would aid in developing a biological profile of decedents.

Positive Identification

The method for developing a positive identification from the teeth involves comparing antemortem dental records with the results of a thorough postmortem dental examination. Generally, these analyses are accomplished after initial treatment has removed any remaining soft tissue. In addition, osteological analysis has resulted in a potential match so that all records of dental work (i.e., written documents, radiographs, dental casts, photographs) have been obtained from the decedent's dentist. Barry Fisher and colleagues (1987) present a readable account of the methods used for comparing antemortem and postmortem dental records and what constitutes a comprehensive examination of the dentition of deceased persons. Because of its completeness, their article is summarized here, with additions from other sources as noted.

A comprehensive dental exam involves gathering information on no less than five characteristics of the teeth. First, a thorough inventory should be made, documenting both the teeth that are present and those that are absent. If supernumerary dentition (extra teeth) is encountered during this process, these also should be noted. This information can be recorded on inventory forms and/or on sketches of the dentition. Second, restorations such as **amalgams** (fillings) and prosthetics such as bridges and dentures (whether full or partial), as well as crowns, should be identified. The location of these features should be noted both within the dentition (e.g., on the lower first premolar) and within the tooth (e.g., on the bucco-mesial corner). Third, any pathological conditions such as caries (cavities) and cracks or breaks should be documented, as should exterior discoloration or tartar buildup.

Fourth, malocclusion (there are several systems for categorizing the types of malocclusion; see any dental textbook for more details) or peculiar spacing should be noted, as well as the type of bite. Three bite types, illustrated in Figure 18.6 are recognized: **overbite**, where the upper anterior teeth occlude in front of the lower teeth; **underbite**, where the lower anterior teeth occlude in front of the upper teeth; and **edge-to-edge**, where the edges of the upper and lower anterior teeth meet when occluded (Bass, 1995). Fifth, x-rays of the teeth should be taken, which correspond to any radiographs that are available from the antemortem records. This is usually the **bitewing** radiograph that usually is comprised of the upper and lower molars and premolars from each side.

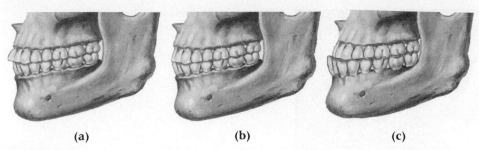

(a)   (b)   (c)

FIGURE 18.6 Common bite types in human dentition: **(a)** overbite, **(b)** edge-to-edge, **(c)** underbite.

After the postmortem dental exam is completed, the positive identification of an individual can be achieved by comparing exam results with documents obtained from the dentist of the purported decedent. This is achieved by determining consistencies between the pre- and postmortem information. The number of consistencies needed for this process varies with the situation. In some cases, a single unusual trait may be enough for this purpose (e.g., a unique feature, either natural or prosthetic, in a single tooth). However, in most instances, consistencies between the antemortem and postmortem records must be absolute. The exception to this involves cases for which there is a high amount of concordance between the records and any inconsistencies that exist are explainable. Thus, if it can be proved that differences of errors in the records are the result of additional dental work for which records are not available, a positive identification may be acceptable.

The comparison of records is performed in a step-by-step manner. The first step involves matching the written records. In most cases, there will be perfect agreement as to number of teeth, placement of prosthetics, presence of pathological conditions, and type of bite (including any malocclusion). Bradley Adams (2003) has shown the importance of this part of the analysis. He discovered that the patterns of missing, filled, and unrestored teeth were so individualistic that a positive identification from this examination alone may be possible. He demonstrated that, in a sample of over 19,000 people, the only pattern that appeared with any regularity was the presence of all teeth (except the third molars) in an unrestored condition. All other patterns appeared with a frequency under 1%. He argues that some patterns are so rare that the probability of an incorrect match is small enough to assume a positive identification.

Despite this, a number of problems can cause discrepancies to appear, even when decedents are being compared to their correct antemortem records. First, not all dentists record the work that they perform nor do they document the state of the dentition of their patients; poor record keeping can be a major problem in some cases. Second, although in the United States dentists are required to keep records for not less than 2 years (many keep them longer), sometimes these documents are discarded early. Third, errors can occur in written documents. Although these sometimes can be fixed by using other sources of information (e.g., radiographs, photographs, casts), not all errors in antemortem written records will be possible to correct.

Even with complete dental records, pre- and postmortem comparison may not be easy for several reasons. First, dentists use different methods of coding teeth. Thus, obtaining agreement between records using the **Zsigmondy** method (which designates individual teeth by letters) and records using the **Fédération Dentaire Internationale** (FDI) method (which uses two numbers for each tooth) is both challenging and prone to error. Second, postmortem information may indicate that more work was done than documented in the antemortem records. This usually indicates either that the latest work was not reported by the dentist or that the work was done by another provider, whose records have not been (but need to be) obtained. Conversely, postmortem information may indicate that less work was done than indicated by antemortem documents. This can be due to teeth with amalgams being extracted, problems in the postmortem examination, or antemortem charting errors.

After the written records have been shown to agree, or all discrepancies explained, antemortem photographs, casts, and dental appliances (if available) should be compared with their postmortem counterparts. By placing the dentition side by side with either of these two sources, concordance can be obtained by noting the size, number, and spacing of teeth and the configuration of the cusps. Dental work that was performed after the photographs were taken or casts made is the greatest cause of nonconcordance between these two sources. With dental appliances such as dentures or dental plates, the prosthesis can be reassembled in the mouth to ensure concordance between the biological and mechanical points of contact (see Figure 18.7).

The last step in the comparison process involves obtaining agreement between pre- and postmortem radiographs, especially in the contours of amalgams. This is considered to be the best method for establishing positive identity in skeletonized remains. Because the probability that persons would possess exactly the same amalgam profiles is infinitesimally small, a match between antemortem and postmortem filling contours is given the same credence as fingerprints. (In a very real sense, a single radiograph depicting highly idiosyncratic restorations is more valuable than all written records; see Box 18.2 for an example.) Another advantage to this method is its availability. Because x-raying is a routine part of dental work, antemortem radiographs almost always are present in dental records. The bitewing is particularly useful because the method for obtaining this radiograph has been standardized (i.e., it is always taken from the buccal aspect and one is taken for each side of the dental arcade).

The matching of pre- and postmortem contours of amalgams is performed by placing the radiographs side by side (Figure 18.8a) and comparing the corresponding fillings point by point. Starting at one corner, agreement between the shape and dimensions of the profiles is noted by proceeding either clockwise or counterclockwise. In some cases, the two are measured to ensure agreement; in other cases, the radiographs can be superimposed to ensure concurrence. After the contours have been so examined, the crown sizes and shapes and the root shapes, the outline of pulp cavities, profiles of crowns and roots, and outlines of the trabecular bone can be used. Similarly, other prostheses that appear in radiographs can be compared, such as the result of

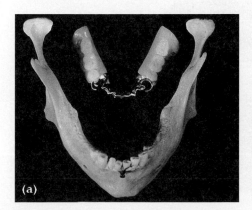 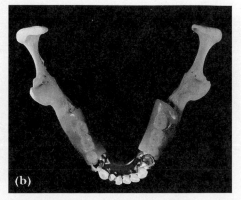

FIGURE 18.7 **(a)** Comparison of a dental plate with the lower jaw of a person. **(b)** Reassembly indicates matching between these structures. (Photos by Julie R. Angel; specimen courtesy of the University of New Mexico–Albuquerque, Maxwell Museum of Anthropology, #99)

BOX 18.2
The Bat-Wing Filling

Mary Manhein (1999) describes a case in which a single, unique amalgam (filling) was sufficient to provide a positive identification. Her example involved a heavily weathered human skeleton represented by an arm bone, leg bone, part of a skull, and the lower jaw. From these, she was able to develop a demographic profile that was found to match a 17-year-old White girl who had been missing for over 5 years. Since the maxillae had not been found, only the teeth of the lower jaw could be used for odontological analysis. In addition, only one of these teeth contained a filling; however, the configuration of this restoration was especially odd.

The amalgam in question, located in one of the molars, was shaped like a bat with wings when viewed in x-ray; that is, it had a vertical center section, with horizontal sections spreading from each side. After obtaining antemortem radiographs from the dentist of the girl as well as from the dental remains, the configurations of the fillings matched. Although this was slender evidence, the shape of the amalgam was so distinctive that a positive identification was accepted. When confronted with the evidence that the body was that of his victim, the perpetrator confessed to murdering the girl and accepted life in prison without parole.

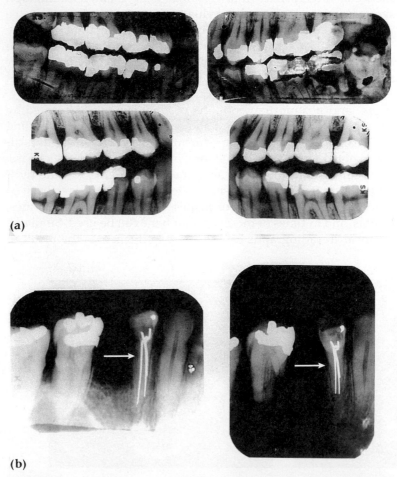

(a)

(b)

FIGURE 18.8 Postmortem *(top)* and antemortem *(bottom)* radiographs for positive identification: **(a)** bitewing radiographs; **(b)** unique dental appliance *(arrow).* (Photos by Julie R. Angel; radiographs courtesy of Dr. Homer Campbell, State of New Mexico, Office of the Medical Investigator)

endodontic procedures (see Figure 18.8b), bridges, and crowns. Finally, the location and shape of caries, especially if the antemortem x-rays were taken shortly before death, can be used in this process.

Other features of the dentition, dependent on the habits of the person, may add weight to a positive identification. For example, pipe smoking can cause wear facets unrelated to mastication to appear on some teeth (especially the premolars). Also, smoking in general can cause abnormally severe staining. Similarly, grooves on crowns from holding materials, such as thread by tailors and nails by carpenters, also can be present and useful. Finally, anomalous conditions such as enamel hypoplasias may aid in this process. These defects can be either areas of thinner enamel (e.g., pits and lines) or areas of discoloration. Because they are indicative of childhood stress (e.g., severe acute disease), family or medical records may document an incident that could be the causative factor.

MISCELLANEOUS TECHNIQUES

In addition to those described above, there are a number of other methods by which a positive identification can be achieved. One such method involves **identification by exclusion**. In cases for which there are multiple bodies and the identification of all the victims are known (e.g., airplane accidents for which passenger manifests are available), this technique can be used when all but one person are identified. In this situation, it is reasonable to assume that the last skeletal remains must be the remaining unidentified person. These types of identifications have been used most successfully in the crash of small airplanes involving only a few persons. Generally, the intense burning following aircraft accidents disfigures human bodies to the point of making identifications difficult. Thus, if one of two or two of three persons can be distinguished using the methods described above, the remaining person can be identified by exclusion if the osteological evidence is in agreement with antemortem biographical information. A final method of positive identification that has gained popularity over the last years is DNA testing. The general approach is to recover DNA from the soft tissues, bone, or teeth of a forensic case and compare it with that of purported family members. Although plagued by problems of degradation of DNA chains due to taphonomic forces, this method is considered as reliable as fingerprints and radiographic comparison for obtaining a positive identification. For a more detailed discussion, the reader is directed to Lee and colleagues (1998) and Mundorff et al. (2009).

Summary

1. Forensic anthropologists recognize two types of identifications: positive and probable.

2. Any unique skeletal characteristic documented in antemortem records and present in postmortem skeletal or odontological structures has the potential to provide a positive identification of human remains.

3. Radiographs of the sinuses of the skull (especially in the frontal) have been used successfully to obtain a positive identification.

4. Any unique characteristic of the skeleton visible in antemortem radiographs potentially can result in a personal identification.

5. The combining of multiple sources of information, including the likeness of a skull superimposed on an image of a face depicted in premortem photographs, can add weight to the probability of an identification.

6. Forensic odontology is the study of the dentition in forensic situations.

7. Although they analyze dentition, forensic odontologists have the same goals as forensic anthropologists; that is, they attempt to determine demographic characteristics and cause of death and to obtain a positive identification of decedents.

8. Identification from dental remains requires comparison of antemortem records (e.g., paper documents, radiographs, photographs, casts) with the dentition of the deceased.

9. The configuration of amalgams (fillings) is so distinct between different individuals that matching between pre- and postmortem radiographs is considered proof of identity.

10. Miscellaneous methods for obtaining a positive identification involve the use of any characteristic that is distinct enough that, when used in conjunction with the basic demographic profile, it uniquely identifies an individual.

11. Identity by exclusion can be used in cases of multiple bodies where all persons but one have been identified.

12. Positive identification can be obtained by comparing the DNA from purported relatives with that recovered from the soft and hard tissues of a forensic case.

Exercises

1. An intact skull is discovered, which is determined to be a Black male between 20 and 40 years of age. If a missing person matching that description was once treated for a head injury at the local hospital, what steps should be taken to obtain a positive identification?

2. If radiographs of the side of the head of a person and bitewings from the local dentist are available, how could a positive identification be achieved?

3. Of the methods presented in this chapter for obtaining an identification, which is the least accurate and why?

4. Considering the method presented for comparing the skull and a picture of the face of an individual, what characteristics of the picture of an arm would be used to compare it to a skeletonized upper limb?

5. Considering the answer given in Exercise 4, how accurate would the identification based on that arm be?

6. What are the components of the frontal sinuses that are used to obtain a positive identification? Considering the information presented on maxillary, ethmoid, and mastoid sinuses, could a similar system be developed for these structures? Should such a system be developed and why?

7. In forensic odontology, the characteristic most often considered as conclusive proof of identity is the configuration of the tooth amalgams. Discuss why this is so and why general observations on the placement and number of fillings might not necessarily lead to a positive identification.

8. Why is the size of bones seen in radiographs not considered proof of identity, whereas the configuration of internal structure (e.g., trabecular bone) is?

9. Which of the demographic characteristics is least likely to be determinable from the teeth? Explain your answer.

10. Given what has been presented in this book to this point, list other characteristics of the skeleton that may be useful (under the right circumstances) for obtaining a positive identification.

19

Conclusion

The last topics to consider before ending this book involve subjects that have not been described earlier and issues, not previously discussed, that pervade all previous chapters. Four such areas can be identified. First, the ethical responsibilities of forensic anthropologists will be described; the main ethic of this discipline is the honest presentation of data and opinion so that the judicial process is neither falsely exaggerated nor unnecessarily hampered. Second, a description of the final report will be presented; because this is the terminus of most skeletal analyses, its general layout and contents deserve explication. Third, forensic anthropologists are being asked to offer expert testimony (by attorneys for both the prosecution and defense), so the aspects surrounding courtroom appearances are explained. Fourth, a discussion of the future of forensic anthropology is presented.

ETHICAL RESPONSIBILITIES

Given the gravity of the situation surrounding the deaths of individuals, forensic anthropologists cannot take their role in the forensic process lightly. Because the life or liberty of accused persons may hinge on their findings, forensic anthropologists must ensure that their work neither falsely implicates the innocent nor prevents the prosecution of the guilty. In addition, the identification of a victim affects the peace of mind of the decedent's relatives. These persons sometimes wait years to learn of the fate of their loved ones, so the accurate assessment of identification and proper notification of the family must also be undertaken with the utmost seriousness. Thus, persons engaged in this profession have an ethical responsibility to ensure that their work uses the best available methods for full assessment of the remains, that the process is carefully done, and that the accuracy of the identification and accompanying information (e.g., factors related to manner and cause of death) is unquestionable. Some forensic anthropologists (Blau 2009) go so far as to say that physical anthropologists should not undertake forensic work unless they have received advanced training from one of the institutions specializing in forensic anthropology (e.g., the Forensic Anthropology Center at the University of Tennessee, Knoxville) and have been certified (e.g., Diplomates of the American Academy of Forensic Anthropologists; see Chapter 1). In this way, forensic anthropologists will ensure that their work does not impede the judicial process or harm the families of victims. This section is divided into two parts; the first deals with the ethics that surround the profession of forensic anthropology, while the second deals with personal ethics of the forensic anthropologist.

Professional Ethics

The professional ethics of forensic anthropology (and all the forensic sciences) have three components (Burns, 1999): respect, confidentiality, and honesty. **Respect** involves treating the remains and the families of the decedents not only with the respect due to all human beings but also with the sensitivity due to anyone who has endured the loss of a loved one. This aspect of ethics renders inappropriate the use of "gallows humor" to ease the nervousness of forensic workers. **Confidentiality** involves refraining from communicating case findings to others before they have been made public by the proper authorities. Because forensic anthropologists often are among the first persons to analyze osteological remains, they are in a position to provide information to outsiders early in a forensic investigation. This creates a temptation to discuss issues surrounding (especially high profile) cases that must be resisted (Snow, 1982). (Moreover, it must be remembered that it is medical examiners, coroners, and law enforcement officials who are mainly responsible for statements to the press in these types of investigations.) Finally, **honesty** involves providing a complete and accurate assessment of forensic cases, without contributing information or opinions that cannot be substantiated by data. This is so important that it constitutes part of the code of ethics outlined in the Bylaws of the American Academy of Forensic Sciences. Honesty in forensic anthropology has two components: the recognition of the difference between evidence and opinion and the accurate assessment of levels of certainty.

The evidence–opinion dichotomy is one of the most important distinctions in forensic anthropological analysis (or any branch of forensic medicine). Although forensic anthropologists are allowed to offer opinions in their role as expert witnesses, they must be able to distinguish between data and interpretation, a part of all scientific inquiry. As seen in earlier chapters, **evidence** in forensic anthropology consists of the physical remains (skeletons) of individuals. A bone that can be held in the hand and examined closely is evidence (data). **Opinion** encompasses any interpretations about the remains developed from the methods used by forensic anthropologists.

From this starting point, observations are made on bones that can fall on either side of this dichotomy, with some representing evidence and others opinion. For example, observations that fall within the realm of well-accepted information can be considered evidence. These include statements such as "the skull is complete except for the mandible, which was not recovered" or "the right femur is broken." However, other observations must be considered opinion. These include statements such as "the skull exhibited large browridges" or "the fracture to the right femur occurred around the time of death."

After all relevant observations have been made, forensic anthropologists offer opinions concerning the person represented by the remains and the significance of various observations. Most of the chapters of this book describe the methods by which forensic anthropologists formulate these opinions from the skeleton. Thus, statements concerning the probable ancestry, sex, age at death, stature, and time since death represent the opinions of forensic anthropologists. Similarly, facial reproduction and possible occupation of decedents represent opinion.

The second aspect of levels of certainty involves recognizing the differences between the three types of opinions: speculation, possible, and probable. **Speculation** is a statement that is based on few or no data. In this type of opinion, forensic anthropologists use their experience as forensic investigators to provide an opinion on a subject for which no information is available. Workers should avoid offering these types of opinions unless they are specifically asked or they are very experienced (Stanley Rhine, personal communication). In addition, these opinions should not be put in writing.

The second level of certainty involves offering an opinion on a characteristic or event that is **possible**. This has a higher certainty than speculation, but still represents an unlikely situation. Thus, phrases such as "possible, but unlikely" indicate that an opinion is possible, given the full variety of events that can occur in the world, but is too unlikely to be taken seriously. For example, there was an instance where a child was born with a full set of deciduous dentition (Michael Charney, personal communication), rendering an odontological estimate of age many years too high for this individual. Although this is a documented event, it should not prevent forensic anthropologists from determining age from tooth eruption; such events are too rare to invalidate the general procedure.

Finally, **probable** is the word used for opinions with the highest level of certainty that can be applied to any data determined from the human skeleton. Within this last category, levels of certainty can be further subdivided such that some statements can be taken as an opinion indicating **general tendency** (e.g., the majority of females have a wide subpubic angle), while others indicate **certainty** (e.g., the configuration of tooth amalgams indicates a positive identification).

Determining the placement of an opinion between the general tendency and certainty is a skill needed by all forensic anthropologists. For example, as described earlier, ancestry is one of the most difficult attributions to make from the skeleton. Thus, an opinion of this demographic characteristic must be considered less reliable than an estimation of sex, which has a higher likelihood of correct assessment. Similarly, a judgment concerning time since death must be considered less accurate than a calculation of stature. When conveying the accuracy of these types of opinions, several approaches can be used.

First, **levels of probability** can be attached to assessments of the demographics of individuals represented by skeletons, as well as the circumstances surrounding their deaths. Thus, statements can be made such as "I am 95 percent certain that the decedent was between 35 and 45 when he died." Unfortunately, this conveys a level of certainty that is not necessarily supported by data. All probabilities in forensic anthropology are based on the samples of skeletons that provided the information from which standards of demographics and other osteological features were derived. Because it is unknown how representative these samples are of modern populations, such statements convey a precision that cannot be proved. Similarly, statements such as "the decedent was five foot ten, plus or minus two inches" conveys a certainty that is more exact than warranted. (See Klepinger and Giles, 1998, for a fuller discussion of this topic.)

A second method for stating a level of certainty involves not using set **statistics** (e.g., minimums and maximums) when offering an opinion on characteristics that can be described in numeric terms. Thus, statements such as "she was in her mid- to late twenties when she died" convey an uncertainty that is less confining than "25 to 30." Similarly, **word qualifiers** can be used instead of probability levels. For example, statements such as "it is unlikely that he was over six feet tall" leaves open the possibility that the person's stature was over this maximum.

Unfortunately, indistinct extremes and word qualifiers mean different things to different persons. A study by M. A. Nakao and Steve Axelrod (1983) of the meaning of word qualifiers among physicians and nonphysicians revealed differences in terms that are heavily used by forensic anthropologists. For example, they found that the word *often* meant a probability level around 0.4 to physicians, but around 0.59 to nonphysicians. Similarly, the qualifier *characteristic* meant 0.20 to physicians, but 0.37 to nonphysicians. (Readers probably have their own meaning for these terms that would add more ambiguity to that discovered by Nakao and Axelrod.)

One last method of offering opinions involves talking in terms of consistency and inconsistency. Use of the word **consistent** imparts an agreement with a possibility that is less confining than a numerical range. Statements such as "consistent with homicide" or "consistent with age of mid- to late forties" convey that a meaning is both restrictive and nonconfining. Conversely, **inconsistent** imparts a disagreement with an interpretation.

BOX 19.1
Ethics in a Case of Death by Strangulation

Angel and Caldwell (1984) describe a case in which the expertise of an anthropologist was extensive enough to provide evidence of cause of death. As outlined in Boxes 14.2 and 15.2, the case involved a young adult female whose remains exhibited trauma to the laminae of the sixth cervical vertebra. Because both the anterior and posterior sections displayed breaks, it was concluded that a strong force compressed the soft tissues of the neck to the extent that the side of the neural arch was fractured. Given the strength of the force necessary to inflict this type of injury, Angel and Caldwell concluded that it was reasonable and ethically sound to assume that the young woman died from strangulation. They go on to state:

A commonsense description of the "weapons" recovered, linked to the postmortem anatomy of the deceased (not going beyond the physical evidence in any way), is more credible and persuasive to a jury than an aggressive expert opinion on the cause of death. No anthropologist lacking direct experience in the examination of bone fractures at death, in addition to a detailed knowledge of anatomy, should ever take on a skeletal case of this kind.*

*From L. J. Angel and P. C. Caldwell, Death by Strangulation, in *Human Identification* T. A, Rathbun and J. E. Buikstra, eds., 1984, p. 174. Courtesy of Charles C. Thomas Publisher, Ltd., Springfield, IL.

It is similar to the phrase *incompatible with,* which can be used for judgments that do not fit within what is known in forensic anthropology. Thus, phrases such as "inconsistent with a person over six feet tall" or "inconsistent with suicide" impart a disagreement with a possibility that does not transgress the bounds of the known.

Considering the preceding discussion, the demarcation between data and opinion is one of the most important distinctions that forensic anthropologists must make. In a like manner, it is just as important that these workers be able to express an expert opinion in proper terms so that levels of certainty are not overstated. This can be done only if these specialists understand the limits of their knowledge and of the science of forensic anthropology so that their opinions meet the *Daubert* guidelines and do not exceed the data on which they are based (see Box 19.1 for an example). By knowing these, forensic anthropologists will not be accused of misconduct when providing expert testimony during legal proceedings. Similarly, they will avoid getting involved in offering opinions on topics out of their area of expertise.

Personal Ethics

Soren Blau (2009) presents a fine discussion of the personal ethical dilemmas faced by forensic anthropologists when performing of their work. Her work is transformed here into a discussion of six issues, moderated by personal ethics, that should be considered by all professionals in the field. First, political and social aspects must be considered when undertaking work in foreign countries; this involves understanding the customs of the indigenous people as well as a host of other issues such as doing work without leaving an infrastructure that allows these people to perform their own work in the future. Second, forensic anthropologists must decide if they should undertake an investigation when conditions are such that the quality of their work would be negatively affected. In many recovery site areas, there are no facilities for analyzing skeletal remains and no hope of moving the remains to such a facility. Third, the rights of the victims' families must be considered because some families may not want outsiders touching the remains of their relatives or may not want the closure that such investigations can bring (i.e., they may wish to believe their loved one is only "missing"). Fourth, forensic anthropologists who are morally opposed to the death penalty must decide if they should participate in an investigation if the jurisdiction in which the case resides would execute persons convicted of the crime. Fifth, in some places in the world, the lives of the investigators may be put in danger by persons opposed to the uncovering of the crime. Sixth, justice from an investigation occasionally causes distress among innocent persons, such as the children of a parent who murdered the other parent. All of these aspects must be considered by forensic anthropologists before becoming involved in an investigation. Importantly, it must be remembered that a decision to not participate may mean that the perpetrators of a crime may not be brought to justice.

THE FINAL REPORT

All the information provided in previous chapters has lead to the development of the ultimate product of any forensic anthropological investigation, the final report. This is the written document provided to medical examiners, coroners, law enforcement officials, or other legal authorities that states the results of the skeletal analysis. The final report should be as accurate and complete as possible, leaving the reader with few unanswered questions concerning the results of the investigation. Just as importantly, the report should give the impression that the forensic anthropologist is both competent and conscientious. (This is an extension of the ethic of honesty when providing information on decedents.)

Generally, the report can have two main parts. The first is a one-page **summary** that briefly describes the results of the skeletal analysis; this should be a part of any report that is excessively lengthy (Snow, 1982). The summary is useful because it provides the pertinent information in a brief and readable format without cluttering the results with unnecessary detail. If included in a report, it should contain the case number, date and investigator's name(s), and subheadings for each topic of the forensic anthropology protocol (Figure 19.1). The second part should provide a description of the methods used and a detailed discussion of the results obtained from the analysis. This section should be longer and more complete than the summary so that readers can get particulars on the steps completed during the forensic anthropological examination. Burns (1999) presents a useful outline of the six sections that should comprise this part of the report.

Section 1 should contain the **background of the case**, including information on names, dates, and places as they apply to the case. This section would include how the forensic anthropologist was summoned, what work had been done prior to this summons, and who was present during the analyses. These are the prosaic but important details that should be included in all forensic anthropologists' notes concerning a case. In section 2, the **general condition of the remains** should be described, with emphasis on the amount and condition of soft tissue present and the state of preservation of the osteological material. Any photographs of the body included as an appendix to the report can be referenced here. Section 3 should contain a complete **inventory** of the osteological and odontological remains, including a judgment as to the number of individuals present. In section 4, each of the four aspects of demography (i.e., **ancestry, sex, age at death**, and **stature**) should be presented in separate subsections that fully describe the means by which these characteristics were determined. Section 5 should contain information on **antemortem**, **perimortem**, and **postmortem injuries** using photographs, line drawings, and other appropriate supportive material. The sixth section should comprise any **recommendations for further testing** that are outside the realm of forensic anthropology or the abilities of the researcher (e.g., DNA analysis). This section can include suggestions concerning searches of missing persons files from different geographic locations (e.g., the skeletal evidence indicates that the person was from a different state than the one in which the remains were discovered) or ethnic enclaves

FIGURE 19.1
Executive Summary of
Simulated Case.

Summary of Skeletal Analysis

Case Number: 2000-Bern-10

Prepared by: John Smith, Ph.D., Professor of Anthropology

Date: January 10, 2000

The following summary presents the major findings of the analysis performed by the investigator on the human skeletal remains recovered with the above-given case number. The major findings of my analysis follow (refer to subsequent pages of this report for more detailed information):

Condition: Approximately 90% of the skeleton was found; the missing parts included the bones of the left hand and both feet. Most of the soft tissue was missing and there was evidence of carnivore gnawing on both distal tibiae (shinbones).

Time Since Death: Between 6 months and 1 year.

Ancestry: Black.

Sex: Female.

Age at Death: Between 30 and 35 years.

Stature: 5 feet, 2 inches, to 5 feet, 8 inches; average 5 feet, 5 inches.

Trauma: The skull has a half-inch circular hole to the right temporal bone and a large, irregular opening on the left side of the skull. The defects and their characteristics are consistent with a wound caused by a large-caliber weapon discharged into the right side of the head of the person around the time of death.

Unique Characteristics: The skeleton contains some anomalies of no forensic significance that may assist in the identification of this individual. Ribs 4 through 8 on the right side deviate inward to a greater degree than those on the left side.

that should be approached for information on the decedent. After these sections, any supportive photographs and tables should be attached as **appendixes**.

In cases of genocide investigations, the final forensic anthropology report would be accompanied by a report of the chief archaeologist and chief pathologist (Klinkner, 2008). The forensic anthropology report would be similar to that described above, that is, demographic profile with information on antemortem, perimortem, and postmortem alterations to bone. The chief archaeologist's report would contain information on artifacts found with the human remains, most importantly any that relate to the events at death (e.g., ligatures, blindfolds). The chief pathologist, who is tasked with assigning cause of death, would present information on this for all decedents, where information exists. These reports present the scientific evidence that helps to define the "forensic truth" (Klinkner, 2008) concerning the deaths of the victims and form a key element to the prosecutions case against the defendant(s). Because of its key role in this process, the forensic experts, including the forensic anthropologist, must seek to be objective and present truth that is independent of ultimate purpose.

COURTROOM TESTIMONY

In recent years, forensic anthropologists increasingly are being called to offer expert testimony in criminal and even civil court cases. As this practice increases, so does the need for these professionals to have a clear understanding of the steps involved in this process. Robert Sundick (1984) and Macief Henneberg (2009) present readable accounts of what forensic workers can expect when becoming involved in courtroom testimony.

Because these works cover the main aspects of this process, they will be summarized here. (See also Chapter 2 of Stewart, 1979.)

When contacted by law enforcement agencies (e.g., police, sheriff) or legal offices (e.g., district attorney, attorney-at-law), forensic anthropologists should identify themselves as experts in the field of human skeletal identification with an emphasis on forensics. At this time, a fee appropriate to the affluence of the jurisdiction should be requested as a means of reimbursing the anthropologist for time spent in the case and to enhance the credibility of the subsequent analysis. (All other experts in forensics require such a fee.) Also important at this contact is maintaining the chain of evidence by signing for any remains presented for analysis and ensuring the security of these remains while in possession of them. At this point, careful notes on all aspects of the examination should be started. These include records on the skeletal material, and observations and opinions formulated during analysis. In addition, more mundane details such as date of contact, case number, type of contact (i.e., phone or personal visit), name(s) of contact person(s), and the substance of conversations should be included. When constructing these notes, it is important to make them both readable and accurate, because they can be subpoenaed by a court of law.

If a courtroom appearance for the purpose of offering expert testimony is requested, forensic anthropologists must ensure that the date and time do not conflict unnecessarily with other duties (there usually is some leeway in the scheduling of witnesses). A **pretrial meeting** with the contacting attorney is important so that the testimony is properly guided (e.g., covers only appropriate subjects) and improper questions are avoided (e.g., In your opinion, what was the cause of death?). In addition, the credentials as an expert witness can be presented at this time. Also, the forensic anthropologist should give a short description of the nature of the discipline so that the limits on information resulting from osteological analyses can be established. Proper attention to these details during this meeting will avoid unanswerable questions in a courtroom that make it appear that the entire science of forensic anthropology is too inexact to be taken seriously.

After the preliminaries, the actual courtroom appearance takes place. Several considerations should be contemplated when planning this event. First, forensic anthropologists should dress in such a way that they convey the image of a forensic professional. Second, an attitude of confidence without arrogance should be adopted that conveys a sense of a capable authority in the field. Third, terminology used during testimony should be appropriate to the courtroom personnel, especially the jury. Because the jury is usually the intended audience of any expert testimony, neither overly complex terms nor overly simple language should be used.

The testimony itself involves three and possibly four phases: establishing qualifications, direct examination, cross-examination, and (possibly) redirect examination. **Establishing qualifications** involves a review of the forensic anthropologist's education, background, publications in the field, membership in professional organizations (e.g., American Academy of Forensic Sciences), certifications (e.g., Diplomate of the American Board of Forensic Anthropology), and experience in casework. Presentation of the qualifications at the beginning of testimony establishes the credibility of forensic anthropologists to the judge, who must rule on their acceptability as expert witnesses. In addition, the establishment of credibility helps to ensure that the jury both will listen to and believe their testimony.

Direct examination, performed by the contacting attorney, is the time during which the forensic anthropologist presents the evidence and opinions concerning the human remains. It is here that the method for determining time since death, demographic characteristics, and perimortem trauma are presented in a manner understandable to the jury and other courtroom personnel.

> **BOX 19.2**
> **An Unusual Effect of Trial Testimony**
>
> Maples and Browning (1994) describe a court-room testimony that had unusual results. Maples was providing expert testimony against Tim Burgess, a person accused of killing and dismembering his landlord. The decedent's body was discovered with shotgun blasts to the buttocks, abdomen, and neck. In addition, the legs had been amputated through the femora using an unorthodox method. First the soft tissue of one of the thighs was cut through with a hunting knife, after which the same instrument was used to try and cut through the bone. When that proved inefficient, the perpetrator severed both legs with single blows of an axe. All these injuries were identified by Maples by examining the bones. While providing testimony on the grisly details of the murder and dismemberment, Maples observed the following behavior of the accused:
>
> All the while, Burgess was fidgeting in his chair. After I finished my testimony, and the medical examiner was beginning his, the accused motioned to his attorney. A whispered conference ensued. At the end of it, Burgess's attorney asked to approach the bench.
>
> Burgess wished to change his plea to "guilty." His attorney explained that Burgess found the demonstrations of the death and dismemberment of his former landlord so true to life, so evocative of the real event, that it was recalling memories too horrible for him to bear.*
>
> _____
> *From W. R. Maples and M. Browning, *Dead Men Do Tell Tales*, Doubleday, New York, 1994, pp. 73–74, with permission.

After this testimony ends, usually the opposing attorney will **cross-examine** the forensic anthropologist (see Box 19.2 for an example) in an attempt to **impeach** the testimony given during direct examination. Impeaching testimony involves finding inconsistencies in the evidence offered or proving that the methods used are inadequate. Inconsistencies can occur between the present testimony and any previous testimonies, as well as between the final report and notes taken during the examination of the remains. Similarly, the methods used to arrive at expert conclusions might be questioned by citing other experts or reference books.

Finally, **redirect examination** is a chance for the consulting attorney to clarify issues brought up during cross-examination to avoid unnecessary loss of credibility. In all these testimonies, it is important that the conclusions drawn and the opinions rendered do not exceed those allowed by the data.

FUTURE OF FORENSIC ANTHROPOLOGY

As of this writing, the future of forensic anthropology is considerably brighter than when the first edition of this textbook was published. Within the medicolegal community, this discipline is becoming a known and utilized source, thanks mainly to the early efforts of Ellis Kerley and Clyde Snow, but now to the efforts of the many professionals in the field. There are a number of forensic anthropology programs that offer advanced training in various universities around the United States as well as elsewhere in the world. Law enforcement officials have become more aware of what can be told from human bone, and they are more likely to call a specialist when these remains are encountered. Similarly, officers of the court are increasingly becoming more likely to call on forensic anthropological expertise when preparing for, or while conducting, trials.

Unfortunately, the situation in academia is less favorable. Although human osteology and skeletal biology are still considered legitimate areas of study, the more applied science of forensic anthropology is less acceptable. Part of this stems from the tendency among academicians to look down on any work that is not "pure research" (Maples and Browning, 1994). Whereas the less practical issues of human evolution and variation are admired and prized, applied anthropology in general and forensic anthropology in particular are not considered by some as legitimate subjects of study.

This situation is unfortunate. Forensic anthropology had its start in academics through the efforts of Wilton Krogman, who taught in universities most of his life, Ellis Kerley, also an academician, T. Dale Stewart from the Smithsonian, and others. In addition, all practicing forensic anthropologists have received their training in academic institutions, and many of them hold primary teaching appointments in universities and colleges. For academia to turn its back on this profession now would be tantamount to stating that this field, ably started by fine academic scholars, no longer deserves the respect of the institutions that gave it its start.

Another point of support for forensic anthropology deals strictly with practical issues. From the standpoint of everyday life, forensic anthropologists probably perform the most important work in biological anthropology today. Although the search for human ancestors and the study of modern human variation are significant, they pale in importance to the role performed by forensic anthropologists when providing an identification of a missing loved one. During a forensic investigation, the families of decedents do not care about how humans evolved or what the skeletons of ancient populations say about how extinct peoples lived. They simply want the peace of mind that comes from knowing the fate of their loved one (even if that fate was through nefarious means). And it is forensic anthropologists who start and occasionally end the process that results in the identification of human skeletal remains. For this, they deserve the admiration and respect of academics as well as the community as a whole.

Summary

1. Forensic anthropologists are guided by three ethics when engaged in a forensic investigation: respect, confidentiality, and honesty.
2. Honesty involves deriving as much information from the skeleton as can be determined, without exceeding the bounds of forensic anthropological knowledge.
3. Forensic anthropologists must be aware of the differences between evidence and opinion, as well as levels of certainty when offering opinions.
4. The final report should contain all information derived from the skeleton that is useful to law enforcement officials and others when searching for missing persons or when determining the circumstances under which they died.
5. Although courtroom appearances are not common, forensic anthropologists must be aware of the steps involved in offering expert testimony in a court of law.
6. Forensic anthropology as a discipline is becoming more acceptable to members of the jurisprudence community, while becoming less acceptable to some persons in academics.

REFERENCES

Adams, B. J. (2003). Establishing personal identification based on specific patterns of missing, filled, and unrestored teeth. *Journal of Forensic Sciences,* 48(3):487–496.

Adams, B. J., Herrmann, N. P. (2009). Estimation of living stature from selected anthropometric (soft tissue) measurements: Applications for forensic anthropology. *Journal of Forensic Sciences,* 54(4):753–760.

Albanese, J. (2003). A metric method for sex determination using the hipbone and the femur. *Journal of Forensic Sciences,* 48(2):263–273.

Albanese, J., Eklics, G., Tuck, A. (2008). A metric method for sex determination using the proximal femur and fragmentary hipbone. *Journal of Forensic Sciences,* 53(6):1283–1288.

Alunni-Perret, V., Muller-Bolla, M., Laugier, J. P., Lupi-Pegurier, L., Bertrand, M. F., Staccini, P., Bolla, M., Quatrehomme, G. (2005). Scanning electron microscopy analysis of experimental bone hacking trauma. *Journal of Forensic Sciences,* 50:796–801.

Alves Cardoso, F., Henderson, C. Y. (2010). Enthesopathy formation in the humerus: Data from known age-at-death and known occupation skeletal collections. *American Journal of Physical Anthropology,* 141(4): 550–560.

Anderson, B. (2007). Statistical basis for positive identification in forensic anthropology. *American Journal of Physical Anthropology,* 133(1):741–742.

Anderson, D. L., Thompson, G. W. (1973). Interrelationships and sex differences of dental and skeletal measurements. *Journal of Dental Research* 52:431–438.

Anderson, J. E. (1963). The people of Fairty. An osteological analysis of an Iroquois ossuary. *Bulletin of the Natural History Museum of Canada,* 193:28–129.

Angel, L. J., Caldwell, P. C. (1984). Death by strangulation. In: Rathbun, T. A., Buikstra, J. E., eds. *Human Identification. Case Studies in Forensic Anthropology.* Springfield, IL: Charles C. Thomas.

Arismendi, J. L., Baker, L. E., Matteson, K. J. (2004). Effects of processing techniques on the forensic DNA analysis of human skeletal remains. *Journal of Forensic Sciences,* 49(5):930–934.

Austin-Smith, D., Maples, W. R. (1994). The reliability of skull/photograph superimposition in individual identification. *Journal of Forensic Sciences,* 39:446–455.

Baker, P. T., Newman, R. W. (1957). The use of bone weight for human identification. *American Journal of Physical Anthropology,* 15:601–618.

Barach, E., Tomlanovich, M., Nowak, R. (1986a). Ballistics: A pathophysiologic examination of wounding mechanisms of firearms: Part I. *Journal of Trauma,* 26(3):225–235.

Barach, E., Tomlanovich, M., Nowak, R. (1986b). Ballistics: A pathophysiologic examination of wounding mechanisms of firearms: Part II. *Journal of Trauma,* 26(4):374–383.

Baraybar, J. P. (2008). When DNA is not available, can we still identify people? Recommendations of best practice. *Journal of Forensic Sciences,* 53(3):533–540.

Barbian, L. T., Sledzik, P. S. (2008). Healing following cranial trauma. *Journal of Forensic Sciences,* 53(2):263–268.

Bartelink, E. J., Wiersema, J. M., Demaree, R. S. (2001). Quantitative analysis of sharp-force trauma: An application of scanning electron microscopy in forensic anthropology. *Journal of Forensic Sciences,* 46:1288–1293.

Bass, W. M. (1984). Time interval since death: A difficult decision. In: Rathbun, T. A., Buikstra, J. E., eds. *Human Identification. Case Studies in Forensic Anthropology.* Springfield, IL: Charles C. Thomas.

Bass, W. M. (1987). Forensic anthropology: The American experience. In: Boddington, A., Garland, A. N., Janaway, R. C., eds.*Death, Decay, and Reconstruction: Approaches to Archeology and the Forensic Sciences.* Manchester, England: Manchester University Press.

Bass, W. M. (1995). *Human Osteology. A Laboratory and Field Manual.* 4th ed. Columbia, MO: Missouri Archaeological Society.

Bass, W. M. (1997). Outdoor decomposition rates in Tennessee. In: Haglund, W. D., Sorg, M. H., eds. *Forensic Taphonomy.* New York: CRC Press.

Bennett, K. A. (1993). *A Field Guide for Human Skeletal Identification.* Springfield, IL: Charles C. Thomas.

Berg, G. E., Ta'Ala, S. C., Kontanis, E. J., Leney, S. S. (2007). Measuring the intercondylar shelf angle using radiographs: Intra- and inter-observer error tests of reliablity. *Journal of Forensic Sciences,* 52(5):1020–1024.

Berrizbeeitia, E. L. (1989). Sex determination with the head of the radius. *Journal of Forensic Sciences,* 34(5): 1206–1213.

Berry, A. C., Berry, R. J. (1967). Epigenetic variation in the human cranium. *Journal of Anatomy,* 101:361–379.

Berryman, H. E., Symes, S. A. (1998). Recognizing gunshot and blunt cranial trauma through fracture interpretation. In: Reichs, K. J., ed. *Forensic Osteology, Advances in the Identification of Human Remains.* 2nd ed. Springfield, IL: Charles C. Thomas.

Berryman, H. E., Smith, O. C., Symes, S. A. (1995). Diameter of cranial gunshot wounds as a function of bullet caliber. *Journal of Forensic Sciences,* 40:751–754.

Bierry, G., Le Minor, J., Schmittbuhl, M. (2010). Oval in males and triangular in females? A quantitative evaluation of sexual dimorphism in the human obturator foramen. *American Journal of Physical Anthropology,* 141(4):626–631

Black, T. K. (1978). Sexual dimorphism in the tooth-crown diameters of the deciduous teeth. *American Journal of Physical Anthropology,* 48:77–82.

Blackburn, A., Knüsel, C. J. (2006). Hand dominance and bilateral asymmetry of the epicondylar breadth of the humerus: A test in a living sample. *Current Anthropology,* 47(2):377–382.

Blau, S. (2009). More than just bare bones: Ethical considerations for forensic anthropologists. In: Blau, S., Ubelaker, D. *Handbook of Forensic Anthropology and Archaeology,* Chapter 37. Walnut Creek, CA: Left Coast Press.

Boucher, B. J. (1957). Sex differences in the fetal pelvis. *American Journal of Physical Anthropology,* 15:581–600.

Brooks, S. T. (1955). Age at death: Reliability of cranial and pubic age indicators. *American Journal of Physical Anthropology,* 13:567–597.

Brooks, S. T., Suchey, J. M. (1990). Skeletal age determination based on the os pubis: A comparison of the Ascáadi–Nemeskéri and Suchey–Brooks methods. *Human Evolution,* 5:227–238.

Brues, A. M. (1977). *People and Races.* New York: Macmillan.

Buck, S. C. (2003). Searching for graves using geophysical technology: Field tests with ground penetrating radar, magnetometry, and electrical resistivity. *Journal of Forensic Sciences,* 48:5–11.

Buckberry, J. L., Chamberlain, A. T. (2002). Age estimation from the auricular surface of the ilium: A revised method. *American Journal of Physical Anthropology,* 119(3):213–239.

Buikstra, J. E., Ubelaker, D. H. (1994). *Standards for Data Collection from Human Skeletal Remains.* Fayetteville, AR: Arkansas Archeological Survey Research Series 44.

Burke, T. W., Rowe, W. F. (1992). Bullet ricochet: A comprehensive review. *Journal of Forensic Sciences,* 37:1254–1260.

Burns, K. R. (1999). *Forensic Anthropology Training Manual.* Upper Saddle River, NJ: Prentice Hall.

Burns, K. R., Maples, W. R. (1976). Estimation of age from individual adult teeth. *Journal of Forensic Sciences,* 21:343–356.

Byers, S. N. (1984). Non-fusion anomalies of the human postcranial skeleton. Unpublished manuscript.

Byers, S. N., Akoshima, K., Curran, B. K. (1989). The determination of adult stature from metatarsal length. *American Journal of Physical Anthropology,* 79(3):275–279.

Byers, S. N., Churchill, S., Curran, B. (1989). Determination of stature from metacarpals. *American Journal of Physical Anthropology,* 79:275–279.

Byrd, J. E., Adams, B. J. (2003). Osteometric sorting of commingled human remains. *Journal of Forensic Sciences,* 48:717–724.

Byrd, J. E., Adams, B. J. (2009). Analysis of commingled human remains. In: Blau, S., Ubelaker, D. *Handbook of Forensic Anthropology and Archaeology,* Chapter 15. Walnut Creek, CA: Left Coast Press.

Calce, S. E., Rogers, T. L. (2007). Taphonomic changes to blunt force trauma: A preliminary study. *Journal of Forensic Sciences,* 52(3):519–531.

Cameriere, R., Ferrante, L., Mirtella, D., Rollo, F. U., Cingolani, M. (2005). Frontal sinuses for identification: Quality of classifications, possible error and potential corrections. *Journal of Forensic Sciences,* 50(4):770–773.

Cameriere, R., Ferrante, L., Molleson, T., Brown, B. (2008). Frontal sinus accuracy in identification as measured by false positives in kin groups. *Journal of Forensic Sciences,* 53(6):1280–1282.

Castellano, M. A., Villanueva, E. C., von Frenckel, R. (1984). Estimating the date of bone remains: A multivariate study. *Journal of Forensic Sciences,* 29:527–534.

Cattaneo, C., Porta, D., Gibelli, D., Gamba, C. (2009). Histological determination of the human origin of bone fragments. *Journal of Forensic Sciences,* 54(3):531–533.

Charney, M. (1974). Individual identification from human skeletal material. In: Wilber, C. G., ed. *Forensic Biology for the Law Enforcement Officer,* Chapter 13. Springfield, IL: Charles C. Thomas.

Charney, M., Wilber, C. G. (1984). The Big Thompson flood. In: Rathbun, T. A., Buikstra, J. E., eds. *Human Identification. Case Studies in Forensic Anthropology.* Springfield, IL: Charles C. Thomas.

Cho, H., Stout, S. D., Madsen, R. W., Streeter, M. A. (2002). Population-specific histological age-estimating method: A model for known African-American and European-American skeletal remains. *Journal of Forensic Sciences,* 47:12–18.

Cho, H., Stout, S. D., Bishop, T. A. (2006). Cortical bone remodeling rates in a sample of African American and European American descent groups from the American Midwest: comparisons of age and sex in ribs. *American Journal of Physical Anthropology,* 130(2):214–216.

Christensen, A. M. (2005). Testing the reliability of frontal sinuses in positive identification. *Journal of Forensic Sciences,* 50(1):18–22.

Ciapparelli, L. (1992). The chronology of dental development and age assessment. In: Clark, D. H., ed. *Practical Forensic Odontology.* Oxford, England: Wright.

Coon, C. S. (1969). *The Living Races of Man.* New York: Alfred A. Knopf.

Cornwall, I. W. (1956). *Bones for the Archeologist.* New York: Macmillan Press.

Correia, P. M. M. (1997). Fire modification of bone: A review of the literature. In: Haglund, W. D., Sorg, M. H., eds. *Forensic Taphonomy.* New York: CRC Press.

Craig, E. A. (1995). Intercondylar shelf angle: A new method to determine race from the distal femur. *Journal of Forensic Sciences,* 40:777–782.

Croft, A. M., Ferllini, R. (2007). Macroscopic characteristics of screwdriver trauma. *Journal of Forensic Sciences,* 52(6):1243–1251.

Crowder, C., Austin, D. (2005). Age ranges of epiphyseal union in the distal tibia and fibula of contemporary males and females. *Journal of Forensic Sciences,* 50(5):1001–1007.

Curran, B. K. (1990). The application of measures of midfacial projection for racial classification. In: Gill, G. W., Rhine, J. S., eds. *Skeletal Attribution of Race: Methods for Forensic Anthropology.* Anthropological Papers 4, Maxwell Museum of Anthropology, Albuquerque, NM.

Dabbs, G. R. (2009). Is Dwight right? Can the maximum height of the scapula be used for accurate sex estimation. *Journal of Forensic Sciences,* 54(3):529–530.

Dabbs, G. R., Moore-Jansen, P. H. (2010). A method for estimating sex using metric analysis of the scapula. *Journal of Forensic Sciences,* 55(1):149–152.

Daegling, D. J., Warren, M. W., Hotzman, J. L., Self, C. J. (2008). Structural analysis of human rib fracture and implications for forensic interpretation. *Journal of Forensic Sciences,* 53(6):1301–1307.

Danforth, M. E., Thompson, A. T. (2008). An evaluation of determination of handedness using standard osteological measurements. *Journal of Forensic Sciences,* 53(4):777–781.

De la Grandmaison, D. L., Brion, F, Durigon, M. (2001). Frequency of bone lesions: An inadequate criterion for gunshot wound diagnosis in skeletal remains. *Journal of Forensic Sciences,* 46(3):593–595.

De Vito, C., Saunders, S. R. (1990). A discriminant function analysis of deciduous teeth to determine sex. *Journal of Forensic Sciences,* 35:845–858.

Di Maio, V. J. M. (1993). *Gunshot Wounds. Practical Aspects of Firearms, Ballistics, and Forensic Techniques.* Boca Raton, FL: CRC Press.

Dirkmaat, D. C., Adovasio, J. M. (1997). The role of archaeology in the recovery and interpretation of human remains from an outdoor forensic setting. In: Haglund, W. D., Sorg, M. H., eds. *Forensic Taphonomy.* New York: CRC Press.

Ditch, L. E., Rose, J. C. (1972). A multivariate dental sexing technique. *American Journal of Physical Anthropology,* 37:61–64.

Dixon, D. S. (1982). Keyhole lesions in gunshot wounds to the skull and direction of fire. *Journal of Forensic Sciences,* 27:555–566.

Downs, J. C. U., Nichols, C. A., Scala-Barnett, D., Lifschultz, B. D. (1994). Handling and interpretation of crossbow injuries.*Journal of Forensic Sciences,* 39(2):428–445.

Drusini, A., Calliari, I., Volpe, A. (1991). Root dentine transparency: Age determination of human teeth using computerized densiometric analysis. *American Journal of Physical Anthropology,* 85:25–30.

Dudar, J. C. (1993). Identification of rib number and assessment of intercostal variation at the sternal rib end. *Journal of Forensic Sciences,* 38(4):788–797.

Edgar, H. J. H. (2005). Prediction of race using characteristics of dental morphology. *Journal of Forensic Sciences,* 50(2):269–273.

Eisele, J. W., Reay, D. T., Cook, A. (1981). Sites of suicidal gunshot wounds. *Journal of Forensic Sciences,* 26:480–485.

Falys, C. G., Schutkowsky, H., Weston, D. A. (2006). Auricular surface aging: Worse than expected? A test of the revised method on a documented historic skeletal assemblage. *American Journal of Physical Anthropology,* 130(4):508–513.

Fanning, E. A. (1961). A longitudinal study of tooth formation and root resorption. *New Zealand Dental Journal,* 57:202–217.

Fazekas, I. G., Kosa, F. (1978). *Forensic Fetal Osteology.* Akademiai Kiado, Budapest.

Fenton, T. W., Birkby, W. H., Cornelison, J. (2003). A fast and safe non-bleaching method for forensic skeletal preparation. *Journal of Forensic Sciences,* 48:274–276.

Fenton, T. W., Stefan, V. H., Wood, L. A., Sauer, N. J. (2005). Symmetrical fracturing of the skull from midline contact gunshot wounds: Reconstruction of individual death histories from skeletonized human remains. *Journal of Forensic Sciences,* 50(2):274–285.

Finnegan, M. (1978). Non-metric variation of the infracranial skeleton. *Journal of Anatomy,* 125:23–37.

Fisher, B. A. J., Svensson, A., Wendel, O. (1987). *Techniques of Crime Scene Investigation.* New York: Elsevier.

France, D. L. (1998). Observational and metric analysis of sex in the skeleton. In: Reichs, K. J., ed. *Forensic Osteology. Advances in the Identification of Human Remains.* 2nd ed. Springfield, IL: Charles C. Thomas.

Fully, G. (1956). Un nouvelle méthode de détermination de la taille. *Ann Méd Lég,* 35:266–273.

Fulton, B. A., Meloan, C. E., Finnegan, M. (1986). Reassembling scattered and mixed human bones by trace element ratios. *Journal of Forensic Sciences,* 31:1455–1462.

Galera, V., Ubelaker, D. H., Hayek, L. A. C. (1998). Comparison of macroscopic cranial methods of age estimation applied to skeletons from the Terry Collection. *Journal of Forensic Sciences,* 43:933–939.

Galloway, A. (1988). Estimating actual height in the older individual. *Journal of Forensic Sciences,* 33:126–136.

Galloway, A. (1999). *Broken Bones: Anthropological Analysis of Blunt Force Trauma.* Springfield, IL: Charles C. Thomas.

Galloway, A., Snodgrass, J. J. (1998). Biological and chemical hazards of forensic skeletal analysis. *Journal of Forensic Sciences,* 43:940–948.

Galloway, A., Birkby, W. H., Jones, A. M., Henry, T. E., Parks, B. O. (1989). Decay rates of human remains in an arid environment. *Journal of Forensic Sciences,* 34:607–616.

Garn, S. M., Lewis, A. B., Kerewsky, R. S. (1964). Sex differences in tooth size. *Journal of Dental Research,* 43:306.

Garn, S. M., Lewis, A. B., Swindler, D. R., Kerewsky, R. S. (1967). Genetic control of sexual dimorphism in tooth size. *Journal of Dental Research,* 46(supplement):963–972.

George, R. M. (1987). The lateral craniofacial method of facial reconstruction. *Journal of Forensic Sciences,* 32:1305–1330.

Gilbert, B. M. (1973). *Mammalian Osteo-archaeology: North America.* Columbia: The Missouri Archaeological Society.

Gilbert, B. M. (1976). Anterior femoral curvature: Its probable basis and utility as a criterion of racial assessment. *American Journal of Physical Anthropology,* 45:601–604.

Gilbert, B. M., Marin, L. D., Savage, H. G. (1981). *Avian Osteology.* Laramie, WY: B. Miles Gilbert.

Gilbert, R., Gill, G. W. (1990). A metric technique for identifying American Indian femora. In: Gill, G. W., Rhine, J. S., eds. *Skeletal Attribution of Race: Methods for Forensic Anthropology.* Anthropological Papers 4, Maxwell Museum of Natural History, Albuquerque, NM.

Giles, E. (1970). Discriminant function sexing of the human skeleton. In: Stewart, T. D., ed. *Personal Identification in Mass Disasters.* National Museum of Natural History, Smithsonian Institution, Washington, DC.

Giles, E. (1991). Corrections for age in estimating older adults' stature from long bones. *Journal of Forensic Sciences,* 36:898–901.

Giles, E., Elliot, O. (1962). Race identification from cranial measurements. *Journal of Forensic Sciences,* 7:147–157.

Giles, E., Elliot, O. (1963). Sex determination by discriminant function analysis of crania. *American Journal of Physical Anthropology,* 21:53–68.

Gill, G. W., Gilbert, B. M. (1990). Race identification from the midfacial skeleton: American blacks and whites. In: Gill, G. W., Rhine, J. S., eds. *Skeletal Attribution of Race: Methods for Forensic Anthropology.* Anthropological Papers 4, Maxwell Museum of Anthropology, Albuquerque, NM.

Gill, G. W., Rhine, S. (1990). Appendix A. A metric technique for identifying American Indian femora. In: Gill, G. W., Rhine, J. S., eds. *Skeletal Attribution of Race: Methods for Forensic Anthropology.* Anthropological Papers 4, Maxwell Museum of Natural History, Albuquerque, NM.

Glaister, J., Brash, J. C. (1937). *Medico-Legal Aspects of the Ruxton Case.* Edinburgh: E. & S. Livingstone.

Goss, C. M. (1973). *Gray's Anatomy.* Philadelphia: Lea & Febiger.

Gordon, C.C. and others. (1989) 1988 anthropometric survey of U.S. army personnel: Methods and summary statistics. Technical Report NATICK/TR-89/044. Natick, MA: U.S. Army Natick, Research, Development and Engineering Center.

Gruspier, K. L., Mullen, G. J. (1991). Maxillary suture obliteration: A test of the Mann method. *Journal of Forensic Sciences,* 36:512–519.

Gustafson, G. (1950). Age determinations of teeth. *Journal of the American Dental Association,* 41(1):45–54.

Haglund, W. D. (1997a). Dogs and coyotes: Postmortem involvement with human remains. In: Haglund, W. D., Sorg, M. H., eds. *Forensic Taphonomy.* New York: CRC Press.

Haglund, W. D. (1997b). Rodents and human remains. In: Haglund, W. D., Sorg, M. H., eds. *Forensic Taphonomy.* New York: CRC Press.

Haglund, W. D., Reay, D. Y., Swindler, D. R. (1988). Tooth artifacts and survival of bones in animal-scavenged human skeletons. *Journal of Forensic Sciences,* 33:985–997.

Hall, D. W. (1997). Forensic botany. In: Haglund, W. D., Sorg, M. H., eds. *Forensic Taphonomy.* New York: CRC Press.

Harris, E. F., McKee, J. H. (1990). Tooth mineralization standards for Blacks and Whites from the middle southern United States. *Journal of Forensic Sciences,* 34:859–872.

Hart, G. O. (2005). Fracture pattern interpretation in the skull: Differentiating blunt force from ballistics trauma using concentric fractures. *Journal of Forensic Sciences,* 50(60):1276–1281.

Haskell, N. H., Hall, R. D., Cervenka, V. J., Clark, M. A. (1997). On the body: Insects' life stage presence and their postmortem artifacts. In: Haglund, W. D., Sorg, M. H., eds. *Forensic Taphonomy.* New York: CRC Press.

Haviland, W. A. (1997). *Anthropology.* 8th ed. New York: Harcourt Brace College Publishers.

Hefner, J. T. (2009). Cranial nonmetric variation and estimating ancestry. *Journal of Forensic Sciences,* 54(5):985–995.

Henneberg, M. (2009). The expert witness and the court of law. In: Blau, S., Ubelaker, D. *Handbook of Forensic Anthropology and Archaeology,* Chapter 40. Walnut Creek, CA: Left Coast Press.

Hermann, N. P., Devlin, J. B. (2008). Assessment of commingled human remains using a GIS-based approach. In: Adams, B. J., Byrd, J. E., eds. *Recovery, Analysis, and Identification of Commingled Human Remains,* Chapter 13. Totowa, NJ: Humana Press.

Hillier, M. L., Bell, L. S. (2007). Differentiating human bone from animal bone: A review of histological methods. *Journal of Forensic Sciences,*54(2)249–263.

Hinkes, M. J. (1990). Shovel shaped incisors in human indentification. In: Gill, G. W., Rhine, J. S., eds. *Skeletal Attribution of Race: Methods for Forensic Anthropology.* Anthropological Papers 4, Maxwell Museum of Anthropology, Albuquerque, NM.

Hoffman, B. E., McConathy, D. A., Coward, M., Saddler, L. (1991). Relationship between the piriform aperture and intalar nasal widths in adult males. *Journal of Forensic Sciences,* 36:1152–1161.

Hoffman, J. M. (1979). Age estimations from diaphyseal lengths: Two months to twelve years. *Journal of Forensic Sciences,* 24:461–469.

Hooton, E. A. (1947). *Up from the Ape.* New York: Macmillan.

Hoppa, R., Saunders, S. (1998). Two quantitative methods for rib seriation in human skeletal remains. *Journal of Forensic Sciences,* 43:174–177.

Horvath, F., Gardner, K., Siegel, J. (1993). Range of fire estimates from shotgun pellet patterns: The effect of shell and barrel temperature. *Journal of Forensic Sciences,* 38:585–592.

Huelke, D. F., Darling, J. H. (1964). Bone fractures produced by bullets. *Journal of Forensic Sciences,* 9(4):461–469. (A definitive reference on effects of bullets on long bones.)

Hughes, C. E., White, C. A. (2009). Crack propagation in teeth: A comparison of perimortem and postmortem behavior of dental materials and cracks. *Journal of Forensic Sciences,* 54(2):263–266.

Humphrey, J. H., Hutchinson, D. L. (2001). Macroscopic characteristics of hacking trauma. *Journal of Forensic Sciences,* 46:228–233.

Hunt, E. E., Gleiser, I. (1955). The estimation of age and sex of preadolescent children from bones and teeth. *American Journal of Physical Anthropology,* 13:479–487.

Hunter, J., Roberts, C., Martin, A. (1996). *Studies in Crime: An Introduction to Forensic Archeology.* London: B. T. Batsford Ltd.

Ingalls, N. W. (1927). Studies on the femur. I.I.I. Effects of maceration and drying in the white and the Negro. *American Journal of Physical Anthropology,* 10:297–321.

Irish, J. (1997). Characteristics of high- and low-frequency dental traits in sub-Saharan African populations. *American Journal of Physical Anthropology,* 102:455–467.

Isçan, M. Y., Loth, S. R., Wright, R. K. (1984). Age estimation from the rib by phase analysis: White males. *Journal of Forensic Sciences,* 29:1094–1104.

Isçan, M. Y., Loth, S. R., Wright, R. K. (1985). Age estimation from the rib by phase analysis: White females. *Journal of Forensic Sciences,* 30:853–863.

Jackson, D. M. (1996). *The Bone Detectives.* Boston: Little, Brown and Company.

Jankauskas, R., Barakauskas, S., Boharun, R. (2001). Incremental lines of dental cementum in biological age estimation. *Homo,* 52:59–71.

Jantz, R. L., Hunt, D. R., Meadows, L. (1995). The measure and mismeasure of the tibia: Implications for stature estimation.*Journal of Forensic Sciences,* 40:758–761.

Jason, D. R., Taylor, K. (1995). Estimation of stature from the length of the cervical, thoracic, and lumbar segments of the spine in American whites and blacks. *Journal of Forensic Sciences,* 40:59–62.

Joyce, C., Stover, E. (1991). *Witnesses from the Grave.* Boston: Little, Brown, and Company.

Kagerer, P., Grupe, G. (2001). On the validity of individual age-at-death diagnosis by incremental line counts in human dental cementum. Technical considerations. *Anthropologischer Anzeiger,* 59:331–342.

Kerely, E. (1965). The microscopic determination of age in human bone. *American Journal of Physical Anthropology,* 23:149–164.

Kerely, E. R., Ubelaker, D. H. (1978). Revisions in the microscopic method of estimating age at death in human cortical bone. *American Journal of Physical Anthropology,* 49:545–546.

Klepinger, L. L., Giles, G. (1998). Clarification or confusion: Statistical interpretation in forensic anthropology. In: Reichs, K. J., ed. *Forensic Osteology Advances in the Identification of Human Remains.* 2nd ed. Springfield, IL: Charles C. Thomas.

Klinkner, M. (2008). Proving genocide? Forensic expertise and the ICTY. *Journal of International Criminal Justice,* 6:447–466.

Klippel, W. E., Synstelien, J. A. (2007). Rodents as taphonomic agents: Bone gnawing by brown rats and gray squirrels. *Journal of Forensic Sciences,* 52(4):765–773.

Knudson, J. W. (1972). *Collecting and Preserving Plants and Animals.* New York: Harper & Row.

Komar, D. A. (1998). Decay rates in a cold climate region: A review of cases involving advanced decomposition from the medical examiner's office in Edmonton, Alberta. *Journal of Forensic Sciences,* 43:57–61.

Komar, D. A., Lathrop, S. (2008). The use of material culture to establish the ethnic identity of victims in genocide investigations: A validation study from the American Southwest. *Journal of Forensic Sciences,* 53(5):1035–1039.

Komar, D. A., Potter, W. E. (2007). Percentage of body recovered and its effect on identification rates and cause and manner of death determination. *Journal of Forensic Sciences,* 52(3):528–531.

Krogman, W. M. (1939). Guide to the identification of human skeletal material. *FBI Law Enforcement Bulletin,* 8:3–31.

Krogman, W. M. (1962). *The Human Skeleton in Forensic Medicine.* Springfield, IL: Charles C. Thomas.

Krogman, W. M., Iscan, M. Y. (1986). *The Human Skeleton in Forensic Medicine.* 2nd ed. Springfield, IL: Charles C. Thomas.

Lamendin, H., Baccion, E., Humbert, J. F., Tavernier, J. C., Nossintchouk, R. M., Zerilli, A. (1992). A simple technique for age estimation in adult corpses: The two criteria dental method. *Journal of Forensic Sciences,* 37:1373–1379.

Langley, N. R. (2007). An anthropological analysis of gunshot wounds to the chest. *Journal of Forensic Sciences,* 52(3):532–537.

Lee, H. C., Ladd, C., Scherczinger, C. A., Bourke, M. T. (1998). Forensic applications of DNA typing, Part 2: Collection and preservation of DNA evidence. *American Journal of Forensic Medicine and Pathology,* 19:10–18.

Levine, L. J. (1972). Forensic odontology today—a "new" forensic science. *FBI Law Enforcement Bulletin,* August 1972.

Listi, G. A., Bassett, H. E. (2006). Test of an alternative method for determining sex from the Os Coxae: Applications for modern Americans. *Journal of Forensic Sciences,* 51(2):248–252.

London, M. R., Hunt, D. R. (1998). Morphometric segregation of commingled remains using the femoral head and acetabulum. Paper delivered to the 67th annual meeting of the American Association of Physical Anthropologists.

Love, J. C., Symes, S. A., (2004). Understanding rib fracture patterns: Incomplete and buckle fractures. *Journal of Forensic Sciences,* 49(6):1153–1158.

Lovejoy, C. O., Meindl, R. S., Mensforth, R., Barton, T. J. (1985). Chronological metamorphosis of the auricular surface of the ilium: A new method for the determination of adult skeletal age at death. *American Journal of Physical Anthropology,* 68:15–28.

Lovell, N. C. (1989). Test of Phenice's technique for determining sex from the os pubis. *American Journal of Physical Anthropology,* 79:117–120.

Lucy, D., Aykroyd, R. G., Pollar, A. M., Solheim, T. (1996). A Bayesian approach to adult human age estimation from dental observations by Johanson's age changes. *Journal of Forensic Sciences,* 41:189–194.

Lundy, J. K. (1988). Sacralization of a sixth lumbar vertebra and its effect upon the estimation of living stature. *Journal of Forensic Sciences,* 33:1045–1049.

Lynn, K.S., Fairgieve, S. I. (2009). Macroscopic analysis of axe and hatchet trauma in fleshed and defleshed mammalian long bones. *Journal of Forensic Science,* 54(4) 5:786–792.

MacLaughlin, S. M., Bruce, M. F. (1990). The accuracy of sex identification in European skeletal remains using the Phenice characters. *Journal of Forensic Sciences,* 35:1384–1392.

Manhein, M. H. (1999). *The Bone Lady.* Baton Rouge, LA: Louisiana State University Press.

Manheim, M. H., Listi, G. A., Leitner, M. (2006). The application of geographic information systems and spatial analysis to assess dumped and subsequently scattered human remains. *Journal of Forensic Sciences,* 51:469–474.

Mann, R. W. (1993). A method for siding and sequencing human ribs. *Journal of Forensic Sciences,* 38(1):151–155.

Mann, R. W., Bass, W. M., Meadows, L. (1990). Time since death and decomposition of the human body: Variables and observation in case and experimental field studies. *Journal of Forensic Sciences,* 35:103–111.

Mann, R. W., Symes, S. A., Bass, W. M. (1987). Maxillary suture obliteration: Aging the human skeleton based on intact or fragmentary maxilla. *Journal of Forensic Sciences,* 32:148–157.

Maples, W. R. (1978). An improved technique using dental histology for the estimation of adult age. *Journal of Forensic Sciences,* 23:764–770.

Maples, W. R. (1984). The identifying pathology. In: Rathbun, T. A., Buikstra, J. E., eds. *Human Indentification. Case Studies in Forensic Anthropology.* Springfield, IL: Charles C. Thomas.

Maples, W. R. (1986). Trauma analysis by the forensic anthropologist. In: Reichs, K. J., ed. *Forensic Osteology Advances in the Identification of Human Remains.* Springfield, IL: Charles C. Thomas.

Maples, W. R., Browning, M. (1994). *Dead Men Do Tell Tales. The Strange and Fascinating Cases of a Forensic Anthropologist.* New York: Doubleday.

Marciniak, S. M. (2009). A preliminary assessment of the identification of saw marks on burned bone. *Journal of Forensic Sciences,* 54(4):779–785.

Marks, M. K., Bennett, J. L., Wilson, O. L. (1997). Digital video image capture in establishing positive identification. *Journal of Forensic Sciences*, 42:492–495.

Martin, D. L., Goodman, A. H., Armelagos, G. J., Magennis, A. L. (1990). *Black Mesa Anasazi Health: Reconstructing Life from Patterns of Death and Disease.* Carbondale, IL: Center for Archeological Research, Southern Illinois University.

Martiniakova, M., Grosskopf, B., Omelka, R., Vondrakova, M., Bauerova, M. (2006). Differences among species in compact bone tissue microstructure of mammalian skeleton: Use of a discriminant function analysis for species identification. *Journal of Forensic Sciences*, 51(6):1235–1239.

McKenna, J. J. I., Jablonski, N. G., Fearnhaed, R. W. (1984). A method of matching skulls with photographic portraits using landmarks and measurements of the dentition. *Journal of Forensic Sciences*, 29:787–797.

McKern, T., Stewart, T. D. (1957). Skeletal age changes in young American males, analyzed from the standpoint of identification. Technical report EP-45. Headquarters, Quartermaster Research and Development Command, Natick, MA.

Meadows, L., Jantz, R. L. (1992). Estimation of stature from metacarpal lengths. *Journal of Forensic Sciences,* 37:147–154.

Meadows, L., Jantz, R. L. (1995). Allometric secular change in the long bones from the 1800s to the present. *Journal of Forensic Sciences*, 40(5):762–767.

Megyesi, M. S., Nawrocki, S. P., Haskell, N. H. (2005). Using accumulated degree-days to estimate the postmortem interval from decomposed human remains. *Journal of Forensic Sciences*, 50(3):618–626.

Meindl, R. S., Lovejoy, C. O. (1985). Ectocranial suture closure: A revised method for the determination of skeletal age at death based on the lateral-anterior sutures. *American Journal of Physical Anthropology*, 68:57–66.

Meindl, R. S., Lovejoy, O. C., Mensforth, R. P., Walker, R. A. (1985). A revised method of age determination using the os pubis with a review and tests of accuracy of other current methods of pubic symphyseal aging. *American Journal of Physical Anthropology*, 68:29–45.

Metzger, Z., Buchner, A., Gorsk, M. (1980). Gustafson's method for age determination from teeth—A modification for the use of dentists in identification teams. *Journal of Forensic Sciences*, 25:742–749.

Mittler, D. M., Sheridan, S. G. (1992). Sex determination in subadults using auricular surface morphology: A forensic science perspective. *Journal of Forensic Sciences*, 37:1068–1075.

Montagu, M. F. A (1947). A study of man embracing error. *Technological Review*, 49:345–362.

Moorrees, C. F. A., Fanning, E. A., Hunt, E. E. (1963a). Formation and resorption of three deciduous teeth in children. *American Journal of Physical Anthropology*, 21:205–213.

Moorrees, C. F. A., Fanning, E. A., Hunt, E. E. (1963b). Age variation of formation stages for ten permanent teeth. *Journal of Dental Research*, 42: 1490–1502.

Moore-Jansen, P. M., Ousley, S. D., Jantz, R. L. (1994). Data collection procedures for forensic skeletal material. Report of Investigations 48, University of Tennessee, Anthropology Department, Knoxville, TN.

Morse, D., Crusoe, D., Smith, H. G. (1976). Forensic archaeology. *Journal of Forensic Sciences*, 21:323–332.

Morse, D., Duncan, J., Stoutamire, J. (1983). *Handbook of Forensic Archaeology and Anthropology.* Tallahassee, FL: Rose Printing.

Mulhern, D. M., Jones, E. B. (2005). Test of revised method of age estimation from the auricular surface of the ilium. *American Journal of Physical Anthropology*, 126(1):61–65.

Mundorff, A. Z., Bartelink, E. J., Mar-Cash, E. (2009). DNA preservation in skeletal elements from the World Trade Center disaster: Recommendations for mass fatality management. *Journal of Forensic Sciences*, 54(4):739–745.

Murad, T. A., Boddy, M. A. (1987). A case with bear facts. *Journal of Forensic Sciences*, 32:1819–1826.

Murphy, W. A., Gantner, G. E. (1982). Radiologic examination of anatomic parts and skeletonized remains. *Journal of Forensic Sciences*, 27:9–18.

Murray, K. A., Murray, T. (1991). A test of the auricular surface aging technique. *Journal of Forensic Sciences*, 36(4):1162–1169.

Nakao, M. A., Axelrod, S. (1983). Numbers are better than words: Verbal specification has no place in medicine. *American Journal of Medicine*, 74:1061–1065.

Nawrocki, S., Pless, J., Hawley, D., Wagnes, S. (1996). Fluvial transport of human crania. In: Haglund, W. D., Sorg, M. H., eds. *Forensic Taphonomy.* New York: CRC Press.

Nickerson, B. A., Fitzhorn, P. A., Koch, S. K., Charney, M. (1991). A methodology for near-optimal computational superimposition of two-dimensional digital facial photographs and three-dimensional cranial surface meshes. *Journal of Forensic Sciences*, 36:480–500.

O'Brien, T. G., Kuehner, A. C. (2007). Waxing grave about Adipocere: Soft tissue change in an aquatic context. *Journal of Forensic Sciences*, 52(2):294–301.

O'Halloran, R. L., Lundy, J. K. (1987). Age and ossification of the hyoid bone: Forensic implications. *Journal of Forensic Sciences*, 32:1655–1659.

Ohtani, S., Yamamoto, T. (2005). Strategy for the estimation of chronological age using the aspartic acid racemization method with special reference to coefficient of correlation between D/L ratios and ages. *Journal of Forensic Sciences,* 50(5):1020–1027.

Olivier, G. (1969). *Practical Anthropology.* Springfield, IL: Charles C. Thomas.

Ortner, D. J., Putschar, W. G. J. (1981). *Identification of Pathological Conditions in Human Skeletal Remains.* Smithsonian Contributions to Anthropology 28. Washington, DC: Smithsonian Institution Press.

Osborne, D. L., Simmons, T. L., Nawrocki, S. P. (2004). Reconsidering the auricular surface as an indicator of age at death. *Journal of Forensic Sciences,* 49(5):905–911.

Ousley, S. (1995). Should we estimate biological or forensic stature. *Journal of Forensic Sciences,* 40:768–773.

Overbury, R. S., Cabo, L. L., Dirkmatt, D. C., Symes, S. A. (2009). Asymmetry of the os pubis: Implications for the Suchey-Brooks method. *American Journal of Physical Anthropology,* 139(2):261–268.

Owers, S. K., Pastor, R. F., (2005). Analysis of quantitative methods for rib seriation using the Spitalfields documented skeletal collection. *American Journal of Physical Anthropology,* 127:210–218.

Owsley, D. W., Ubelaker, D. H., Houck, M. M., Sandness, K. L., Grant, W. E., Craig, E. A., Woltanski, T. J., Peerwani, N. (1995) The role of forensic anthropology in the recovery and analysis of Branch Davidian Compound victims: Techniques of analysis. *Journal of Forensic Sciences,* 40(3):341–348.

Owsely, D. W., Webb, R. S. (1983). Misclassification probability in dental discrimination functions for sex determination.*Journal of Forensic Sciences,* 8:181–185.

Paine, R. R., Brenton, B. P. (2006). Dietary health does affect histologic age assessment: An evaluation of the Stout and Paine (1992) age estimation equation using secondary osteons from the rib. *Journal of Forensic Sciences,* 51:489–492.

Parsons, T. J., Weedn, V. W. (1997). Preservation and recovery of DNA in postmortem specimens and trace samples. In: Hagland, W. D., Song, M. H., eds. *Forensic Taphonomy.* New York: CRC Press.

Pearson, M. P. (1999). *The Archaeology of Death and Burial.* College Station, TX: Texas A&M University Press.

Perzigian, A. J., Jolly, P. N. (1984). Skeletal and dental identification of an adolescent female. In: Rathbun, T. A., Buikstra, J. E., eds. *Human Identification. Case Studies in Forensic Anthropology.* Springfield, IL: Charles C. Thomas.

Peterson, B. L. (1991). External beveling of cranial gunshot entrance wounds. *Journal of Forensic Sciences,* 36:1592–1595.

Phenice, T. W. (1969). A newly developed visual method of sexing the *os pubis. American Journal of Physical Anthropology,* 30:297–302.

Pickering, R. B., Bachman, D. C. (1997). *The Use of Forensic Anthropology.* Boca Raton, FL: CRC Press.

Pollanen, M. S., Chiasson, D. S. (1996). Fracture of the hyoid bone in strangulation: Comparison of fractured and unfractured hyoids from victims of strangulation. *Journal of Forensic Sciences,* 41:110–113.

Pollanen, M. S., Bulger, B., Chiasson, D. S. (1995). The location of hyoid fractures in strangulation revealed by xeroradiography. *Journal of Forensic Sciences,* 40:303–305.

Pope, E. J., Smith, O. C. (2004). Identification of traumatic injury in burned cranial bone: An experimental approach. *Journal of Forensic Sciences,* 49(3):431–440.

Prag, J., Neave, R. (1997). *Making Faces: Using Forensic and Archeological Evidence.* College Station, TX: Texas A&M University Press.

Randall, B. (1991). Body retrieval and morgue operations at the crash of United Flight 232. *Journal of Forensic Sciences,* 36:403–409.

Rathbun, T. A., Buikstra, J. E., eds. (1984). *Human Identification. Case Studies in Forensic Anthropology.* Springfield, IL: Charles C. Thomas.

Raxter, M. H., Auerbach, D. M., Ruff, C. B. (2006). Revision of the Fully technique for estimating statures. *American Journal of Physical Anthropology,* 130:374–384.

Raxter, M. H., Ruff, C. B., Auerbach, B. M. (2007). Technocal note: Revised Fully stature estimation technique. *American Journal of Physical Anthropology,* 133(2):817–818.

Reeves, N. M. (2009). Taphonomic effects of vulture scavenging. *Journal of Forensic Sciences,* 54(3):523–528.

Reichs, K. J., ed. (1986). *Forensic Osteology: Advances in the Identification of Human Remains.* Springfield, IL: Charles C. Thomas.

Reichs, K. J. (1989). Cranial suture eccentricities: A case study in which precocious closure complicated determination of sex and commingling. *Journal of Forensic Sciences,* 34(1):263–273.

Reichs, K. J., ed. (1998a). *Forensic Osteology, Advances in the Identification of Human Remains.* 2nd ed. Springfield, IL: Charles C. Thomas.

Reichs, K. J. (1998b). Postmortem dismemberment: recovery, analysis and interpretation. In: Reichs, K. J., ed. *Forensic Osteology Advances in the Identification of Human Remains.* 2nd ed. Springfield, IL: Charles C. Thomas.

Rhine, S. (1970). *The Beginnings of Mankind, A Laboratory Notebook.* Fort Collins, CO: Robinson-Warfield.

Rhine, S. (1984). Facial reproduction in court. In: Rathbun, T. A., Buikstra, J. E., eds. *Human Identification. Case Studies in Forensic Anthropology.* Springfield, IL: Charles C. Thomas.

Rhine, S. (1990a). Coming to terms with facial reproduction. *Journal of Forensic Sciences,* 35:960–963.

Rhine, S. (1990b). Non-metric skull racing. In: Gill, G. W., Rhine, J. S., eds. *Skeletal Attribution of Race: Methods for Forensic Anthropology.* Anthropological Papers 4, Maxwell Museum of Anthropology, Albuquerque, NM.

Rhine, S. (1998). *Bone Voyage.* Albuquerque, NM: University of New Mexico Press.

Rhine, S., Curran, B. K. (1990). Multiple gunshot wounds of the head: An anthropological view. *Journal of Forensic Sciences,* 35:1236–1245.

Rhine, S., Sperry, K. (1991). Radiographic identification by mastoid sinus and arterial pattern. *Journal of Forensic Sciences,* 36:272–279.

Riddick, L., Brogdon, B. G., Lasswell-Hoff, J., Delmas, B. (1983). Radiographic identification of charred human remains through use of the dorsal defect of the patella. *Journal of Forensic Sciences,* 28:263–267.

Rodriguez, W. C., Bass, W. M. (1983). Insect activity and its relationship to decay rates of human cadavers in east Tennessee.*Journal of Forensic Sciences,* 28:423–432.

Rodriguez, W. C., Bass, W. M. (1985). Decomposition of buried bodies and methods that may aid in their location. *Journal of Forensic Sciences,* 30:836–852.

Rogers, T. L. (2005). Recognition of cemetery remains in a forensic context. *Journal of Forensic Sciences,* 50(1):5–11.

Rogers, T. L., Allard, T. T. (2004). Expert testimony and positive identification of human remains through cranial suture patterns. *Journal of Forensic Sciences,* 49(2):203–207.

Rogers, T. L., Saunders, S. (1994). Accuracy of sex determination using morphological traits of the human pelvis. *Journal of Forensic Sciences,* 39(4):1047–1056.

Romero, J. (1970). Dental mutilation, tephination, and cranial deformation. In: Stewart, T. D., ed. *Handbook of Middle American Indians,* Volume 9: *Physical Anthropology.* Austin, TX: University of Texas Press.

Ross, A. H. (1996). Caliber estimation from cranial entrance defect measurements. *Journal of Forensic Sciences,* 41:629–633.

Rowe, W. F. (1997). Biodegradation of hairs and fibers. In: Haglund, W. D., Sorg, M. H., eds. *Forensic Taphonomy.* New York: CRC Press.

Ruff, C. (2007). Body size prediction from juvenile skeletal remains. *American Journal of Physical Anthropology,* 133(1):698–716.

Sauer, N. J. (1984). Manner of death: Skeletal evidence of blunt and sharp instrument wounds. In: Rathbun, T. A., Buikstra, J. E., eds. *Human Identification. Case Studies in Forensic Anthropology.* Springfield, IL: Charles C. Thomas.

Sauer, N. J. (1998). The timing of injuries and manner of death: Distinguishing among antemortem, perimortem, and postmortem trauma. In: Reichs, K. J., ed. *Forensic Osteology, Advances in the Identification of Human Remains.* 2nd ed. Springfield, IL: Charles C. Thomas.

Sauer, N. J., Simson, L. R. (1984). Clarifying the role of forensic anthropologists in death investigations. *Journal of Forensic Sciences,* 29:1081–1086.

Schaefer, M. C., Black, S. M. (2007). Epiphyseal union sequencing: Aiding in the recognition and sorting of commingled remains. *Journal of Forensic Sciences,* 52(2):277–285.

Schmid, E. (1972). *Atlas of Animal Bones.* Amsterdam: Elsevier.

Schour, M. (1941). The development of the human dentition. *Journal of the American Dental Association,* 28:1153.

Schutkowski, H. (1993). Sex determination of infant and juvenile skeletons: I., morphognostic features. *American Journal of Physical Anthropology,* 90:199–205.

Sciulli, P. W., Pfau, R. O. (1994). A method of estimating weight in children from femoral midshaft diameter and age. *Journal of Forensic Sciences,* 39:1280–1286.

Sharma, B. R., Singh, V. P., Harish, D. (2005). Neck structure injuries in hanging—Comparing retrospective and prospective studies. *Medicine, Science and the Law,* 45(4):321–330.

Shean, B. S., Messinger, L., Papworth, M. (1993). Observations of differential decomposition on sun exposed v. shaded pig carrion in coastal Washington state. *Journal of Forensic Sciences,* 38:938–949.

Shepherd, K. L., Walsh-Haney, H., Coburn, M. U. (2010). Surgical sutures as a means of identifying human remains. *Journal of Forensic Sciences,* 55(1):237–240.

Shkrum, M. J., Green, R. N., McClafferty, K. J., Nowak, E. S. (1994). Skull fractures in fatalities due to motor vehicle collisions. *Journal of Forensic Sciences,* 39:107–122.

Smith, O. C., Berryman, H. E., Lahern, C. H. (1987). Cranial fracture patterns and estimate of direction from low velocity gunshot wounds. *Journal of Forensic Sciences,* 32:1416–1421.

Snedecor, G. W., Cochran, W. G. (1967). *Statistical Methods.* 6th ed. Ames, IA: Iowa State University Press.

Snodgrass, J. J. (2004). Sex differences and aging of the vertebral column. *Journal of Forensic Sciences,* 49(3):458–463.

Snow, C. C. (1982). Forensic anthropology. *Annual Review of Anthropology,* 11:97–131.

Snow, C. C., Luke, J. (1984). The Oklahoma child disappearance cases of 1987. In: Rathbun, T. A., Buikstra, J. E., eds. *Human Identification. Case Studies in Forensic Anthropology.* Springfield, IL: Charles C. Thomas.

Snow, C. C., Gatliff, B., McWilliams, K. R. (1970). Reconstruction of facial features from the skull: An evaluation of its usefulness in forensic anthropology. *American Journal of Physical Anthropology,* 33:221–228.

Snow, C. E. (1948). The identification of the unknown war dead. *American Journal of Physical Anthropology,* 6:323–328.

Snyder, R. G., Burdi, A., Gaul, G. (1975). A rapid technique for preparation of human fetal and adult skeletal material. *Journal of Forensic Sciences,* 20:576–580.

Sognnaes, R. F., Gratt, B. M., Papin, P. J. (1985). Biomedical image processing for age measurements of intact teeth. *Journal of Forensic Sciences,* 30:1082–1089.

Spitz, W. U. (1980). The road traffic victim. In: Spitz, W. U., Fisher, R. S., eds. *Medicolegal Investigation of Death,* Chapter 15. Springfield, IL: Charles C. Thomas.

Spradley, M. K., Jantz, R. L., Robinson, A., Peccerelli, F. (2008). Demographic change and forensic identification: Problems in metric identification of Hispanic skeletons. *Journal of Forensic Sciences,* 53:21–28.

Steadman, D. W., Adams, B. J., Konigsberg, L. W. (2006) Statistical basis for positive identification in forensic anthropology.*American Journal of Physical Anthropology,* 131(1):15–26

Steadman, D. W., DiAntonio, L. L., Wilson, J. J., Sheridan, K. E., Tammariello, S. P. (2006). The effects of chemical and heat maceration techniques on the recovery of nuclear and mitochondrial DNA from bone. *Journal of Forensic Sciences,* 51(1):11–17.

Steele, D. G. (1970). Estimation of stature from fragments of long limb bones. In: Stewart, T. D., ed. *Personal Identification in Mass Disasters.* Washington, DC: National Museum of Natural History, Smithsonian Institution.

Steele, D. G., Bramblett, C. A. (1988). *The Anatomy and Biology of the Human Skeleton.* College Station, TX: Texas A&M University Press.

Stephan, C. N. (2003). Facial approximation: An evaluation of mouth-width determination. *American Journal of Physical Anthropology,* 121:48–57.

Stephan, C. N., Davidson, P. L. (2008). The placement of the human eyeball and Canthi in craniofacial identification. *Journal of Forensic Sciences,* 53(3):612–619.

Stephan, C. N., Henneberg, M. (2003). Predicting mouth width from inter-canine width—A 75% rule. *Journal of Forensic Sciences,* 48:725–727.

Stephan, C. N., Henneberg, M., Sampson, W. (2003). Predicting nose projection and pronasale position in facial approximation: A test of published methods and proposal of new guidelines. *American Journal Physical Anthropology,* 122:240–250.

Stephan, C. N., Huang, A. R., Davidson, P. L. (2009). Futher evidence on the anatomical placement of the human eyeball for facial approximation and craniofacial superimposition. *Journal of Forensic Sciences,* 54(2):267–269.

Stephan, C. N., Simpson, E. K. (2008a). Facial soft tissue depths in craniofacial identification (Part 1): An analytical review of the published adult data. *Journal of Forensic Sciences,* 53(6):1257–1272.

Stephan, C. N., Simpson, E. K. (2008b). Facial soft tissue depths in craniofacial identification (Part 2): An analytical review of the published sub-adult data. *Journal of Forensic Sciences,* 53(6):1273–1279.

Stephens, B. G. (1979). A simple method for preparing human skeletal material for forensic examination. *Journal of Forensic Sciences,* 24:660–662.

Stevens, S. S. (1946). On the theory of scales of measurement. *Science,* 103:677–680.

Stewart, T. D. (1962). Anterior femoral curvature: Its utility for race identification. *Human Biology,* 34:49–62.

Stewart, T. D. (1979). *Essentials of Forensic Anthropology.* Springfield, IL: Charles C. Thomas.

Stewart, T. D. (1983). The points of attachment of the Palpebral Ligaments: Their use in facial reconstructions on the skull. *Journal of Forensic Sciences,* 28:858–863.

Suchey, J. M., Katz, D. (1986). Skeletal age standards derived from an extensive multiracial sample of modern Americans. *American Journal of Physical Anthropology,* 69:269.

Suckling, G. W., Herbison, G. P., Brown, R. H. (1987). Etiological factors influencing the prevalence of developmental defects of dental enamel in nine-year-old New Zealand children participating in a health and development study. *Journal of Dental Research,* 66:1466–1469.

Sundick, R. I. (1984). Ashes to ashes, dust to dust, or where did the skeleton go. In: Rathbun, T. A., Buikstra, J. E., eds. *Human Identification. Case Studies in Forensic Anthropology.* Springfield, IL: Charles C. Thomas.

Sutherland, L. D., Suchy, J. M. (1991). Use of the ventral arc in pubic sex determination. *Journal of Forensic Sciences,* 36:501–511.

Sutter, R. C. (2003). Nonmetric subadult sexing traits: I. A blind test of the accuracy of eight proposed methods using prehistoric known-sex mummies from northern Chile. *Journal of Forensic Sciences,* 48(5):927–935.

Symes, S. A., Berryman, H. E., Smith, O. C. (1998). Saw marks in bone: Introduction and examination of residual kerf contour. In: Reichs, K. J., ed. *Forensic Osteology, Advances in the Identification of Human Remains.* 2nd ed. Springfield, IL: Charles C. Thomas.

Taylor, R. M. S. (1978). *Variation in Morphology of Teeth: Anthropologic and Forensic Aspects.* Springfield, IL: Charles C. Thomas.

Todd, T. W. (1920). Age changes in the pubic bone: I, the male white pubis. *American Journal of Physical Anthropology,* 3:285–334.

Thompson, T. J. (2005). Heat-induced dimensional changes in bone and their consequences for forensic anthropology. *Journal of Forensic Sciences*, 50(5):1008–1015.

Todd, T. W., Lyon, D. W. (1924). Endocranial suture closure: Its progress and age relationship. Part I, adult males of white stock. *American Journal of Physical Anthropology*, 7:325–384.

Todd, T. W., Lyon, D. W. (1925a). Cranial suture closure: Its progress and age relationship. Part II, ectocranial closure in adult males of white stock. *American Journal of Physical Anthropology*, 8:23–44.

Todd, T. W., Lyon, D. W. (1925b). Cranial suture closure: Its progress and age relationship. Part III, endocranial closure in adult males of Negro stock. *American Journal of Physical Anthropology*, 8:47–71.

Todd, T. W., Lyon, D. W. (1925c). Cranial suture closure: Its progress and age relationship. Part IV, ectocranial closure in adult males of Negro stock. *American Journal of Physical Anthropology*, 8:149–168.

Trotter, M. (1970). Estimation of stature from intact long limb bones. In: Stewart, T. D., ed. *Personal Identification in Mass Disasters*. Washington, DC: National Museum of Natural History, Smithsonian Institution.

Trotter, M., Gleser, G. C. (1951). The effect of aging on stature. *American Journal of Physical Anthropology*, 9:311–324.

Trotter, M., Gleser, G. C. (1952). Estimation of stature from long bones of American Whites and Negroes. *American Journal of Physical Anthropology*, 10:463–514.

Trotter, M., Gleser, G. C. (1958). A re-evaluation of estimation of stature based on measurements of stature taken during life and of long bones after death. *American Journal of Physical Anthropology*, 16:79–123.

Tucker, B. K., Hutchinson, D. L., Gilliland, M. F. G., Charles, T. M., Daniel, H. H., Wolfe, L. D. (2001). Microscopic characteristics of hacking trauma. *Journal of Forensic Sciences*, 46:234–240.

Tuller, H., Durić, M. (2006). Keeping the pieces together: Comparison of mass grave excavation methodology. *Forensic Science International*, 156:192–200.

Tyrrell, A. J., Evison, M. P., Chamberlain, A. T., Green, M. A. (1997). Forensic three-dimensional facial reconstruction: Historical review and contemporary developments. *Journal of Forensic Sciences*, 42:653–661.

Ubelaker, D. H. (1984). Positive identification from the radiographic comparison of frontal sinus patterns. In: Rathbun, T. A., Buikstra, J. E., eds. *Human Identification. Case Studies in Forensic Anthropology*. Springfield, IL: Charles C. Thomas.

Ubelaker, D. H. (1989). *Human Skeletal Remains*. 2nd ed. Washington, DC: Taraxacum Press.

Ubelaker, D. H. (1992). Hyoid fracture and strangulation. *Journal of Forensic Sciences*, 37:1216–1222.

Ubelaker, D. H. (1997). Taphonomic applications in forensic anthropology. In: Haglund, W. D., Sorg, M. H., eds. *Forensic Taphonomy*. New York: CRC Press.

Ubelaker, D. H. (1998). The evolving role of the microscope in forensic anthropology. In: Reichs, K. J., ed. *Forensic Osteology Advances in the Identification of Human Remains*. 2nd ed. Springfield, IL: Charles C. Thomas.

Ubelaker, D. H. (1999). *Human Skeletal Remains*. 3rd ed. Washington, DC: Taraxacum Press.

Ubelaker, D. H. (2008). Issues in the global applications of methodology in Forensic Anthropology. *Journal of Forensic Sciences*, 53(3):606–607.

Ubelaker, D. H., O'Donnell, G. (1992). Computer-assisted facial reproduction. *Journal of Forensic Sciences*, 37:155–162.

Ubelaker, D. H., Scammell, H. (1992). *Bones, a Forensic Detective's Casebook*. New York: M. Evans and Company.

Ubelaker, D. H., Bubniak, E., O'Donnell, G. (1992). Computer-assisted photographic superimposition. *Journal of Forensic Sciences*, 37:750–762.

Ubelaker, D. H., Ward, D. C., Braz, V. S., Stewart, J. (2002). The use of SEM/EDS analysis to distinguish dental and osseous tissues from other materials. *Journal of Forensic Sciences*, 47:940–943.

Valenzuela, A., Martin-de las Heras, S., Mandojana, J. M., de Dios Luna, J., Valenzuela, M., Villanueva, E. (2002). Multiple regression models for age estimation by assessment of morphologic dental changes according to teeth sequence. *American Journal of Forensic Medicine and Pathology*, 23:386–389.

Vass, A. A., Bass, W. M., Wolt, J. D., Foss, J. E., Ammons, J. T. (1992). Time since death determinations of human cadavers using soil solution. *Journal of Forensic Sciences*, 37:1236–1253.

Walker, P. L. (2005). Greater sciatic notch morphology: Sex, age, and population differences. *American Journal of Physical Anthropology*, 127:385–391.

Walker, P. L. (2008). Sexing skulls using discriminant function analysis of visually assessed traits. *American Journal of Physical Anthropology*, 136(1):39–50.

Walker, P. L., Cook, D. C., Lambert, P. M. (1997). Skeletal evidence of child abuse: A physical anthropological perspective. *Journal of Forensic Sciences*, 42:196–207.

Walker, R. A., Lovejoy, C. O. (1985). Radiographic changes in the clavicle and proximal femur and their use in the determination of skeletal age at death. *American Journal of Physical Anthropology*, 68:67–78.

Walsh-Haney, H. A. (1999). Sharp-force trauma analysis and the forensic anthropologist: Techniques advocated by William R. Maples, Ph.D. *Journal of Forensic Sciences*, 44:720–723.

Warren, J. (1991). Thomas Dwight, M.D., L.L.D., *Anatomical Record*, 5:431–439.

Washburn, S. L. (1948). Sex differences in the pubic bone. *American Journal of Physical Anthropology,* 6:199–207.

Washburn, S. L. (1949). Sex differences in the pubic bone of Bantu and Bushman. *American Journal of Physical Anthropology,* 7:425–432.

Weaver, D. S. (1980). Sex differences in the ilia of a known sex and age sample of fetal and infant skeletons. *American Journal of Physical Anthropology,* 52:191–195.

Wescott, D. J. (2005). Population variation in femur sub-trochanteric shape. *Journal of Forensic Sciences,* 50(2):286–293.

Wescott, D. J. (2006). Ontogeny of Femur Subtrochanteric Shape in Native Americans and American Blacks and Whites. *Journal of Forensic Sciences,* 51(6):1240–1245.

White, T. D. (1991). *Human Osteology.* San Diego, CA: Academic Press.

Whittaker, D. K., Bakri, M. M. (1996). Racial variations in the extent of tooth root translucency in ageing individuals. *Archives of Oral Biology,* 41:15–19.

Wieberg, D. A. M., Wescott, D. J. (2008). Estimating the timing of long bone fractures: Correlation between the postmortem interval, bone moisture content, and blunt force trauma fracture characteristics. *Journal of Forensic Sciences,* 53(5):1028–1034.

Wilber, C. G. (1974). *Forensic Biology for the Law Enforcement Officer.* Springfield, IL: Charles C. Thomas.

Wilczak, C. A., Kennedy, K. A. R (1998). Mostly MOS: Technical aspects of identification of skeletal markers of occupational stress. In: Reichs, K. J., ed. *Forensic Osteology Advances in the Identification of Human Remains.* 2nd ed. Springfield, IL: Charles C. Thomas.

Wiley, P., Heilman, A. (1987). Estimating time since death using plant roots and stems. *Journal of Forensic Sciences,* 32:1264–1270.

Wilson, L.A., MacLeod, N., Humphrey, L.T. (2008) Morphometric criteria for sexing juvenile human skeletons using the ilium. *Journal of Forensic Sciences,* 53(2):269–278.

Wilson, R. J., Herrmann, N. P., Jantz, L. M. (2010). Evaluation of stature estimation using the Database for Forensic Anthropology.*Journal of Forensic Sciences,* 55(3):684–694.

Wormington, H. M. (1947). *Prehistoric Indians of the Southwest.* Denver Museum of Natural History, Popular Series No. 7, Denver, CO.

Yoder, C., Ubelaker, D. H., Powell, J. F. (2001). Examination of variation in sternal rib end morphology relevant to age assessment.*Journal of Forensic Sciences,* 46:223–227.

Yoshino, C., Ubelaker, D. H., Powell, J. F. (1987). Classification system of frontal sinus patterns in radiography. Its application to identification of unknown remains. *Forensic Science International,* 34:289–299.

A NOTE ON PHOTOGRAPHY

I employed 35mm format primarily to keep costs down, using a Chinon CG5 and a Pentax ZX-M on a tripod along with a compressed air release to reduce camera movement. I relied on manual metering to take into account the large exposure difference between the black background and the white bones, and to maintain full depth of field. My main lens was a generic 50mm, with stacked Vivitar extension tubes for the close-ups. Kodak T-Max 100 rated at 100 and processed for 6.5 minutes at 24°C provided high resolution, mid tones, and small-grain negatives. These printed on Ilford Multigrade RC glossy paper, using the Ilford filters—on the whole, grade 2.5 to 3 was sufficient. The lights were primarily photo floods on stands (I used anything from mostly 1 with reflectors, to the occasional 3 for the more complicated shots). On occasion location limitations forced me to use a couple of adjustable desk lamps, which, though a lower wattage and output, were more than adequate. In the field, I used Metz-CT45 strobes as additional fillin lighting to daylight, although any off-the-camera flash would be adequate. Black velveteen, play dough or clay, clamp stands, bean bags, various pieces of white card paper, and tape comprised the rest of my "kit."

Julie R. Angel

INDEX